AF323306

Seduced *and* Abandoned

Obfuscation in Economics

Seduced *and* Abandoned

Obfuscation in Economics

Craig Freedman

World Scientific

NEW JERSEY · LONDON · SINGAPORE · BEIJING · SHANGHAI · TAIPEI · CHENNAI

Published by

World Scientific Publishing Co. Pte. Ltd.

5 Toh Tuck Link, Singapore 596224

USA office: 27 Warren Street, Suite 401-402, Hackensack, NJ 07601

UK office: 57 Shelton Street, Covent Garden, London WC2H 9HE

Library of Congress Cataloging-in-Publication Data
Names: Freedman, Craig, 1950–   author.
Title: Seduced and abandoned : obfuscation in economics / Craig Freedman.
Description: New Jersey : World Scientific, [2025] | Includes bibliographical references and index.
Identifiers: LCCN 2024056956 | ISBN 9789819807390 (hardcover) |
    ISBN 9789819807406 (ebook) | ISBN 9789819807413 (ebook other)
Subjects: LCSH: Information theory in economics. | Economics--Information services.
Classification: LCC HB133 .F74 2025 | DDC 330--dc23/eng/20250311
LC record available at https://lccn.loc.gov/2024056956

British Library Cataloguing-in-Publication Data
A catalogue record for this book is available from the British Library.

Cover Image: Ophelia, 1851-2, Sir John Everett Millais, Bt 1829-1896, Photo: Tate

For any available supplementary material, please visit
https://www.worldscientific.com/worldscibooks/10.1142/14164#t=suppl

Desk Editors: Kannan Krishnan/Pui Yee Lum

Typeset by Stallion Press
Email: enquiries@stallionpress.com

*To Karen, Kathy and Lucy, three charming women
who are too wise to debate the whims of economics.*

When the Ideological Tail Wags the Analytical Dog: The Strategic Destruction of Informative Discourse

> … so there ain't nothing more to write about, and I am rotten glad of it, because if I'd a knowed what a trouble it was to make a book I wouldn't a tackled it and ain't going to no more (Twain 1884:377–378).[1]

Restrained to write strictly in terms of abstractions, while compelled to strategically lace these elusive constructions with an occasional sprinkling of broad generalities, leads an unwary academic only in one dubious direction. Far too soon, by barrelling down this well-trampled highway, innocent researchers find themselves grappling with a severe attack of the dreaded MEGO[2] disorder. A malady that is largely brought on by struggling to make sense of their own convoluted efforts. Fortunately, despite the profession's lurking admiration for discourse that leans toward the esoteric, we actually learn, and even understand, best through the simple medium of storytelling.[3] This humble source of ideas and pertinent insights informs an option which is too often dismissed, if not downright scorned, by a coterie of scientifically preening economists.[4] But representing somewhat of a personal reprieve, my concerns in writing this volume are narrowly defined by more decidedly straightforward objectives. These pointedly exclude a yen to impress or dazzle the economics profession. A competent ability to simply pour out four concrete case studies (before a semi-attentive regiment of readers), amply describes the extent of my own limited goals. Consequently, despite the seeming naivety of following such a course, this direct approach can more easily produce somewhat digestible results by making contested issues entirely tangible and decidedly comprehensible.

Almost accidentally, this book also demonstrates the importance of recycling. Even when viewed from a purely economic perspective, it turns out that previously ignored by-products of research may contain a sprinkling of interesting (and even sparkling) flakes of revelatory insight and information. At the very least, buried within all the more obvious mental dross may lie at least a few precious flecks of valuable material. To freely confess then to an origin story, much of the raw resources that produced this volume actually started life as discarded chapters from another book, now fortunately no longer in my hands.[5] These items were cut, not necessarily because of any quality considerations, but rather because they ultimately proved to be digressions from a given story line. Inevitably, such wanderings eventually failed to be intrinsic to the tale that was being carefully constructed and meticulously shaped.[6] Or in some instances, the finished chapters appearing in the collection before you were the result of thinking through previously unresolved issues.

These matters then almost exclusively arose while puzzling through the content of that previous volume. (The exception being the final case study. This chapter arrived as an unexpected latecomer, spurred by a decidedly negative reaction to a biography.) For instance, Ronald Coase produced what could only be described as a subdued response to George Stigler's questionable transformation of his 1960 paper. The reason for Coase's undramatic reaction created (at least in my mind), a niggling sense of unease, one which was tightly wrapped up in a murky film of mystery.[7] A satisfactory resolution of this perplexity failed to immediately occur to me when cross-examined by my co-author. A workable solution only arrived some months after the publication of that previously mentioned (co-authored) work.[8] Surprisingly, the way forward, which was prompted by the unlikely (but highly recognisable), profile of Alfred Hitchcock, provided an unanticipated bit of assistance. Any previous personal mental struggles were ultimately (and effectively) quelled.[9] Revealed instead were the dangers attached to lazily categorizing the work of any economist. Unfortunately, attempting to carefully understand articles and books proves to be a step too onerous for many practitioners of economics.

In addition to those more obvious Coasian concerns, previous attention had been paid to Philip Mirowski's insights and claims. These particularly included the more forceful conclusions constructed both by him and by his close associates. Perspectives tinged by Mirowski's agenda had been destined to enjoy an entire chapter in the Colander/Freedman (2018) volume. We had initially hoped to focus on the manner in which those authors treated the development (and objectives) of the post war Chicago School. Instead, that path turned out to be one of those railroad sidings that could only serve as an unnecessary detour from that book's final destination. However, with a sufficient passage of time, what sometimes eventuates is the hard-nosed realisation that ejecting ideas from a given book can prove far easier than erasing those themes and concerns entirely from one's thoughts and fixations.[10]

What continued to strike me in the months after publication, was that there were moments when authors such as Mirowski had gleefully embraced a very Chicago rhetorical strategy. In their work, they had conducted a similar series of 'demolition derby'[11] tactical strikes against an array of designated opponents.[12] In their structured attacks, tactics employed quite deliberately were chillingly similar to those that had once enchanted Thomas Sowell as a graduate student. At Chicago, that style had been finely honed by his dissertation advisor (George Stigler). This ability so impressed Sowell that he deliberately included a description of this practise when drawing a quick sketch of his time spent under the tutelage of that advisor.[13] He had become unreservedly fascinated by the lethal eviscerations George Stigler meted out when choosing to completely decimate his chosen targets.[14]

This memory of Stigler's consistently scorched earth approach creates something of a lingering sense of irony when compared to those similar attacks initiated decades later by Team Mirowski.[15] These staunch opponents of all things Chicago, when confronting views they attributed to that particular school, failed to resist the temptation of borrowing generously from George Stigler's own grab bag of critical tactics. These served, as one might expect, to effectively skewer Stigler's own framework and insights. In doing so, Mirowski and his associates blithely ignored the questionable standards employed whenever Stigler (and others) launched such sharp edged attacks. Carelessly disregarded when utilising such tactics is an ugly willingness that favours simply triumphing at all (or any) costs.[16]

Next to grab my attention was Milton Friedman's success at tunnelling his way into this volume, despite lacking an explicit invitation to do so. Characterised by a decided lack of intention on my part, Friedman's definitive appearance eventuality managed to materialise, in doing so almost defying my expectations. To be a touch more precise, when formulating an initial blueprint for this work, his name was nowhere to be found. The subsequent temptation (warily embraced), one that led to Friedman's inclusion, rested (perhaps lazily) on a collection of amorphous bits and pieces shed wilfully from a previous examination of his work. However, it turned out that I was loathe to let even these scattered nuggets go completely to waste.

Though the core topic of this Friedman-centric chapter has remained largely unexplored by most published papers, both Colander and I honed on the same underlying objective driving his seminal 1953 essay. But, we also had agreed to exclude any such discussion from our joint work. Featuring this particular insight in our proposed volume would probably have produced no more than an interesting digression, an amusing outlier that perversely drew attention away from our shared concerns.

But Friedman's methodological attempt (as featured in that 1953 essay), did prove relevant in terms of strategic obfuscation. Perhaps most important to note, at least initially, was that the issue (at the time, or a foreseeable time in the future), never focused on an issue that even vaguely resembled one of Friedman's multitudinous interests. Yet this singular bit of output appeared (with quite a deliberate and timely splash), during a period of critical debate within the economics profession. (We have here either a curious coincidence, or something of a more deliberate and intentional nature.) My concern then was not with the meaning of this now classic work, but with its controlling objective, namely what it hoped to accomplish.

Bluntly speaking, I suspected that there was a driving force behind Friedman's methodology, one which had been (hitherto) insufficiently explored. The miasma of confusion that surrounded his specific intentions, served only to spark my own curiosity. Clearly, or at least to me, a river of subterranean objectives might possibly flow beneath Friedman's placid surface of carefully crafted thoughts. Fortunately, discovering the underlying common thread defining Friedman's unstated objectives managed to resolve this fundamental mystery. (In a rather attenuated fashion, I successfully imitated the Greek hero, Theseus. He was only able to track his own path out of the Cretan labyrinth by means of Ariadne's singular offering. Though unlike Theseus, I skilfully dodged any visceral obligations in completing my search.) In this fashion, I managed to discover the implicit, but motivating, aim driving Friedman's atypical essay.

Any success (on my part), was accomplished, not so much by meeting Friedman's work head on, but by sidling up to it obliquely. Consequently, I deliberately eschewed analysing the actual methodology, or the purported philosophical undergarments, encapsulated within that famous essay. Instead, my selected alternative approach relied on an examination of what Friedman was trying to achieve, rather than stumbling aimlessly over his words, or elusive arguments. However, discovering this goal involved plunging headfirst into largely unexplored territory. The residing hope was that the purpose of his methodological effort might be fortuitously revealed by placing the specific work within a larger contextual framework. The key then to unlocking this niggling puzzle required an almost forensic autopsy of Friedman's larger aims (and those of his colleagues), which helped to define Chicago economics during that post war era.

Hardly surprising, with Friedman still lurking somewhere in my subterranean thoughts, that I was fortuitously struck by the obstructive qualities of Jennifer Burns (2003) recent biography. The volume seemed more an apotheosis of Milton Friedman than an attempt to sketch a three-dimensional portrait of the man. Previously I had assumed that only the Pope (and not some historian of intellectual ideas) had the power to vault an individual into such a heavenly position. The decided lily gilding within that book almost forcefully thrust me into the position of devil's advocate. Burns' photo-shopping of one of the very seminal economists of the twentieth century served to tarnish his very real accomplishments. Her framed portrait depended too heavily on a distinctly, selective employment of evidence.

Retrospectively, the end result of this filtering of my stray thoughts (and previously aborted chapters), revealed a common theme tying these four case studies together. As it turned out, each case could be viewed as reflecting a common rhetorical device. In fact, so common are the discovered tactics that similar methods can often be found in the work of a diverse array of economists. The generality marking their employment holds true no matter into which field these economists might choose to place their plough. Thus the specific articles (and authors) that appear in this volume remain of no intrinsic importance in and of themselves. The intention is not to turn a critical eye on the shortcomings of a targeted set of economists (and especially not on their overweening cleverness). Any one of these cases could easily have been replaced by similar instances, featuring different leading practitioners. Despite any ensuing change of cast, the same series of misleading snares and pitfalls would still make their appearance. Consequently, readers will find themselves barrelling head-first toward a series of inescapable cul-de-sacs, if they are led to view my efforts as attempts to grapple with (and criticise) definitive instances, or persons. However, I state this necessary explanatory caveat while knowing full well that it will largely be ignored by a multitude of critics and readers. (If, of course, I would ever be so bold as to assume the potential existence of such individuals.)

Case studies, especially the ones appearing here, are meant only as representative illustrations of a series of underlying issues. Both the first two instances of obfuscation (described in this volume), require conclaves of undiscerning readers (an indifference to textual meaning). Unfortunately, the potential trap noted in this preface, too easily springs open when larger concerns are casually swept aside to focus instead on individual personages (for instance, drawing a specific bead on an always controversial Phil Mirowski rather than the case he happens to illustrate). This error reverses the focus of the first case study where the tree is ignored (understanding Coase) for the sake of the forest (boosting an ideological objective by means of producing a generalisation).

In any case, a widespread misreading of the intention of this volume will at least partially indict much of the profession for too easily jumping to a convenient conclusion, while exercising only a superficial degree of comprehension. Namely, this reflects a tendency to stubbornly carve out a path noted more for its misconceptions than for its insights. Wilfully sinking into this quicksand of cross purposes manages to ignite a tedious and entirely misdirected series of fruitless debates. What would be entirely missed, if readers remain fixated on these mentioned personalities, is the purpose behind this volume. The book is deliberately focused on four rhetorical strategies, whose predictable result is mainly to obfuscate, rather than clarify, any discussion. These approaches turn out to be frequently nurtured and buttressed by a series of ideological positions covering the full political spectrum. They represent neither a medium of light, nor of insight.

A quick reminder at this point for those readers who have yet to finish their morning cup of coffee. The introduction to the book is defined and represented by its first chapter. The joys that chapter offer lie ahead for the tireless reader. Meaning that those of you who have strayed on to these pages have instead been gulled into reading a common place preface, instead of jumping headfirst into the main stream of discussion. At least from my perspective, a designated preface serves only as a device that allows authors to spout whatever nonsense that may strike their fancy. The expectation is that very few potential readers will actually prove foolish enough to bother with the trivia flaunted in these limited pages. The author here is perhaps optimistically hoping as well that those who bother to crack open the book at this preliminary point won't require prefaces or introductions to be labelled as such. The two are easily distinguishable.

However, as the author of this volume, I do feel obliged to provide a few trigger warnings to assist the faint hearted. Trigger warnings, though controversial, have become increasingly widespread, even if not universally embraced. For this volume, I reluctantly acknowledge the yearning for (or even the necessity to include) a few such red flags. Experience has painfully taught me that I often find myself working at cross purposes to other economists. My approach to writing might be deemed unconventional, or even suspect by much of the profession. In which case, I need to warn readers (especially those with deep set allegiances to the customary practises of more every-day economists), that they might very well stumble across several literary allusions within these pages. Such references have been known to repulse, annoy and antagonise a certain portion of the economics discipline. Paul Samuelson, for one, faced this particular hurdle of targeted opprobrium with stoic patience. He continued to employ such stylistics, despite being scorned for daring to display familiarity with works of a literary nature.

Such indulgence, in the judgment of these ubiquitous critics, betrays an obnoxious impulse to flaunt one's superior knowledge, education and refinement. Consequently (in the past), any such discovered allusions in Samuelson's work were duly categorised as unfortunate examples of an egoistic need to show off. Quotes (or references) of this fashion were scorned as being devoid of any obvious economic validation. But at least implicitly, such critics were conveying the singular idea that there exists but one correct way to compose an economics article. This canonical, rhetorical construction that they alone were privy to, coincidentally seemed to mirror the way in which these omnipresent critics structured their own work. Unfortunately, what such boasted stylistics might have lacked in self-assured pretentiousness was more than counter-balanced by a surplus of arrogance and dismissal. Recognising, however, the need to eschew judgment on any of my potential readers, if literary references (no matter what their source), do tend to annoy, I would suggest skipping lightly over them rather than engaging in a prolonged gnashing of one's teeth. Practising a mere modicum of tolerance may ultimately serve to reduce the vital blood pressure of any of my more tendentious readers.

Related to any discussion of writing stylistics, however, is my own ruling assumption that underwrites the entire extent of this work, namely that my readers are capable of drawing their own conclusions.[17] Consequently, a refusal to bludgeon such readers with explicit signposts and labels should not be confused with some sad attempt to imitate a bogus 'stream of consciousness' technique. What remains my only guiding star in these matters is a deliberate insistence that invited readers not be force fed with a diet of pre-packaged ideas. The intention instead is to avoid constructing a book that resembles predicable episodes rashly snatched from a seventies sitcom series.

Yet another trigger warning (kindly provided for those readers with queasy digestive systems), indicates the forthcoming presence of far too many endnotes. These gem-like meanderings will sometimes be quite lengthy. However, out of consideration for finicky readers, all of these enjoyable digressions will be forcefully exiled to the end of each chapter (as the term 'endnotes' suggests). These offerings can even be discovered at the conclusion of this lowly preface. Personally the author, given free reign over such decisions, would happily opt for footnotes. Doing so would avoid all the bothersome page flipping that endnotes entail. However, endnotes (when allowed to thrive), should make it sufficiently clear to even the least discerning reader that perusing these additions is strictly optional. If such points were unarguably vital for the unfolding of the relevant story, they would have clearly been transposed to the main body of the text. Unfortunately, even this concession may fail to satiate the anger aroused in some readers by endnotes extending beyond the length of two sentences. Their thinking appears to be that since no immediate or direct use is made of such items within the main text, any appearance of these thoughts should be briskly condemned as an example of rhetorical excess. This phobic response seems to offer no other option but to engage in a holocaust of deletion. Like witches in Salem, all endnotes would need to be driven out, drowned, or burned at the stake. Again, the stubborn underlying idea is that there is somehow a unique method of constructing and conveying economic stories. More accurately however, some economists just suffer from an overly fragile (or limited) set of sensibilities.

With the requisite trigger warnings now all in place, the inevitably acknowledgments are made to those who have kindly offered assistance in the formation and ultimate publication of this book. Especial thanks to each and every one of those individuals who patiently sat through my interviews more than two decades ago. However, there are some who have gleefully impaired my progress by paving my way with unwanted stumbling blocks.[18] To all such individuals, I can only hope that they receive their future due in a timely fashion.

Endnotes

1   Producing a book is always a challenge, one never made easier by what is, at times, an almost adversarial and inevitably convoluted contest with those factors in the process that masquerade as helpful assistants. But after surmounting the all too many challenges and snares involved in the preparation and production of this particular volume, I am, once again, tempted to endorse, if fail to always rigorously follow, the wise words (reported in the above quote) that were once uttered by that eminent author, Huckleberry Finn. If I were in fact the rational individual that I sometimes lull myself into believing, I would hold true to my purpose and cease any future attempts at writing. Unfortunately, the wisdom conveyed by first year economic textbooks is sometimes only an imperfect reflection of the world in which we are condemned to operate.

2   My Eyes Glaze Over. This phenomenon often occurs in seminars when presenters opt to bombard their stultified audience with some twenty equations per operative slide.

3   Such a simple and obvious fact required decades of teaching to become fully realised. I may be a slow learner in this regard, but then again, I'm not sure the profession, in general, recognises (or is particularly fascinated by) this modest revelation. Readers with nothing better to do might want to glance at an article, Freedman (2014), which appeared in a particularly obscure journal. (Though it might not be an exaggeration to claim that all journals dealing with economic education are by definition, obscure.)

   Oddly enough (and speaking of all things Chicago), support for my story telling approach comes from Robert Lucas (2011) in a University of Chicago commencement address (9 December 1988). Notice that decades passed before either Lucas (or some journal editor) decided that this unusually charming piece was worthy of publication.

4   Economists who desperately are driven to display degrees of scientific profundity, can often be designated as a group that has difficulty in distinguishing rigor from rigor mortis in their professional work.

5   The book somehow saw the light of day (Colander and Freedman 2018) despite my occasional bouts of obstinacy, as well as compulsive rewriting. If a reader is willing to trudge his or her way through both volumes (the 2018 effort and this curious addition to the literature), I suspect certain points of connection, or affinity, will be discovered, though at times these links are quite distant rather than closely joined. But though a similar methodology (observed rather than predictive) runs through and defines both books, a clear differentiation in their respective objectives separates the two efforts in a sufficiently discernible fashion.

6   This, at least, is my generous evaluation of these by-products. My former co-author might choose to disagree in no unambiguous fashion. Though I suspect that he will prove to be too polite to do so.

7   The issue was initially raised by my co-author, Dave Colander. My own immediate and uninspired response to Coase's tempered response rested on a reasonable assumption. Namely that any peace loving individual would desire to avoid an unwelcome confrontation, particularly one directly involving a colleague. Running afoul of Stigler's caustic wit promised a path littered with attacks and recrimination. But my instant and facile response only displayed a distinct lack of imagination and insight. To fully understand the historical specifics of the case ultimately required a better understanding of Coase's own project and objectives. Depending solely on the personal idiosyncrasies of these two economists led only to an uninspired dead-end.

8   This mystery can be catalogued, for those compelled to toy with such exercises, as a classic case of 'the dog that didn't bark.' The reference is, of course, to the classic Sherlock Holmes story of confusion, chicanery and deceit, 'Silver Blaze'.

> Gregory (Scotland Yard detective): Is there any other point to which you would wish to draw my attention?
> Holmes: To the curious incident of the dog in the night-time.
> Gregory: The dog did nothing in the night-time.
> Holmes: That was the curious incident (Doyle 1893).

9   Here, an unexpected appearance of Hitchcock's cinematic employment of the MacGuffin acts as a crucial catalyst.

10   As Charles Baudelaire insists in 'Le Cygne' (*Fleurs du mal* – 1857):

> la forme d'une ville
> Change plus vite, hélas! que le coeur d'un morte

11   For those who refused to fritter away significant portions of their youthful years, a demolition derby is a purely American invention. Such events are generally witnessed by those with a sustained predilection (and weakness), for mindless violence. As a variation of a 'last man standing' gambit, these contests pit a number of junk autos warring against one another. Each gleefully rams into the most vulnerable potential victim with the focused homicidal intention of destroying, or at least fatally demobilising, all and any one of them. The last car still moving, though by this time quite arthritically, is declared the winner. Stigler's approach then is to bash head-on into any particularly noisome opposing theories, in order to simply flatten and destroy them. Nothing slyly subtle characterises Stigler's attempts to totally demolish opposing (and personally repugnant) views.

12   Mirowski and his associates also shared the same sense of urgency when apprising the need to annihilate opponents judged to be critically dangerous.

13   The October 1993 edition of *The Journal of Political Economy* is largely devoted to remembrances of George Stigler, who had long served as one of its editors. Thomas Sowell provides a short memoir of his student experience with George Stigler. He was a graduate student in the economics department while attending the University of Chicago. (Sowell also managed to survive having Stigler as his dissertation chair – barely.)

> Few, if any, areas of economics, have a much confusion, circular reasoning, definitional traps and fervent nonsense as industrial organization. It was the perfect place for Stigler to conduct a Demolition Derby. Nor was he hesitant about the task. Theories like "monopolistic competition" and "countervailing power," which were treated reverently at Harvard (where they originated), were eviscerated by Stigler (Sowell 1993:787).

14   An argument can be mounted that Stigler's sharp wit provided an extra (perhaps misleading) gloss to his hard earned reputation. Certainly Mark Perlman, who co-wrote (along with Charles McCann) the definitive obituary on George Stigler in the *Economic Journal* (1993), held a somewhat sceptical view of Stigler's actual talent. Perlman was a graduate student at Columbia University during George Stigler's faculty tenure there.

> I think that I agree with your points on our Boy George, but I wish you were not so intense on the topic. Stigler's attacks are now mainline economics; and I think that the way to counter the mainline is simply to laugh at it. "Surely one cannot take Professor Stigler, the Nobel Laureate, really seriously – he is clever, even amusing, but to those of us to whom the good Lord has never revealed The Light, Stigler's approach is on the scale of sophistication (1 to 10) debatably 6.9 although on days when I feel stimulated by callow youth, I've even been known to give him a 7.1. My trouble, which invariably I later regret, is that I am always overgenerous to glibness."
>
> Socialist rhetoric has always lacked humour, a most unfortunate aspect of the socialist Weltanschauung.
>
> All kind regards.
>
> Sincerely yours,
>
> Mark Perlman (e-mail to the author, 16 October 1995).

15   Throughout this volume, 'Team Mirowski' is a shorthand that will serve to denote Philip Mirowski and his like-minded associates. In particular, the relevant colleagues in thought will turn out to be Robert Van Horn and Edward Nik-Khah, who share many of his own concerns.

16   Graham Richardson, a noted Australian politician of the 1980s, defended his skull cracking tactics as simply doing whatever it took to achieve a

desired end. In truth, the lingering suspicion was that he immensely enjoyed crushing opponents. The sport enjoyed by doing so (cracking skulls), was a genuine end in itself.

17 The desire throughout this volume is to treat readers as adults, rather than as toddlers with short attention spans. Achieving this goal requires eschewing the oft favoured formula of telling readers what you intend to do, what you are doing and then what you have done.

18 To paraphrase Nietzsche, whatever doesn't kill me makes me increasingly annoyed.

References

Baudelaire, C. (1857). *Les Fleurs du mal*. Paris: Auguste Poulet-Malassis.

Burns, J. (2023). *Milton Friedman – The Last Conservative*. New York: Farrar, Giroux and Straus.

Coase, R. H. (1960). "The problem of social cost", *The Journal of Law & Economics*. 3(1): 1–44.

Colander, D. and Craig, F. (2018). *Where Economics Went Wrong*. Princeton: Princeton University Press.

Doyle, A. C. (1893). "Silver blaze", in *The Memoirs of Sherlock Holmes*. London: George Newnes.

Freedman, C. (2014). "1001 micro nights", *Australasian Journal of Economics Education*. 11(1): 21–43.

Friedman, M. (1953). "The methodology of positive economics", in *Essays in Positive Economics*. Chicago: University of Chicago Press, pp. 3–47.

Lucas, R. Jr. (2011). "What economists do", *Journal of Applied Economics*. 14(1): 1–4.

McCann, C. Jr. and Mark, P. (1993). "On thinking about George Stigler", *The Economic Journal*. 103(419): 994–1014.

Sowell, T. (1993). "A student's eye view of George Stigler", *The Journal of Political Economy*. 101(5): 784–792.

Twain, M. (1884/2009). *The Adventures of Huckleberry Finn*. Camberwell, Victoria, Australia: Penguin Books.

Contents

Paving the Road to Hell –
An Economist's Guide[1]

L'enfer est plein de bonnes volontés ou désirs (Saint Bernard of Clairvaux (c. 1150)).

Like most of my scattered writing, the impetus for this volume came unexpectedly, perhaps even in what should be labelled as an almost random fashion. As noted, in respect of the many readers who justifiably think looking at a preface is time wasted, here follows a bit of a confession to explain the fashion in which this book happened to arise. The volume grew unexpectedly from a stand-alone (and originally quite a lengthy) article. The initial result was a case study that focused on a particular aspect of Ronald Coase's work. The actual germination of the idea expressed was nurtured by a rather expedient demand. At an ill-planned moment I found myself in want of a conference presentation. That impetus created a quick, if not entirely expert explanation of a key aspect of Coase's most well-known work. To accomplish this end, I resorted to a time honoured academic tactic. Namely, by imitating any good environmentalist, I recycled and reconstructed some previously discarded jottings. These discards originated in discussion, as well as a number of preliminary drafts (written as possible chapters), of a joint effort I undertook with Dave Colander (2018).[2]

Unfortunately (or perhaps fortunately), each of these proposed additions to that volume turned out, on later inspection, not to sufficiently align with the developing theme of that co-authored book. But if nothing else, a career misspent endeavouring to make my way through the cul-de-sacs of economics has sharpened my instinctive habit of thrift. Consequently, when in a state of desperation, the orphaned material of my previous efforts were re-examined, I was surprised to discover, within these bits and pieces, a certain heretofore unrecognized theme. Such a discovery should hardly have produced a frisson of either shock or pleasure, given that certain consistent and underlying concerns often dominate the thoughts and efforts of many practising economists.

Therefore, given some careful analysis, these themes (with only a smidgen of prodding) managed to bubble their way to the surface of my jumbled thoughts. In fact, these initial oddments were no hodgepodge of misrelated themes. Specifically, the common pentameter discernible throughout, though appearing more as a palimpsest rather than chiselled for all to discern, emerged as a thread emphasizing the pitfalls common to most practising economists. But whether the presented material (the four case studies within this volume) would be examined judiciously (and not superficially) by potential readers was always far from clear. A rudimentary examination might characterise those discarded drafts as being minor explorations in the neglected field of history of economic thought.

But though the material is historically based, these studies proved to have a much wider application if removed from that narrowly restrictive context. The book does, in fact, focus on case studies from the history of economic thought, a field which remains a rather marginal and bedraggled neighbourhood that perhaps only a complete devotee could truly love. But fortunately, the cardinal sins elucidated and exposed in the following four case studies apply more generally. Its inherent topicality extends to work encompassed by any area of economic analysis. Besides, all phases of economics eventually become history, as will those assiduously engaged in its creation as a discipline. Dismissing work simply because of its historical nature is no more than an easy, but definitely unfruitful, option to embrace.

The first then of these four moments (case studies) in the history of economics dissects what appears to be the kerfuffle caused by mistaking a MacGuffin for a theorem, or what happens when papers are read to suit an *a priori* perspective.[3] But the more extended, underlying theme throughout the Coase case study aims to explore the dangers that adhere to an obsessive impulse to categorize economists and their work. Meaning that readers have nurtured a habit of coming to a work with a fixed vision. They repeatedly err by doing so, rather than shouldering the responsibility of carefully sifting through the words and individual objectives of each article or book. Only by doing so can a deep understanding of the intended meaning enclosed within each work be achieved. In contrast, the act of pigeon-holing nurtures quite the opposite result. Instead of enlightenment, an approach of this nature provides a non-shiftable buttress serving to support prior preconceptions.

This compulsive cataloguing of economists into distinct and competing tribes leads most readers astray. Any obsessive sorting of this type manages to provide the profession with a ersatz sense of comprehension. Meaning that economists should never confuse themselves with botanists. Non-ending division gains neither insight nor understanding, but instead tends to discourage careful reading and analysis. To reiterate, the available alternative to approaching each paper de novo, is a type of gravitational laxity which tends to fortify any pre-existing view (despite the existence of counter arguments and evidence). Consequently, cataloguing authors into separable tribes provides definitive blinders that serve to hinder possible insights. Theories and articles by designated opponents are simply dismissed, once their tribe of origin is determine. This lazy option continues to appeal to readers despite the fact that the assignment of any author to a particular group is often carelessly and inexactly accomplished.

Unfortunately, bad habits are not so easily broken. Keynes in his landmark work, began by describing his 'long struggle of escape' (1964:viii), a sort of confession about the process of writing *The General Theory*.[4] The point made being that we all operate out of convenient and comfortable conventions and traditions. These mental easements become such a part of the environment in which we operate that we tend to cease being aware of our own prior convictions, or how insidiously they mould (and can shape) our work.

> Now, what you have to understand with somebody like Allen Wallis, and so to a degree those people who were in his circle, is that Allen Wallis had the sharpest priors – I'm using the language of Bayesian probability – of anybody I ever knew.[5] Almost no new data could change his view for this reason. On the other hand, if he thought of somebody as a dangerous, or an incompetent thinker, but Jimmy Savage[6] assured him that the man was very smart and had good judgement that carried more weight with Allen Wallis than a two-year study of the person's vitae and an audit of his writings. There's an in-group of the good guys and the much larger out-group (Conversation with Paul Samuelson, October 1997).

But this is a path that can all too easily lead to serious distortions in the way in which we observe and calculate our empirical data. As Keynes claims, it is a struggle to escape from the allure of received wisdom (and easy habits). But it is always equally a battle worth attempting. Awareness then of exactly what composes our *a priori* certainties becomes a crucial bulwark of theoretical or empirical reasoning. In fact, if economists wish to avoid the decided drawback of lazy thinking, the intrinsic bias associated with categorical perspectives needs to be explicitly recognised and reduced. Such ideological convictions, when too strongly held and ascribed to, will unfortunately colour all and any evidence. Whatever might be discovered within a theory or article will only manage to buttress positions which are already firmly established. Bluntly speaking, in such cases, no possible (or imaginable) evidence will ever sway these given *a priori* positions. The goal of reading becomes a search and destroy mission rather than an exploration of different (and even opposing) approaches and thoughts. Therefore empirical research for such determined advocates like George Stigler and Gardiner Means could only serve to re-enforce their pre-established (and diametrically opposite) visions of how the world worked.

> People take particular stands early in their career and they're steadfast, I have to admit that. They are not wishy-washy. No amount of empirical evidence will persuade them to change to a different point of view. Would there be some evidence that would have persuaded George on this? I'm not sure. He believed, he really believed that prices responded to short-run market demand. Was there any evidence that would have caused George not to believe that prices responded to short-run market demand? I can't help you on this. I don't have any reason to believe that he did believe there was any evidence for that. But it was not a question that came up in our daily work.[7]
>
> *Because, on the other side, it is hard to see what would have persuaded Gardiner Means on the opposite side.*
>
> Gardiner Means was also not a man likely to change his views (Conversation with James Kindahl October 1997).[8]

But as indicated, categorical thinking (and reading with an intent to destroy), tend to bleed into one another. The boundary between the two rhetorical strategies is at points quite fluid. Consequently, dealing too exclusively in the broad but comforting world of convenient categories and classifications can assist in destroying an opponent's work, while dodging the core issues actually raised in a specific paper. This form of faux criticism (claiming to be exercising a neutral, critical eye) forms the basis for the second of the volume's case studies.[9] Thus Stigler felt free to savage Chamberlin's method of aggregation, while employing not dissimilar methods when it suited his purposes. In an immediate respect, there is a severe aggregation problem which stains the entire profession. Stigler could scoff (in the peculiarly lethal fashion he had mastered) at Chamberlin for his concept of monopolistic markets (and the incipient aggregation problem of jamming together unlikely market sectors). But Stigler blithely employed the same discredited method in his minimum wage paper (Stigler 1946). There he blithely talked about a non-existent aggregate labour market, when examining the effect that imposing a minimum wage level might exert on such a mythical market.

In other words, Stigler could gleefully crucify Chamberlin for the sin of aggregating incompatible markets, while not being fussed by falling into much the same trap. There is of course nothing resembling an aggregate labour market, but rather lots of small, local ones, namely different types of labour performed in very different markets. To paraphrase Stigler's attack in his Chamberlin (1949) lecture, how is it possible to aggregate the demand for bar tenders in Kansas City with the demand for neurosurgeons in West Palm Beach, Florida. The cumulative effect of a minimum wage could cause the effects on the multitude of individual markets to largely cancel each other out or to augment the result. Moreover, the result would logically change as the structure of the individual markets altered over time. Like Chamberlin, Stigler is convinced that such a heuristic simplification can provide some useful insight. Those harbouring unkind thoughts might suspect that a double standard was being implicitly employed in this case.

In fact Stigler, though a stickler for consistency in theory and thought (as well as nursing a burning desire for theoretical comprehensiveness), seemed capable of harbouring certain blind spots. Such convenient moments might occur, if by claiming them, Stigler advanced his agenda. (Here it is impossible to evaluate the extent that such behaviour was done consciously.) For instance, Stigler gave explicit credit to his sometime colleague, Harold Demsetz (1968) for demolishing to a great extent monopoly theory. In his analysis, Demsetz did define the standard approach of market competition as being observationally pervasive. But he extended competition within monopoly markets as well, by establishing a sort of end around the intuitive meaning of the word.[10] Though competition might be entirely absent within the market, there might be competition for the monopoly position defining that market. In other words, even though there might be room in a market for only one firm to effectively operate, that position could be open to competitive bidding. Competition in this case consists of contracting out to those who prevail in the auctioning off of those desired positions. If the bidding is competitive, Demsetz boldly claimed that the resulting outcomes would be similar to those achieved by the dynamics of competitive markets.[11]

Yet one peculiar aspect of Demsetz' mechanism (required to yield a competitive equivalent result), bears an eerie (and no doubt unwanted) resemblance to John Kenneth Galbraith's much earlier construction of countervailing power (1952). This idea was mercilessly demolished, if not cruelly ridiculed, back in 1954 by the same George Stigler at an American Economic Association meeting. There he dismissed Galbraith's concoction in a presentation entitled 'An Economist Plays at Blocs'.[12] Stigler's memory (like those possessing the sharpest of minds), can be fortuitously selective without any deliberate or conscious strategy underlining such actions. In his auto-biography, Stigler praises his protégé, Demsetz, for a supposed Galbraithian trespass (the employment of countervailing power) committed many decades before.

In effect, Stigler when sensing a credible threat to his conception of price theory, sought to demolish, rather than to understand a given work. Thus he would search for any weakness or bit of sloppy writing hidden in any presentation. If possible he would construct a strawman version of the actual opposing theory, one which he could easily (and at times gleefully) disintegrate. In something of a deliberate flip, I indicate how Mirowski and his associates have attempted to employ Stigler's own strategy against his own work and that of his colleagues. But as with Stigler, this search and destroy technique delivers more heat than light, controversy rather than insight.

As the third offering of the volume's constrained bounty, Chicago's obfuscation strategies are explored further. A given article is capable of containing an objective not easily discerned by the casual reader. In essence, the work is something of a wolf in sheep's clothing, or as labelled in this volume, a poison apple. A less digestible theory (or insight), is conveyed veiled by a seemingly obvious assumption. To elucidate this idea, Friedman's famous (and only) work on methodology (1953) is yanked out of the mothballs and closely examined. The focus is not on the argument that can be discovered in the essay itself, but rather the precise target of Friedman's methodological excursion. The rhetoric and analysis encased in the article becomes (under a broader perspective), merely the means to a more fundamental end. To discover (or at least partially reveal) such intentions is that chapter's objective, providing the case study with an illustrative value., This goal is attempted by explicitly ignoring the accumulated literature that has evolved, since it deals almost entirely with Friedman's talking points and contentions. These located in his methodological pastiche need to be largely ignored, if Friedman's operative objective is to be discovered and analysed.[13] The explicit issues raise in the essay act more as a traditional red herring that throw the inquisitive hunter off Friedman's hidden intention,

The cascade of strangled arguments (and counter-arguments) that followed the publication of Friedman's work reflected (unintentionally and largely only distantly) a buried agenda that lay permanently camouflaged. Friedman's actual (as opposed to ostensible) purpose behind this bit of methodological wading, remained unimpeachably obscure throughout the ensuing debate. Stated bluntly, the essay was meant to reshape the profession's agenda. The operative intention was to effectively harness a growing methodological debate (circa the late 1940s – early 1950s), deemed to be dangerous. Friedman aimed to redirect professional debate away from attempts to challenge the validity of commonly employed assumptions. Thus the reality of such controversial assertions became (under his direction), largely immaterial. To be precise, those assumptions supporting the theoretical scaffolding of Chicago style price theory required, not exactly, shoring up, but attention needed to be diverted away from testing the viability of all such struts.[14]

Friedman in a sense simply extended Stigler's (1949) brief gloss on the issue. No matter who one wishes to award a major share of credit for these ideas, upon examination the end result seems more of a joint project, for which Friedman received the lion's share of credit. His name alone marks the essay that moved the profession.[15] That the purpose of these methodological musings was to act as a catalyst shifting the direction and tone of debate is best supported by the fact that neither Friedman nor Stigler deigned to be sucked into the ensuing maelstrom of debate that followed publication. Mission accomplished, the ensuing discussion encapsulated little of interest or enchantment to either one.[16]

Stigler, in fact would come to drop his heavily Knight influenced methodological chapter from the opening phase of subsequent editions of his textbook.[17] If anything, such a continuing omission reflected a distinct lack of any abiding interest in that area of inquiry, as was equally the case for Friedman. Realistically, his textbook restructuring can also be construed as yet another step in his ongoing distancing from the views of his teacher, Frank Knight.

> When I [Gary Becker] was a student I thought Knight was great, but my opinion of Knight went down over time. The reason why mine went down, I knew was the same as George's. Knight makes a lot of strong assertions, but when you ask 'why, why' a lot of his things don't hold up so well. I think Stigler began to get disappointed (Gary Becker conversation with the author, October 1997).

His relationship to Knight perhaps raises at least a faint parallel with his stance *vis-à-vis* Alfred Marshall. Stigler, throughout his career, can be described as remaining a loyal, but faithless supporter of Knight as he was of Marshall (see Hart 2020).[18] Though perhaps in the case of Knight, Stigler was far more explicit in refuting (and discarding) Knight's approaches (particularly his income distribution ideas). His stance on Marshall can be classified as something of a continued misconception, rather than an accurate rejection. In the case of Knight, Stigler not only at times manage to misconceive Knight's meaning, but also based his rejection of Knight on his own constructed misconceptions.[19] Simply put, these ideas ran counter to his own viewpoints. Though his takes on Knight (as with Marshall) always build on what appear to be reasonable starting points.

As with Stigler, Friedman also often lulls a reader's suspicions by offering shiny and easily digestible assertions that ultimately leads one to embrace more questionable assumptions.[20] The goal when creating such poison apples is never to enlighten potential readers, but to close off controversial debate while guiding them step by step to a desired conclusion. As this volume attempts to elucidate, rhetorical obfuscation isn't identical with economic enlightenment. The objective when employing such strategy (as already indicated) is one of creating the heat of debate rather than the light of insight. In essence the goal is to confuse rather than clarify. Such tactics are intrinsically intended only to distract from controversial and opposing ideas.

The last (and late comer to this list of obfuscation) is perhaps an illegitimate second cousin to the 'strawman construction' detailed in the second essay. Though it depends on a bit of prestidigitation on the part of an author, rather than a reader's sleight of hand. In the biography discussed (Burns 2023), the writer starts off with a preconceived picture of the subject of her work (Milton Friedman). The mechanics of such constructions are not unlike the workings of a jigsaw puzzle. A fixed and inviolate frame is filled with predetermined pieces. When properly fitted together (recreating the deviser's original plan), that precise design (or picture) is predictably assembled. In much the same way, Burns shapes her evidence (while discarding those which maintain an awkward fit), in order to serve up Friedman as a hero of sorts. In doing so, she does Friedman himself no favours. Better to display all vices and virtues than to serve up a confectioner's delight, suppressing what lies beneath the glossily produced surface.[21]

When taken then as a whole, the four cases are intended to display the disruptions achieved by employing obfuscation instead of transparency. In essence, nothing positive is accomplished when intentions (and meanings) remain hidden (whether deliberately or not). Readers and writers both let each other down by diverting understanding into camouflaged cul-de-sacs.

Endnotes

1   The author is well aware that there is a difference between the number one and the number two. For those fond of multiplicative reasoning, the latter figure is twice the former. No doubt perspicacious (and morally offended) readers have therefore jumped on the fact that this is the second preface. Or to be blunt, that there are twice as many prefaces as are usually discovered in such volumes. No doubt some will take great umbrage at this flagrant disregard of the rules of publishing. For most readers, one preface is already one too many. Adding an additional effort is viewed as clearly violating an unwritten law of good sense and judicious moderation. But in reality, there is no hard and set reason why an author can't indulge in as many prefaces as he or she sees fit. Unless they are excessively egomaniacal, no reasonable author would expect anyone to actually read a preface. These written oddities survive more as throwaway pages, which can equally exist to entertain the writer even more than the put upon reader. Consequently, I feel no shame at adding an additional preface. To emphasise, readers are under absolutely no obligation to even skim through them. Simply flip through to the introduction and little, if anything will actually be lost.

2   I may be misleading the reader a bit here. The Coase case study derived from that noted co-authored book (Colander and Freedman – 2018). Thus its immediate origin aligns with that of the other two case studies. However, the Coase case represents the resolution of a question left largely unanswered in that volume. Namely, a certain challenge posed by Dave Colander for which I supplied a rather flimsy response. However, that two of the other case studies began as discarded chapters as previously mentioned remains largely correct. The final case study came more as an extremely negative reaction to the Burn's (2023) biography.

3   For those readers lacking cinematic impulses, a MacGuffin is a term beloved by film-maker Alfred Hitchcock. The term encapsulates the idea of a filmic device or catalyst that facilitates the plot of a film without itself being of any moment in and of itself. Thus, the actual statue of the Maltese Falcon in the film of the same name is of no import. The figure could have been the Armenian Bear (or the Mongolian Monkey), without changing anything essential to the film itself. However, without the existence of such a mythical figure, the film's plot would have been left dead in the water. The characters in the film need a central motivation, which the supposedly fabulous statue manages to supply.

4   The entire paragraph is worth repeating since Keynes suggests the rare mindset required to escape the tentacles of conventional discernment that would otherwise impede any productive progress. Clearly the process of attempting to uproot ingrained habits of thought (either in one's own minds or others), is not a task to be taken lightly.

> The composition of this book has been for the author a long struggle of escape, and so must the reading of it be for most readers if the author's assault upon them is to be successful, – a struggle of escape from habitual modes of thought and expression. The ideas which are here expressed so laboriously are extremely simple and should be obvious. The difficulty lies, not in the new ideas, but in escaping from the old ones, which ramify, for those brought up as most of us have been, into every corner of our minds (Keynes, 1964:viii).

5   Allen Wallis was a Chicago graduate student at the same time as George Stigler and Milton Friedman. (Wallis and Stigler were together 1933–1935.) Though Wallis, like Friedman, never received doctorates from Chicago. All held similar economic and political outlooks, initially viewing themselves as equivalent to a three musketeers' type of friendship. Upon reuniting at Chicago in 1958 they composed this bit of doggerel.

> Twenty-five years for the tale to unfold
> Yo-ho-ho and again there are three
> Walgreen was good and Kempton was bold
> Yo-ho-ho and again there are three (Friedman 1993:771).

Though perhaps, given all the 'yo-ho-ho' business, they saw themselves as more closely resembling a pack of buccaneers.

6 Jimmy Savage (Leonard James Savage) was a statistician who co-authored (with Milton Friedman) a seminal paper on subjective probability (1948).

7 James (Jim) Kindahl (1970) was one of Stigler's co-authors. Kindahl and I dove behind the curtain provided by published work to explore how the sausage of economic research is at times heavily spiced with previously marinated ideological beliefs.

8 Published in *The American Economic Review* in 1946, this analysis of the effect of the minimum wage on employment is in fact a response to the work of Richard Lester (1946), (The exchange is made somewhat notable by having Stigler largely talk past Richard Lester's concerns, while backing his contentions with some curious statistical analysis.) The Chamberlin piece published in 1949 was initially delivered as one of five lectures to the associated good and great of the London School of Economics and Politics in 1948. The proximity of dates shows that even the sharpest of minds can surrender to cognitive dissonance when the moment is propitious.

9 The actual case study turns the tables a bit with the focus targeting the Chicago School, while using Chicago's own burnt earth approach. Phillip Mirowski (and those closely associated with him), happily supply the ammunition for this sustained attack on Friedman, Stigler and Director.

10 The idea is that technology may create natural monopolies where operating one big firm yields that most efficient result, as long as the firm is somehow restricted from commanding monopoly pricing. A classic example is a public utility, like a company tasked with supplying a city's water.

11 Such a competitive outcome, according to Demsetz, would be achieved by auctioning off the monopoly position for x number of years. In a competitive auction, the winning bid would have to offer reliable, quality service at the equivalent of a competitive price. Failure to meet such contractual standards would mean penalties and loss of any future contract. The supposition is that a correctly drawn and monitored contract could achieve the same desired result as that associated with competitive markets.

12 For those desiring an understanding of the search and destroy method of faux criticism, Stigler's 1954 presentation provides an excellent starting point.

13 For those so inclined, an almost forensic, detailed trudge through Friedman's extended argument can be found in a relatively recent work by Squires (2018). Though, the debates over the work go back for many decades.

14 The tradition of dismissing, rather than addressing, a question is something of a radical strategy that would continue to survive at Chicago. As one simple example, Eugene Fama (1980) in a well cited paper dealt with the principle-agent conflict endemic to corporate life by simply denying

the existence of any such agency relationship. By banishing existence, any fruitful debate must automatically die as well. Consequently, in the case of Friedman, by dismissing the credibility of assumptions as a non-issue, that debate could also be dismissed out of hand. The hope was to redirect discussion to the points constructed by Friedman (and of course Stigler).

15 Milton Friedman himself was not reluctant about awarding his close friend George Stigler his rightful due.

> Milton Friedman: I had written the methodology paper, which was later formally published. This preceded, by three or four years, the earlier versions. And he refers in one of those lectures to the fact that we had been talking about it.
> *Yes. And how influential were you in each other's thinking on this matter?*
> Milton Friedman: We were very influential. I think there's no doubt that my work would have been different if I hadn't been influenced by George and George's work would have been different if he hadn't been influenced by me (Conversation with Milton Friedman, Rose Friedman and Aaron Director, August 1997).

The crucial exchange of letters between the two bears out the irrefutable collaboration.

> In a way, the better the hypothesis the greater the extent to which it simplifies, the more sharply will its assumptions depart from reality (Letter from Milton Friedman to George Stigler, November 19, 1947 in Hammond and Hammond 2006:65).

As Mark Blaug (Stigler's dissertation student at Columbia) remarks, in class, Stigler plugged this point of view.

> It was a kind of (what shall I call it) a poor man's Popperism. I mean it is basically Karl Popper's falsification with a tremendous emphasis on prediction, etc (Conversation with Mark Blaug, April 1998).

How Stigler ultimately felt about Friedman garnering all the attention in this regard is unknowable. As always, Stigler guarded his inner feelings carefully, dismissing any hint of jealously though Mark Blaug suspected some residual grain of resentment remained.

> And I later realised, discovered this because I asked him, that he and Milton Friedman talked about all these things. Milton however just ran away with it. George Stigler always slightly resented the fact that the entire world learned all this stuff from Milton Friedman, when in fact, if you look at the order of precedence, George Stigler was slightly ahead in this sort of attitude to the testing of hypotheses (Conversation with Mark Blaug, April 1998).

In a similar fashion, Stigler dismissed with a joke Friedman's 1948 Chicago appointment, a position presumably assured to Stigler.

> So the professorship was offered to Milton Friedman, and President Colwell and I had launched the new Chicago School. We both deserve credit for that appointment, although for a long time I was not inclined to share it with Colwell (Stigler 1988:40).

16 Celebrating 50 years of this truly seminal work in 2003 at the annual AEA conference, Milton Friedman (connected by phone to the relevant session), could blithely affirm the views he expressed 50 years earlier. Those who listened carefully could easily infer that not only did his position remain adamant, but that perhaps he hadn't given much, if any, thought to the issue in half a century.

17 David Kamerschen and Deepa Sridhar (2009) produced an interesting examination of the various editions of Stigler's textbook, noting particular changes and the reasons that generated them

18 Chicago, under the Friedman-Stigler aegis, prided itself as one of the lone outposts still upholding the economic verities revealed by Alfred Marshall.

> Or for that matter in England, where the conventional kind of Marshallian price theory went to hell. I mean Marshall invented a lot of that stuff. [laughs] Yet it was gone by World War 2. You couldn't learn it there. You had to come to the US to learn about it. That was shocking.
> *Stigler certainly saw himself in the Marshallian tradition.*
> Yeah. Friedman too. All those Micro-Economists, and I guess I'm a student of theirs, feel that way. I think younger people don't feel themselves so attached to that tradition. They are more concerned with the strategic aspects of theory. They're attracted to political economy, game theory and so on. They've become fairly divorced from that Marshallian tradition (Conversation with Sherwin Rosen – October 1997).

In Stigler's dissertation (later his 1941 published work), he makes this unabashed admiration clear.

> Alfred Marshall ranks so high among the greatest figures in Anglo-Saxon economics that it is still almost presumptuous to praise his accomplishments, and indeed there is little need for doing so … Marshall was almost incomparably superior to his immediate predecessors and his early contemporaries in the profundity and originality of his thought, and in the breadth of his vision (Stigler 1941:61).

Yet, not unlike his view of Coase (or of Smith), Stigler somehow moulded what he found in Marshall's writing to buttress his own *a priori* perspective. Stigler seemed to become somewhat peeved when he discovered elements in Marshall of which he heartily disapproved. "Was it expedient to attempt to achieve (as Marshall did) a high degree of realism, without first establishing the very much simpler theory of stationary economics" (Stigler 1941:63). As Hart points out:

> Stigler was well aware that Marshall's 'economic biology Mecca' was incompatible with his own agenda t promote, market and defend the traditional theory of competitive price theory. Despite being a staunch defender of Marshall's heritage, Stigler epitomised the faithless follower of Marshall's tradition (Hart 2020:411).

19 Stigler adamantly rejected any redistributive policy. His direct reasoning, from early on (in his dissertation chapter on Clark), insisted that such efforts must necessarily change incentives for the worse. For that reason he defended productivity ethics (the consequence of competitive markets) as yielding not only efficient, but equitable outcomes. Thus he rejected what would seem to be Knight's obvious objections to such results. For one, he took exception to Knight's claim that income is distributed largely according to inheritance and luck. Stigler would have none of this and simply ridiculed Knight's position. (Though it might be argued that Knight's position aligns more closely with common observation.)

> The fact that more than skill and effort go into remuneration – that in Knight's example bearded women get good circus jobs simply by not shaving – is not enough to dismiss productivity ethics (Stigler 1982:19).

20 Friedman, a master of debate (and exceedingly quick on his feet), would try to trap an opponent by initially obtaining an agreement on a seemingly non-controversial assumption (what is referred to in the volume as a poison apple).

> But I always said, if you want to win an argument with Milton, you have to disagree with his first premise. When he says one and one is two, you have to say, "no". [laughter] Because, from then on Milton will not make a mistake in logic, he will present some overwhelming evidence and he will be witty and charming and you *will* be devastated. I mean there are people who are just very convincing presenters (Conversation with Claire Friedland, October 1997).

21 Filmgoers with see parallels here with David Lynch's classic film, *Blue Velvet*.

References

Burns, J. (2023). *Milton Friedman – The Last Conservative*. New York: Farrar, Straus and Giroux.

Demsetz, H. (1968). "Why regulate utilities", *Journal of Law & Economics*. 11(1): 55–65.

Fama, E. (1980). "Agency problems and the theory of the firm", *Journal of Political Economy*. 88(2): 288–307.

Friedman, M. and Leonard, J. S. (1948). "The utility analysis of choices involving risk", *Journal of Political Economy*. 56(4): 279–304.

Friedman, M. (1953). *Essays in Positive Economics*. Chicago: University of Chicago Press.

Friedman, M. (1993). "George Stigler a personal reminiscence", *Journal of Political Economy*. 101(5): 768–773.

Galbraith, J. K. (1952). *American Capitalism: The Concept of Countervailing Power*. Boston: Houghton Mifflin.

Galbraith, J. K. (1954). "Countervailing power", *American Economic Review Papers and Proceedings*. 44(2): 1–6.

Hammond, J. D. and Claire, H. H. (eds.) (2006). *Making Chicago Price Theory*. London: Routledge.

Hart, N. (2020). "George Stigler: Marshall's Loyal, but faithless follower", in Craig, F. (ed.) *George Stigler: Enigmatic Price Theorist of the Twentieth Century*. London: Palgrave Macmillan, pp. 391–421.

Kamerschen, D. and Deepa, S. (2009). "The theory of [competitive] price according to George J. Stigler", *Journal of the History of Economic Thought*. 31(2): 181–200.

Keynes, J. M. (1964). *The General Theory of Employment, Interest and Money*. New York and London: Harcourt Brace Jovanovich.

Lester, R. (1946). "Wage diversity and its theoretical implications", *American Economic Review*. 28(3): 152–159.

Stigler, G. J. (1941). *Production and Distribution Theories*. New York: Macmillan.

Stigler, G. J. (1946). "The economics of minimum wage legislation", *The American Economic Review*. 36(3): 358–365.

Stigler, G. J. (1949). "Monopolistic competition in retrospect", in *Five Lectures on Economic Problems*. London: Longmans, Green & Co. Ltd., pp. 12–24.

Stigler, G. J. (1954). "The economist plays with blocs," *American Economic Review Papers and Proceedings*. 44(2): 7–14.

Stigler, G. J. (1982). "The ethics of competition: The unfriendly critics", in *The Economist as Preacher*. Chicago: University of Chicago Press, pp. 14–27.

Stigler, G. J. (1988). *Memoirs of an Unregulated Economist*. New York: Basic Books.

Stigler, G. J. and James, K. (1970). *The Behavior of Industrial Prices*. Washington: NBER Books.

Failure to Communicate:
The Not So Gentle Art of Talking
Past One Another

Another damned, thick, square book! Always scribble, scribble, scribble! Eh, Mr. Gibbon? (Attributed to Prince William Henry, Duke of Gloucester and Edinburgh, 1781, upon receiving the second (or third, or possibly both) volume(s) of *The History of the Decline and Fall of the Roman Empire* from the author.)

'Yikes!' as any self-respecting economist would be reluctant to exclaim, "Not another contentious scribbler eager to detail the disreputable shortcomings of the economics profession. An unwelcomed and undesired malcontent intent on displaying these mostly fabricated faults in all their many-hued colours. Ho, tedious hum" would be the response grudgingly elicited from most of the tribe of practising economists. Even worse (and far less interesting), the author of these pages seems determined to (at least occasionally) root around in the historical dust for answers. Presenting potential readers with a rationale for simply dismissing a book (in this fashion) is never strategic. Nor is it the author's intention. But in fact, such a negative categorisation would be entirely misleading. Perhaps ironically, a careless rejection of that kind would serve to perfectly demonstrate the problems discussed in this volume.

At odds with such predictable assumptions, the question posed within these numerous pages focuses on the role transparency plays in economic writing (or more precisely its dour side – obfuscation). That reduces my initial task to simply convincing readers that this is not yet another standard critical volume larded with the usual carping about the shortcomings of the profession. Instead, the communication blockage at the heart of the described problems serves only as a literal drag, one that inhibits the the progress that the profession should be hoping to see. But unfortunately, the very sensitive nature of this volume's critical edge almost insures that it will be entirely disregarded. Questioning the essential reading and writing agility of the profession (claiming that it is subpar) seldom composes a winning strategy, or at least not for those seeking the sweet rewards of recognition and acclaim. Consequently, a tendency towards obfuscation (either intentionally or not) continues to hinder fundamental flows of ideas, since these unsavoury faults are too often left basically unexamined. Transparency is often honoured only in the breech. My intent then is not to engage in an indulgent outing of nit-picking but to raise some serious doubts about communicative levels residing in the discipline.

Moreover, the method chosen to explore these neglected regions hardly strengthens the revealed argument. By definition, any use of case studies (as occurs in the following chapters) as an explanatory method unfortunately tends to place the historical narratives in the past. That is (by definition) when such events occurred. There is no escaping time, even for (and amongst) the striving ranks of academic economists. Unfortunately, a seeming option of setting a case study in a future period would turn any effort into science fiction, which is a territory best left unexplored. The danger however of directly employing past economic efforts almost inevitably places such a discussion in a dusty (and largely ignored) bin labelled history of economic thought. But this is exactly the narrow categorisation that I am hoping to avoid and disavow. The very label induces what is commonly known as a confirmation bias. Readers tend to find exactly what they expect to discover when steered (*a priori*) in a selected direction. Avoiding the facile label 'history of economic thought' within this context becomes vital, if misinterpretation is to be avoided. Employing that defining term has the unfortunate effect of putting a narrow focus on what is in fact a broader work.[1] The issues discussed in these case studies are not meant to be viewed as simple historical artefacts. The problems discussed via these case studies, as I hope to demonstrate, still actively plague the profession.

Moreover, in the recent past, such critical judgements (or what has sneeringly been known as fault finding) have seldom been met with anything resembling an enthusiastic response. Certainly, they are rarely honoured within the narrow boundaries that define the discipline. Sadly (or perhaps not so sadly), this distinctly tepid response reflects the widespread view that such repeated attacks are nothing more than a flow of bilious and interminable outpourings lacking any serious content. Even worse, they appear to lack any viable conclusive solutions to the posed infirmities. Consequently, the bulk of these previous critical efforts have threatened to unintentionally mimic the actions of that liver-loving eagle (a masquerading and transformed Zeus), featured in Greek mythology. The semblance can be discerned in the repetitive nature of these actions, critical as well as mythical. Both of them, no matter how often repeated, refuse to yield a conclusive result. (Though in the mythical alternative, the inflicted pain and suffering can be counterpoised to the ineffectual impact of academic criticism.)

Driven by some largely unexplored impulse, these critics of economics, as well as the pantheon of Greek gods, all seem deplorably addicted to acts which are commensurate with nearly interminable repetition.[2] Unfortunately, the result of such efforts manages only to sustain a precarious status quo, with the same prior equilibrium almost mindlessly re-established. (For those scattered, but devoutly mythologically minded readers, Zeus' avatar, according to legend, would fly daily to a designated rock (somewhere in the Caucasus) to which the Titan, Prometheus, was chained.[3]) The eagle's sole obsessive objective was strictly limited to devouring the liver of the imprisoned Prometheus. The liver, however, would single-mindedly regenerate each and every night.[4] This unlimited regeneration made such daily visits a categorical requisite, offering a punishment firmly attached to an infinite degree of repetition.[5] The allocated pain and punishment so studiously inflicted was intended to linger on for at least an eternity, leaving no chance for the memory of the original deed to fade or the crime to be forgiven. In the carefully constrained world of Greek myths, once anyone displayed the temerity to sin against the Gods, his or her goose was terminally cooked.[6] A reprieve of any sort remained simply inconceivable, a potential plea ruled entirely out of the question. This total inability to provide a pathway leading back to forgiveness composed part and parcel of this detailed, but other-worldly, package of ancient justice.

However, in the less notorious case of economists, the response offered to its critics (though equally predictable) differs radically from that beloved by Greek mythology. (No livers have been recorded as being lost, or devoured, due to the construction of risible theories, or faulty methodologies.) Instead of inflicting even momentary pain and damage, the profession has been seemingly anesthetised against any form of serious self-criticism, completely impervious to repeated attacks, no matter how anatomically incisive. Moreover, the profession has implicitly discovered that maintaining this status quo requires remarkably little effort from any one of its members. Decades ago (Freedman, 1993), when I was not quite so ancient, I explored the curious mystery of why so much of economics was so badly written. (The solution ran parallel (to a certain extent), to Sherlock Holmes' observation of the non-barking dog.) My perception, at that time, was that the plague of bad writing largely reflected an inability to read, which was widely spread amongst the profession.

This current investigation further explores, at least to a degree, a possible reason why this basic skill (reading and writing – carefully and thoughtfully) remains so limited. To some degree, ideas that should flow freely are either deliberately, or accidentally, impeded through an array of obfuscatory devices. The strategic purposes possibly played by impeding transparency and understanding reveal a tendency to sloppiness (by at least some), economists, as well as hidden (and more nefarious) objectives. Clearly, if such habits and usages do exist, they must aid some unstated purpose. Understanding the reasons behind such tactics, as well as the subsequent damage inflicted, forms a central theme of this volume.

Certainly, the profession displays an absence of any discernible shame in being wrong, or even in ignoring its aggregate mistakes. Consequently, the effect that any stream of unforgiving critical analysis (no matter how dour) might have on the discipline has come to mirror the annoyance a stray midge might inflict on a random camper. Namely, such intrusions merely parallel that of a slightly annoying insect that insists on buzzing around one's ear. This absence of any penalty reliably attached to repeated ideological transgressions by its practitioners allows the profession, at times, to steam contentedly down a wrong track without enduring any serious strictures, or censure. Though routinely an unwelcome event, such criticism, though perhaps (at times) mildly disruptive, remains risibly forgettable. As a result, many of the same criticisms against economic verities have been repeatedly levied over the passing decades without imposing any noticeable effect on its myriad of practitioners, or on their output.[7] In the case of economics, the mythological eagle returns only to be confronted by an effective avian repellent.[8]

Admittedly, even at its worst, such personal misapprehensions (or critical rejections) are not quite comparable to having one's liver eaten in a repetitious fashion. Still, for the author, an exhibited lack of comprehension by potential readers would signal an unfortunate failure. Meaning an inability (on the part of potential readers) to break through a careless, but rather shallow, understanding of the book's central argument. (The failure deservedly shared between reader and author.) No matter how justified such a total rejection might appear to be (at least from some perspectives), this predictable response serves to emphasise the futility of attempting fundamental criticism.[9] In a not entirely dissimilar way, having one's liver repeatedly devoured must inevitably become tiresome, notwithstanding the attached pain.

This feeling of repetitive non-achievement does make futility a serious side effect of essaying criticism of any kind. To underline this point, allow me to unfold an actual anecdote. Many years ago, while toiling away as a graduate student, I accepted a year's position at San Francisco State in a battle to retain whatever remaining shreds of sanity I had left. As a mere adjunct instructor, I was banished from the heart of the buzzing Business School to dwell somewhere on the campus fringes. My office mate was a recent Berkeley English Department PhD who had completed a dissertation on Dryden. In desperation, he had agreed to try to teach business students the lost art of writing. One lazy afternoon, I suggested that his role paralleled that of Sisyphus.[10] He in turn leaned back in his chair, shaking his head wearily. 'At least Sisyphus got to roll the boulder up the mountain.' Even senseless repetition (the ever-present feeling of going nowhere) can encapsulate different categories and classifications of frustration.

In essence, branding analysis in this reductive fashion (the sin of facile categorisation) is simply an efficient way to dismiss the importance of any such work. The underlying logic behind such a move is straightforward to those economists who in fact dabble in these fields. Any attempt to educate the discipline, so that it might appreciate such endeavours, must leave these economists with feelings similar to those endured by the poor, benighted Dryden scholar. Unfortunately, though critical essays were once a common feature in major professional journals, they now attract limited, if any, respect. This art has fallen in repute, much as had the family of *Tess of the D'Urbervilles*.[11] Instead, such efforts are viewed as something of an indulgence, suitable only for those nearing retirement, possibly an honourable alternative to taking up an irrational interest in intensive gardening.[12]

Thus, both the historical and some of the critical elements that define the employment of the four case studies are purely incidental to the purpose they serve. That these specific past cases are presented is simply a facet of their illustrative power. But in a very determinative sense, the entire field of history of thought clearly illuminates the difficulty of clear communications in the field of economics. In essence, the little that the profession bothers claiming to know about its own subject (or even about its particular methodology) is dominated by a dubious oral tradition and the sordid world of indifferent textbooks. Consequently (returning to the liver-loving eagle analogy), no matter how many times evidence is clearly presented to demonstrate that for Keynes, sticky prices remain a saving grace instead of a fatal hindrance, this misconception about Keynes and the bane of sticky prices continues.[13] (In any competition between accuracy and myth, myth inevitably triumphs.) Much the same can be said of the scattered references remaining in the literature that deign to mention any of the towering figures of the profession. The discipline continues to communicate only what it deems to be necessary, carelessly disregarding the deliberate intentions of any given economist.[14]

> Jacob Viner, whose vast and honest erudition has long been my despair, once told me that the average modern reference to the classical economists is so vulgarly ignorant as not to deserve notice, let alone refutation. I shall not give examples, but famous economists have made breathtaking misrepresentations of Malthus on population, Ricardo on value, and so on (Stigler, 1982:214).[15]

Communicating is difficult (if not impossible), even (or perhaps especially) with those who can boast of being highly educated. To be blunt, if hell is other people, then trying to talk to them represents the pitchforks of everyday life. Observing this incontrovertible reality is hardly a new (or daring) supposition. Economists on the whole have not been known for their ability to communicate. (This inability sadly extends to both those who read, as well as those who write economic articles.) Perhaps the observed standard of writing is too often tortuous because fundamentally, economists also lack the ability to read critically, at least with a sufficient level of dexterity (Freedman, 1993).[16] In essence, economists are too often motivated by an alternative agenda (one that relegates understanding to a level of insignificance), when confronted by a published article.

Unfortunately, what can be most compelling to those who adopt critical stances is not a strong desire to closely investigate an argument (or comprehend), the thinking displayed by some fellow economist.

Instead, prior to reading an article, many economists already know what they will discover in it. They too often uncover exactly what they expected to find. All that is then required is a relatively quick flick of the chosen article into one of the numerous pigeon holes that the profession has created. Labelling involves employing terms that are seldom questioned since everyone assumes they know what these labels signify.[17] Perhaps even worse, reading is sometimes done not for any enlightenment but simply to effectively destroy what has been written. The result more closely resembles a demolition derby than an attempt at critical reading. (Though readers alone are not solely at fault in creating spirals of obfuscation. The writer is hardly immune from the allure of deliberate concealment.) In selected cases, the underlying objective of an author can be artfully (and deliberately) camouflaged.

The same fundamental rhetorical obfuscations that plague the following four specific case studies then manage to invade every nook and cranny of economic research. Namely, they assist the ideological tail of economics to periodically wag the more substantial body of the discipline.[18] Preconceptions running through a tunnel of *a priori* conclusions inevitably produce predetermined results.[19] This filtering process necessarily skews the very value of what is ultimately produced. But this objective is best advanced by deploying certain rhetorical strategies. The ideology is forced to lurk within, without being allowed to completely reveal itself. But, whether such obfuscation is always deliberately conscious is impossible to determine.

Given the potential importance of such work (communication being unquestionably essential to any discipline), investigating this particular peril is actually best performed through the use of actual examples (case studies). The clarity obtained is certainly sharper than when depending on abstract generalities. In which case, the implied strategy employed throughout this work is one of diagnostically presenting these missteps (and bits of rhetorical camouflage), as they have actually been employed by noted economists (or caused them to be misrepresented). These cases serve as a concrete instance of a sort of invidious gangrene limiting communication within the profession. The cases also provide some of the propelling incentives and reasons that compel economists to view such strategic paths of obfuscation as presenting enticing options, when employed as rhetorical strategies. Unfortunately, this volume represents only a very preliminary effort rather than anything like a definitive work. The problem is laid out rather than resolved.

But, if I am correct in seeing these failings as a serious deviation currently plaguing the profession, as presenting an almost intractable problem, a start should best be made. Though to be honest, any such derived insights can only comprise a stab at an initial analysis of this particular quandary. However, such preliminary work can still provide a compelling, if not fully formed, autopsy of the problem. These fundamental misperceptions and sleights of hand do occur across the board within the profession. Nor are they limited to any specific political persuasion, ideology or attached methodology. Consequently, the examples chosen are not presented in order to indict specific economists or groups of economists.[20] I only delve into matters where I believe that I have garnered something of a comparative advantage. Accordingly, I attempt to remain silent when faced with my own ignorance. Other equally valid case studies remain to be explored. But I must leave it to others to unearth these parallel cases and examples and not presume more than I actually know.

> Most economists would say 'How do you spell 'gold'? And then they'll tell you what we should be doing about gold or anything else that you can imagine (Conversation with Paul Samuelson, October 1997).

What I will label as my Four Fundamental Pillars of Distortion (a deliberate muddling of communication and comprehension) are therefore distinctly exemplified in the work of an array of prominent economists. (They travel across contrasting political positions as well as opposing ideologies, rather than being consigned to any specific perspective.) Again, those examples presented in the following chapters need not be the worst offenders by any evaluation. These examples are instead employed based simply on the clarity provided by each given case. (Notice that the four constructed categories tend to blur into one another, with each case tending to reinforce the other in an unfortunate symbiotic relationship. The individual case studies presented depend more on which particular error tends to dominate in each example.) Notice that when unfolded, two of the categories will deal with misjudged readings of economic material, while the other two look towards misdirected writing. The four provided strategies can be easily described as follows:

- The Categorisation Trap/The Perils of Group Identity
- Reading with an Intent to Destroy/Critical Analysis as a Weapon of Mass Annihilation

- The Poison Apple Peril/Camouflaging One's Intentions
- Pretty Pictures

Certainly, any perceptive reader will identify these failings as sadly intrinsic to human psychology, where unrecognised needs and desires distort more rational thought. But in the actual cases under examination, I will purposely refrain from treading heavily into the field of armchair psychology. Within such landscapes, I cannot pretend to be an expert but just someone with decidedly questionable opinions. Instead, I will refrain, as best as I can, from letting my attention stray outside the bounds defined by the underlining economic issues.[21]

I. The Categorisation Trap/The Perils of Group Identity

To begin with, categorisation in human behaviour is a failing that approaches the smell and flavour of original sin.[22] This automatic response of clumping things together (be they people, ideas, or even paper clips) provides a convenient way to identify (or dismiss) groups without considering their individual components.[23] Categorisation sadly acts as an almost perfect fertiliser for favoured ideological and marketing concerns, whether such discriminatory preferences are recognised consciously or not. Dismissal, at its extreme level in the academic world, doesn't quite reach the level attained by some self-righteous, Bible-thumping Calvinist preachers. Within the confines of such churches, the self-satisfied religious leaders seem to take visceral pleasure in imagining designated sinners burning eternally in hellfire.

Unfortunately, even sans the detour to the inferno, the lack of any real incentive to judge individual efforts as singular episodes, causes much to be lost and hidden within a soggy swamp of generalisation and miscommunication. Such alluring shortcuts seem to exist as a facilitating means for paving the roads of insight with fundamental misunderstandings and fruitless resentments. These deliberately clogged highways remain naturally enticing (or they would not pose a problem). They offer convenience without demanding much in terms of effort or thought. Unfortunately, the conclusions achieved are almost always intrinsically wrong-headed.[24]

Generalising in this fashion can also serve as an effective, and certainly efficient, device for destroying an opposing theory or paper. Armed with such precise directives, readers inevitably find in a work exactly what they were prepared to discover. The result leaves given writers grossly misunderstood or even transformed (fundamentally hijacked), in order to justify some alternative objective. Thus, an economist (and his or her associated work) can be carelessly tossed into a bin labelled, Neo-classical, Marxist, New Keynesian, Behaviourist, New Institutionalist or New Classical. (These compose just a handful of the almost infinite (and ever-burgeoning) number of labels found plastered over the work performed within the profession.) Other economists seemingly accept, or carelessly dismiss, the writings of such individuals based almost entirely on this reflexive pigeon-holing.[25]

Even more misleading is the fashion in which an economist can win renown for a theorem that represents the antithesis of his or her own intentions, simply by first being tossed into a specific, well-worn category. The 'Coase Theorem', from this perspective, becomes an intriguing mousetrap ingeniously engineered by George Stigler to advance his own agenda.[26] (Advocated as a supposed encapsulation of Coase's very lengthy 1960 work but more practically meant to reflect Stigler's ideas, thoughts and objectives.[27]) In this instance, Coase appears to be a victim of the company he kept. Being continually tarred with the same ideological brush, it was subsequently easy to simply include Coase as a subscribing member of the Chicago School, one who abided by the same prescribed methodology and analysis as did Friedman or Stigler.

> What I showed in that article, as I thought, was that in a regime of zero transaction costs – an assumption of standard economic theory – negotiations between the parties would lead to those arrangements being made which would maximize wealth, and this irrespective of the initial assignment of rights. This is the infamous Coase Theorem, named and formulated by George Stigler, although it is based on work of mine. Stigler argues that the Coase Theorem follows from the standard assumptions of economic theory. Its logic cannot be questioned, only its domain. I do not disagree with Stigler. However, I tend to regard the Coase Theorem as a stepping stone on the way to an analysis of an economy with positive transaction costs. The significance to me of the Coase Theorem is that it undermines the Pigouvian system. Since standard economic theory assumes transaction costs to be zero, the Coase Theorem demonstrates that the Pigouvian solutions are unnecessary in these circumstances. Of course, it does not imply, when transaction costs are positive, that government actions (such as government operation,

regulation or taxation, including subsidies) could not produce a better result than relying on negotiations between individuals in the market. Whether this would be so could be discovered not by studying imaginary governments but what real governments actually do. My conclusion: Let us study the world of positive transaction costs (Coase, 1994a:10–11).[28]

Ronald Coase, in this instance, had already accumulated a lengthy and well-documented academic history even before embracing the comforts of the University of Chicago in 1964. His methods and approach to economic research were easily identified. If fully understood, they distinctly differentiate his style of research from the approach advanced by the Chicago School of Friedman and Stigler. Yet lazy categorisation easily identifies Coase with his Chicago colleagues. Meaning that far too many economists think they understand Coase's objectives and methods while grasping only a Chicago-infused perception. However, if his actual work is examined with an open mind, from the 1930s on, his distinctive interest in pricing theory was evident. So also was his disinclination to accept theoretical work at face value, or to be fobbed off by generalisations formed within an abstract context.[29] A plausible, or even convincing, story was not sufficient to necessarily pacify him into acquiescence. Solid evidence was always required to sufficiently buttress a convincing argument. Meaning that acceptable evidence could only be derived from the specific case under investigation.

Consequently, he might view a logically coherent cobweb pricing scheme as a clever construct but one that might not be applicable within existing markets. (The sizzle of theoretical bacon mollifies no appetites.) Such a pricing scheme, when tested, could abysmally fail to explain actual specific cases. In validation, his empirical papers with Fowler (1935a, 1935b, 1937) seemed to indicate a result opposite to what the cobweb theory claimed to unequivocally predict. In this case, the actual analysis performed by Coase and Fowler was based instead on the relevant workings of the prices attached to the pig market rather than purely on the construction of a theoretical model. (Namely, this analysis was based on what the actual stubborn prices were, rather than what the prices should be according to a plausible abstract construct.)

I don't know whether you knew I worked with Fowler on working out what people's expectations were. Well, if you read Muth's article on rational expectation, you will find a reference to me there, as one of the first people to have a sort of rational expectations idea.[30] What we were concerned with was this. In those days, there was something called a cobweb theorem. The name was invented by Nicky Kaldor.[31] It is based on the idea that people assume that existing prices and costs are going to continue as is. So Fowler and I took the pig industry and we showed that it wasn't true.[32] We showed that it wasn't true, because what you had was a market for two types of pigs. You had breeders and feeders. I think that in a lot of these sorts of industries, you still do. Anyway, there was a market for young pigs. Now, one knew in a general sort of way what the costs were of feeding. Well, the price that they paid for young pigs would reflect what they thought the price of the pigs, once fed, would fetch. So you could work out what people's expectations were. We showed that when prices were exceptionally high, they thought they would fall, and when they were low, they thought they would rise, and so on (Conversation with Ronald Coase, October 1997).

In which case, when Coase first introduced his sense of market transaction costs in his famous paper on the firm (1937), he sought to utilise basic pricing theory in order to explain observable facts about fundamental decisions. Or simply put, if using markets was in fact costless, there would be absolutely no reason for firms to exist.[33] Markets which sufficiently reflected a multitude of individual choices would provide a comprehensive explanation of all observed economic results. Moreover, when mounting any one of his basic arguments, Coase was never one to value dazzling technique over more solid usefulness. Consequently, his work on transaction costs, first developed in that 1937 paper, depended on employing, in a very practical fashion, a system of comparative marginal analysis.

> Businessmen in deciding on their ways of doing business and on what got produced have to take into account transaction costs. If the costs of making an exchange are greater than the gains which that exchange would bring, that exchange would not take place and the greater production that would flow from specialisation would not be realised. In this way transaction costs affect not only contractual arrangements but also what goods and services are produced (Coase, 1994a:9).

Coase's focus on actual markets and the operative pricing system never really ceased. His near obsession is once more unarguably on display in his 1946 paper on marginal cost pricing. Arthur Cecil Pigou, who would become something of a negative inspiration for his work, helped to focus Coase's analysis. This nexus is evidenced in not only that 1946 paper but even more so in his seminal 1960 work on social cost. Again, the idea of simply accepting commonly held (or lazily categorised) truths at face value would continue to run contrary to his own way of thinking, as well as to his research strategy.[34] From Coase's standpoint, Pigou's claims, or at least those consistent with his work, needed to be critically examined instead of simply swallowed as a sort of canonical basis for conducting pricing analysis.[35]

A central problem from Coase's perspective was logical policy jumps made from theoretical bases. This fallacy afforded a superficial justification for connecting theory directly to applied policy. (Specifics, when operating from this perspective, seemed almost deliberately ignored, while generalised categorisations dominated instead.) In essence, in the Pigouvian scheme of applied analysis, once a theoretical difficulty was discerned and classified as a market failure, the only corrective alternative was a government-imposed solution.[36] Unfortunately, the unfailing pursuit of that one singular path could deliberately cause other possible (and quite pragmatic) market pricing regimes to be ignored. Such lazy thinking might mean that alternative paths offering better resolutions of such detected problems would remain unexplored. Moreover, hidden assumptions needed to be unearthed. For instance, implicitly, in Pigou's analysis, government intervention was also assumed to have a marginal cost of zero. Clearly, Pigou's analysis required the rarefied environment where crucial effects were consistently costless. In raising questions about such generally accepted policy resolutions, Coase was indirectly reflecting the bone-deep scepticism established by Frank Knight to broadly based 'truths'.

> Professor Pigou's logic in regard to the roads is, as logic, quite unexceptionable. Its weakness is one frequently met with in economic theorizing, namely that the assumptions diverge in essential respects from the facts of real economic situations (Knight, 1953:163).

However, the same question still remains, as it does in each case study within this volume. Does such miscomprehension matter in the course of economic analysis? After all, the same mistaken approach to the work of an individual economist might be frequently repeated. But simple identification of a failure doesn't ensure that such a discovery actually demonstrates the presence of an effective communication distortion or even a significant misunderstanding. The mere existence of such bumps might not lead to seriously skewed analytical results. If in fact these issues are instead truly insignificant, then for the professional economist (or casting even a broader net, for the policy maker), a failure to comprehend Coase's intent, for example, would appear to be largely irrelevant. Certainly, George Stigler, who managed to create a great deal of confusion by inventing the Coase Theorem (an attempt to facilitate his own economic agenda), seems largely unfussed by possibly misinterpreting the intent of Coase's work (or any parallel failures of comprehension). Though if understanding past economists carries little or no clout, in a similar fashion, comprehending the current work of practising economists might also be of small import.

> Just as a student of differential calculus would learn little if he turned to Newton or Leibnitz or Lagrange, so a student of price theory is unlikely to learn from Adam Smith or, in a work a century later, from Alfred Marshall. When I say that this is the prevailing answer, I mean both that it is the practice of modern economists and that the practice does not interfere with brilliant scholarly careers. A young economist who believes that Adam Smith was the Smith who founded the Mormon faith will only provide innocent amusement outside of Utah, at no cost to his professional status (Stigler, 1982:215).[37]

Unfortunately, the problem presented by distracting attention and understanding by means of categorisation goes far beyond the case of Ronald Coase and the purported Coase Theorem. This fundamentally flawed analytic approach leads economists to talk past one another as they attempt to control rather than facilitate debate. Making it almost effortless to dismiss opponents (simply by tossing them into disposable dustbins), might succeed in spurring academic competition between opposing camps. But such objectives are accomplished by successfully lowering the average comprehension of specific economic articles. Even at the very best of times, with generosity blanketing the landscape, the meaning someone wishes to convey can remain stubbornly elusive. Consequently, constructing impenetrable meshes that actively distort and destroy communication tends to advance ideological agendas rather than economic insight.

> This means, on the one hand, that an economic writer requires from his reader much goodwill and intelligence and a large measure of

co-operation; and, on the other hand, that there are a thousand futile, yet verbally legitimate, objections which objectors can raise (Keynes, 1973:469–470).

As Keynes pointed out, communication is difficult, if not at times seemingly impossible. Complicating such needed attempts to break through one's standard solipsistic isolation, the associated obligation to achieve even a minimal level of mutual good will is usually sufficiently daunting in and of itself. This gulf of potential misunderstanding nurtures the second deadly strategy of communicative obfuscation. Communication becomes practically unreachable if a critic is only intent on turning the researcher's words into potent weapons that can be boomeranged back at their own creator. The problem then isn't limited only to those who habitually nit-pick, the obsessive fault finders driven by the desire to tear down what others have constructed. This perverse objective also fosters those who are driven to deliberately create a universe inhabited by non-existent but highly volatile nits. Such customised reading of any specific output is accomplished by dropping a critical anvil (smashing arguments within a given article) as often, and wherever, it is possible, even if objections have to be deliberately fabricated. Pursuing this strategy often demands a complete annihilation of an article, even if the offending elements have to first be misinterpreted and transformed into fragile artefacts. In such circumstances, reading critically transforms itself into the equivalent of reading with an intent to destroy.[38] In contrast, the term 'constructive criticism', in a better (more, well-intentioned) world, would be recognised as an unnecessary source of redundancy.

Often, these illusory versions of a theory or article are swallowed whole by the profession. Unfortunately, for too many economists, even the simple act of reading, with some degree of actual comprehension, poses a continuing source of befuddlement. Many years ago (1993), I concocted a modest article that attempted to explain the puzzling fact that most economists seem to be incapable of writing in anything like an adequate fashion, or at least one capable of capturing a reader's interest. My suggestion, at that time, was that the compelling reason for this shortcoming lay with the fact that these prolific economists had never actually learned how to effectively read in the first place. (A quote from Walt Kelly, of Pogo fame, in that article proved apropos.[39] So apropos to communication failures that it will be used again in one of the case studies. *Pogo* recognition, most likely, extends only to older readers, with long memories of that ancient, but revered, comic strip. The exact quote is as follows: "I'd write my Congersman, if he could read, if I could write." As in that quote, the fault lies with both the readers and the writers.)

In a sense then, this book is an accumulation of many of the ideas that were initially explored almost three decades ago. The four off-kilter strategies and interpretations highlighted here boil down to failures to communicate either for reasons that remain largely unintentional, or in other cases to strategies that tumble decidedly into the intentional basket. Consequently, despite George Stigler's professed view and flippant dismissal in his academic memoir (1982), it does matter that so many in the profession misunderstand the intentions and methods championed by Ronald Coase.

This extensive failure reflects the prolonged faltering of the required determination needed to bridge the inevitable gulfs created by faux communication and ingrained misunderstanding of an array of economic thought. Ideas and theories can become somehow perverted, driven by ulterior objectives or subconscious ideological goals. Even when such errors and trespasses are innocently committed, these tendencies still manage to effectively undercut beneficial communication. Instead of exchanging ideas, the disregard as well as overall disinterest in ferreting out the exact meaning contained by published research, encourages a transformation of any subsequent debate and discussion into something resembling strategic positioning. Economists act instead as designated champions attempting to eviscerate opposing theories, rather than accepting the arduous challenge of trying to comprehend them. Economics, when masquerading in this guise, deteriorates into no more than an entertaining, but vacuous jousting tournament.[40]

Consequently, any attempt to grapple with the meaning hidden in the work of Ronald Coase should not be viewed as a simple diversion, one comparable to playing trivial pursuits. (Name the 19th-century economist who was beaten with a slipper.) Rather, it is a prime example of how the persistent error of categorisation (and of indifference) can lead economists astray. By simply tossing Coase down the chute and into the Chicago laundry bag, his actual approach to economics (and particularly economic investigation) is too often lost in the shuffle. Perhaps this is why over the years Coase himself became increasingly frustrated with the profession's response to his work. Coase (discussed at some limited length in Chapter Two) saw himself as a Classic Liberal who conscientiously tromped down a similar path to that previously blazed by Frank Knight.[41] As such, he tried manfully not to blur the line separating the abstractions of economic theory from the specifics of applied policy.[42]

> There are several reasons why the approximate character of theoretical economic laws and their inapplicability without empirical correction to real situations should be especially emphasized as compared, for instance, with those of mechanics. … The limitations of the results have not always been clear, and theorists themselves as well as writers in practical economics and statecraft have carelessly used them without regard for the corrections necessary to make them fit concrete facts. Policies must fail, and fail disastrously, which are based on perpetual motion reasoning *without the recognition that it is such* (Knight, 1971:11).[43]

As pointed out, Coase was highly sceptical of what he quite acidly termed to be no more than 'blackboard economics'. This abstract approach promoted conclusions dependent solely on the underlying logic of an argument. At best, such foundational statements floated only on top of an over-generalised statistical foundation. Specifics, within this perspective, were no more than distracting and annoying bits of flotsam. Instead, performing like some demented Gertrude Stein simulacrum, this approach proclaimed reductively that 'a market is a market is a market', dismissing discernible differences and specifics as being merely trivial. Unfortunately, at least to Coase, conducting this relentless search for generality by engaging solely with abstractions would too often lack any serious validity, or prove incapable of providing a generous pinch of usefulness. In essence, ignoring specifics in order to better market universals may ultimately sow only confusion. In any case, such strictly theoretical thinking remains reliably inconsistent with the methodological approach Coase favoured. He had the maverick audacity to assume that investigating a specific market meant understanding the nuts and bolts of how that market actually operated.[44] But lumping Coase with the Chicago School successfully washes away this key differentiation. In essence, lazy categorisation can smother understanding.

Moreover, for Coase (as opposed to Stigler or Friedman), possession of such knowledge wasn't simply some idle form of amusement. Specifics were not only important but also central to applied research. In this sense, broad generalisations (when clumsily applied) could be distracting and confusing rather than capable of providing even an evanescent glimmer of enlightenment.[45] Thus, at least for Coase, the generally accepted understanding of Pigou, and his work, could become perversely inspirational given the right contextual environment. The drive to improve, or possibly correct, Pigou's thought provided Coase with a sturdy theoretical scaffolding, an evolving roadmap, suggesting much of the direction his future investigations would take. Pigou, at least in Coase's evaluation, seemed to dependably favour the purely theoretical over the applied actual, which steered the profession blindly down policy dead-ends. Such an inclination stood in direct opposition to Coase's own tendencies. Making sweeping statements *ex cathedra* failed to either convince or amuse Coase throughout his lengthy career. In his work, he consistently appears more interested in pragmatically discovering solutions that might work, instead of prejudging answers and justifying foreordained results. The useful, in his estimation, was to be preferred to the theoretically optimal, at least when investigating actual economies.

Coase then while surely being at Chicago was not in any simple way 'of Chicago'. To start from that prejudgement is to overlook what he has to offer. Coase certainly spent almost half his long life in Chicago (1964–2013), though he was always attached to the Law School rather than to either the Business School or the Economics Department. However, he interacted (and spent a good chunk of his academic career while in Chicago) with founding Southside figures like George Stigler and Gary Becker. He admired their work and the insights that broadened and deepened the discipline, especially the theoretical neighbourhood.

Politically his ideas ran closely parallel to those associated with the Chicago School of Economics during the Stigler–Friedman–Becker heyday.[46] For many economists, that proved sufficient to carelessly toss him into the identical category. He was tarred with the same popularly conceived brush of market activism that defined the leading Chicago figures. Thus, his work is most often placed in the same pot created over the years by the towering characters defining the Chicago School approach to economics. But, such an evaluation dismisses as inherently trivial, the way in which an economist actually works and thinks, what might be broadly considered to be the practical methodology that he or she actually employs. Coase, for instance, failed to completely swallow Chicago's nearly cult-like veneration of the rational decision-maker. In the writ according to Becker, this absolute construct provided an almost universal explanation for each and every outcome.

> When you say it [Coase's views on rational behaviour] is un-Chicago, you mean that it is an unmodern Chicago view. Because Frank Knight was at Chicago, and I was brought up more on Knight than I was on any

of the others. And my views were quite consistent with what he says. They're not consistent with what George Stigler, Gary Becker, and Richard Posner say. Posner condemns me because I don't think people maximize utility (Coase in Hazlett, 1997:3).

What is sometimes forgotten by those instinctively opposed to these erected Chicago economic scaffoldings is that rejecting his conclusions and results does not automatically require a similar dismissal of Coase's approach to economics. His conservative policy inclinations should be separable from the applied methodology of his work. Political leanings (or positions) are never the sole determinative judgements evaluating an individual's work. These are more a matter of differing interpretations of the available evidence, or of ideological predispositions. Ideally, then, a theme validated by Coase's methodology involves keeping well away from what might be termed the George Stigler conundrum. Namely, an approach that presumes to know not only what questions to ask, but also knowing the answers to those very same questions beforehand. Coase instead sought to determine, to the best of his ability, the validity of propositions deemed to be true by logic alone, or even by simple assertion. What everyone knows to be true may not be, at least not until thoroughly investigated. Faith is never a useful scientific determinative. Thus, for example, despite decades of being labelled as an example of a pure public good, no one had carefully examined the specific case embodied by the lighthouse (Coase, 1974). Checking the facts that could underwrite this sweeping claim simply languished. Nor was the ability to construct a convincing 'just so' story, to be deemed as serious proof of a general proposition. Needing something to be true never made it so *a priori*.[47]

Examining the way in which Coase, while ostensibly remaining a well-known figure, largely escaped any serious comprehension by the bulk of the profession serves merely as an example of a wider failing. Within this volume, it is employed solely as a case study rather than as a conclusive analysis. The example provided only sketches out the dangers associated with falling into the booby trap represented by categorisation. The investigation does not pretend (or propose), to be anything resembling a definitive study of Ronald Coase himself. The example's importance lies in the way it illustrates a particular strategy of obfuscation. Any insights into Coase, or his work, remain mere by-products. As previously emphasised, shoving someone's output and research into a convenient category creates something of a research loophole. Pigeon-holing becomes a device by which to promote, whether consciously or not, an array of ulterior objectives seemingly unrelated to the actual work under consideration. By using this type of categorisation to conveniently box and broadly label whatever actually is being conveyed, an author's work can be casually condemned and dismissed, or equally, lauded, for extraneous reasons.

In effect, such an alternative goal can be efficiently accomplished without bearing the attached inconvenience of reading any of the relevant work, or making do with a superficial browse. Certainly, it relieves the obligation of examining such material carefully, or conducting an array of more mundane efforts, with anything resembling an open mind. Categorising allows a focused reader to prejudge, which in turn allows such readers to discover quite comfortingly that the examined work yields and meets every pre-ordained expectation. Consequently, thrusting an opposing economist into a defined cage can prove to be a useful, yet highly destructive critical tool, promoting the sin of obfuscation. Inevitably, that almost careless level of annihilation has proven to be the inevitable result, of anyone resolutely reading all research solely with the intent of decimating a contrary argument.

II. Reading with an Intent to Destroy: Critical Analysis as a Weapon of Mass Annihilation

VOGON GUARD: Resistance is useless!
FORD: You can shut up as well!
VOGON GUARD: Resistance is useless!
FORD: Oh, give it a rest! Do you really enjoy this sort of thing?
VOGON GUARD: Resistance is......what d' ya mean?
FORD: I mean does it give you a full satisfying life? Stomping around, shouting, throwing people out of spaceships?
VOGON GUARD: The hours are good (Douglas Adams: *A Hitchhikers Guide to the Galaxy*).

As briefly touched upon before, if we bother to read carefully what purports to be critical evaluations of theories and research, at least some of these efforts seem to be driven by unmistakably malign motivations.[48] Strawmen (flammable and easily incinerated versions of a structured theory) are deliberately constructed, only to have their desiccated remnants, carted away in the form of smouldering ashes. Consequently, a committed misuse of economic analysis, but one distinguishable from categorisation, occurs when viewing economics as akin to a peculiar zero-sum jousting tournament, or some other obscure sporting contest. Constructing, and subsequently discovering, strategically placed weaknesses in ersatz versions is pursued not for the purpose of expanded understanding, or entertaining a simple discussion of underlying and intrinsic ideas. The overriding ambition driving such strategies is clearly a desire to eviscerate (and eliminate) theories standing stubbornly in opposition to a preferred approach. Thus, the error of categorisation can at times blend easily into reading research with an intent simply to destroy. (As noted, categorisation can provide an efficient method for dismissing unappealing frameworks.) In which case, ostensible searches for knowledge can instead encourage an unplanned detour into an alternative universe where good must perennially battle and destroy evil.

> Oh, he [George Stigler] was a true believer. He wouldn't like that term. But put that in because he thought in that sense. He was absolutely convinced that he was right. It wasn't a doctrinal battle. It was a battle of facts. I almost said good and evil.
>
> *And those facts?*
>
> He was sure. But then some people are sure that God is on their side. He was absolutely sure the economy was on his side and if research was properly done it would show this. He really believed that he understood how the world works. And the way the world works had been shown to him by the theory of price (Conversation with James Kindahl, October 1997).

Coincidentally, the case study constructed to investigate the 'reading with an intent to destroy' trap is again Chicago based.[49] But this case turns the previous Midwestern perspective on its head. The narrative unfolded focuses not on the use Chicago makes of this strategy (though eminent members of this faculty were past masters of the technique). Instead, the portrait detailed is one that evaluates those very same tactics when they are employed to eviscerate the Chicago School itself.[50] In a display of tit for tat, Philip Mirowski and his associates allow targeted Chicagoans, like George Stigler, to embody what they widely characterise as neo-liberal thought. By the defined lights of these authors, Chicago represents an uncompromising fount of policies that support (whether intentional or not) social discord and oppression. (Harking back to the previous discussion, note that the search and destroy missions subsequently conducted begin by creating a dank pigeon-hole into which designated opponents can be entombed.)

Whether it may be legitimate to attack an opponent in the same fashion as those opponents employed remains an open question. Unfortunately, it pushes into territory where justice is weighed against revenge. (Perhaps this even edges into the ethical, a configured abstract happily eschewed by most economists.) However, when 'reading with a distinct intent to destroy', more heat than light will inevitably be the by-product, if not the targeted result.[51] In any case, undoubtedly questionable is the presence of any proposed rationale daring to claim that one side's repeated interpretive trespasses automatically condones a reciprocal degree of blurring. In this instance, the line separating useful from purely destructive criticism is not one that should be legitimately (or carelessly) crossed. Nor, for that matter, is deliberately erasing or blurring that line ever seriously justified.

Unfortunately, both sides of the ideological divide are wont to engage in exactly this act of intentionally provoked conflict by mounting deliberate attacks. Each set of combatants presumably convinces themselves that they have somehow conscripted armies of golden angels to cheer them on. Supposedly, these tame seraphs act as mere judicial spectators, arrayed along some hallowed neutral side-line. Such assured confidence in the principles and goodwill of the undertaken campaign fails to obliterate the political exigencies and ideological battles brewing behind any contrived smokescreen. Such flimsy diversions serendipitously offer a supposed rationale for outright aggressive behaviour that is only meant, ultimately, to mislead. Sadly, any valid examination of this strategic rhetoric would be forced to consign such attempted defences of this approach to the shallow end of the logic pool.

Published research can then become the raw material that allows these eager inquisitors (Grand or otherwise) to frame a story that appears sufficiently convincing. The aim and result of such inquisitorial forays are to induce a guilty verdict rather than focusing on producing anything resembling a set of striking or valuable insights. The objective underlying such strained efforts veers noticeably away from investigation and moves instead towards condemnation and dismissal. Viewed from a certain tangential perspective, the intention of these critical economists might (with a dollop of generosity) even be judged to be noble. Evil, even if only in the eye of the beholder, should always be responsibly battled and stymied whenever possible. But distorting the work opposed to one's predilections manages to ultimately undermine the very validity of those who travel down this route of attack. Doing, 'whatever it takes' might seduce these champions into rationalising the shape their efforts assume.[52] But the very seductiveness of their cause, which induces an eagerness to flatten and destroy, seems to ultimately cloud their judgement.[53]

Mirowski and his associates don't seem to desire to either analyse or comprehend what they oppose (at least not to any sufficient depth), as to simply destroy it. Consequently, they begin their chosen crusade by first tar-brushing selected opponents like George Stigler with the dire label of 'neo-liberal'.[54] Such attempts at pigeonholing, according to their own interpretation of this particular category, successfully discover a veritable cesspool of evil intentions befouling the very bowels of the profession. Equally, despite their propensity to 'read with an intent to destroy', their motivations might also justifiably be classified as pursuing poison apple tactics in order to effectively sway their readers. Under the guise of constructing a critical analysis with which to evaluate a prevalent framework, these academics are instead intent on easing a Trojan horse past those who would act as gatekeepers of the discipline.[55]

By tying Stigler and his Chicago colleagues with the tainted label of neo-liberal, they hope to chip away at the credibility of these economists. To undermine these opponents, they choose to focus strictly on ideological debating points rather than the constructed arguments driving such research. The unannounced intention seems to favour shifting focus away from the economic analysis performed, as well as whatever questions those investigations might legitimately raise. Dragging a discussion towards a quicksand of demise reveals the true purpose of any concerted attack. Though the strategies involved in each case are distinguishable, it is easy to see how the slipshod results yielded by categorising, can slip easily into the cul-de-sac of reading with an intent to destroy. Or, with a similar twist, how such attempts can bleed seamlessly into a more sophisticated poison apple strategy, where it is the author who is guilty of misleading his or her readers.

III. The Poison Apple Peril/Camouflaging One's Intentions

However, the apple had been made with such cunning that only the red part was poisoned. Snow White was eager to eat the beautiful apple, and when she saw the peasant woman eating her half, she could no longer resist, stretched out her hand, and too the poisoned half (Grimm and Grimm, 1992:202).

Surprisingly to some, the appearance of poison apple strategies is not particularly unusual in the endless byways provided by economic literature. They exist as persuasive outbursts that are coated in guile, or facilitated by ingenious attempts at planning. If anything, they are far too commonplace in the literature to even be widely noted. Such strategic offerings have positioned themselves too close to the norm in economics, resulting in an almost lazy disinterest in this otherwise important issue. But the same tactic manages to thrive in other fields and locales as well. In that minefield labelled politics, few would accept today that the Iraq invasion under George W. Bush was simply an attempt to remove an imminent threat posed by Iraqi weapons of mass destruction.

Consequently, it is not necessary to be a full-fledged devotee of conspiracy theories to recognise that this particular American adventure in the Middle East was driven by quite other unstated objectives. Weapons of mass destruction provided a simpler selling point at that juncture in time than other alternatives. (The marketing of the invasion began while the attack on the New York Twin Towers was still fresh in most American minds. The timing made the decision seem all the more exigent.) Invading was marketed as purely a self-defence measure tied to a seemingly imminent threat posed by global terrorism. The expectation of those packaging (and selling) this attractive piece of motivation was that other, more contentious, goals could be slyly slipped by a guileless public while remaining hidden within this more conducive guise.[56]

The intent behind the construction of these deadly apples, especially as it pertains to the most tempting of them, is often complex and not without a degree of subtlety. The very opaqueness of the underlying subtext tends to repel any deep dive into its hidden depths by requiring an excess of effort and discernment. (Such apple-based strategies deliberately shy away from any degree of transparency.) Though examining the details of any argument (as well as its logical structure) is always vital, getting distracted by minutiae and peripheral details may lead the unwary down an unnumbered array of fruitless paths.[57] However, despite these deliberately imposed difficulties, the underlying task for any self-respecting analyst remains one of ferreting out the sometimes hidden implications of the theory presented. Once a reader does become thoroughly conversant with the structured mechanism driving a given argument, by initially accepting the proposed theory as valid, the resulting responsibility is to trace out the exact implications often hidden behind a set of theoretical curtains. To resolve such a puzzle, the debated research often needs to be placed within an appropriate contextual framework.

For example, the much-cited work by Alchian and Demsetz (1972) appears to offer a straightforward rationale for the existence of firms. It relates a 'just so' story explaining how the logic of (and rationale for) firms might (or must) have evolved and come into being.[58] But the year it was published is not insignificant. The early 1970s saw a continuation of the upheaval of the 1960s. (Actually, what is often thought of as 'the sixties' in its more romantic and ideological facsimiles doesn't begin in 1960 and end in 1969. Once again, categorisation provides a false template of knowledge and certainty by trying to boil down a series of complex events into manageable simplicities.) Standard neo-classical analysis (or price theory) was being widely challenged during the period bracketing the late sixties and early seventies.

Associated attacks were also launched against the perceived system of market capitalism (and especially private property). Alchian and Demsetz (1972) provided what at first glance might appear to be a serendipitous counterpunch to such revolutionary trends. The argument presented seeks to demonstrate that firms, by their very architecture, provide both efficient and equitable outcomes. Such an institutional structure is shown to be beneficent, thus correcting any badly misinformed notion of capitalism being something akin to a predatory incubus. But these corporate arrangements are revealed to do much more. They also unflinchingly defend private property and the associated market system that supports it. Firms then exist to solve core agency problems (allowing for specialisation). They do so by providing the scaffolding required for private markets to exist and even flourish. These (in contrast to public markets) form the foundation of economic growth and viability. Not at all coincidentally, a key assumption provides a foundation for the article. This assertion is presented as though it were a common notion, allowing it to act as a quintessential poison apple that successfully drives an ideological house of cards.[59] The authors' deft construction manages to provide what can only be understood as the foundational pivot for their argument but one that is carefully camouflaged within a wad of innocuous packaging.

Consequently, when the limelight is deliberately turned on Milton Friedman's famous (1953) *Essay on Positive Economics*, another classic example of employing a poison apple strategy is revealed. The case demonstrates an instance of where what you see isn't what you get. Friedman's focus ostensibly fixes on what appears to be a purely methodological quandary. His approach, at first glance, seems to fall into a quite familiar and conveniently ploughed furrow of economic thought. However, the actual interest evinced by Friedman in such methodological niceties appears to be, subsequently, evanescent at best. His seemingly intensive methodological obsession springs almost spontaneously to life immediately following the first 1947 Mont Pelerin meeting.[60] A sort of conservative jamboree of leading intellectual lights that shone only on the political right, this initial gathering was attended by Milton Friedman, George Stigler and Aaron Director (academics who would help to engineer the Chicago counter-revolution). Each would subsequently go on to play either key, or at times more peripheral, parts in cleverly constructing shiny new poison apples that the economics discipline would be unable to resist.

Consequently, when examined more intensely, Friedman's literary stab at what he labels 'positive economics' closely resembles a tactical pose. This disguised attack (the poison apple) is deliberately launched against the nominated forces of collectivism, the threat explicitly identified by the Mont Pelerin Society. Friedman's attempt at a methodological construct seems irredeemably meant to influence (and even eliminate) some of the widespread debates that clearly dominated that era but not by meeting them head-on. One aspect of the ongoing struggle between identifiable camps of economists focused on the reality of the assumptions that continued to underpin widely accepted economic theories. Questioning the nature of such assumptions was viewed as potentially eating away at the very foundation of standard price theory (particularly the version espoused at Chicago). Hence, even the conceivable existence of such debates was perceived as posing a present danger to the discipline, at least by those subscribing to the Mont Pelerin creed.

The Chicago-based fear was that any extended (and legitimate) scepticism concerning those questionable assumptions might provide a degree of credence to alternative (and opposed) theories. In other words, more realistic assumptions might be better aligned to the structure of Keynesian theory in those post-war years. Consequently, shoring up the foundational structure of traditional price theory provided a present (and future) staging platform for attacks directed against approaches conducive to a more collectivist policy approach. For those first few decades of the post-war period, what existed in textbooks and classrooms was a cobbled-together portmanteau theory of economics where the micro and macro components refused to easily adhere to one another. Certainly, Friedman's methodological efforts didn't provide a final death knell to such debates. (Though one suspects that Friedman would have been delighted at such an outcome.) Friedman's tactics, at best, only diverted attention away from potentially dangerous investigations, which had the audacity to evaluate assumptions according to their reality.[61] Waving a red flag at the profession succeeded by diverting attention away from more fundamental issues towards a morass of pseudo-methodological debates.

However, despite Friedman's best efforts, Keynesian (and aligned) perspectives did not suddenly crumble with the 1953 publication of his methodological foray. But this essay did represent an important way station leading to the subsequent triumphs of the 1980s. In the same way that although the battles of Leipzig and Borodino fail to entirely encompass the Napoleonic Wars in their entirety, these battles still remain as important historical mileposts. In this sense, understanding Friedman's goals in constructing his methodological cul-de-sac does not lack a certain historical vitality. Nor do his tactics for achieving such goals remain negligible but rather stand out as a masterclass in obfuscation.

Friedman, in providing a classic example of a poison apple strategy, constructed an approach that successfully retained a large degree of resonance for decades. Its long-lasting impact is at least partly due to the clever way in which the argument is constructed. The poison apple hidden within the essay managed to largely slip quietly past the gatekeepers of the profession. Quite naturally, nothing could be more useless than a poison apple that instantly disintegrated at the first sign of careful examination or a version that automatically raised alarms.[62] Certainly, Friedman thrived on creating controversy, although the profession, at times, has appeared too obtuse in recognising the fundamental position played by this tendency.[63] Due to his deliberately high-profile style, however, he could dependably expect that attention would be paid to his efforts. Any one of his contentious theories (or utterances) would dependably be exhaustively raked over with the finest of fine-tooth combs by both opponents and supporters.

Consequently, the sweep of his constructed arguments managed to cleverly divert attention away from any underlying objectives hidden by his carefully crafted poisoned apples. Instead, professional focus latched on to the minutia of his methodological arguments. By strategically camouflaging his objectives, Friedman could disguise the true nature of some of his more controversial constructions. Opponents who got stuck into his logical tar babies became bogged down and subsequently trapped into debating the details of his theories rather than probing his more implicit goals. The army of economists that chose to take Friedman on became naively trapped within a veritable quicksand of philosophical trivia. By this means, subsequent debate was then successfully shifted to a more conducive terrain (at least from Friedman's perspective). Doing so meant that Friedman's artfulness served to create an effective distraction, pointing the profession down a played-out mine shaft that failed to yield any valuable ideas. Bickering over endless theoretical details inevitably diverts attention away from potentially more fruitful and perhaps exceptionally troublesome avenues of research that might succeed in bolstering opposing perspectives. Friedman managed to set at least part of the profession chasing after a will-of-the-wisp.

> Most economists, and all bankers, will challenge Friedman's conclusions – in fact, a fair number will challenge them even before they learn what he has written (Stigler, 1975:29).

Evidence ultimately points to a fairly solid conclusion in terms of the construction and employment of poisoned apples. Milton Friedman (1953) almost certainly harboured an ulterior motive in constructing his methodology (produced with the thoughtful assistance of George Stigler). The time and context of its publication provide a clear indication (or at least a useful hint) of his implicit purpose. That Friedman was engaged in a broad-based version of the Mont Pelerin project (to restore his conception of the foundations of Classical Liberal thought to predominance within the field of economics and beyond) seems indisputable. Certainly, acting as an advisor to the Goldwater (1964) campaign was hardly accidental or inconsistent with Friedman's broader strategy. Nor did his television series (or his best-selling books) stray far from this objective.

His life reflected his overarching crusade, not unlike the lifelong crusade conducted by his contemporary Billy Graham. Although, in Friedman's case, he preached salvation through the miracle of markets. However, again like Graham, throughout his endeavours, he remained one of the truly outstanding marketers (the ultimate persuader or spinner) that the economics profession would ever manage to produce. Friedman embodied the rare gift that enabled him to sell anything, including a wide variety of notions, to the general public. He was someone who could deftly sell water to a drowning man while rationalising the propriety of doing so. Moreover, he was willing to speak and persuade at the proverbial drop of a hat. The defeat of collectivist thought became almost an obsession in his intensive quest to champion liberty and freedom.

However, that he had no longstanding or continuing passion for methodological issues is painfully evident when examining the arch of his career. He was silent as the tomb after the 1953 publication of his ultimate thinking on the matter. Even more so, despite the subsequent furore over the meaning of his essay and its implications, he refused to respond to any of the legions of critical work that sprung up like weeds in a vacant field. Further, this passing interest in methodology arose in a maddeningly convenient fashion and abruptly subsided with the publication of his sole methodological effort. The essay saw daylight at exactly the same time as questions were arising, questions focused on the foundations of price theory. This bit of timing would appear to incorporate an otherwise rather remarkable random coincidence. Lastly, we need to evaluate in some depth the results of Friedman's efforts. One of the ways in which we mark a tree is by its fruits.

The 1953 essay had at least two clear results: First, it did seduce the profession into a largely unproductive (and unresolved) methodological debate that diverted attention away from the issue of assumptions. (More ink was spilled in arguing over his contentions than on the more central issue regarding the nature of assumptions themselves.) Second, as George Akerlof (2020) has noted, it helped stack the deck away from what the profession would come to dismiss as a soft approach to economics (to some degree derided as being too descriptive, or lacking in statistical evidence). The noticeable and accelerated drift was towards what might be considered to be a hard perspective. (Proponents would henceforth stick a heavy thumb on the discipline's evaluation scale, by overwhelmingly labelling (or categorising) this conveniently designated method as being the only true scientific alternative. All other approaches would be tossed in the rejected dustbin labelled unscientific.[64]) The end result was a distinct shift over time to a position where generating testable predictions became the *sine qua non* of economics. Only assumptions that forcefully supported this approach would henceforth matter. More importantly, the quality (or reality) of those starting points ceased to carry any decisive significance.[65] Other such considerations could conveniently be dismissed out of hand (and banished out of mind).

> Second, hardness bias reduces the ability to challenge existing paradigms. According to the usual procedures in economics, as in science more generally, old ideas are only rejected when they are shown to be inferior in tests against new ideas. Since Friedman's (1953) classic essay, it has become all but uncontestable that new theories need to generate *testable predictions*. This belief may seem innocuous; but, in

point of fact, it involves rejecting softer tests of theories, such as those that evaluate models based upon the qualities of their *assumptions* as well as the quality of their *conclusions*. It especially entails exclusion of evidence from case studies, whose detailed evidence can be highly informative concerning context and motivation. While harder tests with statistical data may be a gold standard, restricting the set of permissible tests reduces – perhaps greatly – the ability to test theories. Hence, bias toward the hard makes us too accepting of existing theory and insufficiently willing to be self-critical as a profession (Akerlof, 2020:408–409).

IV. Pretty Pictures

Deepfakes (a portmanteau of 'deep learning' and 'fake') were originally synthetic media productions which have been digitally manipulated to deceptively and convincingly replace one person's likeness with that of another. The term, coined in 2017 by an anonymous Reddit user, has been expanded to cover any videos, pictures, or audio made with artificial intelligence to appear real, by fabricating observably realistic images or audio of individuals who do not exist (Wikipedia, https://en.wikipedia.org/wiki/Deepfake).

Too often (in this case, once would be too often), authors start writing with a pre-conceived script that has to be meticulously followed. Meaning that the facts and evidence they encounter have to be shaped to fit into an inflexible frame, or simply discarded. This operative pattern should never happen, let alone be tolerated, or even nurtured. Without first acknowledging the problem, as well as possible methods for resolving this diversion, attempts to impede this method will always fail to get off the ground. Basically, the final case study investigates what happens when implicit objectives hijack the duty to communicate honestly and transparently. But what makes this problem insidious is that it would seem to be largely unrecognised by the perpetrators themselves.

The case study chosen deviates from the rest in that it is based on a lengthy biography written by a non-economist (the author is a historian of intellectual ideas). But what the author, Jennifer Burns (2023), does in cinemascope (using a broad canvas), others do in miniature. In fact, what she does is to create a reality that is a second cousin to the strawman confections previously discussed. But where those were engineered to destruct (and in doing so undermine a theory), Burns intends to enhance reality. In essence, the lily is heavily gilded, perhaps to advance a deeply held ideological position. But without a serious psychological analysis, or perhaps even hypnosis, the exact motivation can never be exactly pinpointed.

For whatever reason, Burns turns Milton Friedman's life into a hero's journey.[66] Briefly, such a schematic generally starts with an obscure individual who is driven to achieve greatness. Through his (or less often her) superior intelligence and drive, the hero overcomes obstacles, as well as the entrenched forces opposed to his advancement. Despite setbacks, the hero always triumphs as the story fades out. The obfuscation committed in this biography is that it resembles a legitimate recounting of Friedman's life without that resemblance being strictly legitimate.

Being a historian of some substance, the research is more than thorough. The structure and unfolding of her tale are skilfully accomplished. That is what makes the method frankly dangerous. For the general reader, the portrait would likely prove to be entirely convincing.[67] Even in the case of most academics, the bulk of the narrative would prove palatable. That is exactly the problem posed when a clever author chooses obfuscation, whether deliberately or not. In this case, readers are left with a carefully composed but ultimately skewed portrait of a seminal 20th-century economist. Friedman did help shape the economics of his time. But he was a complex individual, not some simple hero. Like any human, he made mistakes and was sometimes on the wrong side of a political issue. The motivations driving his thoughts and actions were not always obvious or clear. He deserves a sympathetic but painstaking investigation, not merely a pretty picture that at first glance seems to adequately describe (and examine) his life. Curiously enough then, where Friedman himself would sometimes resort to obfuscation in his writing (as documented in the previous chapter), Burns feels comfortable using a similar approach when detailing his life in her lengthy biography.

Consequently, whether obfuscation is conscious or unconscious is impossible to determine in any given instance. But clearly, such methods, when strategically applied, can benefit the individual economist, if not the profession as a whole. If you add to this unfortunate mix the urge to market one's ideological wares, the hidden objective in some economic writing depends upon bending communication to a specific goal. What then this volume investigates is a problem that to some extent limits the discipline by diverting it down abandoned spur lines.

> I do not think it is practical to write an elaborate work on the working of economic process in modern society on a completely "objective" basis ... Anyone who could do so would be pathological, and the pathology would be likely to extend to his selection of premises – It is always necessary to begin somewhere, but where one begins can have great influence on where one ends up – and on his decisions as to what are facts and what myths. In so far as is possible, value judgements, should be labelled as such, but their systematic exclusion is, I am convinced not in practice either possible or desirable. They should not be concealed, they should not be eccentric, and they should not be elaborated or didactically pressed (Viner quoted in Van Horn, 2011:291f41).

Endnotes

1   Unfortunately, the history of economic thought is not a field regarded seriously throughout the profession. Implicitly, it is allocated to those aged members who now lack the vitality to accomplish anything more productive than a spot of gardening.

2   In the case of Greek mythology, interminable punishment seemed the objective. Forgiveness was rarely on offer. The parallel case in economics (repetition without resolution) seems to reflect either ego or the delusion that such work could be an effective catalyst for change.

3   For those economists whose entire grasp of Greek mythology derives from ogling *Xena: Warrior Princess* as teenagers, Prometheus (forethought) is credited with creating the human race out of clay (others may think of more suitable and accurate material). Whether he employed inferior clay in completing this unusual task remains for the reader to decide. Prometheus ends up on that rock as punishment for stealing fire and giving it to his human creations. Punishment within the Greek circle of Gods was usually structured to fit the crime and to be unrelenting. As previously mentioned, forgiveness (or restitution) was out of the question. These extreme forms of retribution were meant to serve as a stark learning experience be they enforced on Gods or humans. Clearly, this theft by Prometheus was considered to be so dangerous and vile (at least by Zeus) that no amount of punishment could ever

prove sufficient. Such an eternal aim is easily accomplished when faced with a regenerative liver inside an eternal being.

4   For the ancient Greeks, the liver was regarded as the centre of the soul and the source of emotions. Greek myths are overloaded with various sins against the Gods and their subsequent punishments. The aim of these judgements (as mentioned) repetitively emphasised the idea that the punishment should fit the crime. The sentences tend to be notably harsh while also lasting into eternity. In the myth noted, Zeus consumes the very passion that motivated Prometheus. Zeus not only repetitively destroys that passion but uses it to fuel his own wrath on a daily basis. Running afoul of the ruling power structure thus leads to one's eternal damnation. In a hierarchal world, the symbolic lesson of obedience could not be delineated more clearly.

5   The story either displays the existence of an infinitely patient eagle or one with a decided taste for liver.

6   Many of these myths simply detailed why and how each goose was deliberately sautéed.

7   As a test of this hypothesis, see if it is possible to name any theory, despite having at times been discarded, that was not eventually resurrected, even if reformulated in a more appealing fashion. For centuries, economists have been the great recyclers of theories and suppositions.

8   At this very early stage in this current narrative, it might not be inappropriate to directly intervene in what will shortly become a gusher of words and ideas. I follow the path hacked out by Henry Fielding (*Tom Jones*) by indulging in this no longer fashionable conceit. But a short confession of this author's perspective on style and fashion in economic writing might help clarify what is to come in this volume. Frequently, throughout an extended, but ill-spent, career, I have stumbled across referees who claim (without reservation) that there exists but one canonical method for writing economics. Moreover, these fortunate experts claim that they alone have been gifted with this vital knowledge. Their assurance in this matter is such that any deviation from this received template deserves unmitigated and unending scorn. (As such, these referees are not much different from the unforgiving eagle that ripped the liver out of the immobile Prometheus.) Sadly, such stylised thought is not that different from earlier pedants who insisted that left-handed students learn to write only with their right hand (defenders of a God-given norm). However, such unified and intolerant approaches deliberately scorn individualised talent. They exalt instead the skills of some representative styled agent, who is to be imitated without question. The result often tends towards a predictable level of mediocrity. In fact, when this lauded canonical writing style is revealed in its full glory, it turns out to have too many points in common with the notes blackmailers compose by cutting out individual letters from newspapers and magazines.

In fact, this scornful style of criticism, beloved by too many referees, has deep roots in the history of the profession, a sort of 'tall poppy syndrome' that inflicts the discipline. Paul Samuelson, for instance, was often denounced for employing literary allusions in his books and articles. Such scholarship was deemed to be pompous and inappropriate by numbers of critical economists. (Lacking an ability to effectively evaluate a theory often reduces a critic to the base level of *ad hominins*.)

9   Alfred Marshall, for example, delighted in excluding from serious consideration, anyone who lacked approved credentials. Their thoughts on economics were simply dismissed without any serious consideration. See Marshall's attacks on George or Hobson. (This is not to say that these personalities were correct, but that failure to gain a set of approved degrees, doesn't automatically invalidate ideas.)

10   Yet another famous image from Greek mythology. Sisyphus, the Greek King of Ephyra, was characterised by being something of a trickster, famous for escaping from impossible situations. When finally consigned to the Underworld, Hades (ruler of the Underworld) sought punishment for that lifetime of tricks and cons by having Sisyphus condemned to perform an endless task that offered no escape. (Many readers may recognise the similarity attached between the task to which Sisyphus was condemned and any attempt to teach economics.) No amount of cleverness could avoid the inevitable failure following each day's fruitless efforts. His predictably unsuccessful attempts to complete a seemingly simple objective meant that the boulder would predictably escape his grasp and roll back down the incline, forcing him to repeat the operation over and over again. In essence, the punishment symbolised that there existed no avenue through which to atone for offending against the Gods. For Sisyphus, finally, possible escapes no longer existed.

11   Those antipathetic to the novels of Thomas Hardy might satisfy their curiosity by sitting through the film version instead.

12   Certainly, Milton Friedman seemed to dismiss this field of study as a suitable option for any serious economist. Barely redeemable, only if a dearth of viable research avenues dominated.

> Beginning with the 1930s, there was a period of very active work on economic theory, macro and micro, in both areas. What became prestigious was work in a kind of economic theory, namely pure and largely mathematical oriented. And it did not really have any considerable history. Now that period of change and development, that excitement, has disappeared. We are now in, what I would say is, a relatively flat period of additions to the structure. So today, you either have to be an extraordinarily good mathematician, or else there is nothing else for you to do but the history of economic thought. I'm saying that there is sort of a balance wheel here. If there are exciting

things being done in a theory, an interesting and exciting thing to do with the structure of the body of economics, that's what will attract the top young economists. They'll be drawn away from the history of economic thought or similar fields. On the other hand, if it's a dry period, so far as really adding to the structure of economic thought is concerned, all of a sudden, everybody is interested in such things as the background of Stigler of Keynes, of Samuelson (Conversation with Milton Friedman, Rose Friedman and Aaron Director, August 1997).

13   The need to cultivate and mainly sustain the specious myth of sticky prices is hardly an unfathomable mystery. Making sticky instances of prices the defining condition of Keynesianism effectively served to domesticate Keynes. Transformed from a general theory, the actual broad scaffolding constructed by Keynes could be conveniently crammed into the highly constrained space of a special case. Instead of a fortuitous source of stability, sticky wages become a garden variety of market failure, one capable of improvement, or even of resolution.

14   Glaring mistakes in interpreting the works of famous authors are to be expected rather than providing anything resembling a cause for surprise. Oral and textbook traditions provide the usual background that sustains, at best, only the most casual understanding of classic works. Unfortunately, the more serious readers also tend to prejudge and find in any work what they have always expected to locate there. Minds do have a tendency to edit and rearrange an actual text so that it fits cosily into pre-prepared categories. This bit of scholarly legerdemain has continued to redefine Keynes and misstate his understanding of the labour market.

> *The General Theory* makes clear that money wage stickiness is not in Keynes' opinion the ultimate cause of involuntary unemployment; indeed, due to the adverse effect of falling prices on demand, involuntary unemployment might possibly be more severe in its absence … What to Keynes was a minor assumption in a theory rationalizing business cycles is now interpreted as the key assumption (Akerlof and Yellen, 1987:137).

15   George Stigler, a major figure in the field of History of Thought, sometimes seemed to think of his efforts when indulging in such studies as something of a guilty pleasure. His attempts to defend such pursuits (1969) come off sounding somewhat lame, or at least half-hearted. In fact, at moments, Stigler could paint time spent focused on the past as being downright dangerous.

> He really believed in modern orthodox price theory, markets and all that. It is perfectly true that if you believe that then (a) you don't need the history of economic thought (b) the more history of economic thought you know the less you'll be inclined to believe the latest modern economics. Therefore, scepticism in any form is to some extent a bad thing. You know, the more

doubt that you acknowledge on any subject, the more sceptical you will be that you really have the truth. The less you know, of course, the less you will believe, but you will be sceptical even of your own clearly held beliefs. At some level, Stigler was very tempted by the idea that it might be better that you don't have any doubts that you really believe in things. He is tempted by the allure of the true believer. Of course, he is much too sophisticated to come right out with it. You need to remember all he had invested, an enormous amount of intellectual capital and scholarship, in the history of economic thought (Conversation with Mark Blaug, April 1998).

16   The supposition that economists can't write because they can't basically read was made a number of years ago by the author of this piece (Freedman, 1993). A potential chasm exists between thinking one can read (in terms of comprehension) and actually being able to do so. Perhaps this is somehow linked to the delusion that people can easily communicate with one another.

17   In politics, terms like 'socialist', 'fascist', 'communist' or even 'Marxist' are tossed about with abandon. The temptation is to insist that those who use such labels first define them, before being permitted to employ them.

18   Although many of my other efforts have dealt with the insidious effect of ideology on the professional output of economics, that particular investigation remains largely outside the bounds self-imposed on this work. Here the focus is rather on those rhetorical devices and habits (the things that economists do) that serve to impede communication and understanding within the profession.

19   For instance, it is not completely inaccurate to claim that George Stigler possessed an uncanny knack for sensing and formulating core economic questions but the unfortunate habit of knowing the answers to those very same questions prior to any research or investigation.

20   If, as some believe, the past is prologue to the future, this point will be widely ignored since the names involved will tend to drown out the purpose of employing them. Many other economists could have been substituted for the chosen few in this volume. The intention is not to analyse, let alone attack, any specific individual. These examples simply represent a means to an end, their importance as a demonstrative illustration. Plus, even the finest of economists have their own particular Achilles heel rendering them vulnerable to attack. That the selected economists surveyed in these pages may have chosen to deliberately hide their intentions, or eschew any real attempt to comprehend the work of their specified opponents, is entirely peripheral to the objectives pursued in this book. Consequently, assigning blame or praise to individuals remains a diversion rather than a relevancy. Nor should particular economists be faulted if his, or her, work is misconstrued due to ingrained, but lazy, habits shared by a majority of readers.

21   Too many economists suffer badly from the unreclaimed urge to be a Professor Know-it-all in each and every happenstance. Cynically, one reason driving the unalloyed pleasure most economists derive from locating unintended consequences within any given event (especially those flowing from policy decisions), is the self-satisfied feeling of implied superiority. (Namely, didn't you realise 'x' would happen? You must be either naïve, or dense, not to have anticipated that unfortunate consequence.) Far too often, the shouldered responsibility of clearing up any inevitable confusion is delivered with a distasteful side order of sneering. This menu item consists of some superior economist gleefully informing the lay public that everything they think they know is in fact completely wrong. The preening economist, posing as omniscient, has done much to effectively undermine the public reputation of the profession.

22   Those who strive to achieve ideological purity in the economics profession often become prey to nurturing a dubious stance, namely a tendency to embrace one sided scepticism. The group that could be assigned to a rightward pull on political matters tend to believe in a distinct version of original sin, enabling them to dismiss collectivists as at best a gaggle of naïve fantasists. Policy that intrinsically depends on human generosity is viewed as fundamentally flawed. Perhaps Dennis Robertson best encapsulated this position with the following question and response. 'What do economists, economize? Love' (1956:154). The focus in this case is an (almost) obsession with individual accountability and responsibility. Given this puritanical mix as a starting point, the result is inevitably seasoned with a dash of added disdain, as well as a pronounced repulsion towards any collective action.

> The liberal conceive of men as imperfect beings. He regards the problem of social organization to be as much a negative problem of preventing "bad" people from doing harm as of enabling "good" people to do good; and of course, "bad" and "good:" people may be the same people, depending on who is judging them (Friedman, 1962:12).

The other extreme, with their vision ever leftward, believes in the power of collectivism with an evangelical like certainty. They are not too distant in temperament from Holden Caulfield, the lead character in *The Catcher in the Rye* (Salinger, 1951). He is something of a cynical innocent in that he somehow manages to nurture an unwavering faith in the purity of young children, while disdaining almost everything else. Caulfield grieves that the young are inevitably corrupted by their institutional environment. Such an attitude is undeniably sweet but not particularly evidential. This perspective is based more on hope and illusion rather than on experience, or any clear grounding in reality. Consequently, strong ideological views find that categorisation is able to represent something of a protective haven from opposing ideas. Within such sound-proof walls, almost any justification for dismissing disparate views is strongly substantiated. Moreover, those who scrupulously search for reasons to be offended by opposing views are also seldom disappointed. Prejudging effectively saves the fuss attached to undertaking the tedious process of understanding a given text or alternative view.

23   An evolutionary impetus for such behaviour need not be too highly speculative. There basically appears to be a human inclination to search for (and adopt) a specific group identity. As mentioned, such a state does then lead to an 'us' versus 'them' mentality. Those outside one's circle of comrades, or duly recognised society, can be summarily dismissed, or even openly despised. If we allow ourselves to think in terms of the prehistoric era, humans tended to live together in small, limited tribes. Loyalty, the willingness to defend one's own and reject, or even battle, those outside one's closely defined circle assisted in basic survival. In evolutionary terms, survival is always paramount. Nothing is achievable if one's tribe effectively vanishes. (Alternatives to tribal survival include such grim options as servitude or death.) It is then hardly fanciful to imagine that this ritual bonding within a group became hardwired for evolutionary reasons, a trait that clearly enhanced survival probabilities.

24   This generalisation itself verges on being yet another poorly substantiated generalisation.

25   To be more exact, this type of pigeon-holing inevitably influences the way in which economists read a paper. The process of categorising may, in fact, encourage economists to read a work solely motivated by a desire to simply destroy it. Actual understanding of a given work is often much more difficult and far from urgent.

26   At this point, it becomes useful, if not entirely necessary, to offer an initial reminder that will be repeated and forcefully re-emphasised in the first case study. The intention in that chapter is not so much to explore Coase (or the Coase theorem), as to use this instance of misunderstanding to be indicative of a common impediment to understanding and communication. The errant pigeon-holing of Coase is selected merely as a convenient instance that manages to illustrate the issue at hand rather than as the focus of a specific investigation.

27   Stigler, himself, felt he was honouring, rather than distorting, Coase's intentions. Essentially, it is unclear whether George Stigler ever entirely grasped the sweep of Coase's broader project, starting with his famous 1937 paper on the firm.

> He [George Stigler] makes a number of remarks which are sort of coming to the entry point, as it were of the subject. When he reprinted that thing of his,

that the 'division of labor is limited' [Stigler 1951], or whatever the phrase is, 'by the extent of the market', he adds in a footnote of the reprint that he ought to have referred to my article [Coase 1937]. Well, I'm not sure that he ought to have referred to the article. I didn't want him to worry. But I think there was a feeling that he might have missed something (Conversation with Ronald Coase, October 1997).

28   One curious, but useful, way of thinking about Stigler's construction (of a hypothetical 'Coase Theorem') is in cinematic terms. Hitchcock was fond of using the term 'MacGuffin' to describe an object necessary to motivate the plot of a film without itself being of any real importance. The actual statue of 'The Maltese Falcon' in the book and film of the same name could have equally been a pink flamingo. Nothing in the story or script would have been forced to change. Similarly, in the Hitchcock film *Psycho*, the money stolen, which sets the plot in motion, is itself insignificant. Something had to be snaffled to lead Janet Leigh to the Bates Motel, but the exact nature of the missing goods remains strictly irrelevant.

In fiction, a MacGuffin (sometimes McGuffin) is an object, device, or event that is necessary to the plot and the motivation of the characters, but insignificant, unimportant, or irrelevant in itself. The term was originated by Angus MacPhail for film, adopted by Alfred Hitchcock, and later extended to a similar device in other fiction (https://en.wikipedia.org/wiki/MacGuffin).

29   A decided proclivity to embrace value theory over dull fact (or reality) is encapsulated in a famous New Yorker cartoon. The cartoon displays a bearded economist at a blackboard covered with an endless mathematical model. Chalk in hand, he boldly raises the core economic question to his colleague: "That may be all very well in practice, but does it work in theory?"

30   Muth's famous article appeared in 1960.

31   Kaldor invented the name in a 1934 article in the then newly established *Review of Economic Studies*. [The graphical model resembled a spider's cobweb. Economists tend not to waste any effort by constructing imaginative labels for their theories. Most economists remain intractably unmoved by poetic yearnings.] The journal itself grew out of a desire by young English economists of that era to have an outlet for their more mathematical approach to economics, an approach not then fully appreciated by the editors of the staid *Economic Journal*.

32   Ronald Fowler was a fellow student with Ronald Coase at the London School of Economics. Not having studied economics at LSE, but instead taking a commerce degree, Coase attributes what he knew about the subject to fellow students like Fowler, as well as his most influential teacher, Arnold Plant. Coase attended Plant's seminar while at LSE. Those interested in the pig market (or becoming a prosperous pig farmer) should see

Coase and Fowler (1935a, 1935b, 1937). Or, they could decide to actually raise pigs to gain the ultimate in confirmation.

> I had not studied economics at LSE and had picked up what I knew about economics from discussions with a fellow commerce degree student, Ronald Fowler, with students who were economics specialists and through attendance at a seminar with Arnold Plant, who was a Professor of Commerce (Coase, 2006:258–259).

33   For Coase, in fact, the firm (as a recognisable firm) fails to exist in standard microeconomic theory. The firm, like consumers, simply reacts to readily available market data. No actual decisions are taken, nor do individuals exist who are responsible for decision making. They are simply defined dot points.

> The consumer is not a human being but a consistent set of preferences. The firm to an economist, as Slater has said, "is effectively defined as a cost curve and a demand curve, and the theory is simply the logic of optimal pricing and input combination. Exchange takes place without any specification of its institutional setting. We have consumers without humanity, firms without organization, and even exchange without markets (Coase, 1988:3).

34   As opposed to those with more ideological leanings, his displayed scepticism was never purely one sided. Claims, even from those who outside observers would lazily categorise as his allies, were never taken on faith by Coase.

35   Pigou's approach, transformed into standard textbook theology, tackled decreasing cost industries only from an unarguably logical perspective. Efficient pricing demanded that price be set by and regulated according to marginal cost. In a competitive marketplace (faced with falling costs), this became inoperative since attempting to do so would relegate total revenue to a sum insufficient to cover total costs. Accordingly, and certainly logically, the deficit created by such economies of scale would best be alleviated via government subsidies. Coase, in particular, references a 1938 work by Hotelling as an exemplar of such reasoning (Coase, 1946:169).

36   Coase would not be reluctant to point out that textbook solutions ignore the clear fact that such government interventions refuse to operate at a zero transaction cost level. Theory and associated policy tends to embrace a predilection for a more amnesiac mind-set, as far as this element is concerned.

37   Even from the limited bit of geography that Stigler is staking out here, the statement, if not exactly wrong, seems incomplete and certainly unsatisfying. Considered only from the narrow perspective of career advancement, a substantial knowledge of the discipline's past is neither necessary nor sufficient in and of itself. But this fails to negate the possibility that an

individual would be a more thoughtful and even (measured by some scales) a better economist by gaining a deeper understanding of the past. This would seem to be the case if the individual strives to be more than a competent technician. The same would be true for the mathematician who might get a better idea of how to think about mathematics (and its associated problems), as well as other pertinent issues, by trying to comprehend the works of Newton or Leibnitz. (After all, even serious chess players are assiduous in studying the past games played by various grandmasters.) Seeing how problems were conceptualised and tackled in the past can hardly be deleterious, or a complete waste of time. Consequently, a misunderstanding of Coase, from the blinkered perspective provided by Stigler, might seem to be bereft of any meaningful consequences. But perhaps such a misunderstanding would eventually, and subtly, shape the tracks that the discipline follows or the policies it opts to pursue.

> If a physician mishandles a number of patients, there is the danger that they will lose their lives. If a teacher interprets a poem to his students in an impossible manner, "nothing further happens." But perhaps it is good if we speak more cautiously here. By ignoring the question concerning the thing and by insufficiently interpreting a poem, it appears as though nothing further happens. One day, perhaps after fifty or one hundred years, nevertheless something has happened (Heidegger, 1967:53–54).

38   For clarity, the four dubious strategies cited in this volume are separated and kept distinct. But it is obvious that one often bleeds into the next. Strategies and communication techniques that embrace all four are consequently far from a rarity. Though in the Coase example presented, no conclusive evidence exists of others attacking him specifically, or seeking to eviscerate him to any extent. (Instead, most of the withering fire has targeted the ersatz version of Coase created by George Stigler.) However, lumping Coase in with the Chicago School is a rather broad and sloppy act of categorisation that appears to be committed based largely on the allure of convenience, or just plain, lazy thinking. Many critics and supporters of the aforementioned, and woefully labelled, Coase Theorem employ this formulation as a jumping off point to discuss the Chicago School (whether favourably or not). Perhaps such a focus might better serve as a convenient excuse to air their own understanding (or misunderstanding) of transaction costs, given Coase's identification with the idea. Unfortunately, Coase's distinctive methodology often gets lost in the fervid shuffle of discussion driven by ulterior objectives.

Coase himself has pointedly attempted to explain how even ostensible supporters like Richard Posner, have attributed unjustified ideas and positions to him that simply fail to have any identifiable basis. In the case of this constructed theorem, we can clearly discern how displaying such labelled buckets as 'The Chicago School' actually incorporate a number of not perfectly compatible perspectives. Posner seems to have simply assumed what Coase should be thinking, rather than taking the time to stop by his Law School office and ask him. (Both held positions there.)

> My first reaction on reading Richard Posner's [1993] paper was one of amusement. It recalled to my mind Miss Elliot's description of Alfred Marshall's lectures on Henry George. She said that Marshall reminded her of a boa-constrictor that had slobbered over its victim before swallowing it (Marshall [1947:35]). In saying this, I had no intention of equating Posner with Marshall, still less with any kind of snake. Although I must confess that the wicked thought did flicker through my mind as I studied this paper with more care and ceased to be amused (Coase, 1993:96).
>
> The trouble with Posner, to use a phrase of Frank Knight's, is not with what he doesn't know but with what he knows that "ain't so" (Coase, 1993:98).

39   Readers who fail to be those of an elderly persuasion (and who are too lazy to google the answer) might be sufficiently curious to discover that *Pogo* was a satirical comic strip back in the dark ages of the 1950s and 1960s (though officially running from 1948 to 1975). *Pogo*, a possum, is perhaps best remembered for the quote, 'We have met the enemy and they are us.' Notice it is a quote that is quite applicable to any historical era, including the present one.

40   The Chicago approach assumes that the market for ideas works much like any other market. Since competitive markets are theoretically constructed to yield optimal results, so too should the market for ideas. But there is a basic fallacy underwriting this bit of logic. Markets at best deliver those goods and services most adopted to the demands of their relevant consumers. The resulting output then is simply best adapted to its environment rather than somehow correctly evaluated as an example of what is defined as being the best, or as some sort of an optimal result. In the same way, the marketplace for ideas may deliver a result that need not be true or good but suits the consumers of those theories, such as professional economists.

> It may be that in the long run good ideas do surface but they surface faster, if written in a persuasive fashion. Moreover, bad ideas may be put persuasively. And they may gain the necessary threshold. However, taking that same analogy in competition among ideas, there is a presumption, although not a certainty, that in the longer run, the good ideas are going to compete out the bad ideas. But that may take a long time and may not even always operate. There's nothing necessary about that. Nothing guaranteed about that (Conversation with Gary Becker, October 1997).

41   He did not show quite the same aversion to mathematical formulations (or econometrics) that often appeared in thoughts expressed by Knight.

> There is much in Posner's paper with which I disagree such as his assertion
> that I object to econometric studies (Posner [1993, 79]). In fact, much of my
> early work was econometric (Coase, 1993:97).

42   Though like many of his Chicago colleagues (Friedman, Stigler, Director
and a number of others), Coase did conclude that there had been an excessive degree of government intervention in the economy. However, unlike
his supposed compatriots, he based this judgment on his specific investigations (and those of others) into the results such public policies had achieved.
In contrast, he recognised that there was no *a priori*, theoretical basis for
making substantial policy claims. In essence, his methodological approach
eschewed knowing the answer to a posed question prior to any actual investigation. Otherwise, theory can be used as a tool to ram through preferred
policy positions. In essence, theory becomes no more than a rhetorical,
rather than an investigative, device, a mere handmaiden to ideological
leanings.

> I explained [in 'The Problem of Social Cost'] that there were costs involved
> in making market transactions and that consequently there were reallocations
> of factors of production which would, of themselves, raise the value of pro-
> duction but would not take place when the costs of the necessary transactions
> exceeded the gain in the value of production that would result. Such realloca-
> tions of factors can also, of course, be brought about by government regula-
> tion. Now government regulation also has costs – and government regulators
> may have in mind ends other than raising the value of production. But the
> opportunity is there for government regulation to improve on the market. I
> wrote that "direct government regulation will not necessarily give better
> results than leaving the problem to be solved by the market or the firm. But
> equally, there is no reason why, on occasion, such governmental administra-
> tive regulation should not lead to an improvement in economic efficiency"
> (Coase, 1994b:61–62).

43   Please note that selected quotes that appear in the four case study chapters
may also appear in this introduction. This strategy of deliberate repetition
manages to agitate some editors (and readers) who nurture a distinct allergy
to seeing something more than once. As well, some critical readers, who
read with an intent to destroy, may hungrily latch on to such repetitions,
like barnacles cementing themselves to a wooden ship's hull. Unambiguous
joy seems to attend the discovery of such repeated quotes. These supposed
faux pas are readily concocted to represent a legitimate avenue through
which an entire volume of work can be dismissed and discredited. (The
implied conclusion is that the unequivocal appearance of sloppy editing
reflects an inexcusable amount of sloppy thinking and analysis.) My suggestion is that these would be critics get over themselves. If someone is
reading only with the intent to destroy and demolish, the point then arises

as to whether doing so ranks as anything that approximates to a legitimate effort. Surely readers who remain stubbornly uninterested in trying to understand what they have read could find a more productive use for their time. Consequently, be forewarned that the technique is deliberate and quite conscious. Disagree with it if you must, but there really is no reason to mention it or to make a fuss. Though, if your desire is to appear fatuous, so be it. Of course, by pointing out this small oddity, I am deliberately tempting fate by almost encouraging any such potential reader to focus on this supposed transgression (and other irrelevant issues) with an almost laser like precision. The process of self-selection and sorting is always revealing (and sometimes even amusing).

44   Coase's compulsion to examine the way in which firms and industries actually operated, or his tendency to dive into historical archives, started early in his career. In 1932, he was awarded a Cassel Travelling Scholarship by the University of London. He spent that time in the US, touring plants and talking to plant managers. In essence, his quest was to understand the following neglected question. Namely, if prices were sufficient to coordinate economic output and activity, where did firms, planning and management fit in?

> I found the answer by the summer of 1932. It was to realise that there were costs of using the pricing mechanism. What the prices are have to be discovered. There are negotiations to be undertaken, contracts to be drawn up, inspections to be made, arrangements to be made to settle disputes, and so on. These costs have come to be known as transaction costs. Their existence implies that methods of coordination alternative to the market, which are themselves costly and in various ways imperfect, may nonetheless be preferable to relying on the pricing mechanism, the only method of co-ordination normally analysed by economists (Coase, 1994a:7–8).

45   Again, Coase's perspective on abstraction was equally misunderstood as being some deviation (or perversion), from Chicago orthodoxy. He certainly objected to abstraction for abstraction's sake. This tendency is what he dismissed as 'blackboard economics'.

> Posner [1993, 76] also refers to my "dislike of abstraction." This is wrong. It is true that I said in my Warren Nutter lecture that the assumption of our theories should be realistic. "[R]ealism in assumptions forces us to analyse the world that exists, not some imaginary world that does not" (Coase [1988a, 65]). But I go on to say: "It is, of course, true that our assumptions should not be completely realistic" (Coase [1988a, 65]).

46   Though like his Chicago colleagues, he was wary when it came to approving additional government interventions, his reasoning was far from perfectly aligned with their thinking. As the editor of the *Journal of Law and*

Economics (1964–1982) he had seen a multitude of articles detailing government inefficiency in operation. Yet his reasoning for a smaller government goes back to the thinking first displayed in his 1937 paper on the firm. Essentially, just as a firm could expand past the point of producing a net positive marginal product, so too could government. The exact size and extent determining when a government had overreached its mark was an empirical rather than a theoretical question.

> I have come to the conclusion that the most probable reason we obtain these results is that the government is attempting to do too much – that it operates on such a gigantic scale that it has reached the stage at which, for many of its activities, as economists would say, the marginal product is negative. We would expect to reach this stage if the size of an organisation were allowed to expand indefinitely. I suspect that this is exactly what has happened (Coase, 1994b:62).

47 An interesting example of Coase's refusal to accept a persuasive, but evidence light, story comes in his 2006 article examining the absorption of Fisher Body by General Motors. In a well-cited piece, Klein *et al.* (1978) couldn't resist trimming an historical event to substantiate their preferred theory. The fact that it took decades for someone to examine the validity of this widely accepted story elucidates an almost ineradicable disregard the profession has for examining the nuts and bolts of specific events. Among economists, economic history, industry studies and other fields that contain a large descriptive component are, like the history of economic theory, fields that attract little attention, or award a limited quantum of recognition (or honour) to their labourers.

48 Such approaches are unfortunately all too common within referee reports. Ideally, these evaluations are meant to assist a researcher to improve his or her output. Unfortunately, too many academics, when called to perform this role, instead view it as an opportunity to demonstrate their own superiority by undercutting a paper in sometimes irrelevant fashions. (For those vaguely interested, see Freedman, 2000.)

49 It will turn out that all four cases are Chicago based. Let me again emphasise that this focus doesn't imply, or pretend to imply, that Chicago represents some cesspool that fosters such misanalysis or shady strategies. I could easily have shifted to different perspectives (or alternative locales) and found much the same tendencies. Chicago, for me, just happens to represent a more familiar terrain. Within these illustrated case studies, lie no hidden subtext or malicious intent.

50 There is more than a Shakespearean whiff of being hoisted on one's own petard. Or perhaps even a dash of Mafiosi payback can be sensed, without any extended effort to do so.

51   I confess that here I am obliquely referring to the book (1989) that first brought Philip Mirowski to the well-earned attention of his profession. Curiously enough, I would be tempted to suggest that in that volume, Mirowski attempted to demonstrate that neo-classical economics had been guilty of what I have labelled as the third cardinal sin – employing a poisoned apple. In essence, Mirowski's claim was that economics had been less than open (or honest), in describing what it had to offer, or the basis on which it had been built. The profession, knowingly or not, has too often used a bit of camouflage to conceal its true intent.

52   Those willing to do whatever it takes sometimes prove reluctant in admitting that they actually enjoy diving headfirst into this strategic pool of bullying and one-upmanship. For academics, nothing is more pleasurable than showing off their brilliance, demonstrating how much more clever they are compared to lesser beings in the profession. Thus, shredding an opposing theory or article yields pleasures unconnected with advancing truth, improving the discipline or taking tea with one's elderly grandmother.

> Nor, perhaps, are we wholly satisfied with what Samuelson calls our own applause – indeed we cannot be confident that this applause is unaffected by our policy positions. I concede to Samuelson, nevertheless, that to a scientist educated hands make more melodious applause than ignorant hands, but too often the educated hands seem to be sat upon by educated asses (Stigler, 1976:354).

53   In passing, it may be useful simply to repeat that there is an associated, and definitely much more, tawdry thrill attached to utterly demolishing an opponent. In academia, the desire to show off one's own cleverness often rears its far from attractive head. Test this proposition by having the willingness and tenacity to sit through an academic seminar. Vanity within such settings comes in all forms and shapes.

54   As previously indicated, labelling can prove deadly. Once someone is labelled as a wife beater, misogynist or racist, further discussion is largely at an end. Proving what you are not is difficult, if not at times impossible. Any incident, no matter how possibly unintended or even innocent, can be used with damning intent.

55   As explained elsewhere, the terms 'poison apple' and 'Trojan horse' are employed almost inter-changeably. Possibly, some obscure difference exists, if one wants to imaginatively excavate deeply enough, but pragmatically, what term appears is more likely a reflection of a mostly whimsical choice.

56   Naively, failure of the implicit scenario that was to follow the invasion was never seriously contemplated. Thus, the invasion failed to underwrite either the ostensible justification proposed to the public, or even the host of more implicit reasons that were actually driving the decision.

57   Robert Solow famously dismissed the idea of rational expectations by laughing at the very idea that underpinned the theory.

> Suppose someone sits down where you are sitting right now and announces to me that he is Napoleon Bonaparte. The last thing I want to do with him is to get involved in a technical discussion of cavalry tactics at the battle of Austerlitz. If I do that, I'm getting tacitly drawn into the game that he is Napoleon. Now, Bob Lucas and Tom Sargent like nothing better than to get drawn into technical discussions, because then you have tacitly gone along with their fundamental assumptions; your attention is attracted away from the basic weakness of the whole story. Since I find that fundamental framework ludicrous, I respond by treating it as ludicrous – that is, by laughing at it – so as not to fall into the trap of taking it seriously and passing on to matters of technique (Robert Solow quoted in Klamer, 1983:146).

58   'Just so' stories appear with a degree of frequency in economic articles. These enter in the guise of concrete examples or applications. When examined more closely, they reveal themselves to be the way in which economists think the world should and thus has operated. Logic is largely substituted for evidence. In essence, from an economic perspective, this is the way the world should have unfolded, if it had not stubbornly refused to play by self-imposed economic rules. However, whether such nominated events actually occurred often fail to be investigated. In other words, you don't read Kipling (1902) to explore natural history. The information provided by such sources fails to confirm any hypothesis suggested by a more exact scientific discipline.

59   The labour market is simply assumed to be no different than any other market. In essence, the opportunity cost of any exchange in this market is implicitly taken to be equal for each side of a labour contract. To be more precise, switching costs for employers and employees are magically assumed not to differ.

60   Encouraged by Hayek's (1944) *Road to Serfdom,* this 1947 mountaintop meeting sought to counter the then intellectual dominance of what its members viewed as a dangerous drift towards collectivism and authoritarianism. For this embattled group (or at least embattled in their own eyes), liberty and freedom were at stake in (and at the heart of) their struggle. The dangers identified were as real to these participants as those which had been posed by the recently defeated Nazi Germany.

> If the society's members were troubled by the difficulty of reconciling capitalism and social traditions, they were equally preoccupied with a second challenge that Hayek's philosophical project entailed: the need to clarify the complex relationship between capitalism and democracy. Many of them believed that the central attributes of participative governance, including democracy and freedom of speech, had developed concurrently with and

largely because of the emergence of the market economy. One of the central virtues they attributed to the market was its capacity to loosen restrictions in other areas of life, and they asserted that "political freedoms" and "economic freedoms" were closely and necessarily entwined (Burgin, 2012:116–117).

Linking freedom to free markets would become Milton Friedman's unchanging and near sacred gospel from the first Mont Pelerin meeting through the rest of a very lengthy life. (He died in 2006 at the age of 96.)

> NPQ: So you see the march of liberty and free markets going forward into the 21st century, not taking a detour backward in China or elsewhere?
>   Friedman: Yes. The world as a whole has more or less embraced freedom. (Friedman, 2006:5).

61   As would later be the case with rational expectations, Friedman's essay enticed the profession, or at least a healthy section of it, into a virtual briar patch of technical and philosophical issues. Doing so helped shift the terms of methodological debate away from what both Friedman and Stigler considered to represent much more treacherous terrain.

62   Imagine Snow White being presented with an apple that had worms crawling out of it. The Evil Queen would have been immediately dispatched to a boot camp for remedial treachery.

63   Some individuals are compulsive stirrers. They are not content unless they can rouse contention in others. For academics like Friedman or Stigler, the very worse fate their work could face would be to have their efforts simply ignored. In this, they were not unlike Milton's (the poet, not the economist) Satan. Like Satan, they just couldn't help themselves.

64   The use of categorisation as an easy means to dismiss approaches summarily, hand again rears its dubious head.

65   Abstraction and generality came to dominate, with specific differences seen more as a diversion than entailing critical and determinative information. Detailed information (depending on specifics) was characterised as no more than a minor distraction, a cask full of anecdotal trivia.

66   A description of what a cinematic journey of this type entails is described, at length, in that concluding chapter. Except in the case of hardened cinema fans, a repetition of this common film feature would most likely be seriously unwelcome.

67   A bit of speculation here is hard to resist, though it never leaves the realm of 'no more than speculation'. The publisher of the Friedman biography is not an academic press. The suspicion remains that it is meant to appeal and sell to the general public. There might even be some distant hope to interest film studios into purchasing the movie rights with Danny DeVito slated to play Milton Friedman (at least in his later years). In which case, transforming Friedman's life into a hero's journey would be entirely logical.

References

Akerlof, G. (2020). "Sins of omission and the practice of economics", *Journal of Economic Literature*. 58(2): 405–418.

Akerlof, G. and Yellen, J. (1987). "Rational models of irrational behaviour", *American Economic Review – Papers and Proceedings*. 77(2): 137–142.

Alchian, A. and Demsetz, H. (1972). "Production, information costs, and economic organization", *The American Economic Review*. 62(5): 777–795.

Burgin, A. (2012). *The Great Persuasion*. Cambridge: Harvard University Press.

Burns, J. (2023). *Milton Friedman – The Last Conservative*. New York: Farrar Straus and Giroux.

Coase, R. H. and Fowler, R. F. (1935a). "Bacon production and the pig-cycle in Great Britain", *Economica* (n.s.). 2: 142–147.

Coase, R. H. and Fowler, R. F. (1935b). "The pig-cycle: A rejoinder", *Economica* (n.s.). 2: 423–428.

Coase, R. H. and Fowler, R. F. (1937). "The pig-cycle in Great Britain: An explanation", *Economica* (n.s.). 4: 55.

Coase, R. H. (1937). "The nature of the firm", *Economica* (n.s.). 4(16): 386–405.

Coase, R. H. (1946). "The marginal cost controversy", *Economica* (n.s.). 13(51): 169–182.

Coase, R. H. (1960). "The problem of social cost", *The Journal of Law & Economics*. 3(1): 1–44.

Coase, R. H. (1974). "The lighthouse in economics", *Journal of Law and Economics*. 17(2): 357–376.

Coase, R. H. (1988a). "How should economists choose?", in *Ideas, Their Origins and Consequences*. Washington, D.C.: The American Enterprise Institute.

Coase, R. H. (1988b). *The Firm, the Market, and the Law*. Chicago: The University of Chicago Press.

Coase, R. H. (1993). "Coase on Posner on Coase: Comment", *Journal of Institutional and Theoretical Economics*. 149(1): 96–98.

Coase, R. H. (1994a). "The institutional structure of production", in *Essays on Economics and Economists*. Chicago: The University of Chicago Press, pp. 3–15.

Coase, R. H. (1994b). "Economics and public policy", in *Essays on Economics and Economists*. Chicago: The University of Chicago Press, pp. 47–63.

Coase, R. H. (2006). "The conduct of economics: The example of Fisher Body and General Motors", *Journal of Economics and Management Strategy*. 15(2): 255–278.

Freedman, C. (1993). "Why economists can't read", *Methodus* (*The Journal of Economic Methodology*). 5(1): 6–23.

Freedman, C. (2000). "Do economic journals obey economic prescriptions", *The Review of Industrial Organization.* 17(4): 371–384.

Friedman, M. (1953). *Essays in Positive Economics.* Chicago: University of Chicago Press.

Friedman, M. (1962). *Capitalism & Freedom.* Chicago: University of Chicago Press.

Friedman, M. (2006). "Free markets and the end of history", *New Perspectives Quarterly.* 23(1): 37–43, http://www.digitalnpq.org/archive/2006_winter/friedman.html (14/02/2006).

Grimm, J. and Grimm, W. (1992). "Snow white", Zipes, J. (tr.) in *The Complete Fairy Tales of the Brothers Grimm.* New York: Bantam Press, pp. 196–204.

Hayek, F. (1944). *The Road to Serfdom.* Chicago: University of Chicago Press.

Hazlett, T. W. (1997). "Looking for results", Reason.com. January 1: 1–8, http://reason.com/archives/1997/01/01/looking-for-results (04/09/2013).

Heidegger, M. (1967). *What Is a Thing?* Chicago: Henry Regnery Company.

Hotelling, H. (1938). "The general welfare in relation to problems of taxation and of railway and utility rates", *Econometrica.* 6(3): 242–269.

Kaldor, N. (1934). "A classificatory note on the determination of equilibrium", *Review of Economic Studies.* 1(1): 122–136.

Keynes, J. M. (1973). *The Collected Works of John Maynard Keynes: Volume IV.* London: Macmillan.

Kipling, R. (1902). *Just So Stories.* London: Macmillan Publishers.

Klamer, A. (1983). *Conversations with Economists: New Classical Economists and Opponents Speak Out on the Current Controversy in Macroeconomics.* Totowa: Rowman and Littlefield.

Klein, B., Crawford, R. G., and Alchian, A. A. (1978). "Vertical integration, appropriable rents, and the competitive contracting process", *Journal of Law & Economics.* 21(2): 297–326.

Knight, F. (1953/1924). "Some fallacies in the interpretation of social cost", in Boulding, K. and Stigler, G. (eds.) *Readings in Price Theory.* London: George Allen and Unwin Ltd, pp. 160–179.

Knight, F. (1971). *Risk, Uncertainty and Profit.* Chicago: University of Chicago Press.

Marshall, M. (1947). *What I Remember.* Cambridge: Cambridge University Press.

Mirowski, P. (1989). *More Heat Than Light.* Cambridge: Cambridge University Press.

Muth, J. (1960). "Optimal properties of exponentially weighted forecasts", *Journal of the American Statistical Association.* 55(290): 299–306.

Posner, R. (1993). "The new institutional economics meets law and economics", *Journal of Institutional and Theoretical Economics.* 149(1): 73–87.

Robertson, D. (1956). *Economic Commentaries.* London: Staples Press Limited.

Salinger, J. D. (1951). *The Catcher in the Rye*. Boston: Little, Brown and Company.

Stigler, G. J. (1951). "The division of labor is limited by the extent of the market", *Journal of Political Economy*. 59(3): 185–193.

Stigler, G. J. (1969). "Does economics have a useful past?" *History of Political Economy*. 1(2): 217–230.

Stigler, G. J. (1975). "The tactics of economic reform", in *The Citizen and the State*, Chicago: The University of Chicago Press, pp. 23–38.

Stigler, G. J. (1976). "Do economists matter?", *Southern Economic Journal*. 42(1): 347–354.

Stigler, G. J. (1982). *Memoirs of an Unregulated Economist*. Chicago: University of Chicago Press.

Van Horn, R. (2011). "Jacob Viner's critique of Chicago neoliberalism" in Van Horn, R., Mirowski, P., and Stapleford, T. A. (eds.) *Building Chicago Economics*. Cambridge: Cambridge University Press, pp. 279–301.

Theorem or MacGuffin[1]: Finding a Way Through the Coasian Muddle

Two roads diverged in a wood, and I –
I took the road less travelled by,
And that has made all the difference (Frost 1916:1).

I. The Sesame Street Gambit – the Intrinsic Problems of Pigeon-Holing[2]

Wyrd bið ful aræd (destiny is all)

In a more perfect world, this opening section would not be required. These words would remain clearly superfluous and simply never appear. Such a desirable environment would imply that this pesky prologue of sorts would remain an unseen explanation, one whose absence would prove entirely unlamented by any potential reader.[3] But forced to inhabit a neighbourhood noted and dominated by miscommunication, the forthcoming story that will unfold in this chapter demands something of a roadmap to keep readers' attention from straying too far. The hope is that many of those unknown, but potentially pesky, readers can be gently enticed to travel down an unfamiliar road, even if not perfectly graded, but one that requires at least a minimum degree of comprehension. Despite my own personal cultivated dislike of such preambles to an actual event (I'd prefer the action to start at the get-go), any attempt to minimize the risk of reading at cross purposes cannot be an effort that is entirely wasted. Consequently, the discussion that lies before you must commence by cataloguing two major (but closely related) errors that economists commit when purporting to read articles or books. Such missteps are often discoverable in a wide array of economic analyses, all of which display a noticeably befuddled understanding of a given text. Both of these failings, unfortunately, nurse and sometimes nurture even broader and more dangerous extensions and applications that bleed into everyday life. In essence the discussion focuses on an academic subclass of a much broader problem.

One discerned fallibility is the inescapable desire (and even the desperate need) for 'group identification'. Forms of this human desire (or possibly weakness) can be recognized as almost something of a ubiquitous phenomenon.[4] More broadly, concrete examples manifest themselves in the ostentatious display of religious affiliation, rabid but narrow nationalism, overtly virulent racism and even down to an unreasoning and fanatical support for local sporting teams. Such identification can remain largely benign, resulting only in true believers meeting and communicating together, buying paraphernalia (flags and bumper stickers), or even generating beneficial charity drives as a supportive device. But the ugly side of such human desires are too often perverted into fostering uglier objectives. Wars, prejudice and discrimination all flow from the persistent need to identify 'the other', those outside one's group, who by definition are somehow less human than those within. Even seemingly innocent sporting events can turn into a contested war in all but name, with outbreaks of football hooliganism and other unsavoury elements added to an already indigestible recipe of violence. In other words, group identification makes it all too easy to be dismissive of anyone lying outside the nominated group.

Consequently, group identity has long found a comfortable home within the economics discipline. Such an urge manages to provide convenience, efficiency and even psychic support to designated members. This need to pigeon hole, or catalogue perceptions, simplifies the requisite judgments bestowed on any given research work. Defining economists and their output in this fashion allows for facile prejudgments based mainly on allegiances and a preconceived sense of certainty. Thus the profession seems to have increasingly splintered into factions, each planting its own flag as representative of the sole source of economic wisdom. Yet economists are not botanists, cursed with a categorical imperative to catalogue. There are no exigent or compelling reasons that would justify a pursuit of categorization with such a degree of focused and unrelieved zeal. This urge appears to be ruled more by vanity and divisiveness than by utility based rationality.

Consequently, economics has sliced itself into ever narrower and proliferating camps. There are now Neo-Classicals, Classicals, Neo-Liberals, Keynesians, Post-Keynesians, Neo-Keynesians. Austrians, Marxists, Post-Marxists, Institutionalists, New Institutionalists, Behaviouralists, and many, many more. Benefits from slotting work into predetermined pigeon-holes flow accordingly. Staking one's allegiance to a convenient and congenial flag allows for an automatic dismissal of work lying outside the ambit of one's own sanctified circle. Thus papers can be rejected as Marxian drivel, or standard Neo-Classical propaganda. By forcing research and analysis into certain preconceived configurations, we can reject (*a priori*) the gist of all and any alien arguments that might appear. Even when opponents deign to read the work of others, opting not to dismiss such views out of hand, these opposition articles inevitably yield only that which the predisposed reader expects to discover.

For example, an economist may find himself (or possibly herself) to be widely identified with the Chicago School approach. For most of the profession that serves as a sufficient determination to either embrace or reject his or her research instantly.[5] The essential point is that this need to pigeon-hole can blind the reader to the actual work of an author by generating a powerful and unalterable prejudgment. (Perhaps this failing should be labelled 'the fallacy of expectations'.) The created smokescreen of received wisdom inevitably clouds any forthcoming conclusions. The only method for successfully avoiding such a whirlpool of misunderstanding is to ignore labels and judge each work on its own merits. This statement is so obvious that it goes without saying and appears indisputable. Unfortunately, this rational approach to communication must be repeatedly emphasized, since although not truly debatable, the actual action of avoiding prejudgment is often stubbornly ignored.[6]

Closely related to the prejudgment error is the related misstep of evaluating an author solely by the company he or she keeps. This might be referred to as 'being tarred with the same brush' or perhaps being defined by 'the company one keeps'. Here, a small personal anecdote may help (or at least provide a momentary diversion). When I was young and still impressionable, I can remember my mother lecturing my sister on being careful about the company she kept. She was warned away from becoming close friends with what my mother labelled as girls who were 'fast'. (Here I am almost dead certain that my mother wasn't referring to those young women who participated in track and field.) The idea was that my sister would be identified as having the same sort of behaviour exhibited by her friends, whether or not any truth attached to the matter.

Putting these two related issues together allows us to analyze a core problem underlying the confusion associated with the work of Ronald Coase, an eminent economist whose work remains widely misunderstood.[7] He was undeniably at Chicago (nearly half of his very long life, though residing within the Law School rather than the economics department).[8] He also spent most of his professional time in the company of such stalwarts of the Chicago School as Milton Friedman and George Stigler. Even more so, his policy views usually ran parallel with those of Friedman and Stigler.[9] Yet to thoroughly understand his work, you need to grasp more than his erstwhile affiliation. Comprehension of his methodological approach is equally necessary. A careful examination of Coase's perspective aligns him more with Classical Liberals, such as Frank Knight, rather than those of the post war Chicago School.[10] In other words, while Coase was at Chicago, he was not of the Chicago School of Economics. His approach to economics ran down an alternative track.

Approaching Coase as just another Chicago Boy leads to a radical failure to grasp his methodology or clearly understand his analysis. It allows others, though sometimes in good faith, to exploit Coase's work for their own purposes. No clearer case of this type of (*uber alles* employment of ideologically driven) insight can be found than in the perspective constructed by George Stigler when formulating his infamous Coase Theorem. This was Stigler's well known reading, and ultimate transformation, of Coase's 1960 paper, *The Problem of Social Cost*. It is from this reading that the misnamed and misdirected 'Coase Theorem' derives. In fact Stigler's construction stems from his efforts to hijack Coase's paper for his own purposes, rather than any attempt to encapsulate the articles essential objectives.[11] That Stigler could successfully accomplish this misdirection stems from a facile dumping of Coase into the voluminous Chicago School pigeon hole.

II. Prelude to Misadventure – The Huck Finn Conundrum

It seems to me that when you get to his [Stigler's] later work, say with Becker, you know what the conclusion is going to be before you start the argument. In a sense, you're assembling arguments to support a conclusion. I mean, that may be unkind and untrue but it's an impression. And, it's even more so in the work of Richard Posner. Have you read any of that? It seems to me that the plot is always the same, and the characters stay fixed (Conversation with Ronald Coase, October 1997).

The story of the eventful dinner at the home of Aaron Director (Chicago) remains well documented by George Stigler (1988),[12] as well as too many other available sources. That revelatory moment of triumph, when the scales of dissimulation and confusion fell from the assembled eyes of a conclave of doubting academics, has been rendered dramatically by one of its more notorious participants. In his autobiography, George Stigler (1988) conjures up the nearly mythical story of that now famous gathering, where Coase single-handedly challenged and changed the minds of a cohort of Chicago's finest economists. Drama though, does not necessarily underwrite verisimilitude.[13] In Coase's understanding, his argument was primarily focused on transactions costs, a discussion advanced by employing a direct and unambiguous application of the marginal cost curve.[14]

His initial target in that paper was a specific and prevailing Pigouvian model of external costs. Presented was a version of Pigou's thinking, at least as understood within the profession and often appearing in textbooks. This model blithely failed to recognize such transaction costs, but instead implicitly analyzed the problem of externalities as if transactions costs were simply nonexistent.[15] Coase opposed this approach by persistently arguing that if one assumed the total absence of transaction costs, then one should expect any externality to be effectively handled by inter-agent bargaining. Consequently, if there are no transactions costs, then there is no relevant need for government intervention.[16] Externality problems would be simply internalized by the relevant participants. Unfortunately, this state of zero transaction costs clearly runs counter to Coase's objective in constructing his more comprehensive argument. However, by ignoring the obvious, such fundamental claims become almost entirely superfluous once processed through the methodological millstones favoured by the Chicago School.[17]

Consequently, if his work is read carefully (by first removing any Chicago installed goggles), Coase is found to favour a more open-minded, skeptical approach to questions involving externalities. Directly eschewed is any legal or moral notion of assigning blame by identifying a transgressor or formulating anything resembling a universal policy assumed to resolve all issues.[18] Rather, the driving rationale is simply a pragmatic one. The operative imperative is to discover, through careful empirical investigation, the most efficient response to a given (and rather specific) situation. No *a priori* judgments need apply.

> *Interviewer:* The place the Coase Theorem comes into play most often is when talking about pollution. The pollution problem has been seen in a very different light because of the Coase Theorem.

> *Coase:* It should be seen in a different light, but I don't see why you needed the Coase Theorem to do it. The pollution problem is always seen as someone who was doing something bad that has to be stopped. To me, pollution is doing something bad and good. People don't pollute because they like polluting. They do it because it's a cheaper way of producing something else. The cheaper way of producing something else is the good; the loss in value that you get from the pollution is the bad. You've got to compare the two. That's the way to look at it. It isn't the way that people look at it. They think zero pollution is the best situation (Coase 1997:2–3).

The use of the Coase theorem to support a narrow, market approach to economics serves as a useful demonstration of the crafted style and categorical logic that the Chicago School employed to sell its beliefs and ideology. The implemented vision reveals a policy based agenda. The supporting framework is structurally anchored to a universal and seemingly unimpeachable system of markets and decision making. (Actors are defined as rational agents performing within a competitive and constrained market topography.) The emphasis remains firmly on the tactical advantage to be gained by adhering to a given approach. The underlying logic similarly eschews any potential explanatory benefits that might be afforded by alternative or heavily conceptualized responses. Fidelity to a proven path remains the unspecified goal. Therefore, as stipulated by George Stigler, any focus on the sharp deviations that the Coase Theorem nurtures from the original is deemed to be largely inconsequential (despite being a clean-cut departure from the intentions of its assumed creator). Instead, this conceptual transformation represents Stigler's deliberate attempt to buttress his own critical vision.[19]

Consequently, the way in which the Coase Theorem subsequently evolved into a key building block in policy debates is worth exploring. A targeted investigation may also be instructive by reflecting the manner and extent to which the Chicago School deviated from the approach that defined Classical Liberalism. Examining this discrepancy simultaneously highlights an alternative perspective that has been largely forsaken.[20] Equally important is that such analysis demonstrates how Coase could be identified with an extraneous theory, by simply tossing him into a common pot labelled 'The Chicago School'. Doing so successfully immunized readers against the ideas and approaches Coase intended to underline.

> Similarly ideological is the way he [George Stigler] lit on Ron Coase and read the Coase theorem incorrectly, much to Coase's own amazement.[21] Coase never realized there was a theorem there. That's all a wonderful example of ideologically inspired criticism and also a perception of the subtle weakness of economics. This, from an economist who otherwise would, of course, have denied that ideology had any role to play in advancing the role of economics (Conversation with Mark Blaug, April 1998).

The difference here is far more subtle than may appear initially. Stigler, like Coase, did not believe that transaction costs were ever strictly zero. The issue instead rested on the verisimilitude markets possessed in resembling those more theoretical versions underpinning the model of perfect competition. This construct formed the basis for Chicago style price theory.[22] Coase professed to be an agnostic in this matter, a 'Doubting Thomas' who needed to examine the specifics of the world on a case by case basis. He preferred feeling the actual and specific wounds rather than depending on any strict act of faith. There remains a vast gulf between logical wounds or even wounds of faith and the actual bleeding variety. In contrast, Chicago, and particularly Stigler, saw their surroundings as approximating, or running closely parallel to, the world limned by perfect competition. Markets, in this perspective, acted to resolve externalities since inherently ingrained incentives provided sufficient rewards for discovering solutions to any quandary.[23] In essence, from within this perspective, the Coase Theorem indicated that transaction costs did not create serious barriers to the efficient working of markets. In which case, ignoring them would not traduce either economics or policies based on that constructed bedrock.[24]

> Well that's a very strong externality. Because if you don't get vaccinated you endanger others. I think that this is one of the reasons that Coase's work was so important to George. Coase's work indicated that an awful

lot of things which *were* externalities or had the *potential* to be externalities might be handled in a non-governmental way. I know there is a problem with Coase. I've read a lot about the literature based on Coase for Stigler's "Law or Economics" article because that deals specifically with Coase.[25] And it was very interesting. Many people interpreted Coase as saying it only works with *zero* transaction costs, and that wasn't how *I* interpreted Coase. Not that I'm anybody, but I thought that Coase was saying that to the *extent* that transaction costs are important, markets will be *less* effective, but not that you had to have zero. A lot depends upon how you interpret that one item. If you have to have 'zero', we don't have any 'zeros'. Now the Coase approach worked to some degree. You see that once again we have some empirical issues to test and measure. How much are the transaction costs that we do have? What mechanisms are at work to get rid of them? The way George saw the economy was as one in which the market *constantly* was adapting to all the non-market deficiencies that so much of the profession were concerned with. He knew that they were out there, that externalities were out there. However, he said, "Look, the market's rushing in every moment to take care of them. Here's Coase opening this big door for the market to rush in." And *that* was what George was focused on, starting perhaps in 1960 or '61, whenever it was that Coase gave his famous talk. George described in his memoirs that wonderful talk in which he said that everybody in Chicago who was there was wrong and Coase was actually right. George was focused on the way the market marches in to *eliminate* the externalities, to work *around* them to make them a market problem instead of a non-market problem. I think I've quoted him in my memoir as saying something like, 'externalities are what the market has not *yet* eliminated.' That's not an exact quote but in my memoirs I do have the exact quote. You see he saw the market as *the* force. He was looking at the other side of the market, at how the market may provide an appropriate solution. He said he saw this arbitrage going on all around him. Whenever there was a situation that somebody could take advantage of to make money he would. That was what solved a lot of these problems (Conversation with Claire Friedland, October 1997).

A. *Knight's Disciple – The Persistent Un-Chicagoan*

When you say it is un-Chicago, you mean that it is an unmodern Chicago View. Because Frank Knight was at Chicago, and I was brought up more on Knight than I was on any of the others. And my views were quite consistent with what he says. They're not consistent with what George Stigler, Gary Becker and Richard Posner say. Posner condemns me because I don't think people maximize utility (Coase 1997:3).

In 1964, Ronald Coase migrated to Chicago from the University of Virginia. He was the designated, and a not inappropriate successor, to the law school position previously cultivated under the watchful eye of Aaron Director, after an initial, and brief, appearance by Henry Simons. Coase was (and remained) a Classical Liberal, writing and working consistently in that tradition. Inherent in that approach, was his critical conclusions which confirmed, from his perspective, the failure of the entire Pigouvian framework. For Coase, this approach failed to capture the nuances of the arguments that had been constructed either to attack or defend the nature of markets.[26] He proceeded to expose those conceptual flaws in his seminal 1960 article. The driving mechanism displayed, seemingly combined a fundamental employment of marginal cost techniques with the insight that in any operative market economy, transaction costs shaped outcomes. The strategy of conjuring up a world lacking any shred or remnant of such costs exists as no more than an extended thought experiment. Coase's intention throughout is to direct a conceptual spotlight on the basic issue of transaction costs, not to upholster the comforts of some theoretical lounge.

In essence, he eschews any more Stiglerian style obsession that insists upon the long run ability of the market mechanism to resolve any and all conceivable problems or conflicts of interest.[27] Maintaining a Coasian coloured approach would require a more practical and possibly productive economic analysis of specific markets. Such a distinct variety of analysis would demand, at least initially, a careful evaluation of the relevant transaction costs operative under a given environment and set of circumstances. Policies, under this more pragmatic imprimatur, could only proceed from what, arguably, the state of the world might be, rather than what any analyst might insist that state should be. Coase, in his 1960 examination, was once again guided by Knight's version of Classical Liberalism (and an opportune level of good sense).[28]

There are several reasons why the approximate character of theoretical economic laws and their inapplicability without empirical correction to real situations should be especially emphasized as compared, for instance, with those of mechanics. ... The limitations of the results have not always been clear, and theorists themselves as well as writers in practical economics and statecraft have carelessly used them without regard for the corrections necessary to make them fit concrete facts. Policies must fail, and fail disastrously, which are based on perpetual motion reasoning *without the recognition that it is such* (Knight 1972:11).

The basis for Coase's seminal work (1960) finds its immediate inspiration in a paper published a mere year before. In "The Federal Communications Commission" (1959), he attempted to examine the tacit agreement (widely held within the profession), that radio and television channels were public goods to be allocated only by the federal government. In essence, there existed an explicit assurance that any reliance on a market price mechanism must inevitably fail. In response, Coase instituted a skeptical examination of this particular instance of regulation and the reasons why it existed.[29] His strategy largely consisted of placing the history of such legislation, up to the current state of regulation (as of 1959), under his critical microscope. The result of such a focused investigation fails, in Coase's estimation, to discover anything that resembles a compelling case for regulation, despite standard (and almost universal) claims to the contrary.[30]

> It was indeed in the shadows cast by a mysterious technology that our views on broadcasting policy were formed. It has been the burden of this article to show that the problems posed by the broadcasting industry do not call for any fundamental changes in the legal and economic arrangements which serve other industries. But the belief that broadcasting industry is unique and requires regulation of a kind which would be unthinkable in the other media of communication is now so firmly held as perhaps to be beyond critical examination. The history of regulation in broadcasting demonstrates the crucial importance of events in the early days of a new development in determining long-run governmental policy. It also suggests that lawyers and economists should not be so overwhelmed by the emergence of new technologies as to change the existing legal and economic without first making quite certain that this is required (Coase 1959:41).[31]

The fruition of this concrete and specifically targeted line of thought and approach, clearly evident in the FCC paper, reached its natural development the following year after that fateful dinner at Aaron Director's house.

Like that previous article, the full working out of Coase's argument also appeared in the *Journal of Law and Economics*, debuting as *The Problem of Social Cost* (1960). The article, to a healthy extent, incorporates a clear application of Knight's unvarnished skepticism, entailing a refusal to uncritically accept any tenet of economics, no matter how firmly established. Such assertions, (economic truths that everyone knows) viewed from this entrenched, arms-length perspective, were assumed to be guilty and highly suspect until carefully examined and completely exonerated.

> Knight was a man of formidable character as well as intelligence. He was fiercely independent, and insisted upon a critical and searching examination of all matters intellectual. I suspect that he approached even the multiplication table with initial scepticism (Stigler 1991:1).

Coase specifically refused to transform his social cost argument in such a fashion that government intervention could (and should) never be appropriate or required. Sustained conclusions, in this Coasean context, could never remain completely independent of all and any surrounding circumstances. Nor was it permissible to calculate any *a priori* estimate of either the necessity, or even likelihood, of such intervention. If forced to hold fast to his professed principles, Coase would honestly have to confess to have harboured doubts more appropriate to an agnostic on these matters. Such an extreme version of *laissez faire* policy would have directly violated his method of economic thinking, a stance sustained consistently throughout his career.[32] He fully recognized that when faced with a total absence of transactions costs, not only does such an environment prohibit the necessity for government intervention, but it equally fails to induce any serious substantiation requiring either markets or the mechanisms they are able to offer.[33] According to Coase at least, under such conditions, people will obviously use available resources individually in a manner that will maximize possible value. Doing so remains clearly in their own self-interest.

> The law of property determines who owns something, but the market determines how it will be used. It's so obvious to me that I couldn't understand the fuss. All it says is that the people will use resources in the way that produces the most value, that's all. I still think it's an obvious point. You wouldn't think there was a need for a Coase Theorem really (Coase in conversation with Hazlet 1997–1998:25).

Completely specified inter-agent agreements could perfectly substitute for the role performed by market exchanges. However, the inherent existence of transaction costs negates the usefulness of applying any such fanciful model to serve as a practical basis for forming economic policy. Instead, as Coase stubbornly insisted, policy should preferably be negotiated on a case by case investigation of the relevant specifics of each and every instance under examination. Coase's argument, developed over his lengthy academic career, took aim directly at the broadly maintained acceptance of a Pigouvian stylized framework of economic welfare. His papers were not intended primarily to mount a persuasive argument either for or against government intervention. The goal, instead, was a concerted attempt to rethink the basic methodology used to buttress regulation, rather than to knit together a working condemnation of all such external interference.[34]

> What I showed in that article, as I thought, was that in a regime of zero transaction costs – an assumption of standard economic theory – negotiations between the parties would lead to those arrangements being made which would maximize wealth, and this irrespective of the initial assignment of rights. This is the infamous Coase Theorem, named and formulated by George Stigler, although it is based on work of mine. Stigler argues that the Coase Theorem follows from the standard assumptions of economic theory. Its logic cannot be question, only its domain. I do not disagree with Stigler. However, I tend to regard the Coase Theorem as a stepping stone on the way to an analysis of an economy with positive transaction costs. The significance to me of the Coase Theorem is that it undermines the Pigouvian system. Since standard economic theory assumes transaction costs to be zero, the Coase Theorem demonstrates that the Pigouvian solutions are unnecessary in these circumstances. Of course, it does not imply, when transaction costs are positive, that government actions (such as government operation, regulation or taxation, including subsidies) could not produce a better result than relying on negotiations between individuals in the market. Whether this would be so could be discovered not by studying imaginary governments but what real governments actually do. My conclusion: Let us study the world of positive transaction costs (Coase 1994d:10–11).

For Coase, economic theory had nothing either directly or categorically to say about whether a government should, or should not, disrupt market mechanisms. Instead, he supported an approach essentially incorporating a fundamental aspect of Classical Liberal thinking, at least as filtered through such economists as Frank Knight. Coase's argument, sustained by case studies, examples and critical logic contended that assuming away transaction costs, excluded any model, no matter how intricately constructed, from being relevant to actual policy discussions. Such thinking remained incapable of resolving whether government intervention would make a positive difference given a specified set of circumstances. (Market problems persistently fail to exist in the abstract. Government administrators must face irritatingly specific issues, not average or general ones. In much the same fashion, parents, at 3 A.M. must deal with an actual infant, not some mythical average, or representative, offspring.) For Coase, intelligent decision making consequently had to be evidence based, rather than theoretically valid. Even more so, ideological imperatives are best deliberately ignored, rather than left to dominate policy construction.[35]

> I wrote that "direct government regulation will not necessarily give better results than leaving the problem to be solved by the market or the firm. But equally there is no reason why, on occasion, such governmental administrative regulation should not lead to an improvement in economic efficiency" (Coase 1994a:62).

Coase's approach, left room for 'too much' as well as 'too little' government. *A priori* judgements were not let in either through the front or back door, disallowing the attempt to mold observations so that they would align with preordained conclusions. Both logic and evidence insisted on such stipulations.[36] This perspective closely followed the Classical tradition – theory and models were primarily used as aids to judgment, not definitive guides to policy. Coase stubbornly exhibited such open-minded intentions. His dislike of jumping from theory to policy was announced explicitly and repeatedly.[37]

> What is studied is a system which lives in the minds of economists but not on earth. I have called the result "blackboard economics," The firm and the market appear by name but they lack any substance. The firm in mainstream economic theory has often been described as a "black box." And so it is. This is very extraordinary given that most resources in a modern economic system are employed within firms, with how these

resources are used dependent on administrative decisions and not directly on the operation of a market (Coase 1994d:5–6).

Stigler however, seized upon this Coasian argument, which did manage to persuasively undercut the stark Pigouvian style approach. Pigou's widely presented method (at least in textbook fashion) also insisted on moving directly from theory to policy.[38] But Stigler failed to disassociate himself from the same fundamental error dominating textbook discussions of externalities. In practice, he proved to be just as agile in basing conclusions on theoretical constructs as any of his East Coast opponents (perhaps even more skilled at times.) Stigler chose instead to forcefully encapsulate a lengthy article, bulging with abbreviated case studies, into a slogan length dictum. His newly hatched catechism of faith transformed a methodologically alternative argument into one that followed the modernist instinct to move inevitably from theory to policy. Stigler's striking difference from the rejected Pigouvian stylized method lay distinctly in his conclusion, rather than the route chosen to arrive there.[39]

Stigler's reformulation, which he neatly labelled the Coase theorem,[40] effectively buttressed a policy that commanded his unswerving *a priori* support. The predictably embraced dictum, insisted on a policy that would inevitably leave the market to deal idiosyncratically with any problems. With logic nestled safely under the Chicago ideological umbrella, Stigler was assured that unhindered markets must achieve (almost by definition) an efficient outcome.[41] Thus, what occurred was a nearly deliberate misinterpretation of the argument Coase provided. Stigler failed to focus on the need to incorporate transaction costs when formulating policies. Instead, he chose to largely interpret the article's arguments as underwriting a framework that would effectively demolish the problem posed by externalities.[42] For Stigler, his reframing, if not outright reformulation, of Coase demonstrated the preordained conclusion that markets were capable of taking care of even the most troublesome issues. The market mechanism was essentially self-correcting since from Stigler's perspective, it simply had to be.[43]

Using his carefully tailored version of Coase's work, Stigler adapted a purpose constructed argument to serve as a permanent bulwark against government intervention.[44] Coase's insight, or strategic ploy, was now transformed into the irrefutable Coase's Theorem. This device sported an implacable insistence that in the absence of transactions costs, externalities should never be conceived as a problem awaiting a solution.[45] The Pigouvian externality analysis, hitherto a thorn in the side of market fundamentalism, could now be effectively extracted. Price theory became capable of providing both a necessary and sufficient reason for supporting an unconstrained laissez faire policy, leaving little, if any, room for government intervention. While technically (and nearly by definition) true, the Coase Theorem was simultaneously irrelevant for any direct policy application.[46]

The theorem unfortunately implied that in the absence of those same transactions costs, there would be no need for markets – people would just freely negotiate all agreements among themselves. (A universal swap-meet could well define economic activity.) But for opposing mainstream economists to challenge Stigler's creation and its tacit policies, they would have to be willing to backtrack on their own foundations. Essentially, these academics would need to confess the errors of their own proverbial transgressions. Critics would be obliged to admit that the Pigouvian framework, the construction that they had so carelessly embraced as a model and way of thinking, failed equally to propose any direct policy applications, or at least any legitimate options. To effectively defeat, or undermine the Chicago position, they were obligated to surrender and discard their own predispositions. To accomplish this singular objective, these economists would have to willingly turn their backs on the policy methodology they had previously embraced with such fervour.[47]

Stigler's invention of a Coasian theorem inevitably proved to be highly contentious, given its indisputable role as a rhetorical ploy. Stigler habitually courted such controversy strategically, the worst reaction (given his perspective) being one of indifference. For Stigler a total lack of response equated to a virtual stab through the heart.[48] However, when viewed from a more practical perspective, both market and government solutions inevitably involve a set of specific attributes and conditions. These arrive predigested with permanent assumptions strictly attached to them. Unfortunately, in such cases, abstract theory manages to persistently triumph over available evidence, or even basic usefulness. This perspective deliberately avoids promoting the more reasonable Coasian position that real world decisions need to be made on a case by case basis. Instead, this 'through the looking glass' transformation offers the seemingly tantalizing gift of delivering intransigent policy absolutes. Since the profession instinctively lumped Coase as just another pea within the Chicago pod, marketing the Coase theorem as a digest of his thought became all too plausible.

Under Stigler's skillful stage crafting, Coase's Classical Liberal position was goosed into transcending any imposed constraints. Offered instead was a rhetorical basis that proved capable of supporting an array of preferred market mechanisms. Mainstream Pigouvian style models, faced with an attack constructed under the aegis of Stigler's Coase Theorem, could only hope to counter this torrent of logic by cannibalizing its own underpinnings.[49] Unfortunately, would be opponents objecting to the Stigler steamroller, proved equally reluctant to surrender the comforts of their own scientifically bolstered version of modernism. Consequently, they almost deliberately failed to place anything resembling an effective spoke in the wheels of the opposing Chicago ideological express. They more often than not tried to wiggle through this conundrum by lumping Coase with Stigler and focusing on the theoretical viability of the more visible Coase's Theorem.

B. *Laissez Faire Uber Alles: Or at Least, Whenever Appropriate*

> Of course governmental action, if effective, limits freedom, and few of us are anarchists. It should not be necessary to argue either for or against laissez faire in principle. The issue lies in the amount of freedom, or of control, and the kinds, which depend on circumstances (Knight 1967:782).

Coase's consistent message in his written and printed work views transaction costs as fundamental to analyzing any market economy.[50] Because of such inherent frictions, universal principles, those obtained by the science of economics, cannot be appropriately applied directly to each and every market, especially if time and place specifications are simply ignored. Policy conclusions based on this brand of 'blackboard economics' are bound to mislead and are in a crucial sense absurd.[51] The only fruitful response to the unfortunate inconvenience of transaction costs is to examine each situation on a case by case basis, before suggesting possible policy responses. Any such conclusions inevitably entail at least a modicum of judgment. These decision points necessarily generate differences of opinion, even when assisted, if not aided and abetted, by truckloads of statistical evidence. (Data consistently refuses to speak for itself, no matter how closely observed.) Thus Coase recognised the necessity for getting his hands dirty, something that Knight welcomed without necessarily indulging in the practice himself.[52]

Though trained in the 1930s, not unlike Stigler or Friedman, Coase was never tugged in the direction of any version of the stark modernism that arose during that decade and especially in the following post war period. Though he was hardly averse to the employment of statistics, utilizing them during a period when the available tools made such strategic employment a genuine challenge, he never quite bought into the same waltz that took the Chicago School by storm. Those dance steps dictated that each acolyte: formulate a hypothesis, test the hypothesis, and derive policy from the resulting theoretical model. Thus Chicago, with George Stigler doing service as the engineer driving an unstoppable theoretical locomotive, campaigned relentlessly for the employment of statistics and quantitative methods as being the only path to scientific certainty.

> I was sitting with Aaron Director at the time when he [George Stigler] gave his Presidential address and we did look at one another at the time to try to see what each one thought about all of this (Conversation with Ronald Coase, October 1997).

In this respect, Coase remained an outlier in the profession despite his growing reputation during the latter part of his career. He became best known for a theorem he neither created nor promoted. Equally, he stood apart from the theorem's implied objective. He was a loyalist to the Marshallian tradition as inculcated in him by his LSE teachers, Edwin Canaan and especially Arnold Plant. Thus he remained, in his own odd way, methodologically impervious to the furor that seemed to overturn economic methodology after the war. This scientific modernist perspective planted its initial roots in the 1930s and managed to triumphantly sweep away most remnants of Classical Liberalism in the post war period. Certainly, Coase dug in his heels when presented with the sort of strategic methodology formulated by Friedman and Stigler. Such a construct, in his view, was simply unworkable.[53] Though unarticulated in his own analysis, the unavoidable implication is that Friedman's positivist approach is more rhetorical positioning, than anything approaching serious methodology.

> If all economists followed Friedman's principles in choosing theories, no economist could be found who believed in a theory until it had been tested, which would have the paradoxical result that no tests would be carried out. This is what I meant when I said that acceptance of Friedman's methodology would result in the paralysis of scientific activity. Work could certainly continue but no new theories would emerge (Coase 1994b:24).

However, in the 1930s at least, Coase was not quite the oddity he would become at a later date. Classical Liberalism still largely dominated the discipline, especially among older academics. Many in the profession continued to follow Marshall in taking a cautious approach to theory, wary of imposing a physics-like agenda on the discipline. In his presidential speech to the American Economic Association, a future colleague of Stigler's (John Maurice Clark) was willing to sum up the past and present by reminding his audience of crucial limitations inherent in theoretical approaches. (Contrasting Clark's presidential speech with that of Stigler's, almost thirty years later, reveals to a considerable degree the transformation of the profession's methods and approaches.)

> … while a picture of perfect equilibrium deals in its way with forces which are at work in the actual world, the form in which it presents these forces will almost inevitably need to be modified when we move on to the task of studying them as they actually operate (Clark 1936:4).

For Coase, empirical work embraced more than simply the sort of statistical practices that seems to define modern day economics.[54] From his perspective, humble facts and observations also played a significant role. In sum, sheer elegance and convoluted presentation in model construction, and testing, did not equate with suitability for application. Rigor could be rightfully redefined, at least from this perspective, as containing a desired degree of persuasion using the least amount of resources. His reliance on empirical detail appears to have been largely overlooked by those who seemingly embraced his work (or claimed to do so). Consequently, though supposedly supportive of Coase, neither Stigler nor Friedman seemed to have adequately grasped his basic focus or objectives.[55]

> *He doesn't seem to have ever been very interested in Coase's '37 work on the firm and transaction costs. Is that correct, and why? Why is that of no concern?*
> Milton Friedman: I don't really …
> Aaron Director: I never thought there was anything in it. But George always said, that well, you've got to start somewhere and that was as good a place as any.
> *Because I know, in none of his [Stigler's] work, is there any interest in that aspect. I mean it seems to me that Ronald Coase has always stressed going out and looking at firms.*

Milton Friedman: And where do you see him doing that? The industry work that Ronnie did is a study on the British Broadcasting industry (1954) and …

Aaron Director: The post office (1961).

Milton Friedman: Yes, the post office … but none of that had to do with the issue of what determine the boundaries of a firm. His '37 article said essentially that market transactions involve transactions costs. If you have fewer transaction costs by doing it within a firm than you do within a firm. If you have more, etc. But to the best of my knowledge, none of his later work really answered that question (Conversation with Milton Friedman, Rose Friedman, Aaron Director, August 1997).

What is interesting here is the narrow interpretation of Coase's methods and his work, particularly the role that transaction costs plays.[56] Like their friend and colleague, George Stigler, they simply don't appear to comprehend Coase's purpose in employing his chosen framework. As previously mentioned, their respect seems largely dependent on a group misunderstanding of his *Social Cost* (1960) paper. His other work was not really contiguous with their own methodology or understanding of economics.[57] Common ground was only shared (at least to some degree) within the realm of ideology, although unlike the Chicago contingent, Coase did not seem to claim an equivalent firm grasp on the inner workings of the world. Coase largely parted company with his Chicago colleagues in this sense, since his Classical Liberal approach shunned such absolutes. Consequently, he was unable to wholeheartedly subscribe to an unswerving core faith in rational decision-making, which seemed to sustain much of the work done at Chicago.[58]

I don't say people are wholly irrational. I have said that almost the only thing we can say about consumer behaviour is, if you raise the price of something, people will demand less. And that we know, but it doesn't follow that because a person does less foolishness when the price is high for foolishness that you don't have foolishness. The foolishness follows the universal law of demand. The greater the price you have to pay for being foolish, the less you do (Coase 1997:3).

In some ways, though perhaps straining for a literary correspondence, Coase is not dissimilar from another English compatriot, one who over the centuries since her death was often misunderstood, especially by male authors. Jane Austen sketched her novels in miniature, unlike the grand historical romances that made her contemporary literary figure, Sir Walter Scott, that era's most popular novelist. Chicago in the post war period obsessively hunted the Snark, as depicted by Lewis Carroll (1876/1962).[59] Only the universal that opened all locked passages (and resolved each and every matter of importance) was deemed worthy of their efforts. In contrast, Coase appeared to harbour less grandiose goals. He seemed uninterested in how markets should operate or mandating the way that people should make their decisions. Instead, he remained endlessly fascinated with the challenging task of delving into the specifics comprising the actual world. His self-imposed requirement was to sift through the available evidence for what might compose the evidential case. He proved ever reluctant to embrace a contention that was purely theory based, or a policy deduction dependent on logic alone.

His innate modesty perhaps makes the parallel between Coase and Austen appealing. Austen failed to be much of an enthusiastic fit for the ensuing Romantic era, which gained momentum soon after her death (1817).[60] Coase, in turn, was swamped by a post war modernist methodology. Though, a handful of more perspicacious authors, such as Trollope or Bronte, did not fail to recognize Austen's specific and unusual talents, such insights did not reflect the more general standards defining that period. In a parallel fashion, Coase, at least in the later period of his career, may eventually have gained some more insightful enthusiasts.[61]

> I have likewise read one of Miss Austen's works, *Emma* – read it with interest and with just the degree of admiration which Miss Austen herself would have thought sensible and suitable – anything like warmth or enthusiasm, anything energetic, poignant, or heartfelt, is utterly out of place in commending these works: all such demonstrations the authoress would have met with a well-bred sneer, would have calmly scorned as outré and extravagant. She does her business of delineating the surface of the lives of genteel English people curiously well; there is a Chinese fidelity, a miniature delicacy in the painting: she ruffles her reader by nothing vehement, disturbs him by nothing profound: the Passions are perfectly unknown to her; she rejects even a speaking acquaintance with that stormy Sisterhood; even to the Feelings she vouchsafes no more than an occasional graceful but distant recognition; too frequent converse with them would ruffle the smooth elegance of her progress (Bronte 1850).

Perhaps, an increasing number of economists these days are able to separate Coase's work from that of the Chicago School. (Though, it might be foolhardy to bet on that supposition.) At least in her own day, Austen did receive some (but only some), limited recognition from the major literary figures of her time. Scott, an author of almost unlimited popularity in that era, did not fail to recognize Austen's worth. Unfortunately, in contrast, the Chicago School itself never fully fathomed the game Coase insisted on playing. The respect paid to this Nobel Prize winning economist may largely have been based on a misconception. Rowing against the stream (as Coase was wont to do), meant a willingness to be misunderstood (though not equally an acceptance of being so), even by those who profess to be one's esteemed colleagues.

> Also read again, and for the third time at least, Miss Austen's very finely written novel of _Pride and Prejudice_. That young lady had a talent for describing the involvements and feelings and characters of ordinary life, which is to me the most wonderful I ever met with. The Big Bow-wow strain I can do myself like any now going; but the exquisite touch, which renders ordinary commonplace things and characters interesting, from the truth of the description and the sentiment, is denied to me (Scott 1826).

C. *One Example Does Not a Universe Create: Classical Liberalism in Practice*

> Now take an economics textbook. It's more or less the same. Exposition improves, techniques improve. There is a lot more illustrative material that didn't exist before, but anyway Y that's my view, so the empirical work doesn't seem to change a vision, or hasn't in economics, but I don't know why. It's very tricky, this whole business of how ideas emerge and subjects change, and so on (Conversation with Ronald Coase, October 1997).

An all too common mistake, based on this example of an alternative to the dominant path Chicago forged, would be to dismiss the significance of the case that Ronald Coase presents. Coase has been presented here as representing an incontrovertible and identifiable example of applying a Classical Liberal approach to economic policy formulation. (A perspective that somewhat divorces him from the more didactic constraints of the

Chicago School proper.) The consequent error that is easily committed involves confusing, if not emphatically muddling, a specifically defined ideology with a much more broadly based methodological approach. An inevitably misdirected deductive logic would then automatically identify the similarities in the topological reaches of both Chicago and Virginia based policies. (Even though congruent policies need not reflect a methodological alignment.) The common thread of attachment would reflect a variety of laissez faire liberalism, one that largely originated in the nineteenth century.[62] Such thinking unfortunately, quickly leads any researcher barreling down a futile spur line of analysis.

Conforming to such a convenient (policy based) categorization would clearly (and unnecessarily) resuscitate the fallacy of universalizing in an overly precipitous fashion. In essence, ideological and political prescriptions efficiently define and delineate the economics trade. In which case, differing approaches to economics can be dismissed as being of only, at most, peripheral concern. All that matters, when accepting that fixed perspective, are the end points reached, rather than the route taken. The convincing factor behind this analytic twist would necessarily rely on only a very limited number of cherry-picked examples. Conclusions reflecting this self-validating perspective would more closely resemble wish fulfillment, rather than research based on any available evidence. Such a casually committed misstep would blithely incorporate a forced identification of methodologies (or economic approaches), with preferred policies. Methodological discussion, within this context, can quickly become reduced to a mere shred of camouflage, or perhaps simply regarded as an outright (and profitless) diversion. Even granted the existence of distinctly different perspectives, or approaches, if they are tied to (and automatically deliver) the same set of policies, then methodological differences are often considered to be a fundamentally meaningless foray into cataloguing and quibbling.

Exploring such deviations may continue to be mildly entertaining, without ever yielding anything of substance or importance. Ideological stances in these cases will seemingly exert much more leverage than categories of professed research methods. Consequently, a reasonable conclusion would maintain that methodologies lack either theoretical or any other conceivable type of leverage in policy construction (they don't effectively matter). Like the truism that held for ancient Romans, all roads lead to the same destination. Yet on closer examination, while it may be true that (as pointed out), different methodologies can lead to the same policy prescription, equally true is the fact that employing the same methodology need not lead to a specific (or foreordained) policy outcome.

Any attempt to provide proof of this methodological dismissal would inescapably claim that both the Chicago and Virginia style of methodological approaches yield very similar conservative, or right wing, policy perspectives. Since results are assumed to be the only valid assessment in economics, getting bogged down by differentiating and analyzing paths to the same end, is summarily dismissed as a matter of pure diversion. Buying into this one dimensional conclusion, however, simply reflects a misunderstanding of the issue actually under discussion. The manner in which an economist perceives the practice of economics and economic research does not dictate a set of prescribed policies. Empirical evidence never speaks for itself, but instead needs to be interpreted. Differences in interpretation inescapably yield varying policies. (Additionally, ideological biases place an unwanted thumb on any evaluation.) The issue is how such evidence is weighed. In which case, perspectives do matter. The controversy under discussion here (once intentional blinders are removed), centres on theory determined policy versus that which is carefully adjusted for the specifics of time and place. In essence, one size should never be made to dependably fit all.

The focus then in this particular examination of Coase and the Chicago School is deliberately indifferent to any specific ideology prejudging results. Undoubtedly, such *a priori* frameworks often drive the formation, and particularly, the targeted marketing of specific policies. Instead, the relevant concern here is attached to the proposed relation between economic theories and policy formation. Theory in the Classical Liberal analysis has nothing definitive to say about devising an appropriate policy, namely one that would achieve a very concrete objective in a specific environment. The science of economics is then not to be considered as some sort of mechanical sausage machine capable of spitting out an array of all-purpose policies. The resulting implication is that applied analysts should never be excused from carefully investigating the specifics of relevant individual markets and firms.

Consequently, the implicit imperative is for these researchers to get their hands dirty by pawing through each and every available detail.[63] Observations, and closely considered empirical work, should necessarily become an indispensable component, one that is prominently displayed in the toolkit of the profession. Undertaking such activities is not to be dismissed as composing some mere category of busy work and drudgery only suited to those with mediocre abilities and aspirations. Inevitably, those who are tempted to reject the methodology of Classical Liberalism for perceived ideological reasons, turn out to be as equally wrong-headed as those accepting it to support contrary ideological stances. To simply reinforce the inherent dangers of tarring with the same brush in the field of economics, Coase's key contributions remain hidden and obscured unless he is definitively separated from Chicago orthodoxy. His insights otherwise have the tendency to be hidden in the jumble-box of Chicago School ideas.

As pointed out previously, Coase's published work is spangled with often detailed investigations of specific items, whether they be pigs, post offices, the BBC, or the Federal Communications Commission. (I leave it to the reader to draw distinctions between these topics.) In line with John Stuart Mill, but unlike his colleague, George Stigler, he declined to view broad-based or universal economic rationality as encompassing the entire boundaries of economic inquiry.

> Political economists generally and English political economists above others, have been accustomed to lay almost exclusive stress upon the first of these agencies, to exaggerate the effect of competition, and to take into little account the other and conflicting principle (custom). They are apt to express themselves as if they thought that competition actually does, in all cases, whatever it can be shown to be the tendency of competition to do. This is partly intelligible, if we consider that only through the principle of competition has political economy any pretense to the character of a science (Mill 1967:242).

Coase modestly accepted any evidence he deemed legitimate, validating historical (as well as psychological) evidence when appropriate.[64] Unlike George Stigler, who adeptly shaped statistical evidence to fit the boundaries of his pre-ordained jigsaw puzzle, Coase proved willing to paw among the specifics provided by dusty historical records. His efforts represented an attempt to determine what actually occurred in the past, rather than assuming that the world worked in line with his own modeled realities.[65] While Stigler considered such details of industries and firms to be superfluous, Coase focused on these intrinsic particulars, rather than relying on abstract theorizing.[66] By embracing this Classical Liberal perspective, policies instead become dependent on operative specifics, rather than theoretical conclusions.[67] The danger remains that by ignoring the dominant institutional constraints of a given era, the resulting conclusions would insure that policy recommendations would inevitably lack any compelling logical (or practical basis) for subsequent specific applications.

> Economics has been becoming more and more abstract, less and less related to what goes on in the real world. In fact, economists have devoted themselves to studying imaginary systems, and they don't distinguish between the imaginary systems and the real world. That's what modern economics has been and continues to be. All the prestige goes to people who produce the most abstract results about an economic system that doesn't exist (Coase in conversation with Hazlet 1997–1998:27).

D. *The Economist as Spelunker: Exploring the Nitty Gritty of Evidence*

> In my long life I have known some great economists but I have never counted myself among their number nor walked in their company. I have made no innovations in high theory. My contribution to economics has been to urge the inclusion in our analysis of features of the economic system so obvious that, like the postman in G.K. Chesterton's Father Brown tale, "The Invisible Man," they have tended to be overlooked. Nonetheless, once included in the analysis, they will, I believe, bring about a complete change in the structure of economic theory, at least in what is called price theory or microeconomics. What I have done is to show the importance for the working of the economic system of what may be termed the institutional structure of production (Coase 1992:713).

One way to comprehend the approach Coase adopted in his work, and its relation to Classical Liberalism, is to look at two of his articles which are strictly empirical in content. Both efforts however remain devoid of the standard statistical testing that represents, almost in its entirety, what economists are wont to categorize as empirical analysis. According to the Chicago School, theoretical hypotheses are proposed and then submitted to a test by statistical ordeal. If deemed verified, conclusions, including policy recommendations, are then allowed to flow. Coase instead, often sought to verify commonplace ideas that were virtually accepted as being logical necessities, given the way in which economists insist that the world must operate. Coase, in practice, carefully exhumed evidence that definitively undermined seemingly unarguable verities. This predilection remained a significant trait for those papers previously discussed, including his most well-known efforts (1937, 1960). In many cases, he unsurprisingly targeted Pigouvian ideas of private versus social welfare functions, including conceptions of public goods and the implied policies attached to such notions.

Amplifying this method, in his 1974 examination of lighthouses, Coase directly sheds an empirical floodlight on the textbook problem of public goods. Given that these are non-rival and non-exclusionary goods or services, governments, according to textbook theory, are obliged to unquestionably insure their existence. The private sector is peremptorily excluded from lines of provision given the nature of the output required. Such an unquestioned public policy conclusion is provided with an assured academic imprimatur of approval, leaving the responsible economist to remain comfortably ensconced in his or her office armchair.[68] Conveniently, deductive logic in this case takes over to an extent that effectively excludes the necessity for checking the historical record. The widely held supposition under these circumstances is that evidence need not apply, or even forlornly tap on the door. To effectively pinpoint this professional stance, Coase quotes Samuelson's textbook as a convenient reflection of the discipline's unquestioned faith in unverified theory.

> … in the lighthouse example one thing should be noticed: The fact that the lighthouse operators cannot appropriate in the form of a purchase price a fee from those it benefits certainly helps to make it a suitable social or public good. But even if the operators were able – say, by radar reconnaissance – to claim a toll from every nearby user, that fact would not necessarily make it socially optimal for this service to be provided like a private good at a market-determined individual price. Why not? Because it costs society *zero extra cost*. To let one extra ship use the service; hence any ships discouraged from those waters by the requirement to pay a positive price will represent a social economic loss – even if the price charged to all is no more than enough to pay the long-run expenses of the lighthouse. If the lighthouse is socially worth building and operating – and it need not be – a more advanced treatise can show how this social good is worth being made optimally available to all (Samuelson quoted in Coase 1974:359).

Notice the common preoccupations displayed in this 1974 piece. Previously (1946), Coase had explored what he came to consider as the myth of marginal cost pricing. But in this specific example of a public good, economic wisdom appeared willing to claim, despite lacking any historical, or verifiable, facts that the private sector and lighthouses maintained no contiguous borders. In the lighthouse example, readers are rigidly instructed by economists to deny the wisdom of private enterprise since users cannot be excluded (property rights not preserved). Even more tellingly, at least according to standard theoretical analysis, the marketplace, in this case, would be unwilling to supply any additional beams of light at a zero price. A deliberate refusal, despite the marginal cost of doing so remaining resolutely at an indicative price of zero. (By definition, non-rival goods must be priced in such a fashion.) Consequently, only government funded activity could claim the prize of theoretical efficiency, if the textbook logic is to remain undisputed.

> Economists had always used this as a service that had to be provided by governments. How could a private provider ever be paid for it? So without government operation you wouldn't get lighthouses. My usual practice is to look into what actually happens, and if you look into what actually happens you discover that there's a long period in which lighthouses were provided by private enterprise. They were financed by private people, they were built by private people, they were operated by the people who had the rights to the lighthouses, which they could bequeath to others and sell (Coase in conversation with Hazlet 1997–1998:28).

Coase refuses to simply accept this reality, despite the overwhelming evidence that to a plethora of economists, these conclusions are indisputable.[69] He proceeds to poke an inquisitive finger into the solidity of such claims (governments must build, own and operate these edifices) by examining the historical record which refuses to be logically dismissed. Within the coterie that most closely defines the academic realm of economics, grubbing through piles of mouldering paper for the facts of a matter lies beneath the dignity to which most members of the profession aspire. They deliberately view themselves as inhabiting and exploring a higher realm of knowledge. But almost perversely, careful examination (unfortunately for the self-assured reasoning populating textbooks), indicates that in Britain at least, private ownership and operation of lighthouses did exist at one time. This indisputable fact would seem to fatally undercut the theoretical foundation upon which the stated policy is based.[70]

> From 1838 or some such date, I can't remember it, the lighthouse people
> were bought out and compensation was given. Samuelson says that no
> one would build a lighthouse with the idea of making a fortune. Actually
> people did build lighthouses and did make a fortune (Coase in conversa-
> tion with Hazlet 1997–1998:29).

Notice that Coase consistently failed to claim that such evidence supported any conclusion regarding the best option for constructing and
maintaining such edifices. Again, his Classical Liberal ethos would not
permit such a leap of unfounded faith. But it laid to rest the claim that only
governments can supply such a service simply by categorizing lighthouses as being an indisputable public good.[71] As Coase implies, the real
policy challenge lies in discovering the best method for providing and
pricing this particular service, given the specifics of the case.[72]

> The system apparently favoured by Samuelson, finance by government
> out of general taxation has never been tried in Britain. Such a govern-
> ment-financed system does not necessarily exclude the participation of
> private enterprise in the building or operation of lighthouses, except in a
> very attenuated form and would certainly be quite different from the
> system in Britain which came to an end in the 1830s. Of course, govern-
> ment finance would be very likely to involve both government operation
> and government ownership of lighthouses. How such governmental
> systems actually operate I do not know. Bierce's definition of an
> American lighthouse – "A tall building on the seashore in which govern-
> ment maintains a lamp and the friend of a politician" – presumably does
> not tell the whole story.
>
> We may conclude that economists should not use the lighthouse as
> an example of a service which could only be provided by the govern-
> ment. But this paper is not intended to settle the question of how light-
> house service ought to be organized and financed. This must await more
> detailed studies. In the meantime, economists wishing to point to a ser-
> vice which is best provided by the government should use an example
> which has a more solid backing (Coase 1974:376).

In a similar fashion, the second related case takes aim at the predilection of economists for backing up their theories with 'just so' stories.[73]
Thus a long running predilection within the profession has been to promote ersatz examples that serve to vivify and seemingly prove their

underlying theoretical constructs.[74] These often repeated fables appear to put meat on what would otherwise remain as theoretical bare-bones. In this category, if the described incidents failed to occur or lacked the grace to manifest themselves in the fashion demanded, the economist's implicit response is to implicitly suggest that 'it should have happened'. We are immersed then, just as in the realm of policy, with accepting that the envisaged theoretical tail in this case should continue to wag the historical or evidentiary dog. In much the same way, films often advertise, or preface their screening by claiming that they are based on a true story. Such an assertion supposedly provides a gloss of verisimilitude to the cinematic fiction that the film would otherwise lack.

A false degree of credence becomes associated with what is no more than a dramatic reconstruction. Unfortunately, avoiding this predicament carries no more weight in economics than it does within cinematic endeavours. In the notorious business case Coase tackled, with his usual skeptical vision, he re-examined a specific chunk of business history. The tale constructed around this event had managed to become an anecdotal nugget that approached a gospel truth in the repertoire of standard economic illustrations (specifically within the field of industrial organization).

Historical fact, meaning an event that is difficult or even foolish to dispute, states that in 1926 General Motors merged with Fisher Body at a time when closed bodies on cars were overtaking the demand for open roadsters. This takeover occurred as the demand for cars with closed bodies grew. The open issue that requires adjudication is why this historical fact unfolded at this time. In 1978, Klein, Crawford and Alchian, used this undeniable occurrence to illustrate their theory of 'hold-up' as the prime motivating force behind vertical integration.[75] Their fashioning and explanation of the story behind such a corporate marriage was seemingly moulded to form a useful illustration highlighting the express needs of the theory presented. Thus the validity of the explanation lay in the manner in which it so snugly accorded with their suggested hypothesis. In a perverse fashion, the theory justified or explained the events rather than having the historical record supporting the theoretical construct.

As with many such tales, subsequent repetitions of these verities, embedded in print and in the classroom, often manages to transform any given story (these conveniently jury-rigged explanations) into unalloyed (and unquestioned) facts. The story could be said to have wormed itself into the discipline's oral tradition.[76] Yet because of these noncontroversial factual facades, for a number of decades, no economist felt compelled to actually examine the historical record in order to distinguish mythmaking from business history. When others, including Coase, did so, questions were raised and the solidity of this particular example began to crumble. The previously untarnished story seemed to suddenly edge distinctly over into the realm of historical fiction. From the Classical Liberal perspective, preferred descriptive history and theoretical imperatives consistently fail to shape the contours created by the past. This simple idea continues to hold, no matter how hard economists are wont to squeeze them into a more desirable shape.

> It is commonly said that in 1926 General Motors was led to acquire its supplier of automobile bodies, Fisher Body, because Fisher Body held up General Motors. It is claimed that Fisher Body did this by locating its body plants far away from the General Motors assembly plants and by adapting inefficient methods of production, thus increasing both the cost of producing bodies and the profits of Fisher Body under its cost-plus contract. This tale is factually incorrect. What General Motors acquired in 1926 was the 40 percent of the shares of Fisher Body that it did not already own. Furthermore, Fisher Body did not locate its plants far away from the General Motors assembly plants. It is also most implausible, for many reasons, that the Fisher brothers would have used inefficient methods of production. There is no evidence that a holdup occurred (Coase 2006:16).

Coase then has far too frequently been forcefully shoved into the wrong pigeon hole leading to a misunderstanding of his work. When we are forced (or inspired) to examine the existing evidence, it is impossible to deny that Coase was at Chicago for nearly half of his life. Nor is there any dispute that he was a close colleague of such Chicago luminaries as George Stigler, Milton Friedman and Aaron Director. But it is almost as easy to demonstrate that Coase was not 'of Chicago'. Though sharing a similar political perspective, his approach to economics (his methodological position if we insist on being overly grown-up) radically differed from that espoused by his lunch mates. Simply categorising or classifying Coase as a card carrying member of the Chicago School is to wilfully misinterpret and fail to understand his thinking. The imperative to categorise meant that Coase's insights were largely buried, much to his own frustration. By choosing this simpler alternative, members of the profession deliberately opted to travel down the most unencumbered path available, rather than struggling to comprehend a specific position. In contrast, respecting Coase's methods and approaches to economics entails no equal necessity to support his ideological leanings or his evaluation of available evidence. However, Classical Liberalism does require that his results be taken seriously and not dismissed simply because they fail to be congenial to some conflicting set of *a priori* values. (Certainly, rejecting Coase out of hand due to some imagined 'Chicago stain' is a simple act of frivolity, rather than thoughtful evaluation.)

Instead, the initial obligation of those who dissent from a given perspective (such as that presented by Coase), is to attempt to seriously understand the basis of the argument provided. Only then can it become appropriate to ferret out any weak links and the possibility of misinterpreted evidence. Employing the spirit of James Stuart Mill or Albert Hirschman tends to provide a better guide for broadening understanding.[77] (To follow the guidance of Hirschman entails choosing voice, instead of the more categorical options of either loyalty or exit. Voice requires a serious engagement in what must become mutually respectful argument.) In essence, academics would need to consciously foreswear engaging in zero sum controversies by ending their incessant categorising. Dismissing an opponent out of hand advances little in the way of insight, or productive policy outcomes. Gladiatorial displays within academic arenas are intended merely to decimate and bury opposing theories and ideas, rather than exploring them. These modes of debate seek instead to simply substantiate, without either deepening or certainly improving, a given set of ideological perspectives.

I know in that same piece, 'How do Economists Choose', you start off by referring to Warren Nutter and then you quote the line from Frank Knight about how in order to achieve objectivity you need competence, integrity and humility.[78] Do you think George Stigler had humility?

Ronald Coase: He didn't show it. He may have had it, but it wasn't that apparent. He always appeared confident, sure of himself, but in a way that suggests to me a sense of insecurity. I don't know whether others felt that, but I did. He was always very nice and kind and helpful in many ways. Always. But I often wondered how far he agreed with what I was saying. I think he thought I was all right, but a little odd (Conversation with Ronald Coase, October 1997).

Endnotes

1   For those who haven't wallowed in the pleasures provided by classic Hitchcock films, a MacGuffin is a term often employed by Alfred Hitchcock to describe an element central to his directorial strategy. The purpose served by this particular mechanism is that it efficiently defines a specific plot device employed only to drive the plot of a film, while remaining trivial in and of itself. Thus the search to discover the meaning of 'rosebud' propels *Citizen Kane* despite remaining, of and in itself, essentially insignificant. (Nothing changes by making the sled into a bicycle or pogo stick for instance. Though a bike (let alone a pogo stick) employed during a Colorado winter might prove to be a dubious proposition.) In the same fashion, the film *The Maltese Falcon* would cease to exist without the sought for statue, though the specific form or history of that statue has no intrinsic importance in the unfolding of the story.

2   Decades ago, I published a paper linking the almost contagious failure of economists to write in a clear, persuasive fashion with a corresponding inability to read. (I introduced the argument with a timeless quote from Walt Kelley, the creator or the comic strip *Pogo*. "I'd write my Congersman if he could read, if I could write.") This ubiquitous inability to read is solidified by the tendency of many economists to pigeon-hole all and any published work, prior to, or even without actually, reading a particular article or piece of research. Doing so doubtlessly allows these prickly readers to find in each work exactly what they would expect and need to discover. This particular process is prized, since it can be successfully accomplished without actually attempting to fathom the constructed argument within the designated article. Consequently, this dubious approach allows readers to definitively reject or accept (though largely to dismiss) any piece of work with an alarming and almost automatic efficiency. In some sense, employing such a mechanism is unarguably effective and thus appealing. Unfortunately, doing so cuts off any meaningful debate or fruitful means of communication. Pigeon-holing of this type deteriorates into defending or attacking pre-existing positions, instead of exploring and refashioning ideas.

3   The author is generally less than receptive to prologues. There has been a fashion in crime fiction, for too many decades, of equipping each novel within this genre with a prologue. These tend to annoy rather than entice. My response when spotting one is to think, 'Just get on with the story telling and stop the blather.'

4   The idea that humans, seemingly by necessity, seek their identity in groups is encapsulated in this well-known quote by Aristotle. The idea is as old as philosophy and perhaps thought itself.

It follows that the state belongs to a class of objects which exist in nature, and that man is by nature a political animal; it is his nature to live in a state. He who by his nature and not simply by ill-luck has no city, no state, is either too bad or too good, either sub-human or super-human (Aristotle 1962:28).

The same idea was later picked up by Nietzsche and largely misunderstood. His *ubermensch* represented a human capable of providing his own sense of identity. Namely, such a person did not require the recognition by, or shared identity, of others. (For those who enjoy a bit of philosophical obliqueness, Nietzsche's *Thus Spoke Zarathustra* (1883) might prove rewarding.

5   As explained in the next chapter, such articles are read only with a concentrated intent to destroy. Understanding is eliminated as a guiding purpose. Instead, such research is explored merely to find a method employed or a careless instance that can be leveraged into a wholesale dismissal of the author's work. Sometimes even a mere typo seems sufficient.

6   The bulk of economists toiling away in the discipline seem sadly unaware of the problem, even when they should know better. Pigeon-holing (cramming economists into a convenient box) proves seductive due to its ease and efficiency. In this fashion, what 'everyone knows' about given figures, a sort of oral tradition transmitted in lectures and textbooks, gets perpetuated. A recent referee report I received with some amusement summarily dismissed the following recorded exchange as insignificant.

> *There is an article he [George Stigler] wrote, or it could have been a talk. I can't recall it straight off. He addressed this ideal of specializing. First he looked at interdisciplinary studies and then within a given field. He took a very standard economic view of it. Yet the problem remains, namely how far can you actually push that line of thought? Or the issue might be, do you want to push it at all? Of course, if you go back to Smith, he would say, 'Yes, it's very useful.' But equally, if you get too narrowly specialized the workers in his famous pin factory become absolute dolts, because they can only do a very limited part of the production process.*
>
> Sherwin Rosen: No. That was Marx (Conversation with Sherwin Rosen, October 1997).

Rosen was pigeon-holed as lacking scholarly expertise on Smith, thus reducing this exchange to a level of insignificance. Consequently the self-proclaimed Smith expert acting as designated referee, by misapplying his purported expertise, only demonstrated an ability to entirely miss the obvious point. Of course it is true that historians of thought (like far too many academics) reflect a tendency to become overly focused on their narrow specialty, blinding them to the elephant in the room. They forget how small a chunk of the larger landscape their work represents. Even worse, practitioners of history of thought often blind themselves to how little the rest of the profession knows or cares about their little scholarly corner.

Rosen was a very able economist, and unlike many of a more recent vintage, conversant with Smith. But even when dealing with a thoughtful practitioner, the tendency to fall back on lazy classifications and labelling comes to the fore. Namely, Smith is defined by self-interest and Marx by exploitation of workers. Most economists will fall back on these simplicities even though it would be an easy task to find quotes in Marx with which even a hardcore Chicagoan would concur if they were presented anonymously. Consequently the very point made by featuring Rosen's exchange is that even well informed economists prefer simplified classifications.

This response is then intensified if the economist in question has an ideological point to pursue. Someone like George Stigler, a certified historian of thought, felt able to chastise Smith for not being the Smith he required, namely the pure Smith defined only by a focus on self-interest.

> In the political scene no corresponding search is made for the effective principles of behaviour. Therefore reforms must be effected, if effected they can be, by moral suasion. At best this is an extraordinarily slow and uncertain method of changing policy; at worst it may lead to policies which endanger the society. Of course erroneous and undesirable public policies arise out of failures of comprehension as well as out of the efforts of self-serving groups, but there is little reason to accept Smith's implicit assumption that the main source of error is ignorance or "prejudice" (Stigler 1982b:143).

The urge to narrowly classify and dismiss with pleasure led the same referee to toss out an exchange with Marc Blaug, considering Blaug to also be an insufficient authority on Smith.

> He [George Stigler] liked *The Wealth of Nations*. I think *The Theory of Moral Sentiments* is very hard. It is not really easy to marry up with *The Wealth of Nations* because it presupposes that trust is crucial. To put it very succinctly, orthodox price theory works best when all the traders are anonymous on opposite sides and unlimited. Once there are personal relationships, which of course there are inside any firm, and as there are between traders in any well-defined market, the situation changes (Conversation with Mark Blaug, April 1998).

But the referee's rejection in practice exemplifies the problem. In a bit of one-upmanship, the focus is on Blaug's credentials rather than on the statement itself. The wider point which the referee ignored is that such cataloguing and dismissals are not limited to the work of long dead economists. The same source of misunderstanding and rejection can be readily performed on the work of those who are far from dead (or at least claim to be so).

The consequence is that any useful understanding of a specific work is often obfuscated by the dominating power of lazy classifications.

7 Those readers intent on searching for some perceived shortcomings in this effort, will no doubt notice that there is clearly lacking in this text anything resembling a review of the extensive literature surrounding Coase. Nor is there even a more specialized presentation of the many words, insightful or otherwise, that have been bestowed on George Stigler's clever and devious encapsulation of his thought (commonly known as the Coase Theorem). To incorporate such a role call would just be bowing to tortuous convention while diverting attention away from the point being made. To undertake anything like such an endeavour would be straying wildly away from my stated objective. However, those who might become interested in exploring such more detailed options will find that they can easily locate a number of excellent investigations on this topic simply by conducting a quick internet search. But expecting such work to be done by this paper's author would immediately point to a serious misconception of the ruling objective behind this chapter. If in fact I complied with such an expectation, I would be doing no more than trying to cravenly oblige a group of suspected, though anonymous critics. In effect, I would only then succeed in muddling the story that I am attempting to unfold. Pandering to misunderstanding is seldom a serious virtue.

8 He arrived at Chicago from the University of Virginia in 1964, remaining there until his death in 2013. Originally from England, Ronald Coase was born in 1909. Even for an economist, Coase enjoyed an unusually long and productive life. (I have for years nursed a completely unproven conjecture that the life expectancy of an economist is significantly longer than that representing the appropriate societal average. Economics somehow provides its denizens with a synthetic fountain of youth.)

9 Unfortunately, these undeniable facts encourage less careful readers to apply the 'duck' rule of thumb – 'if it looks like a duck, sounds like a duck, then it's a duck'. But just because Coase looks like a Chicago School product, seems to sound like a Chicago School member, this is still an insufficient basis for transforming him into a prime grade Chicago follower. A less than careful researcher, may end up listening only for duck like quacks, while turning a deaf ear to everything else.

10 The term 'Classical Liberal' of course represents a category. I would seem to be contradicting myself. Sometimes though it is difficult when communicating not to utilise the shortcut provided by categories. But here what is meant by 'Classical Liberal' is best represented by the economist, John Stuart Mill.

11 Equally important to note is the lack of any evidence that this hijacking was intended to be deliberate or intentional. George Stigler remained convinced

that he had grasped the essential idea behind Coase's work (thus naming it in Coase's honour).

12   George Stigler presents the evening as a triumph of market logic over poorly examined textbook verities. But a key to understanding Coase's insight was widely missed. The largely unrecognized impact of that evening's debate remained buried by having the subsequent focus of inquiry shifted quite sharply away from the article's original direction. Initially unremarked in the ensuing debate was Stigler's willingness to jump, from his formulation of a fundamentally ersatz Coase's theorem, directly to a set of implied policy recommendations. Instead, Stigler in his strategically remembered account presents a more romantic and historical snapshot where truth inevitably triumphs over false belief.

> We strongly objected to this heresy. Milton Friedman did most of the talking, as usual. He also did much of the thinking, as usual. In the course of two hours of argument the vote went from twenty against and one for Coase to twenty-one for Coase. What an exhilarating event! (Stigler 1988:76).

This description fits rather snugly with Stigler's almost sweet, but nearly ingenuous belief in Edwin Canaan's dictum that in the long run truth wins out. "However lucky Error may be for a time, Truth keeps the bank and wins in the long run" (Cannan 1903:392).

13   Even the scientific yearnings characterising economics often surrender to the demands of professional mythmaking. In such instances, the ruling dictum coincides with the sentiments expressed in John Ford's classic western, *The Man Who Shot Liberty Valence*. "No, sir. This is the West, sir. When the legend becomes fact, print the legend."

14   In contrast, Coase has recollected that during that fateful dinner, only Arnold Harberger managed to actually understand what he was attempting to do (Conversation with Ronald Coase, October 1997).

> I remember at one stage, Harberger saying, "Well, if you can't say that the marginal cost schedule changes when there's a change in liability, he can run right through." What he meant was that, if this was so, there was no way of stopping me from reaching my conclusions. And of course that was right. I said, "What is the cost schedule if a person is liable, and what is the cost schedule if he isn't liable for damage?" It's the same. The opportunity cost doesn't shift (Coase 1997:2).

The habit of thinking in terms of transaction costs, while employing a straight-forward application of the marginal cost concept is not original with his 1960 paper. Certainly a similar approach appears in his earlier, but equally famous paper on the firm (1937a). Coase in his insights and methodology seemed to remain an unabashed hedgehog throughout his lengthy career. Though in fact, transaction costs were not the one big thing he knew.

The concept served more practically, only as a set of useful goggles helping him to understand a number of very specific things about given economic phenomena. Perhaps then, Coase was more of a fox (knowing many little things) who successfully masqueraded as a hedgehog.

15   Pigou was careful to note the limitations of his framework. Later users of his welfare framework, such as Lerner, or even Samuelson, were less finicky. See Pigou, 1920.

16   Given Coase's world of positive, and often significant transaction costs, the importance of property rights and the role played by government bureaucrats immediately come to the fore. Also, often overlooked, is the cost of legal proceedings. Implicitly assuming zero legal costs is a convenient, but completely fatuous, attempt at buttressing market efficiency.

> If we move from a regime of zero transaction costs to one of positive transaction costs, what becomes immediately clear is the crucial importance of the legal system in this new world (Coase 1994d:11).

17   The confused relation between the Stigler formulated 'Coase Theorem' and Coase's intentions reflects a particularly unproductive level of muddle. In the realm of chemistry this state of bewilderment would be comparable to one that stubbornly confused the produced chemical reaction with the catalyst essential to producing that specific chemical outcome. More precisely, what textbooks inevitably attach to Coase's name, perhaps being the sole knowledge many economist have about the Nobel awarded economist, exists as no more than a Hitchcock style MacGuffin in the actual article itself. (How carefully such articles are read, or if they are perused at all, is yet another question perhaps best left unresolved.) The formulated Coase Theorem then is simply employed as a plot device, a starting point that initiates the story that Coase wants to tell. The terminology itself (a MacGuffin) was devised and employed by Alfred Hitchcock to describe his own plot devices. Essentially they existed as a means to an end, necessary, but in and of themselves only of negligible importance.

For instance, in Hitchcock's film *Psycho*, the money that Janet Leigh steals at the commencement of the film serves merely as a convenient mechanism to deliver her to the dubious environs of the Bates Motel. But, if viewed from the perspective that Stigler uses to analyze that seminal 1960 article by Coase, the film would best be understood as a story about a trusted employee who came to a bad end. Such an unfortunate result ensued, according to this peculiar interpretive method (one that ignored the whole intent of the film, focusing instead on a limited slice only), due to her inability to resist temptation. The featured moral that is spelled out, achieved by focusing on the MacGuffin employed rather than on the film itself, is a simple and almost trite homily. To repeat, if limited to this narrow analysis,

Pyscho conclusively demonstrates only that crime does not pay. By focusing solely on the MacGuffin, such an insight is eminently defensible. However, maintaining this view manages to deliberately ignore approximately two-thirds of the actual film, which could consequently be logically dismissed as no more than an extravagant waste of time and effort. In other words most of the film can be catalogued as simply extended bombast.

In much the same fashion, Stigler's formulation of Coase's intentions deftly ignores the bulk of the article, reducing it to nothing more than unremarkable space filler. Stigler, whether deliberately or not, allows the MacGuffin of the article to become the fulcrum point, and the very essence, of Coase's thought. Coase raised no objections to the structure of Stigler's theoretical formulation. In a world of zero transaction costs, Coase regards it as self-evident. But Coase actually employs that mechanism simply to eliminate the validity of Pigou's formulation. Clearly given this perspective, the crux of the matter doesn't reside in the existence of externalities, but rather the presence of transaction costs. Once Pigou is properly dispatched, Coase can then examine the very concrete world where positive transaction costs serve to define the problems presented, as well as specifically tailored solutions. The stark differences in Stigler's and Coase's methodological approaches to economics could not be laid out with greater surgical precision. For Coase, the thought experiment, which serves as a prologue to his purpose, is strategic by nature. In direct contrast, Stigler regards the abstract and general formulation of his theory as that which composes the heart of the matter. This difference nicely defines what separates the two methodologically. Coase is Knight's disciple for whom an impermeable 'Chinese Wall' separates the world of theory from that of practical policy. For Stigler, there is an almost romantic temptation to veer into a Hegelianism by identifying the real with the ideal (or the entirely rational). Consequently, the differentiated responses to the same material properly act as the equivalent of a forensic autopsy. Close examination succeeds in revealing the very different styles of economics practiced by these two famed, but quite dissimilar, economists.

18   An irreducible tendency persisted within these Chicago-style ramparts, one which stubbornly resisted Coase's basic methodology. (Coase's approach harked back to the Classical Liberalism of Frank Knight, rather than the post war reconstruction of Liberalism engineered by Stigler, Friedman and Director.) The lack of universal dictums offered within the Coasean literature represented a failure when judged from the Chicago perspective. This verdict at least accorded with the standard scientific analysis favoured within the Chicago School. Such a specific (and nitty-gritty) approach was not seen by Stigler or Friedman as offering a possible path to practical policy applications. In sharp contrast to the Chicago style of exploration, work

such as Coase's (1974) detailed analysis of lighthouses in Britain exists as a preliminary exercise in understanding the possible economic roles government might play in a world of positive transaction costs. This investigation deliberately eschews the pure world of theoretic models, whether proffered by those perched on either side of the political spectrum. (Theoretical lighthouses have never lighted the paths of any ship.) By choosing instead to follow this path, Coase slips away from the strictly constrained world defined by abstraction and generalisation. What is revealed can only be termed suggestive, rather than conclusive. Such modest investigations lack the sweeping vistas generally favoured by the Chicago boys.

19   Care must be exercised at this point to emphasize the total absence of any malevolent objective on Stigler's part. Machiavellian manipulators and creators of spidery conspiracies lack any coherent role to play in the unfolding of the depicted events. No evidence of dishonourable intentions have ever been conveniently unearthed. Their potential existence and discovery are dubious at best. Rather, this is simply the way George Stigler was capable of comprehending the world, or perhaps needed to do so. The theorem represents just one reflection of Stigler's unwavering conception of the economy. Given his underlying understanding of Coase's (1960) work, if anything, Stigler was being aboveboard and generous by recognizing Coase as the originator of this soon to be famous (if not at times infamous) theory.

> I christened the proposition the "Coase Theorem" and that is how it is known today. Scientific theories are hardly ever named after their first discoverers (more on this later), so this is a rare example of correct attribution of a priority (Stigler 1988:77).

20   Another Chicago trained economist who remained much more closely aligned to the Classical Liberal tradition, especially as envisioned by Frank Knight, was one of his few PhD students. James Buchanan created what might best be labeled as a Constitutional approach to constructing economic theory. Buchanan eschewed the temptation of arguing for markets by marshalling standard economic models to perform the heavy lifting. Instead, he fashioned broader, more institutional, arguments that supported the notion of free markets and laissez faire. But precisely because he chose to move in that direction, one that ran counter to the period's *Geist*, his arguments failed to exercise the degree of influence wielded by his erstwhile Chicago School counterparts. His public choice work (especially as influenced by Gordon Tullock (1962)), provided insights that were more easily reducible to mathematical analysis. This peculiar version of political economy was thus more tractable and closer to the profession's desired objectives. Consequently, this was the wedge of Buchanan's work that managed to gain a noticeably greater level of support and associated impact.

21   To underline this point, the textbook formulation, the one familiar to students, is not explicitly stated anywhere within Coase's 1960 article. What became widely known as Coase's Theorem is more correctly the creation of George Stigler in his subsequent interpretation of the paper. Some economists have objected that such a formulation conveys neither the content of the article nor Coase's intention. Coase himself has raised doubts repeatedly as to whether Stigler understood his work or the objectives delineated within it.

> But you know our relationship was very cordial, very friendly, but I didn't know, half of the time, what he thought about me. You know it was respect, but how far? (Conversation with Ronald Coase, October 1997).

22   The core Chicago insistence that economic agents simply respond to market signals translates into an absence of any sustained private economic power. Price theory, viewed from this angle, eliminates monopoly issues from any serious public debate. Substituted for this menace, is the ever encroaching reach of government. Consequently, intervention is targeted as an inefficient (and inequitable) distortion of market distribution and allocation.

23   The shorthand for this notion is that 'no fifty dollar bill is left on the sidewalk'. People are on the lookout for, and eager to exploit, any opportunity which would leave them better off. Markets are structured to provide rewards for economic activity which (as a result) removes any blockages, those which tenaciously restrict profitable exchange. Consequently, externalities in George Stigler's parlance are merely problems that markets have yet to solve. The key to this system is a strong belief in rational economic decision making. From a Becker-Stigler perspective, Chicago offers a theory of decision making firmly founded on an unwavering faith in rationality. (Notice that even if not strictly true, under the provision of 'as if', the assumption could become entirely operable.)

> But as I said, he [George Stigler] really believed in the rational mind. You'd show him some example of an irrational behaviour and he would show you that it can't be true.
> *Almost by definition ...*
> Almost. Almost. It's getting more and more, more and more part of him as he got older actually, this whole view. He insists it's rational. He would tell you, 'There is some rational explanation for it. It's just that you haven't looked completely into it and found it' (Conversation with Sam Peltzman, October 1997).

24   Coase clearly delineated his differences with Stigler in his Nobel Prize speech. He never assumed that it was his role to enter into anything resembling a confrontation over the validity of Stigler's formulation that Stigler insisted on labelling the Coase Theorem. Given the hedged assumptions

forming the foundation of that proposition, little of interest can be said about actual free flowing exchanges occurring in such a non-existent environment. But the point of Coase's work is to target the necessity of vacating that world when transaction costs cease to be negligible. Stigler, as well as Friedman, never proved to be particularly interested in making such a jump. The incentives for doing so would fail to eventuate, given the set of inflexible ideological constraints that hemmed in any explorations undertaken by Stigler or Friedman. Stigler saw a quite different potential in Coase's work, one that was not necessarily consistent with that harboured by Coase himself.

> Then he [Coase] goes off to America, gives that session in Chicago, and is told there is a theory in what he has written. It's really funny. He himself describes, you know, his surprise. 'What is this Coase's Theorem?' Then, once he understood it, he says that it is false, that it's not a theory. This is an incredible story of intellectual development, of discovery. A man is shown what he believes. Only then is he fully aware of what it is. After he is shown what he believes, he is kind of horrified by it. To think that transaction costs could ever be zero. It's ridiculous. But out of it all has come the idea of transaction costs (Conversation with Mark Blaug, April 1998).

25 "Law or Economics" is Stigler's spectral article from the grave, published 1992 in the *Journal of Law and Economics*. (An earlier version was actually presented at the University of Virginia Law School in April 17, 1990 when presumably, he was still alive. Seminars are seldom séances.) The article is a bit disjointed as if he wanted to make several separable points about the use of economic reasoning to understand legal matters. But the article does underline some key issues he was still grappling with at the time of his death. Some points clearly delineated in this piece even seem to contradict, to some degree, arguments advanced in his earlier work. His starting points are not only consumer sovereignty, but the decisive nature of rational decision making in a market economy. Stigler boldly explores this terrain while down playing the importance of transaction costs or the problem of rent seeking. (Both are mentioned, but only in passing. They fail to coincide comfortably with Stigler's main themes and ideological desires.)

Rationality simply rules. When substituting his own 'Coase Theorem' for Coase's actual thought, he employs Coase's example of the grain farmer and cattle rancher to support his firmly held notion that exchange is rationally based on a strict cost to benefit approach. Using a textbook style of counter-factual reasoning, Stigler claims that if the farmer and rancher were making foolish decisions then, "I would buy the two enterprises and reap a capital gain from an efficient reorganization" (Stigler 1992:457). In a perfectly rational world of competitive markets any chance at arbitrage is instantly exploited and thus eliminated. Resources inevitably flow to those who can make the best use of them. Or in Stigler's words, use those scarce resources efficiently. Rationality ensures the fruition of this desired objective (especially in a world where transaction costs are relatively insignificant).

> That cannot be the entire story, however: human behaviour is not as rigorously deterministic as a multiplication table. There are some people who do not care for wealth, more who do not reason well, and vastly more who are incompletely informed. These people will not necessarily achieve optimal agreements, and this is specially true in new and unfamiliar circumstances. We do not believe that such people govern important markets; other market participants who love wealth, reason precisely and buy information in optimal quantities will call the tune (Stigler 1992:457–458).

Dismissed, or simply not worth mentioning, are issues like loss aversion, status quo bias, or simply acting based on dubious information, emotion or old-fashioned prejudice. The jump then is quickly made to using a test of time to justify regulatory regimes. (Whether there is a difference between a test of time and old fashioned inertia is never seriously entertained.) Given the unarguable primacy of consumer sovereignty, as Becker and Stigler make clear in their seminal 1977 article, preferences are consequently not a subject of debate. Since in the view of Stigler, economic and political markets (in democracies) operate equivalently then even such apparent inefficiencies as sugar subsidies become justified as the most efficient method for redistributing income to sugar producers. "Lacking a cheaper way of achieving this domestic subsidy, our sugar program is efficient. This program is more than fifty years old – it has met the test of time" (Stigler 1992:459). Unfortunately this conclusion seems to run counter to his earlier analysis of political rent seeking (Stigler 1971). Vested interests with more to gain than a broader mass audience, can simply outweigh consumer preferences. Once such regulations pass, Stigler might argue that it is not in the self-interest of consumers to try to change the existing state, but surely it is not in their interests to pass such subsidies in the first place. A victim of extortion may learn to live with the situation, but simply a test of time fails to redeem the practise as some disguised variety of a public good.

In the same sense, Stigler vacates questions of fairness or justice to the legal profession, leaving questions of efficiency as being the only legal aspect left in the wheelhouse of economists. "The difference between a discipline that seeks to explain economic life (and, indeed, all rational behaviour) and a discipline that seeks to achieve justice in regulating all aspects of human behaviour is profound" (Stigler 1992:463). Yet earlier (1982), Stigler seemed to equate efficiency with equity, by viewing these aspects as simply the inevitable by-products of market exchange. Rational utility maximising is not for Stigler a useful 'as if' assumption. Rather it necessarily exists as a testable hypothesis, which he firmly believed would elicit no other option than its ultimate justification. Moreover, by assuming the ever-present existence of a competitive environment, the end result, given his perspective, is not only efficient, but also a model of ethical behaviour.

> In fact Rawls's proposal of a method of constructing an inductive ethical system, which I briefly described earlier, is exactly the procedure that would show that the ethical system was based on utility-maximizing behaviour. My confidence that the test would yield this result will be disputed by many people of distinction, and that argues all the more for making the test (Stigler 1982:36).

26   In many ways, Ronald Coase was inspired, if only negatively, by Pigou's extensive efforts. As early as 1946 (and as will be demonstrated, even before), Coase took aim at what he saw as basic missteps in understanding the tools economics could provide. Here it might prove useful to remember Coase's practical turn of mind, which proved not to be conveniently ame-nable to purely theoretical efforts. In particular, the modernist spirit in the 1940s had allowed young economists, such as Abba Lerner (1944), to deduce the need for government intervention in markets in which firms enjoyed economies of scale. The science was impeccable. Efficient pricing (and production) demanded marginal cost settings. Economies of scale implied falling average costs and therefore marginal costs lying below average unit ones. Since firms would find efficient pricing to be antitheti-cal to survival (the need to cover opportunity costs), governments were scientifically obliged to step-in to uphold market requirements (to dupli-cate optimum resource allocation). "The amount by which total costs exceed total receipts (the loss, as it is sometimes termed) should be a charge on the Government and should be borne out of taxation" (Coase 1946:169). The interesting problem raised by this early example of model based policy is the lack of any concrete examination of what firms actually do (or could do) when faced with exactly this challenge. Even worse, no indication in either Lerner's work or that of Hotelling (1938) hints at the need to consider other potential pricing choices, or the responses of con-sumers within the relevant markets. Policy formation is instead stripped down to the construction of an economic model with policy directly derived from that model's conclusions. (In such schemes, both firms and government seem to operate in a privileged sphere of zero transaction costs.) But for Coase, the very logic underpinning this broadly accepted analysis is faulty.

> Any actual economic situation is complex and a single economic problem does not exist in isolation. Consequently, confusion is liable to result because economists dealing with an actual situation are attempting to solve several problems at once (Coase 1946:170).

For Coase, the methodology, and unsubstantiated certainty, bundled together with such policy recommendations have an otherworldly quality attached to them. Historical results become unnecessary when markets are expected to align themselves to the constraints imposed by economic science. These cleverly stitched together policies carry with them more than a definite whiff of the methodology deployed by Swift's tailors of Laputa. Imbued with Knight's ingrained skepticism of any such all-embracing plans for improving the world, Coase would have little faith that governments of any stripe or ability would automatically be capable of implementing such immaculately conceived schemes.

> This, he [Hotelling] says, "is an interesting historical question." And he adds later: "When the question arises of building new railroads or new major industries of any kind or of scrapping the old, we shall face, not a historical, but a mathematical and economic problem." Nowhere in Professor Hotelling's article does one find recognition of the fact that it will be more difficult to discover whether to build new railroads or new industries if one does not know whether the creation of past railroads or industries was wise social policy. And it is certainly not absurd to take into account the fact that decisions are likely to be better made if afterwards there is some test of whether such decisions were wise social policy than if such an enquiry is never made (Coase 1946:175–176).

27 Stigler sometimes verges on the boundaries of formulating a mirror version (though implacably defined by the market) of Marx' historical materialism. Individuals passively respond to market necessities, having surrendered all economic power or influence in a Hobbesian type arrangement. In a throwback to the Old Norse Gods, within Stigler's framework, 'Fate is inexorable'.

> I believe, on the contrary, that if Cobden had spoken only Yiddish, and with a stammer, and Peel had been a narrow, stupid man, England would have moved toward free trade in grain as its agricultural classes declined and its manufacturing and commercial classes grew. Perhaps a few years later, but not many (Stigler 1976:352).

28 Unquestionably the key engineers of the post war Chicago School (Stigler, Friedman and Director) broke with Frank Knight (their most influential teacher) on a variety of levels, especially in rejecting the methodology of Classical Liberalism. But what may be surprising is the implicit attempt, at times, to rescue Knight (fitting him, somewhat strenuously, back within the fold) by reinterpreting his views on crucial conceptions (knowledge and uncertainty). The implicit goal of doing so seems to be an attempt to force Knights ideas to align with their own perspective. Hard to fathom is whether Friedman's transformation of Knight at this late date (1997) was

simply a deliberate attempt at cosmetic refurbishing. Equally possible, his actual misunderstanding may reflect an urge or subconscious need to have the observed world coincide with his own preconceived viewpoint. In the same fashion, it is questionable whether Friedman, as well as Stigler, were ever motivated to fully grasp Coase's approach.

The other thing is on uncertainty, the role of uncertainty. Knight of course writes that volume on Risk and Uncertainty. Yet if you read George Stigler, time and time again he wants to marginalize the effects of uncertainty, which is understandable, I think, given his work and what he is trying to do.

Milton Friedman: It's understandable from a different point of view. See I'm a great admirer of Knight, but I think his distinction between risk and uncertainty is untenable.

In what aspect?

Milton Friedman: I believe that it uses a false theory of probability. I believe that the only theory of probability that can hold water is personal probability, the kind of thing that Jimmy Savage helped develop. If you take that approach, you can't distinguish uncertainty from risk. There's no break point. But also, you see, it means that Knight implicitly was working on a definition of probability as a relative frequency. And that misleads people into thinking that there are objective probabilities that you can know. Therefore it leads to a distinction between risk and uncertainty in terms of costs. Knight assumes you know some probabilities and that there's no way you can know others. In a personal probability sense, nobody really knows any probability. There are no objective probabilities.

But is there a continuum of, for instance, how much you'd be willing to bet on one.

Milton Friedman: Well, if I can experiment with your willingness to bet, I can determine your probabilities. There's going to be a war next year. Knight would say that's uncertainty. But in principle, if I can experiment with you, I can find out at what odds you are willing to take a bet that there will be a war next year. And thus I can extract your subjective probability of there being a war and in that sense there's no distinction between risk and uncertainty.

In the sense of subjective probability.

Milton Friedman: At any moment of time, you will in principle have subjective probabilities of any strategic event.

Yes, potentially

Milton Friedman: And I think George was influenced by that approach to probability as well.

So, he basically saw that distinction as a dead end.

Milton Friedman: That's right.

Taking you nowhere.

Milton Friedman: I think it is a dead end. It's received a lot of attention and a lot of people talk about it. But I think it is very, very hard to make a logical

distinction. Where does uncertainty begin and where does probability end, risk end? ... How happy do you think Knight was about that distinction?
Aaron Director: I don't know. I thought he drew his distinction from the fact that you can insure one and you couldn't insure the other. Period. I'm only establishing his belief.
Milton Friedman: That was his belief. You can insure any of them in principle.
Aaron Director: Really?
Milton Friedman: And do.
Aaron Director: I understand that. But we are only talking about what Knight thought about it.
Milton Friedman: And Knight thought there were problems ...
Aaron Director: You couldn't.
Milton Friedman: You couldn't?
That's right. That was his distinction. Uninsurable risk.
Aaron Director: Yep.
Milton Friedman: But if you say all risk is insurable, of course it means nothing.
Aaron Director: No distinction.
If you've got a zero set of uninsurable risks, then it's of no use.
Milton Friedman: If you ask somebody 'I want to make a bet with you' you'll find somebody who'll take your bet, if you advertise widely enough.
If you give them the appropriate odds.
Milton Friedman: Right. And at that point, you've insured the risk (Conversation with Milton Friedman, Rose Friedman and Aaron Director, August 1997).

29 Following Frank Knight's brand of inherent scepticism, Coase proved reluctant to accept *a priori*, professional truths deemed too obvious to be questioned. Theoretical conclusions needed perforce to be compared with observed economic outcomes. Theory itself, when starting from different premises, was productive of alternative paths and solutions.

30 Such work predates Stigler's own pioneering efforts that examined whether regulation actually achieves its objectives (1962), as well as the reason for the existence of such regulations (1971). Notice however, the difference in approaches. Stigler abstracts and makes wide ranging, universal claims. Coase works in miniature, examining each specific case as it comes to hand. Significantly, Coase's articles tend to shy away from staking out any extravagant claims.

31 Notice that this thinking doesn't pre-emptively rule out a need for regulation in this case but rather rules out adopting an *a priori* stance before empirically considering all possible options. If we follow Coase's theory it is only here that differences in evaluating existing evidence may occur.

The relevance of this approach to the current artificial intelligence conundrum seems particularly appropriate.

32   Undoubtedly, if you troll through everything Coase might have written or said, some contradictory elements will surely be identified. However, such discoveries hardly amount to an 'aha moment'. No one is one hundred percent consistent, no matter what pains are taken to avoid such missteps. Deviations do not inevitably succeed in cancelling out or diverting the basic framework of thought constructed over a lifetime of effort.

33   Here it might be useful to distinguish between structural economic models and the dangers of employing policies derived from such idealized constructions. Perfectly competitive markets devoid of any transaction costs eliminate the fundamental reason for the formation of such markets. An economy could, under such circumstances, operate effectively in the guise of one multi-divisional, integrated firm. Distribution could be conducted by means of some central governmental authority or some private monopoly. In contrast, it is useful to remember that Coase took his inspiration partly from Knight, who happily pointed out the absurdities of such a world where transactions or 'frictions' ceased to exist. "… if competition worked without let or hindrance, pure business profit would be annihilated as fast as it could be created" (Clark quoted by Knight 1971:34). But Knight then drives home the difference between the realm of economic models and an operative economy, by pushing this idea of an absence of 'frictions' (or for that matter transaction costs) to a logical extreme.

> This is fallacious even under the assumptions, since the profits of change come largely in the form of readjustments of capital values. The difficulty is, of course, avoided if "friction" be so broadly defined that "perfect mobility" means the absence of all resistance to the human will. But in a world where a breath could transform a brick factory building into a railway yard or an ocean greyhound there would be no need for economic activity or economic science (Knight 1971:34 ftn. 4).

34   Clearly the same approach could be equally employed to limit the extent of unconstrained markets. The Classical Liberal methodology that Coase advanced was, in its untainted version, not associated or defined by any specific ideology.

35   Contrast Coase's approach with that of Chicago where the search for universals dominated. The ruling passion at Chicago, during Coase's decades-long residence, was an imperative to abstract in order to generalize. The generalized hypothesis was then tested, found substantiated and applied generally. As opposed to Coase's perspective, there was a decided preferences for devising and employing a 'one-size-fits-all' approach.

36 Evidence, and particularly statistics, inevitably fail to speak for themselves. Judgement and interpretation are required. Practically speaking, any examination of existing facts requires yet another effort to avoid letting ideological preconceptions shape or rule the resulting conclusions of one's endeavours.

37 Coase never denigrated theory, nor did the economists he admired, such as Frank Knight. The problem however was to meticulously maintain the boundaries separating economic science, or theory, from the practical realm of policy. In the later kingdom, the necessity of ideas working in practice is far more important than having them work in theory.

> Blackboard economics is undoubtedly an exercise requiring great intellectual ability and it may have a role in developing the skills of an economist, but it misdirects our attention when thinking about economic policy (Coase 1988:19).

38 Though George Stigler supported Coase while at Chicago, including lobbying for his Nobel Prize, how much he grasped or cared to understand Coase's approach to economics remains questionable.

> You know the 'Nature of the Firm' that was reprinted in the series which George and Boulding edited. I once asked him about the choice there. And, it was George's choice. They agreed that Boulding should choose half of the articles and George should choose the other half of the articles. So, in a sense it was not a joint effort the selection. And George chose my article. So that, I think, is interesting that he had a sort of general sympathy, a feeling that it was of some importance. And at a time when, I don't think other people did.
> *But he doesn't seem to have actually, himself, done anything in that area.*
> No. He makes a number of remarks which are sort of coming to the entry point, as it were of the subject. When he reprinted that thing of his, that the 'division of labour is limited', or whatever the phrase is, 'by the extent of the market', he adds in a footnote of the reprint that he ought to have referred to my article. Well, I'm not sure that he ought to have referred to the article. I didn't want him to worry. But I think there was a feeling that he might have missed something (Conversation with Ronald Coase, October 1997).

39 Stigler and Coase would have largely agreed on policy recommendations. The tendency then is to lump them together, by focusing only on the final destination they mutually reached. Both would have deduced the existence of too heavy a dollop of government intervention and regulation. But the road which led them to such conclusions in fact varied substantially. Stigler provided a one way turnpike leading only to a single, predictable conclusion. His methodology led to a unique set of policies. Coase's throughway, contained alternative turnoffs. Endpoints would depend on how each specific

navigator read the various traffic signals and provided data. Methods matter as well as ultimate conclusions.

40 The theorem might be better understood if it came supplied with a cinematic tagline: 'a theorem inspired by a Ronald Coase article', or 'based on a published article'.

41 That Stigler chose to title that chapter of his autobiography 'Eureka!' easily reveals a not so well hidden agenda. Samuelson also saw a bit of sleight of hand being performed by the Chicago contingent.

> But Stigler and Friedman jumped on to Ronald Coase and felt that the Coase doctrines about transaction costs and property rights - just get the property rights right then *laissez-faire* could be relied upon - was the lifeline that they sought. Now, all that I know about this part of the story is what's called the Coase Theorem. And that's a coinage of Stigler's. I don't think Coase knew what his theorem was. There's great argumentation as to whether there is a theorem (Conversation with Paul Samuelson, October 1997).

42 Stigler's long time researcher, Claire Friedland best sums up Stigler's views on externalities.

> George was focused on the way the market marches in to *eliminate* the externalities, to work *around* them to make them a market problem instead of a non-market problem. I think I've quoted him in my memoir as saying something like, 'externalities are what the market has not *yet* eliminated.' (Conversation with Claire Friedland November 1997).
>
> He described externalities as that for which there are no transactions *at the present time* (Friedland 1993:781).

43 From Stigler's chosen perspective, perfect competition represented not a possible theoretical model, but 'the model' that accurately mirrored working, concrete markets. At least the resemblance was close enough to be practically employable for direct policy configurations.

44 It would be foolish to simply dismiss the rhetorical value of the 'Coase Theorem'. The formulation served as an effective way to dismiss the idea of market failure (and to focus by default on government failure), or at least on the need to consider such a possibility seriously. The intent here is not to denigrate the scientific aspect of his work. However, Stigler valued his scientific efforts not only for their contribution in buttressing the underlying economic framework he clearly preferred. The craftily formulated theorem particularly gained traction as an effective platform for marketing Stigler's *a priori* vision of how the economy works. In a similar sense, although Stigler studiously championed the value of quantitative methods, he often used his own empirical research more as a rhetorical device than as an engine of discovery.

> The interesting thing is he was a great enthusiast for quantitative methods. So, it doesn't seem altogether consistent. But he certainly was. On the other hand, he knew what the answer was going to be. He just regarded it, as I say, as a way of persuading other people (Conversation with Ronald Coase, October 1997).

45   That which Stigler forcefully shaped into his 'Coase Theorem' was no more than Coase's adroit use of a MacGuffin. The standard idea of externalities is usually formulated in a zero transaction cost bubble. Coase demonstrated that in such an environment, externalities fail to pose any problem to a market economy. The difficulty to be overcome then lies only in the existence of positive transaction costs, rather than the existence of externalities. The heuristic formulation of a world of zero transaction costs exists as a method for motivating Coase's essential examination of the place of transaction costs in determining outcomes and formulating policies. This stratagem then is simply a device that serves to clear away the basic confusion surrounding the idea of externalities, at least given Coase's pronounced perspective. In and of itself, the formulation, which endures as the 'Coase Theorem', is essentially trivial. Consequently, Stigler, for whatever reason or motivation, essentially managed to confuse the actual article with the article's functional MacGuffin. Economically, confusing the two is equivalent to a film critic discussing the height and weight of the Maltese Falcon statue, while ignoring the actual film.

46   The validity of the Coase Theorem as a scientific construct is inevitably debatable. In one sense, it is no more than a tautology, capable of shedding only limited light on the issue at hand. (In a seemingly unlimited wedge of literature on its scientific validity, a useful place to start is with Cooter (1982. 1987)) But the formulated theory itself has been challenged periodically. In discussing it, Coase's erstwhile colleague Lester Telser (though admittedly residing on the other side of the Midway), dismissed the scientific formulation by referencing the theory of the core (Conversation with Lester Telser, October 1997). However, while a debate over Stigler's theoretical conception is no doubt legitimate, becoming immersed in such a discussion distracts from Coase's original intention in the actual cited article. (Though Coase's article loses much of its impact if it fails to explode the traditional role of externalities.) The simple idea, once again, is that Stigler's obsession with the MacGuffin successfully sidesteps Coase's purpose or idea. Stigler persistently had trouble finding useful insights laying outside the boundaries defining his own ideological preconceptions.

47   The almost instinctive reaction was simply to attack its scientific validity, a strategy also readily employed by counterparts at Chicago when faced with policies objectionable from their own perspective. Supposedly, destroying the theory meant destroying the detested policy it supported. However,

except by committing to a voluntary leap of faith, undercutting this particular scientific formulation provided no conclusive direction for pragmatic policy construction. What did, or did not, occur in an alternative universe of zero transaction costs need not necessarily constrain, or even channel, the interactions within actual market environments.

48 Stigler was an inveterate stirrer. Nothing spooked him quite as much as being confronted with silence. For a brief period he alternated in writing a column for *The Business Monthly* with Robert Solow. (Surprisingly, or perhaps not that surprisingly, one of his closest friends.) Stigler threw in the towel after a few attempts. Despite assuming controversial positions in each of his columns, they all failed to elicit a single response from the journal's readers. This event proved to be more than Stigler could bear.

> He was a bit of a provocateur. He liked upsetting people. I told you he wrote that column for *Business Month*. After a year went by, nobody had criticized it. They didn't get any letters to the editor. And you know, he had said so many outrageous things: that insider trading is really okay, that sort of thing. He said things meant to upset people. Well, he gave it up. He wasn't having any fun. He wanted people to criticize his ideas and then he wanted to come back with his rejoinders. You know, he wanted to have a little controversy (Conversation with Claire Friedland, October 1997).

49 In a private conversation (October 1997), Coase suggested that at that famous dinner it was only Arnold Harberger who had seriously grasped both his intentions and the associated employment of marginal analysis. When asked about the 'Coase Theorem' he agreed that Stigler had transformed his argument into something that wasn't exactly there. Coase stated "He was always very nice and kind and helpful in many ways. Always. But I often wondered how far he agreed with what I was saying. I think he thought I was all right, but a little odd" (Conversation with Ronald Coase, October 1997).

50 To further emphasise the structure and intention of Coase's (1960) work, the world of zero transaction costs is created to clear away previous misguided analysis. (Or at least misguided from Coase's long standing perspective.) If with zero such costs, externalities pose no problem, than economists are misled by obsessing about the existence of such observed phenomena. For Coase, pollution is not the problem. Rather it is the presence of positive transaction costs that create market distortions, not the existence of this or any other externality.

51 Taking refuge in the world of 'as if' provides little in the way of a reliable refuge. Comparing the economics of zero transaction costs to that of physics fails to pass muster. Assuming a frictionless world is not an entirely imaginary leap since vacuums can be created, or observed in outer space

with results recorded. Nor is dealing with the interactions of physical items in any way comparable to dissecting the objectives and actions of emotion ridden humans. Thought and lab experiments remain only distant cousins as far as evidentiary certainty goes.

52   If one is willing to assume a sufficiently cynical perspective, then a distinct temptation exists to contrast the difficulty, and associated labour, involved in adopting a more Coase-like approach to policy construction. Compare this alternative to simply embracing theoretical conclusions as unequivocal guides for all aspects of economic policy. Given a need for career advancement, amid increased competition for even a base level of recognition, time constraints alone favour the theoretic (or scientific) path to policy formulation.

53   The reference is to Friedman's (1953) solitary attempt, though an influential one, to analyse economic methodology. Even today, many economists would remain familiar, in some vague fashion, with this work. However, relatively few would be aware of Stigler's (1949) essential, if perhaps not equal, contribution in formulating this methodological roadmap.

54   Certainly he wasn't reluctant to use statistics when and if he deemed it to be appropriate to do so. At the very start of his career, he investigated the expectations driven pricing model first formulated by Nicholas Kaldor (1934). Using actual pricing statistics, instead of assuming the way in which pig farmers (in this case) should operate, Coase and Fowler (1935a) were able to raise serious doubts about the efficacy of such a model. Doing so, consequently raised serious doubts about any agricultural policy based on such theoretical assertions.

> In those days, there was something called a cobweb theorem. The name was invented by Nicky Kaldor (1934). It is based on the idea that people assume that existing prices and costs are going to continue as is. So Fowler [a fellow student with Ronald Coase at the London School of Economics] and I took the pig industry and we showed that it wasn't true [1935a, 1935b, 1937a]. We showed that it wasn't true, because what you had was a market for two types of pigs. You had breeders and feeders. I think that in a lot of these sorts of industries, you still do. Anyway, there was a market for young pigs. Now, one knew in a general sort of way what the costs were of feeding. Well, the price that they paid for young pigs would reflect what they thought the price of the pigs, once fed, would fetch. So you could work out what people's expectations were. We showed that when prices were exceptionally high, they thought they would fall, and when they were low, they thought they would rise, and so on (Conversation with Ronald Coase, October 1997).

55   The point is that while Coase was certainly at Chicago for many decades, he was really never of Chicago in the sense of conforming to the Stigler-Friedman perspective. The dangers of lumping Coase with other leading

Chicago figures involve a tendency to overlook Coase's actual contribution. Reading with prior expectations almost inevitably leads to attempts to jam Coase's square pegs into rounded Chicago School holes.

> *He did seem as he worked with Gary Becker to push the ideal of self-interest more and more.*
> And rationality. George didn't like my piece that I wrote on 'Economics and The Contiguous Disciplines' (1994e).
> *Yes, I've read it. It's good work.*
> He didn't think so.
> **What was his problem?**
> Well, I didn't actually ask him. He indicated his displeasure by saying - you know, it had been written for originally, and then given at, a conference in Germany. He said it would have been better if it had been written in German.
> *I suppose he didn't care for it.*
> He didn't care for it. This must mean, I think, and this may be of interest to you, that he didn't understand it (Conversation with Ronald Coase, October 1997).

56   The distinct suspicion is that Friedman, Stigler or even Director would expect some method of forming an abstract hypothesis that could then be tested. Coase, instead, offers more of an Easter egg hunt for existing transaction costs in a specific instance or situation. Policy would subsequently flow once a reliable identification was complete. This is particularly contrary to the Chicago mindset of 'once and done'. In the world in which Coase operates, transaction costs, for a myriad of reasons, can be expected to change over time.

57   The difficulty such luminaries as Stigler and Friedman seem to have had with Coase's methods might be a simple misunderstanding of intentions. They were apt to try to fit work into predetermined configurations. (In terms of this paper's argument, falling into the fallacy of categorization.) Difficulties arose when grappling with an approach that ran counter to theirs. Consequently, Coase provided the proverbial square pegs for their round theoretical holes. This mismatch led to Coase's erstwhile colleagues and friends glossing over the actual contours of his efforts. In contrast, their imperative was to abstract from observed phenomena in order to generalize, reflecting an unalloyed obsession with the generation and application of universal laws. In a throwback to the myth of Procrustes, and his formidable bed, in Chicago, one size was reflexively made to fit all. Coase, in contrast, insisted on the importance of specifics, of working in miniature while honouring the divergence of specific cases and observations. However, all of the Chicago cognoscenti, including Coase, did hold similar political views and usually supported aligned policies. Perhaps this led these Chicago compatriots to implicitly transform Coase's work into something a bit more

palatable to their narrowly, cultivated tastes. Consequently, they would naturally find it difficult to swallow the true intent of his output, or to give the work its complete due.

58   As an extreme Chicago instance, George Stigler became more and more convinced that rational decision-making not only supplied a necessary, but also sufficient explanation for any observation.

59   Obsessive pursuits come in all sizes and shades. Most lack the dignity of Ahab's single-minded pursuit of Moby Dick. Under Lewis Carroll's quizzical gaze, the hunt for the Snark occurs at a distinctly different level.

> They sought it with thimbles, they sought it with care;
> They pursued it with forks and hope;
> They threatened its life with a railway share;
> They charmed it with smiles and soap (Carroll 1876/1962:123).

60   Another unlikely parallel links Austen to Coase. (Despite the fact that it would be difficult to imagine Ronald Coase as an ardent suitor in a proper English novel, though a more likely one than either George Stigler or Milton Friedman.) Austen's best loved novel, *Pride and Prejudice* (1813), is driven by the unintended consequences derived by acts of hasty categorization. *First Impressions*, the novel's initial working title, clearly conveys this fundamental concept. Both Elizabeth Bennett and Fitzwilliam Darcy initially dismiss each other by means of an act of lazy pigeon-holing. Darcy driven by his pride and Elizabeth Bennett by an incited rush of prejudice. They both see each other as a representative type, rather than as a more complex and individual personality. Such cataloguing makes any true evaluation of specific characteristics difficult, if not impossible. Time (and a whole novel of complications) are needed before both parties grow into a more mature perspective.

61   Late in his life, Ronald Coase was still pushing, against the odds, for a change in the profession's basic methodology. He continued to search for a new, more practical perspective.

> But, it means that we have to get the vision first and then do the empirical work. I've just been involved in the starting of a new society, The International Society for the New Institutional Economics. And the inaugural conference was held last month in St. Louis. I wanted to have a small meeting, but we invited some people and they told other people and they told still other people and in the end we had 200 people come from all over the world. No one from Australia, but someone from New Zealand, and I know there were people from Russia, and China, Taiwan, all the European countries and so on. So there is a lot of dissatisfaction with the present state of economics. It's not dominant, but there's a lot of it and its widespread (Conversation with Ronald Coase, 1997).

62   The Virginia School of Economics, now widely unrecognized as such within the profession, flourished at the University of Virginia from the

mid-1950s through most of the 1960s. Pioneering in areas like Public Choice, Law and Economics, as well as Constitutional Economics, much of the work done would only flourish later at other institutions. The Department included such luminaries as James Buchanan, Gordon Tullock, Ronald Coase, G. Warren Nutter and Robert Tollison among others. These economists saw themselves, more or less, as operating within the spirit of Classical Liberal Economics, or at least that spirit as defined by Frank Knight. (Buchanan, of course, was one of Knight's few students.) The Department largely lost the support of the University Administration. These officials stubbornly viewed the constituted department as being too old fashioned and out of sync with current economic thought. (Administrators tend not to be overly concerned with weighing current fads against long run verities.) Coase left for Chicago in 1964, with Buchanan decamping for Virginia Tech by 1968. Boettke (1987) provides some interesting insights into this once and future school.

> They thought the work we were doing was disreputable. They thought of us as right-wing extremists. My wife was at a cocktail party and heard me described as someone to the right of the John Birch Society. There was a great antagonism in the '50s and '60's to anyone who saw any advantage in a market system or in a nonregulated or relatively economically free system (Coase in conversation with Hazlet 1997–1998:27).

63 Perhaps, rather than forcing observations and events to be wedged tightly into preconceived categories, anything resembling a general, or even universal, statement should be teased out of many detailed examinations of specific cases and even then only employed as a tentative rule of thumb.

64 Though in some aspects an extreme example, it might prove useful to examine the contrasting understandings, offered by Coase and Stigler, of Smith's view of humanity. George Stigler almost carelessly dismissed any psychological factors as extraneous to economic analysis and to its directly derived policies. Given his fixed, almost Kantian schemata (his corresponding vision of how markets operated and individuals choose), such psychological considerations could only be ruled peremptorily out of court.

> If one were to seek a major economic theory whose existence depended directly and essentially upon prior work in another field, he would find few likely candidates. Putting aside for a moment the methodological fields of statistics and mathematics, there is in fact no important candidate. A theory of behaviour, such as our profit maximizing assumption implies could have come from psychology, but of course it did not. In fact Smith's professional work on psychology (in the *Theory of Moral Sentiments*) bears scarcely any relationship to his economics, and this tradition of independence of economics from psychology has persisted despite continued efforts from Jennings ... to Herbert Simon and George Katona to destroy it (Stigler 1960:44).

Coase sharply parted company with his erstwhile colleague in regard to psychology and the role Smith's two great works play in formulating a workable conception of human behaviour. "Well, you know my argument [regarding *The Wealth of* Nations and *The Moral Sentiments*] is the opposite" (Conversation with Ronald Coase, October 1997).

> It is sometimes said that Smith assumes that human beings are motivated solely by self-interest. Self-interest is certainly, in Smith's view, a powerful motive in human behaviour, but it is by no means the only motive. I think his analysis does not weaken but rather strengthens his argument for the use of the market and the limitation of governmental action in economic affairs (Coase 1994c:95).

65   Evidence that failed to assume required topological arrangements, and to align closely to Stigler's orthodox price models, could be summarily dismissed as simply unreliable. Such anomalies automatically commandeered further investigation with existing evidence subsequently interrogated, or more precisely water-boarded, until these errant observations surrendered to deduced logical outcomes.

> He was absolutely convinced that prices were flexible from Day 1. That was clearly his *a priori* intention. It was more than an intention. It was his belief. In the true believer sense. He really believed that. The very first interview we did was with a big firm. We have to keep this all anonymous, but it was a large firm in the Chicago area. That doesn't give very much away. Yes, perhaps there were more then than there are now. Anyway, the essence of it was that the people there absolutely denied anything about price flexibility, hidden discounts or things like that. They put out a price book and that was that. Everybody paid the same price. There were quantity discounts that were clearly stated in this price book. Anyone who bought large quantities got the large quantity prices, and small quantities got small quantities prices. George Stigler was clearly disappointed in that. He came back and he told me, 'Well, we'll get to the bottom of this' (Conversation with James Kindahl, October 1997).

66   Any significant overlap in the methodologies employed by Coase and the Chicago School were not ever clearly in evidence. Stigler, for instance, sought to isolate commonalities within markets by abstracting away from any specifics. But for Coase, crucial understanding could often lie hidden in such details.

> He was not really interested in what firms did or really what the political parties did, although he writes about it, what their effects were on registration and so on. He sort of studied them from the outside. But why political parties were organised the way they were, which is an interesting question in itself, he never investigated (Conversation with Ronald Coase, October 1997).

67 A famous essay by Isaiah Berlin (1953), *The Hedgehog and the Fox* draws its title from a fragment attributed to the Ancient Greek poet Archilochus: πόλλ' οἶδ' ἀλώπηξ, ἀλλ' ἐχῖνος ἓν μέγα ("a fox knows many things, but a hedgehog one important thing"). In the case of George Stigler and Ronald Coase appearances mostly deceive. Stigler, who superficially seems to have jumped from one topic of research to the next, upon examination has obsessively reduced all observations to meditations on rational choice and perfectly competitive markets. Coase, on the other hand, appears transfixed by the single idea of transaction costs, but in practice his work depends upon his knowing many specific things, rather than one all-encompassing concept. George Stigler in action becomes the dominating hedgehog pretending to be a fox, while Coase remains the eternal vixen disguised as the indefatigable hedgehog.

68 Economics is rife with what might be thought of as one sided scepticism. In the example Coase examined, once a lighthouse is labelled a public good, private provision is automatically dismissed as suboptimal, if at all feasible. Government provision, from this perspective, becomes the sole alternative. But in this bit of logical analysis, questions involving the costs of government provision are conveniently ignored. (In Coase's terms, the relevant transaction costs are deemed to be at a relentlessly zero value.) The perennial problem of government failure is simply ignored. Unfortunately, serious market proponents display an equal absence of anything resembling a balanced view. The starting point in their favoured approach is to emphasise the costs of government provision, but ignore the transaction costs of private market supply. Coase, no matter what his ultimate conclusions, starts from a more reasonable agnostic position. (Or, he at least attempts to achieve that more balanced stance.) Policy deductions depend on whatever specific evidence is available. This basis allows reasonable differences, given that judgments are never identical. What is essential here is not Coase's conservative position, but that his method rejects any predetermined conclusions. Such a perspective does avoid the sort of obsession with universals, in which economists like Stigler, Friedman or Samuelson are wont to traffic. Perhaps a core reason why Coase's Chicago colleagues largely failed to understand his intentions, rested on his focus with specifics, rather than abstract generalisations.

> I don't reject any policy without considering what the results are. If someone says there's going to be regulation, I don't say that regulation will be bad. Let's see. What we discover is that most regulation does produce, or has produced in recent times, a worse result. But I wouldn't like to say that all regulation would have this effect because one can think of circumstances in which it doesn't (Coase in conversation with Hazlet 1997–1998:26).

69   That economists could talk so confidently about lighthouses, which they had never investigated, nor even perhaps viewed, is reminiscent of Frank Knight's favourite quote by Josh Billings, a nineteenth century humourist, who during his time rivalled Mark Twain in popularity. "The trouble with people is not that they don't know but that they know so much that ain't so."

> Samuelson says I was wrong and he was right and he froths at the mouth when people talk about the lighthouse example. He says Coase is wrong; he doesn't overcome the free rider problem. Who are the free riders? The foreign ships going past the British coast which do not call at a British port. Using Samuelson's approach what do you do? Do you ask the foreign governments to give you a subsidy? Do you tax people in Britain because the foreign ships are getting help without paying for it? What do you do?
>
> My approach is to compare the alternatives. People like Samuelson like to set up a perfect world and say that the market does not bring us to this point and imply that the government should do something. They stop their analysis at that point ((Coase in conversation with Hazlet 1997–1998:28).

70   To clarify, Coase doesn't attempt to demonstrate the superiority of the private sector in building and operating lighthouses. Whether governments or private ownership yield a preferred outcome is left unresolved. Established is the undeniable fact of private sector lighthouses. Given the cost incurred by governments in building and operating such establishments (neither governments nor markets operate in a backyard of zero transaction costs), which is the better option is hardly self-evident. The inevitable conclusion from examining Coase's lighthouse efforts is that theoretical universals will not be decisive in determining specific cases.

71   Apropos of nothing in particular, the family of the author Robert Louis Stevenson (commencing with his grandfather) was famous as being the foremost lighthouse engineers in Scotland. They designed and constructed many of the more famous lighthouses in the nineteenth century and largely succeeded in lighting up the Scottish coast. (Not being a lighthouse connoisseur, I am unable to explain what exactly might make a given lighthouse famous.) An interesting bit of lighthouse liturgy, though not particularly economically decisive as regards either Coase or Stigler.

72   The problem, once again, lies in the confidence with which economists expound on subjects of which they actually know very little. "Most economists would say 'How do you spell 'gold'? And then they'll tell you what we should be doing about gold or anything else that you can imagine" (Conversation with Paul Samuelson October 1997). In the same vein as Coase's 1974 paper is an article produced by Steven Cheung (1973). Again, a textbook example employed to demonstrate an unarguable positive externality involved the pollination performed by bees for at least some primary crops. Economists logically deduced that lacking enforceable property

rights, the contribution provided by these ever buzzing bees was simply unpriced. However, Cheung found that upon examination, beekeepers and farmers had come to mutually beneficial arrangements effectively negating the assumed positive externality aspect of such pollination. Theory in such cases can underestimate the ability of actual individuals to resolve difficulties projected by assured abstract constructions. The idea (of just asking the relevant principals) seems to have largely escaped the notice of many economists.

73 Relatively early in his career, George Stigler faced (and most likely ignored) the charge of being more fabulist than researcher. Immediately following the war, Stigler and Friedman engaged in their only published collaboration. They were contracted (for financial gain) by The Foundation for Economic Education to produce a pamphlet on the controversial rent control policies that were being enacted. (Put in place to supposedly aid returning veterans and other renters trying to negotiate a constrained supply of available apartments.) The result was *Roofs or Ceilings? The Current Housing Problem* (Friedman and Stigler, 1946). An ongoing controversy attached to the writing of that pamphlet with the designated paymasters evaluating some remarks as being too left-wing. (The exchanged letters between the two economists, and those of V. Orval Watts and Leonard E. Read of the Foundation, can be found in Hammond and Hammond, 2006.) However, one resident of Boston, Harold C. Harlow was left less than impressed by their efforts and responded with a characteristically 'outraged' letter:

> My dear Mr. Stigler:
>
> I was highly interested to read of what you had to say concerning rent ceilings in your pamphlet "Roofs or Ceilings", for I cannot conceive of professors in good standing in Economics never having learned how to do research, or having used it, perjure themselves and it and still remain in good standing.
>
> In turn I should like to ask you a few questions: where did you get your facts, – or maybe that's why you called it a "theory". Did you poll anyone who was not a veteran to find how many of these "others" are now doubling up too? Are you living in a university house? Have you taken in veterans? Have you inspected housing for students and families, already tripling up to pay the present high rents – these very rents which you say will be the only ones to be really effected by rent rises: new tenants (sic) (recent figures over 3 million) and those without leases. Did you consult with any social scientist as to your theory's effects on standards of living (records show the effects of a housing shortage back before 1936); did you consult with any political scientist as to the results of its use by the National Association of Real Estate Boards.

> If your students still have respect for your opinions after having read your pamphlet, I feel sorry for them – not you (Letter from Harold C. Harlow to George Stigler, November 7, 1946; Special Collections, Regenstein Library, University of Chicago).

74   In a sense, creating these bits of potted history is equivalent to a form of reverse engineering conducted in order to advance specific economic objectives. Given a theoretical position, researchers troll economic and business history for cases that can be moulded to fit preconceived conclusions. Actual evidence, which might support these claims, is deemed to be superfluous.

75   Unfortunately, this might not have been the only case of Armen Alchian's affinity for 'just so' stories. At least that would have to be deemed as a plausible evaluation, if a letter dated July 13, 1971 from one R. M. Brown, Senior Industry Planning Administrator at that time for IBM, is accurate. (In fact, believing that Mr. Brown would bother to write a detailed private letter to an academic which contained assorted falsehoods is not highly credible.) In which case, it might prove instructive, or at least amusing, to reproduce the pointed communication in its entirety. The issue creating contention appears to be a textbook instance where Armen Alchian used IBM's supposed pricing policies as an historical example of tied pricing

> Dear Mr. Alchien [sic]
>
> A student in one of your class has pointed out some gross inaccuracies in the text content of UNIVERSITY ECONOMICS – Second Edition, regarding monopolistic practices of the IBM Corporation (chapter 18, pp. 331, 332).
>
> For the sake of accuracy in your journalistic endeavours, I would like to point out that:
>
> - IBM does not, and has never, required its customers to buy IBM cards only. (Check the source of supply at U.C.L.A.) Anyone can legally enter the market and can, in fact, get engineering specifications on the paper stock itself and detailed machinery and manufacturing specifications from IBM, even though patents are held by this corporation.
> - IBM machines can be rented or purchased.
> - IBM has never had a discriminatory pricing structure. (The card-count theory can only be termed an author's contrivance.) Special discounts are allowed to educational institutions. Certain large government contracts are subject to bid – otherwise, you as an individual would pay precisely the same price to rent or purchase IBM machines as would General Motors.

> If there is a Third Edition, I would hope that as a responsible reporter, you will correct your text – even though it may make your economic thesis somewhat less convincing (Letter from R. M. Brown to Armen A. Alchien [sic] July 13, 1971; Special Collections, Regenstein Library, University of Chicago).

76   Perhaps these stories are the oral equivalent to what is commonly known as an ear worm in music. These are songs that somehow bury themselves into your brain and stubbornly refuse to leave.

77   The reference here is to Hirschman's (1970) book *Exit, Voice, and Loyalty.* The Chicago School of Friedman, Stigler and Director seemingly recognized only the bivariate market options of either accepting or rejecting an exchange. In a similar manner, these Chicagoans viewed the viable available options as a matter of either remaining in a given organization (loyalty) or departing from it (exit). Opposing perspectives (theories running counter to the Chicago approach) were to be decimated and overrun rather than analyzed and discussed. Opponents were to be vanquished rather than persuaded to embrace alternative views. Hirschman in his work puts forward the often neglected option of trying to change the existing status quo by voicing one's dissent and arguing one's view. The controlling idea is to persuade with reasoned argument and evidence rather than to bully opponents into submission. Positive sum games are given a reasonable amount of credence in such an approach.

78   The exact quote is "The presuppositions of objectivity are integrity, competence and humility", (Knight quoted in Coase 1994b:15).

References

Aristotle (1962). *The Politics*. Sinclair, T. A. (trans.) Harmondsworth, Middlesex: Penguin Books.

Austen, J. (1813). *Pride and Prejudice*. London: T. Egerton, Whitehall.

Berlin, I. (1953). *The Hedgehog and the Fox*. London: Weidenfeld and Nicolson.

Boettke, P. (1987). "Virginia political economy: A view from Vienna", *Market Process*. 5(2): 7–15.

Bronte, C. (1850). "Letter of April 12th to W. S. Williams", http://www.pemberley.com/janeinfo/janeart.html#swscott1 (08/08/2016).

Buchanan, J. and Gordon, T. (1962). *The Calculus of Consent*. Ann Arbor: The University of Michigan Press.

Cannan, E. (1903). *A History of the Theories of Distribution and Production in English Political Economy 1776–1848* (Second Edition). London: P.S. King & Son.

Carroll, L. (1876/1962). *The Annotated Snark*. New York: Penguin Books.

Cheung, Steven, N. S. (1973). "The fable of the bees: An economic investigation", *The Journal of Law and Economics*. 16(1): 11–33.

Clark, J. M. (1936). "Past accomplishments and present prospects of American economics", *American Economic Review*. 26(2): 1–11.

Coase, R. H. and Ronald, F. F. (1935a). "Bacon production and the pig-cycle in Great Britain", *2 Economica*. 142–147.

Coase, R. H. and Ronald, F. F. (1935b). "The pig-cycle: A rejoinder", *2 Economica*. 423–428.

Coase, R. H. and Ronald, F. F. (1937a). "The pig-cycle in Great Britain: An explanation", *4 Economica*. 55.

Coase, R. H. (1937b). "The nature of the firm", *4 Economica*. 386–405.

Coase, R. H. (1946). "The marginal cost controversy", *Economica*. 13(51): 169–182.

Coase, R. H. (1954). "The development of the British television service", *Land Economics*. 30(3): 207–222.

Coase, R. H. (1959). "The Federal Communications Commission", *The Journal of Law & Economics*. 2(1): 1–41.

Coase, R. H. (1960). "The problem of social cost", *The Journal of Law & Economics*. 3(1): 1–44.

Coase, R. H. (1961). "The British post office and the messenger companies", *The Journal of Law & Economics*. 4(1): 12–65.

Coase, R. H. (1974). "The lighthouse in economics", *Journal of Law and Economics*. 17 (2): 357–376.

Coase, R. H. (1988). "The firm, the market and the law", in *The Firm, the Market and the Law*. Chicago: The University of Chicago Press, pp. 1–33.

Coase, R. H. (1992). "The institutional structure of production: The 1991 Alfred Nobel memorial prize lecture in economic sciences", *American Economic Review*. 82(4): 713–719.

Coase, R. H. (1994a). "Economists and public policy", in *Essays on Economics and Economists*. Chicago: The University of Chicago Press, pp. 47–64.

Coase, R. H. (1994b). "How should economists choose?", in *Essays on Economics and Economists*. Chicago: The University of Chicago Press, pp. 15–33.

Coase, R. H. (1994c). "Adam Smith's view of man", in *Essays on Economics and Economists*. Chicago: The University of Chicago Press, pp. 95–136.

Coase, R. H. (1994d). "The institutional structure of production", in *Essays on Economics and Economists*. Chicago: The University of Chicago Press, pp. 3–15.

Coase, R. H. (1994e). "Economics and contiguous disciplines", in *Essays on Economics and Economists*. Chicago: The University of Chicago Press, pp. 34–47.

Coase, R. H. (1997). "Looking for results", *Reason.com*. 1(1): 1–8. http://reason.com/archives/1997/01/01/looking-for-results/ (04/09/2013).

Coase, R. H. (2006). "The conduct of economics: The example of fisher body and General Motors", *Journal of Economics and Management Strategy*. 15(2): 255–278.

Cooter, R. D. (1987). "Coase theorem", in Eatwell, J., Murray, M., and Peter, N. (eds.) *The New Palgrave: A Dictionary of Economics* (First Edition). Oxford: Palgrave Macmillan, http://www.dictionaryofeconomics.com/article?id=pde1987_X000351doi:10.1057/9780230226203.2205 (04/05/2017).

Cooter, R. D. (1982). "The cost of coase", *The Journal of Legal Studies*. 11(1): 1–33.

Freedman, C. (1993). "Why economists can't read", *Methodus* (*Journal of Economic Methodology*), 5(1): 6–23.

Friedman, M. and George, S. (1946). *Roofs or Ceilings? The Current Housing Problem*. Irvington-on-Hudson: Foundation for Economic Education and National Association of Real Estate Boards.

Friedman, M. (1953). *Essays in Positive Economics*. Chicago: University of Chicago Press.

Frost, R. (1916). "The road not taken", in *Mountain Interval*. New York: Henry Holt & Co., p. 1.

Hammond, J. D. and Claire, H. (2006). *Making Chicago Price Theory*. New York: Routledge.

Hazlett, T. (1997–1998). "Looking for results – Ronald Coase talks to Thomas Hazlett", *Policy*. 13(4): 24–30.

Hirschman, A. O. (1970). *Exit, Voice, and Loyalty*. Cambridge: Harvard University Press.

Hotelling, H. (1938). "The general welfare in relation to problems of taxation and of railway and utility rates", *Econometrica*. 6(2): 242–269.

Kaldor, N. (1934). "A classificatory note on the determination of equilibrium", *Review of Economic Studies*. 1(1): 122–136.

Klein, B., Robert, G. C., and Armen, A. A. (1978). "Vertical integration, appropriable rents, and the competitive contracting process", *Journal of Law & Economics*. 21(2): 297–326.

Knight, F. H. (1967). "Laissez Faire: Pro and Con", *The Journal of Political Economy*. 75(6): 782–795.

Knight, F. H. (1972). *Risk, Uncertainty and Profit*. Chicago: University of Chicago Press.

Lerner, A. (1944). *The Economics of Control*. London: Macmillan.

Nietzsche, F. (1883). *Also Sprach Zarathustra*. Chemnitz: Verlag von Ernst Schmeitzner.

Muth, J. F. (1960). "Optimal properties of exponentially weighted forecasts", *Journal of the American Statistical Association*. 55(290): 299–306.

Pigou, A. C. (1920). *The Economics of Welfare*. London: Macmillan and Company.

Scott, W. (1826) "Journal Entry, March 14", https://janeausteninvermont.wordpress.com/2009/03/13/sir-walter-scott-on-austen-march-14-1826/ (08/08/2016).

Stigler, G. J. (1949). "Monopolistic competition in retrospect", *in Five Lectures on Economic Problems*. London: Longmans. Green & Co. Ltd., pp. 12–24.

Stigler, G. J. (1960). "The influence of events and policies on economic theory", *The American Economic Review, Papers and Proceedings*. 50(2): 36–45.

Stigler, G. J. (1971). "The theory of economic regulation", *The Bell Journal of Economics and Management Science*. 2(1): 3–21.

Stigler, G. J. (1976). "Do economists matter?" *Southern Economic Journal*. 42(3): 347–354.

Stigler, G. J. (1982a). "The ethics of competition: The unfriendly critics", in *The Economist as Preacher*. Chicago: The University of Chicago Press, pp. 27–37.

Stigler, G. J. (1982b). "Smith's travels on the ship of state", in *The Economist as Preacher*. Chicago: The University of Chicago Press, pp. 136–146.

Stigler, G. J. (1988). *Memoirs of an Unregulated Economist*. New York: Basic Books.

Stigler, G. J. (1991). "Memorial service for Ethel Verry", mimeo. 28(10): 1–2.

Stigler, G. J. (1992). "Law or economics", *Journal of Law & Economics*. 35(10): 455–468.

Stigler, G. J. and Claire, F. (1962). "What can regulators regulate? The Case of Electricity", *Journal of Law & Economics*. 5(1): 1–16.

Stigler, G. J. and Gary, B. (1977). "De Gustibus Non Est Disputandum", *American Economic Review*. 67(1): 76–90.

The Dalek[1] Perplex:
Reading with an Intent to Destroy

And if you wrong us, do we not revenge? If we are like you in the rest, we will resemble you in that (William Shakespeare, *The Merchant of Venice*).

I. Evisceration as Pure Bliss: Applying Demolition Derby Tactics as an Analytic Methodology[2]

This means, on the one hand, that an economic writer requires from his reader much goodwill and intelligence and a large measure of cooperation; and, on the other hand, that there are a thousand futile, yet verbally legitimate, objections which an objector can raise. In economics you cannot *convict* you opponent of error; you can only *convince* him of it. And, even if you are right, you cannot convince him, if there is a defect in your own powers of persuasion and exposition or if his head is already so filled with contrary notions that he cannot catch the clues to your thought which you are trying to throw to him (Keynes 1973:470).

In the long defunct comic strip 'Pogo'[3], a frog is pictured complaining to his mate, "I'd write my congressman – if he could read, if I could write." In a manner that closely imitates those swamp creatures, economists on the whole, have not been known for their ability to communicate in a precise (and easily comprehensible) fashion. Perhaps their writing is too often tortured because fundamentally, they lack the ability to read critically, at least with a sufficient level of dexterity. In essence, when reading, economists are too often led (if not dominated) by implicit agenda, especially when confronted by published articles (and books). At such moments, a strong desire to understand the thoughts posed by another fails to predominate. Such tendencies are steamrollered by less salubrious objectives.

Instead of approaching with an open mind (or at least a vague resemblance to one), economists appear to reach a definite conclusion, prior to actually reading a designated article. Constrained by these circumstances, such readers will predictably discover precisely what they expected (and needed) to find in each item. This strategy can be easily facilitated by flicking the article's author into one of the many convenient (and available), pigeon holes. It matters not whether the label reads neo-liberal or post-Marxist. In this fashion, any article can be quickly dismissed (or accepted), without the bother of meticulously searching for any serious level of comprehension. This default mechanism allows a proto-antagonistic reader to carefully comb articles for points that effectively permit the demolishment of a despised article. The aim is to find a fissure that provides destructive leverage, rather than gathering insights that might allow a scintilla of understanding to shine forth.

Even the writer of this volume hasn't always succeeded in resisting the allure offered by educated nit-picking, whether done on a grand scale or not. The joys of showing off one's intellect should not be undersold. Still, this insidious objective that may drive a reviewer is often cleverly camouflaged, refusing to be easily disinterred. Critical analyses, informed by a distinctly supercilious attitude, may masquerade as serious scholarship, if not examined too carefully. In this fashion, pure negativity and outright antagonism can be dressed up as balanced evaluation, even while remaining controversial. The potential rewards from this approach, may for some economists, outweigh any more principled obligations. At its worse, this lingering problem could reflect a simple lack of goodwill within the profession. But in that case, this state of affairs would be far from remarkable. Any group in which ambition dominates, can easily foster a dangerous level of opportunism. The right conflux of circumstance, namely one where scoring points off another practitioner becomes a rewarding tactic, serves to encourage the habit of approaching an article with the intent of destroying it, whether by foul means or fair. The result is a somewhat lamentable common practise that predictably generates more heat than light. (Yes, the title of Mirowski's breakthrough book has been deliberately employed.)

As pointed out, it is unfortunate, yet sadly true, that economists tend to find in any work they might stumble across, exactly what they need to see and to discover.[4] That critical claim may represent too broad of a characterization to openly avow, seeming to convey a veritable slur on a profession that harbours pretensions to scientific rigour. Yet many, perhaps even numerous, academics appear to be in thrall to the practice of vindicating their own perspective by distorting an opposing text. This malingering problem inevitably intensifies when driven by ideological objectives. Even those individuals generally deemed to be reputable economic icons have not been entirely reluctant in employing this strategy. Adopting such an approach provides (unfortunately) an all too tempting (and convenient) method for disembowelling any of their designated opponents. Consequently, hidden hopes for nurturing a mutually beneficial journey of discovery (when reading the work of others), if effectively corrupted in this fashion, become forlorn. Instead, the profession is forced to confront a battlefield displaying fought over (and contrary) interpretations. On this uneven playing field, words and methods are measured and employed strategically. Intentions reflect strategies that are far more suited to the cut and thrust of the court room, rather than the academic common room. What prevails is a terrain defined by gladiatorial sandpits where winning appears to be the dominant, and perhaps the only, contested objective.

To a certain degree then, reducing critical reading, to a literary form mimicking a demolition derby, confounds any pretence of desiring a clear measure of communication. Obfuscation becomes the preferred operative mode. Clearly some forms of thought and approaches should be attacked and destroyed whenever possible. (Though what these might be are inevitably a matter for fierce debate.) But these moral or principled attacks differ sharply from anything within the realm of strictly scholarly pursuits. In that arena, communication and understanding are foremost. A simple, guiding rule of thumb is that understanding always needs to precede objections. In which case, collaboration and discussion, rather than combative aggression, should determine the carefully composed (and measured) actions of academic participants. Given these criteria, the temptation to reactively immolate opponents must be strictly resisted, especially when paired with the acute desire of showing-off one's innate cleverness.

Consequently, reading economic articles, when coated with a prior malicious intent, becomes in effect simply a reflection of gratuitous cruelty. In fact, the basic foundation on which such combative competition is built, seems to be fatally flawed. The defence of this approach largely rests on a quasi- Social Darwinian view. In that realm of thought, the result of a brutal, no holds competition is bound to yield insight and truth.[5] In essence, a sort of trial by fire uncovers and destroys falsehoods and faulty thinking. A clear example of applying this method was constantly exhibited in George Stigler's famed Industrial Organisation workshop where Deirdre McCloskey once viewed a presenter brought to tears after his paper was cut to pieces.[6]

> There's a blood and guts attitude here in Chicago about Economics. That's what makes the Chicago School. That's what I think the Chicago School is about … He [George Stigler] had this workshop. People had their knives out. I participated in some of them. I think people were using George's example. No prisoners were taken in other words. [laughs] And everybody just jumped in. It was just *chaos* those work-shops. [laughter]A paper was never given. It was just discussed. It was taken apart. And it was *breathtaking*. [laughs] It was totally breathtaking (Conversation with Sherwin Rosen, October 1997).

To generalise, destructive reading offers at least three variations. Nit-picking for potential errors has been briefly mentioned. Basically the strat-egy here is to punch so many holes into a paper that the argument sinks on its own weight. In some sense, this is the most straightforward method observable. But there are at least two other more sophisticated options, which take alternative paths (though seeking the same objective). Strawmen versions of the originals can share a resemblance to the actual theories, while being fundamentally flawed. In essence these narratives are created so that they can be easily destroyed. These straw creations prove to be as highly flammable as anticipated. The end result, once again, is a theory deposed, though not necessarily comprehended. However, if the first two paths present daunting challenges, a more disreputable option is available to those who are desperate, lazy, or basically unprincipled. Though in most cases, the perpetrators seem unaware of the dubious neighbourhoods they willingly enter. Character assassination provides a simple distraction to the main game of analysis. The ruling principle here is that bad people produce bad theories. Consequently, if the moral viability of a theorist is undercut, so will that person's ideas. Though the logic here is dubious, the strategy remains enticing with at least some damage occasionally accomplished.

All of these stated options survive in a Darwinian world of struggle. In a far from attractive sense, too many economists seem to view the profession through zero sum tinted lenses, or at least in terms of an elbows-first competition. Given this context, advancement in the academic ranks can be effectively bolstered by maliciously hobbling the standing of others. A competitor's stumble advances one's own career. Locked then into this Hobbesian world,[7] the medium of official communication (the academic journal article), is instead transformed into a location which nurtures denigration. By starting with an antagonistic approach as a default position, papers are read, but not comprehended. Purported critical reading becomes no more than a search and destroy mission, meaning an attempt to find errors (for instance), in order to shred the validity of alien papers at all costs. This particular intention can lead, at best, to a certain level of unproductive nit-picking (as previously noted), or even more darkly, to a serious misreading of the text.

Consequently, reading preformed as a combat sport produces abundant warmth, but insufficient clarity. The result might even be humorous, or in a perverse way an attempt to display a degree of cleverness, but nonetheless heavily tinged with an element that is essentially ugly. Assisting these dark tendencies is the way in which the profession has, over the years, divided itself into competing armies, operating under different banners. Friedman's 'good eggs' (for instance) seemed to exist (mainly) in order to battle wrong-headed collectivists. Given this vision of treacherous terrains, the output of a competing army has to be immediately viewed with suspicion.

> He [George Stigler] would come across empirical work which was contradictory to other empirical work. Somehow it always seemed to him that the empirical work which favoured his side was done better than the empirical work which didn't (Conversation with James Kindahl, October 1997).

This *a priori* bias has been previously explored. In the last chapter, the reflexive art of pigeon-holing was extensively discussed. The practise was recognised as incorporating a distortion common to economic analysis. (Perhaps for some readers, the examination was judged to have continued to a wearying length. Authors can unfortunately be cruel, uncaring task-masters, even when harbouring the best of intentions.) Consequently, if only to a limited extent, the following discussion flows unmistakably from that previously examined hypothesis, namely the inherent human need to develop some form of intellectual comradeship (a group identity).

The linkage derives from the way in which relevant material is read and digested by those sporting similar ideological leanings.

Both categorising, as well as reading with a deliberate intent to destroy, define shortcomings in comprehension that block an author's ideas from earning the right to an undistorted transmission. Obfuscation can too easily triumph over communication. In essence, posed by that previous chapter is the lingering existence of a warped intellectual drive. This *sui generis* imperative comes to reflect a near obsession with the need to classify and relocate theoretical positions, as much as possible, into convenient, pre-existing categories. But the purpose in doing so is quite simple. Whether consciously or not, such a set-up allows for an almost automatic dismissal of opposing theories and approaches. Similar motivations drive those who pick up presented research with the sole purpose of destroying, rather than comprehending it.

This indivertible tendency not only exists in the economics profession, but may, at times, even dominate and distort far too many economic debates and investigations. This intransigence is especially intellectually destructive when conducted at levels that strategically miss the rigorous mark. Ruled by this persistent drive, one compelling a substantiation of group identity, individuals are effectively tempted. Even self-regarding economists, subconsciously (or even consciously) self-enrol in these competing and sharply antagonistic tribes.[8] The observed result, however, is that by hewing to such self-selected (and often ideologically defined) platforms, adherents sanctify the ability to peremptorily dismiss, or at times successfully destroy, contrary views that they find distasteful. To sum up, if the previous chapter focused on the ways in which an economist locates and targets opponents, this one explores a strategy employed to successfully incinerate those discovered targets. (The third and fourth chapters explores a more subtle bit of weaponry, one reserved for the acknowledged virtuosos of the profession. More significantly, while these two chapters focus on slanted reading, the third and fourth explore an author's prerogative.)

The ineradicable, but ideological, aspect of this process promotes a tendency which allows a practitioner to place a judicious spin on any material. An underlying, core body of dogma reliably powers this slanted perspective. Achievement is accomplished by camouflaging these preconceptions in an evasive manner, while seeming to explain away an array of contrary research. The required sleight of hand requires an ability to wear down, dismiss and even ridicule opposing ideas without allowing any overt, ideological agenda to shine through the cracks lying within the professed surface objectivity of intent. In practice, grinding down the opposition in this fashion involves a complementary and implied, simultaneous defence of one's own home truths. This desired result can be handily achieved by simply dismissing all and any alternatives. The constraints imposed by strict group solidarity, effectively encourages self-pledged members to focus, completely undiverted, on decimating any opposing theories.

Given what is judged to be at stake, the use of any convenient (even if destructive) method is deemed not only necessary, but justified as well. This narrowly defined goal of selective immolation can be efficiently accomplished by perusing available research only with the implacable objective of destroying the target so designated. Economists, in this respect, come to more closely resemble conquistadors, rather than simple academics. But this strategy does lack a certain boldness. A certain whiff of compulsive nit-picking (and narrow vision) adheres to the method. For instance, a transfer tarring defines the leverage gained by this careful combing of every paragraph. Namely, if the author is careless (and sloppy) about small matters, then the theoretical core of the article must be similarly riddled with faults.

Consequently, conducting search and destroy missions for perceived errors is the more obvious route to travel if the goal is strictly to undermine the validity of an opponent's article. A more sophisticated option, however, is to conjure up a classic strawman version of the original position. The flimsy construction is forced to resemble, at least to a less than exacting reader, a valid interpretation of the article's logic and conclusion. This bit of obfuscation allows a despised position to be tactically destroyed by simply igniting the ultra-flammable material composing the strawman argument. The initial sleight of hand when accomplished effectively pawns off a specially created (but entirely ersatz) version as reliably mirroring the original. The adopted procedure does not attempt to banish an article (or its author) by making a thousand small (but direct) cuts. Instead, the objective is to deliver one definitive knock-out blow capable of destroying the entire hypothesis constructed within the article. The entire edifice of that article seemingly collapses.[9]

What the selected case study attempts to demonstrate is that these convenient (if strawman-like) interpretations of theory and economic models, are fashioned by creative, but still distorted readings of an examined text. (In which case, the implied terms of debate (or engaged discussion), engendered by a specific work, have been deliberately shifted from their originally intended locations. They now occupy a terrain deliberately contoured for purposes of demolition. This terminal destination is reached by employing narrowed textual understandings that mislead (rather than enlighten), the targeted reader. (As a result, subsequent discussions can be artfully deflected away from the core purposes of the original authors.) These revised (and contrived) versions are often fabricated by employing deliberately flimsy logic. Such ersatz theoretical constructs come pre-structured with attached fault lines. Interpretive creations (defined by their congenital flaws), reflect the underlying purpose driving such supposedly objective recapitulations. In essence, the ultimate goal rests on the hope that the flawed doppelganger, once conjured up, will yield a highly destructible phantasm. The resulting legion of academic ghosts and pale shades come in a variety of fashions. No matter what their configurations, they have been known to scare away (and replace) the genuine versions. (The process of substitution is clearly apparent in textbook versions of these originals. Neither the versions of monopolistic competition, or the kinked demand curve, displayed in those glossy pages closely resemble the constructed theories devised by either Chamberlin or Sweezy.)

Sometimes these contrived versions can be propagated in the form of a soporific and misleading oral tradition, namely one capable of gaining widespread credibility within the profession itself. (Mythmaking in this communicative form may be both conscious and intentional. Or, these fables may reflect a more unconscious accumulation of small misinterpretations.) Such a transformed understanding, no matter what its specific origin, seldom hews strictly (or sometimes even loosely) to any referred text. Nor is there any discernible motivation that might drive a concerted attempt to do so. The unacknowledged assumption is that these claims (or interpretations) will not be closely checked (or scrutinised). Instead they become what 'everyone knows', namely something so obvious that discussion becomes unnecessary. An unwelcome spurt of rectitude would only encourage those conspirators responsible for such distorted constructions to deny or distract, frantically shoring up an already weakened position.[10] Unfortunately, economic fabulists of this variety are only infrequently exposed and almost never convicted.

Instead, these fabricated textual understandings serve as useful simplifications (in the hands of ideological allies) that manage to undermine the original text. As pointed out, these ersatz versions present a tidy theoretical structure that is capable of being conveniently replicated by textbook writers (passing on this confected wisdom to future generations).[11] Textbooks come to incorporate a consensus view of what every economist supposedly should know about a given work, author or subject.[12]

However, they continue to actually serve this function without necessarily being staked firmly to the original text (at least not in any reliable manner). The textbook presentation poses as consensus knowledge, while at best only providing the most superficial of insights.[13] (Educational tools, produced to sell, must appeal to the widest possible audience, meaning they must try to eschew controversy.)

Thus a given (but skewed) presentation, under the guise of innocent propagation and dispersion, can simultaneously destroy the essence of an idea (or theory), by creating an ersatz doppelganger in place of the original. Such chimeras can then appear as a textbook's version of commonly accepted economic wisdom.[14] The means to decimate that which one's own tribe finds distinctly distasteful (and even potentially dangerous) motivates these combative incursions. (As explained in a previous chapter, at least some economists tend to be open-minded, identifying with any number of different economic factions. By nature, they are unwitting adherents of polytheism. Though most of the more tribal economists adhere religiously to their one true faith. Unfortunately, open-mindedness doesn't necessarily promote academic success.)

II. Ideology as the Anti-Christ – The Case of Neo-Liberalism

The Chicago School is famous not merely for its contributions to economics per se, but for its attempt to apply economic methodology to a range of problems (Mirowski, Philip and Dieter Plehwe 2015:xxi).

The prevalent type of obfuscation examined in this chapter can be highlighted by focusing on a single case example. The chosen illustrative instance is, of course, only a representative example. The purpose of utilising this method is only to illuminate a specific issue, not to criticise or attack any particular economist. But, the recent formulation of neo-liberalism (by those who wish to attack this created conception), typifies some of the key aspects defining this type of obfuscation, namely reading with an attempt to destroy. Remember, as previously noted, this strategy can embrace a number of forms, whether fossicking for purported errors, or constructing an ersatz version that is easily immolated.

Given the ongoing tribal dynamic that often drives cases of obfuscation, the somewhat amorphous conglomeration of ideas and poses (that has been labelled as neo-liberalism), draws both its staunch defenders as well as a host of obsessed foes. For those dedicated to disembowelling a despised position (such as neo-liberalism), aim is carefully taken to erode its underpinnings by constructing a negative portrait of this apparently abhorrent movement. Conveniently, the Chicago School (or the way in which these opponents conceive of that department), provides a convenient representation of the evil incarnate that they choose to attack.[15] (Many people nurse their own tailored version of what the Chicago School entails. In other words, the tenets of this school can easily, and often, be unwittingly burlesqued. Opponents find strength by nurturing specific distortions about the department and its denizens.)

As a result, few foes of neo-liberalism would welcome having their firmly held, preconceived notions about this targeted faction, disturbed by facts, let alone uncomfortable evidence. In obsessing about those on the other side of the battlefield, these ideological warriors attempt to shift and constrain all subsequent debate and discussion. They feel compelled to forcibly slant the commentary flow into an advantageous direction. Consequently, those who deign to joust with these designated opponents, compose arguments that transpose that debate onto more conducive terrain, as was previously noted. Simply put, these evangelists want to focus on certain aspects of any question and avoid others.

Ironically, whether consciously or not, these dedicated opponents are also inveterate connoisseurs of pigeonholing. Predictably, they employ tactics parallel to those already enshrined in a well-thumbed playbook. Ironically, the strategy, which these warriors seem to unconsciously embrace, appears to mimic the approach developed (over a concentrated lifetime of activity) by their own designated arch villain, George Stigler.[16] Despite this unacknowledged commonality, Stigler continues to represent, for many of these ardent critics, a deep dyed embodiment of all the failings the Chicago School supposedly embodies.[17] Consequently, critics (often residing on the political left) have simultaneously recognised and deplored the economic approach and ideology established there. The institutionalised ideology prevalent in Chicago is often deemed as comprising the very fountainhead of the neo-liberal faith.

In reaction, those who view themselves as inhabiting the very forefront in this battle against neo-liberalism, almost automatically approach the work of George Stigler with a good deal of distaste. Opponents appear to particularly dislike Stigler's insistence that economic barbarians (of the left) were at the very gates of rational analysis, threatening to disrupt proven scientific analysis. Moreover, Stigler fancied himself as some sort of self-appointed, plumed warrior valiantly staving off the hordes of mindless collectivists undermining personal freedom. He saw himself as standing between these authoritarian attempts to gain a decisive degree of domination over both academia and government policy.[18] (Stigler was convinced that most European governments were already lost causes.)

Given these dire circumstances, any conceivable means could justifiably be employed without restraint, as long as they could successfully defend the fundamental ramparts composing self-defined liberty.[19] Economically, these attempts to thwart the hordes of barbarians at the gate were underwritten by the collected wisdom contained within Chicago style price theory. This panoply of unconstrained strategies and desperate defences, forged against the untutored masses of collectivism, were not only permissible, but even bordered on the exigent, at least from Stigler's perspective.

Composing the very core of Stigler's personally perceived mission (his all-purpose justification), lay a set of proposed grounds (and a basis) for economic and political liberty. This vital battle could not pause for scruples (or other niceties), that might impede a comprehensive and fair evaluation of opposing views and theories.[20] Such a careful, respectful and even generous approach clearly lacked the effectiveness required to quell dangerous heresy. Like the infamous Daleks featured in the Doctor Who dramas, these tribes of ideologically driven economists, attacked what they designated to be dangerous thought. Regiments of academic stalwarts, boasting implacable tribal loyalties, seem mostly, if not entirely, motivated by the need to totally exterminate all perceived opposition. Half measures, given such looming dangers, were deemed to be clearly inadequate. The panoply of heretical threats (posed to personal freedom and liberty), proved too consequential to warrant either generosity or genuine attempts at objectivity.

Thus, although purporting to be a balanced, critical stance, these fierce ideologues were in fact reading aberrant material with a distinct intent to destroy. No serious inclination existed (nor even significantly appeared as an objective) that encouraged open-minded comprehension. Targeted texts would be appropriately analysed in terms of a prior objective. These academic road warriors intended to eliminate, rather than to understand (or possibly entertain), opposing views. There is a difference between searching for a key to unlock any intended meaning and simply blasting open a theory with a flame thrower. Consequently, what occurs under these circumstances, is not some simple market for competing ideas, one which would winnow out faulty thinking and promote only that which is the strongest and most sustainable. (That rationale is quite naturally the unimpeachable cover story that allows perpetrators of this technique to largely avoid general condemnation.)

Contrary to their stated rationales, those who engage in this practice promote a misrepresentation of an opposing idea or theory. These sometimes fanciful creations can exert a lasting effect in defining the actual evolution of any set of contested ideas.[21] (Inserting preferred perspectives into an academic discourse exists as the controlling purpose of those would be critics. The concerted objective is to effectively dismiss selected texts by employing scorched earth methods, while claiming to be offering a fair evaluation.) As a result, perspectives which may contain at least the germ of a useful insight, end up instead summarily dismissed by a majority of the profession. (Assuming, of course, the presence of a successful marketing campaign by those targeting such theories.) Acting on the basis of their received misconceptions, the profession, as a whole, can operate as if they understood a given controversial approach without actually bothering to carefully consult the relevant primary sources.[22]

> No question about it. Because what meets market demand, may have an element of so-called truth in it in the sense that what people think better organises the world for them, about how do we know what shapes events and so on, would presumably be one of the factors (and we hope an important factor) in determining legitimacy. But it wouldn't be the only factor. We would need other factors. And where these other factors dominate you'll get other results. That's why you get fads and fashions in ideas and so on that don't have lasting value. They will still be meeting the marketplace of ideas and I would say, I think that is right (Conversation with Gary Becker, October 1997).

The purpose then of this chapter, or at least a hoped for result, is to display the dangers of employing a zero sum mentality when reading research output. Under these prescribed terms, any controversial article (or even tentative theory), becomes fodder for targeted attacks. Simply destroying offending material can be the strategic intention lurking behind such targeting. The objective is not to gain understanding or offer critical improvements. An opponent's loss is, from this given perspective, the attacker's gain. As previously mentioned, the best method for tackling this issue requires a detailed case study. (Underlining the explored study is the explosive academic landscape that these obfuscative examples create.) Often providing a detailed (and very concrete), instance of a problem succeeds in illustrating an issue more effectively than relying on broad brush generalities.

One potential pitfall, however, is the predictable need to deal with readers who insist on nominating the subject of a case study as the objective of an article. These would be critics manage to confuse a device providing a useful sketch of a widespread problem, with an attempt to pillory specific people.[23] An involution, or at least a definite distraction, occurs where issues of secondary importance appear to forcibly grab centre stage away from the more explicitly intended themes. As something of a prophylactic against such foreseeable outcomes, I can only emphasize that the intention here is not to barbeque the reputations of any economist (alive, dead or somewhere in between). Consequently, any reader who instead insists on focusing attention on specific individuals (residing within this case study), serves only to shift the terms of debate onto more arid terrain. Such territorial digressions represent an attempt (intentional or otherwise) to hijack the relevant and intended discussions informing this chapter.

Analysis is instead forced to head in a direction where it was never meant to wander, into the sort of quicksand defined by a mere quibbling over personalities. Of course, posting warnings about such pitfalls will not effectively insure that such errors are not subsequently committed. 'Wet paint' signs repeatedly fail to repel the inevitability of unwanted finger prints. Still, with the hope that at least some readers will notice (within themselves), any latent tendency pointing in this direction, such signalling of intent becomes an obligation, even if a somewhat hapless one.

This particular case study then, attempts to present and analyse a straightforward issue involved in understanding and interpreting economic thought and theoretic presentations. To some economists at least, unacknowledged, ideological constraints can force suspect theories to unintentionally present themselves in rather Byronic terms. Such ideas can be twisted so that they are widely comprehended as being, 'Mad, Bad and Dangerous to Know'. If such labelling is broadly propagated, even oozing into the professional subconscious, these distorted theoretic interpretations can lead economists, and any derived economic policy, badly astray. Only occasionally, are red herrings in this mode entirely unintentional.

Ancient and rooted prejudices do often pass into principles; and those propositions which once obtain the force and credit of a principle, are not only themselves, but likewise whatever is deductible from them, thought privileged from all examination (Bishop Berkeley quoted in Kline, 1980:160).

Fortunately, there does exist an array of approaches that permit investigators to effectively measure the presence of smoke and mirrors. They pose obstacles to be overcome in order to prevent being misled. The distractions presented are intended to camouflage any theoretical distortions. When bending texts in this fashion, compounded dangers arise. Such misdirection requires forcing these facts into preconceived patterns of thought. Bits of a theory can be cherry picked from articles and rearranged to yield a preconceived interpretation. Specifically, an ersatz display of criticism can become an exercise demanding that available jigsaw pieces (either consciously or subconsciously), be manually hammered into a given prefabricated frame. The object is to retell a specific, ideologically based tale.[24]

Certainly, stirring up controversy in this forceful fashion need not generate any useful illumination or interpretive analysis. Reading with an intent to destroy can often only create a counter-productive muddle, one which confuses rather than clarifies. (The goal being to forestall any informed debate.) A desired degree of muddle can be achieved by deliberately shifting the focus (or even the terms), of debate, moving them instead toward landscapes that are more aligned to specific pre-ordained objectives. These carefully designed attacks are aligned only with the limited goals of the stirrers and disrupters. But considered more dispassionately, such determined attempts to shift comprehension may ultimately shipwreck all potentially viable conversations, guiding them instead to what will prove to be less than fertile landscapes. The design of such crafted criticism is to shut down, rather than nurture debate.

For instance, when faced with theories authored by those he readily categorized as left-wing collectivists, George Stigler reflexively viewed their presented perspective as unalterably warped.[25] In essence, before even starting to consider a work, he could dismiss it as 'bad economics'. In which case, the only task to accomplish was the theory's complete and unredeemable incineration, a sort of euthanasia of faulty thinking. Consequently, such theories, evidence or provided statistical work must, by definition, be entirely lacking in any redeeming characteristic whatsoever. (Given the conclusions such articles advanced, any provided evidence must be at best dubious, if not unsubstantiated.)

Or to be more exact, whatever the intention of those provocateurs might be, such ideas were inherently dangerous, posing a continuing threat to individual liberty.[26] Given the presence of such incipient danger, Stigler felt justified in employing whatever means it might take to exorcise this unarguable threat from every aspect of academic life, let alone, broader society. In which case, Stigler deemed (whether consciously or not) that he was perfectly justified in weaponising his analysis, honing the critical edge of his forceful attack. These deadly thrusts were precisely aimed at the vital heart of what he regarded as incorrect (and thoroughly dangerous) theory.[27] Again, the aim was genocidal in intent, an eradication, rather than constructing a critical, if thorough rejection.

To reemphasise, in his view, the ideas presented were not only blatantly wrong, but implicitly posed a distinct threat to individual choice and freedom.[28] Fortunately, Stigler's critical imperative nurtured a perspective that proved sufficiently flexible when faced with challenges to neo-classical price theory. Such flexibility allowed his perspective to mould any circumstance to his preferred perspective. This strategic ability enabled Stigler to implicitly legitimise some questionable shifting of the terms defining established debates. Defeating a despised argument could be substantially assisted by deftly re-establishing the core definitions providing the foundation of any controversy.

As pointed out, contested theories are simply strategically shifted onto a more congenial landscape. The new terrain fails to provide a viable environment for the spotlighted theory. But such contests could at times resort to multiple lines of fire. The struggle could descend to the personal, the realm of the ad hominem. Stigler's estimation of the stakes at risk seemingly authorised the launching of personal, as well as logical, attacks against opposing theorists. From a zero sum perspective, a stance to which he implicitly subscribed, winning always remained the constraining (and possibly only) goal.[29] Consequently, Stigler was also far from averse to creating fragile caricatures of any and all associated theories created by these perceived opponents. Nor did he consistently shun sharp and dismissive personal comments about those supporting alternative positions and views.

Therefore, this strategy, whether consciously mapped out or not, translated into an intent to destroy the very logic providing the underpinnings of an opposing ideology. Using whatever it might take to achieve this goal was in this sense entirely justified.[30] But rhetorical warfare, for instance, is not necessarily symbiotic with the sort of probing analysis that can generate useful insights.[31] Attacks of this nature are almost guaranteed to become heated without shedding much in the way of useful light, especially when attention is turned on the individual author, rather than on the relevant work. To illustrate this specific problem, attention in this chapter is focused on the Chicago School, but not as the central protagonist of the case study. Instead, the case study focuses on the efforts of Philip Mirowski, Robert Van Horn and Eddie Nik-Khah. Particularly, the emphasis is only on the work they produced that excavates and evaluates the neo-liberal contributions made by the post war Chicago Department. The trio have employed such output as the basis of a lethal attack mechanism. The primary aim motivating their critiques has been to ultimately undermine what they have repeatedly labelled to be 'neo-liberal thought'.

Unfortunately as will be demonstrated, economic analysis does not thrive when reduced to a sort of extended jousting match. Economists themselves are not knights in shining, or even rusted, armour. The idea that trial by combat yields either truth or justice remains a fanciful figment, unless one is willing to believe that the pointed lances of the winning combatants are guided by some higher, beneficent hand. But this is equivalent to becoming convinced, against all available evidence that law courts exist to mete out justice, rather than performing as an umpire in a zero sum contest of wills. When economics becomes weaponised, those engaged become willing to adopt any convenient strategy simply to defeat an opposing viewpoint. Victory can, at times, be awarded to the strong, rather than to the wise. The result is a profession which, on the whole, becomes all the poorer for doing so.

III. Down the Rabbit Hole

Down, down, down. There was nothing else to do, so Alice soon began talking again (Carroll 1974:16).

'Curiouser and curiouser,'[32] as Alice was prompted to remark on her stroll through the contrary logic of Wonderland. Such a skewed perspective serves to characterise some of the more recent work that evaluates the contributions achieved by the post war Chicago School. A particularly interesting path to explore requires a bit of stealthy stalking down a path blasted out by Philip Mirowski and his compatriots. These adventurers have doggedly attempted to explicate the Chicago School, and the associated neo-liberal faith that seems to surround it. But any close examination of their work makes it difficult to overlook the common characteristics that seem to emerge whenever opposing ideologies square off against one another. The resulting confusion can more aptly be described as not so much an intellectual exercise, but rather a no holds barred, fight to the death. The strategies unconsciously employed, at least in a handful of their work, mirror those favoured by Demolition Derby competitors.[33]

The imagined picture of opposing economists peddling their ideological convictions, much in the same fashion that racers manoeuvre their automotive junkers, is unnervingly accurate. In both cases, their shared objective demands that they both gleefully crash destructively into each other's opponents. In an all or nothing challenge, dedicated combatants belonging to this genus, fiercely compete with the sole intention of leaving naught but a single vehicle still struggling to retain its mobile condition. On an ideological, as opposed to an automotive level, such an advertised clash of ideas seems to describe, to some degree, both the strategy honed over the decades by George Stigler and that which Team Mirowski[34] employs as it seeks to decimate neo-liberalism. Academically, the ingrained purpose is a continuing attempt, on their part, to undercut the very basis and justification for Stigler's counter-revolution. (George Stigler has evolved for them into a convenient embodiment of all things neo-liberal.) Tactically, nominating Stigler as a representative chief architect of this ideological strain allows for a more closely targeted attack on an opposing ideology. Simpler to take aim at just a single personality than to try to personify the entire Chicago Department of that era into some constructed average, or even median. (Doing so would require a deliberate steamrolling of the distinct differences that existed among the Chicago faculty.)

As a consequence of becoming the object of their focused targeting, Stigler's meticulous theoretical constructions are summarily dismissed by these modern day vampire hunters.[35] The idea is to eviscerate the theoretical base supporting what they consider to be unconscionable policies. This ritual disembowelment seeks to deliberately categorise Stigler's theories as a basket of ramshackle ideas deserving only to be tossed permanently away. For these practising deconstructionists, such ersatz theoretical facades represent no more than the bankrupt ideology of neo-liberalism itself. Even worse, these Chicago style fancies (when placed under the lens provided by Team Mirowski's powerful microscope) reveal themselves to be tarred with a heavy (and rather distinct) whiff of self-dealing and corruption. (In essence, the logical glue that should hold theories together is absent. Plus the creators themselves are badly stained by terminal conflicts of interest. As an additive, corruption doubly invalidates the manner in which these leaders of the Chicago School confronted the theories and ideas of their opponents.)

Consequently, their version of Chicago's past history, based to a large extent on their associated archival work, becomes inevitably weaponized when cultivated under the Team Mirowski operating agenda. The results provided by such a pre-planned immersion into the depths of Chicago theorising, does fortuitously unearth more than a few fascinating insights. Not surprising, since they are all talented researchers. However, their chosen approach can only encourage future investigators to more willingly allow the less rigorous tail of ideology to vigorously wag the more bulky dog of analysis. Given this less than salubrious petri dish of objectives that shapes their investigations, some of the Team Mirowski research may be terminally biased by their less than benevolent intentions. Accordingly, the leading and initial question required when confronted by any similar work is best answered by evaluating the underlying aims driving a given group of researchers.[36]

In which case, it is difficult to accept, even on a superficial level, that tying the Chicago School to a warts and all depiction of neo-liberalism is either a coincidental outcome or something resembling an irreversible bit of linkage. Note that 'neo-liberal' has become (especially in some circles on the left) a term to be spat out pejoratively. This response closely resembles the manner in which 'neo-classical economics' can become a label of opprobrium among blinkered opponents of that approach.[37] However, as Mirowski admits, those that he categorizes as practising neo-liberals don't themselves employ that terminology to distinguish their views, or at least haven't bothered to do so since the early 1950s. At that time, the term was employed only tentatively and then almost instantly discarded. The category and its decidedly negative connotations have been specifically crafted by opponents residing on the left of the political spectrum.

Again, the label seems to have risen out of an ideological need, a convenient shorthand, or strategic tool, used to instantly discredit an opposed perspective.[38] Basically, the term encapsulates a specific ideological clash between two implacable positions. In contrast to the use of the term neo-liberal, neo-classical seems a label acknowledged by a much wider range of economists (although differences exist in its exact characterization). However, what is incorporated by using the term neo-liberal, and what is compacted and composted within that label, remains much more contentious. Perhaps even insisting that the controversy (and at times furore) ignited by this term is far from accidental, would not be a claim too far.

Curiously, these self-proclaimed critics of neo-liberalism seem in turn enamoured by the same tactics their opponents used successfully against the 'collectivists' of an earlier era. In fact, one of the godfathers of this self-designated approach, George Stigler, over a number of decades refined a two prong attack on any suspect theory. These targets included not only what he considered to be outré economic constructs, but those that he deemed to be dangerous. Dangerous, not simply because they directly countered the 'tight prior equilibrium' analysis offered by Chicago price theory.[39] But also potentially treacherous, because these despised alternatives seemed, for a time, to be not only theoretically viable, but also gaining a respectable number of adherents within the profession. Stigler's straightforward and direct objective was always to thoroughly shred the targeted theory itself, assisted by constructing an easily destructible counterfoil of the actual proposed framework.[40] Keep in mind the sort of lemma underwriting the logic behind this strategy. Namely, that the most effective way to destroy a policy was to render its theoretical base devoid of cogent rationality, or persuasive evidence.

For those, like Stigler, who had acquired a distinct taste for verbalised Demolition Derbies, this tactic, lacked a degree of sufficiency. Simply decimating an unwanted (or objectionable) approach proved not to deliver a necessary guarantee that it had been rendered impotent. More obsessive combatants tended to complement a theoretical prong of attack with a deliberate attempt to create some personal shade that they could direct against their target. The strategy operated by lumbering an opponent with a dubious moral compass. Anthropological and ethical excavations supported attempts by these academic warriors to question the very motives (and even the moral character), of those choosing (in their evaluation) to perpetuate entirely indefensible ideological constructs. These opponents were at least implicitly judged guilty of propagating destructively distorted theoretical perspectives. In their hostile evaluation, defending such constructs was largely motivated by personal gain, or other less than salubrious motives. What else but bad intentions, or sporadic idiocy, could otherwise encourage the purveying of such obvious falsehoods, at least when judged by the minds of these academic battlers?

Consequently, those targets residing on the opposite frontier of an economic dispute attracted a specific categorical imperative. Opposing economists of this ilk were judged to deserve nothing less than a strategic dipping into, or at least a light coating of, smeared sleaze. Even *ad hominin* attacks were permitted, given the context (and associated dubious attached motives), of the relegated targets. To be more precise, charges of personal career advancement as an underlying motivation, allied with the stink of crass financial gain, might be effectively riveted on to any ideologically opposed and affronting economist. In this fashion, creating a convenient whiff of stagnant corruption serves to successfully undermine an opposing position.[41] The strategy has the appreciated side benefit of shifting attention away from the theory and policy side of the debate. In essence, bad behaviour must necessarily lead to bad theoretical constructs.[42] Once the charges were thoroughly sown, both theory and associated policy could then be allowed to self-incinerate.

As a last, and almost desperate, resort for those working the dubious seams afforded by dwelling on personality disorders, there always remained a dredging up of veiled charges encompassing elitism, anti-democratic leanings or outright authoritarian proclivities. The aim behind badging such offenders would appear to be an attempt to undermine the validity of any proposed approach by fracturing the character of its creator. Guilt by association is fashioned by gambling that a certain desired emotional, rather than a logical, response will be elicited.[43] Though rationally, the quality of an argument should never rest on the character of its proponents, preventing the formation of such a connection can prove difficult, if not impossible. (Certainly there is no necessity for research on smoking to be automatically flawed, even if underwritten by tobacco money. Though admittedly, such analysis would necessarily come under particularly close scrutiny.)[44] Consequently, weaponizing economic thought, whether by the wholesale employment of opportune strawman arguments, or employing ninja-sharp personal attacks on offending opponents, is a dubious path down which to nutritionally forage.[45] Neither method of attack is likely to avoid producing fatally flawed analysis. At its worst, an insight free zone is effectively created.

A. *A Wizard of Oz Revival (Strawmen Meet Their Match)*[46]

> We can sympathize with an impatience for those who use the term "neoliberalism" as a blanket swear word for everything they despise, or a brainless synonym for modern capitalism. The problem of conflating globalized capitalism and neoliberalism after the era of social liberalism amounts to the over-specification problem and refrains from considering (neoliberal) hegemonic constellations (Mirowski and Plehwe 2015:xvii).[47]

The prickly problem confronting Team Mirowski (and earlier George Stigler) is tightly bound to framing the most effective response when faced with theoretically wrong economic ideas (perceived as such, or actually so). At least from their inalterable perspective, such disreputable ideas in turn nurture a groundwork that buttress (and motivates) danger-ous policy directions. A tempting solution to this dilemma is to utilise a seeming analytic and neutral device, namely, delivering an even-handed critical evaluation of any controversial theory. However in practise, such criticism can instead be transformed into a form of lethally infested writ-ing. A façade of detached evaluation can serve to camouflage a buried aim that seeks instead to burnish a distinctly ideological outcome. Under such circumstances, the initial tactic employed to carry out this focused strat-egy often requires the creation of a highly simplified (or even a carica-tured) version of the targeted theory itself. The hidden aim is then successfully accomplished by demolishing these easily imploded straw-men counterparts. These semblances of the original theory (or model), reflect a distorted version of the actual framework.

The actionable strategy employed tends to be straightforward and even obvious to the careful reader. (Though these readers are not their target audience.) Any overt subtlety of design (or convoluted intention), when constructing these faux theories, would only confuse, or even impede, the effective marketing required for a convincing level of success.[48] The aim is consistently to demolish, not to raise some serious doubts, or to objec-tively question. Under those circumstances, the sought for, unambiguous dismissal of the targeted work, can then be delivered shorn of any poten-tially mitigating circumstances. (The targeted theory, as judged in these mock trials, is found to be undeniably guilty, lacking any redeeming fea-tures that might soften the blows of criticism. Though the verdict is unsur-prising, if we are willing to keep in mind the ruling objective determining this bit of ersatz evaluation.) At some (hard to distinguish) point, an econo-mist driven by such goals, can transform him or herself into a crusader, or even a Quixote tilting at windmills, seeing threats where none exist.[49] Dangers that are mostly borne out of ideological necessity.

However, the fact that the delivered verdict appears irredeemably harsh fails to also imply that the underlying critical intention of this 'demolition derby' effort, entirely lacks benign intentions or motivations. (The perceived threats entwined around these opposition theories are judged to be too serious to remain unchallenged.) The offending position that is so vigorously attacked (one which is buoyed by an alternative theory or framework) might (given the right circumstances), be legitimately classified as grossly incorrect or even downright dangerous.[50] (Societal threats often thrive if simply ignored, or allowed to expand their roots deeply into a culture's thinking.) Operating within the rigid constraints provided by such a perspective (whether legitimately or not) creates both motivation and justification for employing whatever means are available to annihilate an offending theory. From this perspective, such threats must be nipped in the proverbial bud.

The alluring, albeit facile, solution to combatting such a perceived threat is to substitute a classic strawman version for the more complex original. Such measures act as a sort of self-exploding, clockwork device. The constructed effigy does, indeed must, contain a rough resemblance to the more detailed physiognomy of the actual theory, while skilfully avoiding its essence. The ersatz version must ring true with the bulk of lackadaisical readers, especially those that can't be bothered to read an original source.[51] Given this contrived architecture, the targeted theory becomes easy to attack, if not capable of collapsing at the first critical glance provided. The articulated strawman version is cleverly fragile. The carefully revealed Achilles heel is easily targeted, with the model itself rendered so as to largely lose any sense of tenacious coherency. Undoubtedly, this approach may prove to be a reliable recipe for ideological point scoring. The strategy does provide an expeditious strategy for inflicting irreparable damage on one's opponents. But unhappily, such a chosen methodology does tend to obfuscate the issue at hand, rather than to clarify any conflicting ideas.[52] This option is clearly the preferred path for those who gleefully transform the process of research into nothing more than a zero sum game of noughts and crosses, where only winning the battle remains significant.[53]

In seeking then to cast a defining light on practises, methodologies and ideological positions that appear repugnant, economists can imperceptibly slide into behaviour that too closely resembles the very strategies they ostensibly deplore. In this instance, the individuals composing Team Mirowski intently attempt to disembowel what they consider to be a representation, though a particularly virulent one, of neo-liberalism. Namely, their stated intention is to attack the rationales and logic emanating from the Chicago School. Unfortunately in doing so, they fail to consistently avoid the tactics employed by members of the school they excoriate. For instance, George Stigler when demolishing opposing theories (and theoreticians), namely those finding fault with Chicago style price theory, would imaginatively create ultra-flammable straw man versions of the targeted and despised approaches.[54] These depictions, whether consciously constructed to do so (or not), seem designed to produce a maximum conflagration at the merest flick of a critical stare.

But a careful reading of Stigler's work equally indicates his apparent lack of awareness of the drivers behind his own strategy. (He would, most likely, honestly deny the existence of such a deliberate blueprint.)[55] Like many others who came before him, he managed to discover in these offending texts exactly what he needed to dredge up. For him, such semblances were then identified with his existing theoretical reality. Consequently, Stigler appeared to believe in the validity of his own creations, though his contrived portraits were born out of necessity rather than in an attempt to ape a degree of strict accuracy. This transformative conduit is then the type of muddy sluice into which Team Mirowski occasionally dives. They wilfully plunge down this track, while simultaneously constrained by their own ideological imperatives.

Given such a perspective, opposition theories (those automatically prejudged as being disreputable) are manhandled (and forcibly transformed) until they are able to successfully fill out a predetermined silhouette. By doing so, a more complex and incisive understanding of the spotlighted theory could be decisively avoided. The genuine version systematically is transformed into a seductive substitute. This convenient construction relies heavily on a simplified (and stripped down), narrative that demands a far simpler composition. The fable-like bundle of ersatz analysis could even be reduced to a tale centred on the character of the author, rather than the theory itself. The targeted opponent would then turn out to be somewhat of a corrupt and deceitful villain. An unreliable academic who through his (seldom a 'her') own maladroitness, or sheer ignorance, managed to endow a topic with a mist of confusion, rather than the clarity the presumptive attacker upheld. Understanding the theory under evaluation (at least in a fair-minded manner), never primarily (or even perhaps incidentally) motivated a subsequent analysis or balanced presentation. The objective instead was a nearly Dalekian imperative to 'exterminate' at all costs a dangerous interloper.[56] Stigler preferred the Carthaginian solution of scouring such theories from the face of the earth.[57]

Effectively, a theory could also be pre-emptily damned simply by tarring it with a despised categorisation. In which case, a certain wariness should be adopted when considering the pseudo-scientific categorization employed. A strong, ideological imperative often lies hidden behind seemingly orthodox analysis. Consequently, identifying a given economist with a specific methodological approach is all too often tinged with an aspect of tribalism, a 'which side are you on' mentality. Such categories then serve as a convenient shorthand device through which to praise (or to excoriate), a designated economist based on what is essentially an ideological litmus test.[58]

> If he [Joseph Ben-David of Israel] were willing to work on this, however, he has the right abilities and the right ideology …
> He [Arrigo Levi – Journalist of *La Stampa*] is not of our persuasion but also he is not hopeless (Letter Milton Friedman to George Stigler 30 September 1971).

Despite possible objections to the contrary, the Chicago School has been most closely defined, both publicly and within the profession, by the policies it subsequently formulated and those that it promoted.[59] Undoubtedly, key figures such as Milton Friedman and George Stigler might differ on the value of the public promotion of policies.[60] But even Stigler, certainly in his invited presentations to receptive audiences (and within his less formal papers), as well as more implicitly in his formal articles, took noticeable policy positions. Though he would no doubt claim that any implied or explicit position taken was soundly based on his foundational scientific work. It is however true, that at a certain superficial level, both Friedman and Stigler assiduously differentiated their work between what they considered to be essentially scientific efforts and periodic discussions that were clearly focused on policy issues. Nonetheless, there was always a strange, almost serendipitous, congruence between their consistent policy inclinations and the associated economic science that inevitably happened to perfectly buttress their positions.

In contrast, both of them tended to label institutional and historical evidence as being incorrigibly unscientific. Therefore, such supportive material, if only as a defence of scientific rigour, needed to be rejected out of hand. "I don't believe that empirical work owes much to either institutionalism or historicism" (Letter from George Stigler to Donald Patinkin, June 28, 1976). Despite such objections (as well as the danger of being condemned as dramatically unscientific), evaluating the Chicago School's impact on the profession (extended perhaps to a wider context that includes both society and the economy), offers a formidable challenge. Such work almost demands selecting policy as a logical starting position for any serious investigation.[61] Certainly Mirowski and his cohort have been perfectly justified in focusing on policy as a viable entry point, when attempting to explain the true contribution provided by those Chicago denizens. Equally, if these critics muster the audacity to play strictly according to Chicago rules (goose and gander principle), doing so would at a minimum entail undermining the theoretical basis of those despised Chicago policy positions.

Thus to better market their destructive excavations, Mirowski and his team (including Van Horn and Nik Khah) have employed a seemingly innocuous term, neo-liberalism, to cover a multitude of policy sins.[62] Quite conveniently, labels can provide a rhetorical fulcrum for shaping opinion by attaching a vaguely defined measure of opprobrium to those who are forcibly caught within such a purposely defined net.[63] The objective behind employing such a label as 'neo-liberalism' originates in trying to highlight a strain of market fundamentalism that has become synonymously linked to that term. Chicago gained a post war reputation by, in part, almost deifying markets and the role that they are seen to play within a given economy. Certainly, most economists, justifiably, tend to give a great deal of precedence to markets (be market friendly), but the level that allegiance takes does matter. Over the years, Chicago has become associated with an insistence on eschewing, or even dismissing, the possibility of private economic power, while lauding the efficiency of markets in an unswerving fashion. Consequently, almost all economic woes are exclusively attributed to the misguided expectations attached to government intervention. Though, such a position (if pushed only a bit farther) can veer dangerously close to representing a step too far in the world of economic thought.[64] In essence, we venture into the territory of unhinged ideology.

B. *Defining Neo-Liberalism*

So we must ask: Where in the writings of Hayek and the Chicago economists is to be found any support for the theses that corporations can do no wrong or that international agencies overseeing trade should make themselves subservient to the wishes of transnational corporations? It is here that citations should have been provided, yet none are (Caldwell 2011:326).

As previously sketched, reading with an intent to destroy implies finding a simple way to dismiss or destroy an offending work. To emphasise once more, the objective is not to understand or analyse, but rather finding a point where destructive leverage can be exerted. One method is to look for positions defined by extreme statements and illogical strands. These findings are then woven together to display a more easily debunked version of a given framework. If done with sufficient expertise, the construction almost collapses of its own accord. Add to these fabrications, views attributed to one's opponent (but resting on subjective interpolations of intent), that yield a version of market fundamentalism shorn of all existing ambiguities. The position under such conditions is rendered absurd. By taking this kamikaze approach, lines are drawn that induce only partisans to join the debate. Complexity is ruled out with more extreme views dominating. As previously indicated, the process fails to yield any useful enlightenment.

Thus when looking at the way in which Team Mirowski characterises neo-liberalism, some key points emerge. A list that concisely defines the Mirowski Inc. view of neo-liberalism, is fortuitously supplied by Bruce Caldwell (2011:324-325).[65] The compilation that he claims to derive from Team Mirowski's own writings is sufficiently comprehensive to provide a workable blueprint of the particular perspective pushed in that list. The cataloguing effort describes the offensive nature of Chicago neo-liberalism (at least as defined by Mirowski and his associates). Notice though, that the very terminology (and approach) deployed within such an extensive listing tends to overlook any substantial differences that divide given combinations of these Chicago stalwarts. Such broad strokes, by definition, become unnecessarily misleading at times.[66] The urge to generalise, breeds a distinct tendency toward over simplification, especially when the imperative is to categorise in this directed fashion. Some of these proposed characteristics merely lack a useful measure, rather than being strictly incorrect and thus easily dismissible. Team Mirowski is generally too careful to fall into that particular trap. However, the strategic question to keep in mind when wading through this list is the nature of the points chosen and the manner in which they are presented.

Consequently, the assault on neo-liberalism, driving this defining list, contains within its core an ulterior motive. Despite ostensibly collecting and distilling the available evidence gleaned from Team Mirowski's attacks, preventing an ineradicable whiff redolent of conspiracy theory from poking through its neutral structure proves impossible. The implicit intentions lurking behind Team Mirowski's efforts lead to disparate puzzle pieces being bound together in a flimsy, make-do fashion. Purpose rather than logic holds the parts together. The exercise of list making can't resist revealing a negative indictment, whether or not this was Caldwell's conscious intention. (Team Mirowski presents the heart of neo-liberalism as being riddled with inextricable corruption. The intentional melding together of corporate and political leaders with selected Chicago neo-liberal theorists (acting in the supposed role of policy midwives), plays out as a somewhat questionable attempt to uncover devious intentions and downright skulduggery.) But upon examination, such explorations by Team Mirowski reduce to an attempt to deem such academics guilty merely by association. What these critics deliver is no more than a clear example of the dangers associated with using the same brush to tar a selected target. The accomplished aim is to condemn a group of economists for associating with a demonised crowd.

However, on closer examination, many of these neo-classical propositions listed from the Team Mirowski perspective, do not immediately appear to harbour any inherently nefarious intent. Instead, they appear to be predictably conservative dictums. In essence, they would only be judged guilty of nakedly flouting a pronounced right wing viewpoint.[67] But at least some of these neo-liberal characterisations, as specified, do edge close to being dismissible caricatures of conservative ideology, though perhaps not so extreme as to be instantly disqualified as terminally distortionary. Many of these borderline contentions manage to slip through as seemingly plausible, if lacking a touch or two in accuracy.[68] Nonetheless, Team Mirowski's presentation of this agenda seems deliberately devised to hobble neo-liberalism by slathering the provided positions with a decidedly negative gloss. Doing so is a matter of applying just the proper degree of spin on these statements that leaves them with a faint, but clearly, discernible stench. While appearing to be straightforward and non-controversial, they remain just sufficiently off-centre. (For clarity, what follows is not intended to be a verbatim account, but rather an interpretive summary of Caldwell's list. The result is an adequate rendition of Team Mirowski's approach when evaluating neo-liberalism.)

Nonetheless, readers are encouraged, and certainly not dissuaded, from foraging within the original sources, both Caldwell's more extensive list and the relevant work produced by Mirowski and friends.)

- Neo-liberalism in this rendition starts with a critique of State reason
  - Notice that there is a consistent emphasis, in this account, on what States get wrong and why they do so. Focus is deliberately moved

away from gauging any market limitations in a relentless attempt to concentrate attention on the potential malevolence of the State. The criticism presented may be approximately correct, but the affect provided remains definitively one-sided. Thus the standard presentation can be considered skewed without being simply false.

o However, the opposite problem also exists, appearing in work slanted more to the political left. In essence, simply rejecting this focus on government failure, could possibly lead to a parallel, though opposite mistake of focusing only on market failure. Namely in each case we are left with a one-sided form of scepticism. Thus when attacking neo-liberalism, it is useful to remember that the noticeable motes discovered in one targeted set of eyes are not exclusive.

o Though government failure is a common thread in the work of neo-liberal economists, such claims would be stretched too far by representing all neo-liberals as holding identical views on this subject. Thus George Stigler and Aaron Director would be at one end of the possible spectrum of views on this topic, with other members of the same camp holding less absolutist positions.[69] In essence, those tarred with the neo-liberal brush are not necessarily also extreme libertarians.

• Neoclassical economics is a good representation of the capacities of the market as an information processor

o At least in his later years, George Stigler, for example, appeared to consider perfect competition as a reasonable reflection of actual market activity. This conclusion easily migrates toward a creed maintaining that what is, is efficient. Markets reward efficiency. Consequently inefficient results cannot be sustained over time. Clearly those who utilize resources more efficiently will by definition be adequately rewarded for their effort. Thus the market is the ultimate sorting mechanism. A more colloquial version would claim that fifty dollar bills are incapable of being left on the ground. Opportunities, by definition, are always exploited within the neo-liberal perspective. Embracing this position would automatically make any subsequent State intervention an anathema, given that such action must inevitably distort market incentives.

o Starting from this position, such government action could only cause an existing efficient result to deteriorate. Or, equally detrimental impede the inevitable movement toward such an outcome. However, this representation exists only as one possible interpretation of the tenets of neoclassical theory. Many economists would argue that this approach need not be presented in quite the conveniently narrow (or absolute) fashion that Team Mirowski prefers. Though doing so (distorting in this manner), does represent a useful way in which to present these ideas, at least if the subsequent aim is theoretical annihilation. Essentially, extreme presentations are more easily dismissed and destroyed. Therefore tactically, opposing theories are made to appear as exaggerated constructs. More to the point, despite the confidence with which this doctored version of neo-liberalism is presented, neoclassical perspectives (even the branch labelled Chicago price theory) are not quite as unified or simple-minded as Mirowski and his associates conveniently imply.[70]

- Politics exists as a form of market activity that remains analogous to the more familiar sphere of its economic mirror image. (Easy to think of this characterisation by adopting a Gertrude Stein type of consciousness, namely that 'a market is a market is a market' wherever and whenever it appears.)
  - Caldwell interprets Team Mirowski as identifying neo-liberalism as being the mouthpiece that promotes corporate objectives (an oddly pseudo Marxist approach on the Team's part). They see neo-liberals as seeking to grab and consolidate political power, while being consistently suspicious of any true element of democracy. (In this view, neo-liberals falsely coat democratic processes with a strategic varnish of authoritarianism.) The implicit equation supposedly employed by neo-liberals insists that elements, ostensibly presented as promoting democracy, simply disguise a series of deliberate shoves toward restrictive collectivism. In this mysteriously revealed neo-liberal dictionary, collective action inevitably promotes authoritarian regimes.
  - But not only is democracy misused as a means to mislead. In an equally skewed defining equation, Mirowski and associates charge neo-liberalism with disguising a preferred elitist power structure by dousing it with meritocratic bouquets (meritocracy equals elitism under this formula). Ironically, both sides of this battle label the other as being essentially undemocratic and edging toward totalitarian forms of government. Such punch and counter-punch edges

dangerously close to the level of three year olds sticking their tongues out at one another. As investigated below, these preferred claims by Team Mirowski are at best precarious. Disagreement, rather than reliable concordance, often mark the positions of those individuals identified as being in this despised neo-liberal camp. (One of their prime offenders, George Stigler, would seem to make at least the authoritarian claim problematical).[71] The available evidence seems too often stretched to accommodate Team Mirowski's pre-existing positions.

- Government ordering is predicated on the appropriate government of the self, namely a strict application of defined rationality. (The relation to the previous point should be clear.) In essence, government decisions reflect the rational choices of individuals.

  o Individual rational decision making is the stratum on which the Chicago system (or neo-liberalism in Team Mirowski speak) is founded. Certainly the ineradicable foundation of consumer sovereignty is the widely acknowledged basis for all subsequent analysis. Though to be precise, Chicago thinking is not focused on actual individual actors, but rather (a somewhat mythical) representative rational actor. These are the constructs which form the basis for the structural framework composing Chicago price theory. Stated, occasionally explicitly by George Stigler, is the principle that government intervention by distorting incentives erodes something equivalent to the moral fibre defining a given society. (Individuals inevitably react rationally to those changed incentives created by this outside agency.) Stigler worried that government operatives would happily trade off the liberating pleasure of freedom for the proposed drabness of greater income equality. However, even when focused solely on the Chicago point of view, there is a marked aspect of carelessness in transforming George Stigler into the department's representative economist.[72]

> But we are persuaded that an economic system will not help us to move in the right direction unless it grants both opportunity and responsibility to the individual: the very uncertainty of our ultimate ethical goals dictates a wide area of individual

> self-determination. We are not able to supply a blue-
> print of the ideal life, but we are persuaded that even
> if it were known it would be ideal only for the person
> who individually and knowingly and voluntarily
> accepted it. It is not necessary, however, to know what
> is best; it is enough to know what is better (Stigler
> 1949:8).

Certainly redistribution of income (Stigler's persistent bete noire), given this perspective, can only damage the economy. 'National output as presently measured can and usually will fall when a new redistribution of income is instituted, because it is costly to redistribute income' (Stigler, 'Precis of Adam Smith Lecture' *undated draft*, University of Chicago, Special Collections).

o Caldwell may overstate a touch when summarising this case, but Team Mirowski tends to muddle and even blur the distinction between Chicago pricing models and the broader concept of neo-classical theory. (At times the distinction between the Team Mirowski concept of neo-classical theory and that of neo-liberalism is not sufficiently maintained.) There is a tendency in their critical attacks to market Chicago's particular perspective as equivalent and completely encompassing the structure and boundaries of neo-classical economics. (In Team Mirowski's defining vision, Chicago represents the heart and soul of neo-liberalism, while Chicago price theory is essentially another name for the neo-classical framework. The two terms, in that case, must be one and the same.) However, presenting this relevant issue more accurately, Chicago offers a version, rather than the entirety, of that particular neo-classical framework. (Nor did the varied faculty at Chicago ever adhere to quite the lock-step perspective that Mirowski and associates ascribe to the constituent members. As emphasised in the previous chapter, such categorisation can become a lazy device for dismissing unappealing ideas.)

• Corporations can do no wrong given competitive market dynamics. The reasoning here is quite straightforward. Competition causes corporations to use resources in the most efficient manner. Those that don't will have difficulty, over time, in surviving. Inefficiently used resources will then be bid away by those that can employ those resources more efficiently to yield a greater return. In essence, the market is an efficient sorting machine given no outside interference. Again, highlighting an extreme version of this theory, as if in some fashion representative, does facilitate subsequent critical attacks on neo-liberalism. (Simple minded constructs are often more fallible than their complex brethren.) The strawman strategy devolves into cherry picking these more extreme examples and stitching them together. Sewed properly, these disparate pieces can pose as resembling a general consensus, one upheld by the neo-liberal approach to policy.

- o This stance argues against any sustained instance of private power which could skew economic outcomes. If such an assertion is accepted, then market competition erodes attempts at collusion and effectively punishes inefficiency. Therefore, in a modern dress version of the survival of the fittest, what is, must be efficient. Or, what the market has dared to ordain, let no man set asunder. (Notice, this logic forms the substratum of much of Aaron Director's perspective on anti-trust policy as developed while at the Law School at Chicago. An actual shift in anti-trust enforcement was largely influenced by Robert Bork (1978), one of Director's protégées, during his reign at the Law School. This policy transformation would subsequently take place during the Reagan administration and continue with modifications for more than thirty years.[73]) Though the profession (including suspected neo-liberals) has gradually modified this univocal 1980s approach.

- Corporate interests are preserved, by disciplining individual nation-states, through the agency of international initiatives. In essence, international agencies are there to accomplish what corporations cannot do singly or by collusion.

- o For Team Mirowski, international agencies (the IMF, World Bank, WTO and others) have been completely co-opted (captured) by capitalist or more precisely corporatist interests. (Again, Mirowski and associates manage to identify neo-liberalism in a one to one fashion with George Stigler. Here the reference is to Stigler's (1971) work on regulation. Though internationalised in a manner that Stigler may or may not have supported.[74]) Team Mirowski estimates that such institutions exist only to enrich the elites and entrench their accumulated privileges. Holding to dark conclusions of this nature would imply a belief in a deliberate (and quite complex) conspiracy.

(Readers can fill in the blank by naming whatever shadowy elite group they prefer at this point.) In which case, the institutions' officially stated objectives act as no more than a ruse hoping to deflect an unwary and naïve public away from the underlying truth. Again, a determined validating of such conspiracy styled conclusions would require a narrow focusing only on those actions that appear to fit this preconceived design. Equally convenient, if support for such a hypothetical framework is to be maintained, would be the intention to ignore (consciously or not) anything that didn't fit this pre-established, conspiratorial pattern. In essence, this approach rejects, out of hand, the potential complexity involved in these cases. Grey areas need not apply given Team Mirowski's black and white representations.[75]

- The Market (suitably re-engineered and promoted) can always provide solutions to any ostensible problem seemingly caused by The Market in the first place. This framework, if legitimate, becomes fundamentally self-sustaining. (No need to beseech the market to heal itself or provide deliberate outside assistance to assist such a process.) Notice that this peculiar rendition shifts a more extreme version of neo-classicalism into a conveniently created representative centre

  o George Stigler was fond of saying (approximately) that markets set themselves only those problems that markets can solve effectively and efficiently. In contrast, while markets move on a path to resolve such issues, government intervention (manipulated by vested interests) steadily move an economy away from desirable resolutions. This pat formula simply ignores Stigler's later work in which the public's preference for a specific form of income redistribution, via the political market place, cannot legitimately be questioned but must instead be acknowledged. Given this perspective, if economic markets adequately reflect consumer sovereignty, so must political markets as well. Policy that passes the test of time cannot rightfully be questioned, since such positions merely mirror the public's preferences. In a sense, this is the logical extension of the core of the Becker/Stigler paper (1977) as made explicit in Stigler (1992).

> He was interested, I would say primarily, in a particular sort of puzzle and it's a typical Chicago puzzle.

> And I don't mean that in any bad way, it's the sort of
> puzzle that the Chicago School's presuppositions
> require. Show me an apparent anomaly, something
> that does not seem to be explicable using the Smithian
> apparatus or the Marshalian apparatus and I will show
> you that it can be explained that way. That was exactly
> the sort of thing that George went looking for
> (Conversation with Robert Solow, November 1997).

Even this summary of the Caldwell synopsis list can be boiled down to a simple phrase. Mirowski and his associates are equating neo-liberalism (and similarly Chicago) with the dictum that 'Corporations should be allowed to run free.' From a certain narrowed perspective such a tag cannot be automatically tossed aside. To a degree, and especially among certain of the key players in this drama, support for a type of laissez faire policy is not without a degree of accuracy. Milton Friedman's (1970:17) often heard argument that corporations do good only by pursuing profits falls neatly within this cartoon-like version of neo-liberalism.

> In a free-enterprise, private-property system, a corporate executive is an
> employee of the owners of the business. He has direct responsibility to
> his employers. That responsibility is to conduct the business in accord-
> ance with their desires, which generally will be to make as much money
> as possible while conforming to the basic rules of the society, both those
> embodied in law and those embodied in ethical custom (Friedman
> 1970:17).

Yet this strategic box, which Mirowski and associates construct to define and house neo-liberalism/Chicago, deftly obliterates the context of at least some of this supposedly corporate point of view. One of Stigler's major points in his 1970 paper on regulation is to display the unintended Japanese aspects of his regulation theory. The Nipponese connection is to the *tatamae* (the appearance) versus *honne* (the reality) of the regulatory process. In essence, although regulation appears to be promoting social welfare, the reality is that it serves to advance or protect business interests instead. This potentially dangerous nexus between business and government was noted as far back as Adam Smith. He would have been heavily influenced by the 1772 Parliamentary hearings into the corrupt dealings of the East Indian Company. (Robert Clive of The East India Company distinguished himself with his reply when questioned about the large sums of money that had flowed into his personal coffers while in India. 'I stand astonished at my own moderation'.

Certainly the 'gilded age' in the US (the post-Civil War years through the 19th century), reflects the growing links between government and corporate America.[76] Both major parties (Republican as well as Democrats) were under the thrall of business interests.[77] In essence they funded the politicians who then reflected corporate and banking needs. (Not to speak of corporate leaders who were themselves in Congress or members of the Cabinet.)

> Between 1887 and 1890, as the embittered La Follette recollects, there was launched a renewed and tremendous offensive campaign for more and more rights and privileges by the "struggling railways," the "infant industries," and aggregations of private capital, everywhere nourished and grown strong upon government favour and now gathered in a solid community of interests. Not only did they seize upon natural resources and strategic monopolies, but parties, legislatures, courts, Congress was "overwhelmed" (Josephson 1938:447).

The danger then to competition and the welfare of consumers came, at least given this historical perspective, from the inevitable link between business and politics. Such a claim is hardly speculative. The fact of this indisputable link largely shaped the US economic evolution, especially in the last two decades of the nineteenth century. The argument then could be posed that the neo-liberal objection to regulatory action, and other such stated limitations to an aggressive regulatory regime, is the creation of a non-transparent back door that encourages corporate and financial economic power. In essence, this inevitable distortion of the market mechanism doesn't bode well for social welfare. Looking then through the Chicago end of the telescope, even the more recent craze for deregulation is no more than a sham. In the strict Chicago view, such reconstructed policy only reflects a shifting leverage between different self-interested parties.[78] "But surely George would have explained it in terms of the change in the perceived self-interest of the parties, of course" (Conversation with Milton Friedman, August 1997).

However, the clear problem created by attaching neo-liberalism to corporatism should be obvious. The nexus identifying these designated Chicagoans with the idea of letting corporations run free opens a trap door that enables Mirowski and company to drag out perceived and speculative motivations for Chicago's unbending support of the business sector. A simple twist of available records can sniff out illicit connections and flagellate seemingly outright instances of corruption. Opened up by this manoeuvre, is the potential for wholesale character assassination. Academically, by effectively sinking the theorist, the theory itself can be made to flounder. This created opportunity to destroy a reputation irrepressibly peeks out from beneath a muddle of confused evidence. Conditions can be intensified by adding a further welter of academic obfuscation. In essence, circumstantial evidence is awarded an untoward weight. Castigating the aims and purposes of those leading Chicago lights by tarring them with a corrupt lustre can be far more effective than attacking the relevant policies directly. The aim is to allow others to connect corrupt individuals to biased policies. Corporate minions are implicitly charged with constructing made to order theories. Therefore, drilling down incessantly on the corporate bent of Chicago's theoretic base, opens up the possibility of reducing an entire academic department to the position of paid flacks. But before entering this realm of putative character assassination, it may prove useful to more closely examine the imposed simplifications used by the Mirowski team to yoke Chicago (and neo-liberalism) so inescapably to corporate imperatives.

Given the previously described agenda (as detailed by Caldwell), it is reasonable to argue that this description of neo-liberalism (and what Team Mirowski loves to hate about it) has been oversimplified. (Again, remember the fashion in which the principle position (as listed), boils down to a simple dictum of letting corporations run free.) By embracing this route, the Team gains the ability to construct a more vulnerable target for their subsequent investigations (and ultimate deconstruction), of neo-liberalism. The goal when employing such analysis is to pull off something of a high wire act without breaking a sweat. Namely, they need to closely and continually identify neo-liberalism with a post war Chicago School dominated by Friedman, Stigler and Director (and later Gary Becker). The justification for this deliberate strategy is that they are then handed the ability to identify Chicago as the pressure-cooker that produced a post war counter-revolution against the then dominant Keynesian framework (along with its subsequent variations). This bit of prestidigitation reduces Chicago's thrust to shape the dominant economic perspective to a one dimensional effort that simply identified anything reminiscent of collective policy (or action), as a threat to individual freedom and liberty. Doing so creates a targeted method for undermining neo-liberalism by creating a highly reduced version of the original.

Team Mirowski could then more easily drive home their own aims and objectives by making neo-liberalism's opposing intentions suspect. Once formulated (and simplified) by Mirowski and company, this created neo-liberal program allowed Chicago to be conveniently charged with providing the petri dish that cultured neo-liberalism (characterised as nefariously evil). By doing so, this derived portrait allowed Team Mirowski's depiction of Chicago to comfortably stand in for (and be in fact equivalent to), those tenets espoused by neo-liberalism. But at the same time, such a strategic construction cannot be simply accepted, based only on a dubious indictment. Nor can an associated condemnation, lacking clear validation, be equally approved. The implied contention that this labelled neo-liberal perspective has dominated (and continues to dominate), economic theory, but more particularly economic policy, lacks the conviction that Team Mirowski assigns to it. This necessary policy leverage is crucial to their framework. It ultimately provides neo-liberalism with a significant degree of anointed economic and political power. Shorn of any string pulling ability, neo-liberalism would shrink to become some will-o'-the-wisp that has managed to enthral only a small group of radical economists. Thus the validity of this charge becomes fundamental. The attention Team Mirowski devotes to Chicago style omnipotence effectively inflates the importance of neo-liberalism. A particularly obsessive focus is established by placing this economic tribe at the very rudders of the ship of state. Their ideology (enveloped within a given perspective), monopolises and steers policy. They are viewed as controlling what Team Mirowski forcefully labels as an evil, but effective, empire.

In essence, Mirowski and his cohorts construct a world seemingly infected by the scourge of neo-liberalism. The seeds of this evil, at least accordingly to this version, deliberately planted at the start of the Reagan administration, due to the Chicago transplants that found a home there. The same approach is claimed to still define the policy terrain in the US and in much of the developed world. This particular strategic twist, which provides Mirowski and company with the target they require, can only succeed by nominating Chicago as the dominant force in shaping this brand of economic thought. As a result, the designated department that succeeded in marketing neo-liberal policy to the rest of the profession, can (jujitsu-like), be cleverly reversed into becoming neo-liberalism's Achilles heel. (Chicago, under this scheme, becomes simultaneously, both the strength and weakness of neo-liberalism.) If the Chicago project can somehow be destroyed, using whatever means necessary, the neo-liberal empire of policy and thought crashes as well. Thus the equating of Chicago with neo-liberalism can now be viewed as displaying strategic intention.

Consequently, in their campaign to take down neo-liberalism, Mirowski and his friends have erected something of a Jenga-like construction as the chosen mechanism. The seeming impregnable tower, representing neo-liberalism, collapses once a critical Chicago-shaped block is successfully removed. Notice that prior to this forced crumbling of their targeted theoretic structure, Team Mirowski have carefully transformed the targeted ideology into an unstoppable dark force. Consequently, the previous historical triumph of this evil empire, as insisted upon in their own convenient retelling of this tale, helps to construct neo-liberalism as an unquestionably terminal threat to society (and especially to human rights). Spotlighted, from a carefully developed angle, Team Mirowski can then shine forth as dragon slayers, the fearless Beowulf to the profession's dreaded Grendel. (You cannot seize the heroic spotlight without the overbearing presence of fearsome villains.)

However, a germ of validity does define this equating of Chicago with neo-liberalism. From the very first Mont Pelerin meeting onward, Friedman, Stigler and Director were intent on transforming the traditional Classical Liberal approach away from its post-war decay. Their intention in producing this preferred shift was to direct economics toward a more modern encapsulation that would still honour what they defined as the essence of this creed. In essence, they championed the protection of individual liberty (supposedly threatened by what appeared to them to be a drift toward left wing collectivism).[79] Such stated idealism was to remain paramount, acting as an unalterable axiom for all future discourse. Their Chicago brand of market fundamentalism then arose out of an assumption that markets formed the necessary basis for, and groundwork of, individual liberty, essentially encapsulating Milton Friedman's idea of being 'free to choose'.[80]

> The widespread use of the market reduces the strain on the social fabric by rendering conformity unnecessary with respect to any activities it encompasses. The wider the range of activities covered by the market, the fewer are the issues on which explicitly political decisions are required and hence on which it is necessary to achieve agreement. In turn, the fewer the issues on which agreement is necessary, the greater

is the likelihood of getting agreement while maintaining a free society (Friedman 1962:24).

In direct contrast, the Team Mirowski approach doggedly drains the Chicago position of any and all subtlety. As suggested, their annotated edition of that perspective could be reduced to the idea of 'letting corporations run free'. Reading with an intent to destroy almost demands that a resulting interpretation is essentially over-egged. The version presented by design displays a sufficient number of easily recognisable cracks each one capable of undermining the presented theory. Thus, subsequently watching this carefully constructed version self-implode seems inevitable, when a replicant theory is deliberately composed along such identifiable fault lines.[81] However, much of Team Mirowski's characterisation depends on liberally employing a scheme centred upon broad categorisation. The implied requirement is the production of a carefully curated (but generalised), version of an average Chicago School denizen.[82] (The Team find convenient by-passes that allow the Chicago idea to be conveniently shaped to achieve their own specific objectives.) Done skilfully, the result can prove persuasive (especially to less than conscientious readers), but more often than not also deliberately misleading. Differences and important subtleties are papered over, effectively hidden from sight and barred from any further discussion. Simplified replicas usually prove much easier to disembowel.

Unfortunately, such an elementary version of complex theory lacks a certain degree of buoyancy. Often, marketing the preferred simplification requires that differences between those lumped together as denizens of the Chicago School should be largely ignored. Instead, any convenient core similarities that Team Mirowski chooses to emphasise are magnified, all the better to amplify any cracks or weaknesses. Surreptitious cherry picking yields a pleasing, but often misleading, concatenation of evidence, chosen largely for its ability to fit preferred presuppositions, while driving home designated objectives. Essentially then, once Chicago and neo-liberalism are conclusively welded to a form of corporatism, the next step a destroying angel attempts is to explain the motivation behind this cooperative venture. Here, Mirowski and his associates have set the opposition up for a form of total and irretrievable demolition. Moreover, this tactic allows the attack to shift seamlessly away from controversial theoretical aspects to more damning personal ones. To remind the reader, articles and theories are primarily examined with an intent to destroy foremost.

The next step in this process is to succinctly drive home the accusation that Chicago's virulent form of corporate defence is not a principled (or theoretic) one. The motivation driving this response is rather driven by personal advancement, greed and corruption (the unholy trinity). Team Mirowski takes aim at neo-liberal policy and theory by launching an ad hominin attack on their version of the targeted defenders.[83] Tarring academics with corruption, misconduct and dishonesty, can offer the more direct (and easier) option than proving a theory to be bankrupt. Such a psychological weapon, when deployed, ominously warns that only bad policy can possibly flow from bad people. In essence, shoot the messenger before he or she can deliver a tainted message. Otherwise only malicious intent would urge an academic to launch personal rather than professional attacks.

C. *Darker Byways – Sewing Together Seeming Connections*

> But the man had hereditary tendencies of the most diabolical kind. A criminal strain ran in his blood, which, instead of being modified, was increased and rendered infinitely more dangerous by his extraordinary mental powers. Dark rumours gathered round him in the university town, and eventually he was compelled to resign his chair and to come down to London, where he set up as an army coach. So much is known to the world, but what I am telling you now is what I have myself discovered (https://www.arthurconandoyle.com/professormoriarty.html).[84]

Unfortunately, focusing on only the actual (or even a self-modified) Chicago theory and policy platform proves to be insufficient for Team Mirowski. They perceive an assumed need to diversify their attack on Chicago and the associated scourge of neo-liberalism. Presumably by spreading one's net wider, more convincing results will ensue. Parallel to some of the occasional strategies employed by those at Chicago, they prefer to discover elements of conspiracy and corruption behind the formation of Chicago's structural approach. In which case, these authors opt for a story-telling device beloved by novelists and screenwriters alike. To ginger up the story they unfold a narrative (which further consolidates random chunks of the framework), allowing Team Mirowski to conveniently discover a hulking, influence pulling villain. (The proverbial explanatory rabbit expertly pulled out of a carefully selected sorting hat.) This fatal economic nemesis reliably belongs to the familiar 'spider weaving its web' variety of evil doers, though this essential mastermind predictably remains effectively hidden from view. Or at least the true power of this plotter is almost magically concealed from all but the most perspicacious of neo-liberal hunters.

In essence, the Team has a natural inclination to locate (and if necessary create), its own version of an identifiable Ernst Stavro Blofeld. They are fundamentally in need of a black-hearted miscreant, one aided and abetted by an equally shadowy SPECTRE type of organization, if they are to blow neoliberalism forever out of the water.[85] Successfully linking the two together would stamp a guilty verdict on the nefarious machinations committed under the seemingly blameless banner of orthodox economics.[86] The veil of hypocrisy would finally be effectively stripped away. While doing so does not explicitly dictate edging into the realm of conspiracy theory, Team Mirowski would seem willing to sail uncomfortably close to those treacherous shoals. Here one can easily note the affinity many hardened ideologues have for such theoretical will-of-the-wisps.[87]

Advancing their continuing campaign against neo-liberalism, Team Mirowski have fortunately, at least for their purposes, discovered a more than adequate vehicle for furthering their ends. As will be seen further on in this piece, at least by those readers who make it that far, conspiracy when attached to a specific group can be employed to conduct a destructive character assassination. Attacks of this type can be aimed at any group of designated opponents. As a rationale for stooping to these levels, this tactic is deliberately attempted against those who are branded as the irredeemable champions of this neoliberal framework, deemed to be inescapably dangerous. In essence, the battle is far too important to stop at niceties.

The strategy employed is simple and direct. Nothing can be more excoriating to carefully cultivated, academic reputations than to be branded as being mere intellectual lackeys, willing to slavishly carry out the multifarious objectives of the corporate elite. As pointed out, the goal is to reveal this motivation as the only convincing explanation for adhering to such a corporatist philosophy. Evidence arrives in the form of a usefully malleable target, the Mont Pelerin Society. (Not quite a smoking gun, but the best available option.) Much like the Illuminati, this group is elevated, to the requisite pinnacle of skulduggery and conspiracy. Simultaneously, what would appear to be a stodgy assemblage of conservative academics and hangers-on, receives an unacknowledged injection of behind the scenes plotting and power. This designated Society metamorphoses into a menacing conclave of academic guns for hire. Even of greater convenience, this largely archaic Society turns out to be cheerfully populated by many of the leading lights residing in Chicago, a remarkable (if not unforeseen) coincidence. This fortunate congruence sets the desired linkages in place for the subsequent attack.

Not then for Team Mirowski the complex and carefully researched story developed by Burgin (2012), one which they feel entitled to casually dismiss.[88] Instead, the Pelerin Society is elevated from its very inception into a univocal force for the world's moneyed interests. Team Mirowski fails to entirely resist the temptation of fabricating a story that serves to highlight the malevolence emanating from a tightly woven conspiracy. Moreover, the constructed tale is one of a society that achieved its dominating influence by employing strategic manipulations, moves that rival those performed on a chessboard by an acknowledged Grandmaster. In essence, the indictment manages not only to invalidate the legitimacy of neo-liberalism (or at least leave its reputation fatally tainted), by casting doubt on the motives of those who created that structure. These objectives (strained through the Team's pre-constructed sieve) are almost summarily judged to be indefensible. Again, they are seen legitimising the aims of its corporate funders. The primary bit of targeting is in turn overlaid with a companion attack (the inevitable dollop of corruption and malevolence). Such an aggressive, no quarter given, evaluation would probably surprise even the most thick-skinned, Chicago academic. This smearing of personal integrity would most likely be dismissed as reflecting nothing less than a case of unwarranted effrontery.[89] Even for a hardened Chicago denizen, this would appear to be a step too far.

Undeniably, the Mont Pelerin Society did reinforce and encourage existing tendencies among members by putting them in contact with other like-minded individuals. That was unquestionably the intention of bringing a group of old-styled liberals together. The gathering was meant to assist a disparate bunch of right-wing intellectuals dispel the rather dismal fear that they belonged to a hopeless and ever shrinking minority in the immediate post war period. Liberalism, according to the basic tenets held by the Mont Pelerin Society, had to be reformed in order to meet the demands of modern society.[90] The nineteenth century version featuring a laissez faire policy was reckoned to have reached a terminal dead end. Though the lasting irony here is that ultimately, this deliberate reformation of liberalism turned the classical variety into a caricature of itself. The version that was incubated (and flourished) at Chicago, for example, can perhaps best be imagined as something of a fundamentalist version of 19th century ideas, at odds with any post war trends. The twist being that laissez faire, instead of undergoing a reformulation, had been elevated and transformed into a universal policy. The approach was now based entirely on Chicago style price theory and the ultimate primacy of markets.

Undoubtedly, the leading lights at Chicago may have explicitly conceived their task as one of reformulating the type of Classical Liberal economics exemplified by John Stuart Mill. These would-be, counter-revolutionaries seemed to dream of and desire a sort of Renaissance of intellectual thinking. They were convinced that they had the tools to build a template that would dispel the dark and stupefying clouds brought on by Keynesianism and its associated collective propaganda.[91] To update these proven and time validated principles of what they conceived to be Classical Liberalism, they were more than willing to jettison some key aspects of this approach. By doing so, they believed that they still could maintain what existed as the treasured core, or essence, of such a doctrine, while performing a bit of overdue remodelling. (The approach needed a distinct modern look if it was to compete with the newer, post war doctrines.)

Unfortunately, Team Mirowski's detailing of the rise and machination of Chicago only sporadically focuses on what would appear to be more vital analytical issues. Instead, they too often are carried down less fruitful, but more alluring, bypaths, what would appear to be distractions away from the operating principles defining neoliberalism. Consequently, no matter how interesting the attraction of these explorations might be, they at best represent only fascinations of the distracting variety. They basically fail to shed new light on the vital keys that might unlock the mysteries of the post war Chicago School. You might shy away from giving such representatives as Aaron Director or George Stigler a hug, but their congeniality has little to do with the validity of their presented doctrine.

By analysing various fragments of the Chicago past (depending almost entirely on archival letters, memos and drafts), Team Mirowski have managed to piece together what would appear to be a wide-ranging and complete historical account. Their journey through the relevant archives seems to go a long way toward providing a compelling impression that supports the inevitability of post war events, as well as the inexcusable deviousness of the Chicago brigade. But this imaginative compilation turns out, on closer examination, to be a complexly intricate framework without a strongly viable foundation. Being able to leap upon a conveniently reassuring archival statement is in no way the equivalent of finding a modern day Rosetta Stone.

Unfortunately, this vaunted key unlocks no subterranean secrets. To no reliable degree does a single (and seemingly solo) expression of an idea (or even passing thought) qualify as one that miraculously unveils and unscrambles previously incomprehensible mysteries. Employing a lone document in such a fashion seems to signal that this particular piece of evidence should be accorded pride of place simply because it solidifies some preferred narrative.[92] In essence, its importance is based solely on its ability to buttress some pre-conceived perspective. In which case, the future imperative for researchers would evolve into single-mindedly cherry picking only that evidence that fits neatly into a preconceived jig-saw puzzle. Pieces that fail to glue together a predetermined theory would be simply discarded, no matter how consequential they might appear to be. Unfortunately, elevating one convenient archival find to the status of a Stiglerian revelation can offer only limited, and possibly dubious, rewards. Consequently, believing that a particular artefact consistent with one's own preconceived views is the heretofore lost key capable of unlocking the hidden secrets of George Stigler's heart seems more that a touch far-fetched.

If the actual facts are more carefully considered we see instead only a confluence of events, some of which are simply more random than care-fully planned. For example, Aaron Director gaining a permanent home at the Chicago Law School through Simons' death. Stigler finding himself being somehow rejected in 1946 for a Chicago faculty position. Friedman unexpectedly gaining the perch instead, based on the whimsical idea that Stigler, as opposed to Friedman, was too empirical. In turn that decision may have resulted from the fact that Robert Hutchins, Chancellor of the University of Chicago, who was supposed to interview Stigler was unable to do so due to illness. It was in fact his substitute (President Ernest Colwell) that found Stigler unsatisfactory.[93] Even Mirowski and his com-patriots would shy away from claiming that Hutchins' temporary indispo-sition was fated by the omnipotent gods of reactionary neo-liberalism. (Or even worse that Simons somehow sacrificed himself for some greater ideological crusade.) Nonetheless, outcomes could be envisaged as much altered had not Director, Friedman and Stigler eventually arrived at the same campus.

The inclusion of Friedman and Stigler at the first Mont Pelerin meet-ing, which admittedly greatly influenced their thinking, cannot seriously be classified as a predestined event.[94] Nor was it an automatic given that the Volker fund would pay their travel expenses to that key meeting.

Moreover, if Stigler had been offered the expected 1946 position, it is far from certain that he also would have managed at some point to be appointed to the Walgreen professorship. (Friedman was not.) The Walgreen money (starting with his 1958 appointment) provided him with the ability to use the attached research funds.[95] This flood of money helped to facilitate core investigations, which formed in part, the foundation of the Chicago approach. Thus Bruce Caldwell's objections to the inevitability of the rise of neo-liberalism at Chicago cannot be so easily dismissed, even if it tends to undercut the claims of Team Mirowski.

> What about the chance elements? Simply put, they were everywhere in this story. Had there been no *Reader's Digest* condensation of *The Road to Serfdom*, Luhnow, who from VHM's [Van Horn/Mirowski] account does not strike one as a deep reader, would probably never have heard of F.A. Hayek. The story of how the condensation came to be is itself also rather remarkable: Apparently Harry Gideonse had a chance encounter with a press staffer on the train into Chicago one day, and suggested that a copy of *The Road to Serdom* be sent to Max Eastman. Eastman, former editor of *The Masses* and enthusiast for the Russian Revolution, but by then a roving editor for *Reader's Digest*, was so impressed with the book that he offered to do a condensation. What if Gideonse had missed his train that morning? Note too that Hayek's manuscript had been offered to three other presses, all of which had turned him down, before it was sent to Chicago. It might well have been rejected by Chicago too, given the distinctly ambivalent first reader's report by Frank Knight. It was the second report by the socialist Jacob Marschak that convinced the press to take a chance on the manuscript … Thus the unlikely trio of Harry Gideonse, Max Eastman, and Jacob Marschak were in their own ways all bit players in the creation of the Chicago School, for without them Hayek would not have talked before the Detroit Economics Club on April 23, 1945 (Caldwell 2011:306–307).

The term (neo-liberalism) itself, reiterated repeatedly by Team Mirowski, seems to provide little clarification as to the purpose or motivating reason behind the rise of the post war Chicago School. Its use can instead be considered as somewhat dismissive in purpose, given that those who are brushed with this all enveloping designation, do not themselves accept such a categorization.[96] Neo-liberal might have been a term toyed with by those opposing what they denoted as left wing collectivism. But the designation simply gathered dust for decades. We can employ a rule of thumb, which simply states that a one-sided acceptance of any such terminology clearly implies that the label is being used in a derogatory, or dismissive, fashion.[97] On a superficial level, the term is innocent of any perverse or pejorative connotations. Those at Chicago and elsewhere simply set out to transform classical liberalism, to carve out a place for this doctrine in the post war world of the 20th century. They were true believers rather than hardened conspirators.

Starting with the first Mont Pelerin Society meeting (and subsequently elsewhere), these individuals may have attempted to construct a 'new liberalism'. However, somehow seen through the goggles provided by Team Mirowski, this objective becomes associated, even if only obliquely, with a type of conspiracy reeking of perdition and manipulation. To tell a convincing story, the hidden objective driving such a narrative must loom larger and be more pernicious than any explicitly professed goals. The hidden heart often proves to provide a more fascinating alternative focus. Easily discoverable, explicitly stated aims inevitably become decisively and convincingly dismissed as no more than simple camouflage. (The rotten heart motivating the reality of the matter must be skilfully hidden from all but the eyes of the cognoscenti.) Thus much of what is published and easily obtainable is simply exiled from any serious consideration.

There may even come a point where Team Mirowski's focus on the Mont Pelerin Society tips over to reflect an unhealthy level of obsession, though that in itself would seem to be something of an extreme suggestion. Marketing an unstated, yet implicit ideological stance, may require investing certain powers and strategic planning to one's opponent, whether or not such an attribution is entirely legitimate. Under such an imperative (or operating within a narrow, but unstated, agenda), straw figures can come to replace more complex and hard to grasp realities. Thus in this telling of the origin of the Chicago School, these authors don't simply create a simplistic bugaboo, one that is capable of dismissing the professed opponents of these economists. Team Mirowski is driven to not only specify, but to explain Chicago's support of corporatism in the darkest, possible terms. That neo-liberalism, under their censorious eyes, has already been thoroughly condemned as lacking any defensible economic foundation (or even simple humanity), is deemed insufficient. They still feel the necessity of going even further. Team Mirowski's unwavering aim remains the total annihilation of this self-designated evil theology. To accomplish their predetermined ends, they embrace, not so much the joys of performing a critical evaluation, but instead choose the critical equivalent of nuclear obliteration.

To do so, Team Mirowski pounces on a dictum beloved by journalists and fictional detectives, namely they doggedly pursue a conveniently discovered money trail. Once accomplished, they can then proceed to piece together a more damning and dismissive narrative. Nothing else could possibly be both more explanatory and incriminating than introducing money as the motivating factor. The problem posed in pursuing this option is one that Team Mirowski never convincingly settles. Difficulties arise from a pressing need to transform the funds and resources, which the Chicago School managed to corral, into a sort of eminence grise that defined the movement itself. 'Money may talk', but the fundamental assertion that it always dictates, is a generalization that takes analysis at least a step too far. A nefarious, grant wielding, corporate power that managed to advance its goals by using these academics as pawns, is (at times) implied in their narration. Damning claims can (of course) always be finessed, but you can't entirely divorce yourself from their existence. They exist as bombshells, carefully laid for maximum effect.

Consequently, at least according to the scenario created by Team Mirowski, the rise of Chicago (along with the Frankenstein type monster thus created (neo-liberalism)), was not only lubricated by, but also predominately driven by monetary flows. Unfortunately, the evidence they muster to support such an audacious claim, appears heavily based on an unreliable strategy invoking guilt by association. The perceived danger discovered (the one lurking at the core of neo-liberalism), leads Team Mirowski to mirror the very methods previously employed by those despised Chicago economists. The perceived urgency created by the spreading propagation of neo-liberalism seems to justify Team Mirowski in employing whatever tactics that might come to hand. Justifying in this fashion is roughly derivative of a 'whatever it takes' philosophy beloved by cynical politicians.

> Neoliberalism, then is not generally used as a term of approbation. The doctrine purportedly provides a rationale for powerful transnational corporations who wish to utilize the power of the state to advance their own interests. The chief desideratum of transnational capital is a stable global economy, which ensures both a steady supply of resources for the production process, and a steady supply of consumers for the purchasing

of goods. Corporations accordingly use international organizations like the World Bank, the WTO, and the IMF, as well as the military power of strong states (and in particular the United States) to enforce the ideology of the market and to spread Western (especially consumerist) values (Caldwell 2011:308–309).

D. *Follow the Money: Knuckle-Dusting the Chicago School*

It is possible, and in fact usually the case, that an intellectual can please his customers without recourse to professing beliefs he does not actually hold, or other dishonourable practices (Stigler 1976:347).

The core problem evoked, when indulging in a bit of destructive reading, is a discernible shift (in the terms of debate), away from discussing any major issues. These are the concerns that should produce the greatest long term impact on both theory and policy. (Or worse, it effectively impedes such a discussion from occurring.) A dominant strategy, actively pursued by Team Mirowski, appears to be overly grounded on an eagerness to destroy the validity of Chicago School type policies at all costs. (Given the exigency of action, niceties be damned.) This aim, if driven by critical inquiry, poses no serious problem. Any policy needs a thorough examination and evaluation. Flawed policies should be demonstrably revealed as inadequate, or even counter-productive. However, seeking to do so by demolishing the probity of those who devise and market these views, presents a more questionable path to traverse.

There is a parallel here with the way in which the Chicago School itself often operated. By its own methodology, those at Chicago was forced to undercut opposing policies by lethally eviscerating the theories that provided them with ground cover.[98] Part of this process involved whittling away at the reputation enjoyed by their opponents.[99] Thus Friedman (1974) attempted to shrink Keynes from a towering figure of the profession into a decorative garden gnome. Keynes in this sculptured reading became a minor quantity theorist who had contributed only the rather insignificant idea of the liquidity trap to the received wisdom of the discipline.[100] Nor did these Chicagoans exhibit any compunction in linking the policies advocated by the more mainstream economists they battled with warnings of the potentially dangerous limitations such polices posed to individual freedom and liberty.

Both Team Mirowski and the Chicago School seem to display an all too frequent fondness for playing the man, rather than the policy. Such motives appear as deliberately camouflaged under the pretence of performing a legitimate, critical evaluation. In contrast, the Classical Liberal perspective focused more on the policy agenda presented, without being distracted, at least not to the same degree, by the ideology supporting alternative approaches.[101] (There are no defendable grounds for automatically dismissing a Chicago based policy.[102]) Making such an evaluation doesn't negate the sanctioned practice of having each side of any given policy debate argue the available evidence. But when ideology is the driving force, both contentious groups are capable of arguing past one another, shaping facts to match preordained conclusions.

This deliberate strategy of befuddlement can only be further confused by an almost inevitable escalation into character assassinations that is boxed and delivered in every fashion imaginable. (The academic sneer of superiority is not an infrequent occurrence.) Classical Liberals would attempt (or at least claim they were seriously trying) to eschew any conclusions prior to examining the available, detailed evidence. (Rather than seeking a method for sanctifying preordained conclusions.) They would at the very least attempt to familiarise themselves with the specific details surrounding each case, eschewing a rush to some prescribed judgment. Personal attacks would not be deemed even implicitly acceptable, though at times this barrier would inevitably be breached. But it would fail to become a ruling principle.

Unfortunately, this tendency to overstep, without the benefit of supporting evidence, is illustrated by a quote (see below) from Team Mirowski (in this case Mirowski and Van Horn (2015)). Charges are simply flung scattershot in this example and labels gaily pinned to perceived vulnerabilities. The outright charge (Friedman is accused of being an intellectual for hire), is perhaps one of the most damning accusations that can be levelled at any academic. Consequently, such charges should be undertaken with a considerable dollop of trepidation, absent of any incipient glee. Putting the claim in some sort of context, imagine, hypothetically only, manufacturing a similar inflammatory charge against the members of Team Mirowski.

Any fair-minded economist, one operating in an imagined rational world, would quickly dismiss such an accusation as outrageous. This type of insidious charge would seem to serve only as a convenient distraction from the essential issues being questioned. However, the basis for rejecting the charge of self-dealing should never depend on which side of the ideological fence such authors inhabit. Team Mirowski is not to be judged automatically innocent simply because these academics happen to be bereft of any substantial corporate backing while advancing their attacks. Nor are their targets inevitably guilty simply for enjoying corporate funds.

> Crude argumentation of this ilk proved wildly popular in the American arena, as evidenced by the fact that the book [*Capitalism and Freedom*] has never gone out of print. Friedman accomplished what Hayek never did and what Director was apparently incapable of doing. The *Road to Serfdom* is an intricate and subtle tract compared to its confident bromide. But the major difference is that *Capitalism and Freedom* wore its own provenance on its sleeve; it was *proud* to be the work of an intellectual for hire, because all human discourse was essentially just a sequence of disguised market transactions[103] (Mirowski and Van Horn 2015:167–168).

As pointed out, Friedman and his erstwhile Chicago conspirators should not be judged guilty simply due to their corporate links. (In the Team Mirowski distorted mirror, these Chicago based denizens often appear as being both bankrolled and controlled by corporate dark money.)[104] The simplicity of such strained logic in either case is fortunately self-cancelling (or should be) to all but the most closed minds. Cash from any source (even of the corporate persuasion), is not automatically or legitimately to be transformed into prima facie evidence of any ethical trespass. The conclusions of many economists tend to embrace the predictable. But this fails to prove that corporate funds are pulling any strings. These donors would be unlikely to expend resources for conclusions antithetical to their corporate goals. This obvious imperative only indicates that such money isn't spent randomly or indiscriminately. (Corporations do not necessarily seek unbiased research or evidence.) Such obvious corporate strategy is quite different than claiming that economists will simply switch his or her views in order to gain a measure of desired funding. Vehicles travelling down parallel roads are not guiding one another, or necessarily determining each other's path.

To view any one of the trio, composed of Friedman, Stigler and Director, as bending easily to their paymaster's voice is to determinedly ignore the relevant cantankerous personalities involved.[105] As Van Horn

(2010) clearly illuminates, Aaron Director was perhaps born with a permanently contrary nature. With a chip firmly planted (or implanted) on his shoulder, Director revelled in the ability to proclaim that something just wasn't so.

> Aaron Director was extremely conservative. Why, I don't know. By the time I knew him he was already like that. And he was an iconoclast. But he didn't develop new data with respect to industrial organisation. He didn't develop and articulate new theories. He just said that the conventional belief wasn't so (Conversation with Paul Samuelson, October 1997).[106]

Sketching the curmudgeonly figure of Aaron Director as someone who would do the bidding of his paymasters would badly skew and ignore his inherent personality.[107] Even the story Mirowski and associates want to tell (as one that decisively points the finger of guilt) leaves Director as someone who stalls and fudges without delivering exactly what his funders wish. Financial backing was of course welcomed, as it would have been by any group of academic economists including Team Mirowski. Funds allowed other similar minded researchers to be hired and increased the research output supporting a distinct line of inquiry. Academia doesn't escape the dictum of money being power. But during his long life, finding examples of Director doing the bidding of anyone, at any time, for a bundle of cash seems to be distinctly wanting in either evidence or credibility.

Admittedly, Team Mirowski does acknowledge the responsibility of delineating a clear line of causation and control running from the Volker Fund (that financed what was then termed 'The Free Market Study' at Chicago), to the placement of Director at its head. Doing so is logically the initial step towards buttressing their stated string pulling hypothesis. Events are accordingly carefully recast to provide a desired top down ordering. The objective is to portray neo-liberalism as no more than a convenient front for corporate interests. Consequently, they determinately transform Director's indisputable failure to live up to his contractual Volker responsibilities into a clear reflection of nefarious actions in an almost conspirator-like fashion. These imagined connections, quite naturally, are viewed as lurking somewhere just below the surface, explaining why they are not normally recognised.

The connective bridges, when exposed by Team Mirowski, reveal the clear stench of Chicago's subservience to its named paymasters. In other words, readers are implicitly induced to detect at least a faint whiff of collusion associated with these dealings. Of course, the initial idea behind the Free Market Study (and its corporate funding) was for Director to simply transform Hayek's *Road to Serfdom* (and its subsequent influence), into an American friendly version. This derivative work was to be published as the *American Road*. But the way in which Director's contractual failure is logically resurfaced by Team Mirowski remains puzzling. Somehow, not delivering on his promises becomes solid evidence that Director predominantly focused on carrying out his paymaster's objectives, rather than tending to his own druthers.[108] Such a conclusion smells contradictory, or at least lacking in any tight logical reasoning. Rather, wishful thinking appears to be driving the argument.

Fortunately, in terms at least of funding considerations, the objectives pursued by Director and his colleagues were consistently evaluated as being aligned with that of the Volker Fund. This determination was advanced by those financing the project, which would effectively explain the funding continuation. However, the existence of a reliable flow of cash need not be interpreted as obeisance. Instead, the events can more simply be viewed as Director successfully dodging undesired responsibilities, talking his way out of potential difficulties. In essence, such outcomes seem all too consistent with Director's discerned character traits. Simply put, Director proved sufficiently slippery when dealing with his erstwhile corporate funders. By acting in a strategic fashion, he was able to placate these moneyed individuals, while he pursued the initiatives that actually aroused his interest. A reasonable conclusion would view Director as largely doing what he wanted. This alternative reality would undermine Team Mirowski's rather peculiar view of what 'calling the shots' actually means. Director's actions then are not quite equivalent to deliberately shaping one's work to match dictated objectives. Despite all their efforts, Team Mirowski continually fails to develop any singular convincing evidence demonstrating that the principals at Chicago willingly changed their positions to suit any of these nominated moneyed interests. Instead, Team Mirowski unfortunately resort to a Chicago style strategy, namely that by definition whatever is observed (or examined), must be reshaped in such a fashion that it automatically proves a pre-existing position.

For instance, if someone always intended to travel from Chicago, Illinois to Gary, Indiana on the first of May 1952, while only subsequently agreeing to deliver a message to a friend's relative in Gary, a legitimate conclusion would not be that the trip was undertaken at that friend's behest.

Rather, the two goals simply happened to coincide. The requisite individual was nominated to act in the role of a messenger simply because of a prior and independent commitment. Yet, even though the noted academics at Chicago appeared to be following their own inclinations (ones clearly etched in their articles and speeches), these events are somehow transmuted by Mirowski and associates, even if not explicitly, into work demanded by their designated paymasters. To even hint at such a curious conclusion seems to serve no other purpose than to mislead and distract away from a potentially more useful focus on the relevant contested theories and policies. The strategy appears to be one of attacking the work by questioning the character and legitimacy of its authors. (Tainted authors produce dubious output.)

> Most notably, Aaron Director did not fulfil his original obligation to finish the *American Road* by the spring of 1952, nor did he ever. … Nevertheless, the Volker Fund took the long view and helped Director and other Free Market Study members to revise the classical liberal doctrine and propagate the result through both technical and popularized outlets. Thus, in spite of their contractual failure in 1952, Director and the Free Market Study had pleased the Volker Fund in other ways as evidenced by its continued largesse (Mirowski and Van Horn 2015:166).

Thus Mirowski and Company feel compelled to weave an intricate web of conspiratorial intersections in order to achieve a level of belief that is sufficiently convincing. Or at least, they throw up a sufficient number of distractions to the point of potentially swaying sceptical readers. (Otherwise they fall into the classic trap of preaching to the choir.) Undoubtedly, they perform useful and even admirable work in tracking the movements of the key players at the initial inception of the Chicago School, as well as the funding that helped to jumpstart their activity. But unfortunately, Team Mirowski betrays the additional need to construct more shadowed and hard to discern regions, where questionable rationales are allowed to dominate. These intricate terrains are displayed, with supposed innocence, as the inevitable outcome of their quest.

Team Mirowski visualises, somewhat in advance of any actual discovery, a discernible motivation that would inevitably drive both these Chicago academics and their corporate paymasters. The tendency is to unearth exactly the proof needed to validate their core assumptions. Unfortunately, the revealed linkages flowing from the designated funders to the amoral academics, are not so much established, as simply asserted. Unlike Pinocchio, who wanted to be a real boy, these targeted Chicago economists are depicted as wallowing in their shameful academic servitude. Consequently, none of these examined Chicago denizens ever display a desire to break the golden strings controlling their research programs. These inhabitants of the South Side never, according to the slant provided by the Team Mirowski concoction, wanted to be real (independent) economists. Instead, we are offered something of a dystopic fable, devoid of any admirable characters, let alone heroes.

At times the analysis becomes almost obsessed with following the trail of financial funding. This solitary track is ploughed so deeply that all else remains, at best, only of secondary importance. Establishing that money flowed from conservative business interests to a select set of academics is unquestionably of interest. However, such findings fail to imply that these contributions conclusively dictated, or even shaped, the views or research performed by the fortunate recipients. This bit of strained logic exists as a leap that requires more evidence than Team Mirowski seem able to present. A simpler, and perhaps more compelling, explanation would discover that funding inevitably flows to those economists whose established research parallels those of the funders' objectives. Given the range of positions held by economists, it is not a feat of legerdemain to find a select set that shares one's own vision of the world.[109] Even the clash, reported in some detail of the Volcker foundation's dissatisfaction with Aaron Director's accomplishments, does not seem centred so much on Director's policy views, but rather on his failure to deliver his contracted work as promised. Not surprising, since Director seemed to take something of a perverse delight in not publishing.

Nor does transforming Hayek into the equivalent of some sly grandmaster effectively reinforce, to any substantial degree, the pointed conclusions, upon which Team Mirowski insists on pedalling. Though playing an important role in the early post war years, Hayek's influence within the Chicago School itself remained negligible. But to tell a good story, tinged heavily with hinted at conspiracies and whispers down dark corridors, a kingpin has to either be found or forcibly constructed. Mirowski and Co seemed obsessed with Hayek (as they are also almost possessed by the impenetrable shadows cast the Mount Pelerin Society.). The elevation of all things Hayek comes without distinguishing, to any sufficient degree, between those events that shaped the impetus facilitating the creation of post war Chicago and those that occurred subsequently.

At odds with the story Team Mirowski weaves, Hayek never received entry into the Economics Department at Chicago, nor was he particularly welcomed there.[110] The *Road to Serfdom* did perform an almost MacGuffin style role in setting up the post war Chicago School, without simultaneously setting Hayek up with a leading economic role to play at Chicago. Difficultly in subscribing to Hayek's apparent apotheosis arises when attempting to pinpoint any direct subsequent influence Hayek might have exerted over those in the economics department during the subsequent decades.

> He [George Stigler] wasn't sympathetic to the Austrian approach … because I've heard him make remarks about some of them. He thought some of Hayek's stuff was good, particularly his work on knowledge and ideas. Other than that, I don't know if he thought so much of most of Hayek's philosophical stuff to tell you the truth. But he liked, respected Hayek. I can't remember any explicit conversations, but I think George felt these modern Austrians, what were they adding to what we knew about economics? I think he felt they weren't adding much to what we knew. Hayek's paper on knowledge was good. Schumpeter's theory of economic development he probably thought was good. I know he thought highly of Schumpeter (Conversation with Gary Becker, October 1997).

No indicative evidence that Team Mirowski is able to present, sufficiently supports their grand story that corporate dictation composed the backbone of research at Chicago. Their apparent desire is to tell an almost predestined story, one which has all necessary, individual components fitting ever so snugly together. Accepting the result, unfortunately, requires the necessity of either overlooking, or dismissing, a number of potentially random shocks that could easily have changed the face of the department. Thus an aura of inevitability is employed to virtually bury a number of decidedly unpredictable events.[111] To begin with, Lange could have remained at Chicago instead of going back to Poland, thus failing to create a departmental opening. That position seemed, at least initially, to be destined for Stigler rather than Friedman. Would that have made a difference, namely having Stigler in Chicago from 1946 and Friedman elsewhere?[112] Samuelson, who initially accepted an appointment to Chicago, could have actually returned to his old haunts on the South Side instead of backing out after a brief period of reconsideration. Certainly it is difficult to imagine that this would not have made a subsequent difference, including the distinct possibility of not having the Cowles foundation decamp to Yale.

To endorse the tale spun by Team Mirowski then it is essential to downplay anything that might be classified as a random event, while identifying research funding with an equivalent pay to play motif. Naturally, accepting corporate research money, or any funds linked to vested interests, raises a red flag. The ever present indication of a potential case of academic malfeasance can't be ignored. Yet, the only scholarly responsibility in this case seems to be a willingness to reveal such sources and allow others to evaluate the significance. Transparency should effectively dispel the suspicion of any tinge of corruption. Naturally, stories can be easily spun focusing on an assumed willingness to trim results and conclusions to meet the objectives of biased paymasters. In such cases, the researcher is often depicted as being motivated solely by narrow self-interest.[113] More realistically, though indirectly, if funded economists failed to please their underwriters, then additional funding would simply not be forthcoming.[114]

Essentially, in such cases the funder would be deemed to have chosen poorly in terms of achieving a preconceived objective. Therefore, research that can be attached to funding transactions should not automatically be deemed equivalent to a clear act of producing tainted analysis to fit a corporate budget. Again, Mirowski and Co appear to be taking a conscious leap from correlation to causation. Consequently, to simply condemn such activity on an *a priori* basis may implicitly display some discernible urge to blacken reputations by employing the process of association. In these cases, the brush is dipped deeply into the tar pit before slathering it over the selected target.

Experience, however, demonstrates that money will flow inevitably to those who display a certain preferred track record. But this expected result should be insufficient to conclude that anything resembling a corrupt linkage between parties has occurred. (On display are necessary, but hardly sufficient, levels of causation that would be required for any convincing finger-pointing to occur.) There are undoubtedly very few saints, and certainly not even many permanent inhabitants who might be construed as being pure of heart. At least this has proven to be the case among those that are recognised as working down in the mine pits of economic research. But even in a profession packed with morally constrained individuals, the mere fact of corporate funded positions should not automatically negate the work they accomplish. If only saints were effective operatives, little if anything would ever have been achieved within the discipline.

> I have already argued that within narrow limits these goals are compatible: the society wants and will benefit from increments of the objective knowledge of economic life. A few men actually adhere only to this type of work, eschewing all pronouncements on matters of current policy. ... These near-saints of scholarship are wholly unknown to the public, and not always well-known within the profession. Frank Knight was an approximate illustration of this rare type (Stigler 1976:353–354).[115]

The issue of culpability must remain one judged almost entirely by motives. Accepting corporate funds is no more equivalent to a guilty confession than accepting money from the non-neoliberal side of a political debate. Would Team Mirowski have expressed the same trepidations over a conference featuring eminent environmental economists financed by wealthy green donors? Would such a gathering underwritten by corporations like REI that sell camping and other outdoor equipment undercut the research accomplished by these economists? In both cases, funders might be profoundly disappointed if faced with a negative research outcome. Environmentalists quite obviously would be reluctant to ante up funds to well-known climate change deniers. That conclusion doesn't automatically imply that such backing fatally taints research produced with the assistance of corporate specific financial support. Suspicions may prove to be quite appropriate, but not to the degree where *a priori* judgments can legitimately drive conclusions. Otherwise, the use of broad classifications, added to a focus on supposedly damning aspects, deteriorate into a scavenger hunt for ways and means to demolish a despised opponent or ideology. Concurring with this approach, even implicitly, means allowing marketing notions to dominate careful analysis. Or, attempting to strike emotional, rather than intellectual, notes for ideological objectives.

In the same fashion, corporate interests have often shown an almost instinctual revulsion when faced with any government incursion that limits their business operations.[116] Simultaneously, numbers of economists have traditionally focused on the unintentional consequences of such government intrusions. Chicago, in particular, has specifically adopted this stance when evaluating the role that government is obligated to play. Consequently, corporate interests are prone to be magnetically attracted to

South Side economists. The theoretic disposition of such academics makes the links developed and formed highly predictable. Mutually fulfilling relationships of this kind should be entirely unsurprising. But though their existence is commonplace, such connections should not automatically be labelled as conclusively corrupt.[117]

Lacking any reliable evidence of dubious corporate connections, an able researcher like Eddie Nik-Khah (2014) still can't resist the allure of attaching nefarious implications to all such funded work. He indisputably turns up a goodly amount of circumstantial evidence, while prosecuting a case against what he terms 'neo-liberal pharmaceutical science'. (The analysis implicitly starts with a prejudgment of guilty as charged. Therefore, once classified as an offending neo-liberal, the analysis of Peltzman's work follows a well-worn path.)

Undoubtedly (and not unsurprisingly) the economic research in this area, as in many other corresponding regulatory environments, when performed by the denizens of Chicago, confirms an almost automatic tendency to label the status quo, over regulated. Such a result, is entirely to be expected given the operative tenets of the Chicago School. Unfortunately, in order to further demonise this expected result (tagging such analysis with the black tar of collusive guilt), Nik-Khah (2014) focuses on a single, long running pharmaceutical battle. He restricts his attention solely on the Federal Drug Administration's power to provide a green light for newly developed drugs. Expectedly, pharmaceutical companies inevitably judge the process to be unnecessarily convoluted and overly long. The lengthy procedure predictably eats into their corporate profits. These added costs provide them with more than a sufficient justification for hankering after speedier approval. Since an argument based on profits would be publically rejected (being more than a bit medically dubious), any convincing contention must centre instead on welfare considerations.

Consequently, the public must be demonstrably better off if the process is accelerated, allowing useful drugs to become market ready more rapidly. From a perspective moulded to fit this targeted conclusion, lives could inevitably be saved under such a revised regime. Equally, but not emphasized quite as readily by pharmaceutical companies, bringing drugs to the market without sufficient testing and documentation can also imperil lives. Subsequent pharmaceutical disasters historically abound. Think, to begin with, of the drug thalidomide and then start listing many other instances. There is no basis for leaning either way *a priori* without a sufficient supply of reliable research. Logic alone points decisively down neither avenue. Therefore, it should come as no surprise that major pharmaceutical companies would look to Chicago for validation. At a minimum, targeted funds inevitably flow only to those known to display an unshakable faith in the marketplace and a corresponding settled scepticism of government intervention. Pharmaceutical companies have their distinct objectives, meaning that they cannot be expected to fund research likely to be at odds to those aims. In this sense, the research completed by such economists would not be motivated by a deliberate attempt to seek financial advantage for pharmaceutical companies, but would be driven instead by an implacable belief that letting markets decide almost always yields public benefits.[118] Given this perspective, the reverse side of this belief would unquestionably assert that governments distort incentives and favour vested interests.

Thus critics are guilty of taking an unwarranted leap of faith when being reflexively dismissive of the work Chicago conducted in this area, if the justification for suspicion is solely the supposed taint of corporate money. These studies may be entirely off base, but rejection should be thoroughly grounded on the available evidence and analysis, not the character of the researcher.

It was with a spirit of defiance toward the FDA that on 4 and 5 December 1972, pharmaceutical corporations, clinical pharmacologists, legal scholars, and economists participated in the Conference on the Regulation of the Introduction of New Pharmaceuticals, held at the University of Chicago. … The Chicago School of Economics, which included not only the economics department but also the Graduate School of Business (GSB) and the Law School, were newcomers to pharmaceutical policy debates. Chicago scholars assumed primary responsibility for organizing the conference. Faculty advisors involved in drafting the conference proposal included Kenneth Dam, Harold Demsetz, Milton Friedman, Reuben Kessel, Richard Posner, and George Stigler. Stigler and Posner were especially important to the conference efforts. Stigler arranged for his former student Sam Peltzman to produce a paper on the 'costs' of the Kefauver–Harris Amendments, pledged funds from his Walgreen Foundation to finance Peltzman's research, and oversaw its progress; The purpose of the conference was not to carry out a balanced evaluation of the 1962 Amendments but to subject them to a multidirectional attack. For over a decade, the Chicago School had been the epicenter of skeptical studies of the 'governmental control of economic life'. It previously had placed electricity and securities regulation in its cross-hairs. Led by Stigler, Chicago scholars now turned their attention to pharmaceuticals. (Nik-Khah 2014:492).

The idea that Peltzman, for instance, simply served corporate, rather than ideological, ends runs counter to what can be deduced from his work and what he himself undoubtedly believes. "If that's what the evidence is, that is what it is and we have to, we *have* to, you know at the end of the day, if we are convinced that that is what the evidence is, that is the truth. Not our pride. Our pride is not the truth" (Conversation with Sam Peltzman October 1997). A position that assumes that those who take a Chicago-like stance deliberately dissemble in their work and pronouncements would seem difficult to prove in even a semblance of a convincing fashion. Instead, all that anyone determined to blacken an economist's character (using these diversionary tactics), can hope to accomplish is a simple piling up of circumstantial evidence. The most viable result of this process only encourages the additional construction of such cases. These ad hoc stories unfortunately have more in common with the sort of complex intaglios beloved by conspiracy theorists than solid evidence or reasoning. Trafficking in strained circumstantial denouncements share far too little with the more sober models that are widely subscribed to by the bulk of practising economists.[119]

Thus evaluating an economist's work via the agency of personal character smears seems to be a road best avoided. Those who commit themselves to such tactics may only be hoping to shift the terms of debate to more favourable ground. (Or, at the very least, distract the focus of discussion away from unfavourable elements.) In essence, character assassination can be substituted for a failure to effectively disembowel an objectionable theory. Otherwise, credence would unfortunately be granted to those who dismissed (and may still dismiss) John Stuart Mill as being simply entirely enthralled to, and mentally captured by, Harriet Taylor. (This diversionary tactic envisions Mill as a very unlikely, aging sex slave.) In a parallel fashion, the art produced by those possessing an unquestionably dubious character could, given this broad leeway, be permanently exiled without bothering to evaluate the work itself (Richard Wagner anyone?). An economist's character or motives may be an interesting line of inquiry (humans do love gossip and all things personal) without providing a shred of insight into a work itself.

But work done in the ever ambiguous field of History of Economic Thought should primarily focus on the work itself (as should any economic analysis). Ad hominins, or kitchen sink psychology, need not apply, or be deemed at all relevant. As the Chicago School would happily explain, motives (which remain unobservable) are impossible to deduce with any desired degree of certainty. The available observed evidence, and what can be usefully concluded from it, depends on the underlying work that produced it. Research isn't invalidated because it is conducted by a less than admirable individual, or group of individuals. In which case, the war waged so vigorously against neo-liberalism by Team Mirowski is not advanced by reducing Chicago ideology to the status of objectionable money grubbing. Equally, as will be shown, it is not enhanced by further derogation of character and motive, namely labelling Chicago's efforts as deliberately elitist and criminally anti-democratic.

> If however I saw data based on responses to questions like: 'How do you feel this morning? What do you feel about Richard Nixon? Did your wife and you have an argument this morning?' I don't pay attention to *that* kind of data. There is this definite bias in Economics. You see what people *do,* not what they say. Because, you can never competently judge their motives, or what is in it for them. [laughs] You've got to study their behaviour, pure and simple (Conversation with Sherwin Rosen, October 1997).

E. *Friedman is Just Another Word: Chicago and the End of Democracy*

> True there have been developments that have widened men's freedom, but most of these owe little or nothing to govt. & I believe you understate the extent to which freedom has been curtailed. The reason you do, I believe, is because the kind of freedom you & I think of have never been important to more than a small number of people and that kind of freedom has so far fared relatively well (Letter from Milton Friedman to George Stigler, September 1, 1965).

There exists an alternative policy story that might prove to be more accurate when examining the stated case of neo-liberalism. (Discounting the attempt to undermine the reputations of Chicago economists by hurling charges of corruption as broadly as possible.)[120] Offering this equally lethal perspective might even prove to be more effective in undercutting the claimed scourge of neo-liberalism. (Many, but not all, of these attempts aim to provoke more of an emotional, rather than rational response.) However, hewing to a more reasoned basis might involve focusing on the way in which the Chicago School fits into the post war modernist movement. The essence of this particular story is a decided dismissal and rejection of the Classical Liberal approach to economics, at least insofar as such lines of thought extend to methodological issues. In essence, this is an argument about the way that economics should be conducted. Such a methodological and historical break becomes particularly vivid in the case of Chicago, since those that drove the school's formation were carefully nurtured in exactly that traditional liberal mode of analysis.[121] However, the attention displayed in their work is not on how policies are derived, but on the nature of those policies themselves. As previously pointed out, Team Mirowski seems determined to delegitimise these neo-liberal proposals no matter what it may take to do so.

That may be why the dubious connection between theory and policy (creating policies for specific situations from generalised theories) might fail to catch their attention. For whatever reason, this particular critical highway is not one down which Team Mirowski cares to traverse. Not that their careful, fruitful research and scholarship doesn't lend itself to that particular twist, as well as other alternative investigations. But they seem uninterested in exploring the potential depths presented by their material. Mirowski and his associates at times seem unwilling to pursue their research at an arm's length level of examination. They find themselves instead distinctly repelled by Chicago promoted policies (and the attendant perceived damage which these have inflicted). The result of this almost subliminal repulsion has apparently generated an unfortunate outcome. They choose the more precarious route of closely targeting the personalities and tendencies of a set of selected economists, letting economic analysis to play, at best, a secondary role.[122]

As pointed out, Team Mirowski seem eager to display the personalities and individual frailties of their targets, rather than strictly limiting their critical gaze to the confines of theory and policy. Their work certainly is laser focused on undercutting and invalidating the scourge of neo-liberalism by whatever means possible. Assuming the role of medical diagnosticians, Team Mirowski has detected a perceived economic poison in the body politic. This polluted stream of policy projections is identified as composing the chief output that seeps relentlessly out of the Chicago South Side. Namely, they pinpoint a destructive political and social perspective that commenced at the dawn of the post war period. In their eyes, this neo-liberal chain reaction had left a decimated society in its wake, one which would require intensive and immediate remediation.[123] The recognition of these dire consequences then justifies whatever steps Team Mirowski deems to take to counter such a noxious movement.

Clearly Mirowski and his compatriots opt to sidestep the potentially flawed methodology that produces aberrant policy formulations. They forego this approach, although they deem such policies to be reprehensible, if not downright malignant. Instead, for whatever reason, they are drawn toward sullying the motives and the reputations of those that constructed the fundamental architecture of neo-liberalism.[124] Opting for this simpler alternative poses few strands of mystery. Instead of cutting their way through logical thickets, an easier critical path lies in simply unearthing evidence that these academic warriors operated as intractable ideologues. The argument here would be to connect such unshakeable tenets to an expected strain of bias running throughout their theories, positions and suggested policies. In effect, the claim would be that those at Chicago unintentionally biased their results due to what they adopted as their own exigent objectives.

But this remains yet another road untraveled. The path taken, diving into character assassination, remains a somewhat fraught (and not easily justifiable) option. Unhappily, Team Mirowski cannot hope to avoid an ineradicable problem by pursuing their more personalised strategy with such a single-minded determination. Continuing down a potentially explosive character driven critique is difficult without ultimately descending to the personal level. They seem to be inevitably drawn to employ what at best only skirts the tacitly forbidden region defined by *ad hominin* remarks. Despite all the potentially compelling reasons, why such an option should be almost universally rejected, Team Mirowski shows no reluctance in embracing, what a famous film labelled 'the dark side'.

Once such tactics are embraced without noticeable compunction, Team Mirowski feels comfortable in characterising the founding of the Chicago School (and the key players at the time) as irretrievably corrupt, if not fundamentally dishonest. In their considered estimation, what purports to be an academic enterprise, was born in (and continued to be wedded to) clear cut venality. Consequently, they perform like some reincarnated Bernstein and Woodward team, focused on cracking the veneer hiding a Watergate-style of malfeasance. To achieve the desired reveal, Team Mirowski relentlessly follow a perceived trail of suspicious grants and funds. The aim is to reduce the history of the Chicago School to not much more than a puppet show (or a distinctly Noh drama), by assuming the role of interpretive masters of the observed theatre. According to this interpretation, from its very inception, the Chicago agenda was not only funded, but shaped, by corporate largesse and corporate interests. These academics then were compelled, whether consciously or not, to perform as reliable mouthpieces for their financial backers.[125] Team Mirowski seems to intentionally shift its focus away from far more likely and otherwise thought provoking explanations. These more rational alternatives would avoid any dark hints of dubious conspiracy theories that figuratively involve midnight payoffs accessorised by black bags bursting at the seams with wads of corporate cash. But other approaches would be much drabber, lacking the same inherent fireworks, as painting them with the dark tar of corruption.

However, a perfectly adequate response to attacks of this nature has been sufficiently blocked out decades ago by George Stigler, one of Team Mirowski's true bêtes noirs. The Team might have benefited greatly by approaching such a paper with deadly seriousness. (This very point has been previously noted. However, the idea itself cannot be sufficiently repeated and emphasised.) The logic of Stigler's argument is certainly compelling and difficult to simply brush-off. Namely that there seems little need to openly bribe academics to take positions conducive to a given corporate agenda.[126] All a vested interest of any stripe or flavour would need to do is to locate the appropriate academic already espousing such preferred views. There is no discernible need for direct corruption.[127] In terms of integrity, no reputable economist, or certainly very few, is known to have directly shifted positions according to the whims of his or her current paymaster.[128] Vested interests then, find no need to explicitly corrupt (as opposed to exploiting) the varied grab bag of practicing economists. However, the very nature of the profession, one that encompasses a sufficiently diverse and divergent group, would allow any corporate interest to shop around for and find an appropriately matched view to champion their preferred position. Nor would it appear exceptional for an economist to fiercely market his or her honestly held viewpoint in order to gain such advantageous recognition. (The obvious bonus is the generous research funding such actions may attract.)

Each economist has a variety of views, and let us assume for a moment that they come directly from heaven or hell. Unless one of us is singularly narrow in his inventory of views, some of the views appeal to some people and some views to others, and the audiences to which they appeal vary widely in size. It would be astonishing if we did not cultivate those views which had the largest audience. Indeed, it would be difficult not to cultivate these views because they are precisely the views that one is asked most often and most remuneratively to expound. I will be asked on occasion to denounce regulatory bodies, which I can do with tolerable knowledge and adequate sincerity, but no one solicits my related views on the methods of granting of degrees by universities (Stigler 1976:347)[129]

Notwithstanding this obvious observation, Team Mirowski stubbornly persists in focusing on questions of character. In much the same way that Milton Friedman implicitly dismissed Keynes as a minor quantity theorist,[130] so does Team Mirowski reduce Chicago to a mere puppet show where the ventriloquist dummies tout the wares of their corporate masters. If the aim is to undermine Chicago as a bastion of neo-liberalism and its attendant evils, and by doing so question the legitimacy of that particular worldview, the end result is largely unsatisfactory. Evidence for this supposition, the strong hint that output, like tailored suits in Hong Kong, are produced to order, proves to be sadly lacking. Certainly, merely displaying the source of the discovered funding that underwrote the Chicago School's research is almost by definition insufficient, unless pure innuendo is accepted as reliable evidence.

Team Mirowski does deftly illustrate the fact that the funding behind the origin and growth of the Chicago School emanated from sources which Team Mirowski carefully label as 'dubious' and 'undesirable'. Not that the importance of those funds in financing the research and promotion of corporate friendly policies can be denied. That Hayek, Friedman, Stigler and others of that cohort actively sought these buckets of cash is painstakingly detailed without eliciting any real shock or surprise. Naturally, funds are more likely to flow to compatible sources. However, what is missing from this extensive financial detective work is any evidence of cause and effect, namely that the work produced was produced to corporate order. This is much more difficult to demonstrate since corporate sponsors would have almost automatically funded those whose work accorded best with their objectives. But as emphasized, this needn't reflect on the validity, or scrupulousness, of the research itself.

Team Mirowski might instead want to consider a counter-factual. Suppose Friedman's infamous helicopter money was to swoop over the University of Chicago, descend and hover first on top of the Economics Department and then at the Business School. In this fashion, the dream of each and every money hungry researcher (encompassing a considerable proportion of this population) would miraculously materialize. Unlimited and untied funds would then become available, so that each and every faculty member within these establishments could follow their hearts' desires (assuming that they were endowed with such an organ). Believing that under such conditions, Chicago's research output would somehow radically transform is a supposition that many observers familiar with the tendencies and follies of the institution might find difficult to swallow. (Even if this mouthful of pure assertion was lovingly coated in garlic aioli and mounted on a just baked, everything bagel.)

That corporate money did indeed flow to Chicago due to the School's research proclivities would be difficult, and entirely fruitless, to deny. However, the assertion that these economists slavishly tailored their output to placate the fiendish demands of their corporate masters seems an assertion resting on the folk inference of always finding fire in the vicinity of smoke. Sometimes the origin of that smoke is just a cheap cigar. In other words, this faith requires believing that corporate money equals corporate control, a claim seeming to lack any solid foundation. No such coercion would be required, given that both sides of the contractual arrangement held integral objectives. No need then to manipulate when the task is simply to locate congenial economists. Doing so would hardly prove to be an onerous task. Just as any politician can locate economists sympathetic to some given set of policies, so also can moneyed interests find similar supporters of their partisan views. In a sense, Team Mirowski is taking a proverbial leaf out of the Chicago strategy book. Chicago stalwarts, employing any means possible, sought to disqualify Keynesianism, identified as being imbued with a dangerous spirit of collectivism. In the same way, Team Mirowski, by employing similar strategies to drive a stake through the black heart of neo-liberalism, hopes to eviscerate an ideology the members see as impoverishing society.

F. *Sunshine Patriots – The Scourge of Subversive Doctrines*

Patriotism is the last refuge of the traitor (Samuel Johnson)

This aforementioned academic demolition derby, conducted as a no-holds-barred round-robin, proceeds by concocting a series of reputational charges against Chicago's master builders. Unfortunately, this concerted attempt by Team Mirowski seems to fall short of accomplishing the desired auto-da-fé of the neo-liberal creed. A desperate example of such exterminating tactics is displayed in their branding of George Stigler. From their deliberately eccentric perspective Stigler, and the economic framework he helped to develop and to which he adhered, is transformed into an elitist creed. He is charged with being at the heart of a movement that perversely devised a regrettably anti-democratic societal architecture. What makes this charge a touch ironical is that George Stigler, in his more casual essays (1963) and throughout his career (see his Tanner lectures (1981)), consistently charged intellectuals residing on the left as being haughtily imbued with an inbred sense of disdain for the common people they pretended to embrace. In essence, Stigler might have very well viewed the Team Mirowski attack as a classic case of projection.[131]

From Stigler's perspective, such self-selected tribunes of the left were guilty of thinking they knew what was best for people. But in fact, these self-styled crusaders were more interested in elevating their own self-importance.[132] Under this collectivist perspective (the supposedly benevolent gaze provided by a Nanny State), the working class became no more than the proverbial means to an end. However, just as such a broad based (and evidence deficient) claim was hardly inspiring when issued by George Stigler, levelling the identical charge against him turns out to be equally dubious.

> Departing from classical liberals, such as Henry Simons, *neo*liberals concluded that markets required political organization to be brought into existence, and required protection from the public to be maintained. To achieve these tasks, they became activists, which took multifarious forms during the ascendency of neoliberalism. Unlike classical liberals, they denied the strict separation of economics and politics. They sought to take over the state for the purpose of bringing into existence their version of an ideal market society and protecting it from the public. And neoliberals required a strong state to advance their program (Nik-Khah and Van Horn 2020:424).

Much of the support for this contention rests on a bit of archival legerdemain. A curious claim made in much of Team Mirowski's work on neo-liberalism is the sanctity of archival findings (or a curated set of such discoveries). Almost dismissed (and certainly awarded much less credence), is published work, or especially material that is generally categorised as oral history. The world through Team Mirowski style lenses is viewed in almost classic Japanese terms. All the published work that is most accessible is what the Japanese would term as *tatemae*, namely outside appearance intended to hide rather than explain. Archival work (especially that undertaken by Team Mirowski) uncovers the *honne* of such characters, the hidden reality reflecting true intent and meaning. They insist that readers can therefore rest assured in regards to Stigler's elitist, anti-democratic intent, based on one such excavated archival memo, which in their opinion effectively reveals this hidden truth. (Stigler had otherwise managed to keep such sentiments hidden in all his published work, talks, conversation, interviews and even offhand remarks. However, as in any detective novel, one fatal slip existed to be discovered.) An unstated assumption in this case demands that readers ignore the observed fact that Stigler was never known to filter any of his remarks. If it registered on his brain, even a passing idea flew immediately out of his mouth. Yet, somehow contrary to decade's long character traits, Stigler kept this one dark secret almost perfectly hidden.

> The goal was to undermine the ideal of the state governed by democratic consensus. In an unpublished memo, Stigler proposed that one way to address the democracy problem would be to contribute skeptical studies of democracy: such work would, in his words, "shatter the fond hopes of the scholarly professions." Many studies that fell within the "governmental control" project – studies of the determinants of the size of government, pressure group models, economic theories of political agency, historical studies of the origins of popular regulatory policies, to name but a few – served this end (Nik-Khah and Van Horn 2020:435).

Leaping feet first upon a convenient archival statement should not be regarded as discovering the equivalent of a Rosetta Stone, a code breaking device that unveils and unscrambles previously incomprehensible subterfuge. Making this assumption seems to be a practice that is unlikely to yield any durable insights, having instead a distinct tinge of being entirely self-serving. Even someone who could strive for intellectual consistency like Stigler, fails over a long career to continually strike one precise note in an unwavering manner. So it is hardly surprising, or shocking, to find, even among archival material, contradictory thoughts and statements. For the undemocratic charges to stick, a researcher would need to possess solid evidence that George Stigler was chronically duplicitous. Accepting such a conviction would entail dismissing all written works and interviews, especially those which run counter to a pre-sold hypothesis, as so much distracting camouflage. Doing so would appear to require quite an unwarranted leap, driven largely by an overly fervid imagination. Such assertions, alleged about Stigler's undemocratic designs, seem to indicate that this piece of archival evidence is to be accorded pride of place simply because it solidifies some preferred narrative. In essence, the approach boils down to the idea that everything other researchers thought they knew has now been proven wrong. Not an impossible conclusion, but one that is simply less than likely.

Consequently, little of value is gained by elevating one archival discovery to the status of a Stiglerian Rosetta Stone. Believing that a particular artefact, conveniently consistent with one's own preconceived view, is the heretofore lost key (capable of unlocking the hidden secrets of George Stigler's heart) seems more that a touch far-fetched. Archival material demands interpretation. Such analysis needs to be placed within a wider context. Otherwise you raise these documents to the same idealized platform on which Stigler placed empirical testing. Fetishizing one aspect of research, while dismissing all contrary evidence, will seldom yield reliable insights. Convenient bits of information will be clung to with the same desperate grasp awarded a life preserver in a stormy sea. In neither case (of idealising one single source of information) do the facts speak for themselves.

At best, archival material can provide an overview (or offer a few insights) of what happened, according to the viewpoints of those involved at that time. Such an approach does not necessarily deliver an appropriate why (or even a material what) determining the driving force behind a relevant set of events. There is an almost unavoidable sense conveyed that the material presented may have been cherry picked to fit a preconceived blueprint. Archives, like any other empirical data, can be viewed through the predetermined lenses of categorical necessity. But Team Mirowski maintains on principle that archival material, though seemingly not all such written components of that realm, reveals more than any careful analysis of other available published record.[133]

One of the reasons there has been so much confusion about the orientation of the Chicago School is that scholars and commentators have focused mostly on its members' published work. But it is necessary to look beyond the published work of individuals to understand economics imperialism – and, for that matter, to understand the Chicago School. This chapter draws from and synthesizes previous research that has made extensive use of such archival evidence, including private correspondences and unpublished manuscripts, to bring to focus often-overlooked dimensions of the Chicago School, and hence reveals the imperialistic motivations and forays of Chicago neoliberals (Nik-Khah and Van Horn 2020:424).

A major problem with this approach, lies in not really examining George Stigler's theoretical construction of what he conceived as composing the political market place. Either Stigler's actual position is ignored by Mirowski and his associates as not worth exploring, or simply dismissed as somehow deceptive. Stigler's actual work is interpretively tailored to the point where it projects a menace, but one that contains an intentional attempt to mislead the rest of the profession. Whatever the motivating aspect behind Team Mirowski's tactics may be, to declare Stigler or Friedman as undemocratic, for espousing a political marketplace bounded by self-interested individual decisions, remains an unjustified reach.[134] Fundamentally, such a perspective chooses to ignore what their documented stances actually seem to be, as well as the clearly differentiated positions they espoused in regard to public policy.[135] Especially in his later years, Stigler wrestled with what he would come to categorize as the paradox of legitimacy.

But he was very much concerned about how you could call something inefficient in the political arena. We do have a democracy, more or less, we have representative government. Then how can something that has been allowed to happen be inefficient? After all, that government has allowed some programs to go on and on, year after year. The sugar program was sixty years old, the anti- trust law was over a hundred years old by the time George died. If it reflects the public demand for it, how can we call it inefficient? I think *that* is part of the answer to your question 'what do we let the government do?' It's not an answer. It is something that he was worried about. Something he was thinking about. How to reconcile consumer sovereignty, or voter sovereignty, with his previous notions of inefficient government? Can we say this is illegitimate if the public wants it? Is that consistent with our extreme position on consumer sovereignty, which is that no matter what horrible things the public wants, as free market economists we can never question it. That's certainly one of the basic principles of neo-classical economics.

Consumer sovereignty is both the end of the story and the beginning. And we don't argue with the consumer, no matter how self-destructive these demands are or how inappropriate. Anyway, if you want consumers to be free to choose in the market place, how can we argue with them in the political arena where, in a sense, they are acting as consumers too? Well, in his last years he was writing frequently about this.[136] In any case, the problem of government was something George was giving a lot of thought to before he died. This is entirely different from looking at it from the old Adam Smith point of view, 'here's the proper role of government.' There was protection, for instance, the case for an army. Then during the next two hundred years we tried to decide whether Adam Smith was correct or if there was some category that we should take out or put in. George presented an entirely different view of it (Conversation with Claire Friedland, October 1997).

Stigler's position flows as a logical product of his adamantine conviction that market choice was essential to maintain liberty and freedom within any given society. If that sense of consumer sovereignty within the marketplace is extended to political democracy, then there is no real recourse, but to acknowledge the resulting outcome. In the same sense that Becker and Stigler (1977) argued that the preferences of consumers couldn't, or at least shouldn't, be judged, Stigler (1992), speaking as it were from the grave, conceded that the public will had to be dominant, no matter the perceived efficiency loss, or impact of the consequences. As a classic example, Stigler proposed that sugar subsidies, having been in place for more than 50 years, reflected the public will and an implicit approval of the resulting distribution of income. Though quite naturally, from the perspective of any economist (and certainly from Stigler's viewpoint) such subsidies remained incapable of any rational economic defence. Such a stance was completely understandable however, given George Stigler's almost compulsive need to be consistent and paste universality onto his structural framework.

No matter what difficulties might pertain to such a train of analysis, it can hardly be equated with elitism, or any dictatorial tendencies. Consumer sovereignty as the ruling tenet at both the economic and political level doesn't sound much like authoritarianism or even a close cousin.

Disagreement with Stigler is more than possible when focused on this constructed substratum of belief. Stigler's compulsive drive for theoretical consistency is clearly on display in this instance. However, to repeat, equating Stigler's intentions with a rock ribbed authoritarian tendency represents a leap dependent too heavily on limited and debatable evidence.[137] A critical stance in this instance doesn't require a corresponding thrusting of the rejected perspective into some maelstrom defined by fascism, or other debateable ideologies. In essence, the charge against Stigler is that he somehow camouflaged his authoritarian desires by insisting on the fundamental importance of individual choice. (On the surface, freedom of choice and dictatorial government doesn't appear to make for congenial partners.)

> There are people outside of Chicago who read him this way. With Becker it is even more powerful. It's all part of Becker's stuff about optimality and redistribution. Outsiders kind of read both of them as, 'This is kind of the senescence of the Chicago school. They have become toadies for big government, apologists for big government.' And I could see why. It is a really subtle kind of distinction we are making here between the two. But look, if you're going to regulate, conditional on wanting to redistribute income, I can't tell you that this is wrong. So, if I don't like it, if I tell you it's wrong, it has to be because I don't like the resulting redistribution (Conversation with Sam Peltzman, October 1997).

We are perhaps in danger here of entering a minefield that can only spottily distinguish between the realm of unintended (as opposed to intended), consequences. As conceived by Team Mirowski, the unintended consequences of the neo-liberal project may be judged as being unfortunately anti-democratic, a process fostering an undesirable degree of corporate power. (The increasing imbalance of income distribution registers as a co-distortion.) However, unless we are deliberately delving into the shadowland of hidden intentions, only by taking an imaginative leap can Stigler, Friedman or Director be charged with the sort of elitist label that Mirowski and his associates dangle enticingly over the work and efforts of the Chicago School.[138] Certainly following in Hayek's steps, the issue of information gained increasing prominence under the gimlet eyed watch of the Chicago denizens. Still, while determinately trying to transform the very nature of classical liberalism, the baby of consumer sovereignty remained snugly undisturbed, floating happily in the warm bathwater of

Chicago price theory. Difficult then to grasp how improved information flows necessarily contradict this cherished idea of consumer sovereignty, the supposedly indispensable yearning for freedom of choice. That Chicago saw one as a substitute for the other seems fanciful at best.

> Moreover, neoliberals revised their understanding of what markets accomplished. They praised markets not because they gave people what they wanted – that is, for their allocative properties – but instead for their purported epistemic virtues. They reconceived markets as information processors, which produced and conveyed knowledge. Indeed, they insisted markets were the most powerful information processors ever known to humankind (Nik-Khah and Van Horn 2020:426).

To re-emphasize, Team Mirowski displays an unfortunate proclivity for using the same, or at least similar, dubious tactics employed by those they choose to attack. Both Stigler (1963, 1975, 1982b, 1982c, 1989b) and Friedman wrote scathingly about the collectivist tendencies of intellectuals, the media and other self-regarding artists of varying talents and positions.[139] The irony then is that parallel tactics are repeatedly employed on both sides of the political spectrum. For instance, those cemented to the right of the political kaleidoscope can always find nefarious complicity and deliberate misrepresentation lurking in the mainstream media.[140] The proof (of such subsequent accusations) seems to lie in these spurned outlets stubborn refusal to echo conservative, or right-wing positions. (They don't simply broadcast what such listeners want to hear.) Further, for these righteously and fully bootstrapped conspiracy theorists on the right, these journalists wield deliberately sharpened hatchets aimed against right-wing attempts to uncover the truth. Within this idiosyncratic world view, the relevant targets (beloved by mainstream media) are directly dictated by those hidden corporate powers that surreptitiously pull the relevant purse strings.

Thus, for those denizens camping out on the right, rather than producing factual news, these selected information distorters produce output that is directed only toward influencing mass opinion into a prescribed set of channels. In quite an unfortunate, but similar manner, for Team Mirowski, the existence of the Mont Pelerin Society provides the needed skeletal framework over which they can weave convenient left wing fables. The Society is a gift, a gratuitous eureka moment that admirably serves to provide a reliable and consistent target for their wrath. The membership of so many Chicago types in the Mont Pelerin Society serves to clinch the proof for Team Mirowski. Again, guilt by association (tarring with the same brush) replaces logic and evidence. So many right wing ideologues meeting together must by definition, spend their time weaving democracy throttling conspiracies. From this perspective, analysis is reduced to the proposition that nefarious types enrol in nefarious organizations.

Curiously, they adopt a similar Chicago technique in finding collectivist plotting and conspiracies wherever they might cast their glance. (This becomes reminiscent of the McCarthy era idea of 'Reds under the bed'.)[141] The Mont Pelerin group becomes the embodiment of an elitist and undemocratic collective dedicated to transforming society so that it closely reflects their own narrow objectives. The targeted organization, the fount and breeder of the neo-liberal prescript, is depicted in a fashion that dragoons this group into becoming a collectivist conspiracy resembling Ian Fleming's black hearted SPECTRE organization. As sketched, the Swiss assemblage lacks only the chilling figure of a Hans Stavro Blofeld, inevitably accompanied by his white cat happily purring with something of a sinister hiss (the cat, not Blofeld). For Team Mirowski, a mysterious and secretive collective (secluded behind an opaque and purposely distorted curtain) pulls the real operative strings of power. Neutered marionettes, such as Milton Friedman or Friedrich von Hayek, are mere diversionary figures.

> Consider Angus Burgin (2012), who tries hard to elevate Milton Friedman as the last great Mont Pelerin intellectual leader, which in our view gets things exactly backwards. Friedman was the fox, not the hedgehog, making strategic arguments in the short term with little concern for long-term vision or consistency. ... Burgin misses the ways in which Friedman, just like Hayek, regularly put himself at the service of the larger group and the common neoliberal cause, mediating between competing camps ... Not the individual intellectual giant, the paladin of collective individualism, but rather the organizational secretary and the political fixer at the service of the networked collective (Mirowski and Plehwe 2015:xiii).[142]

Again, Team Mirowski mimics Chicago style tactics in adopting a perspective paralleling a simplified Marxist approach, one which insistently denies the effectiveness of all individual efforts. For Chicago denizens, individuals merely respond to market imperatives, just as in simplified

Marxism. Outcomes can reflect no more than the underlying class conflict. In this scenario, individuals act only reflexively. (In each case, categories of individuals respond reflexively to sets of given incentives.) Team Mirowski indicts those denizens of the Chicago School as composing only a pale reflection of the (implicit) collectivist, neo-liberalism promulgated by the Mont Pelerin Society. The defence of freedom espoused by the Society is no more than a ruse covering its authoritarian leanings. (In essence, it provides an academic façade that bestows legitimacy upon its parent organisation.) As the dark, obfuscating screens fall before our eyes, Team Mirowski is now in a position to indict the global conspiracy lurking behind a phantasm of respectability. Yet the case for this conclusion (Chicago reflecting the will of Mont Pelerin), seems flimsy, given that neither Stigler nor Friedman seemed to view the Society in exactly the same reverent manner as Team Mirowski.[143]

Though offered as an evidence backed opinion, the Team Mirowski judgment appears to clash directly with an opposing view, one openly expressed in the 1970s by the supposed pawns of the Society. From this Chicago perspective, the very organisation supposedly plotting the right-wing counter-revolution, the erstwhile vanguard defending against all and any leftist tendencies, had come to no longer actually serve a viable, or at least a definitive, purpose. This piece of archival evidence would appear to run counter to the Team Mirowski theme. In that story, the invisible might of the Society incubated and nurtured an irrepressible battalion of neo-liberal missionaries. These warriors continued to work (through the decades) as one unified thought collective to flatten any opposition. They were determined that their commonly conceived goals would triumph (a sort of Jesuit battalion of the twentieth century). Unfortunately, such a striking conclusion remains, at the very least, debatable and perhaps indefensible.

> I would like to say, however that you attribute more unanimity and influence to the Mont Pelerin Society than I do. I should also add, I suppose, that Friedman and I both urged the termination of the Society with the present meeting but were over-ruled by a large proportion of past officers. I have confidence, therefore, that although some of us are surely wrong, some of us are surely not doctrinaire (Letter from George Stigler to Bertrand de Jouvenal May 1, 1972).

Evidence then needs always to be evaluated carefully, since it never speaks for itself. The issue is not only the meaning and intent a given piece of evidence conveys, but which bits you choose to polish and present, as opposed to those that are tossed back into the sea of undifferentiated data. The tendency is to privilege those items that support a preconceived case. Thus it is far from difficult to trip over the line supposedly separating analysis from conspiracy theories. The issue is not to question the willingness of Team Mirowski to avoid this trap. The focus instead should be on whether (in their eagerness to convict the Chicago School of the same malfeasance they attach to neo-liberalism), conclusions are weighted to tip the scale. Team Mirowski's opinions on the matter are clear, but the ability to fearlessly evaluate one's own work may be rarer than many individuals are willing to admit. "The necessity of distinguishing the building of a thought collective devoted to politics from a conspiracy theory is one major theme of this volume" (Mirowski 2015:449).[144]

Consequently, they feel compelled to brand the Mont Pelerin Society as more than an organization devoted to changing political opinions. Although, Team Mirowski would undoubtedly shy away from territory that too closely borders the irresponsible region defining paranoid conspiracy theory. Unfortunately, too much of Team Mirowski's research carries the distinct viewpoint (or at the very least conveys a suspicious slanted whiff), that would gleefully reduce the Society to being no more than a corporate front. In essence, a society that is no more than an academic styled ornamentation hiding its true workings, machinations and objectives. Uncovered by Team Mirowski is the Society's supposed wilful role as no more than a financial sycophant promoting big business. Corporate money consequently becomes the lifeblood underwriting the ongoing campaign of societal transformation. The revealed purpose of its strivings is one that has for decades sought to germinate and bolster a strategy that plasters a beneficent face onto the goals of naked, vested interests. The result of such conscious plotting (backed by unlimited financial flows) has successfully transformed neo-liberalism from a fringe obsession into an accepted, and even dominant, ideology. Money, not compelling logic, provides the origin of neo-liberalism's success.

To combat this evil (not unlike the urgency felt by those at Mont Pelerin opposing collectivism from the left) Team Mirowski seem not at all unwilling to traffic in character assassination, as previously described. Thus the messenger, as well as the message, is demonized (again reminiscent of the Chicago approach). Upon searching this output, we can easily recognize an inability to avoid rehashing some standard tropes often used to damn Chicago style neo-liberalism. Team Mirowski cannot, for instance, resist the siren call, if only in passing, of connecting Friedman with Pinochet's Chile.

> One notorious incarnation of the neoliberal double truth doctrine was the participation of numerous MPS members and affiliates in the coup that toppled the elected government of Salvador Allende in Chile in 1973. Milton Friedman spends a good chunk of his autobiography attempting to excuse and explain his actions away (Mirowski 2015:445).[145]

Without trying to excuse any of Friedman's choices, clarification identifies the fact that such a broad brush approach muddles, rather than clarifies the relevant issues. (As previously mentioned in the last chapter, tarring with the same brush should automatically set off alarms.) For Chicago, Chile was Arnold Harberger's pet project, not Friedman's.[146] Certainly Friedman visited and provided his usual, one-size-fits-all macro-policy advice.[147] But that is not equivalent to supporting or outright condoning Pinochet's transgressions and the horrors attached to his regime. From his own perspective, Friedman was basically a missionary fired by a fervent belief in market fundamentalism. Like any engaged (if not enraptured) missionary, he travelled enthusiastically throughout the world, spreading his gospel to whatever economically benighted part of the globe would be willing to host him. (This need to evangelize, probably extended to supermarket openings, or to wherever needy groups of the unenlightened were gathered.)

Accordingly, in the seventies he would pop up in South Africa, as well as various communist countries, in his attempt to battle what he saw as the forces of economic ignorance. He firmly believed that unlocking economic growth provided the opening for individual liberty. In his defence, it is not entirely unreasonable to cite the transitions of South Korea and Taiwan from the restrictions of an authoritarian (if not dictatorial) state to more open democracies. Both these cases rode the wave of economic prosperity. It may also be useful to note that despite whatever Friedman's true feelings might have been, he did not openly applaud the regressive governments he visited. This position contrasts with those of economists like Joan Robinson who did not stint in her praise of Mao and the Cultural Revolution. (Earlier examples of the leftist tendency to praise the Soviet Union, or those on the right who saw Nazism as a welcomed wave of the future, transgressed far more than the worse efforts of Milton Friedman.)

For both George Stigler and Milton Friedman, markets promoted consumer sovereignty.[148] It is possible (and almost inevitable) to take issue with the sort of choice and individual freedom such opportunities provide. But the policies they pursued and promoted do not automatically convert to a belief in, or support for, some variety of elitism or even an attempt to buttress anti-democratic tendencies. Thus statements that Team Mirowski dredge up and highlight to support their case are more ambiguous than they perhaps hope. In fact, such evidence seems instead to be reassuringly uncontroversial, sentiments that rouse little suspicion of any pronounced elitist tendencies.

> Let's be clear, I [Milton Friedman] don't believe in democracy in one sense. You don't believe in democracy. Nobody believes in democracy. You will find it hard to find anybody who will say that if, that is democracy interpreted as majority rule. You will find it hard to find anybody who will say that at 55% of the people believe the other 45% of the people should be shot. That's an appropriate exercise of democracy … What I believe is not a democracy but an individual freedom in a society in which individuals cooperate with one another (Friedman quoted in Mirowski 2015:445).[149]

Thus to conclude for instance that seeing markets as an efficient processor of information somehow precludes or lessens the perspective that markets effectively provide individual consumers with what they want seems baseless. For Stigler or Friedman, markets were grounded in consumer sovereignty because they were the institutions, or mechanisms, most capable of efficiently processing information and in this sense linking buyers with the appropriate sellers. Nor does the insistence that individuals, rather than the collective State, tend to be more aware of what their needs and wants might be, automatically reek of anti-democratic tendencies. Consequently, the bite of Team Mirowski's accusation seems largely toothless.

> Moreover, neoliberals revised their understanding of what markets could accomplish. They praised markets not just because they gave people what they wanted – that is, for their allocative properties – but instead for their purported epistemic virtues. They reconceived markets as information processors, which produced and conveyed knowledge. Indeed, they insisted markets were the most powerful information processors ever known to humankind (Nik-Khah and Van Horn 2020:426).

G. *All That's Brillig Isn't Wabe: The Importance of Checking Your Ideology at the Door*

And hast thou slain the Jabberwock?
Come to my arms, my beamish boy!
O frabjous day! Callooh, Callay!
He chortled in his joy (Lewis Carroll).

Without pushing our analysis too far, it might be fair to say that Mirowski and Company display a certain definite fondness for occasionally indulging in the sport of castration, at least when confronted by a particular nemesis.[150] For his part, George Stigler seems also to have enjoyed the frisson provided by demolition derby when battling with (what he deemed to be) unredeemable nonsense. Almost coincidentally then, the steps taken by Team Mirowski manage to often image, or at least are closely reminiscent of, those taken by their avowed Chicago opponents. Consequently, like many other economists, they prove to be not entirely averse to crossing (if only sporadically) the line that should always separate careful, critical analysis from its bastard brother, namely reading with an intent to destroy.

Upon examination, Mirowski and his associates fail to adequately resist this enticing alternative when launching their attacks. They instead, eagerly take a series of calculated, tactical steps. Initially, to shape any further discussion, they create a simplified version of the Chicago research program. This carefully staged drama produces a deliberate identification of these neo-liberal economists as being no more than corporate apologists. All the mountains of research and theory produced by this South Side Empire is instead boiled down to one fundamental slogan, namely the categorical imperative commanding government to 'let corporations run free'. In essence, Team Mirowski delivers a stripped down theory generating a simple policy.

The next step assayed is to follow up by questioning and exploring the possible motivations that might induce such a controversial stance. It is at this juncture that Team Mirowski relies on the tried and true backbone of economic explanations, the universal drive to focus strictly on individual self-interest. By closely following this one unwavering pole star, the denizens of Chicago are inevitably transformed into corporate flacks, at least according to Team Mirowski. The conclusive hammer blow is now ready to fall. Define narrow self-interest as equivalent to amassing mounting sums of money, and the integrity of these academics is cooked. From this perspective, Chicago, thirsting after corporate funding to prop up their research, insured that their considerable output mirrored the wishes of these corporate sources. To the charge then that their paymasters controlled these Chicago puppets, the verdict brought in by Team Mirowski is 'guilty as charged'. In essence, they paint a picture in which Chicago provided a respectable academic front for corporate objectives. Therefore, the neoliberal theory produced by such corrupt individuals can simply be dismissed out of hand. Demonstrating that the associated authors were deeply corrupt automatically invalidates any of their work, if we accept this line of argumentation.

The almost transparent sleight of hand here is that this bit of categorisation allows an abrupt dismissal of any argument, while failing to perform any of the heavy lifting attached to diving deeply into a specific work. Only a willingness to consider work with something resembling an open mind can yield useful insights. Needed is an understanding that critically it is necessary to first gain a thorough understanding of a given work before focusing in on any perceived flaws. Instead, complex articles are simply given the boot by identifying the author's name with some recognised category of thought. Then again, when attempting to disembowel a work, the sole reason for even momentarily shifting attention to an opponent's intent is essentially a search that locates and constructs a method for destroying those theories and articles. Although here it is necessary to backtrack and remind any persistent reader, once again, that the insidious tradition described is far from specific to the one example employed in this chapter, or to the researchers named. Finding other suitable candidates, also guilty of displaying this urge to destroy, rather than understand, opponents would pose no problem. All too many reputable and honoured economists have engaged in this pastime before and will continue to do so in the future. What has been presented is not a specific cancer, but a plague common to the profession as a whole. Ultimately it serves to hinder, if not effectively impede, understanding and communication within the discipline.

With this in mind, it should by now be somewhat clear that Team Mirowski's problems arise whenever a similar effort is channelled to irrigate unrelated environments. Simply put, an author's work is hijacked to foster preconceived ideas and purposes. In essence, the associated obfuscation is attached to work that is repurposed to serve an ulterior goal, work that is even deliberately misread. As an example, a misreading (or multiple misreadings) of the classics of economic literature is certainly nothing new or unorthodox. Everyone implicitly conveys the appearance of understanding these classic works and authors seemingly by osmosis alone. Over the years, an almost impregnable oral tradition has developed within the profession of adorning research with a limited smattering from the classics of economic literature. A certain degree of faux wisdom and authority can be attached in this fashion, much as a model might employ a touch of rouge to draw attention to her cheek.

The overall goal would seem to be mainly in service of advancing a slate of fixed and prior objectives. Thus it is not so much what economists don't know in a given situation, but rather what they think they know, which turns out to be fatally flawed and without support from the relevant text itself.[151] Unfortunately, people are inevitably influenced by what they have already been told or have read, especially if that action has been performed repeatedly.[152] Consequently they find, if they in fact deign to explore the relevant material, exactly what they expect to discover. This result holds almost uniformly, even if they happen to be among the minority that have made the attempt to diligently read the works that they supposedly have mastered.

An associated conundrum then arises when any such type of dominant oral tradition controls professional discourse. All widely accepted judgments of a given well-known work become buttressed over time to such a degree that even careless opinions slip into the category of certain knowledge. The view then becomes impregnable, even when confronted by any counter evidence, no matter how seemingly indisputable. Thus in this comfortably created universe, Adam Smith promotes untrammelled laissez faire and Keynes places the cause and blame of economic recessions on downward sticky wages. These polished bits of supposed knowledge make the actual words and thoughts of these authors virtually irrelevant. Against these oral traditions, and insights of the lecture hall, there exists absolutely no venue of reasonable redress. We have then reached, within the profession, an inevitable cul-de-sac, where no conceivable argument or textual evidence could possibly sway the minds of economists, or erase a multitude of ingrained prejudices.

But when History of Thought is undertaken or employed, something worse than mental laziness may dominate the best of intentions. Work of this type can become unintentionally hijacked to serve unacknowledged ideological purposes. To promote a favoured party line, or destroy an opposing measure, researchers may interpret a given text in a conveniently damning manner. What in fact is ironical in Team Mirowski's efforts, is the way in which their chosen methods unintentionally mimic the patterns of what they so ostentatiously abhor. The strategy employed when examining the Chicago School, parallels the tactics deftly used by the very neo-liberal ideology these authors so gleefully attack. The issue here is not whether what they label as neo-liberalism is as corrosive as claimed. Nor does the problem lie with the evidence they unearth. There is no suspicion of any intentional altering, or of some deliberate shaping, of what they meticulously produce. On the contrary, much of what is displayed reflects the efforts of careful and assiduous scholarship.

The problem rather stems from an unfortunate, but perennial handicap. Namely that solitary facts remain incapable of speaking for themselves. In this case, the details Team Mirowski have unearthed, too often seem to have been pressure fitted to a pre-existing ideological mould. The result is a presentation that edges uncomfortably close to the structure beloved by conspiracy theories, as they proceed to exert every effort to force all available evidence to form a suitably malevolent picture. However, framing this purposive effort as a positive exercise would seem to prove difficult if not nearly impossible.

The implication is that any practicing economist, should consider the importance of seriously investigating the validity of any given piece of research. The easier option is always tempting and all too available. That alternative involves simply dismissing uncongenial research as no more than corrupt outpourings. In essence, refuting opposing theories by asserting that their sole goal is to gain or maintain financial support for their research projects. The regrettable assumption promoted in this case, is that research is no more than paid for propaganda (constructed to order), for corporate funders. But the source of funding provides little, if any, evidence that the research itself is a simple extension of some corporate agenda. Funds will naturally flow to those economists whose work supports the funder's preconceived interests. Given the range of positions defining the profession, there is really no need to pre-order or even dictate results. A limited amount of investigation will simply locate the relevant economist that fits the bill. So that it would appear to be an unwarranted leap to suppose that research was simply tailored at the behest of these anonymous (or not so anonymous) corporate overlords.

Serving interests that share a common world view need to be distinguished from the more primitive role of a media flack, someone whose primary aim is to spin events and evidence according to corporate wishes.[153]

The assumption of tarring a given group of economists with a corporate brand, even if not explicitly enunciated, is a ploy notable for its inherent cynicism and perhaps even its dollop of duplicity. Targeting corporate complicity might be an obvious move to make, but not when based on highly circumstantial, even if readily available, evidence. When such evidence is more carefully examined, the only supportable conclusion is likely to be one that is far more complicated. Namely, that the way in which these designated Chicago people saw the world, and comprehended it, was simply diametrically opposed to the way that Team Mirowski construct their own understanding. They obsessively viewed the world from the opposite ends of a telescope. This idea of conflicting perspectives is not immediately intuitive, unfortunately. Our natural impulse is to extrapolate fundamentally, if not exclusively, from our own mind set, rather than imagining alternatives.

Team Mirowski has done interesting and valuable work, but ultimately they fail to vanquish the tendency to promise more than they are able to deliver. There is still a tinge of the pejorative in their presentation.[154] Mirowski and his associates often seem to share the same dangerous proclivity that they are eager to attach to the neo-liberal enterprise. They make a complex world so simplified that readers achieve only an illusory, but deceptive set of pre-digested convictions. Even those who dabble directly in the field of economic thought are only academic researchers, neither knights in shining, nor even rusted, armour. These academics should exist as discussants rather than single-minded warriors. Our prime responsibility then is not to transform or set the world aright. Moreover, the idea that a trial by combat yields either something resembling the truth (or a verisimilitude of justice), remains at best fanciful, unless we are willing to believe that the victorious lance is guided by a beneficent Almighty. But such a state would be equivalent to a land where law courts exist solely to mete out the fruits of justice, instead of performing as an umpire in a series of zero sum contests. Courts exist instead as a locale where the best and most convincing story teller may emerge victorious.

Ideally, those toiling in the rocky fields of economics should provide a meticulous explanation of what a specific economist thought and perhaps why he or she was led to such a set of conclusions. Only once such an analysis is firmly anchored (in all of the individual's actual work and thoughts), does it perhaps become appropriate to evaluate any weaknesses within that particular framework. The idea is to understand a particular work, not to exterminate the individual who constructed it. Economists are not members of a pest control unit. Agreement with one's subject is not a requirement, but a reasonable level of respect might be necessary to avoid the worst excesses of pre-judgment and polemics.

The object then of this chapter has been to explain the potential shortcomings of weaponising economic analysis. What appears here is only a case study, which attempts to encapsulate the problem. The intention is not to target (or offend), any specific group of economists or to belittle their premises. (Though I suppose that is an almost inevitable by-product.) A specific, and thus designated, economist may provide a useful example of such a problem, but it is hardly unique to that chosen individual. To once again emphasize the underlying theme, "The trouble with people [economists] is not that they don't know but that they know so much that ain't so" (Josh Billings). Accordingly, the need to market one's views, for reasons legitimate, or less so, can come to dominate in all fields of economics. This trend leads to a tendency to muddle, rather than clarify pending issues.

> Part of it is the persuasion. There's no question. George Stigler, I remember when I was a young person, wired and said 'Selling is very important in your research. So write better. Work on writing because that is important. You've got to sell what you are doing.' I think he's exactly right. You've got to sell what you are doing. It may be that in the long run good ideas do surface but they surface faster, if written in a persuasive fashion. Moreover, bad ideas may be put persuasively. And they may gain the necessary threshold. However, taking that same analogy in competition among ideas, there is a presumption, although not a certainty, that in the longer run, the good ideas are going to compete out the bad ideas. But that may take a long time and may not even always operate. There's nothing necessary about that. Nothing guaranteed about that (Conversation with Gary Becker, October 1997).

The last word then should go to one of the prime targets of Team Mirowski's ire. The link between George Stigler, the Chicago School and what Team Mirowski shuns as neo-liberalism is foolish to deny.[155] However, the seamy side, with distinct whiffs of dark conspiracy, puts these competent (and in many ways admirable), economists on shakier grounds. Stigler himself, in one of his all too rare bouts of self-awareness, perhaps comes closer to the underlying problem. It would seem reasonable to agree with Stigler that economists, for the most part, do not change their views to suit special interests. Economists are not especially venal, but they are human, as even George Stigler was forced periodically to admit. They have egos that need stroking and they nurture *a priori* beliefs, even when these are unacknowledged (or unrecognized), by those who hold them.

> But on the other hand, the motives that drive them and me are not completely clear, either. When we strive to solve a scientific problem, is ambition for our own professional status completely overshadowed by our love of knowledge? I wonder. When we write an article to demonstrate the fallacies of someone else's work, is our hatred for error never mixed with a tiny bit of glee at the display of our own cleverness? I wonder. (Stigler 1963:92)

Endnotes

1   Those familiar with the never-ending BBC series, *Dr Who*, will immediately recognize the Daleks as a strange race of self-propelling, canister-like vacuum cleaners. They persist collectively through the many incarnations of The Doctor as his inveterate foes. A distinguishing characteristic of this group-think race is a propensity, when launching a vicious and unprovoked attack, to chant 'exterminate, exterminate, exterminate' in a mindless (and tuneless) unison. To then glimpse the obvious parallel between the Daleks and those writing with a distinct and bloody minded 'intent to destroy' should not require any great leap of the imagination.

2   This reluctantly written initial section is essentially a required slice of irritating prologue. Quite correctly, Hamlet disdains the use of such prologues as both unneeded and unwanted. Such displays in his opinion are warranted only by a desire to spoil the play itself. ("The players cannot keep counsel; they'll tell all" (Shakespeare1963:103.) These garrulous exhibitions intrude into any narration as essentially a dutiful, but rather tiresome, explanation preceding the gist of an article's central argument. Prologues can consequently operate as an acknowledgment that the author may be confronted by potentially careless (or even hostile), readers. These bits of initial folderol then are introductions that have managed to forcefully intrude their presence, without the courtesy of first receiving a proper invitation. They exist more as a makeshift clarification device than as an incisive set of required comments. In the current instance, they simply exude a reluctant recognition that a lurking danger may be attached to how this specific article might be understood.

The problem lies in the unfortunate fact that merely mentioning the name of Philip Mirowski seems to overcome any more balanced or reasoned response on the part of many readers. The focus of discussion tends to become forcefully diverted onto distinctly alien grounds, or at least that tendency is effectively exaggerated. (Mirowski seems to have achieved, through no particular fault of his own, the unenviable position of being one of the profession's personalized Voldemorts.) To repetitively emphasize here, as well as in later passages, the actual focus, or even peripheral spotlight, is not on Mirowski, the individual and noted economist. To be blunt, the chapter is not at all intended to be about Mirowski. If the name somehow manages to distract any readers, they are welcome to substitute the name Smith, Jones, or Voldermort. Nor is there any intent exhibited, indicating a desire to read his work with an intent to destroy his conclusions, or disparage his perspective. By making this caveat clear, the hope is to ward off a repeat of previous problems I've encountered. Communication cul de sacs have unfortunately formed whenever I have struggled to present some of the ideas incorporated in this paper. Namely, that at least some members of any given audience seem determined to object to an entirely illusory, but in their minds apparently savage, personal attack on the work, life and times of one Phillip Mirowski. (At least their minds became distracted and locked into the nonissue of whether the supposed criticism of Mirowski was valid.) Clearly, sensitivities are easily trodden upon and attention spans quickly distracted. Consequently, knowing that readers are prone to 'miss the concept' (and go trundling down deserted spur lines instead), I am trying my best to flag that danger before the opportunity to misstep arises.

> Rose Friedman: You know, they don't simply say 'that's just my theory that's being demolished' and I'm not going to take this personally.
> Aaron Director: That's not surprising. That's about what I would expect. If people's views are being demolished, they don't like it. They don't say 'oh well, it's just my view' (Conversation with Milton Friedman, Rose Friedman and Aaron Director, August 1997).

Needless to repeat, the issue raised in this paper is intended to focus entirely on a method commonly deployed in economics. No distinctive interest was ever exercised, or intended, concerning any aspect of Mirowski or his work. (As far as I can ascertain, not a shred of personal animosity exists between the two of us. I find much of his work thought provoking and valuable.) In contrast to existing as a type of thumbnail biographical sketch, a case study is meant to be illustrative of a specified issue, rather than a unique instance of it. Consequently, care was taken (perhaps ineptly), to point out that weaponising critical thought, was far from exclusive to Philip Mirowski. Many other authors over the centuries have similarly indulged in such trespasses, including one of Mirowski's own targets, namely George Stigler. My choice of Mirowski and his associates has been based solely on the appropriateness of the example, assisted by my knowledge of all things Chicago. Nor am I attempting to judge others from a supposed position of superiority. I can't honestly insist that my own articles (when it comes to including weaponising arguments) have never wandered over the line and into personal intrusiveness. There is after all, a most permeable barrier (one that is often hard to discern), separating criticism of a specific work from less warranted personal attacks. The ability to resist launching Stigler style zingers often crumbles at the most inappropriate moments. (Being pleased with one's own cleverness is a common academic weakness.)

> Milton Friedman: Those who studied or worked with him have one view and everybody else has another. There's nobody in the world that could make smart cracks faster than he could.
> Rose Friedman: He had a tremendous wit. And it was usually at other people's expense.
>
> *It seems that, sometimes, he didn't know when to pull back.*
>
> Rose Friedman: Yes, basically he really didn't mean to offend people.
>
> *It seems like he just couldn't help himself.*
>
> Rose Friedman: That's right.
> Aaron Director: Who could've with his ability to make wisecracks?
> *Rose Friedman*: He learned after a while.
> Aaron Director: I don't know (Conversation with Milton Friedman, Rose Friedman and Aaron Director, August 1997).

The fact that the practice is conceded to be widespread should sufficiently deflect any potential categorization of the article's intention as being an attack on Phillip Mirowski. In fact, it is quite possible to admire someone's work, but still find him or her guilty of indulging in this unjustified pastime. Even more narrowly, such a reaction constitutes an obsessive response (certainly overly defensive) to employing just a sliver of Mirowski's work as a clear exemplar of a specific problem. But deploying a distorted interpretation that focuses on Mirowski alone, tends to also overlook the fact that this chapter targets, again merely as an illustrative device, not just the tactics sometimes favoured by Mirowski. The argument also covers research fashioned in various combination with authors like Robert Van Horn and Eddie Nik-Khah. (The set of articles, not the authors are what remains of fundamental importance.) Yet, the simple utterance of the name, 'Mirowski' seems capable of sucking the air out of any serious discussion. Perhaps this reaction best conveys the controversial nature of Philip Mirowski's reputation, rather than the intention characterising this particular article. However, the sole interest generated by Mirowski in the following pages lies with those objectives closely associated only with a subset of his employed methods, not with the grand scheme of his work. These flawed approaches, found occasionally in Mirowski, are of interest to the degree to which they are representative of a more widespread problem occurring broadly, throughout economic analysis. Again, as the article will insist, the intention is not to evaluate any specific or broader confabulation of Philip Mirowski's contribution to the discipline. Unfortunately this clarification, which strenuously insists that the focus isn't and was never intended to be on Mirowski, may almost inevitably have the exact opposite effect on some readers. Careful scrutiny of a text is a hard earned skill, rather than a natural endowment shared by the vast majority of the profession.

3   For those readers who are not ancient Americans, 'Pogo' was a satirical comic strip appearing between the years 1948-1975. (Hard as it may be to believe, Americans have been known to successfully dabble in satire.) The strip, set in the Okefenoke Swamp, featured the eponymous 'Pogo', an opossum, and his associated swamp creatures. The strip bravely satirised McCarthy, the Red Scare, and The John Birch Society in the 1950s, as well as communist figures. The most famous quote, as voiced by Pogo himself was, "We have met the enemy and he is us."

4   The issue is not whether such careless (and even destructive) types of reading occur, but why it does and why the practice continues to be so prevalent. One obvious reason was succinctly formulated by Spinoza, centuries ago:

> I know, too, that the masses can no more be freed from their superstition than from their fears. Finally, I know that they are unchanging in their obstinacy, that they are not guided by reason, and that their praise and blame is at the mercy of impulse. Therefore I do not invite the common people to read this work, nor all those who are victims of the same emotional attitudes (Spinoza 1998:8).

This characterisation would seem to be far removed from the more ethereal realm wherein academics claim to dwell. Their very essence, what their vocation demands, is to avoid uninformed, emotional responses. Yet, if ideology is substituted for emotion and impulse, reason once again fails to dominate. As with the foolishly superstitious, those guilty of this failing are not necessarily conscious of their shortcomings. Thee intent here is only to examine the all too frequent academic habit of reading other people's work with the sole purpose of destroying an offending text. Those engaged in this fashion, may either attempt to rationalise their efforts, or simply be unaware of the distortions they've committed. To these campaigners, their efforts are intended only to shed some critical light on what they consider to be dubious academic output.

5   The post-war Chicago School tradition, certainly saw the profession as engaged in gladiatorial combat where opposing views needed to be effectively flattened.

> Milton Friedman: I think you are getting something that is (a) the atmosphere at Chicago, and (b) intensified by Knight. That an academic is concerned not with being diplomatic, not with trying to avoid hurting people's feelings, but an academic is concerned with saying what's right. Telling the truth, or trying to get at it. And if you disagree with somebody you don't say 'well, now there may be something in what you say'
> Rose Friedman: You may be right
> Milton Friedman: You say that's a bunch of nonsense.
> Aaron Director: Exactly. That's not surprising. (Conversation with Milton Friedman, Rose Friedman and Aaron Director (August 1997).

6   Claire Friedland, Stigler's long-time research assistant could be overly generous when evaluating his remarks. But his mordant wit could cut a speaker off at his knees. The target would be able to recover only with the greatest difficulty. This more closely mirrored a love of combat, rather than a simple search for insight.

> As for George's caustic wit, he never let go one of his barbs for the sake of mere oneupmanship. They were always aimed at the target's ideas, not the target himself: even when a workshop speaker asked whether he should deliver his paper standing or seated and George responded, "With a paper like this, under the table would not be inappropriate (Friedland 1983:781).

7   For those without a philosophical bent (or defined by philosophical indifference), Thomas Hobbes described a world without government as existing in a state of nature where life was "solitary, poor, nasty, brutish, and short" (Hobbes 1651:XIII.9).

8   Pointing out the group identity aspect driving this slash and burn approach to criticism, does in no way negate the basic egotism that at times seems endemic to any academic calling.

9   This point requires a bit of reemphasis, since this is the path chosen within the case study examined. Or if direct bombardment proves ineffective, substitute versions of the original can be conjured up. These imperfectly mirrored versions have been crafted to collapse under their own weight. But once this pattern of faux examination is established, subsequent inquests of opposing ideas and theories are accordingly forced to rest on dubious (and perhaps entirely fabricated) exegeses. These subsequently discarded ideas have been effectively scuppered by pernicious transformations. Essentially the originals are effectively undermined by being forcefully contoured to fit into pre-determined moulds. In simple language, the strawman versions of the originals prove to be excessively flammable.

10   As an almost classic example, Milton Friedman offered his 1956 version of monetary theory as an antidote to the theory initially crafted by Keynes. To demonstrate its pedigree (as opposed to the revolutionary nature of Keynes' approach) he tied his thought to an oral Chicago tradition that had supposedly flourished during the interwar period. (This fable made his approach evolutionary, rather than revolutionary.) When thwarted by Don Patinkin's (2003) inside knowledge of the Chicago department, Friedman remained undeterred. He shifted to a direct attack on Keynes, attempting to transform him into a minor quantity theorists. (Supposedly his only contribution was the theoretical liquidity trap. Friedman tried to claim that *The General Theory* was riddled with mentions of that theory.)

11   For instance, textbook explanations of Keynes lean heavily on the existence of sticky wages. Under this interpretation, such imperfections impede market adjustments, strengthening recessionary forces. Yet, Keynes warns against flexible wages as a source of market destabilisation. In essence, textbooks flip Keynes on his head. The consequence of this sleight of hand, is that Keynes' *General Theory* is shrunk to a non-threatening level defined by market imperfections. (Such disappointing results consist of a catalogue of garden variety deviations.) Any revolutionary aspects of his approach are carefully eradicated, leaving the theory thoroughly domesticated. Such imperfections are by definition inherently fixable. Extra doses of applied market forces, with a dash of fundamental principles, is bound to correct such failures. In contrast, Keynes intends to offer not something as trivial as a minor glitch in the clockwork, market mechanism, but rather a fundamental flaw in the market universe.

12   Publishers market textbooks that are capable of generating sales. The direct audience, for these books, is not the students, who must plod through the selected text, but the instructors who insist upon them. Students can only influence such a choice in the most indirect way imaginable. Those who, for reasons unknown, might wish to explore the world of textbooks further, might achieve a modicum of satisfaction by skimming through Freedman (2003).

13   A classic example of recalibrating, and thus undermining, a theory is the transformation of Paul Sweezy's (1939) kinked demand curve. This bit of operational unravelling was performed under the gimlet eye of George Stigler (1947). There is a distinct disjuncture in this text between the simple model and explanation provided by Sweezy, compared to the subsequent incarnation created by Stigler. Even the basic graphic models presented in each article fail to align. The issue in such a case becomes whether the compulsive logic underlying Stigler's recrafting wasn't an intention of destroying (deliberately or not) the legitimacy of a potentially subversive article. Yet the textbook version (that somehow became a standard few pages in all first year volumes for decades), reflected Stigler's, rather than

Sweezy's concerns. For the idly curious, Freedman (1995) explores this dubious episode in the history of economic theorizing. Sweezy, however, never bothered to correct the record in this respect.

> I haven't read it [Stigler's 1947 article]. I don't think I ever did. I don't think I was aware of it actually. I didn't pay much attention to Stigler in those days. I was probably in one of my ultra-left moods, or something like that (Conversation with Paul Sweezy, November 1997).

14 When textbooks regularly featured alternative models such a monopolistic competition, or the kinked demand curve, these were often based on some transformative version of the original. The consensus wisdom of these textbooks were seldom challenged. Few were motivated to return to the original source, while those who did were generally ignored. Textbooks existed to relay the mainstream thoughts of the profession rather than authenticating the original, source theory.

15 How closely the attacks, or defenses, come to sketching, or defining, an actual Chicago School brand of economics is an unresolved issue. Often the debate centers on the University of Chicago's economics department, as it is assumed to have existed from the time when George Stigler returned, until sometime during the Reagan years of the 1980s. Whether the department was ever as monolithic as some critics like to contend, is of course debatable.

16 As with super hero devotees, those publicising the scourge of neo-liberalism divide their attention when selecting their favourite arch-villain. Professional economists focused on this issue may lean more to a figure like George Stigler. Those with shakier economic backgrounds may instead opt for someone more publicly notorious like Milton Friedman. He embodied an economist who sought (and was able to snatch), a portion of the public limelight while still alive. Stigler, though well-known within the profession, tended to avoid the glare of mass acknowledgment.

> On one other personal occasion I remember something related to this question coming up. I was at lunch with Milton Friedman and George Stigler at the Quadrangle Club in Chicago and I was then a very young man. And somehow the younger you are, the more evangelistic you are. So I would debate and argue with people about policy issues and as I recall Milton asked me if I would be interested in going on a tour of some campuses, I think in the Southern United States, to talk on these policy issues. Milton said, 'What have you got to lose by doing this?' And George said at the table to me, 'Only your anonymity.' So, on that occasion, I think he was hinting that maybe I ought to stick to my scientific work. But he was always very respectful of Milton and very seldom, in fact I can't remember an occasion, in which he and Milton engaged in open debate on some issue. That's all I can tell you on this. I think that your description is correct (Conversation with Harold Demsetz, October 1997).

17   To a disturbing extent, Stigler approximates a Don Quixote type of figure, one eager to tilt at windmills, which only sometimes turn out to be giants. His approach to opposing doctrines, especially those that appeared to undermine the basis for Chicago style price theory, was one of obliteration, rather than comprehension.

> Much of his work centered around saving the damsel in distress, neoclassicism, from here attackers: hence his work on the economics of information and his enthusiasm for the Coase theorem (Friedland 1993:780–781).

18   The formation of the Mont Pelerin Society (1947) seems to have energized the Chicago crew who attended. (Certainly this proved to be true for the younger contingent composed of Milton Friedman, George Stigler and Aaron Director.) The looming battle (for those attending this gathering of traditional liberals), was meant to pit these forces of resistance squarely against the then academically dominant collectivists. Those on the left, were identified as the controlling power largely orchestrating the relevant debates occurring within most Western nations. Those snugly ensconced within the rugged Swiss mountains defined their battle as being a life-or-death struggle. From their perspective, they were facing a crisis comparable to the recently completed campaign against Nazi Germany. The threat had flipped from fascism to communism. Liberty (in the form of freedom), was at stake. This bleak doctrine had been recently enunciated by one of the Society's key movers, Friedrich Hayek (1944). The anticipated decay and foreshadowed conflict was detailed in his *Road to Serfdom* classic. A focused 'threat to liberty', became a constant refrain among the members of the society. But mobilizing the opposing forces proved to be inherently complicated. Hayek emphatically complained that "At a time when practically all the movements that call themselves progressive agitate for further encroachments of individual liberty, those who want to preserve freedom are apt to dissipate their energies in opposition. In fighting these liberticide movements we inevitably find ourselves frequently on the same side with those who habitually resist change" (1957:1). Hayek here becoming so agitated at the mortal combat faced in saving liberty from the hordes of mindless collectivists, that he was spurred to invent the word 'liberticide' to characterise the evils contemplated by these opponents. (A word that fortunately never caught fire.) Fifteen years later, the perceived death of liberty still remained a ruling obsession of the Society. Events were persistently interpreted to tell this exact tale. Members, had they managed to discover the temerity to forget this ultimate struggle against tyranny, were reminded of their founding creed in three, seemingly endless sentences:

> The decisive values of our civilization are in danger. In large areas of the world the fundamental preconditions for human liberty and dignity have vanished; in others they are permanently jeopardized by the development of

> political conditions. The rights of the individual and of freely constituted groups are being increasingly undermined by the spread of bureaucratic tyranny. Even the most valuable attainment of Western man, the freedom of thought and opinion, is jeopardized by the spread of ideologies which, as long as they are in the minority, insist on tolerance, only to suppress all other opinions and views once they have come into power (Schmulders 1972:71).

19 As will be noted in the next chapter, terms like liberty and freedom (used often by Stigler, or his colleague Friedman) serve as perfect poison apples. They appear to be innocent (and positive) terms understood and supported by all. Yet they are used ambiguously by skilled wordsmiths like Stigler. In essence, the intention behind employing such terms appears to be an attempt to tar their opponents as enemies of liberty and freedom. (If such people as Stigler and Friedman are whole-heartedly defending freedom with their last remaining breath, what then can be properly deduced about their vehement opponents?) By such repetitive employment of these seemingly simple terms, a more subversive and controversial proposition can be slipped in under the guise of stating the obvious.

20 Basically, bare knuckle rules dominated such academic debates. The self-designated brawlers had no time to honour Marquis of Queensbury rules, even if only in the breach.

21 Whether such misconceptions are constructed deliberately is a different question. Doubt can only surround the idea that such mischievous mummery is anything like an intentional standard of action. Much more likely is the tendency for many readers to find in any book or article exactly what they expected to discover there. Preconceptions have always been the intellectual goggles that play a decisive role when interpreting the work of others.

22 For instance, in 2021 public debate saw the term 'critical race theory' gain a widespread notoriety without either contending side knowing exactly what the term meant. Signifying, that few had read the relevant articles composing the core of that theory. Instead, posed arguments depended on what they thought it might mean, or what such ideologues needed it to mean. The primary source for understanding this oft cited theory seemed based upon unreliable social media postings (perhaps a redundancy), or at best, unsubstantiated second hand reports.

23 To revert back to the thinking of the previous chapter, these cases represent the McGuffins of this volume. They are intended only to motivate a consideration of the issue spotlighted without dissecting such problems in clinical detail. The actual cases presented are not in themselves significant. None are chosen based on the relevant authors of such pieces. Other, equally suitable, examples exist and would have served as effective substitutes. The critical examination at the centre of each case is focused on a particular practice rather than on the practitioners. For whatever reason, all too many

readers have proven unwilling to make this leap. The underlying requirement is an ability to disregard the inevitable cast of characters associated with the specific practices under investigation. Thus you can analyse Ridley Scott's film *Alien* as an example (case study) of the science fiction genre. The emphasis would then be on the components, pace and style that form the basis of a successful film in this category. Other science fiction films like Nolan's *Inception* could provide equally fertile material for this purpose. Or the focus could be on the film itself, not as an exemplar of a genre, but instead with an obsessive focus that is concentrated only on the details of the story. Or even worse, an off-kilter critic might become entangled with the biographical details of a film's director, or its cast members instead. (Whether Ridley Scott seduced Sigourney Weaver would seem to be a joy ride down a defunct spur line, rather than anything resembling an interest in the film itself.)

24   The ancient Greeks had a useful mythological metaphor which carefully encapsulated this human imperative. (Unsurprising, since myths and fables often provided a vital societal service.) In this particular tale, Procrustes, like so many other such figures, laid claim to a divine heritage by being a son of Poseidon. (The Greek gods, unfortunately, appeared to be sexually unstoppable.) But like a number of these personages, he was not without a slight character blemish. He not only worked earnestly as an accomplished blacksmith, but also was an incorrigible thief. According to his own idiosyncratic myth, Procrustes would invite weary travelers to spend the night at his abode. They were offered the chance to luxuriate within the confines of his spare bed. However, once comfortably settled onto this innocently looking apparatus, Procrustes (for reasons unknown) would diligently engineer that all his unsuspecting guests fit perfectly on his proffered bed. Success would require either stretching those who failed to measure to the required length, or amputating any unsightly excess. (Perhaps Procrustes was just a perfectionist who was otherwise devastated by imperfections of height.) Subsequently, after Procrustes had successfully conducted a number of such one night engagements, the itinerant hero Theseus bested Procrustes, undertaking to fit his would be host on to his own treacherous bed. (In this case, the punishment enacted was deemed to fit the crime. This underlying moral can often be located in many of these myths.)

25   Notice how Stigler's approach reflects the ideas explored in the previous chapter. From his approach, opponents are immediately pigeon-holed as belonging to a category composed of dangerous collectivist thought. Consequently, all such work was invariably analysed based on this preconceived perspective. Namely, such work must be destroyed at all costs. The aim then becomes not to comprehend the theory and underlying thinking,

but to discover a leverage point by which to destroy it, or at least render it harmless.

26   Liberty and freedom for Stigler was naturally and intrinsically connected to a distinct sense of personal responsibility. The logic behind rational decision making directly implied that each person could best determine what was individually optimal in any given situation. Consequently, failure, from this fundamental perspective, was intimately connected to the decisions each individual made. African-Americans (or in the 1960s – Negroes) were accordingly not the victims of racism, but rather bore the consequences of their own actions. This judgement composed what for Stigler was the only logical stance, given his prior convictions. Today, Stigler's pointed insights would be viewed as decidedly appalling, as shown by the following excerpt. His reasoning, however, is meant to conclusively demonstrate that in the case of claimed discrimination, any government intervention, as usual, is incapable of resolving a problem traced back to individual responsibility.

> The past is not for us to relive, and no amount of restitution for past injustice by the white man could solve the basic problem of the Negro in America. That problem is that on average he lacks a desire to improve himself, and lacks a willingness to discipline himself to this end. The task of our time has been to make the Negro discontented with himself, not with the white man. Consider employment. The Negro boy is excluded from many occupations by the varied barriers the prejudice can raise, and these must and will be struck down. But he is excluded from more occupations by his own inferiority as a worker, again on average. Lacking education, lacking a tenacity of purpose, lacking a willingness to work hard, he will not be an object of employers' competition. What leader of Negro thought is fostering the ancient virtues of diligence and honesty and loyalty? It is so much easier to seek quotas for Negroes,
>
> Consider the Negro as a neighbour. He is frequently repelled and avoided by the white man, but is it only colour prejudice? On the contrary, it is because the Negro family is, on average, a loose, morally lax, group, and brings with its presence a rapid rise in crime and vandalism. No statutes, no sermons, no demonstrations, will obtain for the Negro the liking and respect that sober virtues commend. And the leaders of Negro thought: they blame the crime and immorality upon the slums and the low income – as if individual responsibility could be bought with a thousand dollars a year (Stigler 1965:11–12).

Stigler himself would doubtless reject the idea that he, in any sense of the word, was an unacknowledged racist. (If a group of people were observed to have failed in achieving a measure of success, the fault must lie within themselves and not society.) Such a judgement is, quite naturally, far simpler to make retrospectively. In fact in this instance, as generally, Stigler was simply carrying out the same logic he applied to all such problems. His unyielding perspective was subsequently shared and applauded by his close friend (and colleague) Milton Friedman. This result was entirely unsurprising given the logic to which they both fervently subscribed.

> Your piece on Negro unrest is magnificent. David [Milton Friedman's son] and a friend of his who is an active student conservative politician were over the weekend and I read it aloud to them. They too thought it magnificent (Letter from Milton Friedman to George Stigler, August 4, 1964).

27   Stigler's prime targets were theoretical constructions that provided alternatives to a system yielding a unique, stable equilibrium. Movements away from such an ideal shifted the resulting distribution. A shift implied that each factor of production would not necessarily receive its marginal product. (Such an unsatisfactory outcome implied that what you put in failed to determine what you received in terms of compensation.) In contrast, competitive markets determined distributional outcomes that were both efficient and equitable. (Resourced were utilised without waste while rewards matched individual contributions.) Posed alternatives, unfortunately, yielded more ambiguous outcomes, providing a wedge through which a government could justify intervention. Such non-Chicago theories (those which didn't champion stable, competitive equilibriums), then posed distinct threats to the liberty and freedom ensured by competitive Chicago inspired markets. Consequently, there was no alternative, but for Stigler to strenuously oppose these dangers, at all costs. Freedom and liberty were not to be surrendered without a fight.

> Evidence of Stigler's attachment to neoclassical price theory is also given by the part of his work mainly critical of the work of others. Price rigidity, administered price inflation, the theory of monopolistic competition, and X-efficiency were prominent targets, and each of them denied the efficacy of the neoclassical analytical framework (Demsetz 1993:800).

28   An almost unresolvable issue is whether Stigler sought to demolish opposing theories because they were wrong, or because he judged them to be dangerous. (Perhaps he subconsciously judged them to be wrong because they appeared dangerous.) Certainly, he dismissed such frameworks as being unquestionably wrong. Part of the brusqueness of his attacks can be judiciously attributed to Chicago style, no holds barred debate.

> Rose Friedman: I don't think George had much tolerance for stupidity.
> Milton Friedman: I don't think you're getting at anything that is really specifically George Stigler. I think you are getting something that is (a) the atmosphere at Chicago, and (b) intensified by Knight. That an academic is concerned not with being diplomatic, not with trying to avoid hurting people's feelings, but an academic is concerned with saying what's right. Telling the truth, or trying to get at it. And if you disagree with somebody you don't say 'well, now there may be something in what you say'

> Rose Friedman: You may be right
> Milton Friedman: You say that's a bunch of nonsense.
> Aaron Director: Exactly. That's not surprising (Conversation with Milton Friedman, Rose Friedman and Aaron Director, August 1997).

But scanning those alternative positions, which became his primary targets, not only did they appear to be dead wrong to Stigler, but dangerous to economic theory and indirectly to economic policy. To a certain degree, they were intrinsically wrong because of the inherent threat they posed to fundamental price theory and the policy it generated. All of these despised alternatives invited government intervention and its subsequent redistribution of income. (Redistribution distorted incentives, incurred the misfortune of, in turn, weakening society's moral fibre.) In effect, to qualify for Stigler's unleashed ire, theories had to be as wrong as they were dangerous.

> Evidence of Stigler's attachment to neoclassical price theory is also given by that part of his work mainly critical of the work of others Price rigidity, administered price inflation, the theory of monopolistic competition, and X-efficiency were prominent targets, and each of them demined the efficacy of the efficacy of the neoclassical analytical framework (Demsetz 1993:800).

29   Attributing Stigler's personal attacks solely to his almost romantic defense of liberty and freedom, however, would be a clear overstatement. Such finely honed barbs were undoubtedly the result, as well, of a sarcastic wit that lacked an active discriminatory filter. If he thought of a remark, it did not fail to go unsaid. Deidre McCloskey is fond of relating an Industrial Workshop incident whereby a presenter was brought to tears by Stigler's barbed remarks.

> Yes, he certainly did. He could make mincemeat out of anyone, because he was so truthfully clever and objective. And the amazing thing is he was never, ever like that on an individual basis. I can see that distorted very much what people were saying about George. I think, that was a flaw in his character. Okay, if he had wanted in one or two sentences to make me look like a jackass, but he would occasionally do that with younger people, or inferior, I don't mean that literally … I mean in rank, people with lower status than him. I thought that was terrible. He would just pounce on them. And I would tell him so. He would agree it was terrible. But he couldn't help himself, he couldn't resist (Conversation with Robert Solow, October 1997).

Nor was he unwilling to go down the personal route in print.

> Of course she [Jane Fonda] knows precious little about nuclear energy, but she knows all that her role requires. If she were to spend a few months (with Edward Teller!) learning more about the subject (or, say, about Vietnam), this learning would simply impair her performance: doubts and qualifications would destroy the simplicity and eloquence of her speeches. To ask her to do

> this is something like asking the case of the Merchant of Venice to make a close and sympathetic study of the actual practices of Jewish moneylenders and then to correct Shakespeare's lines (Letter from George Stigler to the Editor of the Wall Street Journal, August 21, 1979).

30 George Stigler always appeared to attack and destroy from a position of absolute certainty. He had no doubt that he knew how the economic world operated. The opposing collectivists were not just essentially incorrect and misguided, but actively supporting policies and approaches that announced the death knell of individual liberty and freedom. A battle of this import warranted whatever ploys and devices would eradicate dangerous constructs, whether in thought or in action.

> His [George Means] facts were wrong. Wrong. Wrong, wrong. And he knew it. How could they be anything but wrong if he thought the economy was not competitive?
>
> *So, a priori*
>
> It comes pretty close to it, pretty close to it. My guess is that he came to his conclusion from an *a priori* position. But then my guess is that most economists make their judgements on *a priori* beliefs and not on empirical evidence (Conversation with James Kindahl, October 1997).

31 No set of circumstances could possibly condone offering a flimsy substitute for the actual theoretical edifice constructed by a targeted opponent. Particularly when an ersatz version seems to be constituted so that it would collapse when subjected to even the lightest of critical gazes.

32 For those who are sticklers, Alice is prompted to come to such a pronounced conclusion only after drinking deeply from a bottle and telescoping out. "'Curiouser and curiouser!' cried Alice (she was so much surprised, that for the moment she quite forgot how to speak good English); 'Now I'm opening out like the largest telescope that ever was!'" Carroll 1974:21). Like Alice, academics seem prone to forget how to speak good English even when they aren't telescoping out.

33 Tomas Sowell, erstwhile, and much battered student of George Stigler, used the term to describe Stigler's method of dealing with alternative or heterodox theories, at least those that ran counter to, or in some way threatened, Chicago style price theory.

> Few, if any, areas of economics have as much confusion, circular reasoning, definitional traps, and fervent nonsense as industrial organization. It was the perfect place for Stigler to conduct a Demolition Derby. Nor was he hesitant about the task. Theories like "monopolistic competition" and "countervailing power," which were treated reverently at Harvard (where they originated), were eviscerated by Stigler (Sowell 1993:787).

34   A puzzle arises when attempting to concoct a suitable collective term for the three economists under investigation. Since Philip Mirowski remains the senior member of the trio, along with a corresponding longer track record, I will arbitrarily invent the term Team Mirowski to incorporate the three main economists involved in this project, namely, Philip Mirowski, Robert Van Horn and Eddie Nik-Khah. This is not meant to relegate the younger two of this group to some satellite or inferior position, or to denigrate their individual and valuable contributions. I am sure the term Team Mirowski will equally offend all three, so I will risk adopting it despite the numerous and justified objections to using such a bastardised term. Otherwise, I would be tempted to opt for Bruce Caldwell's (2010) choice of simply combining initials, which for some unconscious reason I find distracting. (This shorthand might justifiably be swiftly dumped into any nearby PEA disposal unit. PEA standing for pretentious, esoteric anagrams.) Here the use of the term 'team' most closely denotes the sharing of common objectives to the point of co-authoring several papers together. Though, they each of course have their own concerns and focus. In which case, they could hardly serve as close substitutes for one another.

35   This over dramatic turn of phrase (vampire hunters) is employed due to the way in which these crusaders regard neo-liberalism. The neo-liberal structure is displayed in their writings as parasitical in nature, a vampirish doctrine sucking the vitality out of any society to which it is capable of attaching. It does not take a leap of imagination then to visualise Team Mirowski as figuratively attempting to drive a wooden stake through the beating heart of neo-liberalism. Whether decapitation and garlic also have a part to play is left to the whimsy of any obsessive reader of these idiosyncratic endnotes.

36   For those with only sporadic attention spans, though the case studies and analytic focus displayed in the text appear limited to the history of economic thought, the conclusions are meant to apply to all forms of economic research. The problems identified are not just restricted to a very narrow field of economics. In addition, those writers with heavily ideological objectives often give themselves away by the fashion in which they defend their own beliefs and attempt to destroy opposing viewpoints.

37   As discussed in the previous chapter, categorising a given approach to economics (neo-liberal), seemingly permits a casual dismissal of any work that happens to be pasted with such a label.

38   The right has long used such terms as 'socialist', 'communist' and 'marxist' as catch-all terms of opprobrium. Such labels are used without the slightest attempt to define (or employ) them properly.

39   Melvin Reder (1982), himself a long-time Chicago denizen, probably provides the best guided tour through the thickets of Chicago price theory,

although others (such as one of George Stigler's protégés) might choose to differ.

> Who was it, Mel Reder who wrote a piece in which he said 'the distinguishing characteristic of Chicago economics is 'the tight prior equilibrium'. That was wrong. I told Mel it what wrong, but it is easy to see how somebody could come to that conclusion. There was a 'tight prior' but George [Stigler] believed in it based on the evidence (Conversation with Sam Peltzman, October 1997).

40   At least in Stigler's case, his theoretical versions (and their disparity with the actual theory), seem neither conscious nor deliberate. But there is always a parting of ways, whether small or large, between what economists say they do (or claim they should do) and their actual practice. Intentional misdirection is not deducible after examining the case files of George Stigler. Rather, the truth may lie simply in the fact that people discern in their reading what they need to find. They tend to enter the stage with certain given priors that serve to shape their understanding. That in trying to destroy the perceived achievements of Stigler (as a representative model of what they term to be neo-liberalism), Team Mirowski resorts to Stigler's own less than salubrious tactics. Doing so, creates something approaching irony. And life would be a bit dull without an occasional dose of ironic seasoning. Though in their defense, Team Mirowski might be tempted to justify its approach as 'fighting fire with fire'. However, hope still remains that they would find the moral fibre to resist such enticements. But then again, all isn't always fair in love or economics.

41   Stigler himself was more likely to use his sardonic wit to mock an opponent and his creation. In effect, the style of his attack made his targets feel personally belittled, whether or not this was Stigler's intention. He was a sort of equal opportunity generator of insults. Hurled barbs landed on anyone who might cross his path, as though he somehow lacked the ability to filter out his more mischievous thoughts.

> He could make mincemeat out of anyone, because he was so truthfully clever and objective. And the amazing thing is he was never, ever like that on an individual basis. I can see that distorted very much what people were saying about George. I think, that was a flaw in his character. Okay, if he had wanted in one or two sentences to make me look like a jackass, but he would occasionally do that with younger people, or inferior, I don't mean that literally … I mean in rank, people with lower status than him. I thought that was terrible. He would just pounce on them. And I would tell him so. He would agree it was terrible. But he couldn't help himself, he couldn't resist (Conversation with Robert Solow, October 1997).

42   This illegitimate linkage is similar to those enlightened individuals who insist on shunning the output of a despised artist. From their perspective,

great works should reflect great humanity according to their own evaluated standard. Unfortunately, wonderful writers, painters and film directors can't escape being human, complete with the usual array of unloved flaws. As Ezra Pound has demonstrated, you don't have to be a saint to construct poetry. Nor does Polanski's dubious moral character condemn all his films. The issue is whether such well-publicised boycotting doesn't border on high minded self-indulgence, or virtue signaling.

43   Those readers, the ones at least whose short term memories are still intact, will remember that the problems associated with reflexive categorisation were dredged up in the previous chapter.

44   This caution need not, and generally does not, convey a noxious whiff of inevitable corruption. Tobacco companies are not automatically required to employ financial gain in order to achieve a desired result. They are necessarily sufficiently astute to only choose those researchers with a prior inclination to see any tobacco controversy in a favourable corporate light.

45   Personal attacks reflect, all too often, a basic fragility underlying the critical analysis of an offending theory, or perspective. Resorting to such a stratagem is an attempt to shift the terms of debate onto more congenial territory. The dubious implication provided for such an attack is that somehow a flawed individual will inevitably generate flawed research. The connection attempted is at the very least dubious or probably non-existent. It is the equivalent of dismissing Wagner's music (even without listening to it), due solely to the fact that his personality left much to be desired.

46   Constructing strawmen was an art seemingly perfected and employed by George Stigler throughout his very lengthy career. (Such a characterization should not be taken to imply that this was done intentionally or malevolently. No available evidence substantiates the charge that he viewed his constructs as in any way deliberate misrepresentations of opposing views.) However, Stigler did manage to create a sufficient number of these convenient strawmen to sustain stock company performances of *The Wizard of Oz* for many years to come. Those who evidence a smidgen of idle interest in exploring these ideas, might refer to Freedman (1995, 1998a, 1998b, 2002, 2016) for want of any better alternatives.

47   Criticisms of writing styles are so rife with contradictions (and laced with academic snideness), that shying away from any mention of the narrative construction often appears to be the wisest option to choose. Yet any attempt at writing, at least minimally, should always demonstrate a deliberate desire to communicate. (As author, I do not excuse myself from my own occasional trespasses.) While it may be perfectly acceptable to challenge one's readers, defying them is perhaps a step too far. In which case, adopting the often dense and convoluted prose defining sociology, or any work heavily influenced by the post-modern, deconstructionist movement, doesn't appear to facilitate a desirable level of communication. The very phrasing and

vocabulary employed sometimes erects an unnecessary roadblock for readers, who are then forced to linger outside the environments of certain (deliberately constructed and enabled) language clubs. Consequently, those who are excluded in this fashion become simply (perhaps reasonably) uninterested in investing the time to become initiates of such mysteries. A certain assist could easily be offered to the struggling reader whereby authors generously condescend to ensure that an honest attempt is made to remove incomprehensible difficulties. The concrete benefits of seeming to deliberately undercut one's own narrative (by employing ornate and profuse sentences), can only raise befuddlement. When faced with such created hurdles, those readers who seriously weigh the possibility of investing the necessary time to evaluate Mirowski's work, may start to question the cost. Such moments fortunately remain infrequent in the articles under scrutiny, but still they could easily be excised without any noticeable loss of meaning or even style. I speak as one whose own prose has often been criticized. Authors too often fall in love with their own verbiage.

48   Ideally, the aim is to substitute the ersatz model for the original construction. For example, the kinked demand curve that for decades burrowed its way into introductory textbooks, was not the model devised by Sweezy (1939), but rather the strawman version dreamt up by Stigler (1947). Those who harbour suspicions concerning this issue can refer to Freedman (1995).

49   Sometimes the windmills are dangerous giants (an actual posed threat), but more often such targets only represent a different perspective, or mode of analysis.

50   Stigler limited his wholehearted attacks on offending theories to those that he found to be dangerous, namely potential threats to Chicago style price theory.

> Neoclassical price theory offers no doctrine of rigid prices. Not only are there no rationales for price rigidity in its models of competition and monopoly, but the primary result of price theory, if not its raison d'etre, is to show how the *flexibility* inherent in the price system allocates resources in a surprisingly admirable if not completely perfect manner. A tool of analysis that proclaimed rigid prices, such as the kinked demand curve, must have put irresistible temptation before Stigler (Demsetz 1993:800).

51   Such behaviour may in fact be no more than laziness. However a crucial assumption is often made. Namely, that the published version of the theory attacked must be accurate, or referees would not consent to its publication. Such thinking displays either a certain unfortunate naivety when it comes to academic refereeing, or what is displayed is simply a convenient rationalization of the reader's inherent laziness.

52   This approach had at least a whiff of a holy crusade. Readers can picture Stigler jousting against a delegated black knight, the anointed champion of

heresy and falsehood (to add a spot of melodrama to the description). "Much of his work centered on saving the damsel in distress neoclassicism from her attackers" (Friedland 1993:780). Perhaps this perceived need to play the saviour of economics partially explains the savagery of his attacks on non-orthodoxy. Consequently, Stigler never proved to be satisfied with a simple conflagration of his carefully constructed strawmen. Watching them flame and burn was inevitably insufficient. Stigler needed additionally to stomp on the shriveled ashes of the offending theory and scatter them to the wind. Even that was barely enough, inducing him (at least figuratively) to salt the very earth where once they lay. He proved fond of practicing, most likely quite unconsciously, a Roman-like resolution to any Carthaginian style dilemma.

53   To reiterate, this need not be, and probably is not, an option embraced consciously. Instead, the strawman version may materialize simply because that is what the researcher expected or needed to discover. Such results are much more likely to occur if the opposing work is read with malice afore-thought.

54   Chief targets included such luminaries as Chamberlin, Leibenstein, Sweezy, Galbraith and Means.

55   Stigler's habitual discovery of what he needed to find in the work of others extended even to those he viewed favourably. As explained in the previous chapter, he discovered in Coase the intrinsic MacGuffin, which he christened, 'The Coase Theorem'. In this case, he confused a work's MacGuffin like device for the work's actual objective. But that clever formulation was in retrospect, exactly what Stigler needed to discover in Coase's work.

56   For those who cannot boast of a misspent youth watching one of the permutations of *Dr. Who*, the Daleks were a race of alien beings who mostly resembled a failed and drastically discounted vacuum cleaner model. They are best known for attacking their targeted enemies relentlessly while ceaselessly chanting the phrase, "Exterminate!" (Yes, the use of this term has been previously defined. But, I am counting on the fact that at least some of my readers will have a shortened attention span.)

57   The term 'Carthaginian' peace may ring a distant bell with the more history minded of readers. Following the third Punic war between Rome and Carthage (neither side really understanding the gist of the idea of peace), the Romans destroyed Carthage, killed most of its inhabitants and committed the remainder to slavery. Myth has it that the Romans then salted the earth where Carthage once stood, to ensure that the city would never rise again. There are doubts that such an action ever took place, but it does make a lovely story. However, when it came to salting the earth to exterminate any trace of a theory, George Stigler never proved to be short of an endless supply of shakers.

58   Milton Friedman would often refer to those of a similar perspective (or political leaning), as being 'our kind'. This is reminiscent of the expression 'Our Crowd' used to refer to noted Jewish families memorialized in a book of the same name by Stephen Birmingham (1967). These 'good eggs', to use more of Friedman's terminology, shared a sharp skepticism of anything resembling government intervention. In a mirror like manner, Team Mirowski often seem entirely focused on market shortcomings. More balanced views seem to be truncated by difficult to eliminate ideological goggles.

> The economist Robert Solow once observed that when he listened to his liberal colleague John Kenneth Galbraith complaining about the flaws of markets, he found himself reminded of the virtues. When he listened to Friedman, by contrast, he was reminded of the flaws (Applebaum September 18, 2020).

59   This aspect still survives in part as evidenced by the financial crisis of 2008 and the policy stances by Eugene Fama (Cassidy 2010) and John H. Cochrane (2010). Both insisted that the collapse only fortified their structured theory of market efficiency. The question arises as to what evidence (or event), might cause them to reconsider such implacable stances. Both seem incapable of wavering, let alone bending. They both have proven quite adept at forcing balky bits of evidence to cozily adhere to their preferred frameworks.

60   The urge to categorize and toss all Chicago economists into the same despised black hole is perhaps exemplified by ignoring the differences existing even between the closest of allies. A long running and unresolved dispute placed Stigler and Friedman at opposite corners when bridging the gap between devising economic theory and promoting public policy. (The role played by ideology was yet another clear rift between the two.)

> And he, on more than one occasion asked me the question - he never gave the answer himself and I never knew how to answer the question myself - 'Did I think that Milton Friedman would be remembered most for his polemics on policy or his scientific work on things like the consumption function?' He never gave the answer himself and I didn't know what the answer to that question was. I still don't know what the answer to that question is, but he obviously thought about this issue. This was an issue in his view and I would have to infer from his own behaviour that he was of the opinion regarding his good friend and respected colleague, that Milton's scientific work would be the hallmark by which he was most remembered. But that remains to be seen. The real issue, you know, is whether that's in fact going to be, whether that's going to hold up or not. On one other personal occasion I remember something related to this question coming up. I was at lunch with Milton Friedman and George Stigler at the Quadrangle Club in Chicago and I was then a very

young man. And somehow the younger you are, the more evangelistic you are. So I would debate and argue with people about policy issues and as I recall Milton asked me if I would be interested in going on a tour of some campuses, I think in the Southern United States, to talk on these policy issues. Milton said, 'What have you got to lose by doing this?' And George said at the table to me, 'Only your anonymity' (Conversation with Harold Demsetz, October 1997).

61   Someone like Amidae (2003), in contrast, focuses on (and is perhaps obsessed by) her discovered model of rational decision making in the post war era. She falls into a trap that in some ways has disfigured modern economics. She forcefully fits disparate facts to fit her abstract hypothesis, assuring a perfect validation to her jury rigged conclusion. Doing so, allows her to validate the shot gun type of marriages she so willingly performs between such polar figures as Kenneth Arrow and James Buchanan. Strangely, given her one note theme, any mention of the Chicago School is omitted. For instance, Gary Becker is noticeably absent without leave. This smidgeon of legerdemain resembles an investigator intently focused on the mounds of peanut shells in a room, while decidedly turning her eyes away from the elephant ceaselessly trumpeting his existence.

62   This laundry list composing neo-liberalism might broadly be attributed to the strict market orientation of its proponents, particularly pronounced in someone like George Stigler. Similar to any other ideologues, proponents here tend to be one-sided sceptics. To varying degrees, these Chicagoans are justified in their lack of faith in government activity and intervention. However simultaneously, markets are depicted as almost divinely inspired, when sieved through their own preformed judgment. Required in this case is an act of faith, which demands that since markets reward those who resolve market problems, strong (and perhaps irresistible), incentives exist that will guarantee a solution given sufficient time.

> George [Stigler] was focused on the way the market marches in to *eliminate* the externalities, to work *around* them to make them a market problem instead of a non-market problem. I think I've quoted him in my memoir as saying something like, 'externalities are what the market has not *yet* eliminated.' That's not an exact quote but in my memoir I do have the exact quote (Conversation with Claire Friedland October 1997).

63   In the post war period, terms such as 'socialist or communist' have repeatedly been employed in the US to dismiss political opponents and blacken their reputations. Yet, it is unclear whether much of the American public has ever had a reasonable, let alone a precise, idea of what such terms mean. (The 2020 US election saw the ambiguous resurrection of the category 'socialist' as a convenient, yet meaningless term of condemnation. When

examined closely, there is always a lurking sense that these labels are there to identify 'bad' or 'evil' people, without any real idea as to what makes them objectionable.

64   Ideologically, this is counter-poised to an unsubstantiated reliance that government will almost inevitably act as something of a deus-ex-machina. The State, within this counter-perspective, is ascribed a series of fixative powers, backed by no consistently reliable evidence, other than perhaps hope.

65   Many of the points mentioned are not quite as controversial as Team Mirowski would have readers believe. Though it might be argued that such presentations are always slanted a bit to make such ideas appear, at first glance, to be more extreme than they are. Versions of some of these points are widely held by economists, at least some of whom do not sport a neo-liberal lapel pin.

> But let us accept for the moment that Hayek and the Chicago economists believed that markets help to coordinate dispersed knowledge, that public choice theory helps to explain some of the problems that are associated with democratic governance, that a competitive market environment makes it difficult to sustain a monopoly, and that market solutions when feasible are preferable to command and control solutions. These are not wildly controversial theses, at least among economists (Caldwell 2011:325–326).

66   The problem, once again, is a sort of categorical imperative that impels individuals to classify and categorise no matter how misleading such labelling may ultimately be.

67   Terminology gets tricky here and is often used loosely, especially when dealing with lumpish categories. Friedrich Hayek, a key mover of what Team Mirowski would label neo-liberalism, was keen to distinguish himself from conservatives. They might be necessary allies in the battle against collectivist authoritarianism, but they were not in themselves admirable.

> You may well ask whether the name really matters so much. In a country like the United States, that on the whole still has free institutions, and where therefore the defence of the existing is in general a defence of freedom, it may indeed seem not very significant although often be embarrassing to the libertarian; even where we happen to approve of them because they exist or because we regard them as desirable in themselves. The common resistance to the collectivist tide should not conceal the fact that the belief in integral freedom implies an essentially forward-looking attitude and should in no way be guided by a nostalgic longing for the past or a romantic admiration for what has been (Hayek 1957: 10).

68   The next chapter examines this rhetorical device that uses a bit of sleight of hand to drive home its objectives. Mirowski ostensibly provides an extensive summary of the traits defining the neo-liberal position. But when

examined more closely, each summary point contains a bit of ticking explosive given that his aim is to destroy, rather than comprehend, the targeted ideology. In that following chapter, these attempts are known as poison apples, artfully packaging a controversial position in an innocent seeming package.

69　Even Alchian and Stigler didn't always act in tandem, with Alchian forcefully chiding Stigler for wandering a touch away from the true path. Samuelson characterised Alchian as being 'more Catholic than the Pope" (Conversation with Paul Samuelson October 1997).

70　Steven Medema (2011) skillfully discovers fractures between the price theory promulgated by such architectural Chicago stalwarts as Stigler, Friedman and Becker. If there is an absence of undeniable uniformity among these three, it becomes easier to argue against any crude categorisation of Chicago price theory.

> Whereas Stigler had put scarcity at the center, for Becker "the basis of economics is choice" (1971, 3). From the perspective of the present, these may seem to be two sides of the same coin, but this is not inevitably the case. The study of the allocation of resources can take various forms and can be undertaken sans any specific reference to the individual choice process, as reflected in Mirowski and Hand's observation about Chicago demand theory and Friedman's tendency to focus on the market process absent any explicit underpinnings in individual behaviour. Becker, however, explicitly and specifically put individual choice at the center of the subject. Two decades later, in his Nobel address, Becker gave this even greater specificity, equating the "economic … approach" with the "rational choice approach" (1993, 402) (Medema 2011:161).

71　Once you endow political markets with the same mechanisms as their economic counter-parts, contradictions inevitably arise. In his later years, Stigler could never square the circle of wanting both economic and political market places to reflect consumer sovereignty, while simultaneously limiting the role assigned to government.

> But what exactly would he allow as a proper realm for government? Then he got into this – I remembered his name for it after talking to you – 'paradox of legitimacy' he called it, or sometimes he called it the '*problem* of legitimacy'. At the time of his death, this was one of the problems he was working on. It was *very* much of a concern to him. You have to remember the kind of public persona he had. If something bothered him a lot *I* saw the side of him that said, "I don't know what to do about this problem!" But the rest of the public saw that other side, "Here's what I've *done* about this problem and isn't it convincing." But he was very much concerned about how you could call something inefficient in the political arena. We do have a democracy, more or less, we have representative government, then how can something

that has been allowed to happen be inefficient? After all, that government has allowed some programs to go on and on, year after year.

The sugar program was sixty years old, the anti- trust law was over a hundred years old by the time George died. If it reflects the public demand for it, how can we call it inefficient? I think *that* is part of the answer to your question 'what do we let the government do?' It's not an answer. It is something that he was worried about. Something he was thinking about. How to reconcile consumer sovereignty, or voter sovereignty, with his previous notions of inefficient government? Can we say this is illegitimate if the public wants it? Is that consistent with our extreme position on consumer sovereignty which is that no matter what horrible things the public wants, as free market economists we can never question it. That's certainly one of the basic principles of neo-classical economics. Consumer sovereignty is both the end of the story and the beginning. And we don't argue with the consumer, no matter how self-destructive these demands are or how inappropriate. Anyway, if you want consumers to be free to choose in the market place, how can we argue with them in the political arena where, in a sense, they are acting as consumers too? Well, in his last years he was writing frequently about this (Conversation with Claire Friedland, October 1997).

72   Stigler's belief in rational decision making represents the extreme edge of the Chicago credo. For others, it is more a useful heuristic, a productive way to generate testable theories. However, elevating this stance to the representative departmental belief eases the task of tumbling the entire neo-liberal edifice to the ground. First identify this system with Chicago. In turn identify the Chicago department with George Stigler. What Team Mirowski hopes to create by doing this is a Jenga style of construction. If they pull away one or two of the key components propping up the edifice, then the whole theoretical tower comes tumbling down. Lacking a theoretical basis, derived policy can then be promptly dismissed.

> It's getting more and more, more and more part of him as he got older actually, this whole view. He insists it's rational. He would tell you, 'There is some rational explanation for it. It's just that you haven't looked completely into it and found it' (Conversation with Sam Peltzman, October 1997).

73   Bork (1978), who to a degree harnessed the Chicago thinking of that time, reacted against the post war use of anti-trust policy, rooted in the New Deal thinking of the Roosevelt era. The prime focus of that era, perhaps to an extreme extent, rested on the numbers of competitors and their relevant market shares. This evidence was deemed crucial, if not decisive, when evaluating potential corporate mergers. In contrast, Bork argued that the key litmus test of any such decision should be based on consumer welfare, as well as the resulting levels of competition. Under this formula, there is no *a priori* basis to conclude that a limited number of large corporate bodies

would be invariably incapable of maintaining both of these key objectives. In essence, Chicago raised the objection that large corporations were being punished for being more efficient, while also providing consumers with greater benefits. Stigler's brightest student, Sam Peltzman, makes this position clear in his summing up the evolution of George Stigler's views.

What's happening is that over time the literature, the empirical literature in industrial organisations, which is trying to test whether mergers effect price, whether they raise prices or lower prices, that literature takes a long time to develop. That literature continues through the structure-conduct-performance stuff. It runs into the 80s. You have important stuff in the mid-80s, I would say. In fact it hasn't died down yet. We are still teaching it to our classes. But that literature goes through a transformation. Now, along with this, I think he is maturing as a person. He's getting away from Simons. He begins to understand that there must be good reasons why Eastman Kodak dominates the film industry. Obviously there must be market forces involved. Why wasn't capital flowing into an industry with high basic returns? He is asking himself the kinds of questions that just didn't occur to Simons. A guy like Simons would just say, 'Well, they're too big. Break them up! The text books tell you, the more firms, the better'. And that's it. Simple. End of story. Advertising screws up people's minds, tax advertising and it'll be fine. So, he is beginning to understand that market forces are deeper than simple textbook stories. That's one of the lessons that I learned from him. By the early 60s when I was a student, I understood that the foolish kind of economist is the one who reads a textbook and takes it literally as applying to the world. What we are trying to do with a model is to simplify the world so that we can learn more about what is actually going on. He came to that understanding. Not right out of graduate school. He came to that understanding gradually. The evidence is beginning to be a little bit murky.

You have guys trying, actually showing that there is evidence that Eastman Kodak is dominating its market because it is better. You're seeing high profit margins as the result of low costs, rather than high prices. He is simply becoming aware of all this. It is only very, very gradually that he gets there. This didn't happen all at once. In the late 60s he was still sticking to this traditional idea because he believed that you really ought to have an antitrust policy. Of course, his belief is heavily qualified by that time. There was something called the Neal Commission. I don't know if you are familiar with this. It was a commission appointed by Nixon when he first took over. Phil Neal, who was a law professor here, was the head of it. George was on it. They wrote a report about what should be our policy towards concentration. Basically, what it said was 'Look, anti-trust has often done a lot of harm.' (If I remember correctly, I may have it all wrong at this point, but my memory of it is something like this.) 'Anti-trust has gotten off on a lot of side issues like conglomerate mergers, vertical stops, and vertical restraints. That's all wrong. What anti-trust should focus on is price fixing and concentration. That is, it should focus only on those traditional areas.' Concentration however was still part of the package. It hadn't gone away. Even in the late sixties, he was still ten years away from where he finally came out on that issue, which was very sceptical (Conversation with Sam Peltzman, October 1997).

74 Only a séance, or pure speculation, would be able to validate Stigler's views of these international organisations. Though the idea that the driving interest behind its operatives was self-interest would be consistent with his perspective.

> Milton Friedman: Keynes himself was a good example of this earlier noblesse oblige. And that means that it's worth giving advice to government officials. And of course the truth is that it's not all one or the other.
> Rose Friedman: That's right.
> Milton Friedman: Everybody wants to feel that what he's doing is good for the country.
> Aaron Director: Of course.
> Rose Friedman: Of course.
> Milton Friedman: And there's a limit to the extent to which you can rationalize.
> Rose Friedman: Of course.
> Milton Friedman: And so, it isn't all black or all white. And it is true that George would tend to emphasize, more than I would, the extent to which it was - you're just spitting in the wind if you try to advise governmental officials to do something which has not heretofore been in their self-interest to do. It may be most of the time, but where that comes from, I don't know.
> Aaron Director: Where what comes from? I'm just asking him to say it over again.
> Milton Friedman: Where George's going so far in the direction of not letting anything other than self-interest influence governmental behaviour (Conversation with Milton Friedman, Rose Friedman and Aaron Director, August 1997).

75 That neo-liberals necessary approve of this stated capture of international agencies by corporate interests lacks sufficient clarity. Certainly, government capture by these same interests are not viewed in a particularly positive light. Instead, such a situation provides effective ammunition against attempts by governments to intervene. Namely, that rather than operating in the public interest, governments reflect the objectives of vested corporate interests. But to confuse matters even more, George Stigler, the nominated arch neo-liberal had second, and confusing, thoughts on this issue. If, for instance, voters in the political market place consistently supported such intervention, than the preferences of those voters (analogous to consumers), must remain sovereign.

> It is something that he [Stigler] was worried about. Something he was thinking about. How to reconcile consumer sovereignty, or voter sovereignty, with

his previous notions of inefficient government? Can we say this is illegitimate if the public wants it? Is that consistent with our extreme position on consumer sovereignty which is that no matter what horrible things the public wants, as free market economists we can never question it (Conversation with Claire Friedland, October 1997).

He [Stigler] was not consistent. That's clear. And this inconsistency has led to a lot of misunderstanding. There are people outside of Chicago who read him this way. With Becker it is even more powerful. It's all part of Becker's stuff about optimality and redistribution. Outsiders kind of read both of them as, 'This is kind of the senescence of the Chicago school. They have become toadies for big government, apologists for big government.' And I could see why. It is a really subtle kind of distinction we are making here between the two. But look, if you're going to regulate, conditional on wanting to redistribute income, I can't tell you that this is wrong. So, if I don't like it, if I tell you it's wrong, it has to be because I don't like the resulting redistribution (Conversation with Sam Peltzman, October 1997).

76 Politicians of this era demonstrated no compunction in masquerading as the worker's friend. The high tariff system was portrayed as a device to insure jobs for workers and higher wages. Meanwhile, state militias and federal troops were often employed to break strikes in rather violent fashions. Even the Sherman Antitrust Act of 1890 was successfully deployed for the first time, by then President Grover Cleveland, against striking workers.

> Good men, good citizens, honest law-abiding men, justified themselves in the directorates of … railroads and other public service corporations in spending the money of the corporations to elect senators and assemblymen who would protect them against strike bills (Josephson 1938:409).

The Sherman Act can best be understood as a classic piece of legislative smoke and mirrors. The intent was to address national unrest over private economic power (the trust question), without actually doing so.

> The conduct of the Senate … has not been in the line of the honest preparation of a bill to prohibit and punish trusts. It has been in the line of getting some bill with that title that we might go to the country with. The questions of whether the bill would be operative, of how it would operate … have been whistled down the wind in the Senate as idle talk, and the whole effort has been to get some bill headed: "A Bill to Punish Trusts" with which to go to the country (Senator Orville Platt of Connecticut quoted in Josephson 1938: 460).

In fact, by delving a bit into the history of the late nineteenth century, the politicians/businessmen of that era provide a case study for Stigler's (1971) (at time cynical), view of government regulation. A classic instance of deliberately ignoring the man behind the curtain when analysing legislation. From this perspective, regulation becomes a means to buttress corporate interests. It is then not so easy to condemn Stigler as a corporate stooge. Not, at least, if the necessity of competitive markets form the backbone of his approach. A similar vision, though from the left-wing direction of the political landscape, predated Stigler's more structured view. (See Kolko (1963) for an extensive history of how regulation favoured big business and corporate interests.)

> The Commission [Interstate Commerce Commission], as its functions have now been limited by the courts, is, or can be made, of great use to the railroads. It satisfies the popular clamour for a government supervision of railroads, at the same time that that supervision is almost entirely nominal. Further, the older such a commission gets to be, the more inclined it will be found to take the business and railroad view of things. It thus becomes a sort of barrier between the railroad corporations and the people and a sort of protection against hasty and crude legislation hostile to railroad interests ... The part of wisdom is not to destroy the Commission, but to utilize it (Richard Olney, Attorney General in the second Grover Cleveland administration, quoted in Josephson 1938:526).

77   The Democrats of this period were in thrall to their own set of corporate and banking masters. Not until the initial unrest created by the Greenback, Populist and Labor Union movements did reformist politicians gain some traction, culminating in the Progressive movement before WWI. (Though the aims of the Populist and Progressive movements never perfectly synchronized.) Woodrow Wilson, entering the White House in 1913 as a Progressive, claiming to be the first true Democrat elected since the Civil War.

> This country has never had a Democratic administration since the Civil War. You may think Cleveland's administration was Democratic. It was not. Cleveland was a conservative Republican (Wilson quoted in Josephson 1938:392).

78   The core idea of keeping government at more than arm's length from the marketplace is succinctly explained, once again, my George Stigler's prize student, Sam Peltzman.

> As near as I can tell you, when I discussed it with him, he never objected to my story. Which is better articulated than I'm going to do it now, in a piece I did for the Brookings papers which is called ... I forget the name of it now. In any case, it was basically that Brookings has a conference every year in this type of applied micro-economics with economists discussing their papers. The guy who was running the show at Brookings called me up and basically asked me your question. How can it be, it's the late eighties, we've had basically ten years of this deregulation stuff going on, how can you reconcile what's happened with these theories of interest groups buying

regulation? I wrote a piece. He wanted the whole story. It's articulated there in that article. My take, which as I say I think he [Stigler] accepted, was that the important point of the economic theory of regulation is the redistribution part of it. At the end of the day, if you spread rents around, when the rents disappear, there's no point in having the regulation. That's the point. In part the dissipation of rents is endogenous to the regulatory process. You take the simple story of the airlines in America. I don't know about the rest of the world, but in America, after deregulation you simply had a price war. Under regulation, costs are bound to rise if you divert competition from price to non-price factors. Once that process is finished there's no point to the regulation any more. If in fact, once the dissipation of rents is complete, then you just have a substitution of non-price for price competition. Of course the producers aren't getting anything. The consumers are getting a non-optimal bundle. What's the point of the regulation? That's the way I explained it. I go through cases and I show where that view of the endogenous kind of dissipation of rents works, where it is satisfactory and where it is not satisfactory. But that's the one I articulated. George would go around the country making speeches about this sort of thing. He would ask me for example, "What did 'Y' do?" because he didn't know very much about how regulation actually worked. He would ask me, "Well what is the effect of regulation on the railroads? What do people who worry about this think about it? Or the airlines? Or the trucking industry?"

And I would tell him this kind of a story. He would put it into his speeches when he went around the country. We came to some agreement on it. I mean he accepted, very quickly, that this view that regulation is just bought and sold by special interests at some auction, (some sort of government auction where the prize is set and special interests win it), wasn't complete. He accepted that this was not a completely satisfactory view of the regulatory process. He accepted that. Once you do that, then deregulation does become more, at least more viable, than if you just have the very simple story which says, 'We won, we got our prize. Now all of a sudden, it's being taken away from us?' I mean, can that be accurate? It becomes completely a power game. In which case, there must be some aspect of the underlying politics that has changed. My story was, 'No, the economic background has changed. In very profound ways the economic background has changed, which makes it pointless to have the regulation.' I happen to think that that's very important today, a very powerful force.

My students will tell you that in the mid-seventies, before any of this began, when I talked about banking, for example, I said, 'There is no way this industry can remain regulated. There is no way.' Even airlines, this is true even in airlines where the first response to the dissipation of the rents was to try to make them operate better. I said, 'Look, there is something very funny going on here.' This is the mid-seventies. I can remember very clearly telling my class, that there is something very funny going on. This is something never seen before. A regulatory agency is saying that what we need is more efficiency. I said, 'This is a signal that either one of two things can happen.

> Either the regulators are going to be replaced by other regulators who get off this efficiency kick, or regulation is dying.' Because a view that what they are trying to do is to use exactly what in textbook welfare economics are efficient price signals, efficient resource allocation, can't be correct. That's the view that I came to believe was the wrong view of what regulation is trying to do. Regulation only survives if it has rents to spread around. In the past it used price and entry in the traditional mode. Today it's more complicated. But in the airline case, it had price and entry as its delegated mechanisms. So it's got to create inefficient prices if it's going to do its job. If it's focusing on efficiency, something's wrong. So I knew it then. I had this view already back in the seventies that regulation can put itself out of business (Conversation with Sam Peltzman, October 1997).

79   To a certain degree, they were captives of their own experiences. They had striven to defeat the collectivism defining Nazi Germany. They continued after the war to battle the left-wing collectivism of Communism and its fellow travellers. In their considered opinion, to do anything less was to endanger individual liberty.

80   At stake was a clash involving Friedman's vision of a blazing sun streaming forth the light of liberty, being sharply challenged by an authoritarian 'darkness at noon'. Friedman's struggle rested on his heavily (and continuously), marketed concept of freedom. This simple conclusion should be self-evident, if only from the dedication chosen for his seminal 1962 work *Capitalism and Freedom*. The book is dedicated to his two children, Janet and David. It reads, "To Janet and David and their contemporaries who must carry the torch of liberty on its next lap." From Friedman's perspective, collectivists of any variety, no matter what their claims or promises might be, must inevitably snuff out that treasured light of liberty.

> It is widely believed that politics and economics are separate and largely unconnected; that individual freedom is a political problem and material welfare an economic problem; and that any kind of political arrangements can be combined with any kind of economic arrangements. The chief contemporary manifestation of this idea is the advocacy of "democratic socialism" by many who condemn out of hand the restrictions on individual freedom imposed by "totalitarian socialism" in Russia, and who are persuaded that it is possible for a country to adopt the essential features of Russian economic arrangements and yet ensure individual freedom through political arrangements. The thesis of this chapter is that such a view is a delusion, that there is an intimate connection between economic and politics, that only certain combinations of political and economic arrangements are possible, and that in particular, a society which is socialist cannot also be democratic, in the sense of guaranteeing individual freedom.
>
> Economic arrangements play a dual role in the promotion of a free society. On the one hand, freedom in economic arrangements is itself a

component of freedom broadly understood, so economic freedom is an end in itself. In the second place, economic freedom is also an indispensable means toward the achievement of political freedom (Friedman 1962:7–8).

81 In the film 'Blade Runner', replicants are presented as life-like robots created to perform menial and dangerous tasks. Distinguishing then from their human counterparts raises insufferable difficulties for the unwary. In this respect, the strawman version of neo-liberalism (created by Team Mirowski), is in many aspects, replicant-like. Unless closely examined, it appears to provide a legitimate representation of neo-liberalism.

82 To reiterate, this representative Chicago academic, as presented, suspiciously resembles George Stigler. At points, the discussion seems to shift between a purported general conception of neo-liberalism and a more detailed characterisation of Stigler, as if the later somehow entirely incorporates the former.

83 Sadly in economics, this type of personal slicing and dicing represents nothing particularly new. John Stuart Mill was viciously attacked as being akin to Harriet Taylor's sexual slave. In essence, Mill was no more than her chosen male mouthpiece. Rejecting a theory (or policy), simply due to its origin (who conceived it), commits the avoidable sin of categorisation, as discussed in the previous chapter.

84 In this passage, Sherlock Holmes describes the Napoleon of crime, Professor Moriarity. Holmes refuses to accept that many of the crimes he notes could be merely random events. Instead, he posits the necessity for a central planner that links all of these varied events. Holmes may have erroneously travelled down the shunting leading inevitably to the realm of outright conspiracy theory. In some retellings of Holmes and his cases, Moriarity become a mere figment of his imagination.

85 Those readers who religiously avoid watching films would perhaps be enlightened by streaming some James Bond films. One of the more recent films would prove sufficient.

86 In much the same way, Sherlock Holmes required a brilliant and ubiquitous Professor Moriarity to truly test his mettle.

87 No one should be disturbingly shocked that groups of people attempt to conspire. However, the ability to successfully accomplish these projected conspiracies, to anywhere near their proposed objectives, is badly overrated. The world is much too complex, filled with too many unpredictable and random events to make such outcomes probable, or even possible. Such theories do satisfy the human desire to construct and then live in a world that makes sense to them. As a by-product, these conspiracies are capable of awarding their true believers the desired assurance that they are the unfortunate victims of the machinations of the powerful. Unfortunately,

actual evidence to support these invisible schemes, when carefully examined, proves to be scarce and rather fragile. Instead, what is on offer is a tortuous tying together of disparate and seemingly unrelated strings of events. Thus in this nether world, elite groups such as the Trilateral Commission, the Illuminati or the Bilderberg group are unveiled as composing the real power behind the bland façade of political authority. (Some other readers might prefer grinding their teeth at the mere mention of the World Economic Forum or the meetings of the Bohemian Club.) Even when solid evidence seems to effectively undermine conspiracy claims, belief in them are unalterably maintained. Contrary evidence becomes no more than a confirmation of a little understood, but entirely fiendish, plot. (Absence of evidence is viewed as a demonstration of the plotters power and competence.) The true believers, often for psychological reasons, need to hold on to their favoured conspiracies, despite multiple challenges to their validity. *The Protocols of Zion,* a bit of fiction effectively used to inflame Anti-Semitism, has been shown repeatedly to be a fraudulent concoction of the Tsarist Secret Police. Yet to advance their own agendas, groups continue to maintain the validity of this ersatz document. The propensity to embrace conspiracies seems equally characteristic of ideologues residing on either the left or right side of erected political fences. Even more so, such thinking is desperately embraced by those so far out in the wilderness that their views are difficult to pigeon-hole.

88   Burgin and Mirowski are content to travel down two very different paths. Burgin (2012) completed a compelling, if quite academic, analytical examination of the history of ideas. He traces out the post war response to a then prevailing form of collectivist thought. In a sense, he manages to broaden our understanding of how Classical Liberalism evolved, or was transformed, in the post war period. Mirowski is in this respect, intentionally leading a crusade against the dangers of neo-liberalism, a movement which he see as hatched by the Mont Pelerin Society. Both authors are fascinated by the same post war events, while harbouring two very different purposes lurking behind their efforts. They are essentially motoring down two, not at all parallel, sets of train tracks. In which case, given their goals, Burgin can hardly be faulted for not taking passage on Mirowski's ideological express. The indicated destination displayed, holds little interest for him. Curiously enough, the first time I heard Philip Mirowski speak at a seminar, discussing what would become his 1989 breakout book, *More Heat than Light,* Leonard Rapping lambasted Mirowski for not exploring the topic he found to be more interesting than the one actually discussed. This style of critical attack is a classic ploy that focuses more on what the critic thinks should have been written, rather than taking the time to evaluate what has been actually done. Doing so, allows a critic to simply dismiss disagreeable

research by shifting the terms of debate to more convivial terrain. But this tactic serves simply as a distraction. The task should be judged on whether an author has achieved his or her objective, rather than inserting one's own preferences as the sole standard of analysis.

> Burgin catches glimpses of this larger project from time to time, but opts not to explore the outer reaches of the neoliberal thought collective, such as the crucial orbit of dedicated think tanks and their transnational links, the participation of public relations firms such as Hill & Knowlton in formatting corporate-education programs, the innovation of astro-turfed political movements, the commercialization of science, or the decades-long war on the university. For Burgin, politics is mostly about reasoned arguments: in this, he would disagree with Frank Knight. Hewing to an older genre of individually focused intellectual history, he never really manages to drive home the thesis that Neoliberalism as a movement is ultimately far more concerned with epistemology than economics, with political strategies rather than doctrinal consistency, or the entrepreneurial self rather than macroeconomic models. Hence the "persuasion" of the title may be a little misleading; perhaps "reconditioning" would be more accurate (Mirowski 802).

89 Though Chicago people were never known for having successfully avoided personal aspersions, it is difficult to find an instance where they dismissed opponents as dupes. Dopes perhaps, a judgment made from the heights provided by supposedly residing on superior planes of insight. But they never viewed themselves as dupes of malevolent, vested interests.

> ... a workshop speaker asked whether he should deliver his paper standing or seated and George [Stigler]responded, "With a paper like this, under the table would not be inappropriate (Friedland 1993:781).
> Yes, that's a very strong feeling. It's OK to try game theory. But to stick around for twenty years and come up with a result that anything is possible and then to say that this is economics. This is almost the way George would be talking if he was sitting here. 'Having you and your six friends argue about a lemma, that's progress!' He wouldn't be indignant. He would be laughing. He would be dismissive. Saying, 'You're dopes. You're dopes.' What should you do with them George? 'Exile them to Samoa.' Dismissed with a wave of the hand (Conversation with Sam Peltzman, October 1997)

90 Despite what Team Mirowski might conclude, Burgin (2012) is really the go to book for understanding what issues were swirling around the perceived need to reform Classical Liberalism. A reader will discover a well-reasoned exploration of the contending forces and ideas at the first Mont Pelerin Society conference and those that followed. Members were only in accord on what they single-mindedly opposed in the post war world. Collectivism was the menace. But what might pose as humanity's salvation was a much more open question.

91   It might be more accurate to describe the Chicago movement, not so much as an attempt at counter-revolution, but more as a desire for a restoration of the past. In essence, they saw themselves reimagining, in the form of theory and policy, the working principles of Classical Liberalism. These post war Chicagoans aimed not at going back to the future, but rather restoring an imagined past (though with a few necessary adjustments). The difference specified (between counter-revolution and restoration) is one that distinguishes the English Restoration from its later Glorious Revolution. In the former case, the objective was to restore the Stuart monarchy under Charles II, undoing the restrictions applied by Oliver Cromwell. The latter instance aimed to change the status quo by bringing something new to English governance, rather than reaching back and restoring the past. William and Mary were meant to represent something new. Friedman, Stigler and their associates, Janus-like, looked back into the past in order to proceed into the future.

92   A distinct difference exists between constructing a solid, economic argument and raising doubts in a courtroom of law. Complete certainty is never achieved, even within a fastidiously careful analysis of economic thought. Contrary evidence will inevitably be unearthed. However, such evidence will by definition have more impact in a judicial system, where those charged are assumed to be innocent (until overwhelmingly proven to be guilty). In much of economics, only an approach generally deemed to be a better alternative will have the potential to dislodge an existing theory.

93   Given Stigler's razor sharp tongue and acerbic wit, it is difficult to entirely discount the possibility that at the fateful meeting with Colwell, Stigler succeeded in self-destructing through his predictably unguarded replies. Stigler himself clearly wanted the position. His rejection can't easily be relegated to a classic instance of deliberate self-sabotage. The more likely case is that George Stigler couldn't help being George Stigler. Subsequent attempts to lure him back to Chicago failed until 1958, when he was made the proverbial offer he couldn't refuse.

94   In his 1988 autobiography, Stigler describes his Mont Pelerin experience in a chapter titled 'The Apprentice Conservative'. It certainly can be argued that after the 1947 meeting (appropriately held on 1 April) Stigler's work and research became much more focused. Perhaps the path of this subsequent career can best be discerned in the five lectures he presented at the London School of Economics in 1948. (These were later published in 1949).

95   The Walgreen money allowed Stigler to lure such key economists as Gary Becker and Sam Peltzman to Chicago. (He could top up whatever salaries the University offered with generous research funds.) More diligent and highly skilled researchers would inevitably yield more published papers in high impact journals. Any brand needs the very best writers and marketers if it is to reach a desired, critical mass of acceptance.

He [Stigler] had an enormous grant at that time. And his salary was maybe $25,000 in 1958 dollars. That was what I think he was making per year. *It was one of the biggest salaries in economics.* And he had a grant for a full-time research assistant! (Conversation with Claire Friedland, October 1997). But my real contact with him [George Stigler] began in the 60s when I got to know him. Then I was thinking of coming to Chicago as a Visitor for a year. … I got to get this history right. Yeah, for a visit in '69. I already knew him, and I told him that I was coming. Then, I had to cancel because my first wife was sick. And I had to cancel the appointment. Then at the last minute she was getting better, but I already cancelled the appointment. I wrote to Stigler, this was in September. I said to him, I could come if there is anything open. And he said 'Come. I'll guarantee we'll cover it… cover your income if the Department can't do it.' So it means that I knew him already well enough for that to happen. I can't remember all the details of how I knew him so well. But I came at that time. I came as a Visitor. I got to know him quite well during that year. Attended the industrial organisation workshop regularly, which was very much an eye opener for me. And then, after a lot of hesitation, he and Milton Friedman worked on me a lot, he offered me extra research money if I stayed on. This was Walgreen money and it was a large sum. So he said I could have some research money and I decided to stay (Conversation with Gary Becker, October 1997).

96 As the previous chapter insisted, the urge to categorise (and to tar with the same brush), aggressively pushes aside nuances to achieve point scoring objectives.

97 Contrast neo-liberal with neo-classical, a more widely used label in the economics profession. Though employed dismissively by opponents to this form of economic analysis, proponents accept the later term without the merest show of embarrassment. In the same sense, a mainstream economist falling roughly into this category may at times appear to be the bête noire of an ideologue on either the right or left, but still retains a badge of acceptability to the bulk of the profession.

98 The operational strategy assumes that a tested theory provides the framework for broad policy guideposts. Consequently, according to this mindset, undermine the theory and the dependent policy necessarily crumbles.

99 Personal smears to divert attention away from the theory in question has a long, unfortunate history in economics as previously mentioned. In the nineteenth century, John Stuart Mill was dismissed as weak and unmanly. Even today, there are economists willing to dismiss him as a manipulated mouthpiece for Harriet Taylor's supposedly socialist views.

100 George Stigler often seemed incapable of preventing a sneer from surreptitiously defining his evaluation of any work to which he was vehemently opposed. An early counter-punch against John Kenneth Galbraith's idea of countervailing power was entitled 'The Economist Plays with Blocs'

(1954). Stigler continued to faithfully review Galbraith's output for decades to come, seemingly for the inherent joy of gleefully scoffing at the resulting efforts (1977). Or he could effectively dismiss John Maynard Keynes by deliberately referring to him as 'Lord Keynes'.

> Well, he was very intimidating in his critical approach. Your biggest fear was that he would make a joke at your expense. So one was always somewhat on guard (Conversation with Sherwin Rosen October 1997).

101 Theories and policies are inevitably marketed, since it is the rare economist who remains indifferent to whether his or her theories (or policies), are embraced. Focused marketing unfortunately can easily cross the line into deceptive practices. (Though, these may either be applied consciously or unconsciously. Ambition and what is at stake in winning acceptance blurs awareness of what might otherwise be carefully designated boundaries.) Ideology inevitably has some role to play in the selling process. (Only the dead are completely free of such pre-determined views.) But ideological enticements do not have to necessarily control whatever marketing is deemed to be necessary. Unfortunately, marketing itself remains inevitable.

> *And he [George Stigler] did want to convince people when he wrote.*
> Milton Friedman: Yes …
> *Otherwise, why would you write?*
> Milton Friedman: Yes.
> *If not to convince.*
> Aaron Director: I'm not so sure about that rash statement. [laughter]
> *You don't …*
> Aaron Director: You would write - you would want to write just to first make sure that you yourself understood well, and secondly to show other people …
> *Well, you have to convince yourself first.*
> Aaron Director: Well, yes you have to respect it seriously.
> *Absolutely. But if you're going to convince somebody else, or to explain it to somebody else.*
> Aaron Director: Well, you want to do it even if you didn't want to explain it to anybody else. Even if you wanted to explain it to yourself.
> *Mmm.*
> Aaron Director: And maybe just a few students [laughter]
> Milton Friedman: Now you are already giving up some ground.
> Aaron Director: I'm giving up my ground having paid for it (Conversation with Milton Friedman, Rose Friedman and Aaron Director, August 1997).

102 Notice the reference to the previous chapter. Tarring any Chicago based policy with a toxic ideological label allows opponents to instantly dismiss all such proposals. Any effort attached to a serious evaluation is happily avoided. Using this familiar approach inevitably encourages opponents to talk past one another and avoid the more difficult option of talking to one another.

103 Though there are many faults that could be found and reasonably argued about Friedman's work, this paragraph definitely seems to exist merely to eviscerate Milton Friedman. Unfortunately, sufficient evidence presented prior to this charge, which might support these allegations, remain among the missing. The connection between the Volker funds and Friedman's book is baldly stated, offering no more than the most evanescent connection rather than anything resembling cause and effect. It is true that Luhnow did desire an American version of Hayek's work. There is no doubt about that. Director was commissioned to fulfil this wish. He failed to do so, but Friedman's book came out instead. According to the logic provided by Team Mirowski, Friedman consequently produced his book almost entirely due to the pressure and expenditure provided by the Volker foundation. (No mention is made by Team Mirowski that the book was based on lectures and talks previously delivered by Friedman.) For consistency, Team Mirowski would require that Friedman shaped this already existing material into a book mostly (or even entirely) prompted by corporate directives. In essence, the book would not have existed without direct corporate pressure.

Thus the propinquity of a given event is employed to replace either evidence or logic. Through some opaque transmutation, Friedman's work (in this tailored narrative), becomes christened as a deliberate substitute for Director's non-existent output. Such argumentation will simply not do unless we suspend serious investigative efforts and replace it with innuendo. Moreover, if these claims are read with care, at least a modest impression remains that the authors' intention in providing Hayek with a semblance of praise, exists solely as a backhanded strategy that implicitly denounces Friedman. This intention is only compounded by a lack of any convincing rationale supporting the claim that Director was incapable of producing a volume that would meet Luhnow's objective. Given his history of publishing little, and at best only sporadically, the evanescent book requisitioned by, but denied to the Volker foundation, represents just another one of his many potential, but ultimately unwritten, works. There is nothing discernible that makes this particular non-event different from a succession of other non-events (in terms of publishing), that marked Director's career. One need not be an apologist for Friedman to find the accusations made by Team Mirowski to be simply lacking in evidence. Whatever purpose is supposedly served by making such accusations lacks any serious viability, unless innuendo is transformed into the sole decisive factor when evaluating theories and interpretations.

104 As examined in the previous chapter, such conclusions are a clear application of guilt by association, or tarring with the same brush. Team Mirowski never entertains the possibility that such assertions might depend upon consistently confusing causation with correlation. As previous stated,

corporate interests will inevitably fund congenial research to support their preferred views. Accomplishing these purposes will more often than not entail locating groups of congenial economists, rather than dictating the terms and results of funded research. (Such heavy-handed direction would inevitable undercut the marketable value of such efforts. Corporations would be paying for what is effectively damaged goods.) Based on this logic, an Occam razor style conclusion would accordingly eschew conspiracy-like arrangements. Instead, corporate interests would inevitably advance their cause by sniffing out those economists who harbour similar ideological leanings. Useful hires would simply reflect distinct corporate preferences or leanings.

Consequently, in a letter from Richard Posner (of the Law School) to George Stigler, Posner discusses the employment of academics associated with Stigler's Center for the Study of the Economy and State by Lexecon (Now Compass Lexecon). Lexecon was, and is, a consultancy providing economic research for corporate clients such as General Motors, IBM and Exxon. What should come as no surprise is Lexecon's interest in Chicago consultants, given the general economic views that can be attributed to this group of academics.

> So far as the future is concerned, Lexecon will not attempt to hire any young person newly associated with the Center, such as a Rod Smith; a DeVany (Art DeVany) is I think fair game for us (Lexecon) because his habits, scholarly commitment, etc. are established. (Our reasons for laying off on newcomers are narrowly selfish: once they get accustomed to two incomes, one academic and one consulting, it's difficult to hire them as full-time consultants, as we would have liked to do with Linneman [Peter Linneman].) (Letter from Richard Posner to George Stigler, February 13, 1979).

105 Peltzman is painted as an easily manipulated target, subservient to the wishes of the pharmaceutical industry. (These charges can be discovered by perusing Nik-Khah 2014.) But knowing at least something personally about the man, such behaviour becomes even more doubtful. The attributions made by Nik-Khah appear to depend largely on selected quotes from a limited number of articles. Such a characterisation, on examination, provides a rather faint reflection of Peltzman's aims and behaviour. His career as an expert witness, for instance, failed to get off the ground. "We once tried to hire Peltzman on a project, but he insulted the client, and it fell through" (Letter from Richard A Posner to George Stigler; February 13, 1979 concerning potential recruits for work at Lexecon). (When I inquired whether he wished to edit out any part of a lengthy interview I had conducted with him, he simply advised me to publish it as is.) To paint, or even implicitly depict, Peltzman as some sort of pay to play figure is a bit of a

reach, unless more than coincidental evidence can be unearthed. His career is stubbornly one of calling them as he sees them, though a case might be made that he enters an investigation with a distinct ideological bias. However, even such a more muted claim in that vein may not ultimately hold up under close scrutiny. Stigler's consistent claim of flexible pricing runs at least a bit aground in Peltzman's empirical depiction. "Output prices tend to respond faster to input increases than decreases" (Peltzman 2000: 466). The Peltzman portrayal depicted by Nik-Khah (2014) distinctly jars with reality, since Peltzman never appears to curry the favour of others. As Lucky Ned Pepper says to Mattie Ross in True Grit (2010) in describing her all too blunt speech, "You do not varnish your opinions."

106 Aaron Director remains something of a mystery. One largely unanswered question is the origin of his very conservative (or even reactionary, right wing) perspective. An argument does exist claiming that he underwent a sort of major 'road to Damascus' conversion under the Svengali-like influence of Frank Knight. Proponents point to his prior work with a labour union in Oregon (having taught at the Portland Labor College). This stint occurred before arriving at Chicago, in 1927, as a graduate student. His original purpose was to work with Paul Douglas (then representing a staunch left wing component of the department). He co-authored a volume with Douglas in 1931. Nonetheless, Director would come to refer to his brother-in-law, Milton Friedman, only a touch ironically, as "my radical brother-in-law". He, in fact, wrote to his sister Rose before her marriage to Milton "Tell him I shall not hold his very strong New Deal leanings — authoritarian to use an abusive term — against him" (Friedman and Friedman, 1998:81). An alternative, and newer, view rejects the idea that Chicago blew away misconceived socialists dreams that had cobwebbed his brain. (The theme of a disillusioned leftist becoming increasingly right wing is something of a standard trope.) Instead, this perspective sees him as a consistent contrarian and iconoclast, which would explain his ability to bond with Frank Knight. (For a period, they even shared lodgings together). This view has been ably presented by Robert Van Horn (2010).

> Milton Friedman: Well, Frank Knight had a particular influence on the people who came close to him, including Aaron. Aaron was a disciple of Knight's as well, much more so, in a way.
> Aaron Director: Well …
> Milton Friedman: Would you say you were more or less so than George?
> Aaron Director: Maybe for a while, but not for long.
> Milton Friedman: For a while I would say you were more so. Aaron and Knight once jointly owned a farm in Indiana (Conversation with Milton Friedman, Rose Friedman, Aaron Director, August 1997).

107 Van Horn (2010), who has done breakthrough work by shining a spotlight on the shadowy figure of Aaron Director, should have known better. Director in action, immediately brings to mind the lyrics from the Marx Brothers' film *Horsefeathers* (1932), namely 'Whatever it is, I'm against it'.

108 The idea put forward, seems to conclude that if Director wasn't such a faithful corporate servant, then the cash spigot would have been closed off. Namely, that he could skim by his contractual failure since the work he produced forwarded corporate interests. But Director was simply doing what he chose to do, whether in the presence of corporate cash or its absence. Continual funding hardly indicates anything resembling a state of obedience on Director's part. In fact, it is difficult to conclude anything of relevance based on this incident.

109 In more recent times, we can point to a President Trump finding a trade theory match when hiring the economist Peter Navarro. The story widely related is that initially Trump's son-in-law (Jared Kushner), zeroed in on Navarro by whipping through amazon.com. His investigatory method was limited to searching for a book that would parallel Trump's bellicose claims concerning the Chinese trade menace. Navarro's book apparently provided a satisfactory match.

110 Hayek had an active role at the University of Chicago between 1950 and 1962. Such key figures as Friedman and Director had a four year start on Hayek, having been hired as of 1946. Hayek never interacted directly with the Economics Department, the Business or Law Schools, which in the post war period formed the foundational tripod of the Chicago School. Instead, Hayek was ensconced in the Committee on Social Thought, where his concern focused on matters of political philosophy, not economics.

111 This evaluation of events is perhaps an unwanted side effect of approaching material with conspiracy tinged goggles. The desire to deliver a tight, coherent explanation can sustain an implicit imperative that forces all observed events to fit into one tightly articulated frame.

112 For that matter, given Chicago's relatively low pay, Friedman was not impervious to potentially better offers and might have easily been lured away.

> Machlup was pressing me to consider John Hopkins. As you doubtless know, Smithies turned them down for Harvard. I don't know whether to think about it seriously or not. They would offer 8,000 which with 3,000 to 5,000 from the Bureau makes an enormous differential over the 7,500 plus 4E contract I am scheduled to get next year (7,000 this year). Tell me, from the fullness of your experience, together with my indifference curves, how large a price ought I to pay for the privilege of being at Chicago? (Letter from Milton Friedman to George Stigler Tuesday [April 7, 1948] in Hammond and Hammond 206:80).

113 Likelihood is lacking in such a characterisation. Reality trumpets the fact that it isn't in either the self-interest of the researcher (or the corporate sponsor), to be suspected of deliberately shaping results to meet pre-ordered conclusions. The reputation of the researcher (as well as the research delivered), would be deeply discounted should it become widely viewed as lacking independence. Nor would tainted evidence be of much value to the corporate underwriters. Stupidity abounds in all manner of positions and procedures, but this type of overt corruption would appear to be the exception rather than the rule.

114 A distinction can usefully be made here between buying research and the act of hiring an economist as an expert witness, or even the economist who appears as an expert witness. George Stigler did both, but in his autobiography wondered if in such roles, an economist deserved to claim that title. Given the political process, adequate performance in that category demands that those economists so trapped, display loyalty to a given administrative interest. Though in selecting expert witnesses, only fools would select those whose testimony might contain unwanted surprises. However, this explicit connection is not quite the same as accepting research funding with the proviso that any conclusion must reflect a vested interest in the eventual outcome.

> I conclude – and perhaps I am alone in concluding – that when the economist goes to Washington, he deserves no more credence, and no less, than any other political appointment, and it is mildly deceptive to address him as Doctor of Professor (Stigler, 1988:135-136).

115 At issue here is the precise role to be played by an academic economist, such as those residing within the ovals of Chicago. Though usually speaking as one, Milton Friedman and George Stigler displayed distinct differences in this regard, especially as it extended to public policy. For Friedman, no real issues were at stake. Economic theory was the indisputable foundation for policy formation. (Here he followed the path blazed by the founder of the Chicago Department, J. Lawrence Laughlin. In the emotional Presidential election of 1896, he boldly raised the hobgoblin of inflation to back the gold standard championed by McKinley and the Republican Party. In a similar fashion, Friedman would be active in boosting Goldwater during the 1964 campaign.) For Friedman, universal theory (by abstracting and generalising), translated into a one size fits all policy machine, an approach based on the curative powers of market exchange. In this respect, Friedman was the unambiguous crusader, peddling economic salvation to any and all available audiences. His colleague, George Stigler, took a more nuanced and reticent approach. In some sense, at least in policy matters, the influence of his teacher, Frank Knight, had not entirely dissipated. Stigler was

much more reluctant to preach to the economically unenlightened (the general public or the political class), than was Friedman. In an important sense he tended to dismiss the power of economists to persuade. Though not abstaining from taking policy positions in less formal talks or interviews, he questioned if the performance of these roles (or appearing as an expert witness), were legitimately in the purview of the economist as scientist.

> Or, alternatively, if a pure scientist – one believing only demonstrated things – is asked his opinion on policy, he must decline to answer – and listen to his intellectual inferiors give advice on policy. Hence the role of the pure scientist is terribly painful to assume in economics. Your fiscal article, my minimum wages, all of Henry Simons are impure science, and verboten. Can you mention a single instance of written advice on specific policy from Mitchell? (Letter from George Stigler to Milton Friedman, December 1948 in Hammond and Hammond 2005:96).

116 A corporate laissez faire predilection is, no doubt, a convenient simplification. Rent seeking regulation (under the guise of welfare enhancing measures), is far from uncommon. Corporate entities, especially those with significant market share, may also prefer the stability that long run regulation may provide. Such constraints may deliver additional barriers (in terms of opportunity cost), to would be competitors. In a contrary fashion, additional market uncertainly generates added opportunities for competition, which can nibble away at, or even overturn, any favourable status quo.

117 Someone like George Stigler was convinced that he understood how the world worked. For him, society continued to rotate due to the rational choices made by a myriad of individuals. This undeniable fact was exhibited to him most clearly by the miracle of market efficiency. From his perspective, nothing was left to debate in terms of this issue.

> He [George Stigler] was absolutely sure the economy was on his side and if research was properly done it would show this. He really believed that he understood how the world works. And the way the world works had been shown to him by the theory of price (Conversation with James Kindahl, October 1997).

118 Team Mirowski tends to display an almost automatic suspicion of the motives evinced by Chicago's denizens. This skepticism is supported by what they claim is an almost Chicago-style indifference to public welfare. (Though Chicago economist would vigorously dispute such a charge. Both sides of the debate pose as strict defenders of the public good.) However, unless one posits that either Stigler or Friedman was consistently duplicitous, it is misleading to automatically dismiss their professed belief that markets yield predictable welfare benefits. If anything, their belief is that government interventions, no matter how well intentioned, are ultimately

deleterious to the very people such measures seek to assist. (In this, these Chicago economists revel in the idea of unintended consequences.) Moreover, Stigler and Friedman believed that unlike their opponents, they alone sustained an abiding faith in the wisdom of the consumer. (Thus, these Chicagoans would equally reject the perspective of Team Mirowski as one that deifies the Nanny State. A vision in which a wise and selfless government is required to engineer beneficial outcomes for helpless consumers.) These observations fail to imply that it is not perfectly legitimate to dispute Chicago style assumptions, theoretical structures, or any subsequent policy recommendations. However, doing so should not generate an ingrained suspicion attached to the core motives underlying those professed policy positions. Nor should moral issues be unearthed concerning the intrinsic honesty of the various Chicago researchers.

> The assistance could be much better targeted – now much public housing and other benefits are going to the middle classes. More importantly, the beneficiaries of the negative income tax would be given freedom of choice – to choose perhaps more food or medical care at the cost of less housing. The chief opposition to this proposal has come from the many people who believe that the poor would spend most unwisely. I, like Friedman, do not share this fear, but I do share the fear many have that the negative income tax would be added to, not substituted for, the vast smorgasbord of special policies now in place (Stigler 1988: 156).

119 To briefly clarify, citing ideological biases is a fair critical practice, and even a necessary one. However, claiming venality is quite a different kettle of economic fish. The evidence that any Chicago economist, deliberately changed conclusions, or altered research, in exchange for monetary gain seems, despite the best efforts of Team Mirowski, to be largely non-existent. Nor is it necessary to lodge such a claim, if a critic's true objective is to understand an opponent's work, while evaluating any discovered weaknesses. There remains a vast gulf between sceptical analysis and the automatic urge to disembowel any antithetical theory.

120 The claim advanced isn't that this approach is the story that Team Mirowski should have explored. The suggested point is that critical alternatives to their methods and tactics do exist. Many of these, if done carefully, could succeed in undercutting the validity of neo-liberalism. This objective is the one that Team Mirowski so fervidly seeks. All of these alternatives would successfully avoid an unwarranted detour into the personal ethics of a set of targeted neo-liberals. The core idea that bad people develop bad policies is tenuous, at best, more of a distraction than an attempt at serious analysis. Consequently, shifting the terms of debate onto the boggy ground of ethics, personality and intentions might instead turn out to be a distinctly unfortunate strategy.

121 Team Mirowski accurately designates Milton Friedman, George Stigler and Aaron Director as being the key engineers of the post war Chicago School. However, one commonly shared feature that remains applicable to all three was the influence that Frank Knight exerted on the trio during the interwar period. (It can be argued that to lesser degrees, both Henry Simons and Jacob Viner left their marks on these latter day South Side stars.) Knight, Simons and Viner were trained and operated within a certain version of Classical Liberal Economics. Consequently, Friedman, Stigler and Director were all intimately familiar with this older approach to economics. To a degree, all three of these academics were convinced that they had reformed, rather than deserted, the essential core of Classical Liberalism.

122 Playing armchair psychologist here is seductive. But, it poses the danger of falling into an insidious trap. However, the intention displayed is only one of working backwards, not of psycho-analysing. What Team Mirowski has written on the subject is available for any eyes to pursue. Then one of the many questions that might arise is why they chose to take a given approach. Clearly the intention is to undermine (if not demolish) neo-liberalism. But by attempting to read their available work carefully, it is possible to discern what strategies they adopted to achieve the desired end, as well as which ones are largely missing. Doing so does create something resembling a psychological map.

123 Neo-liberalism, in Team Mirowski's endeavour, serves as something of a portmanteau formation that conveniently encompasses everything that nourishes the long standing rot within the economics discipline. The choice of whipping boys, always convey a certain rhetorical impact. Neo-liberalism (under their auspices), serves as a blanket condemnation for each and every policy that the Team so vehemently rejects. In certain progressive circles, the term 'neo-liberal' conveys the same degree of revulsion that is more commonly reserved for the equally unredeemable label of 'pederast', a crime even hardened criminals supposedly detest. Neo-liberal then is employed as a slur to be spat out pejoratively, much in the manner that neo-classical economics can become a label of opprobrium among opponents. Though as Mirowski admits, those that he labels as neo-liberals haven't used that terminology to distinguish their views since the early 1950s. While neo-classical seems a label acknowledged by most economists (although differences exist in its exact characterization). Exactly what is incorporated by the label 'neo-liberal' (and what it may represent), remains much more contentious.

> Neoliberalism, then is not generally used as a term of approbation. The doctrine purportedly provides a rationale for powerful transnational corporations who wish to utilize the power of the state to advance their own interests. The chief desideratum of transnational capital is a stable global economy, which ensures both a steady supply of resources for the production process, and a

steady supply of consumers for the purchasing of goods. Corporations accordingly use international organizations like the World Bank, the WTO, and the IMF, as well as the military power of strong states (and in particular the United States) to enforce the ideology of the market and to spread Western (especially consumerist) values. (Caldwell 2011:308-309).

124 Because the tendency to jump from general theory to specific policy is common within the economics profession, Team Mirowski prefers to avoid what would involve a detailed evaluation and analysis of neo-liberal policies, backed by their theoretical justifications. Taking these Chicago neo-liberals to the woodshed and roughing them up, is quite naturally more appealing than engaging in the tedium of examining evidence and making a slew of evaluations.

125 Though seeming to be a difference that is only separated by a fine line, this approach is in practice radically different than exploring the impact of Chicago's recommended policies. These may benefit the corporate sector, but for Chicago economists that particular result doesn't preclude improving the general welfare. (Every policy cannot be reduced to a zero sum game played amongst societal classes.) But it is essential then to first fully understand the theoretical basis of their policies, while examining any available evidence that is applicable. To instead brand them, at least implicitly, as malevolent mouthpieces and toadies of the corporate sector, serves to dismiss, rather than trying to understand, the research churned out by Chicago. The process is one of classifying and branding in order to condemn, as explored in the previous chapter. However, out of hand dismissal, stands as a perversion of any recognised economic perspective, or any serious attempt at economic analysis. Such a strategy appears to subvert the purpose of all such research. Name calling has historically failed to create a path to knowledge or enlightenment.

126 If all Team Mirowski wants to say is that the ideological leanings of Chicago economists result in them promoting corporate priorities, then simply spell that out. The corporate financial support just confirms this supposition. But even to imply that these economists are in a pay to play arrangement seems more like a distraction, or a Stiglerean urge to completely decimate a despised theoretical and policy perspective.

127 A clearly corrupt academic would appear to be both more unreliable, while also remaining more expensive. Such hired help might be apt to simply shill for the highest bidder. A complete lack of beliefs, demonstrated by being a gun for hire, is easily linked to money (and considerable sums of it), which may be required if a tamed economist is to be kept in line. Provided the academic could somehow maintain a reasonable standard of reputation.

128 Certainly by definition, a reputable economist would shun such perversions of academic integrity. Those embracing the 'dark side' would automatically

fall from grace, no longer worthy of being considered reputable. A corporate purchase would inevitably depreciate the price paid.

129 Stigler here is specifically focused on policy alone, rather than theoretical matters. In the realm of pure theory (where economics is equated to science from Stigler's viewpoint), the self-interest of an individual academic doesn't supposedly enter (or perhaps is just less detectable).

> Such scientific information is value-free in the strictest sense: no matter what one seeks, he will achieve it more efficiently the better his knowledge of the relationship between action and consequences. (Stigler 1976:350)

Notice how Stigler here tries to resolve the tension between the necessities of a self-interested academic and the objectivity he wants to attribute to the scientist. The pure researcher gains satisfaction and a sense of accomplishment (of doing good) from the process itself, without the associated need for widespread recognition. This tension is never entirely resolved in Stigler's work. Somehow, while individuals are by definition motivated solely by narrow self-interest, economists, though believing this, can still be (almost magically) lifted outside the confines of this restricted boundary. Without becoming too wildly far-fetched, the gift of economics is somehow placed in the same category as the Christian gift of grace.

130 Friedman mounted a running campaign to undercut the validity of Keynesian macroeconomics, including and perhaps especially, its preferred economic policies. One way to do so was to denigrate John Maynard Keynes' stature as an economist. Friedman attempted to transform him from a giant into an inconsequential pygmy. In an extended debate with Don Patinkin concerning the quantity theory of money and Chicago's interwar traditions, Keynes and his achievements in *The General Theory* are reduced to no more than creating a footnote to the quantity theory. For Friedman, Keynes' contribution to monetary theory extends only as far as the concept of the liquidity trap. According to Friedman, Keynes was entirely obsessed with this singular idea, which in Friedman's estimation alone, arises continuously throughout the work. See Freedman (2011) for an overly detailed account of Friedman's strategy. Personal denigration of opponents is however not limited to the efforts of Friedman, or to Team Mirowski. Samuelson felt emboldened to dismiss Marx as a minor Ricardian and an autodidact. Further back, John Stuart Mill was attacked for being effeminate. In each case, character assassination of one type or another is employed to undercut the validity of an economist's work. The terms of debate are ruthlessly shifted away to territory more conducive to an attack. By pointing out personal shortcomings of one sort or another, opponents avoid the much harder task of performing a careful and critical analysis of that individual's thought.

Re 4th edition of *Theory of Price:*

> I congratulate you on restraining yourself from including a picture of Keynes
> and even more on not even mentioning him in your index (Letter from Milton
> Friedman to George Stigler Dec. 16, 1986).

131 Without attempting to place Mirowski, or any of his associates, on the classic couch of psycho-therapy, the idea of projection involves attributing one's own faults and failures to targeted opponents. Politicians often fall into this trap. Former US President Trump displayed a classic case of projection every time he opened his mouth. An observer could chart Trump's own dubious projects and trespasses by simply listing the charges he made while lashing out at his opponents.

132 Stigler spent a good chunk of his career scorning the hypocrisy and elitism of leftist intellectuals. His point was that such anti-market views are fueled mostly by ignorance and prejudice, while being buoyed by an implacable sense of ill-founded superiority.

> In one basic respect I believe that the criticism by the intellectuals is misplaced, and at times even hypocritical. The American economy produces many goods that are vulgar, silly, or meretricious, as judged by standards which I share with many intellectuals (Stigler 1963:89).

What the Chicago Boys and Team Mirowski seem to share is an inability to exhibit a sufficient degree of self-examination. Stigler and Friedman could remain seemingly oblivious to the devastating impact of the McCarthy era on academic freedom, while a decade later remaining terminally alarmed by the actions of leftist leaning students and academics. Only at this later moment, rather than during the earlier one, was an unflinching defense of academic freedom aroused. Friedman would even go so far as to raise the question of whether the connection tying leaders of leftist movements to Jewish ethnicity might be 'bad for the Jews'.

> I have a couple of times given some quasi-popular lectures on the topic 'Capitalism and the Jews' ... The theme is the conflict between the two propositions: (a) No people have benefited so much from capitalism as the Jews. (b) No people have done so much by writing and political action to destroy capitalism. How come? (Letter from Milton Friedman to George Stigler, September 20, 1971).

133 The Stigler archives, for instance, housed at the University of Chicago, contains box after box of material, including troves of letters, drafts of papers and much else. But even the letters saved have a certain difficult to detect bias. One of George Stigler's secretaries at Chicago, explained to me that periodically Stigler would ask her to go through and weed out most of his retained correspondence. However, he would soon find more pressing

matters, which she would need to immediately complete. The winnowing of the letters would stop somewhere early in the alphabet. This scenario was repeated several times during her tour of duty. In which case, the surviving correspondence would be biased by excluding a good deal from the beginning of the alphabet.

Clearly, however, attempting any serious stroll through all that material will involve finding items that appear somewhat at odds with one another. Team Mirowski does little to explain how such material should be weighed. Again, the impression provided by just reading the Team Mirowski material is that a few, quoted archival papers are representative of all the rest.

134 Whether it is accurate is another question. A counter argument based on observational evidence might propose that a decisive segment of the voting public makes their decisions based on an emotional, rather than a self-interested and rational, grounding. Only if you extend the meaning of self-interest to cover all and any decisions can the Chicago School outlook be entirely verified. But by extending, or distorting, the meaning to that extent, the value of making that assumption becomes of questionable validity. Something that provides an answer to everything, in practice provides an answer to nothing. Moreover, such a broad base definition of self-interest would contradict Stigler's own understanding. He rejected the overarching idea that anything someone did simply reflected self-interest. As Stigler said, or should have said, that under that understanding, if you saw someone drinking battery acid, all you could say in response is that the person sure likes battery acid. A statement, not in itself, all that useful, let alone exciting.

135 This fundamental difference stands out even more, since in regard to most issues very little daylight distinguished Stigler's position from that of Friedman.

> George Stigler, who was very critical of people, was almost worshipful of Milton Friedman. And I remember that one of his dicta was that a Milton Friedman theorem was more credible than any other theorem, because everybody picks on Milton. It's an unfair world and so forth, which means that he gets a more rigorous testing than anyone else. Doesn't he have genuinely adulatory remarks in his autobiography about Milton? (Conversation with Paul Samuelson October 1997).

On espousing and trying to influence public policy, there was a decisive gap, as indicated by both oral and written pronouncements. These then would have to be heavily discounted to support the somewhat derogatory portrait etched by Team Mirowski.

> Milton Friedman: And it is true that George would tend to emphasize, more than I would, the extent to which it was crucial- you're just spitting in the

wind if you try to advise governmental officials to do something which has not heretofore been in their self-interest to do. It may be so most of the time, but where that comes from, I don't know.

Aaron Director: Where what comes from? I'm just asking him to say it over again.

Milton Friedman: Where George's going so far in the direction of not letting anything other than self-interest influence governmental behaviour.

Aaron Director: He's not very special in that respect.

Milton Friedman: Whatever …

Aaron Director: I don't know what you're thinking.

Milton Friedman: I'm not objecting to what you're saying, I'm …

Aaron Director: No, state it over again.

Milton Friedman We're talking about the notion that you can interpret government behaviour in the same way that you interpret business behaviour. Equilibrium agreement arising out of individuals pursuing their own self-interest.

Aaron Director: Well, that's why you go into business in a democracy. Government is a type of function. But I don't understand that the government is a separate function. I'm sorry.

Milton Friedman: The political market …

Aaron Director: Yeah.

Milton Friedman: We're talking about the political world, the political market as opposed to the economic one. But in interpreting the political market, George very consistently, interprets the political market as a resolution of opposing self-interests and paid zero …

Aaron Director: No …

Milton Friedman: … tended to give very little attention to the extent to which it arose, out of the desire of the people involved in government, to promote the public interest. That is, I think a far statement …

Aaron Director: Yes.

Milton Friedman: … and he took that position to a greater extent than most other people.

Aaron Director: Did he really?

Milton Friedman: Yes, I think that is true.

Aaron Director: Do you?

Milton Friedman: Yes.

Aaron Director: Hm.

Milton Friedman: And you do too.

Aaron Director: I don't know about that.

Milton Friedman: Well, I think we have come to a dead end there (Conversation with Milton Friedman, Rose Friedman and Aaron Director, August 1997).

136 There are two items, written in the last five years of George Stigler's life that Claire Friedland (his long time researcher) thought might be particularly relevant to this paradox: Stigler, George J. (1986) *The Regularities of*

Regulation. Occasional Paper no. 3. Edinburgh: Hume Institute and Stigler, George J. (1989) *The Political Redistribution of Income* [Die politische Umuerteilung des Einkommens]. Zurich: Bank Hofmann AG.

137 If you examine Stigler's ideas (and those of other Mont Pelerin members), during the early post war period, a commonly held feeling was that they had successfully battled the authoritarian collectivism of Nazi Germany. Consequently, they now felt obliged to strenuously block a similar evil stemming from the Soviet Union.

138 To justify these elitist charges appears to require such a deep dive into the collective Chicago id as would demand an extended séance with Dr. Freud, if we were to ever find our way back to conscious thought.

139 Thus in the days in which Friedman, Stigler and Director pictured themselves as counter-revolutionaries, trying nobly to push back the onslaught of collectivist distortion, they were also given to grumble about the unearned and dubious intellectual dominance achieved by their opponents.

140 The attack on the mainstream media (by right leaning elements), goes back many decades. Although more recently, these grumbles have gained in fervour (at times displaying moments of pure, untethered emotionalism0. However, the proclivity of Chicago style followers to tag the media as collectivists is freely duplicated in pantomime style by Team Mirowski. Somehow, they discover an ability to reinterpret the Mont Pelerin Society as a variant of the classic collectivist enterprise. Given the personalities and bickering attached to the Society's history, doing so requires a certain imaginative leap. (An almost obsessive need to discover someone to blame is required for what might instead be, at least to some degree, a failure within one's own favoured ideology. This tendency mirrors a certain question of eyes and the motes within them.) In a fashion parallel to the foibles of Team Mirowski, Milton Friedman was certainly keen on wrinkling out any perceived collectivist tendencies, or threats, posed by the media, as he scrupulously prepared to host a Society conclave.

> One of the topics we would like to have discussed has to do with the mass media and the trend toward collectivism. Why is it that almost everywhere the great bulk of the contributors to the mass media, the journalist, the radio commentators, the TV performers tend to be collectivists in their orientation? (Letter from Milton Friedman to Raymond Aron, January 5, 1972).

141 No doubt, many in recent times will point out the work of Rupert Murdoch and Fox News. Even more so, the role of social networks and the dark money pouring into that sector are far from fanciful. However, it seems hardly legitimate to project the current situation back through time. Neither now, nor in the earlier era of McCarthy fabrications, is there compelling evidence of the Chicago School knowingly producing bogus research.

Friedman, Stigler and Director (or Becker in later years) thought of their work as a force promoting the general welfare through scientific means, not as advancing the vested interests of corporate entities.

142 In contrast to these claims, it can easily be argued that Burgin (2012) presents a well-reasoned argument backed by a wealth of evidence. Moreover, his work is not so obviously motivated by any clear cut ideological or political agenda. Taking issue with Burgin should be more a matter of disputing his evidence and conclusions, since his intention is not to somehow weaponise history of economic thought. Team Mirowski opts simply to dismiss his work.

143 In this case, Team Mirowski at least conveys the appearance that only certain archival evidence is determinative. Unquestionably, letters running counter to their narrative could be dismissed as consciously duplicitous, but in that case, championing archival research starts to ring quite hollow.

144 A thought collective can seamlessly transform itself into something that more closely resembles a complex conspiracy. What appears to be a useful categorization to explain this reformation of old style liberalism is then tainted by an opposed ideological stance.

145 The idea of a 'double truth' emphasizes the claim by Team Mirowski of the elitist and non-democratic nature of those belonging to the Mont Pelerin Society, as well as its associated Chicago minions. Frankly, this truth would compose a reductionist assertion that the Chicago reconceptualization of liberalism, ostensibly emphasizing individual freedom and liberty, is no more than a glittering charade.

> Hayek hit upon the brilliant notion of developing the "double truth" doctrine of neoliberalism – namely, an elite would be tutored to understand the deliciously transgressive Schmittian necessity of repressing democracy, while the masses would be regaled with ripping tales of "rolling back the nanny state" and being set "free to choose" – by convening a closed Leninist organization of counter-intellectuals (Mirowski 2015:444–445).

This pejorative blackening of motives appears to replicate the worst tendencies of the Chicago School. These efforts, staged by both sides, reduce to a series of school yard tactics where name calling tends to crowd out analysis.

146 Arnold Harberger was the point man for a Chicago inspired set of policies and institutions that would become very controversial in the 1970s and 1980s, lingering even into the present era. He, more than figures like Friedman, were the program's 'father figures'. Friedman, however was the public face of Chicago.

In any case, starting in the 1950s, a select group of Chilean economists were encouraged to do their graduate training at Chicago, aided by grants from the Ford and Rockefeller Foundations (hardly radical right organisations). The program, shepherded by Harberger, would only gain its notoriety after 11 September, 1973. That was when Augusto Pinochet led a military coup against the government of Salvadore Allende. The subsequent economic program instituted was largely constructed by these Chicago disciples. Whether such an economic program favoured the Chilean people, or was weighted toward US multinationals, remains a question of continuing contention. The coup itself was rumoured to have heavily depended on funds made available by the CIA.

> "Chile was not a jewel in 1995, but it's a jewel today," the economist Arnold Harberger says in the documentary *Chicago Boys*. Harberger, an American economist who taught at the University of Chicago from 1953 to 1991 alongside Milton Friedman, was a father figure to the "boys" – a group of Chilean economists who studied at the university in the 1950s. There, they became enthusiastic converts to Friedman's free-market economic philosophies, which they were then given free rein to implement on an unprecedented scale during Augusto Pinochet's dictatorship of Chile. The ideas they brought home from Chicago changed Chilean society forever and made it one of the richest countries in Latin America (Opazo 2016:1).

It is perhaps essential to realize that Chicagoans like Harberger didn't view themselves as simple factotums facilitating corporate objectives. From their perspective, opening a country's economy to the magic of the marketplace was the best, and perhaps only way, to foster economic growth and development. They saw themselves as a force for good, rather than as nefarious operatives taking their marching orders from some profit hungry corporate headquarters.

> Well, I [Arnold Harberger] think I can give you a little story. We in Chicago spawned the so-called 'Chicago Boys', who in turn spawned the revolution of economic policy in Chile, which in turn led to major economic revolutions in other countries in Latin America. So, to me, that's a lot of garbage, the idea to me of being fatalistic about this [policy changes]. You know, I've seen it happen. I've seen the transformation take place, I've seen societies bloom. And this happens in other countries too. It happened in Taiwan, it happened in Malaysia, it happened in Korea, it happened in Australia and New Zealand for that matter. It happened in Spain (Conversation with Arnold Harberger, October 1997).

147 Friedman had a one size fits all set of policies. As a result, he maintained a sort of naiveté that assumed he could perform as an instant expert when dealing with very disparate countries, cursed with quite different problems. His insistence on universality and generalization ignored the alternative that

sometimes, attending closely to differences can prove far more productive in gaining useful insights.

148 Market fundamentalism encompasses the idea of consumer sovereignty. The individual remains the best judge of what he or she might want. This idea harks back to Hayek's view of information and its dispersion. Moreover, this particular train of thought conveniently justifies not placing restraints on individual choice, at least of the market variety. Thus the market place, through this particular chunk of logic, becomes the guardian bulwark defending individual liberty and freedom.

> Consumer sovereignty is both the end of the story and the beginning. And we don't argue with the consumer, no matter how self-destructive these demands are or how inappropriate. Anyway, if you want consumers to be free to choose in the market place, how can we argue with them in the political arena where, in a sense, they are acting as consumers too? Well, in his last years he [George Stigler] was writing frequently about this (Conversation with Claire Friedland, October 1997).

149 A radical act of transubstantiation would be required to see such a statement as dangerously elitist.

150 More fastidious readers will doubtless become annoyed at the repetition of previously stated themes in the following paragraphs. I feel obliged to concede the legitimacy of such concerns. Sadly, however, bitter experience has taught me that you cannot repeat a simple idea a sufficient number of times. Plus as mentioned before, the mere utterance of the name 'Mirowski' seems to completely drown out any of the more central points, or aims, that drive a paper. I realise in advance that no repetitive avowals will successfully drive out the notion (at least for some readers) that this chapter exists solely to attack and destroy all things Mirowski. That such intentions could not be further from the truth will be implicitly ignored by all those who fasten, like recalcitrant barnacles, on reaching an unwavering conclusion. The underpinnings of such an unalterable mindset requires only that the name 'Mirowski' appears at the centre of a critical analysis. Yet, the very essence of a case study means that the specifics of the case presented are not the substantive aim of the study. What is presented is intended to be no more than an illustration of an underlying generalisation. Bluntly speaking, numerous other economists (and selected aspects of their work), would have fit the bill just as adequately.

151 Knight's favourite quote comes in handy here. Given his brutal and consistent scepticism, it is doubtful that he would have approved of Team Mirowski's devices and strategies. "The trouble with people is not that they don't know but that they know so much that ain't so" (Josh Billings).

152 A widely reported study provides evidence that individual understanding can be influenced, if not outright seduced, by prior readings, especially those that project adamantine opinion.

> Simply including an ad hominem attack in a reader comment was enough to make study participants think the downside of the reported technology was greater than they'd previously thought (Brossard and Scheufele 2013:2).

153 This assignment of economists as being no better than corporate puppets is reminiscent, to a degree, of using the term 'mouthpiece' to designate the role and position played by lawyers. As such, lawyers have nothing to say that is of their own making. They simply shape and enunciate the wishes of their current clients.

154 I, no doubt, will be accused of sinning in much the same way. Completely avoiding such missteps seems incompatible with managing to avoid those realms where bland thoughts and writing dominate.

155 One last word may be necessary to re-inforce what might otherwise be missed. The intention here is not to evaluate what Team Mirowski terms to be neo-liberalism. Instead, the attempt is to weigh their evaluation of this particular ideology. The issue then is more one of methodology and balance, rather than the validity of the ideology attacked. In simple language, the intention here is to neither attack nor defend what Team Mirowski term neo-liberalism. Guilt, or innocence, is left undetermined.

References

Amidae, S. M. (2003). *Rationalizing Capitalist Democracy*. Chicago: University of Chicago Press.

Applebaum, B. (2020). "50 years of blaming Milton Friedman. Here's another idea", *New York Times*. 18 September, https://www.nytimes.com/2020/09/18/opinion/milton-friedman-essay.html?action=click&module=Opinion&pgtype=Homepage (18/09/2020).

Becker, G. (1971). *Economic Theory*. New York: Knopf.

Becker, G. (1993). "The economic way of looking at behavior", *Journal of Political Economy*. 101(3): 385–409.

Birmingham, S. (1967). *Our Crowd*. New York: Harper.

Bork, R. H. (1978). *The Antitrust Paradox*. New York: The Free Press.

Brossard, D. and Dietram, A. S. (2013). "This story stinks", *NY Times.com*, March 2, http://www.nytimes.com/2013/03/03/opinion/sunday/this-story-stinks (03/03/2013).

Burgin, A. (2012). *The Great Persuasion*. Cambridge: Harvard University Press.

Caldwell, B. (2011). "The Chicago School, Hayek and neoliberalism", in Van Horn, Robert, Philip Mirowski and Thomas A. Stapleford (eds.) *Building Chicago Economics*. Cambridge: Cambridge University Press, pp. 301–335.

Carroll, L. (1974). *The Philosopher's Alice*. New York: St. Martin's Press.

Cassidy, J. (2010). "Interview with Eugene Fama", *New Yorker*, 13 January.

Cochrane, J. (2010). *Understanding Policy in the Great Recession: Some Unpleasant Fiscal Arithmetic*, NBER Working Papers 16087. Washington, DC: National Bureau of Economic Research Inc.

Demsetz, H. (1993). "George J. Stigler: Midcentury neoclassicalist with a passion to quantify", *The Journal of Political Economy*. 101(5): 793–808.

Director, A. and Paul, D. (1931). *The Problem of Unemployment*. New York: Macmillan.

Freedman, C. (1995). "The economist as mythmaker – Stigler's Kinky transformation", *The Journal of Economic Issues*. 29(1): 175–209.

Freedman, C. (1998a). "No end to means – George Stigler's profit motive", *The Journal of Post Keynesian Economics*. 20(4): 621–648.

Freedman, C. (1998b). "Countervailing egos – Galbraith versus Stigler", *History of Economics Review*. 27(Winter): 50–75.

Freedman, C. (2002). "The xistence of definitional economics: Stigler's and Leibenstein's war of the words", *Cambridge Journal of Economics*. 26(2): 161–179.

Freedman, C. (2003). "Economic textbook: Missing and misplaced incentives", in Freedman, C. and Rick, S. (eds.) *Tales of Narcissus: The Looking Glass of Economic Science*. Hauppauge, New York: Nova Science Publishers, pp. 159–175.

Freedman, C. (2016). "The Chicago School of anti-monopolistic competition: Stigler's scorched earth campaign against Chamberlin", in *In Search of the Two Handed Economist: Ideology, Methodology and Marketing in Economics*. London: Palgrave Macmillan.

Friedland, C. (1993). "On Stigler and stiglerisms", *The Journal of Political Economy*. 101(5): 780–783.

Friedman, M. (1956). "The quantity theory of money – A restatement", in Friedman, M. (ed.) *Studies in the Quantity Theory of Money*. Chicago: University of Chicago Press, pp. 3–19.

Friedman, M. (1962). *Capitalism and Freedom*. Chicago: University of Chicago Press.

Friedman, M. (1970). "A Friedman doctrine – The social responsibility of business is to increase its profits", *New York Times*, September 13, Section SM, Page 17, https://www.nytimes.com/1970/09/13/archives/a-friedman-doctrine-the-social-responsibility-of-business-is-to.html (05/12/2021).

Friedman, M. (1974). "Comments on the critics: Patinkin", in Gordon, R. J. (ed.) *Milton Friedman's Monetary Framework: A Debate with his Critics*. Chicago: Chicago University Press, pp. 158–177.

Friedman, M. and Rose, F. (1998). *Two Lucky People*. Chicago: University of Chicago Press.

Hammond, J. D. and Claire, H. H. (2006). *Making Chicago Price Theory*. London: Routledge.

Hayek, F. (1944). *Road to Serfdom*. Chicago: University of Chicago Press.

Hayek, F. (1957). "Why I am not a conservative", paper presented at the *10th Anniversary Meeting*, St. Moritz, of the Mont Pelerin Society, September 2nd to September 8th. Chicago: Special Collections, The University of Chicago Library.

Hobbes, T. (1651/2015). *The Leviathan*. Oxford: Oxford University Press.

Josephson, M. (1938). *The Politicos*. New York: Harcourt Brace Jovanovich.

Keynes, J. M. (1973). *The Collected Works of John Maynard Keynes*, Volume XIII. London and Basingstoke: Macmillan.

Kline, M. (1980). *Mathematics and the Loss of Certainty*. Oxford: Oxford University Press.

Kolko, G. (1963). *The Triumph of Conservatism*. New York: The Free Press.

Medema, S. (2011). "Chicago price theory and Chicago law and economics: A tale of two transitions", in Robert, V. H., Mirowski, P., and Stapleford, T. (eds.) *Building Chicago Economics*. Cambridge: Cambridge University Press, pp. 151–180.

Mirowski, P. (1989). *More Heat than Light*. Cambridge: Cambridge University Press.

Mirowski, P. (2013). "The Great persuasion: Reinventing free markets since the depression by Angus Burgin", *The Business History Review*, 87(4): 800–802.

Mirowski, P. (2015). "Postface", in Mirowski, P. and Dieter, P. (eds.) *The Road from Mont Pelerin*. Cambridge, MA: Harvard University Press, pp. 417–455.

Mirowski, P. and Dieter, P. (2015). "Preface", in Mirowski, P. and Dieter, P. (eds.) *The Road from Mont Pelerin*. Cambridge, MA: Harvard University Press, pp. ix–xxiii.

Mirowski, P. and Robert, V. H. (2015). "The rise of the Chicago School of economics", in Mirowski, P. and Dieter, P. (eds.) *The Road from Mont Pelerin*. Cambridge, MA: Harvard University Press, pp. 139–178.

Nik-Khah, E. (2014). "Neoliberal pharmaceutical science and the Chicago School of economics", *Social Studies of Science*. 44(4): 489–517.

Nik-Khah, E. and Robert, V. H. (2016). "The ascendancy of Chicago neoliberalism", in Springer, S., Kean, B., and Julie, M. (eds.) *The Handbook of Neoliberalism*. London: Routledge, pp. 27–38.

Nik-Khah, E. and Robert, V. H. (2020). "Shattering hope and building empire: Economics imperialism at Chicago, George Stigler and Aaron Director", in Freedman, C. (ed.) *George Stigler: Enigmatic Price Theorist of the Twentieth Century*. London: Palgrave Macmillan, pp. 421–445.

Opazo, T. (2016). "The boys who got to remake an economy", *Slate.* January 12, http://www.slate.com/articles/business/moneybox/2016/01/in_chicago_boys_the_story_of_chilean_economists_who_studied_in_america_and.html (31/01/2017).

Patinkin, D. (2003/1969). "Friedman on the quantity theory and Keynesian economics", in Leeson, R. (ed.) *Keynes, Chicago and Friedman*, Vol. 2. London: Pickering & Chatto, pp. 123–143.

Peltzman, S. (2000). "Prices rise faster than they fall", *The Journal of Political Economy.* 108(3): 466–503.

Reder, M. W. (1982). "Chicago economics: Permanence and change", *The Journal of Economic Literature.* 20(1): 1–38.

Schmulders, G. (1972). "Ludwig Erhard and the Mont Pelerin society", *The German Economic Review.* 19(1): 71–78.

Shakespeare, W. (1963). *Hamlet.* New York: Signet Classics.

Spinoza, B. (1670/1998). *Theological-Political Treatise.* Shirley, S. (tr.) Cambridge: Hackett Publishing Company.

Stigler, G. J. (1947). "The Kinky oligopoly demand curve and rigid prices", *Journal of Political Economy.* 55(5): 432–449.

Stigler, G. J. (1949a). *Five Lectures on Economic Problems.* London: Longmans, Green and Co.

Stigler, G. J. (1949b). "The economists and equality", *Five Lectures on Economic Problems.* London: Longmans, Green and Co., pp. 1–11.

Stigler, G. J. (1954). "The economist plays with blocs", *American Economic Review Papers and Proceedings.* 44(2): 7–14.

Stigler, G. J. (1963). *The Intellectual and the Marketplace, and Other Essays*: New York: Free Press of Glencoe.

Stigler, G. J. (1965). "The problem of the Negro", *New Guard.* 5(12): 11–12.

Stigler, G. J. (1971). The theory of economic regulation", *Bell Journal of Economics and Management Science.* 2(1): 3–21.

Stigler, G. J. (1975). "The intellectual and his society", in Selden, R. T. (ed.) *Capitalism and Freedom: Problems and Prospects: Proceedings of a Conference in Honor of Milton Friedman.* Charlottesville: University Press of Virginia, pp. 311–321.

Stigler, G. J. (1976). "Do economists matter?" *Southern Economic Journal.* 42(3): 347–354.

Stigler, G. J. (1977). "A certain Galbraith in an uncertain age", *National Review.* 29(05): 601–604.

Stigler, G. J. (1982a). "Economics or ethics?" in Sterling, M. M. (ed.) *The Tanner Lectures on Human Values*, Vol. 2. Salt Lake Cities: University of Utah Press.

Stigler, G. J. (1982b). *American Capitalism at High Noon*. Selected Papers No. 58. Chicago: University of Chicago, Graduate School of Business.

Stigler, G. J. (1982c) *The Pleasures and Pains of Modern Capitalism*. 13th Wincott Memorial Lecture, Occasional Paper No. 64. London: Institute of Economic Affairs.

Stigler, G. J. (1986). *The Regularities of Regulation*. Occasional Paper No. 3. Edinburgh: Hume Institute.

Stigler, G. J. (1988). *Memoirs of an Unregulated Economist*. New York: Basic Books.

Stigler, G. J. (1989a). *The Political Redistribution of Income* [*Die politische Umuerteilung des Einkommens*]. Zurich: Bank Hofmann AG.

Stigler, G. J. (1989b). "Die Intellektueullen und die Markwirtschaft", *Neue Zurcher Zeitung*. 37.

Stigler, G. J. (1992). "Law or economics?", *Journal of Law and Economics*. 35(2): 455–468.

Sowell, T. (1993). "A student's eye view of George Stigler", *The Journal of Political Economy*. 101(5): 784–792.

Sweezy, P. (1939). "Demand under conditions of oligopoly", *Journal of Political Economy*. 47(4): 568–573.

Van Horn, R. (2010). "Harry Aaron Director: The coming of age of a reformer skeptic (1914–24)", *History of Political Economy*. 42(4): 601–630.

Van Horn, R. and Philip, M. (2015). "The rise of the Chicago School of economics and the birth of neoliberalism", in Mirowski, P. and Dieter, P. (eds.) *The Road from Mont Pelerin*. Cambridge, MA: Harvard University Press, pp. 139–180.

Friedman's Just Another Word for Nothing Left to Lose – Poison Apples and Trojan Horses

He [the prince] should, therefore, never take his mind from this exercise of war, and in peacetime he must train himself more than in time of war.... He must also learn the nature of the terrain, and know how mountains slope, how valleys open, how plains lie, and understand the nature of rivers and swamps; and he should devote much attention to such activities. Such knowledge is useful in two ways: first, one learns to know one's own country and can better understand how to defend it; second, with the knowledge and experience of the terrain, one can easily comprehend the characteristics of any other terrain that it is necessary to explore for the first time....A prince who lacks this ability lacks the most important quality in a leader; because this skill teaches you to find the enemy, choose a campsite, lead troops, organize them for battle, and besiege towns to your advantage (Machiavelli 1532 Chapter XIV:375).

> "I do not understand you."
> "Then we are on very unequal terms, for I understand you perfectly well."
> "Me? Yes; I cannot speak well enough to be unintelligible."
> "Bravo! An excellent satire on modern language" (Austen 1818:1138).

I. Seizing the High Ground

Every exertion of physical force if made upwards is more difficult than if it is made in the contrary direction (downwards); consequently it must be so in fighting; and there are three evident reasons why it is so. First, every height may be regarded as an obstacle to approach; secondly, although the range is not perceptibly greater in shooting down from a height, yet, all geometrical relations being taken into consideration, we have a better chance of hitting than in the opposite case; thirdly, an elevation gives a better command of view (Clausewitz 1918/1832:126).

Milton Friedman[1] was a master (even at times something of a magician) when it came to seamlessly shifting the terms of any given debate. Somehow, with a certain tinge of the inevitable, he would manage to capture the decisive high ground that controlled contentious academic and public policy battles. By doing so, he would successfully define the nature of any ensuing discourse. (Though naturally, not even Milton Friedman was capable of being 100% effective.) This feat would be, at times, lethally accomplished, whenever, and wherever, feasible. (Keep in mind however that at Chicago, winning at all costs was one of the ruling cardinal virtues guiding the department. Economics was taken seriously and played unquestionably 'for keeps'.)

Consequently, at a rather early stage in his career, Friedman somehow, almost intuitively, discovered that the key to consistent success (when marketing his preferred views), required an almost unerring ability to skilfully redirect the course of any hotly debated topic. This designated strategy demanded an almost uncanny ability to control the direction that such discussions would take. The key determinant in this redirecting exercise being a knack for shifting such debates onto terrain that would prove more amenable to Friedman's predetermined objectives. Verbal struggles within this category can be won or lost based on no more than a fleeting sleight of hand movement. (To succeed, timing must be precise, or the moment when such redirection is most effective will quickly pass.) In which case, success can (and should) be viewed simply as the oral equivalent of capturing the high ground in the midst of an armed struggle. In such circumstances of verbal jousting, the strongest (whether logical or evidential) argument need not triumph. In an equivalent fashion, simply amassing the most troops (or even fire power) is no guarantee of inevitable military success in lieu of capturing those all-important heights.

If we are bold enough to take a historical plunge, British troops (under Wellington) mastered (and consistently accomplished) one fundamental tactic during the Peninsular Campaign. By controlling the heights of any given battlefield, his army was capable of shooting down on, and picking off, the tightly bunched troops of Napoleonic soldiers. (Fortunately for the British, Napoleon proved to be something of a slow learner, trying to succeed by simply repeating his past triumphs.) The key to victory, in this 19th century case, was an ability to gain a defensible strategic position, one that was not so easily assaulted.[2] Doing so successfully required an ability to dominate an essential geographical area, one from which an ensuing battle could be largely controlled and directed. (On a level battleground, outcomes would be decidedly more unpredictable.) Speaking in a general vein, this strategy continues to reign supreme, whether it is applied to a military action, or (more politely) to a bit of academic jousting. The trick in any comparable war involving words then is to make sure issues are discussed only according to a prejudged order (or fashion) that remains favourable to one's individual aims.[3] (The goal is to discuss a favoured agenda while dodging (or outright ignoring) that of an opponent. This ostensible debating strategy represents something of an implied categorical imperative for all ambitious academics deliberately striving after reputation and approval.) Such strategic manoeuvres are often remarkably, if sometimes even regrettably, successful. But defeating opponents in this fashion comes with the added proviso that it needs be feasible to swiftly relocate the terms of any ensuing debate so that they remain comfortably grounded on more conducive terrain. In essence, an effective control of those ruling heights can often lead to a preferred outcome.

For instance, a relatively neutral focus on a very concrete analytic process, one which painstakingly tests the reality of any assumption employed, can instead (with a smidgen of skill) be shifted to a preferred, more ideologically agreeable, terrain.[4] The initially constructed argument then finds itself resembling an abandoned orphan. In practical terms, a theory judged objectionable can be deliberately relocated to a convenient, intellectual sinkhole. Once reached, ideas, theories and hypothesis find themselves to have been prepared for a final and immediate disposal. In this fashion, a targeted idea is intentionally ensnared in a series of abstract, methodological traps and extraneous considerations. (In simple terms, the goal is to manoeuvre an opponent away from discussing his or her concerns by forcing any debate to be strictly conducted, only according to one's designated terms.[5]) Tactics of this ilk, can (when successfully conducted) cause irksome (or confrontational) issues to conveniently disappear. Any subsequent debate will likely be transformed into a session that is only conducive to trivial pursuits (and remains agreeably off-topic).

As part of his larger rhetorical strategy, Friedman developed a sustained knack for persuading an erstwhile opponent into accepting a seemingly innocent initial assumption, one which, once accepted, would then determine the path or paths any ensuing discussion might take.[6] (Doing so is what is being labelled in this discussion as a 'poison apple' strategy.) Rails had to be deliberately laid down by the self-interested debater so that they would subsequently determine and constrain the future direction of debate or investigation.[7] Opponents would inevitably find themselves in alignment with pre-set rails inevitably leading to a set conclusion. The argumentative journey began, once an opponent implicitly (or almost unconsciously) accepted the imposed terms of debate that would subsequently rule the ensuing discussion. In demonstrating an effective method for countering such tactics, Robert Solow outlined a succinct explanation of why he refused to seriously (or even) discuss the assumption behind rational expectations. He outright rejected any version of such a foundation, no matter what manifestation it might take. Fundamentally, nothing conceivable would induce him to seriously consider that contention.[8] From Solow's perspective, discussing the assumption would imbue it with a degree of unintended credence. In essence, he would risk trapping himself into an unwinnable tar baby-like debate.[9]

> Suppose someone sits down where you are sitting right now and announces to me that he is Napoleon Bonaparte. The last thing I want to do with him is to get involved in a technical discussion of cavalry tactics at the battle of Austerlitz. If I do that, I'm getting tacitly drawn into the game that he is Napoleon. Now, Bob Lucas and Tom Sargent like nothing better than to get drawn into technical discussions, because then you have tacitly gone along with their fundamental assumptions; your attention is attracted away from the basic weakness of the whole story. Since I find that fundamental framework ludicrous, I respond by treating it as ludicrous–that is, by laughing at it–so as not to fall into the trap of taking it seriously and passing on to matters of technique (Solow August 21, 2015). https://equitablegrowth.org/must-read-robert-solow-conversations-economists/. 12/05/2020).

To his credit, Friedman quite early in his lengthy career, displayed a knack for dodging debilitating replies and criticism. He quickly comprehended the advantage that could be gained by cagily shifting his arguments, when too vigorously pressed on an inconvenient point. Deflection can often be more effective than response. To facilitate this constructed strategy, Friedman pointedly winkled out methods that would effectively buttress any attempts that marketed preferred perspectives. Doing so required a very practical tactic. The often elusive commanding heights of any ongoing debate, would need to be located and successfully controlled. Friedman's targeted use of what was in essence a series of finely-crafted poison apples, could make at least some of his more controversial positions easier for opponents (and colleagues) to swallow. Observing Friedman employ this tactic, usually when attacking opposing positions, clarifies both its use and targets. In the case of Friedman, he seems to be endowed with an almost genetic disposition when it comes to disputing in this fashion. Though his natural talents were undoubtedly refined and augmented as he practised this skill within each passing decade.[10] But such a characterisation is quite different than claiming that Friedman consciously, and moreover deviously, deliberately planned to manipulate an outcome by employing a questionable poison apple strategy.[11] Greater insight into methods of active obfuscation can possibly be achieved by not assuming a practised web of skulduggery or moral turpitude.

From all available evidence, Friedman apparently believed in the validity of the arguments he posed. They weren't, by any reasonable evaluation, simply clever dodges or contrived tactics. It is far easier to argue that he intuitively probed for any weakness in an opponent's position. If exploited, such a leverage point might just encourage an unpalatable (and perceived dangerous) opposition theory to self-destruct. Friedman assuredly believed that the arguments he rallied against were fundamentally wrong. So in doing so, he was in no sense posing as some modern day version of a grand Machiavellian Prince. Nor was Friedman even casting himself as a cut-rate, wily Odysseus successfully overseeing the construction of a Trojan-Horse.[12] While comparing him seriously (certainly not judiciously) to an evil queen bent on destroying a youthful rival would be equally absurd.[13] Milton Friedman may never have deliberately set out on any one of his numerous evangelical journeys nursing a clear intention to blur, or even camouflage, the nature of his argument. The simplest assumption to make is that he saw himself making individual arguments against a variety of wrongheaded policies and theories. Ostensibly, his larger purpose was to spread the gospel of free markets, free enterprise and the near sacred freedom to choose.[14] But often what ensues in reality, when fighting individual battles, can differ markedly from our conscious intention.

In actual fact, and perhaps unfortunately, every Thomas More eventually ends up being defined by, and forced to confront, his own personal Thomas Cromwell. While Friedman was preaching his sermon of salvation and the light bestowed by individual liberty, he was equally intent on combating the perceived darkness nurtured by collectivism. Keynes, within this constrained scenario, was viewed as the dark perverter, deliberately providing a carefully paved alternative path, one which could only lead directly to perdition. In almost every move he made, during those post war decades, the spectre of John Maynard Keynes loomed large, though sometimes only barely discernible in the background (almost as distorting static).[15] Consequently there exists in his efforts a pressing, perhaps even overweening, compulsion to obliterate the legacy of Keynes. This implicit touchstone should never be deliberately overlooked when delving into Milton Friedman's objectives.

Consequently, his periodic employment of a poison apple strategy needs to be understood in terms of the post war dominance of that ubiquitous ghost named John Maynard Keynes. Friedman's personal and political *Mein Kampf* was his continuing struggle to dethrone Keynesian economics. (Not due to conscious vanity or egotism, but rather as a serious threat to liberty and freedom. And equally decisive, in Friedman's mind, Keynes was simply wrong.) By constructing the equivalent of a religiously posed battle for the soul of economics, at least figuratively, he aimed for (and achieved) a denouement that resembled a mere simulacrum of an apotheosis.

Accordingly, by the end of an excruciatingly extended marketing process (or more precisely a quasi-religious quest), he had managed to popularise a belief in the sanctity of the existing level of market competition. Friedman pursued his focused agenda (markets equal freedom) while simultaneously transforming himself into a sainted facsimile. In this constructed vision, Friedman could be accepted as a veritable saviour. He (and a few anointed apostles) would prove capable of championing an economic descent into the policy valley that encompassed a dominating (but just) society of blessed competitive markets.[16] In Christian terms, he preached a series of consistent sermons that in their own way promised a wished for end game. Namely, the vision Friedman provided was roughly equivalent to that of the Evangelical Rapture, but one that would arise within these earthly bounds. He cheerfully sermonised about a society conceived in liberty and unswervingly dedicated to the fruits of entrepreneurial exchange.

The underlying foundation of such beliefs was substantiated by his absolute self-confidence.[17] Friedman, like his colleague and friend George Stigler,[18] was convinced that he unequivocally understood exactly how the world worked.[19] Self-doubt (at least openly) failed to play a significant role in his thoughts and presentations.[20] The economic world, at least, undoubtedly operated according to the functioning parts and gears laid out in the theoretical wisdom mirrored by Chicago price theory.[21] As one of its self-anointed champions, Milton Friedman was determined to demonstrate the validity and superiority of this approach. Such assured determination would inescapably prevail, even if it involved steamrolling over annoying anomalies in the observed evidence. Fortunately for the Chicago project, Friedman proved perpetually clever enough to turn any perceived weakness into an acknowledged strength. For instance, the resilience of his 'as if' assumptions were made to rely entirely on the predictive abilities of their associated theories.[22] Thus objections could be deftly finessed, by at times applying a touch of rubber hosing across any resistant or recalcitrant data. Market failures, or outcomes running at cross purposes to efficient expectations, were simply transformed to reveal their underlying compatibility with the desired outcomes.

> He [George Stigler] was interested, I would say primarily, in a particular sort of puzzle and it's a typical Chicago puzzle. And I don't mean that in any bad way, it's the sort of puzzle that the Chicago School's presuppositions require. Show me an apparent anomaly, something that does not seem to be explicable using the Smithian apparatus or the Marshallian apparatus and I will show you that it can be explained that way. That was exactly the sort of thing that George went looking for (Conversation with Robert Solow, October 1997).[23]

It could sometimes appear that Friedman was forcing an assumption on his audience, much like a magician pressing a card on an unwitting dupe. Similar to that variety of entertainer, his compelling objective was an attempt to successfully accomplish a favoured trick in his ever expanding repertoire. However, there is one significant difference that should not be overlooked. The magician realises that prestidigitation isn't magic, but rather sleight of hand. In contrast, Friedman was a missionary at heart, rather than a magician. He believed entirely in what he was peddling, which was in part illuminated and successfully marketed by his undeterred persuasive skill. If he could mesmerise himself, he could certainly turn around and entrance others. Consequently, he could casually slip assumptions past an unsuspecting audience because he held an unwavering belief in their own specific validity.[24] (Friedman, in this fashion, had at least subconsciously developed a proven method for gaining and controlling the high ground available within any debate or argument.)

> Milton Friedman remarked to me long ago that the study of the stability of general equilibrium is unimportant, first, because it is obvious that the economy is stable, and, second, because if it isn't stable we are wasting our time. He should have known better. In the first place, it is not at all obvious that the actual economy is stable. Apart from the lessons of the past few years, there is the fact that prices do change all the time. Beyond this, however, is a subtler and possibly more important point. Whether or not the actual economy is stable, we *largely lack a convincing theory of why that should be so.* Lacking such a theory, we do not have an adequate theory of value, and there is an important *lacuna* in the centre of microeconomic theory (Fisher 2011:35).

The point then of this extended introduction points to a simple fact. The employment of poisoned apples is not intended to facilitate theoretical investigations, or to encourage extended analysis. The purpose of this rhetorical device, as demonstrated (even if unintentionally) by Friedman, is not to open the gates of academic understanding, but by employing a narrower focus, to increase his ability to triumph in debates. The effect of using this argumentative strategy is rather to curtail, or even effectively deter, targeted opponents from gaining an audience. (These alternatives are implicitly, or openly, dismissed as logically nonviable.) Consequently, an illustrative attempt to explore these procedures, can at least begin by describing those that Milton Friedman employed when sculpting his episodes of rhetorical persuasion. Namely those tropes that allowed him to stake out the high ground of economic arguments. Doing so enabled a much more effective range when destroying opposing targets.[25]

By way of an introduction to this technique, two useful, but perhaps contrasting examples of this particular skill are readily available. Each case features a discernible deployment of a poison apple that Friedman's readers, listeners or followers were asked to swallow and thoroughly digest.[26] To emphasise once again, the strategy is focused on employing a seemingly harmless assumption as a vehicle to deliver far more controversial views once an initial acceptance is achieved. It might help then to begin with a simpler case, one where Friedman willingly descends to more popular, or comfortable, forms of argumentation. Such an existing, broadly representative, environment was one within which he could navigate with unruffled comfort. (Some academics find it difficult to speak to, or formally address, any group differing from a strictly professional audience. They are not those who will become listed among the natural popularizers within the economics trade.)

Therefore, in 1976, as part of his never-ending, evangelical barnstorming tours, Milton Friedman found himself in South Africa, at the height of the apartheid regime in that country.[27] The key to the style of argument he cultivated involves an ability to slip assertions pass an unwary listener or reader. These deceptive nuggets are casually passed off during the course of a Friedman argument as being the equivalent of some indisputable, Euclidean common notion. In essence, they are transformed into a statement so obvious that contesting such an uncontroversial construction would only be a reflection of innate contrariness.[28] Part of Friedman's ability to work his magic consisted of the absolute confidence with which he marketed his ideas, whether or not he actually had the knowledge or experience to do so.[29]

In debate, and during a verbal presentation, Friedman was usually so quick-witted that pinning him down to a specific position would prove difficult. Delivering a knock-out punch that destroyed Friedman's position would often turn out to be no more than an ever elusive dream. By the time an opponent had managed to line up and direct an effective counterpunch aimed at a weak link in Friedman's presentation, he would have somehow managed to shift gears and move somewhere else. Instead of flattening Friedman and destroying his argument, an opponent would instead suddenly be attempting to fend off yet another, seemingly random, attack from an unexpected direction. Consequently, battling Friedman meant the risk of being constantly blindsided. The flurry of barbs and quick-witted jabs (not unlike being surrounded by a swarm of hornets) made debating an unwelcome chore for Friedman's opponents. The given difficulty, or challenge, lay in attempting to follow the numerous discrete jumps composing his presented logic.

> My idea of a nightmare is to stand on a stage and debate with him in front
> of the public. I watched him debating at Cambridge with Joan Robinson
> on flexible exchange rates. Unbelievable! I mean, Joan Robinson was
> one of the world's most aggressive, hostile, debaters. He wiped her

> analytically. He wiped her rhetorically. He had the entire audience eating
> out of his hand, after an hour, an hour and a half. An amazing, amazing
> guy. But a madman, a madman. One of the few people I could strangle
> with my bare hands. I feel I could actually do it (Conversation with Mark
> Blaug, April 1998).

Thus (given his mental quickness) the techniques required when addressing the public never strained the limits of his ability to finesse tangled complexities. The public was generally less attuned to the niceties of economic debate. Most simply lacked any substantive grounding in the subject. Consequently, Friedman was seldom ruffled when searching for the perfect argumentative string that could persuade and win over any audience he faced. It should then come as no surprise that on March 29, 1976 when addressing a gathering of 200 businessmen in Durban, South Africa, he could effortlessly market his arguments. Though when facing such an audience, he would naturally need to employ less subtle reasoning then he would if forced to confront a more academic (and less welcoming) gathering. Such niceties of thought and logic simply were not required in this instance. Painfully obvious to any observer, this particular South African audience was more than eager to swallow even the thinnest of gruels that Milton Friedman might dish out. (Not that Milton Friedman ever seriously diluted the cleverness of his messages.) However, he was sufficiently savvy to hone his rhetoric to accord with his audience's attention span and prior knowledge. These, not necessarily, cosmopolitan businessmen were unlikely to demand finely wrought logic or indisputable evidence. Friedman only needed to offer what his listeners wanted to believe. (The challenge presented on this occasion was much like a cordon bleu chef being asked to serve up snacks to an audience of dope-smoking fiends.) Automatic nods could be predictably expected when Milton Friedman asserted:

> There is no country at any time in the history of the world that has been
> able to maintain a free political system unless the greater part of the
> resources of that country were organized by a free, private enterprise,
> capitalist system (Friedman 1976:21).[30]

As is obvious in this passage, Friedman quickly, and cleverly, identifies a free political system (automatically viewed as a democracy in the minds of most listeners or readers) with that of a free, private enterprise, capitalist system.[31] Based on this symbiotic relationship, achieving democracy would seem then to be inevitably dependent on instituting what Friedman would comprehend as being a free, private enterprise system. (Of course given his definition, the desired political system can only be built if grounded on a capitalist substratum).[32] Consequently, extending this logic would make any opposition to such an economic system (his preferred, vibrant form of capitalism) a basic rejection of democracy (an anti-democratic obstructionist). Those who could somehow discover a sufficient dollop of temerity, at least enough to encourage organised dissent from this quasi-syllogism, could then be categorised as harbouring a deplorably authoritarian streak and thus easily dismissed.[33] The effective sleight of hand performed in this bit of strategic jujitsu, is the claim, made with an unwarranted degree of absolute certainty, that Friedman's proclaimed assertion is actually valid, simply because it has been articulated in no uncertain terms.

A stance defined in such a deliberate and confident fashion, remains unshakable, even when upon closer examination, such supposedly ineluctable facts subsequently crumble into no more than bold assumptions. But by indulging in this bit of strategic information marketing, the very assertiveness of Friedman's claim (once made), defies anyone within listening distance, to entertain the slightest possibility of not accepting Friedman's nugget of undeniable truth. At this point, it might be best to take a step back to gain a sufficient perspective on the clever landscape that Friedman manages to create, acting as if he were an amateur topiary magician. In essence, in the artificial environment devised by Milton Friedman, once you willingly enter into it, objecting to his subsequent conclusions becomes self-contradictory. The end points of his arguments are seemingly backed by indisputable logic given the stated entry point. To refuse to follow Friedman along his disputatious trail is to label yourself no better than a lumbering fool. That, at least, is the impression such rhetoric is meant to convey. (This bit of rhetorical sleight of hand is what I have labelled a poisoned apple. A seemingly innocuous assertion, which once swallowed, leads almost magically to less than salubrious conclusions.)

In essence, the widely accepted South African address consists of Friedman finding repeated ways of saying, 'individualism good' 'collectivism bad' to an extremely receptive audience.[34] This goal is accomplished with not much more finesse than the moment in Orwell's (1945) *Animal Farm,* when the wily pigs drum the doctrine of 'four legs good, two legs bad' into the minds of all the relevant farm animals. Consequently, the palatable poison apple that is meant to tempt its listener is created by only vaguely defining key terms and pitching one's speech very precisely to a level of emotional certainty. People eagerly respond to what they think they want (or need) to hear. Given the quicksand that buries any more questionable elements in the logical foundation of his speech, historical assertions are then piled, one on top of one another, in an almost *jenga-like* style of construction. These all serve to buttress Friedman's fundamental claims. In today's digital age, such bold claims could undoubtedly be instantaneously fact-checked and found wanting. Or, to be a tad more realistic, that would be the reaction and subsequent impact for which we could at least vainly hope.[35] But back in the analogue world of 1976, the assumption of general historical ignorance is probably sufficient to float even the more dubious of Friedman's assertions, as well as his somewhat self-serving, reconstructions of the past.

Consequently definitions must appear to sound sufficiently comprehensive, and even quite reasonable, while remaining at the same time somewhat vague. In other words, such constructs can easily be swallowed while simultaneously avoiding anything resembling a more careful evaluation. (These definitions become, at least to a degree, the intellectual equivalent of a *Krispy Kreme* doughnut. The immediate pleasure provided by heavy doses of sugar and fat can be instantly enjoyed. In the longer term any deleterious effects can, with a bit of misdirection, remain determinately buried.) The goal motivating this deliberate strategy is to produce a carefully assembled sound bite lacking any real specificity. 'What you really must mean by free enterprise is a system in which anybody is free to set up an enterprise' (Friedman 1976: 23). A description of this sort manages to convey precious little information or insight. From a logical point of view, property rights, which Friedman predictably extols, must from a certain ironic perspective, be viewed as a serious hindrance to setting up the type of desired enterprises that Friedman describes.

Entrepreneurs, for instance, are necessarily prevented from constructing an enterprise on land owned, or held, by another property owner. Would be entrants are prevented from creating vibrant businesses based on the patented ideas of others. Loans needed to enter a given market are not granted universally. Fundamentally, anyone can set up an enterprise, but only as long as he or she can afford the opportunity cost of doing so. Thus a simple minded effort to define a free enterprise system can slip far too easily into the realm of vacuous statements. In essence, what is presented as an unarguable definition can start to crumble when poked too strenuously. Instead of reasoned insights, Friedman's statements to his overly receptive South African audience are simple platitudes presented as evidential certainties, a veritable bushel of poisoned apples. By offering economic sweets to such an audience, these gleaming poison apples are inevitably devoured quite greedily. This confused notion of a free enterprise system, that Friedman constructs so carelessly, had previously been defined by Anatole France in a much less flattering fashion: "In its majestic equality, the law forbids rich and poor alike to sleep under bridges, beg in the streets and steal loaves of bread" (https://www.reddit.com/r/QuotesPorn/comments/5i4b6j/it_its_majestic_equality_the_law_forbids_rich_and/).

Moreover, courtesy of a shotgun style wedding, Friedman casually compels the notion of free enterprise to share the same ambiguous territory as does his depiction of essential individualism.[36] In Friedman's distinctive calculus of liberty, intractable individualism exists as an unarguable necessity underpinning the basis for freedom of choice. But Friedman feels compelled to enhance the virtues of this preferred option by painting alternatives in the darkest of hues. Consequently, part of the verbal package Friedman offers (at least implicitly embedded in his speech to his receptive South African audience), contains a warning that treasured liberty can be carelessly tossed away. In particular, Friedman feels obliged to excoriate the way in which voters thoughtlessly throw away their birthright freedom by listening to the false allures of collectivism. "And yet, what we have voted for is a restriction on our individual freedom to use our resources as we see fit for our purposes" (Friedman 1976:30). Namely, governments are able to forcefully take away the property of individuals and the right to use that property as they see fit.

This trampling of individual rights take place (at least from Friedman's perspective), by camouflaging such infringements as an honest reflection of the common good. Friedman's implicit aim in employing this rhetorical trope then is conceivably a directed attempt to stoke residual resentment in his listeners. (No one enjoys paying taxes or becoming tangled in regulations.) This goal is driven home by making his audience feel short-changed and simply victimised. Friedman repeatedly spotlights throughout his talk, the way in which governments refuse to adhere to his version of economic common sense (by infringing on treasured individual freedom). By provoking a desired emotional response, Friedman is then able to more easily achieve his disguised goal (a visceral rejection of collectivism).

This objective turns out to require only a discrete muddling of the meanings that accurately defines the terms he subsequently chooses to employ. Doing so is a simple, but effective, first step.[37]

At this point, Friedman would first do well to engage in a focused refresher course on the meaning and purpose of liberty before further amping his rhetoric. He might instead start with the thoughts expressed by John Stuart Mill (1947), a reliable source of Classical Liberalism. By using a more incisive or pertinent definition, the ability to use resources in whatever fashion an individual sees fit must inevitably be constrained by the effect such efforts have on others. Otherwise any subsequent discussion will focus only on arbitrary (rather than free) actions.[38] Individualism (and especially liberty) is never a license to do whatever you want, or to act self-indulgently on the spur of the moment. Such action is not directly antithetical to a five year old stamping his feet and screaming, 'You're not the boss of me.' Freedom, or liberty, ceases to be a viable idea when shorn of responsibility. Consequently, one person's liberty ideally should not impinge on that of another, an idea which carries with it the whiff of some degree of collectivism, or at least collective standards of behaviour.[39] Friedman assumes such clarification to be either superfluous or simply unwelcome, given the sermon he wishes to preach. But by swallowing his ill-defined notions of individual freedom, his audience provides Friedman with a green light to shovel more controversial ideas down their collective mouths. Essentially the proffered poison apple in this case is eagerly accepted and embraced, given the emotional response to the idea of individual liberty and the imminent need to protect one's own property.

Careful examination (plus some quiet reflection) of this example reveals a fundamental and consistent strategy employed by Friedman in particular, but also toyed with by a number of his colleagues. (Needless to say it is not uncommon within the profession itself.) That vision is one of a poison apple that links freedom of choice and liberty to a specific market structure. The initial step in the process is relatively simple. Being in favour of freedom of choice and liberty in the US is equivalent to supporting motherhood or the virtues of apple pie. Few would have the crass bravado of openly barracking for a lack of freedom in the form of slavery or mass repression. (Few openly admit any authoritarian tendencies they may harbour.) Unsurprisingly, this means that not only are Friedman's calls (asking his audience to fiercely defend these basic rights) eagerly (and almost automatically) swallowed by his readers or listeners. But simultaneously, a corresponding economic model is also thoroughly digested, if only *sub rosa*. In which case, it remains difficult to believe that such an incessant drumbeat promoting freedom and liberty is not necessarily riddled with subconscious marketing strategies. (Making such a claim does not, however, undercut the sincerity and faith behind Friedman's consistent employment of such terms.)

However, by successfully dominating the high ground of this ideological battle, he also manages to implicitly label those on the opposing side as lacking (and even devaluing) the respect and devotion due to these indisputable ideas. In particular, opponents are somehow transformed into proponents of authoritarianism and repression. Friedman's opponents become a dark force posing dangerous threats. Thus, shifting the terms of debate on to more conducive terrain can become a standard strategy for placing opponents on the defensive. In an extreme scenario, success in doing so can force those on the other side to somehow explain that their preferred policies do not in fact favour repression.[40] In too many cases it is virtually impossible to prove what you are not. But by employing this style of argument, the poison apple in this case, becomes the equivalent of a loaded question.[41] By backing an opponent into a corner, such views are permitted no room in which to possibly manoeuvre.

To market the overarching cornerstone of his argument, achieved by employing a method that constructs (and insists upon), a suspiciously convenient definition of liberty, Friedman is motivated to unequivocally condemn even the smallest smidgen in the way of government intervention. Viewed from his particular perspective, such intrusions (no matter how seemingly insignificant), cannot help but distort economic and societal incentives. Consequently, he feels obliged to categorise the perceived dangers from even the smallest collective slip as being a step down the proverbial slippery slope. This well-known (but unfortunately overused), declivity (a slope frequently mentioned, but seldom if ever experienced) somehow, magically, leads to a predictable abandonment of freedom, hope and an alarming widespread rejection of cleanliness. To bolster this bare assertion, Friedman then feels compelled to launch a veritable barrage of buttressing factoids to paper over any apparent logical or evidential cracks.[42] These supportive claims are seemingly savoury nuggets procured from economic history, which can be artfully shaped and combined with other more conclusive evidence. Such rhetorical arguments are then moulded in a fashion that is intended only to win over an unreflecting and entirely sympathetic audience.

Friedman's sheet-rocked package of quasi-truths and homely insights that he produces for his South African audience, includes the assertion that the US government illegitimately rips away some 40 per cent of what taxpayers earn.[43] This particular mechanism (according to Friedman) allows an unelected herd of bureaucrats to remove a citizen's ability to use those stolen resources for his or her own direct benefit. Assumed in this statement is the idea that individual judgment is always (rather than simply generally) superior to that of any conceivable collective will. The underlying supposition insists that an individual can always judge, and properly satisfy, his or her needs in a far preferred fashion no matter what the particular set of circumstances might be. It leans heavily on a beginning textbook assumption that individuals can achieve their objectives while disregarding those of everyone else. In essence that each person's utility is entirely independent and self-sustained.

This judgment would have to extend even to cases where an individual's judgment also affects the welfare of others. (Vaccinations, wearing masks during a pandemic, not defecating in public places might be a few of the many instances that signal a clearly perceived need for collective admonitions.[44]) Consequently, Friedman appears to be at least implicitly rejecting the idea that any substantial needs or demands are better met collectively.[45] Foolish, wasteful and corrupt government spending can be easily discovered and highlighted to emphasise this point, while simultaneously deflecting attention away from any potentially desirable collective outcomes. Individual errors, stupidity and other such wasteful actions are similarly ignored, or implicitly deemed to be simply inevitable, without any possibility of outside induced rectification. Given the prevailing economic incentives, the underlying (unbudgeable) belief is that markets will, in time, create an effective solution.[46]

Revealed by his sharply pointed rhetoric is an overwhelming desire, or even need, to market a specific argument. Doing so, unfortunately, often necessitates eschewing all and any complexities which would tend to spoil the story line. Consequently, as a means of reinforcing his cropped snapshots of economic history, Friedman offers to his receptive audience, a series of fractured fairy tales.[47] (Again, audience receptivity has been predetermined by tailoring necessary poisoned apples to his listeners' proclivities.) In some cases he strains credibility, by seeming to allow his audience a glimpse of a carefully submerged truth that lies hidden just beneath the surface of generally accepted opinion.[48] The very outré quality of these revealed narratives is quite capable of enrapturing his already enthralled audience. As a specific bow to his South African audience, Friedman discovers in himself the required temerity (or perhaps even the sheer *chutzpah*) to support the idea that apartheid, as it existed in 1976, was simply a creation of trade unionists.[49] For authority of this less than widely accepted assertion, he relies on the disputed theories of the South African economist, W. H. Hutt.[50]

Besides pandering to the possibly submerged racist bias of his audience (at least to a certain extent) Friedman can't resist returning to the polestar of much of his research, namely his obsession with money.[51] Of course, given that inflation dominated economic discussions in the seventies, this bit of rhetorical persuasion should come as no surprise. Especially since Friedman during this decade helped to parlay his reputation by claiming that he had predicted and wisely forewarned about the coming wave of world-wide inflation. Conveyed through his familiar tornado of charges and accusations focused on monetary malfeasance, Friedman predictably trots out his repeated charge that assigns sole blame for the world-wide depression of the 1930s to the Federal Reserve. From his adamant perspective, this prolonged slump reflected nothing else but the consequences of the multiple and extended mistakes committed by the Central Bank. Unfortunately, the impact of his finely honed rhetoric remains less than entirely persuasive. That the Federal Reserve of that period failed to deal properly with the initial financial panic is an assertion based on rock solid evidence. (Though other economists, much earlier than Friedman produced compelling data to back the same claim.)[52]

However, it is a leap of faith to then insist that dealing adequately with a financial panic automatically precludes any subsequent need to deal with an ensuing economic recession. (The 2008 financial panic was fairly quickly quelled. However, doing so did not prevent the subsequent substantial downturn.) Even more questionable is the idea that in the absence of the Federal Reserve, financial markets could have effectively resolved any such difficulties. The Panic of 1905 perhaps belies that belief. Historically, the lessons learned from that episode subsequently served as a strong impetus for instituting a central bank system in the United States. But such claims by Friedman are all too consistent with the core idea that government intervention only leads to perverse unintended consequences. Such conclusions predictably stem from, the seemingly innocuous assumptions initially accepted by Friedman's attentive audience. Consequently, these unfortunate outcomes, when they occur within the defined sphere of Friedman's universe, are almost entirely dismal yielding only destructive results. However, given the audience he is addressing, such flights of reasoning serve persuasively as part of Friedman's conjured poison apple. (He manages to utilise, if not pander to, his audience's suspicion of government, allowing him to later slide more controversial monetary theory into his presentation.)

Even a multiple blizzard of examples crammed into a limited number of pages (or squeezed into a constrained amount of time) would ultimately fail to convince an appropriately sceptical audience that government intervention is entirely bad per se.[53] But in this specific case, Friedman enjoyed the advantage of addressing a group of true believers (or a near enough approximation of such a group), those defined as eager to swallow the proffered gospel. Fortunately for Friedman, he remained perpetually adept at reading his audience, the undeniable mark of any accomplished marketeer.

Consequently, a true meeting of minds occurred during this South African speech, an example of a preacher expertly orchestrating his receptive congregation. Given that Friedman was a self-admitted Cold Warrior (battling single-mindedly against totalitarianism, guided only by a professed devotion to the sweet cause of liberty), such rococo rhetoric adorning his Durban speech hardly comes as a surprise. But ultimately, when shorn of its rhetorical frills, Friedman's demonstration does little more than indicate that bad government can add nothing worthwhile to either an economy or its associated society. This conclusion is understandably indisputable, with a veritable flood of examples coming easily to mind. Governments quite obviously have repeatedly discovered that generating damage has been far easier than creating and conveying benefits. However, unless Friedman wants to make a further claim that all government actions are equally incompetent, and even malevolent, his blanket identification of collectivism as deleterious remains firmly restricted to the sphere of ideology.

Friedman's favoured, but repetitive, campaign against the evils of collectivism slips soundlessly into his Durban talk, almost without notice. He initially proffers, and the audience subsequently eagerly swallows, a seemingly innocuous, though well-polished, poison apple. Friedman insists on identifying free enterprise markets as composing a sufficient foundation and source of protection for political freedom. Once this thesis is granted by any selected group of listeners, a perceived threat to such markets, real or imagined, automatically is transmuted into a critical battle to defend freedom and liberty. The trap is effectively baited and set since few in the audience would deliberately confess to despising a country that is steeped in liberty and receives the continuing benefits of freedom. (The seeming irony of delivering such a speech in 1970s South Africa is pointedly ignored by all involved. Conspiracies of silence are all too common given a vast array of favourable circumstances.) Consequently, a controversial assumption, in this case, slips in while carefully disguised as a seemingly obvious and indisputable common observation. Such a device constitutes the perfect poison apple.

So far however, we have just examined this rhetorical device at its simplest level. We need to climb further up the ladder of strategic deployment to fully comprehend its operation. Doing so allows us to investigate a more sophisticated use of this seemingly innocent device. We need to progress from the type of popular approach typified by the South African example. This level represents no more than the equivalent of a five-fingered exercise for an experienced campaigner like Friedman. A more serious attempt at creating a tempting poison apple involves the construction of a less explicit (and deliberately more destructive) theoretical attack. (A continuing Chicago School tactic employed in its ideological wars involved undermining a policy by trying to shred its underlying theoretical base). In this instance, Friedman's targeted grenade aligns perfectly with his consistent and continuing campaign to unseat Keynesianism as the dominant economic approach in the post war era. Keynesian theory, when daring to enter the bailiwick ruled by Milton Friedman, becomes more than simply an opposed and despised economic framework. That rejected perspective, when shipwrecked within Friedman's Chicago styled world, is carefully refurbished to symbolise, or act as, a looming substitute for collectivism.

In Friedman's idiosyncratic reading of Keynes' intentions, a pervasive lathering of collectivism greases the slippery slope that eases a country's downward plunge into the black whirlpool of totalitarianism. (A dramatic, and particularly overstated, view of the perceived clash of ideas.) At that forlorn stage, at that point of no return, the public becomes neither free to choose nor free to do much of anything else. From the vantage point of Friedman's intensive insight, this outcome becomes irrefutable. Given that presumed unalterable endpoint, Keynesian thought must then be stopped, not simply because it embodies a fatuous and misleading form of economic thought, but because of the dangerous implications it disguises. This economic theory, from Friedman's perspective, is dogma, the infamous thin edge of the wedge, which will ultimately enfeeble and destroy liberty. In other words, to certain ideological warriors, Keynesianism is a seemingly innocent theory that in fact carries with it, as the rat does fleas, the scourge of the collectivist pandemic.

Given the need to forestall and thwart the more dangerous aspects of this perceived trend, an effective strategy for undermining Keynesian style economics would involve a deliberate recasting of Keynes' contributions. In this case, to trivialise is to triumph. Therefore, in much the same way that a frog is transformed into a handsome prince, Milton Friedman's acid gaze would hope to effectively reverse that process. A giant of economic thought would under this spell be deftly reduced to the state of a harmless dwarf.[54] In a constructed landscape where the prestidigitator's hand is inevitably faster than the onlooker's eye, Friedman would attempt to initially sneak in a seemingly non-controversial assumption (the poison apple). Doing so might allow him to smuggle in with that more savoury titbit, a much more dubious conclusion, at least once the bait is successfully swallowed.

Again, the perpetrator need not be entirely aware of the false pretences inherent in such a strategy. Perhaps thinking of Friedman as almost the victim of his own approach might be helpful. In which case, Milton Friedman's strategic poses can best be understood by using a transitory 'as if' perspective. Namely, a no-fault perspective might clarify matters by viewing such proffered arguments as essentially equivalent to those that are shaped with more conscious deliberation. Substantially, it is always going to be difficult to differentiate, simply from the result of his efforts, the extent to which Friedman might have been consciously aware of constructing this poisoned apple strategy. (Nor does it seem to matter from any but a moral evaluation whether he was.) No one can actually fathom what might otherwise have been produced, simply based on conscious versus unconscious motivations. Such a valid causative factor (judged amongst possible alternatives) would be buried somewhere deep in the progenitor's murky subconscious. By appearance alone, Friedman's observed actions would be difficult to differentiate from hypothetical perpetrators that intended to single-mindedly do whatever it might take to triumph. In essence, Friedman acted 'as if' such a strategy was consciously devised, even if this was not his conscious intent.

The Keynesian campaign then operated by employing two sequential ploys. (Basically, the underlying notion was to have an alternative poisoned apple in reserve if the first didn't prove sufficiently enticing.) The initial attempt offered, closely resembled a basic Trojan horse gambit.[55]

Friedman attempted to ease the way for his proposed monetary theory by linking it to a supposedly revered Chicago tradition. He may (given his own perspective) have succeeded in constructing a more rigorous, and even scientific, version, but he intended that there should be nothing at the core of his framework that might be the cause of any unnecessary alarm. In essence, he flagged that his approach represented nothing that might be viewed as representing a radical departure from received theory. Friedman appeared to confidently welcome an evaluation concluding that he was implicitly presenting time worn and unarguably sound theory. His approach could then be counterpoised to the unproven, and radical, perspective that Keynes had offered. There seems to be, at least some effort, on Friedman's part, to tamp down any perception of excessive controversy being at play in his monetary presentation. The desired appearance that he scrupulously bequeathed to his theory was intended to be the very antithesis of a revolutionary construction. Friedman implicitly labelled his offering as being the judicious (and non-Keynesian) alternative within the field of monetary economics.

When Friedman's proposed linkage with hoary tradition unexpectedly unravelled, becoming hotly disputed by fellow Chicagoan, Don Patinkin, he effortlessly shifted direction. Almost magically Friedman fashioned an alternative justification, while still offering what was essentially a well-polished, poison apple. As pointed out previously, the resistance created when marketing new theories, can be drastically reduced simply by radically dismissing the work of a leading opponent. By creating something of a theoretical vacuum through such a disposal, alternative ideas can more quickly gain a discipline's attention. Thus, when Friedman is seemingly baulked by Patinkin, he then proceeds to take a clear (and undisguised) direct aim at his primary target, John Maynard Keynes. At a quite superficial level, readers are offered what appeared to be a serious re-evaluation of Keynes' work (the poison apple). But at a deeper level, Friedman attempted his supposedly critical analysis by almost deliberately looking through the wrong end of a telescope. By diminishing a towering figure, such as Keynes, Friedman directed a subsequent, almost casual, dismissal of both the man and his theories.[56]

Once again, the poison apple, when accepted, helps ensure that the hidden objective will be validated. Whether Friedman believes he is objectively weighing up Keynes' actual contributions to monetary theory is essentially incidental when framed by a broader scheme that virtually bulldozes through the marketplace for ideas.[57] In effect, Friedman's focus is on torpedoing Keynes as an economist, rather than expending any critical effort to adequately understand his work. (Friedman's analysis is haunted by the suspicion that he damningly starts his examination convinced that Keynes, in both his theoretical approach and policy recommendations, was entirely misguided.) With these objectives firmly in sight, Friedman predictably concludes (by employing an idiosyncratic version of what attempts to pass as a scrupulous consideration), that Keynes is no more than, and at best, a minor quantity theorist. Consequently, Friedman is led to conveniently relegate Keynes' theory, and any subsequent derivative structures, to the infamy of being built upon a questionable flooring composed of theoretical quicksand.

Friedman's vision, in a very definite sense, was meant to be transformative whether or not marketed as such. Given his unalterable perspective of how the world worked, he would inevitably find evidence that confirmed his stoutly rooted, *a priori* ideas. This goal would be dutifully accomplished, even if accomplished by forcefully squeezing the available jigsaw pieces of observation so that they perfectly conformed to a preconceived mould. From a certain perspective, Friedman could even be considered self-delusional, like a magician who somehow comes to believe in his own predictable bag of tricks. However, being so deeply engaged in such a compelling form of self-hypnosis would only make him a more compelling messenger, no matter what he happened to be marketing. Evangelical salesmen are far more dangerous when they are imbued with a faith that renders them completely inflexible in their approach or understanding. Such ideological acolytes become functionally incapable of admitting error, no matter what evidence they chance to stumble upon. Instead, they cleverly fit awkward evidence into pre-conceived structures.[58] Having imbibed the truth, all else must necessarily be reduced to simple falsehoods that can be summarily dismissed.

I sometimes think some of the Chicago people are hopeless. Well, I wouldn't include Milton as among the hopeless because he was smart enough to punch his way out of a paper bag sometimes. But in the end he didn't want to do so. I think that's the case with 100% money, which was just a crotchety part of the first Chicago school. Irving Fisher also embraced it. The only thing it fits into is Milton's later monistic monetarism where, if you have a 100% reserve ratio by law, then you can't have a variable *de facto* reserve ratio and therefore you won't get an additional component in the variance of the money supply. And of course getting a variance in the ups and downs of the money supply is the worst thing possible. Becker, I think, cured him of that. Probably he said, 'Look. You have barriers to money in the banking system and private banking under one disguise or another will inevitably arise. You will simply make the banking system ineffective with a kind of Gresham's Law arising.' And I think Milton quietly changed, he just quietly dropped that. He doesn't particularly announce changes in positions, but instead, lets them just decay away (Conversation with Paul Samuelson, October 1997).

Friedman sought to destroy, or at least undermine, the collectivism that he saw as inherent in the Keynesian approach. To do so, he chose to offer, and tirelessly package, a carefully honed alternative as a valid substitute. To further his aims, Friedman had to devise a method (or strategy) for selling his definitive perspective. Fortunately for him, one of the cardinal rules of marketing is that you increase the acceptance of a product not only by highlighting its virtues, but by shining a bright light on the failures of an alternative option.[59] In essence, by deliberately creating a very low bar to hurdle, Friedman consequently aimed his initial destructive foray at the monetary thinking that formed an essential linchpin in Keynes' theory. Instead of the volatility and uncertainty of the money and bond markets discovered in Keynesian theory, Friedman offered a vision of stability and cohesiveness.[60] In Friedman's universe, a beautifully synchronised, if invisible, market mechanism dependably churned away, managing to efficiently regulate a country's economy. The result was a durable framework that was perfectly capable of providing the necessary self- regulation encapsulated by his version of the quantity theory.

Friedman (2003a/1956) in his seminal monetary work, presented a properly polished poison apple (or perhaps more exactly a Trojan horse) that he politely slipped into the ongoing debate without apparent fanfare.[61] (To be more exact, he would eventually offer two very different poison apples while attempting to quietly inject his monetary theory into mainstream economics.) Initially, at least, his efforts consisted of brandishing his theory as being entirely bereft of any revolutionary impulse. In essence, his ideas were absolutely devoid of any detectable desire to upset the applecart of long standing thought on the subject of monetary economics. Instead, he portrays himself as simply reinforcing time honoured knowledge, rather than forcibly peddling potentially unproven and perhaps even unsound doctrine. (Meaning that he is happy to have his thought defined as sober knowledge based entirely on widely accepted theory. In this particular instance, Friedman insisted that his contribution was only an improved approach to an already existing framework. His suggested perspective (on matters of a monetary nature) is then deliberately tagged as having been nurtured by its deep roots in dominant economic theory. In other words, Friedman is offering a needed enhancement to a widely employed framework that existed prior to any Keynesian style foolishness.)

Consequently, his work on the quantity theory is offered more as a restorative effort, a sort of memorandum to reinstate a long held Chicago oral tradition to its rightful position.[62] (Though it goes almost without saying that in doing this, Friedman is offering a new, improved and vastly more scientific version of traditional thought. Keep in mind that whenever you notice Friedman's name, you may be assured that an expansive marketing campaign will always be on the horizon as well.) Therefore, to polish his rhetorical poisoned apple, Friedman boldly claimed that he harboured a distinct and vivid memory of being inculcated into an exact verbal version of the quantity theory during the relatively brief time he actually spent at Chicago as a student. (More time was spent at Columbia University from whence he gained his degree.) Perhaps instinctively, less likely deliberately, this historical drapery (so visibly deployed) represented a clever strategy to advance his broader aims. Unarguably, anything unwritten is much more difficult to pin down, let alone convincingly disprove, than the printed word.

Friedman is not without a discoverable agenda. (That situation hardly makes him unique, however.) He offers the reader a distinct, and carefully crafted, world. His conveniently dredged up graduate school memories turn out to be quite useful when framed as representing a simple, but true reflection of the past. Consequently, in this hall of constructed mirrors, since Friedman needs to have the past unfold in a distinctly fortuitous fashion, it must automatically be made to do so. But despite Friedman's noticeable marketing skills, his alternative sketch of the 1930s ultimately failed to gain the hoped for traction that he perhaps anticipated. His constructed Chicago scaffolding proved susceptible to a forceful challenge and subsequent dismantling by Don Patinkin. Patinkin's authority rested on having experienced something very similar to Friedman's interwar Chicago experience, not so many years afterwards. (Little reason existed for assuming that those few years saw a radical revision in Chicago's supposed oral tradition or mode of teaching. Moreover, the faculty remained much the same during the relevant period.) Unlike Friedman, Patinkin took careful notes while gaining his doctorate from the University of Chicago. (Friedman waited until 1946, when he received his sanctioned degree not from Chicago, but by way of Columbia University, guidance provided by Simon Kuznets.)

Patinkin, however, in his exchange with Friedman made the fundamental mistake of thinking that when debating with him, logic and evidence would necessarily trump any and all of Friedman's distinct agendas or perpetual proclivities.[63] However, the challenge posed by Patinkin (basically contradicting Friedman's claims) only compelled Friedman to defend his position ever more furiously. When trapped, Friedman would resort to tactics that closely resembled those of a boxer maneuvered into a corner. He attempted to distract attention away from his vulnerabilities by launching a flurry of punches, hoping to eventually slip through his opponent's defences. Not for Friedman a mere covering up, hoping to protect himself by slipping into a defensive crouch. As always, thrown into an adverse situation, he remorselessly preferred to come out storming, using roundhouse punches in the hope of causing his opponent to back off. At the very least he employed this distraction in an attempt to thoroughly confuse, if not entirely muddle, the issue at hand. Friedman's persistent strategy throughout his lengthy career was to seemingly yield no ground, no matter what was thrown at him. The best defence, at least the one consistently favoured by Friedman when parrying arguments, was always an aggressive offence.

> It is hard to imagine an empirical observation that would convince most members of … the University of Chicago to change their minds. My personal view is that if someone holds a view it cannot be dislodged by any conceivable empirical data. Evidence from a data system doesn't convince them. These people have made their decisions already. They've become true believers and no amount of empirical evidence will ever convince them by definition (Conversation with James Kindahl, October 1997).

In response, Patinkin during this polite slugging match, unwittingly falls into Friedman's tactical impulse to construct and perpetuate something of a woozle trap.[64] In this type of low key ambush, a debater ends up constantly backtracking and repeating his or her arguments in the forlorn hope that sweet reason and facts will break through the haze provided by such stout and unyielding resistance. Basically Patinkin keeps finding himself circling back to his starting point in the forlorn hope that logic and evidence would provide effective leverage. In other words, Patinkin is fuelled by the somewhat naïve belief that facts and rational discourse must inevitably overcome pure assertions, no matter how cleverly Friedman's defensive ploys might be hedged. Unfortunately, this stolid piece of wishful thinking turns out to provide only a flimsy shield against the onslaught provided by a slippery, yet single-minded opponent. Friedman's hope appears to reside in having Patinkin tie himself into knots trying to deal with a swarm of circling arguments and attacks.

> Clearly, questions about the history of economic doctrine are empirical questions which can be answered only on the basis of evidence cited from the relevant literature. … My criticism of Friedman is, accordingly, that on many occasions he has ignored the detailed evidence which has been adduced against the views he expresses; and that on still other occasions he has indulged in casual empiricism in the attempt to support his doctrinal interpretations (Patinkin 2003b:123–124).

Friedman though persists with his blizzard of counter-arguments, quite content in Patinkin's words to 'let [policy] wag … theory' (Patinkin 2003b:126). Friedman in his eagerness to erase Patinkin's critiques of his claims, whether deliberately or not, does masterfully muddle what are clearly only associated policy issues with what are purely theoretical matters.[65] As Friedman should have easily recalled, many of the policy recommendations supported by Keynes differed little from those embraced by a number of the prominent Chicago economists of the 1930s. Both sides were perfectly capable of agreeing on a policy of government expenditure (and associated budget deficits) as an appropriate response to forcefully goose the economy out of an extended depression. The real substantial clash was based on the diametrically opposed theoretical frameworks that served as the basis for these identical policy recommendations.[66]

For someone like Simons, expansive fiscal policy could only qualify as something done within the defined constraints of an acknowledged emergency, a necessary short run policy validated only by exceptional circumstances. In contrast, Keynes saw the need for government intervention over a much longer course of time. Given the nature of Keynes' defined investment function, the cyclical nature of any economy would inevitably dictate the breakdown of operative market mechanisms. Downturns, especially severe ones, could not be dodged in any reliable, or predictable, fashion without deliberate guidance. Patinkin, while raising some very legitimate theoretical doubts, makes clear that his objective in doing so is to steer clear of any associated policy matters. He construes that pure theory is in practise potentially separable from suggested responses to more concrete issues. Consequently, he views Friedman as attempting to peddle a questionable theoretical stance in order to substantiate specific policy prescriptions. (If the Patinkin/Friedman debate is more closely examined, the claim can be made that Friedman was at least surreptitiously marketing selected policies, even when ostensibly deeply enmeshed in matters strictly theoretical.) Muddling (wavering between the boundaries defining the separate realms controlled by policy and theory) might be deemed to be acceptable and endearing in the case of Milne's Pooh Bear. However, such debating tactics ceases to charm (and to be not particularly welcome), when evaluating economic frameworks. Friedman, unlike Pooh Bear is not some economist of 'very little brain'.

> ... what interests me now is monetary theory, not monetary policy. These represent two different spheres of discourse. And whatever the relationship between the two, it is clearly not a one-to-one correspondence: different policy recommendations can emanate from the same conceptual theoretical framework; and different frameworks can lead to the same policy recommendation (Patinkin 2003c:319).

As stated, Friedman's (1956) intent is to accomplish a reverse spin in the case of monetary matters by substituting his version of the quantity theory for the then dominant Keynesian approach. To give his poison apple the appropriate gloss, he creates a bit of staged drama that attempts to construct an aura of a restoration clinging to his project. (This ploy should be considered to be step one of his campaign.) Friedman linked his formulation to a long established Chicago tradition, which he alone can manage to clarify and return to its rightful position. This bit of sleight of hand is slyly accomplished by relying on a conveniently remembered oral, rather than written, form of instruction. These unforgettable, intellectual insights, according to the precise memories of Milton Friedman, were unquestionably inculcated in him, during his brief student sojourn at Chicago.[67] When seemingly stymied in his insistence by the objections and pinpoint logic of Don Patinkin, Friedman quickly veered decisively away from the substantial core of evidential objections to his claims. He deliberately chose to divert attention away from a flimsily patched together historical cover story, which he now found himself backed against.[68] (One which offered no obvious escape route hidden within its intrinsic fabric.)

However, this now uncomfortable position was, after all, fashioned only by his suspect memories, which can be easily modified when greater flexibility proves to be more tactically convenient. The initial approach, when necessary, can even be implicitly abandoned without regret. Fortunately, Friedman had yet another poison apple, waiting in reserve, to substitute for the failure of his first tentative foray. (That attempt, his previous Trojan horse effort, was based on greasing the acceptance of his formulated monetary theory by cloaking it in ordinariness.)[69] The second marketing plunge Friedman undertakes is to quietly ease in his monetary perspective by reducing the competing alternative to a matter of trivial insignificance. In essence, what appears to be a viable theory (though opposed to his own position) when critically examined, is shown to be no more than a mirage. This deliberate transformation leaves him unquestionably triumphant if only by default. Friedman, in this case, would command the only theoretical footing that would still remain intact. The focus of his strategy then shifted, quite deliberately, to destroying the competing (Keynesian) theory.

As a polished poison apple, Friedman offers a supposedly objective evaluation of that approach. This proffered analysis only needs to persuade the bulk of a profession whose familiarity with Keynes' thought is at best second hand. But embedded in Friedman's evaluation is his underlying objective. In effect, Friedman is attempting to demolish the prevailing understanding of money that had dominated the post-war period, in order to create a proper space for his own perspective. Propelled by this singular objective, Friedman manages to formulate his attack on Keynes. But strongly associated with and driving this particular skirmish is his implicit, onslaught against collectivism (or at least collectivism as viewed from a Mont Pelerin perspective). If Friedman could effortlessly dismiss Keynesian theory, in terms of its monetary models, the path for his own framework would be left largely unimpeded. Any necessity to ground his wisdom on some contentious previous Chicago tradition would conveniently vanish. If successful in his spot of demolition derby, Friedman would essentially win the contest by default. Though what is striking in both of his focused efforts, is that his intention was persistently hidden beneath a seemingly innocuous objective. (We need to restore a valuable tradition, as his first effort, or failing that, then Keynes as a monetary theorist needs to be meticulously re-evaluated.)

When Friedman is initially caught red-handed by Patinkin, essentially caught in the midst of palming his two-headed tactical coin, he simply doubles down by tossing Keynes into his carefully manicured briar-patch. (Friedman evaluates Keynes, but does so according to his own idiosyncratic approach to monetary theory. No noticeable attempt is made to understand Keynes' actual thought.[70]) To do so, he casually trots down a path that pointedly ignores a stack of abundant, though inconvenient, evidence. Friedman instead carefully substitutes a poorly defined, but basically distracting, subtext to keep his primary monetary argument afloat. By devising a context in which Keynes could be sufficiently diminished, Keynes, along with his rejected theory, could be made to vanish down the proverbial gurgler of historical thought. Friedman, when his initial poison apple (eagerly presented to the profession) failed to gain anything resembling the desired level of enthusiastic acceptance, remained entirely undaunted. In this professional chess match of countermoves, Friedman chose to respond to a temporary setback by exploring the possibility of slipping an even more plausible Trojan horse past the wearied opposition's critical gaze.

Clearly, the initial feint of peddling his quantity theory as a continuation of a revered monetary tradition (as handed down by the assembled interwar Chicago faculty) failed to succeed. Friedman, scrambling to construct an alternative strategy, one which relegated Keynes to the dubious position of being no more than a minor quantity theorist. In essence, the remodelled Keynes is arbitrarily lumped with those who have made a small, and not particularly enlightening, addition to the established corpus of work. A highly diminished Keynes becomes in this perspective an unwilling ally of Milton Friedman, much in the same way that those who fell afoul of the Royal Navy's press gangs could be relabelled as patriotic volunteers.

> The exaggerated claims for the quantity theory have expressed themselves in the attempt (especially by Milton Friedman) to present Keynes' monetary theory not as a new theory, but as a variation of the Cambridge cash balance theory (Patinkin 2003c:317).

Friedman deftly charts his campaign by engineering a curious, but seemingly inoffensive, comparison between Keynes' (1923) *Tract on Monetary Reform* and Keynes' (1936) *General Theory*. Part of Friedman's poison apple is an erroneous, but almost plausible, false equivalence.[71] He appears to insinuate that very little in the way of growth had germinated within Keynes' core thought during those intervening years. Even if judged by others (and by Keynes himself), as being somewhat (if not grossly inaccurate), it is not in and of itself a radical (or freshly constructed) assertion.

> The major points which Milton made is that there is nothing particularly Keynesian about the liquidity preference function, and that the demand for money sections of the *General Theory* are simply a slightly inferior version of Keynes' views in the *Tract* (Stanley Fisher quoted in Leeson 2003: 313).

To clarify, Keynes' 1923 book had been cobbled together from three previously published articles and leaned heavily on the prevailing Cambridge quantity theory of that era. For most careful readers, there is quite a ravine separating the monetary theory of the twenties' book and Keynes' formulation of his liquidity preference approach that dominates the *General Theory*. Friedman though succeeds in deliberately muddling the two by sneaking up on the *General Theory* from an original, and definitely skewed, entry point. In Friedman's version, Keynes in the 1930s (for reasons unknown) became obsessed with the idea of a liquidity trap, or the existence of absolute liquidity preference. That then becomes, from this perspective, the distilled essence of Keynes' intellectual efforts, or at least in Friedman's estimation, Keynes' only original idea.

What makes such an approach decidedly outré, is that Keynes actually mentions the idea more in passing, rather than attempting, in any fashion, to transform it into a mainstay of his theory. Friedman, however, is intent on tactically elevating a relatively minor concept, such as absolute liquidity preference, to a functional role whereby it re-emerges as the essential linchpin for the entirety of Keynes' monetary theory.[72] Only by engineering an unexpected imaginative leap of this sort could Friedman actually elevate this detail into exemplifying the very essence of Keynes' thought. However, in terms of developing a workable poison apple strategy it proved to be extremely convenient.

> One consequence of my rereading large parts of the *General Theory* in the course of writing this reply has been to reinforce my view that absolute liquidity preference plays a key role. Time and again when Keynes

must face up to precisely what it is that prevents a full-employment equilibrium, his final line of defense is absolute liquidity preference. To document this point, I have assembled the relevant quotations in appendix 1 … I do not see how anyone can read through these quotations and come to any other conclusion than that his 'special twist' was highly elastic liquidity preference and that this 'was a key element in Keynes proposition' about the possibility that there might not be a full employment equilibrium even with flexible prices. Patinkin sees the fly on the barn door but not the door (Friedman 2003b:158–159).

Actually it is difficult to comprehend the exact target on which Friedman might have his sights fixed in this suggested analysis. If anything, the actual attempt comes across more like the confused buzzing of an irate hive of bees, than anything conclusive, let along revealing. Friedman's fixation does not rest on any substantial Keynesian barn door, which others have somehow failed to discern. Presented instead are not even any significant fly specks of theory (that might be loitering on that more substantial door). What Friedman offers is a plausible illusion on which to concentrate his analysis. Friedman, unfortunately, seems to fall into a familiar trap of finding in any reading exactly what he expected, or even needed, to discover. To fulfil Friedman's underlying objective, Keynes must be transformed into a run of the mill quantity theorist. That remains the one, overriding goal. Success in this case would mean that his own quantity theory of money might then be regarded as the only legitimate approach available to honest and accomplished economists. Keynes (in Friedman's imaginative retelling of his monetary theory), offers only a trivial twist on the received wisdom offered by the established quantity theory. However, to anyone willing to read and analyse carefully, Friedman would be revealed as a provider of a distinctly skewed presentation. Meaning that his carefully polished version of Keynes' intentions failed to conclusively prove his desired assertion. To reiterate, Friedman himself seems incapable of distinguishing between the fly and the barn door on which the fly sat. Or put more bluntly, he failed to distinguish anything that would run contrary to his prejudged assertions. Since Keynes' contribution must be trivialised to strategically forward his restoration of the quantity theory, Friedman feels compelled to transform Keynes' approach to suit his goals. He strategically chose to artfully box him within a well-worn conventional category (much to Keynes' surprise were he still alive during Friedman's bit of legerdemain).[73] But the catch within this structured attempt to achieve this bit of sleight of hand, is that it required a set of distinct tactical misinterpretations.

Consequently, Friedman methodically buttressed what could otherwise be easily categorised as something of an obsession in the only feasible fashion available. (Having a transparent and implicitly declared goal of simply annihilating Keynes, by whatever means possible, would be a definitive marketing faux pas.) Instead, to make his case, Friedman simply lists what he identified as thirteen relevant quotes proving that Keynes' contribution to monetary economics fails to go past notions of a liquidity trap. The passages are intended to prove the intense focus on this singular concept as a sort of minor addendum to standard quantity theory thinking. These words had been diligently unearthed as conclusive in their intent, though all seemed somewhat hidden within the pages of *The General Theory*. This list of designated quotes was revealed by Friedman as composing a sort of essential key to understanding the text itself. In their entirety they were presented as being capable of unlocking the secret meaning of the book, that which the profession at large had failed to grasp.

Each one of these quotes is presented as a distinct coffin nail that indisputably confirms Friedman's trivialisation of Keynes. Unfortunately, the reality fails (when the evidence is examined) to reflect the hype with which these clues are divulged. Some of these quotes turn out to have nothing to do with the idea of absolute liquidity preference, while others are clearly wrenched out of context.[74] On the contrary, Friedman alone proves consistently capable of finding liquidity traps embedded within each and every paragraph dealing with monetary issues.[75] What then Friedman boldly markets as startling new discoveries, remain instead largely fictitious and even blatantly self-dealing. If indeed this is Friedman's devilishly clever version of a Trojan horse, the flimsiness of his supporting evidence succeeds in delivering the real shock. (His claims appear to rest on the dubious assumption that none of his assertions will be carefully scrutinised.)

Only by taking a true leap of faith could he expect that Keynesians, or even any open minded economists, would let down their critical guard when faced with this type of rhetorical foray. The supposedly ironclad arguments that Friedman provides can be punctured and discarded in turn. Each one could then be simply deported back to his deceptively constructed alternative universe for permanent disposal. All that is required to torpedo his floated liquidity trap hypothesis is a quick reading of the original statements as they appear within the context of *The General* Theory.

Only those choosing to wilfully accept Friedman's assertions at face value would be successfully deceived. Still, it remains doubtful that Friedman, even if confronted by this starkly confronting evidence, would have shifted any of his iron-bound assertions, let alone admitted his errors.[76]

These two straightforward examples, (provided by his South Africa appearance and his bout with Keynes) described here at some length, serve only as an attempt to familiarise the reader with a common strategy. Such an approach has been employed with no little success by Milton Friedman, as well as many other economists. (Notice that the goal is to persuade by obfuscation rather than through clarification.) Whether he was conscious of constructing poison apples as a persuasive device is not particularly relevant in the presented argument. There is in fact little evidence to suggest that he was. (Nothing approximating a Milton Friedman poison apple cookbook, or resembling a confessional, exists.) People, even high-minded academics, tend to use tactics that work to their advantage, without necessarily analysing any attendant details of those specific mechanisms.

How this rhetorical approach developed in Friedman's writing and bravado debating style is an interesting, but ultimately unanswerable question. Clearly, like anyone else, he built on what appeared to work, whether deliberately or even consciously aware of the steps taken. There is, however, a wider purpose in demonstrating the existence of this sleight of hand whether recognised by the promulgator or not. When seeking to quash what both Friedman and Stigler saw as a dangerous methodological controversy, such tried and true devices were already snugly contained within (and readily available from), each one's overflowing toolbox of tricks and devices. Namely, the proper socket wrenches for defensive purposes already existed (all of which were capable of making the fine rhetorical adjustments required for debating purposes). These tools could be successfully employed to buttress the foundations of price theory and consequently tighten the persuasiveness of Chicago style economics.

Therefore, focusing even more intently on the strategic ploys most frequently utilised (while investigating the instance of Milton Friedman's most effective poison apple), requires a somewhat finely detailed context before proceeding further. The controversy in which Friedman's most famous poison apple was deployed must necessarily be associated with an analysable context and a closely associated historical context. In which case, the background that fed the relevant post war debate must have been driven by succinct and discernible motivations. These pre-existing controversies then serve as the unacknowledged catalyst behind Friedman's methodological stratagem in his famous 1953 essay. In effect, a threat was perceived and responded to strategically.

Any useful analysis of this methodological thrust then requires a sufficient understanding of the state of play in those immediate post war years when Friedman's rhetorical strategies were largely conceived and instituted. In which case, it is perhaps wise to initially glance at the turmoil and almost reflexive challenges created during the interwar years. It was during this period that faith in traditional theoretical and social constraints was badly shaken, if not entirely shattered. Friedman would, in the early fifties, choose to balance athwart this cumulative change in professional focus, by attempting to intentionally shift the direction of economic thought and research in a direction more amenable to his explicit objectives. To a degree, he would seek to restore what he viewed as a more substantial (and fundamental) approach to economics. Trying to shape the profession, he would dutifully attempt to dismiss troubling challenges to an imperturbable, market based analysis. Doing so would pose no small challenge.

II. The Empty Box Challenge – A Growing Opposition to Price Theory

> Yet from all his reading and conversations he cannot recall a scene in which anyone opened the boxes and said, with authority and convincing evidence, "Constant Return Industry, hosen: Increasing Return Industry, hats," or used any like words. Nor can he think of an industrial monograph in which profitable use was made of the Laws of Returns in commenting on the things of life (Clapham 1953/1922:119).

> I think it's funny how the orthodox theory of the firm and Marx's value theory, subjective value theory and the labour theory of value, come together. The conclusions of both really have to assume constant returns to scale. The production function becomes a tangent automatically in the case of constant costs. Constant returns to scale in the production function is a necessity, if there is anything else, you get into analytical difficulties. What I want to emphasize is that there is a strange marriage of opposites (Conversations with Mark Blaug, April 1998).

Lost in the trenches of World War I (along with the countless casualties) were the Victorian verities that had structured and constrained society and critical thinking. Movement and dynamics were upending and supplanting customs and manners. Motion pictures were booming at local cinemas. Jazz was introducing previously unheard of rhythms and melodies to music. New notions of time were demoting Newtonian physics, making it into a special case of a framework having a broader and more general perspective. Italian futurism was the most obvious artistic movement simultaneously incorporating both time and motion, but cubism attempted to defy the laws of time and vision as well. Art was tearing apart and reimagining the components of more explicit observation. Dancing and fashions were also increasingly unconstrained and uncorseted, moving more freely to less predictable or at least to less familiar rhythms. Philosophically, Karl Popper questioned the validity of theories and facts while Freud journeyed into the unseen realms of the subconscious. Upheaval was the ruling theme of the twenties, seemingly seeping into every facet of life.

In the realm of economic thought, George Shackle has traced some of the background impulses that questioned formal price theory back to the unsettling impact of the Great War on a younger generation of economists. That war led to a noticeable crumbling of received doctrine and authority of any sort. The self-assurance of accepting knowledge as given and largely indisputable had effectively vanished, along with an untold number of young men.

> But the second of those decades brought to an end the Pax Britannica and the tranquil generation-and-a-half which had favoured and fostered a belief in a self-regulating, inherently and naturally self-optimizing, stable and coherent economic system. When men had got back their breath after the war and turned to apply their conceptual tools to repair the ruins of European organization, their failure (which a few years of endeavour forced them to acknowledge) to bring back the old order of things made them begin to ask for new tools. A new generation of students, which went seriously to college only in 1919 or after, had graduated and begun to think, impelled by new questions and freed in some degree from old preconceptions (Shackle 1967:5).

In this widening re-evaluation, the problems associated with decisively fumbling the apparent issues raised by increasing returns to scale appeared insurmountable. This perplexing quandary appeared to be especially the case when placed within a comparative static framework (the familiar terrain derived from Marshall's authoritative volumes). Any previous solution, seemed to have run aground against a reviving post war culture of ever more frenzied motion and time dislocations. Scepticism was the grace note of the day. Simply dodging the issue seemed no more than a flimsy piece of chicanery. What was now revealed was a not so hidden intent aimed at maintaining a received wisdom, one that had been dutifully hatched as a product of a bygone Victorian status quo.[77] Such reasoning was found to be contradictory, unsupported by (on careful examination), any compelling evidence

> Marshall acknowledged with great candour that he was flummoxed by the problem of dynamic analysis. After discussing the problem of equilibrium with falling supply price he writes; "But such notions must be taken broadly. The attempt to make them precise over-reaches our strength." … There are other indications that Marshall habitually thought of a movement to the right along a supply curve (output increasing) as a movement forward through time. This accounts for the extraordinary importance that he attached to what now seems a mere *curiosum* – economies of large-scale industry in competitive conditions. The reason is that he somehow boiled the effect of technical progress going on through time into the movement down his supply curve (Robinson 1974:41).

More particularly, what had previously been viewed as general cases in physics or mathematics, revealed themselves as only being relevant under certain particular strictures. Einstein's theory of relativity could incorporate Newtonian physics as a special case, while projective geometry had room for three special cases depending on the sum of a triangle's three angles.[78] In this sense, not being bound or constrained by traditional modes of thought might nurture the hope that in a similar fashion, a valuable breakthrough in economic thinking could possibly emerge.[79] Some mode of thought might be found, or constructed, which was more comprehensive, and thus more capable of explaining the cycles and variations that characterised any given economy.

> I shall argue that the postulates of the classical theory are applicable to a special case only and not to the general case, the situation which it assumes being a limiting point of the possible positions of equilibrium.

Moreover, the characteristics of the special case assumed by the classical theory happen not to be those of the economic society in which we actually live, with the result that its teaching is misleading and disastrous if we attempt to apply it to the facts of experience (Keynes 1964:3).

By the 1930s, the economics profession had become more open to alternative approaches. (The world-wide depression presumably acted as a catalyst in bringing this metamorphosis to fruition.) The more mechanical style of employing equilibrium based analysis had come under increasing attack starting in the 1920s. Readiness (a profession hungry for new approaches) was perhaps far more important than evidence in the subsequent rapid embrace that both Chamberlin's monopolistic competition and Keynes' macro/monetary theory received.[80] They were both quickly adopted because both appeared to offer a more intuitive answer than did the standard received theory of the time. The existing doubt already sown, coupled with the general scepticism and disillusionment defining the period after World War I, made this the right time to offer something at odds with the prevailing wisdom of the period. At least the timing was on point, provided such offerings were steeped in the analytic tools of economics.[81] In effect, existing theories were seen as inadequate and were effectively tottering, ready to be displaced by an appropriate alternative. Opportunistically, the stage was set for new theories that would imaginatively appeal to an intuitive sense of time and place.

> This swift adoption of the Keynesian system came about, I believe, because its analysis in terms of the determinants of effective demand seemed to go to the essence of what was going on in the economic system and was easier to understand (at least in its broad outlines) than alternative theories ... The speedy adoption of these new approaches was in large part due to the very unsatisfactory state of the existing price theory. That this was so bad had been demonstrated beyond doubt by the controversies in the *Economic Journal* in the 1920s and perhaps above all by Piero Sraffa's 1926 article. We were therefore looking for ways to solve the dilemmas these discussions revealed (Coase 1994:21–22).[82]

The common idea then that both Keynes and Chamberlin embraced was based on a somewhat pedestrian, yet somehow revolutionary, assumption. Each economist believed that the existing theories, straddling (or being specific to) what Keynes denotes as the fundamental divide between micro and macro theory, was (in effect) a special case masquerading as a more general one. Instead, they insisted in both cases, that there must be some potential theory (or theories) that would encompass the existing wisdom as no more than special cases of a distinctly generalizable framework. Comparing the two, Keynes made a consciously more revolutionary break than that attempted by Chamberlin. What is often overlooked in Keynes' methodological approach is his clear departure from the canonical order perfected by Alfred Marshall. However, when constructing his alternative vision, Keynes discovered a necessity for playing fast and loose with standard marginal analysis.[83] His system is based instead on non-clearing quantity adjustments, not the perfectly domesticated price clearing movements which are notoriously continuous. Discrete jumps inevitably occurred in his system, due to a set of shifting expectations which were only loosely anchored by market mechanisms. The inherent uncertainly of events mitigated fiercely against any clockwork paradigm detailing adjustments, at least when viewed from a Keynesian perspective.

Consequently, heavily laced with such thinking, the two key input markets (capital and labour) must adamantly refuse to operate in the fashion amenable to standard neo-classical economics. Unfortunately, this more revolutionary conception fabricated by Keynes managed to fade and largely disappear following his demise. In his absence, the potentially revolutionary edge of the theory could be more easily domesticated. What was implicitly rejected in these post war years was a theory that depended upon a more ambiguous operative mechanism. The original approach enlisted something of a John Stuart Mill perspective on convention as the theory's somewhat slippery linchpin. Such an amorphous, and seriously non-tractable, package proved to be too exotic for the profession to seriously consider, let alone embrace.[84] As a reaction, many economists deemed it better to diplomatically ignore the methodological implications staked out in *The General Theory*. Instead, the less controversial path taken simply enabled the profession to squeeze Keynes' theory into an ill-fitting corset of neo-classical micro-foundations. In essence, the underlying tacit agreement pretended that a strange, glued together result, featuring a Keynesian head on a neo-classical torso, would be sustainable.[85]

While Keynes deliberately employed the shop-worn tools of standard economics, he tended to use them in a looser, more creative manner. (The necessity for doing so derives from attempting to force what would appear to be a run-of-the-mill version of comparative statics to encompass changes over time. Imposing such a deliberate dose of chaos on a standard, static framework entails a much more intractable, dynamic imperative.) Consequently, in reimagining a marginal efficiency of capital schedule, Keynes is not attempting to reproduce, or measure, a physical productivity rate, one that could be conveniently equated with a real rate of interest. But by failing to do so, Keynes avoids focusing on some simple translation of micro-theory's diminishing returns to a fixed factor. The idea of short-run increasing costs remains, but its link with standard ideas of scarcity is augmented by the necessary addition of expectations. This incorporation occurs necessarily both on the revenue and cost sides. (The mostly neglected discussion of user cost in the appendix to chapter six of *The General Theory* may provide at least a degree of relevant insight that can serve to further this discussion.)

The context in which this analytical tool is employed, fails to describe an instance of, sedately and incrementally, gliding down along a pinioned and unmoving marginal efficiency of capital curve. In standard analysis, a continuous journey of this variety would proceed, nonstop, until the prevailing interest rate is discovered and equated. (A parallel understanding allows economists studying labour markets to inch their way down a marginal product of labour arc in order to discover a defining real wage.) The alternative Keynesian universe, in contrast, features a world where the very movement along such a curve can cause the whole edifice to shift. The system as a whole becomes sensitive to changes. The entire edifice tends to wobble with any serious disturbance. Ostensible movements along a curve feed into expectations of future returns that are directly based upon projections of future levels of aggregate demand. In a similar fashion, interest rates also cease to change smoothly and incrementally. Instead, they are revealed to prefer to proceed in a series of discrete jumps. Marginal ideas become merely a heuristic method of exposition, a possible assistance when engaging in any detailed analysis. Marginalism transforms into a shorthand for talking about or discussing problems, as noted, a useful heuristic, rather than a reflection of any likely reality. For Keynes, marginalism fails to serve as an effective underlying rationale that is capable of propelling a system based on equilibrating and strictly stable curves, whether theoretic or not.

> Changes in the liquidity function itself, due to a change in the news which causes revisions of expectations, will often be discontinuous, and will therefore give rise to a corresponding discontinuity of change in the rate of interest (Keynes 1964:198).

In a similar fashion, the labour market, when examined employing Keynesian eyes, is also distinctly different from the standard supply and demand functions equilibrated by a real wage. In a simple move consistent with his topsy-turvy view of the economy, price clearing labour and capital markets do not determine output but rather the other way around.[86] The level of economic activity (a reflection of effective demand in a demand constrained economy) is the driving force that settles both the question of employment and of capital investment. The idea that workers can, or do, bargain for their real wage is a nonstarter in the world Keynes constructs. Workers cannot effectively bargain for such a wage without concurrently having the simultaneous ability to set the level of aggregate output. Employers analogously find their production plans constrained by their market expectations. Consequently, the real wage that workers receive is the result of contractual negotiations over the money or nominal wage. This factor is then coupled with the actual flow of output resulting from the interaction between aggregate supply and effective demand. (The ultimate planned level of output determining the employment level.)[87]

The agreed upon (negotiated) money wage, like so many other components of Keynes' theory, turns out to be largely based upon conventions, namely those describing the traditional patterns of bargaining. The nominal wage level is acknowledged to be somewhat rigid. Contracts do extend over time, with workers resisting any attempted cutback to their nominal wage.[88] But for Keynes this provides the system with a measure of stability rather than unemployment.[89] On examination, Keynes makes little use of the classical apparatus despite all the attendant superficial trappings and despite his obvious debt to his mentor, Marshall. Rather in using much of the traditional language of economics, he often finds himself entrapped by the very logic he seeks to overthrow. We must therefore pay even closer attention to the thread of his argument. His is not a system where the real wage automatically equates the marginal product of a worker with the marginal disutility of that worker. The decisive action lies somewhere in between. Namely the disutility of a worker provides something resembling a reservation wage while the marginal product exists as a ceiling, limiting wage offers.

Strict adherence to marginal analysis adds very little insight here. The resulting nominal wage, from Keynes' perspective, has more to do with the conventions of bargaining. This perspective runs head on against a fundamental stance that usually underwrites the discipline of economics. The profession held (and continues to hold) an unshakeable belief in supply and demand as being the determinative force behind market clearing positions.[90] Such a perspective would inherently derail most economists from understanding Keynes' focused methodological departures.[91] It remains undeniably the case in standard economic theory that given an absence of market imperfections, prices must adjust to equate supply and demand, much as the sun rises in the east and sets in the west.

Wages, being the cost of labour, are assumed by most economists to perform this price equilibrating function within labour markets. Only the introduction of some institutional constraint, given this perspective, can impede the predictable process of wage adjustment as the driver behind this particular contractual market. Consequently, the desire to preserve a more conventional way of thinking allows for the tempting possibility that with only a small bit of fiddling, Keynes could effectively be stood on his head. In essence, flipping Keynes by inverting his intention only requires the appearance of capturing his thought, while in practise turning his vision upside down. Where Keynes claims that sticky wages provide a modicum of stability to a market system, for the majority of his inheritors these same less than flexible wages come to represent a major stumbling block to anticipated price adjustments. Consequently, to domesticate Keynes, whenever feasible, the employed strategy is to substitute a dose of orthodox thought for the more destabilising approaches favoured by Keynes. Since few economists read carefully, the assumption implicitly made is that this particular sleight of hand which reinstates orthodoxy will go unremarked and largely unnoticed.[92] (Most economists, when confronted by a new perspective, are more likely to feel comfortable with a theory, or at least an approach, that is cloaked in the familiar.)

To a degree, this approach can be categorised as a perverse (or a backfiring) type of poison apple unknowingly employed by Keynes. (At least the unintended consequences were clearly unforeseen.) While seemingly making the work of Keynes more approachable, an alternative (more orthodox) version of his work could be seamlessly slipped into the mainstream of economic analysis. Such thinking, once accepted, did provide a convenient way of dealing with observed labour markets without needing to deny the theoretical building blocks that traditionally define the economic craft. Rather than presenting the profession with a poison apple, had Keynes survived, he would have discovered that his own harsh theoretical antidote to conventional modes of thinking had been sugar coated and rendered somewhat innocuous. In the case of the ensuing transformation architecture of Keynesianism, we are tempted not by a nefarious poison apple, but instead offered the equally misleading (and dangerous) candy-coated apple. The goal in both cases is to replicate a theoretical appearance that becomes capable of tempting other economists to bite and swallow. Notice as well the shared disregard for the reality of the assumptions sustaining the theory.

In contrast to the theory's ultimate utilisation, Keynes intended to establish a more general theory, one which would replace an unnecessarily restrictive classical (or neo-classical) style of thinking. In contrast, a more mainstream approach that focused on sticky money wages merely succeeded in elevating (and misinterpreting) a special aspect, or observed detail, that was folded within the overall arc of a more general theory. For Keynes, workers' resistance to nominal pay cuts (incorporated within such inflexible wages), provides an unintended, but beneficial role. Sticky wages, within a sustainable economy, acted as a stabilising force, rather than performing as an economic stumbling block.[93] Unfortunately the mere mention of wages (whether sticky or otherwise) immediately conjured up (to most economists) the mirage of price (or wage) regimes.[94] By doing so, this distraction succeeded in inverting the quantity adjusted analysis championed by Keynes into one focused, once again, on price equilibration. In this more traditional style of thinking, the standard supply and demand functions of the labour market remain stubbornly paramount. This unrelenting goal of smuggling in the very mode of thought that Keynes claims to be struggling against, persists as the underlying purpose driving such a dislocated application of Keynesian analysis.

In his framework, Keynes never denies the theoretical existence of a real wage which is capable of clearing the labour market. The operative question is instead the role that such a construct actually plays within labour markets. In the world of Keynes, its equilibrating nature however, is demoted to the level of a distinctly special case. The constructed market framework that allows real wages to operate within the confines of a functioning labour market is necessarily clear cut and tightly constrained. In essence, it is not the general case at all. Keynes' logic compels him to issue an explicit denial that actual market forces must inevitably lead to such an envisioned system of real wage adjustments. In a quantity adjusted world, movements in nominal price variables cannot automatically, or even probably, yield a market clearing outcome. Consequently, it is not the lack of flexible wages that prevent labour markets from clearing, but rather an insufficient level of economic activity.

In effect, the process of negotiating nominal wages, added to the prevailing levels of economic activity, yield real wages, but almost as a by-product of these two activities. Placed within a market structure that is widely operative (rather than merely theoretical), involuntary unemployment cannot be cured by nominal wage adjustments. Instead, focusing on sticky (or rigid) wages manages only to create a convenient escape hatch (or a posed distraction) that skirts the issue of insufficient, aggregate demand. Therefore, with sticky wages posing instead as a market friction (or failure) firmly in place, the implications derived from any observed labour market (by denying validity to the non-clearing variety) can be analytically regularised. Any further need to justify the traditional theoretical building blocks that form the basis of the economic craft can now be classified as superfluous.

Methodological faith is restored as supply and demand is once again demonstrated to form the basis of all and any labour market adjustment. (Smidgens of lingering unemployment can consequently be attributed to a market malfunction, namely the catch-all term of sticky wages). Unlike Peter who disowned Jesus three times before the cock crowed, even the young Turks of the 1930s and 40s, striving, ostensibly, to establish a new regime within the profession would not have to deliberately forsake fundamental economic principles or approaches. The fear of excommunication (or overt controversy) would predictably fade. They could pose as revolutionaries without being truly radical. Sticky wages provided the providential 'get out of jail free' card for most of the trade. Economists could be comforted by reinstating a soothing tradition, while simultaneously mouthing their support for the presumptive revolution represented by Keynes' *General Theory*. Cake could be devoured while simultaneously preserving it for future dining.

This essential straddle between the systems, which managed to save the price adjusting methodology of neo-classical analysis, could continue to reign supreme despite sitting on a supressed contradiction. However in a somewhat perverse fashion, by seeming to buttress Keynesian analysis, this domestication of the theory essentially constructed a noticeable Achilles heel attached to the basic architecture of the structure. Inevitably, a flimsy, makeshift arrangement of this type, would allow such a dubious concordat to be successfully breached at a later date. Employing the standard rationale of a market failure meant that Keynesian Theory would be deliberately shaped to accord with a pre-existing, neo-classical foundation.

Doing so meant deliberately forgoing the creation of a more conducive and impermeable microeconomic base. For most of the profession, such a reconstruction was firmly shoved into the 'too hard' basket. Meanwhile, the strategic employment of perceived market imperfections appeared to adequately patch up any serious discrepancies, at least in the short run. Except for those economists intent on imbuing markets with a deliberate touch of divinity, such market failures have traditionally composed a routine and potentially treatable phenomenon for most of the profession. In this sense, economists were assured that they could simply perform minor corrective surgery, as required, on these inherently flawed markets.

However for Keynes, just as a frictionless physical world would be unmanageable, so would one with perfectly flexible wages.[95] In this aspect, it is the grit in the works that allows markets, including labour markets, to operate within a stabilised, concrete reality.[96] His reconceptualization of labour markets is a truly revolutionary move that, as pointed out, has been almost deliberately overlooked.[97] Keynes' very insistence on this point perhaps betrays a premonition that in this respect, neo-classical theory would continue to triumph, despite his best efforts. But if in fact the standard conception of the labour market remained unshakable, the fundamental basis for his own work must eventually crumble. A subsequent failure to have this essential insight widely acknowledged, let alone accepted, would ultimately eviscerate his theory by leaving it open to the type of micro-foundations argument that sustained the 1970s. Deliberately structured Achilles heels almost always prove to be a predictable source of vulnerability.

At the time of its publication, only a limited number of readers seemed to grasp this fundamental departure from orthodox theory. Of Keynes' many vociferous critics that responded to his work, Jacob Viner (1937) is one of the few who seem to have glimpsed the very pivot of Keynes' work as largely turning upon his rejection of standard labour theory wisdom. Dennis Robertson (1973:319) makes an argument similar to that of Viner when defending the position jointly held by both Pigou and himself. Among the virtual blizzard of comments attending Keynes' seminal (1936) work, it is surprising how little focus there is on his central tenet concerning the labour market. Either this point somehow slipped through all the critical examination of supporters and critics alike, or they harboured severe trepidations in engaging with Keynes on this treacherous terrain. Few economists enjoy skating for extended periods over increasingly thin theoretical ice.

What I understand to be the current doctrine is different. It looks to wage reductions during a depression to restore profit margins, thus to restore the investment morale of entrepreneurs and to give them again a credit status which will enable them to finance any investment they may wish to make. It relies upon the occurrence of a lag between the reduction in wage rates and a response in reduced volume of sales at the previous prices, during which interval entrepreneurs find prices to be higher than marginal costs and extension of output therefore profitable, provided buyers can be found for the increased output … They do not contend that this is certain to occur, but on the ground that the chief factor in governing the action of entrepreneurs with respect to postponable expenditure is the current profit status of their operations as compared to their immediately preceding experience, they say that it is a reasonable probability (Viner 1937:162–163).

The extent of such a methodological break from marginalism is perhaps unfortunately hidden by Keynes' perceived need to employ a standard foundation of perfect competition for rhetorical reasons.[98] Keynes' actual methodological break with what he defines as the classical system can more accurately be understood by examining his use of marginality throughout *The General Theory*. As previously examined, though he does not entirely throw out all the bath water along with the baby, at best only a sudsy residue of the traditional approach remains. When laying out his theory, Keynes had no intention of needlessly alienating the profession, which he is trying single-mindedly to woo. Consequently, he doesn't intentionally create auxiliary problems by entirely rejecting the *lingua franca* of the profession. A gloss of marginalism remains, yet employed in a quite non-traditional fashion. The actual use made of marginality is emphatically quite casual, with a more purposive underlying foundation steeped in conventional beliefs and formed expectations instead of marginal mechanics.[99] Unfortunately, Keynes' attempt at slipping the profession something of a poison apple can be judged to be a failure. The attractive language of conventional marginalism floating on the surface of the theory was easily swallowed. Unfortunately, economists almost universally spat out the theoretical core that Keynes had tried to ease through an academic wall of studied resistance. As previously mentioned, his followers candy coated that essence, successfully burying the intended meaning (whether deliberately or not). The initial bite of the apple then was made more palatable (courtesy of Keynes), but unlike the standard poison apple, all subsequent bites became equally palatable under the transformative care of the profession.

As such, the use of marginalism reflects, to some degree, only a rhetorical tactic. Its employment mirrors, to a limited extent, Keynes' failure to realise the full consequences of not making his break from the marginalism of price theory sufficiently clear. (The fact that Keynes presented a quantity adjusted, non-market clearing system as his general case, proved to be an insufficient warning for most of the economics profession.)[100] By adopting this conventional rhetorical stance, in order to persuade his audience, Keynes may have allowed too many economists to declare that Keynes offered nothing radically different, or to reframe his argument within a more traditional structure.[101] As has been noted, the former approach was readily embraced by Milton Friedman. Keynes by employing his clever compromises, unintentionally left his work open to the sort of Trojan horse strategy adopted by those wishing to undermine, or even reverse, what would otherwise be a revolutionary breakthrough.[102]

A similar misunderstanding, deliberate or otherwise, attended Chamberlin's efforts to provide a more general theory of markets. Like Keynes, he was guilty of substantiating his theory by employing more realistic, or amenable, assumptions. (Note here that part of the persuasiveness of both approaches was a shared dependence on more reasonable assumptions. Given such ambiguous circumstances, Friedman's subsequent defence of outcomes rather than assumptions becomes hardly surprising.) Again, Chamberlin's efforts represented attempts to undermine more conventional approaches, which in the 1930s had been judged to have reached a dead end. Like Keynes, he purported to have constructed a more general theory in which perfect competition represented a special case. However, the profession, as a whole, at best seemed to only partially grasp the core of Chamberlin's ideas. Misreading a theory, either innocently or not, can, given the right circumstances, provide an inherent vulnerability. A widely accepted false or misleading version, when enshrined as reality, creates a subsequent opening for future criticism and outright attacks. As was the case with Keynes, this cognitive disjuncture can work in tandem with a continued production of poison apples, as described in this chapter.

More exactly, disguising a misreading as an impartial evaluation is simply a variety of the poison apple strategy. In the case of monopolistic competition, despite the usual textbook pigeon-holing of the theory as just another alternative market structure, such restricted thinking manages to overlook Chamberlin's more ambitious intent. Just as Keynes wasn't willing to offer a specific theory constrained by limiting assumptions, Chamberlin as well was focused on constructing a general theory, an envelope enclosing structures like perfect competition, monopoly or oligopoly. In his own way, Chamberlin sought a comparable revolutionary overhaul consistent with the ruling *Welt Geist* of the 1930s.[103]

In this reconceptualization, such special cases, as perfect competition, or monopoly, are transformed into endpoints along a continuum defined by Chamberlin's generalised theory. Each designated alternative derives from highly specified constraints. In monopolistic competition, in a fashion similar to Keynes' approach, unique equilibria may be absent. (Multiple or even non-equilibria positions are possible as well.) Though unlike Keynes, Chamberlin isn't entirely willing to abruptly forego marginalist thinking, which remains embedded and entwined throughout. However, such conventional aspects of Chamberlin's efforts remains insufficient to assuage Friedman or prevent Stigler's savage rejection. They both recognised the bitter medicine contained within the innocent looking poison apples of these new approaches. (Both Keynes and Chamberlin started with more intuitive assumptions.) Consequently, unlike Joan Robinson's ideas of imperfect competition, at Chicago, the inherent dangers encompassed by monopolistic competition could not be carelessly ignored. Chamberlin's structured approach, with Stigler and Friedman ever watchful for potential threats to established price theory, remains incapable of being dismissed as essentially harmless.

> My recollection is not worth much, but for what it's worth is that the Robinsonian emphasis on the individual firm economics, the analysis of marginal revenue and marginal cost, fitted in very well with what we were otherwise thinking. There were no problems about that. But the Chamberlinian attempt to make it into a theory of the general equilibrium was not. The attempt, as it were, to discuss about closer or less close substitutes in different markets, that kind of thing, trying to talk of an industry of imperfect competitors was not. Now maybe it's only that I'm really going back to George's later discussion[104], but I think from the very beginning that we got on very much less well with that general approach and those preconceptions. That received less support (Conversation with Milton Friedman, Rose Friedman, Aaron Director).

The perceived danger glimpsed in what Chamberlin has to offer, lies in its fundamentally non-equilibrium nature.[105] Though to counter this theoretical departure, Chamberlin's selling point depends on the seeming greater authenticity of the underlying assumptions upon which he builds his grand structure. Moreover, his arrival on the scene proved opportune, as the debate and upheaval featured in the 1920s had seemingly eviscerated the underlying logic of Marshallian analysis as being fatally flawed and unsustainable. In part, such old style analysis appeared to rest creakily on dubious non-observables and highly unlikely assumptions. But contradictorily, the strength offered by monopolistic competition simultaneously contained a point of vulnerability.

The newly formulated theory could be transformed into a fatally flawed 'death star', if that point of weakness were to be effectively exploited. The alternative poison apple, delivered by opponents such as Stigler or Friedman, is intended to turn a strength (the reality of assumptions) into a liability. Success (on their part) entailed having the profession swallow their carefully twisted version of Chamberlin's thoughts. Stigler (1949b), for example, effectively rendered his theory into a trivial and less than productive alternative. Strategically, Stigler's deliberate launching of a precise counter (methodologically inspired) argument would effectively attempt to question the nature and value of more realistic assumptions. By demolishing the appeal of any heretofore hopeful alternative, the intent was to seriously shake any previous acceptance of such an approach. Mobilising a successful attack of this sort therefore, was aimed at pre-emptily dismissing all arguments that might be dependent on the validity of their assumptions. If that validity could be trivialised, the appeal of Chamberlin's argument would sharply diminish.

Friedman and Stigler offered instead an unyielding position which insisted that a methodological miasma had managed to stultify economic thought in an unproductive fashion. Their subsequent back door attack, framed more as a philosophical exercise, sought ultimately to disembowel the persuasiveness of monopolistic competition in terms of composing a general theory. Or viewed more ambitiously, the ultimate hope was to bolster those forces seeking to dismiss it.[106]

> The theory of monopolistic competition had wide influence in economics until the end of the 1950s by which time it became apparent that the doctrine was exhausted. That is to say, numerous economists could play variations on its central theme – that the differences *between* products of the same class (differences in quality, taste, location, associated services, etc., of, say, breakfast cereals or trucks) were prevalent in industry, but

their studies yielded no interesting empirical insights on the workings of industry. The theory was descriptive, not analytical (Stigler 1988: 162).[107]

Consequently, the connection bridging the fierce debate surrounding assumptions in the late 1940s and early 1950s with the sudden interest in methodology that Friedman evinces during the same period, should pose no mystery whatsoever. Again, the fact that after 1953, Friedman walked away from any further methodological discussion, even those centred on his own propositions, conveys an abiding sense of 'mission accomplished'. At least in their minds (Stigler and Friedman), the threats posed to marginalism and price theory had been sufficiently vanquished. The disruption posed by monopolistic competition had to their eyes proved distinctly evanescent. This subsequent lack of interest by the duo provides at least a dollop of credence to the estimation that Friedman's methodological concerns were essentially of the poison apple variety. Namely, that they were created simply to serve as a means to an end. Friedman most likely, deliberately or otherwise, generated a type of unresolvable debate (a virtual endless loop of controversy) to derail the ongoing (poisonous) debate focused on assumptions. (Doing so represented a classic shifting of the terms of debate.) This sense of creating an interminable chatter that would inevitably lead nowhere, continued to encircle his methodological assertions. A deliberate ploy of this variety tended to suck the air out of any claims, or logical arguments, which might have supported evaluating (or even judging) a theory based on the reality of its assumptions.

If science and the arts in the 1930s could explore and create more general approaches and theories to attach to their work, so too could the newly concocted economics of that time. Or at least, that was the optimistic fervour, which attempted to sweep away more limited, existing approaches. Keynes had tried to reduce standard neo-classical economics (in its aggregate or macro respects) to a special case. In somewhat of a parallel fashion, Chamberlin had followed the same route when postulating his breakthrough theory of monopolistic competition. These newly developed approaches seemed to replace the emptiness defining the heart of standard price theory. Such a widely employed, but increasingly criticized, approach appeared to offer no obvious way out from the methodologically critiques raised in the 1920s. However, those who saw themselves as the inheritors and defenders of 'the appearances', the troupe of 'loyal but faithless' Marshallians, were intent on finding some means of pushing back and ultimately burying these bothersome methodological gadflies.[108]

On offer were essentially newly compelling, but dangerous, approaches that lent themselves more easily to the embrace of collectivism. The term became deliberately defined by the defenders of the status quo to identify practically any government intervention with the horrors of authoritarian states (Fascism and later Communism). The same desire, under such conditions, to forcefully internalize any claimed market irregularity would eventually lead Friedman and Stigler to celebrate, and even popularize, their version of Coase's thought expressed in his 1960 paper.[109] To squelch any threat to unrestrained exchange, these true believers, cultured by the snows of Mont Pelerin, were intent on re-establishing the sanctity of price adjusted markets. The culmination of such a continuing campaign would reach its first stage of fruition with Milton Friedman's compelling, and at times fantastical, 1953 essay. Friedman succeeded in sending a compelling methodological debate tumbling harmlessly down a rabbit hole leading to an unproductive Neverland.

III. 'As if' Methodology Mattered – Positivity and Economics

> I should like to offer the general proposition that every important scientific hypothesis almost inevitably must use assumptions that are descriptively erroneous. It is of the very nature of a really important scientific generalization that it provides a simpler rationalization of a mass of facts than was available before. … In a way, the better the hypothesis the greater the extent to which it simplifies, the more sharply will its assumptions depart from reality (Letter from Milton Friedman to George Stigler, November 19, 1947 in Hammond and Hammond 2006:65).[110]

In a sense, Milton Friedman's constant resort to employing a sleight of hand in getting his audience, whether academic in nature or a more general one, to swallow his proffered assumptions is a reworking of an older conundrum. Geocentric or Ptolemaic astronomy, though the dominant astronomical theory for centuries, constantly grappled with an acknowledged imperative to 'save the appearances'.[111] Namely, the task was to align celestial observations with the assumption of a motionless earth residing at the centre of the universe.[112] This perspective could always seemingly be supported simply by piling epicycle on epicycle, and in doing so creating an ever more complex astronomical theory. Or alternatively, a possible option when confronted by this increasing complexity, could be the choice offered by a Tycho Brahe style solution, resorting to a seeming compromise that still involved a continuing retention of the earth as the unmovable centre of the universe. However, in this celestial architecture, other planets would be permitted to circle the sun, which in turn would pay obeisance to the all ruling earth.

Given sufficient cleverness, appearances (or to be blunt, the preferred theory) could always be rescued, if even in an altered, patched together, form. Of equal importance, Ptolemaic theory (or versions of it) was perfectly serviceable. Ships, for instance, could navigate using its implications. This result was a classic 'as if' rationale. It mattered not whether the earth did, or did not, circle the sun. All that mattered was that useful conclusions could be drawn, and calculations derived, by pretending it in fact did. But ignoring the strength of the system's foundation, simply because the attendant predictions were 'good enough', limited future progress in astronomy by sending researchers rushing down the wrong set of tracks.[113]

The idea that there were appearances that required saving was always a misleading form of locution. Behind the veil of apparent communication conveyed by that phrase lay an entirely different objective. But once the poisoned apple of appearances was sufficiently swallowed, retracting this seemingly axiomatic assumption proved more difficult than continued acceptance. In essence, a preferred theory demanded a rigid defence despite an accumulation of contrary evidence. The issue that should be raised in such cases requires a detailing of exactly what appearances must be saved and why. The more contentious, but possibly quite accurate, response might link the preferred appearances to those that promote a given set of theories. Somehow, theoretical verities gather strength over time, all of which tend to support an ever increasing accumulation of narrowly vested interests.

Such self-interested motivation led the Catholic Church in the 17th century to try Galileo for heresy. The intent of the Church (a stellar model of vested interests at that time) was to excommunicate him for the supposed sin of heliocentric thought. The prevailing clerical view of that era insisted on an unswerving attempt to save the appearances surrounding a geocentric world. This approach, according to religious thinking of that period, offered support for the Church's particular agenda and intent. In this mirrored path of thinking, the Earth, and thus mankind, constituted the sole focus of God's creation and irrefutable beneficence. In turn, the

Church was declared to be mankind's only conduit to the Almighty, the one chance of escaping eternal damnation.

Daring to claim that the Earth might play second fiddle to the sun, gravely diminished (at least potentially) the unique role played by the Earth, mankind and thus the Church. The Earth ceased to be God's special creation, or at least uncomfortable questions were raised when examining any quite literal understanding of the Book of Genesis. Even worse, a central role for the Sun could assist in resurrecting, or at least recalling, much older religions, particularly those focused on a solar deity. Competing deities were clearly bad for the ruling ecclesiastical business establishment. Like every other market, the religious one was never entirely bereft of competition. The pontifical hierarchy, buttressed by its professed faith, reacted when confronted with a direct threat. It displayed a predictable unwillingness to relinquish whatever monopoly power it had seized over the years. Certainly the long reformation and counter-reformation period clearly demonstrated the Church's recalcitrance to change.

Consequently, in a similar sense, saving the appearances, at least when viewed through Chicago's precisely ground lenses, translated easily as reflecting a world whose economy works according to the principles laid out by standard neoclassical price theory. Apparent anomalies, by definition, reveal themselves (if analysed properly) as being entirely deceptive.[114] These were no more than puzzles that could be resolved when examined under the light provided by Chicago trained intellects. When exposed to this particular Southside brand of sunshine, such posed difficulties would almost magically disappear.[115]

> I think I've quoted him [George Stigler] in my memoir as saying something like, 'externalities are what the market has not *yet* eliminated.' That's not an exact quote but in my memoirs I do have the exact quote. You see he saw the market as *the* force. He was looking at the other side of the market, at how the market may provide an appropriate solution. He said he saw this arbitrage going on all around him. Whenever there was a situation that somebody could take advantage of to make money he would. That was what solved a lot of these problems (Conversation with Claire Friedland, October 1997).

Unfortunately, what price theory subtly sells as appearances, based on unassailable evidence, fails to automatically repel criticism when analysed under a more conclusive examination. According to these market derived tenets, firms appear to (and do) maximise profits and consumers their utility. These are presented as though they were common notions, especially if viewed using the specially tinted goggles happily supplied by the Chicago School. But accepting this premise effectively muddles heuristic assumptions with indisputable evidence and fact. Undoubtedly, firms do need to generate profits to avoid serious cash flow problems. Narrow self-interest always, to some varying extent, appears lurking within any set of human calculations or decisions. But the degree of reductionist thinking that necessarily defines Chicago price theory, allows for few mitigating circumstances. All observable decisions (and appearances) are breezily attributed to highly structured and limited motivations operating under standardised objectives.[116]

The fundamental goal of profit maximisation fails the test when attempting to masquerade as the equivalent of a Euclidean common notion. To qualify, it needs to resemble something quite similar to a core assumption, one that is virtually self-evident. The practical effect of such an assertion automatically becomes highly foundational. Namely, providing the indisputable type of basis that a system (such as perfect competition) can then successfully build upon. Posing as the equivalent of a common notion, or even as an axiom, implies that attempting to contradict or deny that assumption would necessitate a high degree of perversity. For example, when examining Euclid's elements, a statement claiming that the whole is greater than the part has a brow-beating definitional quality that the idea of firms as profit maximising organisations fail to achieve. To deny the former requires extreme logic bending or a basic redefining of the terms involved. Consequently, while firms as profit seekers appear to carry a reasonable degree of observational weight, profit maximising needs a good measure of Professor Poppins's (sugared for consumption) philosophy to transform a bold assertion into a morsel that insists upon being easily swallowed.[117]

However, contrary to expectations, Armen Alchian (1950/1977) managed to devise a clever spoonful of exactly the required grade of refined sugar. When administered with the proper sleight of hand, and with less than total transparency, his logic underwrites the assertion of profit maximising by providing at least limited salvation for the true believer. His 1950 paper was not only his first notable effort, but certainly a breakthrough insight. No surprise then that his published paper was supported enthusiastically by both Friedman and Stigler.[118] The work turned out to sync perfectly with the 'as if' approach discussed in correspondence between the two. This idea (the 'as if' approach) notably appeared in one of Stigler's five lectures presented at the London School of Economics in 1948 (published the following year (1949b)). Curiously enough, Stigler himself would later author a paper exploring curious examples of breakthroughs occurring almost simultaneously. He would explain such aligned thought as though something at that moment was in the air, readily available to any observant theorist. In which case, those willing to sample and seriously consider such ideas would not surprisingly produce similar theories.[119]

Basically a common, if not overwhelming, unarticulated thread between all this Chicago style work was a sort of agreed to Hobbesian concordat. From this perspective, what dominated any market society was a contract implicitly consented to by the entirety of its economic agents. Politically, Hobbes postulated an arrangement whereby individuals ceded political power to a sovereign in exchange for peace and political stability. The impetus behind such an unacknowledged deal was the bleak alternative offered to those refusing to humbly acquiesce to a Prince or Ruler. As Hobbes puts it, such decentralised, or scattered, foci of power would result in a life that could accurately be described as being, 'solitary, poor, nasty, brutish and short' (https://yalebooksblog.co.uk/2013/04/05/thomas-hobbes-solitary-poor-nasty-brutish-and-short/). Faced with such an 'every man against the other' cataclysm, surrender would present itself as the only sane alternative.

For someone like Friedman (or for that matter Stigler), the market came to represent and play a similar role, as it did for Alchian in his early (1950) paper. Individual economic power was necessarily ceded to the market to insure freedom of choice and the maintenance of liberty. As a result, private economic power could no longer be exerted in an environment defined by its operational absence. Instead, a workable alternative dominated. Economic agents passively responded to market signals (prices) through the irresistible necessity to competitively survive. The fortuitous result of this implicit arrangement, (surrendering economic power) left the agents of this contractual agreement free to choose, in the sense that Friedman repeatedly highlighted. So, in a world determined by an 'as if' perspective, firms appeared as if they were consciously trying to maximise profits. The observational result made the reality of the assumption necessarily irrelevant. Unfortunately, plausible 'as ifs' can fall apart if poked too strenuously.

Given this 'as if' context, accepting profit maximising, though largely at an unexamined level can lead to careless conclusions at best (though this avenue is left unexamined by either Alchian or Friedman). As mentioned, a clear fore-runner of the strategy Friedman (1953) would dutifully employ appeared a few years prior to his methodological adventure. Both papers would attempt to vitiate dangerous methodological investigations that could run counter to this core profit maximising assumption. In Armen Alchian's case (1977/1950), he felt compelled to mount a clever defence of this widely employed proposition, moving it beyond the realm of the purely heuristic.[120] His attempt to preserve the appearances (at least when examined under a Chicago microscope) is to some degree a masterwork of persuasion. The poison apple ploy fashioned to defend the assumption of profit maximisation is an ingenious use of the 'as if' notion Friedman would soon make somewhat infamous.

Alchian begins by offering a charming fairy tale (or more politely a heuristic model) that is easily swallowed, with an evolutionary coating providing it some additional credence. The motivating, but unexpressed, goal employed rests on an analogy that appears to equate market competition to natural selection. This end is achieved by constructing firms engaged in an apparently random decision making process. No matter what the sorting basis may be, in any competitive process winners and losers will emerge. Thus, from a starting array of firms, the acknowledged selection principle for survival (winning) is equated, by definition, to observed success. The evolutionary pair of binoculars used to describe this posited process is validated by insisting that such hypothesised firms act in a distinctly random fashion. A lack of any defined objectives proves to be irrelevant. (Again, even a coin toss produces winners and losers.) Keeping with its evolutionary motif, those firms which happen to best fit the existing economic environment will survive. Profits in the short run increase the chance for survival. Consequently, the key plausible (but entirely necessary) assumption made at this point is to define success as being equivalent to profit maximising. (Though the plausibility insisted upon here might fail to hold up if this assertion was examined more carefully. Credibility is skilfully sustained by the force of its assertion.)

Simply stated, successful firms survive, others do not. Thus even though firms may randomly pursue objectives, only those that consistently maximise profits would over time thrive and continue to exist. These firms would appear 'as if' they were knowingly and deliberately maximising profit due to a natural selection process that is aligned with market competition. By pursuing this logic, at least in this instance, we hit on exactly the same point insisted upon years later by Gary Becker (1991).

Namely that the firms themselves (as represented by their managers) respond to market prices, whether consciously or not. In essence, they act, when examined aggregately, as if they were passive. Firms then need not consciously pursue profit maximisation. But competition (in the same sense as natural selection) insures that those firms act in a convenient 'as if' fashion.

Once a reader willingly accepts the initial (and seemingly innocuous) assumption posited by Alchian, one of his poison apples has been effectively bitten. The identification of market competition with natural selection is the glue holding his argument together. Once swallowed, Alchian's attempt to equate market competition to evolutionary natural selection ceases to appear absurd.[121] If eyed narrowly then, the article's embedded strategy becomes quickly transparent to any astute reader. The underlying, unproven assumption is that when observed and analysed, firms inevitably act 'as if' they profit maximised. Consequently the conscious intent of managers becomes irrelevant. These officials, at least as implied by Alchian, succeed only in deluding themselves by assuming that they are active captains of their firm's fate. As stated, when firms act, their actual decisions represent invisible strings being pulled by their defined market environment. This context in which managers (and their firms) labour must in turn prove to be impervious to their conscious aims. In this sense the weight of realism attached to the assumption of profit maximisation is irrelevant. Questioning this assumption in that manner (as perhaps is the case with all such assumptions) must, by definition, represent a fruitless diversion. The realism of assumptions is rendered operationally meaningless. All that is fundamentally important is that firms operate 'as if' maximising profits was their sole objective.[122]

Alchian, in his 'as if' moment, feels justified when connecting the treadmill-like nature of such an objective to the basic need to survive. (Essentially presented in his 1950 paper is a version of Herbert Spencer's popularised social evolutionary theory.[123]) Firms, viewed from this perspective, have no other viable option than to appear to be passively responding to existing market signals, at least if they value their continued existence. In such an environment, there quite naturally exists a virtual compulsion to at least appear to pursue a rather unitary and unchanging objective. This relation must hold as an observable result, despite management's varying awareness of any such conscious motivation. The underlying logic runs quite simply. Any insufficient flow of cash would inevitably seal a firm's fate over time. They could not survive in a competitive market, causing them to be selected for extinction. Therefore, if not examined too closely, this causative relationship would appear to confirm the assumption of profit maximisation. To persuade his readers, (overriding any doubts created by such logical leaps) Alchian (1950/1977) drives this core idea home in his work with the delicacy of a pneumatic drill. As stated, the compulsion to maximise profits need not be consciously recognised by the firms themselves given the nature of the depicted market forces. Such forces simply provide the observed appearance. However, to the unbiased investigator, the workings of the market would make the results appear 'as if' they were created by individually profit maximising firms.[124] Therefore (within this logical context), the use of the assumption was completely vindicated.

The key then to Alchian's constructed approach is to persuade the reader, in an almost reflexive fashion (and without having the reader fully aware of its importance), to accept his proffered poison apples when they are offered. In essence, the rationale behind the theoretic construct he presents, appears to hold, that is as long as it is not examined too meticulously. Like Snow White entranced by the polished red apple, (but failing to judge wisely)[125] once a reader is mesmerised by the apparent compelling obviousness of the suggestion made, there is no way to easily extricate oneself from the logical web surrounding all the subsequent steps of his argument.[126] At this point, the only viable option is for the carefully constructed evolutionary analogy to be irrefutably swallowed. Once done, any subsequent searches for handsome princes (those with a penchant for enlightenment or given to timely warnings) capable of rescuing the unwary reader will probably prove to convey only a languishing hope. Clarity, achieved by means of dispelling the miasma of carefully crafted argument will never be achieved.[127]

Given a shared Chicago inspired desire to thwart the inroads made by collectivist thought, how then is attention distracted away from pitched arguments that intensely focus on the reality of economic assumptions? Possibly, by conclusively demonstrating that seemingly foundational issues are entirely irrelevant.[128] Namely, at least according to Alchian's (1950/1977) assertions, what decision makers consciously think they are trying to achieve, simply doesn't matter.[129] To establish this theoretical position requires creating a rabbit hole sufficiently attractive to tempt any potential inquisitor to carelessly tumble down into its bottomless depths. Once the reader takes the first ill-fated step, the poison apple strategy can then be activated into a functioning, operative phase.

The leverage mechanism that sets this particular argument in motion is a misuse, if not an outright misrepresentation, of evolutionary theory. Alchian builds his 'just so' version by starting with a misleading interpretation of Darwinian natural selection.[130] The essence of his strategy is a fundamental hijacking of underlying Darwinian principles, though presented in a credible fashion. Created instead is a reasonable semblance to, rather than an accurate reflection of, the natural process by equating the realm of nature with that of market competition. The parallel links, capriciously assembled, are ramrodded through and welded onto the physical world.[131]

> It is not even necessary to suppose that each firm acts as if it possessed the conventional diagrams and knew the analytical principles employed by economists in deriving optimum and equilibrium conditions. The atoms and electrons do not know the laws of nature; the physicist does not impart to each atom a wilful scheme of action based on laws of conservation of energy, etc. The fact that no economist deals with human beings who have sense and ambitions does not *automatically* warrant imparting to these humans the great degree of foresight and motivations which the economist may require for his customary analysis as an outside observer or "oracle" (Alchian 1950/1977:26 ftn. 12).

The underlying problem with this attempt to harness natural selection to the purposes of price theory should be obvious.[132] In Alchian's version, a fundamental issue that refuses to disappear, even when the relevant economic environment is allowed to change in unforeseen ways, is the passive role that must be thrust upon the designated economic agents.[133] Certainly it is a leap of unblinking faith to regard atoms or leaves as conscious actors.[134] Equally, it is rather absurd to ignore the consciousness of human agents, as if they were simply another variety of plant leaves. In contrast to cells or atoms (at least as far as we can ascertain), human consciousness breeds deliberate decisions and specific paths chosen. Though these agents cannot completely control the economic environment in which they operate, they can and do attempt to mould and transform it, leaving a result that is more conducive to their objectives. Simply dismissing such attempts to actively change one's surroundings as a mere illusion, runs counter to available observed evidence. In doing so, the result more closely resembles something of a mystical transcendence than a scientific strategy. If economic agents can partially choose the operative selection process, then some objective system of natural selection no longer strictly dominates. (The exception might be in a one-dimensional version of Herbert Spencer.) Not only must the agents adapt to the prevailing environment to survive, but the option of reconstructing the environment itself is not foreclosed.

However, if not examined too closely, the metaphor of natural selection seems to provide a sufficient starting point, since it remains obvious that without positive profits, firms cannot survive over any extended period. Firms that do earn such profits get to fight out another year's battle, while those that consistently fail to do so eventually get tossed into a dustbin, clogged to the bursting point, with history's business failures.[135] To ram this idea home, Alchian chooses to further fortify his natural selection brainstorm by identifying the idea of success with the idea of survival. Yet, while survival may be a necessary condition for success, it wouldn't appear to be a sufficient one. That is, unless the two terms are acceptably reduced to the level of sharing an identical status.

But by doing so, the term 'success' is then stripped of any significant meaning. Success, as it is usually employed, is a subjective term. (Perhaps it exists only in the eye of the beholder.) Moreover, to be precise, firms don't make operational decisions (or those of any variety), but rather only individuals within the firm are obliged and capable of doing so. How success is measured within these firms is bound to vary, given different individual perspectives. That is, unless a heroic assumption is accepted allocating all firms (and their defined managements) to the unlikely position of being completely identical.[136]

In the absence of such an unlikely (though convenient), assumption, the specific executives making such firm based decisions are likely to have different sets of preferences, even when faced with similar constraints. The ensuing outcomes allow the concept of success to differ, whether or not firms operate in the presence of competitive markets. (Moreover, publicly owned corporations make up a relatively small share of all firms. The majority of markets is characterised by different ownership structures and an array of competitive understandings.) These considerations reduce the attempt to identify survival with success to nothing more than a perfect speculative muddle. The distinct definitional confusion tends to feed the suspicion that Alchian's poison apple may in fact be quite wormy.

Nor is it clear what level of positive profits will enable a firm to be selected for survival. Meaning that Alchian avoids specifying the number of years composing the appropriate survival hurdle for this mysterious achievement of success. For example, being closely attuned to a given economic environment may yield higher than average positive profits in the short run, but leave the firm floundering when that operative environment changes in an unforeseen fashion. In that case, a firm previously earning below average positive profits, or even negative profits, may prosper under a newly installed environmental regime.

Looking at the problem more practically, any firm must make contractual commitments to a variety of connected, constituent groups in order to continue to operate. If they fail to generate sufficient flows of cash to meet those contractual demands, they then have to renegotiate with the relevant groups involved. This process doesn't imply that a cash shortage automatically dooms the survival of any firm. In the US, domestic airline corporations continued to survive through extended periods of history, despite making significant loses. In which case, the necessity of garnering positive profits in each successive period seems an oversimplified basis for determining success (if continuing to survive is the sole criterium). To focus only on the ability to reliably predict outcomes (profit maximisers thrive), in this context dismisses any need to understand how firms, or any other part of the economy, actually works. Given such thinking, an equivalent and valid conclusion would assess astronomers as having stumbled badly when they eventually rejected the Ptolemaic system. That paradigm had performed sufficiently in practise, and could probably have continued to operate sufficiently well enough to satisfy all the practical demands of that particular era (during the heliocentric debates) if only results mattered.

But at this moment, before attempting to digest Alchian's proffered apple, it might be wise to comment that further consideration reveals his stratagem to be even more dubious. If his use of natural selection feels somewhat strained and even initially unconvincing, his further employment of evolutionary style structures appear to verge toward the foolhardy. Moving out onto ever thinner ice, despite the clear risky ground already embraced, counts more as a display of bravado at this rhetorical stage of the argument. The sad reality is that Alchian perpetuates a simple failure to register when an approach has been pushed too far. (In following this path, Alchian comes close to performing a convincing impersonation of Wile E. Coyote.) However, if the starting point of Alchian's theoretical journey has been previously swallowed by his readers, then the further evolutionary embroidery presented in the last part of the article simply solidifies that initial acceptance. His strained parallel bravely equates the core requisites that compose Darwin's theory with somewhat forced constructions that loop back to his original economic contentions.

> All the preceding arguments leave the individual economic participant with imitative, venturesome, innovative, trial-and-error adaptive behaviour. Most conventional economic tools and concepts are still useful, although in a vastly different analytical framework – one which is closely akin to the theory of biological evolution. The economic counterparts of genetic heredity, mutations, and natural selection are imitation, innovation, and positive profits (Alchian 1977:32).

Alchian even manages to tame the pesky intrusion of uncertainty by making it irrelevant. (Uncertainty can act as an irritant making chewing and swallowing the proffered poison apple more provisional.) Certainly, the economic environment and terms of selection are no more (and perhaps much less) stable than those elements composing the natural world. However, from the perspective offered by Alchian, this state of flux is completely irrelevant. Participants involved in this highly structured drama are simply reactive, or even given to purely random decision-making. As mentioned, economic agents are in need of neither foreknowledge nor even a simple acquaintance with the actual rules of the game. (A problem is that what should be a merely heuristic structure for Alchian, quickly bleeds into a facsimile of reality.) The result is that reactions (rather than comprehension or planning), invariably determine outcomes. Under such circumstances, the fact that the future is basically unknowable is of little interest to either the participants, or to the ensuing observable results occurring within this defined space. Survival, as understood within such a highly structured perspective, is forcefully based on selection via the signalling device of positive profits. Those firms that generate positive profits under this new selection regime can be considered the equivalent of successful adapters, no matter the underlying reality.[137]

Consequently, from this idiosyncratic perspective, participating firms that consciously attempt to manage such uncertain environmental shifts are simply dabbling in the irrelevant. To be blunt they are wasting their time in their attempts to read such existential tea leaves, at least if one subscribes to the Alchian rules of conduct. Any supposedly useful information of this variety can be happily ignored and even dismissed by serious investigative economists once they enter into the world of 'as if'.

What matters is the sort of fossicking necessary to fully understand and apply fundamental price theory. Alchian operating in this fashion, manages to successfully work around that which must remain incorrigibly unknown.[138] However, Alchian's uncertainty ploy contrasts sharply with that of Friedman. He prefers a neater and much less complicated device. Friedman opts for the simpler path of wilfully dismissing Knightian uncertainty (uninsurable risk) outright. The concept is deftly labelled by Friedman as simply misconceived, one which carelessly promotes a mistaken perspective.[139]

> In general, uncertainty provides an excellent reason for imitation of observed success. Likewise, it accounts for observed uniformity among the survivors, derived from an evolutionary, adopting, competitive system employing a criterion of survival, which can operate independently of individual motivations. Adapting behaviour via imitation and venturesome innovation enlarges the mode. Imperfect imitators provide opportunity for innovation, and the survival criterion of the economy determines the successful, possibly because imperfect, imitators (Alchian 1977:31–32).

Consequently, given the road blazed by Armen Alchian in this particular attempt at evolutionary prestidigitation, he can be understood as performing a role analogous to that of John the Baptist (at least perceived retrospectively). In that case, Milton Friedman is best viewed from the perspective of inhabiting the subsequent role as a resident saviour of Chicago price theory.[140] In both instances, the goal is to demonstrate (by fabricating a likely and easily acceptable story) that any focus on the nature of the economic assumptions employed must be essentially time wasted. Markets are simply asserted to be capable of selecting the relevant price clearing levels that keep an economy running. Economic agents within such an environment exist merely to respond and adapt to market provided information without any need for conscious recognition of the processes hidden behind a curtain of market complexities.

> These constructed rules of behaviour should be distinguished from "rules" which, in effect, do no more than define the objective being sought. Confusion between objectives which motivate one and rules of behaviour is commonplace. For example, "full-cost pricing": is a "rule" that one cannot really follow. He can try to, but whether he succeeds or

fails in his objective of survival is not controllable by following the "rule of full-cost pricing." If he fails in his objective, he must of necessity, fail to have followed the "rule." The situation is parallel to trying to control the speed of a car by simply setting by hand the indictor on the speedometer (Alchian 1977:29 ftn.14).

In contrast, Gary Becker makes this classic Chicago position, only sketched out at best by Armen Alchian, even more explicit. The apparent realism of assumptions, from the Chicago position, remains, by necessity, largely irrelevant, if not outright misleading. Economic agents, totally unschooled in the intricacies of Chicago price theory, are not assumed to understand how the markets in which they operate actually function. They therefore perform under the false impression that they are steering their own particular organisational ship despite the wheel being completely unattached to the relevant corporate rudder.[141] In truth, their course is instead determined by an intractable pricing current.[142] In essence, what decision makers in a firm think they are doing doesn't fundamentally matter. This issue, in all its splendour, is usefully examined in a short piece published by Gary Becker (1991) in the *Journal of Political Economy*. It serendipitously appeared close to the time of the unexpected death of his close colleague and friend, George Stigler. The article innocently commences with an observed pricing puzzle, which ironically smacks of everyday realism. Though it is quite common for economic ideas to originate from actual existing market elements that seem not to reflect the fundamentals of rational choice (the sine qua non of Chicago thinking).[143] A puzzle is thus presented, which the curious economist feels compelled to solve.

In the case presented, Becker became familiar with two seafood restaurants located near the University campus, but on opposite sides of the same street. The offerings at both are similar and so are the prices. One restaurant is consistently half full while the other usually has people waiting for tables. The oddity in the case, as presented, is that simple competitive forces of supply and demand would seemingly force the prices of the two restaurants to diverge. For instance, textbook economics claims that excess demand forces prices up. Why then does the owner or manager of the popular restaurant not raise prices to clear the market?

Becker responds in the article by using this fortuitous instance to construct a pricing system that will seemingly resolve other similar anomalous pricing situations as well. (Becker in this instance is focused on generalising his specific observation, not unlocking the mysteries of restaurant pricing.) In successfully doing so, market efficiency is maintained despite adverse first impressions. Though when questioned, Becker did claim to have talked with those individuals actually running the relevant restaurants. However, he clearly points out that they would in fact be unlikely to understand the mechanics of the market in which they operated.[144] In essence, they, like other economic agents, simply respond to market prices.

> *I have to say, I was drawn to it because in another, earlier life, I put in five years working in restaurants, doing all sorts of things. In the article, you take the problem presented and you come up with an interesting pricing model that then is more generally applicable. But it's not actually consistent with my experience. You know, I had an alternative explanation. But what struck me then, is a question, I'm sure you've been asked, which is 'Why didn't you just ask the manager of the restaurant?'*

Gary Becker: Yeah. Well, because I had the same view as George, on that issue. That I don't think you can talk with restaurant managers, in fact, about such things. You know they are not trained, they know in a certain deep sense, but they are not trained to articulate why things are happening. But any restaurant owner does in fact recognise it's good if you can get customers to come in and you can lose your audience pretty easily. You know there's unstable demand. Even when you're in the door, you can go out. That, they're all aware of, and so, in that sense they would say, 'sure this is going on.' In terms of pricing and so on, that would be a hard thing for them to articulate. I think that would be a hard thing to get by asking them. So I would have the same view, that yes, I use surveys in labour economics a lot. Surveys may give you suggestions about behaviour but you can't really take that as the same type of evidence. That's my view in that little note. It actually was written, published, just about the time George was close to his death. I think I got it published in 1991 in the *JPE* in the later issues of that year. And he died December 1st 1991. So it was around that time. I'm trying to think if I knew what his reaction to that note was, but I can't really remember (Conversation with Gary Becker, October 1997).

Given this Chicago context, price theory as a sufficient reflection of functioning market economies would appear to harbour serious weaknesses.

A judgment of this sort would still retain its validity, even if a further evaluation of the given framework stopped somewhat short of entirely invalidating such a theoretical pricing perspective. The possibility remains of simply admitting its position as a heuristic, or useful preliminary device, rather than acting as a mirror of reality. But this acquiescence, to a certain degree, requires that the set of what would appear to be curiously unrealistic assumptions exist merely as an attempt to explore the essential requirements for markets to operate optimally. If in fact these assumptions did manage to exist in some unknown, alternative universe, then something closely identical to perfect competition would be the operative force capable of regulating most markets.

The corollary to that deduction can be adequately summarised in order to drive home the essential core conclusion concerning the 'as if' world Chicago has meticulously constructed. Namely, that the degree to which any observable market actually resembles the structure sketched by perfect competition, must correspond to the degree to which the underlying assumptions of that theory continue to hold. Consequently, discovering that some markets may not operate optimally, or anywhere near to that ideal, need not serve to cavalierly dismiss standard price theory once and for all. It can still be viewed as a useful tool, if it is understood to act as no more than an analytic starting point for further investigations. From this perspective, problems can only arise by blindly insisting on equating the ideal with the real in all cases. Stubbornly fitting observations so that they conform to pre-existing conclusions may be satisfying at some unconscious level. Such an operational strategy, unfortunately, will not turn out to be particularly operable or productive.

Sensible deployment of such analysis would correspond more closely with the approach associated with Ronald Coase. His stance favoured conclusions that were more empirically based (evidence verified) than simply resting on some convenient *a priori*. From his perspective, given the fact that markets fail to reflect a theoretical degree of optimality, such sectors might be improved by suffering less government interference or conversely, such failures might demand a larger degree of oversight. Without careful and specific empirical investigation, no obvious path is realistically feasible which would conclusively lead to that knowledge beforehand. Therefore according to Coase, a reasonable resolution to such quandaries could only be provided on a case by case basis.[145] Knowledge of particulars become decisive and these need to be carefully weighed, rather than argued away. Notice that by taking this route, we are moving decisively away from the world of 'as if' where the imperative is to fit all observations into a single, general structure.

However, Friedman and Stigler, for their part, would consistently be less than eager to sanction such a perceived wishy-washy approach, where answers remained unknown prior to any actual research.[146] Launching into such precipitous investigations could potentially yield results that specifically contradicted their unshakeable view of the world. This unlooked for result would be especially the case if the acquired evidence dared to depart from an assured and close correspondence to their steadfast grasp of perceived reality.[147] Consequently, nothing should be allowed, under any circumstances, to undermine, or to alter, their knowledge of how the world worked, or perhaps how it must, in their view, be allowed to work.[148] Neither one of them found it agreeably convenient to condone, let alone encourage, debate that stubbornly focused on the specific legitimacy or effectiveness of any given market.

Acknowledging imperfection was thus comparable to openly allowing as legitimate, intervention by the serried ranks of the feared collectivist Left. To Stigler and Friedman, these opponents represented the often shadowy figures who were determined, in a single-minded fashion, to forcibly strangle the fragile rule of liberty. This inevitable slip into the use of overheated imagery seemed to flow easily into their rhetorical stream of arguments. Such fertile compost served to form the repeated sum and substance of their ideological battles. Those who sowed doubt about market operations were accordingly suspected of feverishly constructing a toxic 'slippery slope' for the unwary. The existence of such traps and ambushes posed by collectivist rhetoric would forever doom the possibility of unconstrained freedom of choice.[149] In contrast, taking an unreconstructed 'as if' approach possessed the distinct strategic allure of transforming the question of legitimacy (the realism of any set of assumptions), into an issue of sheer irrelevancy. The degree to which the evidence for assumptions held, no longer mattered given these methodological suppositions. According to this logical Chicago twist, observable markets, allowed to freely operate, by definition, reflected the tenets of perfect competition. In this fashion, the proverbial thin edge of the wedge (forever eager to dislodge price theory) was effectively blunted.

However, at this point, it may prove useful to step back (taking a needed breathe) in order to trace out a clear connection between Alchian's efforts and the culmination of this strategic brand of theorising under Friedman. By doing so, the art by which poison apples are cultivated may become more clearly revealed. Thus all that counts in the analysis championed by Chicago stalwarts like Friedman, Becker or Alchian is purely observed results. (Though to be strictly accurate, Alchian spent his career at Chicago West, namely UCLA.) To repeat, as Armen Alchian insists, "Success is based on results, not motivation" (Alchian 1977/1950:19)). Implied is the idea that a focus on the validity of assumptions is equivalent to an obsession with the motivation of specific individual agents. In which case, what actually matters is not the activities of some unique firm, but the predictable outcome of a representative one.

> A "representative firm" is not typical of any one producer but, instead, is a set of statistics summarizing the various "modal" characteristics of the population. Surely this was an intended use of Marshall's "representative firm" (Alchian 1977/1950:26).

To emphasise, the goal is to save the appearances, meaning the observed results (or at least a particular Chicago interpretation of such results). In which case, even if firms made purely random decisions there would still be blue ribbons doled out to the declared winners. The results would define exactly who represented the successful cohort. Such evaluation would simply depend on those observed results. The process by which such ends were achieved would then become distinctly irrelevant. Just as in a horse race, there would always be some designated first place finisher, or winner. The actual motivation of the horse would remain unknowable and irrelevant. (Though unlike economists, handicappers would be extremely interested in why that particular horse won that specific race.) Even more importantly, what is observed is also removed from the knowledge or motivation of the bettors themselves. Whether they acted purposely or randomly would be irrelevant to any productive analysis.

> For example, at a horse race with enough bettors wagering strictly at random, someone will win on all eight races. Thus individual random behaviour does not eliminate the likelihood of observing "appropriate" decisions (Alchian 1977/1950:24).

Through this analysis, by accepting the poison apples created by the best and brightest of economists (such as Alchian), readers will inevitably end up by concluding that the fate of the individual firm, over time, should never be a serious matter for the legitimate practitioner. In fact, quibbling over the actual motivation of single firms, or the validity of the assumptions underwriting the theory of the firm, must simply degenerate into a somewhat puerile diversion (entertainment for the hot air specialist). Given then the previously explored preliminary spadework by both Alchian and Stigler, Friedman was more than prepared, in his 1953 article, to permanently banish such methodological questions, condemning such issues into the fires of a limitless inferno.

IV The Poison Apple in Play

> Snow White was eager to eat the beautiful apple, and when she saw the peasant woman eating her half, she could no longer resist, stretched out her hand, and took the poisoned half. No sooner did she take a bit than she fell to the ground dead. The queen stared at her with a cruel look, then burst out laughing and said, "White as snow, red as blood, black as ebony!" (Grimm 1992:202).

For Chicago stalwarts whose belief in the tenets of price theory were unshakeable, the major threat to viewing the supply side of the economy through the lens of perfect competition came from one of Frank Knight's former students, Edward Chamberlin. His 1933 breakthrough work on Monopolistic Competition was quickly embraced, or at least taken quite seriously, by much of the profession. The charm lay in its merging of the perfect competition framework with a monopoly structure. Bifurcating markets into discrete alternatives, (a one or the other formation) served only to confuse the matter (at least from Chamberlin's perspective). This newly hatched (1933) insight claimed that if properly observed, operative markets ran along a continuum with varying degrees of competition attached. Firms did not regulate themselves in some hypothetical seesaw pattern, varying between no market power and total control. Thus in its most commonly recognised version, firms differentiated themselves to avoid the fate of being consigned to the market hell of pure price taking. However, in Chamberlin's formulation, competitors could still enter and exit a particular market freely. This approach appeared to present a pathway out of the quandary first hinted at by Clapham (1922) and driven home by Sraffa (1926).

Perhaps unfortunately, though to no one's surprise, any level of respect for this approach stopped at the borders of the Chicago campus where

Knight particularly rejected Chamberlin's effort out of hand.[150] Little in the way of mystery attaches to the fact that one of Knight's few PhD. students would be moved to mount an attack on this contending alternative.[151] If one of the theory's points of allure was its ability to provide a more realistic basis within its core assumptions, then from the Chicago perspective, this enticement had to be surgically removed from any serious consideration. Poison the root and the rest of the constructed edifice withers according to the logic buttressing these attacks. Thus began a drive culminating in Milton Friedman's 1953 essay.

> It is elementary to all scientists that certain methodological assumptions, which everyone admits are contrary to fact, are indispensable to theoretical reasoning. No one begrudges the physicist the right to ignore friction, and the mathematician is permitted perfect circles no one will ever see. The case for the economic man is just as strong, and had he not been imported into economics, today there would be no science worthy of the name (Stigler 1937:713).[152]

Efforts staged by Friedman and Stigler to undermine any evaluation of the reality of assumptions is not without a history. Such convenient methodology did not appear de novo in Friedman's one great effort to tame, or in effect to nullify, this ongoing debate. The origin of Friedman's landmark (in terms of the impact it had on the profession)[153] 1953 article clearly has its origins in ongoing discussions between Milton Friedman and his close friend George Stigler. (In 1953 Stigler was still exiled at Columbia.[154] Back then, in the pre-digital world, letters were the only practical method for long distance collaborations.)

> *There's an obvious sense that he [Stigler] had been discussing the sort of methodology which you later published. Is that correct, that there had been discussions between the two of you on that topic at the time?*
> Milton Friedman: Sure. I had written the methodology paper, which was later formally published. This preceded, by three or four years, the earlier versions. And he refers in one of those lectures [The London LSE lectures] to the fact that we had been talking about it.
> *Yes. And how influential were you in each other's thinking on this matter?*
> Milton Friedman: We were very influential. I think there's no doubt that my work would have been different if I hadn't been influenced by

George and George's work would have been different if he hadn't been influenced by me (Conversation with Milton Friedman, Rose Friedman and Aaron Director, August 1997).

The letters mentioned were posted in the days that preceded the five lectures Stigler was slated to present before the assemblage of LSE academics in 1948. (Those lectures were later published in 1949.) One of those lectures focused on demolishing Chamberlin's monopolistic competition, a sort of culmination of Stigler's efforts to negate the influence of imperfect competition within the profession. This urge to exterminate contentious alternatives, first noted in his 1937 article, was in part a reflection of his Chicago training (though a distinct deviation from the perspective nurtured by Frank Knight).[155] The overarching intention of Stigler's theoretical approach and practice, focused on the perceived mischief produced when extending any credence, or faith, on a framework determined by the reality of its underlying assumptions.[156] This inflexible perspective implicitly remained the basis of both Stigler and Friedman's future work.

Especially in these early, formative years, the two clearly strategized with one another, but not only by discussing various paths by which they could advance their respective careers and theories. Included in these exchanged missives, especially following the Mont Pelerin meeting, were methods for undermining and ultimately defeating what they saw as a dangerous, collectivist opposition. Stigler makes this operative methodology explicit only when engaged in his obsessive attempt to demolish Chamberlin. However, accomplishing this goal doesn't foreclose the continuing existence of a distinctive underlying methodology in much of his approach to economics. Stigler did not concoct a once off strategy suitable for only one specific occasion. Despite his continued adherence to this approach, after his concerted attack on Chamberlin, Stigler never makes his controversial 'as if' methodology explicitly known.[157] Friedman, on the other hand, would go on to write a much more extended essay devoted entirely to the subject, thus gaining full credit for the approach. His name, not Stigler's, would be forever attached to the idea.

And, he had already revealed the kind of attitude, which I subsequently realized influenced me enormously. It was a methodological position, which, only when Milton Friedman published his famous (methodology of positive economics) article in 1954 [sic] did I then realise he was using the type of argument that sounded exactly like the kind of things

Stigler would drop in his articles. It was a kind of (what shall I call it) a poor man's Popperism. I mean it is basically Karl Popper's falsification with a tremendous emphasis on prediction, etc. And I later realised, discovered this because I asked him, that he and Milton Friedman talked about all these things. Milton however just ran away with it. George Stigler always slightly resented the fact that the entire world learned all this stuff from Milton Friedman, when in fact, if you look at the order of precedence, George Stigler was slightly ahead in this sort of attitude to the testing of hypotheses. It comes out in his articles. By 1952 I had already picked it up. So long before I actually read Karl Popper I sort of knew it all. I certainly knew the essence of it. When I first read Popper it was like, 'Hey, so this is where it comes from.' It didn't come as a surprise (Conversation with Mark Blaug, April 1998).

The unresolved issue that persists, when raking through the details of this favoured approach, remains seemingly unanswered. The sudden interest in exploring methodological thickets arose devoid of any observable motivation or designated inspiration. As always, unexplained mysteries simply raise interesting, and largely unanswered, questions. Clearly the focussed discussion between Stigler and Friedman occurred despite a prior lack of fascination with such an admittedly outré subject.[158] Compounding this inexplicable choice by these usually applied, (nuts and bolts) economists was their quick cessation of interest in the topic. They seemed devoid of any inclination to further consider what had been an intensely debated, methodological issue between the two. As noted, the original discussions of this issue arose prior to Stigler's 1948 rhetorical debut before the LSE faculty. Nothing is then noticeably added to this perspective post Friedman's 1953 essay. Though, no one should be entirely surprised that once published in its fullest form, both Friedman and Stigler mutually concluded that their constructed framework composed the very last and conclusive word on methodological interrogation. No further discussion seemed required in their judgment. But the timing and dates attached to this event indicate an interest extending beyond methodological niceties.

The reason for concluding a literal 'case closed', speaking from a methodological standpoint, must ultimately be entwined with the objectives that were actively pursued. As indicated previously, such goals pursued were neither particularly methodological nor philosophical. To understand, we must examine the relevant context. In this case, as in so many others, providing a contextual overview is paramount, if a mere surface level of comprehension is to be successfully deepened. The practical danger posed to those at Chicago meant that a post-war focus on the validity of assumptions appeared to open the academic sluice gates to heretical challenges. The questions raised and positions taken clearly negated the Chicago version of price theory.[159] For example, these alternatives specifically raised issues with the standard treatment of labour markets. Markets, and specifically labour markets, which could be demonstrated to be neither efficient nor equitable (because of perceived failures) created an almost immediate justification for inviting some degree of government intervention.[160] Such underlying issues ultimately threatened (from this Chicago perspective) the realm of individual liberty as conceived by this academic cohort. An perilous overhang of urgency recognized that such an attack be quickly thwarted (at least based upon the subjectively calculated debits and credits of the case). When performed by Stigler and Friedman this ideological exercise in accounting could entertain only one result.[161] Thus, in this potential policy emergency (with freedom and liberty at stake), any steps taken to forestall predictably dire results were automatically deemed to be legitimate.

> The great tragedy of the drive to centralization, as of the drive to extend the scope of government in general, is that it is mostly led by men of good will who will be the first to rue its consequences (Friedman 1962:3).

Consequently, the real driver behind this methodological foray was in fact Stigler and Friedman's obsessive focus on what they conceived to be a ubiquitous danger. Namely, an almost compulsive response that led them to inevitably define any action they labelled 'collectivist' as automatically composing a distinct threat to liberty. This unyielding piece of fundamentalism became a virtual lodestar for the two in their investigations, certainly in those forays that followed the initial Mont Pelerin meeting. (This particular get together exudes a certain 'road to Damascus' transformative aroma that clings stubbornly to these two novitiates.) Thus what superficially appears to be simply a surprising methodological fancy from Friedman in 1953, actually contains a hidden objective, the strategy (perhaps entirely unconscious) of presenting the profession with an ideological poison apple. In which case, the best way to conceive of this practise may be in terms of a well-worn marketing technique (namely the bait and switch gambit). In simple terms, what the buyer assumes he or she is getting is not what is ultimately acquired.

The objective behind employing such a device is ultimately to persuade by using whatever methods might prove to be most effective. Avoiding a predicable degree of expected pushback from advocating controversial positions may sometimes be achieved by employing the equivalent of a fast shuffle. The controversial sticking point can ideally be camouflaged by wrapping it within a more seemingly innocuous assertion. Meaning the sort of statement that is likely to be accepted almost uncritically, at least if not examined sufficiently closely.[162] Friedman's methodology at first glance doesn't appear to be completely untenable. It projects a certain ring of rhetorical probability. But once enmeshed within the endless loops of its analysis, the profession subsequently found itself heading down a theoretical cul-de-sac. In essence what was created was a philosophical diversion drawing attention away from more relevant investigations.[163]

Professional focus was clearly diverted from a then currently held viewpoint that the reality of assumptions must actually matter. What seemed obvious BF (before Friedman), became (almost miraculously) a completely unresolved, and somewhat unresolvable, dilemma. Any subsequent professional interest in the actual (rather than the purely methodological) debate concerning assumptions rapidly withered. The episode might even be understood as an attempt to end the possibility of any future productive methodological discussions. In this account, Friedman and Stigler succeeded in reanimating a sort of Frankenstein's monster (constructed out of ragged scraps of homespun philosophy), a methodology that was intended to destroy any further methodological debates.

To a considerable extent, Friedman's own foray into methodology was an extended 'as if' experiment, though perhaps performed only at an unconscious level. (Momentarily we will consider Friedman's construction 'as if' it was the basis for a serious methodological investigation.) However, the legitimacy of the devised argument lacks at least some credibility since the subtext driving this interest is neither obvious nor explored. The methodological passion Friedman suddenly shared with George Stigler just somehow magically flared up between the two of them. Any possible explanation is simply mysterious since it can only be described as a research focus that suddenly and essentially vanished almost as quickly as it had blossomed. Tellingly, Friedman at a conscious level proceeded as if he had solved, once and for all the essential methodological problems facing economics.[164] But Friedman was of a generation that displayed scant eagerness to fossick in the sub-basements of their own ids for hidden motivations. Despite the post-war boom in Freudian analysis, Friedman's cohort of tough-minded males seldom went so far as to excavate ulterior motives, let alone possible subtexts.

Consequently, both Friedman and his colleague, George Stigler, developed an intense, but relatively brief, attraction to methodological problems for largely unexplored (and certainly unexplained) reasons. What the two developed was a sort of homespun philosophic version of a methodological discussion, tent-poled by a set of convenient assumptions. Utterly absent was anything resembling a more rigorous or logical structure. What the two concocted existed sans any stated foundation, a system built instead on ready-mixed quicksand. Readers of Friedman's efforts were presented with a structure built itself upon an 'as if' base. Once though Friedman and Stigler had buried, at least to their own satisfaction, the relevance of factual assumptions, they would have viewed their unstated mission as being essentially accomplished. In essence, any compelling reasons for further explorations had entirely vanished.

For those true believers, trained in the Mont Pelerin camp of theology, what was at stake was more than some simple question of economic theory or methodology. The contested ground extended far beyond a mere contest, or even a tussle, for the soul of the economics profession. What unfolded, at least in the case of Friedman and Stigler, was closer to an almost apocalyptic struggle between good and evil.

> Oh, he was a true believer. He wouldn't like that term. But put that in because he thought in that sense. He was absolutely convinced that he was right. It wasn't a doctrinal battle. It was a battle of facts. I almost said good and evil (Conversation with James Kindahl, October 1997).

Friedman, and others belonging to his reconstituted liberal posse, seriously feared that the forces of collectivism were slowly grinding down whatever vestiges of freedom remained. Consequently, there could be no holding back, no available avenue of attack left unexplored, in the service of defeating any sworn enemies of liberty. These hardened cold warriors conceived that they had taken on totalitarianism in the form of Nazism and defeated it unequivocally. This left them experienced and entirely capable (from their own perspective) of thrashing the Soviet threat which was surreptitiously aided and abetted by an unseemly array of leftist fellow travellers (useful idiots as Lenin labelled those on the left).

Their determination did not encourage any conscious or explicit cooking of the books when launching their idiosyncratic liberal project of restoration.[165] Their campaign objectives remained consistent, and entirely loyal, to their vision of how the world worked (at least from their combined perspective). Within, and acting from, that unalterable vision, they fought bare knuckled, carelessly disposing of any Queensbury style constraints or limitations. They battled not by launching some type of defensive counter-revolution, but by resurrecting what they imagined to be a full restoration of a classical liberal era. Though perhaps it was one that only existed in their imaginations and fevered desires. Namely, they sought a return to pre-Keynesian times, or their own recreation of those times. In their efforts, they composed what can aptly be classified as the Pre-Raphaelites of economics. But by adopting this pose, in common with so many other views suffused with romantic nostalgia, they yearned for a kingdom never really achievable.

But this attack on methodology had greater ramifications than simply an effective defence of marginalism, a standard approach providing the backbone of price theory and equilibrium analysis. As pointed out, the post war dominance of Keynesianism had been officially classified at the Mont Pelerin meeting as representing a nefarious slippery slope fashioned by the forces of collectivism.[166] If Milton Friedman was explicitly throwing bombs at the type of macroeconomics that descended from Keynes, Friedman would also at some level recognise that what appeared to be an impregnable post-war structure had a serious Achilles heel. There was a real disjoint between the prevailing macro-economics and the existing micro-foundations reflected by price theory. Thus preventing an alternative micro-economic theory to take root would more likely leave Keynesian theory vulnerable to some future, effectively launched attack.[167] Keynes himself, though to a degree aware of the problem, died before he could properly encourage a development in this direction.

> I thought you [Keynes] were too kind to the 'classical' analysis as applied
> to the individual industry and firm. Unless very artificial assumptions
> (e.g. perfect and instantaneous fluidity of resources) are made. It seems
> to me either wrong or completely jejune. I have been groping all these
> years after a re-statement of it on lines similar in some respect to your

> solution for the system as a whole, stressing in particular 'expectations' and the influence of current and immediately past experience upon them. But I can't make it precise (Shove 1936:1).

To which Keynes replies:

> What you say about the classical analysis as applied to the individual industry and firm is probably right. I have been concentrating on the other problem, and have not, like you, thought very much about the elements of the system. But you ought not to feel inhibited by a difficulty in making the solution precise. It may be that a part of the error in the classical analysis is due to that attempt. As soon as one is dealing with the influence of expectations and of transitory experience, one is, in the nature of things, outside the realm of the formally exact (Keynes 1936:2).

During the intellectual fervent of the 1930s, both Keynes and Chamberlin embraced assumptions in building their theoretical structures that were intuitively more realistic. Given the critical uprising of the twenties and the deepening depression enveloping the world from the late twenties and into the thirties, the existing modes of thought had lost much of their appeal. By the thirties, the profession, let alone the world at large, had become receptive to new theories, especially those with a fresh and more appealing direction.

> Ronald Coase: That's [Keynes' *General Theory*] a very good example. In fact, people have examined a lot of his empirical statements and they've found they were wrong. But that's sort of interesting. Look, the change came so rapidly in England, certainly, and I think in America.

> *And it certainly wasn't by appealing to the empirics.*

> Ronald Coase: No, it wasn't. The monopolistic competition versus perfect competition controversy really swept economics at that time. That was just due to a feeling that, you know, the existing theory was not particularly good, so they switched over (Conversation with Ronald Coase, October 1997).

For Friedman and his associates, such theories were not only wrong, but more importantly quite dangerous. These approaches offered non-clearing, non-equilibrium, or at best a multiple equilibrium analysis of markets. But in particular, if labour markets failed to clear, if workers weren't awarded their marginal products, the standard arguments boosting the efficiency and equity of such markets would in effect dissolve. Doubts regarding the magic of the marketplace invited, or practically demanded, government intervention. Such theoretical constructions were the not so hidden, thin edge of the wedge that provided legitimacy to collectivist efforts. To all stalwarts of the Mont Pelerin Society, collectivism (no matter the initial intentions) brought with it the potential rise of authoritarianism and the attendant loss of liberty. This perceived danger in part explains the ferocity of Friedman's attack on Keynesian economics and its proponents. Consequently, Friedman probed for a potential weakness to the seemingly unified and omnipresent dominance of Keynesian theory, as well as being eternally vigilant to ward off any detrimental challenges to his esteemed Chicago Price Theory.[168]

In which case, one clear strategy for shifting the grounds of debate away from dangerous terrain was to divert attention from the continuing controversy over assumptions. Friedman's aim was to methodologically dispatch that discussion from attracting any serious consideration. Or, at least, to undermine the validity of such approaches. Within this perspective, what might be termed real was superfluous and misleading, the product of smoke and mirrors lacking theoretical rigour. In contrast, part of the attractiveness that helped promote the alternative theories of the thirties was the intuitive appeal of their assumptions, which seemed to align with observable events. If instead, the profession could be distracted into an endless and unresolvable discussion on whether assumptions matter, some of the power behind the attack on traditional price theory could be neutralised and even dismissed. Doing so would not by itself eternally doom either the alternatives presented by Keynes or Chamberlin, but it would certainly weaken their appeal. Keynes' theory could be reduced to one of labour market imperfections (sticky prices). Chamberlin's efforts could be found wanting in terms of producing anything more or even equal to standard price theory. Friedman's (1953) efforts would not then totally destroy these dangerous alternatives, or at least what he deemed to be so, but such attacks could inflict something of a festering wound that would turn gangrenous some two decades later.[169]

The actual impact of this foray into a truncated realm of philosophy certainly accomplished (at least to a considerable degree) its intended objective.[170] Friedman and Stigler managed to produce a bold (and deliberate) attempt meant to shift attention away from a methodological issue that was then a matter of some intense discussion. Doing so required harnessing the power of a rhetorical poison apple. (Remember that the rhetorical purpose of such a device is to obfuscate, rather than clarify.)[171] In their methodological attack, they dismissed, in a peremptorily but believable fashion, any debate focused on the validity of assumptions, an issue that could potentially erode the foundations of standard price theory. But this was accomplished by presenting this foundational dismissal in the guise of a purely hypothetical exploration.

Accordingly, in his famous essay, Friedman (1953) did manage to shift a sufficient amount of the discipline's attention away from continuing a diligent and critical evaluation of the role played by assumptions. Instead, he refocused much of the subsequent debate on an endless discussion of the erudite, but unproductive, alternative he fostered. In essence, the path he methodically constructed, turned out to be a sort of argumentative Mobius strip, turning in on itself without leading to an insightful conclusion. In essence, Friedman persuaded his readers to enter into a deliberately conceived, non-productive debate. But such a seemingly consequential issue, when viewed from this vantage point, becomes no more than a device for camouflaging a quite different objective.

The 1953 essay became, in effect, such a successful distraction that it almost instantly spawned a classic economics joke. (Here the terms classic and joke are used loosely. Economists are not known for possessing a distinctive comical turn of mind.) The sceptical humour flowed directly from the lack of any genuine methodological edge that Friedman's unacknowledged goals successfully provided. Instead, he had other, more pressing, issues in mind when he diverted the profession's methodological discussions onto this carefully structured dead-end spur line. The argument Friedman constructed served as a classic poison apple gambit, one that proved difficult to resist. In this respect, too many economists performed the role of the naïve Snow White. They generally accepted or squabbled over the proposed solution proffered, within the boundaries of his 1953 essay. But like the enticing apple, the essence of the displayed logic appeared to be no more useful as a methodological approach than was the hypothetical Friedmanesque can opener in preying open the mythical can of corn.

> *A physicist, an engineer and an economist are stranded in the desert. They are hungry. Suddenly, they find a can of corn. They want to open it, but how?*

The physicist says: "Let's start a fire and place the can inside the flames. It will explode and then we will all be able to eat".
"Are you crazy?" says the engineer. "All the corn will burn and scatter, and we'll have nothing. We should use a metal wire, attach it to a base, push it and crack the can open."
"Both of you are wrong!" states the economist. "Where the hell do we find a metal wire in the desert?! The solution is simple: ASSUME we have a can opener"...[172]
(https://economicsociology.org/2014/12/27/the-E2%80%AA% E2%80%8Ejoke%E2%80%AC-goes-like-this-a-%E2%80%AA physicist%E2%80%AC-an-%E2%80%AA%E2%80%8Eengineer%E2 %80%AC-and-an-%E2%80%AAeconomist%E2%80%AC-are-stranded-in-the-desert/).

Endnotes

1   Discussion in this paper will almost entirely ignore questions relating to interpretations of content. Any methodological issues that seep out do so more as an unfortunate by-product, than as an essential component of the argument actually examined and dissected. Those interested in methodological spelunking will have much to choose from including Boland (1987), Caldwell (1980), Mayer (1993), Samuelson (1963) and Mariyani-Squire (2017), to name a very few. To paraphrase J.D. Salinger, 'I'm not going to provide you with all that Karl Popper crap about methodology.' For one, I am exactly the wrong person to do so, since I have an inalterable bias against absolutely all prescriptive methodology. Therefore, given my personal, intense dislike of anything resembling this philosophical sink-hole, steering clear of those regions touching on my clear prejudices is perhaps the best, and only wise, course to take. This intense dislike most likely stems from an early, ill-advised reading of Descartes (1701/1966). I found his 'Rules for the Direction of the Mind' to be patently absurd. The effort devoted to prescribing the way in which one should think appears to claim the unenviable absurdity of being presumptuous, while simultaneously achieving a degree of fundamental vapidity. Better to examine how people actually solve problems or craft theories, then to assume there is a one-size-fits-all, optimum path down which all researchers must glide. The purpose then of presenting this case study is definitely not to add yet another critical lump to the mountain of indifferent studies focused on Friedman's methodology. (Nor am I concerned with whether or not Friedman did construct a genuine methodology.) Any such laborious and constrictive effort would rightfully be tossed on to the ever-growing

scrapheap of work, which has masochistically followed Friedman down his purposely, crafted rabbit hole.

> When I was a graduate student we were taught a paradigm of how you do research. I've got to tell you, it's all wrong. It's not the way we operate. We don't sit up here and develop hypotheses and go out and test them. That's just not what we do. George taught me that. Milton taught me that. They're wrong! And I understand that. I'm old enough now to figure out that's not the way we do work (Conversation with Sam Peltzman, October 1997).

2   Success was also the hoped for stepchild in the deployment of the English rifle. Sharpshooters strategically placed on the heights of a battlefield could easily pick off the French troops as they surged upward en masse. Napoleon (perversely) distrusted the new-fangled rifles, continuing to rely on the existing front loaded muskets. Perhaps he thought the precise mechanics of the rifle seeped away too much of the precious French élan, which supposedly guaranteed his triumphs. (The esoteric faith in élan would continue to be part of wrong-headed, but fundamental, French military strategy for centuries after.)

3   A political scientist might speculate that Republican electoral successes have been largely dependent on their ability to control any national debate. Acting in quick response, these politicians locate and embellish areas that depend heavily on emotional cues (the cultural wars). Thus, critical race theory and parent's rights are manufactured into an imagined challenge to a way of life, one which is identified as being under heavy attack. Facts and logic in such cases prove to be only shoddy armour when forced to defend against fabrication and tailored concoctions.

4   For the economics profession, ideology remains, to paraphrase Oscar Wilde 'the love that dares not speak its name.' Economists may secretly be addicted to irreducible beliefs, unable to avoid being enmeshed by these treacherous pitfalls, yet unwilling to confess to the reality of their unyielding hold. In fact ideology, its meaning and role, was one of the rare areas where George Stigler and Milton Friedman clashed. (Perhaps mildly disagreed would be more exact.) Stigler rejected the usefulness of such a construct out of hand. The term, from Stigler's vantage point, was no more than a misleading ploy used to cover one's ignorance on a given matter.

> My self-interest explains part of my behaviour, and the part it fails to explain is called ideology. This is an unsatisfying dichotomy because in a complex world there are always unexplained residuals. The poorer the theory to explain a phenomenon, the larger the role of the residual; (Stigler 1983:1 or 1984:1). [This quote is from an unpublished and undated manuscript held in the Special Collections of the Regenstein Library, University of Chicago. However, it seems highly likely that the letter exchange quoted in what

follows refers to this paper, which Stigler had clearly given to Friedman for comments. Lastly, since the paper itself quotes an article published in 1979, sometime in the 1980s remains as the most likely date of composition].

In contrast, Milton Friedman saw the possibility of reconciling the idea of ideology with the standard self-interest incentive that formed the controlling impetus behind Chicago Price Theory. In essence, the suggestion that economic agents acted according to emotional based beliefs lacked any serious substantiation in Chicago constrained precincts. As he attempted to argue in a letter to his friend George Stigler:

> Most of the public most of the time acts on the principle that "honesty pays." Is that ideology or a perception of self-interest? It is clearly not a perception of narrow self-interest in the immediate case, but as a general maxim for conduct it is reasonable to argue that it is in the long-run self-interest of a randomly selected individual. Surely the role of what you call ideology is in large part a means whereby a society can accept self-denying ordinances which are in the long-run self-interest of the great bulk of participants of the society even though on individual occasions they are not (Letter from Milton Friedman to George Stigler, March 19, 1984, p. 2).

The idea that self-interest was not the instant and ultimate causal factor of all observed decisions would fail to find purchase whenever presented to a tough-minded George Stigler, He batted back Friedman's suggestion by pointing out:

> I don't know how important ideology is, but think it is unimportant. You don't know how important it is, but think it is important. My position is better because I try – feebly and so often unsuccessfully – to use a trusted theory of human behaviour to explain social phenomena. Your position is worse because you try – with marvellous ease – to explain the mysteries by a deus ex machina. I have immense amounts to explain. You will have just as much to explain when you try to give us a theory of ideology (Letter from George Stigler to Milton Friedman, March 29, 1984, p. 2).

5   George Stigler was somewhat notorious for employing such tactics in order to shred an opposing theory. He would construct a strawman version of the original argument in an attempt to pull future discussions away from the contentions of the opposing work. Accordingly, Stigler (1976) proceeded to construct a version of Leibenstein's (1966) x-efficiency theory, fabricated in a manner that allowed it to almost spontaneously self-destruct. Leibenstein (1978), perhaps unwittingly, fell into Stigler's prepared trap by entertaining Stigler's version of his theory (as though it were valid) instead of countering with his own thoughts and ideas. (Or more strategically, Leibenstein could have simply dismissed it as nonsense.) In essence, Leibenstein allowed Stigler to shift the terms of debate onto a more conducive terrain.

(Once relocated, Stigler could proceed to demolish this carelessly constructed version he had deliberately devised.) Those readers burdened with a sufficient degree of curiosity are welcome to further explore this topic (though possibly being confronted by an account which will prove beyond the reader's patience) by digging up (Freedman 2002).

6　Milton Friedman shared the same flare for marketing that is more often found among successful evangelical preachers when they are focused on selling their own particular brand of theological wares. Like them, Friedman would forcefully direct an argument to his desired endpoint, successfully fending off any attempt at flagging down his theoretical express train. By allowing him his initial premises (possibly of the poison apple variety), the subsequent argument too often deteriorated into a vain attempt of avoiding an inevitable conclusion. (This rather careless practice is more commonly known as shooting yourself in the foot.)

> I always said, if you want to win an argument with Milton, you have to disagree with his first premise. When he says one and one is two, you have to say, "no". [laughter] Because, from then on Milton will not make a mistake in logic. He will present some overwhelming evidence and he will be witty and charming and you *will* be devastated. I mean there are people who are just very convincing presenters (Conversation with Claire Friedland, October 1997).

7　Although a given opponent would remain convinced that he was driving the train of argument, the actual tracks down which the train headed had been laid down, at least implicitly by Milton Friedman. Maintaining the illusion of an open debate without a predetermined end was the essential sorcery cast by Friedman. Successful poison apple strategies essentially depend on such acceptance and misdirection.

8　Shifting the terms of debate by pre-defining them is not an unusual strategy in economics. But the skill of those that employ such techniques varies. Milton Friedman's colleague and close friend, George Stigler, was also a master at that particular ploy. His lethal attack on Leibenstein's theory of x-inefficiency (1976) was met by a rather ineffectual defense, one conducted by Leibenstein himself (1978). His repost to Stigler was doomed from the start, since Leibenstein foolishly chose to entrap himself by adopting the very same contentious terms and definitions set out by Stigler in his critical evaluation. Leiberstein strolled willingly into Stigler's deadly ambush. In essence, George Stigler craftily set a seemingly innocent trap for heffalumps, and Leibenstein thoughtlessly fell right into it. A more effective response would have been to reject Stigler's choice of terrain and term settings, rather than being reduced to becoming no more than a captive heffalump. Undoubtedly, a more targeted strategy would reflect an effort to demonstrate the fallacies that Stigler had crafted and employed to buttress his reconstruction of x-inefficiency. In simple terms, when faced with an ideological warrior, always choose to go on the offensive. A defensive position only makes those under attack look weak and rather desperate. In which case, the hapless opponent will find himself faced with someone who is deliberately trying to relocate the terrain of any subsequent battle. To survive such carefully constructed chainsaw attacks, the rule must be to never let the opposing side dictate the terms of debate. (See Freedman (2002) for details.)

9   The tar baby appears in a once, well-known *Uncle Remus* tale. The easily identifiable racial stereotyping has in more recent decades allowed such stories to fall into permanent disfavour.

10   For the idly curious, a sufficient number of YouTube videos exist that demonstrate exactly the rhetorical techniques Friedman used when staging an argument.

11   The idea of accepting a poison apple (or welcoming a Trojan-Horse), is a useful metaphor for swallowing something at face value that is, in fact, potentially dangerous. Readers might be helped by imagining a parallel image of a fish presented with a baited hook. If the fish were capable of foreseeing the consequences of swallowing the hook, instead of just the bait, fishing tackle would be essentially worthless. Clearly employing this strategy harks back deliberately either to the trick played on a proverbial innocent in the Brothers Grimm version of *Snow White,* or the ploy described in the *Illiad,* one which effectively defeated the Trojans. The fundamental error of these victims is in each case demonstrated by their failure to question what may lie hidden beneath a seemingly benign surface. Swallowing a likely sounding assumption, without first salting it with a sufficient sprinkling of skepticism, may prove fatal to a proper evaluation of any proposition or theory. Debating according to the terms set out by one's opponent is equivalent to trying to samba through a minefield. Destruction is almost self-assured. Success under such circumstances is consequently unlikely, with more heat than light being explosively generated.

12   To compare Milton Friedman to the wily Odysseus is more than a bit of a stretch. (Nor would Rose Friedman ever be confused with the patient Penelope.) Clearly no evidence exists to convict Friedman of deliberately scheming to do in his enemies by means of strategic trickery. He may have just been fast on his feet while debating his opponents and quick to spot a decisive opportunity. But he was far from the picture of a commanding general marshalling his troops to decimate an opposing empire. Though he might be decidedly short of stature he somewhat escaped the brutal egoism of a Napoleon. (Yes, Napoleon was actually average height. The shortness myth represented a bit of successful British propaganda.) Nor did he, like

Odysseus, undergo a prolonged journey of self-discovery after a climatic war in which he played an instrumental role. (During his own travails, while attempting to return to Ithaca, Odysseus was stripped bare, both figuratively and literally, of all pretensions and cloaks of disguise.) As the equally undependable Helen of Troy portrayed Odysseus, when once again she had returned to Sparta, little similarity exists between this mythic hero and Milton Friedman:

> Surely I can't describe or even list them all,
> The exploits crowding fearless Odysseus' record,
> But what a feat that hero dared and carried off in the land of Troy where you Achaeans suffered!
> Scarring his own body with mortifying strokes,
> Throwing filthy rags on his back like any slave,
> He slipped into the enemy's city, roamed its streets –
> All disguised, a totally different man, a beggar,
> Hardly the figure he cut among Achaea's ships,
> That's how Odysseus infiltrated Troy,
> And no one knew him at all … (Homer 1996:132).

In the same way, imagining Milton Friedman standing before the equivalent of a magic mirror inquiring the identity of 'the smartest economist of them all' is far from an easy image to embrace. Though actively contesting against and sneering at someone like Paul Samuelson, utter destruction through stealth wasn't quite in his agenda book. However, neither of these Chicago boys could cop a plea that validated anything resembling a complete absence of rancour. In truth, both his colleague, George Stigler, and he himself could be privately quite snide about designated opposition figures. But it is still quite a leap of imaginative gymnastics to recast Milton Friedman as an Evil Queen, let alone transforming Paul Samuelson into a masculine version of Snow White.

> Rumour has it that Samuelson was quite the unsuccessful suave chairman, a la Schumpeter, at the meetings. Sol[omon] Fabricant said he referred to you as an altar boy or something of the sort; I would have relished being there to see your reaction. It may merely be prejudice, but I'm inclined to write him off as an economist. Two of his recent jobs (the Survey article and his essay in the Hansen festschrift) were pure mathematical exposition, as is also his current *Economica* item (which, by the way, has already been done better by Wold), and his textbook suggests that he doesn't know anything that hasn't appeared in the *Survey of Current Business* (Letter from George Stigler to Milton Friedman, January 1949 in Hammond and Hammond 2006:97).

13   Clearly the employment of the term 'queen' here refers to the older, more traditional usage denoting the female ruler of a country. The conjurer of that famous poison apple, subsequently delivered to Snow White, ruled

whatever fairy tale land the Brothers Grimm had thought to create. In essence, the author takes no interest whatsoever in Milton Friedman's possible sexual interests, or whatever associated roles he may have played or endured.

14   Like any tub thumping revivalist preacher, he would market his truths wherever an invitation was extended. To him, spreading the good news, whether it was in Chile, the Soviet Union, South Africa or the United Kingdom, was to him, one and the same in certain respects. He always arrived ready to convert the masses, a virtual Billy Graham of the economics trade. One suspects, perhaps too cynically, that he would have appeared at supermarket openings if these provided him with sufficiently large audiences. The contrast between Milton Friedman and (his close colleague and methodological buddy), George Stigler could hardly be sharper when it came to marketing one's wares to the hoi polloi.

> I was at lunch with Milton Friedman and George Stigler at the Quadrangle Club in Chicago and I was then a very young man. And somehow the younger you are, the more evangelistic you are. So I would debate and argue with people about policy issues and as I recall Milton asked me if I would be interested in going on a tour of some campuses, I think in the Southern United States, to talk on these policy issues. Milton said, 'What have you got to lose by doing this?' And George said at the table to me, 'Only your anonymity.' So, on that occasion, I think he was hinting that maybe I ought to stick to my scientific work (Conversation with Harold Demsetz, October 1997).

Though Friedman's proselytising urges led him to being vilified for advising Pinochet's Chile, that judgment is perhaps a bit harsh. Such condemnation fails to understand what made Friedman tick, his mode of operation and his goals. He was, as stated, an evangelical who firmly believed in the gospel he was spreading. His blinkered, if not single-minded, vision made him overly optimistic, or perhaps even naïve at times. He simply discounted or overlooked those elements in a given situation that was not in synch with his vision. Authoritarian governments were assumed to exist simply as a transitional stage, if only the unshakable grounding of a free enterprise system could be firmly established. For Milton Friedman, such an economic system was the minimum, mandatory requirement for a strong, democratic political system to flourish. From this perspective, liberty and freedom both depended on a chosen market base. Without its prior establishment, attempts at a free, civil society would wither. (One might assume that the interwar Weimar Republic had served to confirm his unshakable beliefs.) This necessity made it crucial for economists, like Milton Friedman, to evangelize for such select systems, ignoring the gruesome points of reality that inevitably attended any practising authoritarian regime. For justification, Friedman could turn to the ex post vindication provided by South Korea and Taiwan. Though when weighing culpability, condemning Friedman while ignoring the past enthusiasms of some left wing economists for the old Soviet Union, or turning a blind eye to Joan Robinson's enchantment with Maoist China, seems hardly justified. Moreover, if one desires a shred of accuracy, the Chicago Boys of Chile were actually protégées of Arnold Harberger, rather than Milton Friedman. Though like Milton Friedman, Harberger was equally convinced of the righteousness of his actions and the associated good it spread.

> We in Chicago spawned the so-called 'Chicago Boys', who in turn spawned the revolution of economic policy in Chile, which in turn led to major economic revolutions in other countries in Latin America. So, to me, that's a lot of garbage, the idea to me of being fatalistic about this. You know, I've seen it happen. I've seen the transformation take place, I've seen societies bloom. And this happens in other countries too. It happened in Taiwan, it happened in Malaysia, it happened in Korea, it happened in Australia and New Zealand for that matter (Conversation with Arnold Harberger, October 1997).

In particular, Harberger is referring to a Chicago inspired set of policies and institutions that would become very controversial in the 1970s and 1980s, lingering even into the present era. Starting in the 1950s, a select group of Chilean economists were able to further their graduate training at Chicago, aided by grants from the Ford and Rockefeller Foundations. The program, shepherded by Harberger, would only gain its notoriety after 11 September, 1973, the date of the Pinochet led military coup against the government of Salvadore Allende. The subsequent economic program was largely constructed by these Chicago disciples within the newly imposed Chilean government. Whether such an economic program favoured the Chilean people, or was heavily weighted toward US multinationals remains a question of continuing contention. Responses to this quandary often reflect only the side of the political fence on which the disputant decides to eventually reside. The coup itself was supported by funds made available by the CIA.

> "Chile was not a jewel in 1995, but it's a jewel today," the economist Arnold Harberger says in the documentary *Chicago Boys*. Harberger, an American economist who taught at the University of Chicago from 1953 to 1991 alongside Milton Friedman, was a father figure to the "boys" – a group of Chilean economists who studied at the university in the 1950s. There, they became enthusiastic converts to Friedman's free-market economic philosophies, which they were then given free rein to implement on an unprecedented scale during Augusto Pinochet's dictatorship of Chile. The ideas they brought home from Chicago changed Chilean society forever and made it one of the richest countries in Latin America (Opazo 2016:1).

15   Ironically perhaps, Friedman's *bete noire*, John Maynard Keynes, showed little reluctance in employing the odd strategic poison apple when he deemed doing so to be necessary. In writing the *General Theory* (1964/1936), he faced an almost insurmountable problem. He had little doubt that what he was writing would be deemed revolutionary, drawing to itself almost instant counter-criticism. But an associated, and more implicit, problem involved a potential attempt by opponents to shift the grounds of debate away from those that Keynes had carefully crafted. By adopting standard market analysis, in particular that of diminishing returns, he hoped to prevent his work from being dismissed as merely the construction of a special case. He managed to avoid this strategic counterpunch, by means of a poison apple. Deliberately framing his argument within a conventional economic architecture provided the key to his solution. To be accepted as a general theory, Keynes needed to demonstrate the inherent flaw in a market based system, even one where perfect competition determined the structure.

> Now I range myself with the heretics. I believe their flair and their instinct move them towards the right conclusions. But I was brought up in the citadel and I recognise its power and might. A large part of the established body of economic doctrine I cannot but accept as broadly correct. I do not doubt it. For me, therefore, it is impossible to rest satisfied until I can put my finger on the flaw in that part of the orthodox reasoning which leads to the conclusions which for various reasons seem to me to be inacceptable. I believe that I am on my way to do so (Keynes 1934 quoted in Marcuzzo 2020: 4).

16   Friedman's perceived battle against the encroachment by the state on individual liberties never diminished. Nor did his ideological perspective ever really waver.

> True there have been developments that have widened men's freedom, but most of these owe little or nothing to govt. & I believe you overstate the extent to which freedom has been curtailed. The reason you do, I believe, is because the kind of freedoms you & I think of have never been important to more than a small number of people and that kind of freedom has so far fared relatively well (Milton Friedman to George Stigler September 1, 1965).
> One of the topics we would like to have discussed has to do with the mass media and the trend toward collectivism. Why is it that almost everywhere the great bulk of the contributors to the mass media, the journalists, the radio commentators, the TV performers tend to be collectivists in their orientation? (Milton Friedman to Raymond Aron Jan 5 1972).

17   This inner (and somewhat inflexible) self-confidence seemed, at times, to largely measure Friedman's own degree of unshakeable self-confidence, one which was based on a rigorous belief in the market methodology that

sustained much of his thinking. He was either oblivious to the faults striated throughout his argument, or at least chose to ignore them. Like many with a pronounced ideological bent, changing his mind proved to be nearly impossible (at least to the point of Friedman recanting or admitting error).

> I sometimes think some of the Chicago people are hopeless. Well, I wouldn't include Milton as among the hopeless because he was smart enough to punch his way out of a paper bag sometimes. But in the end he didn't want to do so. (Conversation with Paul Samuelson, October 1997).

18   Perhaps this poses an appropriate time to acknowledge that George Stigler, like his colleague and friend, was a past master at employing a subtle, poison apple strategy. (Whether this was done deliberately and consciously, or was just an engraved component of his rhetorical forays, must remain unresolvable.) The underlying aim of employing a poison apple strategy is to slide through (during an interchange) a tainted assumption as though simply formulating an axiomatic claim, or at least one not worth questioning. The key to such strategies depends on the fact that they are not easily discernible unless discovered as the result of a deliberate excavation. (Essentially a practiced spelunker is required, one who is willing to carefully sift through every argument searching in each for such deliberately set traps. For instance, during the annual American Economic Association meetings, Stigler (1960) by polishing such an enticing apple, attempted to persuade his listeners (and later readers) that worldly events and economic theory travel along non-intersecting tracks. But to reach this debatable conclusion, early on in his piece, Stigler introduces an untenable assumption as though it was something akin to an established concept, or at least a common notion.

> No such detailed reconciliation of economic theories with their environments, however, is even remotely tenable. When two Englishmen, named Mill and Cairnes, found themselves on opposite sides with respect to the validity of the wages-fund doctrine, both theories could not be mirroring the same reality. If their mirrors were turned to different realities, the environmental explanation of economic theories become too flexible to be useful (Stigler 1960:37).

Notice what Stigler attempts to accomplish here. He is intentionally muddling and redefining the relevant issue so that it will yield his desired result. While doing so, he unfortunately fails to demonstrate convincingly the supposed separation of events from theory, the very conclusion his rhetoric claims. However, he does indicate, though unintentionally, and quite effectively that different theories can be linked to alternative ideologies. The insight that Stigler attempted to explicitly demolish tried to link actual events unfolding in the observable world to simultaneously developing economic theories. In the Mill-Cairnes debate mentioned, the controversy arose when labourers pushed to shorten their work week. This movement by the work force, led employers to argue that a shorter work week would undermine the very rudiments of a sustainable industry. Notice that in this case, both Mill and Cairnes were observing the very same workplace reality. But data when observed fails to speak for itself. It has to be interpreted and those interpretations can, and often do, differ. (Plus ideological inclinations may induce analysts to squeeze observable data into preferred explanatory slots.) Stigler erred in his analysis since there is no reason that competing theories cannot reflect the same reality, only sieved through very different perspectives. In essence, the same data sets can adhere to contrasting theoretical bases.

Think in terms of the development of astronomy. Both Brahe and Copernicus attempted to devise a theory that would explain the observed motion of the planets. They could not help but to observe the same, rather than two alternative heavens. Yet they proposed theories that strictly differed from one another and from those Ptolemaic astronomers who also did their calculations under the same starry skies. (Though one might argue that the quality of the observations employed did differ.) If however we accept Stigler's analysis, both theories could not be correct, since both could not mirror the same reality. That conclusion however does not lead down Stigler's rhetorical lane which would claim that observations cannot shape economic theory. In essence, his example simply lacks pertinence. In a similar sense, during the Great Depression of the 1930s, both Keynes and Simons observed the same events. Both supported similar policies, but they differed greatly in constructing their explanatory theories. The same observations shaped each one's theory, but in a remarkably different manner. Stigler's argument of divorcing theory from reality then is far from self-evident and may even lack any validity. Bluntly speaking, Stigler failed to actually address the stated issue, choosing instead to sidestep it. But what he does contribute is a bit of rhetoric that could easily slide past the inattentive reader and possibly lead to accepting his more controversial contentions. In essence, Stigler actually did no more than to say that the opposing claims held by Cairnes and Mill cannot both be correct. Such a statement would appear to be indisputable, since being both A and not A must be logically unacceptable. But Stigler's stated objective was one of insulating theory from (and contamination by) actual events. This goal unarguably propelled his argument. Consequently his poison apple strategy in this instance is apparent. Somehow by swallowing his non-controversial claim that two opposing theories cannot be simultaneously correct, his readers were to be ultimately led to accept his more dubious assertion insulating theory from external events. Though the swallowed apple is obviously correct, it remains largely irrelevant to the issue at hand. However, it does allow Stigler to build dubious bridges linking that simple statement to less credible conclusions. Such constructed rhetoric is in fact the very definition of a poison apple. (Though in some cases the initial assertion, though superficially plausible, lacks any foundation.)

19   During the years following the first Mount Pelerin meeting, Friedman and Stigler shared a clear vision of the world, a certain weltanschauung, if we prefer to elevate their inviable insight into a perspective infused with a bit of grandeur. This view point would prove to be an unshakable basis for much of their ensuing work.

> He [George Stigler] was absolutely sure the economy was on his side and if research was properly done it would show this. He really believed that he understood how the world works. And the way the world works had been shown to him by the theory of price (Conversation with James Kindahl, October 1997).

20   Both Friedman and Stigler were loath to admit an error. In asserting what they knew to be true, they could be notably abusive. This trait was not uncommon at Chicago, perhaps a reflexive assertiveness absorbed from Knight, their teacher.

> Rose Friedman: I don't think George had much tolerance for stupidity.
> Milton Friedman: I don't think you're getting at anything that is really specifically George Stigler.
> Craig Freedman: No.
> Milton Friedman: I think you are getting something that is (a) the atmosphere at Chicago, and (b) intensified by Knight. That an academic is concerned not with being diplomatic, not with trying to avoid hurting people's feelings, but an academic is concerned with saying what's right. Telling the truth, or trying to get at it. And if you disagree with somebody you don't say 'well, now there may be something in what you say'
> Rose Friedman: You may be right
> Milton Friedman: You say that's a bunch of nonsense.
> Aaron Director: Exactly. That's not surprising. (Conversation with Milton Friedman, Rose Friedman and Aaron Director, August 1997).

21   One repeated weakness that consistently appears in the work of any strong ideologue is a marked preference for one-sided skepticism. Consequently, those on the left tend to avidly discover market failures, but display only limited interest in the potential weaknesses of collective solutions. In a contrary, but parallel, fashion, those aligning with such luminaries as Stigler and Friedman are adept at graphing government shortcomings, but prove loathe to examine market operations with anything resembling a skeptical eye. Instead, like their counterparts, they view their preferred

solutions through the assistance of familiarly rose tinted lenses. In either case, these academics managed to distinguish themselves by knowing in advance, exactly what the answer to their research questions would be prior to any actual investigation.

22   If a reader could become lulled into believing Friedman's devised methodology, issues surrounding assumptions became strikingly irrelevant. Swallowing a seemingly plausible presentation of positive foundations made accepting more substantial issues much easier. In essence, commencing down a given road led a reader effortlessly to a pre-determined conclusion.

23   Both Friedman and Stigler shared the same approach to economics, as well as common policy objectives. Friedman saw the subject much in the same way as Stigler and vice versa. Although Solow names only George Stigler when discussing the Chicago approach, he does indicate that a similar strategy (or even methodology) applies broadly to all dedicated members of the Chicago School.

> Oh, George was a puzzle solver. George was definitely that. As far as George was concerned, I would think that the system building had already been completed by Adam Smith and there was not a hell of a lot of room for him or for anybody else to do that. He was interested, I would say primarily, in a particular sort of puzzle and it's a typical Chicago puzzle. And I don't mean that in any bad way, it's the sort of puzzle that the Chicago School's presuppositions require. Show me an apparent anomaly, something that does not seem to be explicable using the Smithian apparatus or the Marshalian apparatus and I will show you that it can be explained that way. That was exactly the sort of thing that George went looking for (Conversation with Robert Solow, October 1997).

24   At this stage of a designated narrative (namely the start of a 'would be' literary adventure), assigning a proportionate and proper role to Friedman and those belonging to his cohort would seem somewhat imperative, at least if misconceptions are not to be nurtured. Unfortunately, a natural temptation when examining the Chicago School and its counter-revolution (or liberal restoration) proclivities is to become dazzled by the larger than life personalities and the intricate mechanics driving their strategies and objectives. But, falling into that comfortable trap of worshiping rather than investigating, relentlessly draws any analyst into committing a fundamental (and perhaps irreversible) error. But simply rejecting the 'great man in history' approach to analysis, choosing instead from among any one of the viable remaining alternatives, need not imply automatically falling into some sort of Tolstoian mood of fatalism. "The historians, from the old habit of recognizing divine intervention in human affairs, are inclined to look for

the cause of events in the exercise of the will of the person endowed with power but this supposition is not confirmed either by reason or experience" (Tolstoy 1896:1418). Instead, the Chicago (post war) School is better understood by placing it within the professional milieu of that period. Economics, the way in which it was conceived and applied, was rapidly evolving with different perspectives vying for dominance. Policy, the long acknowledged objective of the discipline, was in this enlightened period to be provided by developing a truly scientific basis from which such judgments would flow. To these post war pioneers, science meant quantification. This method alone was the sole vehicle deemed capable of providing this sought after overhaul within the discipline. Chicago, given these undoubted objectives, its ingrained ideological bent (and even the methodology employed), took a path quite distinctive from their compatriots at Eastern schools such as Harvard or MIT. Despite these differences, they both shared the same common vision of an economics discipline with a theoretic, and thus scientific, basis which would determine the foundation of public policy decisions. But they held almost diametrically differing views on most matters, since they persistently saw the world through very contrary ideological lenses. But for an outsider looking in, judgment can have a way of blurring when dazzled by such towering, though ideologically charged, academics. The implication being that even the attention and focus of an honest researcher can be hijacked, to some degree, by the magnetism of these larger than life Chicago figures. The ideology driving the market fundamentalism they espoused could then be overlooked, at least to varying degrees, if camouflaged by more kind-hearted interpretations of their words and intentions. For convenience, whether consciously intended or not, more dubious complications could be opportunistically projected towards (and lost into) the shadows of interpretation. The means employed would then necessitate a certain marketing magic to shift the terms of a discussion onto more convivial territory. The intention would be to divert attention away from prickly and uncomfortable issues. Perhaps the prevailing imperative at Chicago was to simply obfuscate whenever possible.

25   To emphasise the obvious, staking out the high ground isn't intended to denote a grappling for some evidential truth. The term denotes a rhetorical strategic position from which opponents could be defeated, if not annihilated.

26   The idea of accepting a poison apple, or opening up the gates to a certified Trojan-Horse, is to simply grasp the immediacy of an assertion presented at face value, while failing to be motivated to dig any deeper. Implications are notably ignored. The error arises when what may lie hidden beneath that placid surface is not questioned or investigated. Swallowing a likely

sounding assumption without first salting the claim with a decent sprinkling of skepticism, may prove fatal to a serious evaluation of any proposition or theory.

27   James Brown labelled himself as being the hardest working man in show business. An equally comparable label could be pinned to the lapel of Milton Friedman's suit jacket. For him, there was always another frontier of economic ignorance to breach, another country in need of market salvation. Friedman was the equivalent of a Christian soldier in service to a greater good. This dedication, even when cloaked by his relentless showmanship, is not to be belittled or decried. In the South African case described, Friedman delivered his lectures (both words of wisdom and selected bon mots) to predetermined audiences as the guest of the Graduate School of Business, University of Cape Town during March 1976 to April 1976.This experience is tracked in a slim volume produced at that time (Friedman 1976).

28   Friedman was a master of transforming an assertion into an indisputable axiom. (Perhaps not quite fashioned as a deliberate strategy. However, there is every indication that Milton Friedman put an absolute faith in the elixirs he so skillfully marketed.) Friedman was by no means unique in employing such a technique, but he became nearly bullet proof when doing so.

> I mean there are people who are just very convincing presenters. There again, it's personality. Milton of course is a great genius. But even great geniuses make mistakes, and great geniuses lose debates. They lose debates because debating is not necessarily one of their skills. And they make mistakes like anybody else. [laughter] Because, anybody can make a mistake (Conversation with Claire Friedland, October 1997).

29   Besides enjoying almost unlimited confidence in his own select world view, Milton Friedman also managed to display a seeming bottomless supply of patience and stamina in delivering his carefully sculpted truths.

> I was totally opposed to American involvement. Milton was a firm adherent of the bombing of Hanoi. We would have these incredible arguments. Now, I had read quite a lot about Vietnam. I don't think Milton had read anything. I was much better informed. Nevertheless, we would start these arguments at 9:00 o'clock and by 2:00 o'clock in the morning I would say, 'Milton, I just can't go on. I'm tired. I just can't take any more.' And he would say, 'Let me just give you one more argument.' He was patiently prepared to spend eight or ten hours trying to persuade me of the error of my ways. He knew nothing at all about Vietnam, or Communism. This was outside his knowledge. He was always patient, always polite, never got short tempered like I do in an argument, never got nasty. But he was a horrible person to argue with, just a nightmare (Conversation with Mark Blaug, April 1998).

30   At this juncture many of the readers might be momentarily stunned and perplexed due to a blatant contradiction between Friedman's unyielding admonitions and the then reality of South Africa. His example of linking apartheid to a free political system seems to create a pair of extremely uncomfortable bedfellows. However, many of the South Africans sitting in that audience would be convinced that they were participating in a form of Friedman's free political environment. They were, after all, able to scrupulously vote, in fair elections, albeit almost predictably for the National Party, which guaranteed the reassuring security of their preferred apartheid society. Moreover, despite the heavy hand of the government in the South African economy, they no doubt considered that each one of them qualified as valiant capitalists, a variety that was bred in the bone. Any notable success was simply due to their own concentrated efforts and carefully honed abilities.

31   Athenian democracy, which was entirely dependent on the mechanics of a slave economy, seems to have slipped Milton Friedman's mind. Democracy was undoubtedly limited in this city-state. But, a not dissimilar condition also held in the 19th century confines of the United States, which Friedman lionizes, without the slightest hint of hesitation or irony.

32   For Friedman, this was far from an original position. He had developed the same idea at length in his ideologically driven book *Capitalism & Freedom* (1962). This effort, to some degree, merely developed ideas expressed in his previous work and speeches. In his preface (1962), Friedman acknowledges the origin of the book as being "a series of lectures that I gave in June, 1956 at a conference at Wabash College directed by John Van Sickle and Benjamin Rogge and sponsored by the Volker Foundation" (Friedman 1962: i). The book is, in a sense, a compendium of his barnstorming tours of persuasion. To an overwhelming degree, Friedman possessed an unalloyed marketing sense which was in turn fired by a directed drive and a clear set of selected objectives. He might aptly be described as the sort of person who could sell sand to a Bedouin. But an assessment of his well-honed marketing skills is not intended as some sort of flippant denigration of the importance of marketing (for good or for evil) in any profession.

> The thesis of this chapter is that such a view is a delusion, that there is an intimate connection between economics and politics, that only certain combinations of political and economic arrangements are possible, and that in particular, a society which is socialist cannot also be democratic, in the sense of guaranteeing individual freedom.
>
> Economic arrangements play a dual role in the promotion of a free society. On the one hand, freedom in economic arrangements is itself a component of freedom broadly understood, so economic freedom is an end in itself. In the second place, economic freedom is also an indispensable means toward the achievement of political freedom (Friedman 1962:7–8).

33   Notice that this rhetorical sinkhole refers back to the cardinal error described in the South African case study. These issues, though distinguishable, do tend to bleed one into the other. Thus, just as a cocktail of anti-virals are deployed in the treatment of AIDS, so a single strategy will often be insufficient to knock out an opposing idea. Again, by deftly boxing and labelling an opposing stance or theory so that it falls squarely within a disreputable category, that particular opposing theoretical slice is condemned to live a life of desperate futility. Even the most thoughtful position will (under those prescribed conditions) be forever mired in the proverbial dead letter office of ideas. At least, this would be the result if the malevolent process of classifying is performed with any degree of skill and rigour.

34   This simple formulation would seem to denounce any benefit accruing to improvements in public health over the centuries. Certainly, improved sanitation hasn't been derived from the spontaneous actions of individuals or even as a voluntary measure reflecting personal responsibility. In a simple example, voluntary vaccination (based on individual thoughtfulness) is not guaranteed to yield a necessary level of herd immunity. Yet, Friedman here would seem to put himself on the side of today's anti-vaxxers. At least when regarding certain aspects of his recorded stances, there does seem to be policy aspects that remain unrecognized by Milton Friedman, or perhaps overridden by his deep, unconscious rejection of collective action. At times, he simply sees what he wants (or needs) to see.

> Just as an amusement I used to do a little Diogenes-like anthropological study of statistician friends of mine on what their attitude was on cigarette smoking. This was in the years when it had been nominated as an important cause of mortality, excess mortality. Let's say for my money that already the evidence was overwhelming. But this was denied. And when I went to Allen Wallis he said, 'There's nothing to it. Next thing you know they'll be saying coffee causes cancer.' Or something like that. And this was right on my prediction. Before I went to talk to him, I predicted what his response would be. And I remember saying to him, 'Now, what about Milton?' And he said 'Well, Milton agrees with me. However, he has quit smoking' (Conversation with Paul Samuelson, October 1997).

35   Sadly, correcting or even erasing an embraced lie has proven to be an increasingly difficult task in our mystifying digital age. Congenial lies travel at warp speed. Subsequent corrections and rebuttals are often, effectively ignored and disregarded.

36   The common rhetorical sleight of hand (masterfully employed by Friedman) requires an almost careless employment of a term without first bothering to define it. In the academic world, methods of this nature require a pretence that the meaning of such terms are obvious and held in common. Stated definitions are superfluous since the conveyed meaning is unarguable.

Given this carefully crafted context, few readers will subsequently have the courage or sheer audacity to admit ignorance of such an obvious usage.

37   Simply put, Friedman makes his audience feel duped. He accuses them of passively allowing government to steal what is rightfully theirs. In this fashion, ill-defined notions of individual freedom and liberty help Friedman achieve an initial stage of obfuscation. With the groundwork in place, his audience is now primed to further accept even less tethered assertions. The poison apple has been both proffered and accepted.

38   Often devotees of the Chicago School mode of thinking tend to wiggle out of such tight corners by referring such disputes to the relief provided by legal restitution. But here, as perhaps Ronald Coase would remind us, resorting to the law often comes equipped with a large bill of transaction costs attached. The end result depends not so much on justice (let alone efficiency), but on the ability to muster the funds required to hire the most effective legal team. The idea that legal proceedings produce anything resembling justice or some economically efficient outcome seem to be more of a comforting fairy tale fueled by wish fulfilment, rather than a delineation of any feasible reality. In essence, what the Chicago School implicitly posits is an 'as if' legal system, fueled by an invariably instantaneous and cost free transaction process. A whimsical rule of law is assumed to be consistently available to wipe clean any messy and perennially sordid corners of the contractual system. Such a supposition is amusing, but far from coincident with actual systems of justice, which depend more heavily on a country's prevailing income distribution.

39   Part of using a more insightful definition implies that an individual cannot be entirely responsible for all individual outcomes. He or she alone fails to completely own his or her own destiny.

40   Too often, ideological warfare is conducted through strategic labelling. A label can simply be yet another example of a poison pill in disguise. Accepting a proffered label shapes an issue's terms of debate. Thus, instead of an anti-abortion movement, there is a legion of dedicated pro-life proponents. Clearly this is a device for casting their designated opponents as murderers, namely those residing beyond the pale of decency. In response, there is a notable absence of anything purporting to be a pro-abortion movement, but instead one that is pro-choice. Essentially, those who battle to preserve freedom of choice and individual liberty. A similar poison apple dichotomy can be viewed in the gun control versus gun safety argument. Thus, those standing in the way of a favoured moral principle must strategically be painted in the darkest of hues.

41   In essence, how anyone can manage to prove that he or she is not racist or sexist can only continue to be an elusive and hopeless argument. (The

classic loaded question comes in the form, 'When did you stop beating your wife?')

42   Slippery slope arguments remain ingenious by seeming to prove in a logical fashion that any and all change leads only to unmitigated disaster. In other words, even an initial step taken in the proscribed direction encourages the traditional miscreant, or an erring government, to slide inevitably down a hill that is terminally sloped toward perdition. However, upon closer examination it is far from clear that any such argument of this ilk holds water. Nor despite the conviction with which such claims of doom are uttered, is there is any readily available evidence discoverable that might back up such broad claims.

> Discontented people might talk of corruption in the Commons, closeness in the Commons, and the necessity of reforming the Commons, said Mr. Spenlow solemnly, in conclusion; but when the price of wheat per bushel had been highest, the Commons had been busiest; and a man might lay his hand upon his heart, and say this to the whole world, – 'Touch the Commons, and down comes the country!'
>
> I listened to all this with attention; and though, I must say, I had my doubts whether the country was quite as much obliged to the Commons as Mr. Spenlow made out, I respectfully deferred to his opinion. That about the price of wheat per bushel, I modestly felt was too much for my strength, and quite settled the question. I have never, to this hour, got the better of that bushel of wheat. It has reappeared to annihilate me, all through my life, in connexion with all kinds of subjects. I don't know now, exactly, what it has to do with me, or what right it has to crush me, on an infinite variety of occasions; but whenever I see my old friend the bushel brought in by the head and shoulders (as he always is, I observe), I give up a subject for lost.
>
> This is a digression. I was not the man to touch the Commons, and bring down the country. I submissively expressed, by my silence, my acquiescence in all I had heard from my superior in years and knowledge; and we talked about The Stranger and the Drama, and the pairs of horses, until we came to Mr. Spenlow's gate (Dickens, Charles 1850, Chapter 25).

43   This is the type of classic claim, asserted with great confidence, but lacking either a believable source (or failing to supply any applicable definitions) of the terms employed.

44   Clearly with transmissible diseases, individual decisions (to vaccinate, isolate, or take other preventative steps) will affect the health of others. This irrefutable fact can be lost by amplifying emotional appeals supposedly drenched in the sweat and blood of individual freedom and liberty. Individuals may have the right to make their own health decisions, but not those which affect others.

45   Certainly production is not a matter of individual decisions, with firms more closely aligned with activity defined by collective action. Adding to

this initial stumbling block is the apparent dismissal that relative transaction costs might in given cases be more easily reduced by government intervention, rather than by individual decisions. This neglect of a viable alternative implies that mounted within an ostensible constraint (that closely requires market exchange as a determinant of freedom) is a hidden (and controversial) assumption that seems to be conveniently swept under the carpet. Namely, that any necessary legal actions attached to market exchange are both costless and efficient. As Coase pointed out in multiple publications, if transaction costs are zero, any dispute can be magically negotiated away. But such worlds exist only as theoretical constructs. Consequently, Friedman's insistence on the twin requirements of individualism and market exchange as the necessary and sufficient causes of liberty and freedom hits more than a few speed bumps when faced with any standard case of asymmetric information. The problem is further exaggerated when sellers deliberately mislead consumers given the advantages such double-dealing creates. As one of many possible examples, research completed in the early 1970s had already demonstrated the dangers that lead could inflict on children. However, concerted efforts by the lead industry attempted to nullify that research by simply rejecting it in its entirety. Additional distortions were provided by the industry's concerted attempt to cast aspersions on the character of the researchers themselves. (Often when direct, or frontal, attacks are unlikely to succeed, a common strategy is to shift attention away from the relevant issue at hand. In contrast, personal attacks, even when largely irrelevant, often provides a workable strategy of distracting attention away from a given core issue.) Corporate campaigns, though transparently self-centered, can prove exceedingly difficult to squash. Only more than two decades later, was lead actually removed from every-day items such as paint and petrol. This deliberate neglect had allowed damage to mount in the interim. Preventative measures, when they arrived, were government mandated and enforced. Consumer sovereignty, lawsuits or other individual options would have proven to be largely insufficient, serving only as a means to slow walk any meaningful denouement. On a strictly voluntary basis, the likelihood that lead based paint would have been removed from older homes and buildings would seem to be slim. Even farther removed from the realm of the possible would be the construction of a uniform pattern of traffic (vehicles proceeding on the right, or left, side of the road) based entirely on individual and separate choices. (My side, my choice.) The method by which such a result would be obtained remains either fanciful or would require accepting an initial period of carnage.

46   Milton Friedman would most likely subscribe to the thinking of his close friend George Stigler on this matter. Externalities, for example, did not

represent a market failure but rather a problem not yet solved by market forces.

> George was focused on the way the market marches in to *eliminate* the externalities, to work *around* them to make them a market problem instead of a non-market problem. I think I've quoted him in my memoir as saying something like, 'externalities are what the market has not *yet* eliminated' (Conversation with Claire Friedland, October 1997).

47   It might be sufficiently ironic to note that Friedman's obsessive target, John Maynard Keynes, shared with him the unfortunate habit of telling 'just so' stories. Thus the *General Theory* (1964) has convenient historical accounts that serve only to advance his preferred objectives, rather than attempting to elucidate historical events or ideas. (His later chapter on mercantilism contains several entertaining leaps of the imagination.) Like Friedman, Keynes' flexible approach to history is often most striking when he examines the past of his own discipline.

> As a historian of thought in areas in which he was emotionally involved as a protagonist and prophet, Keynes seemed to me to be seriously lacking in the unexciting but essential qualities for the intellectual historian of objectivity and of judiciousness. Even when he was engaged in selecting those upon whom to bestow laurels for having in some degree anticipated his discoveries, his selection seemed to me then, and still seems to me now that I have acquired more knowledge of the older literature, often to have been random when not eccentric (Viner 2003:418).

48   As widely acknowledged, (or at least reflecting something that should be so recognised) motivation for conspiracy theories can best be understood as reflecting a common human hankering. People are reliably titillated and entertained if they believe that they are gaining a glimpse of some hidden truth. These newly won conspiracy recruits can then consider themselves as belonging to a select group of cognoscenti. The pleasure provided by their newly minted, group identity privileges them with an assumed confidence of knowing more, and being wiser, than the general public. The imbued feeling of superiority is not unappreciated by those who buy into a particular conspiracy du jour. Conspiracy theories manage to turn a random and often incoherent world into a comprehensible and alluring entity while providing a yearned for sense of belonging. (Each conspiracy generates its own brood of brothers and/or sisters.)

49   In essence, the argument isn't that white labour unions might very well have supported apartheid, but rather that these unions became the creators and motivating force behind the idea of apartheid, as well as the major support behind subsequent South African regimes that instituted this unwarranted system. The logic implied is that in the absence of such unions,

apartheid would never have been instituted. Clearly, Friedman's grasp of South African history proved, in this instance, to be less than extensive.

50   William H. Hutt (1899–1988) vehemently opposed the rise of Keynesianism, instead propounding his own version of Classical Liberalism. Hutt was a product of Edwin Canaan's London School of Economics in the 1920s, having received a bachelor's degree there in 1924. Gaining no further formal education or degrees, he nonetheless left in 1928 for South Africa to take up the position of senior lecturer at the University of Cape Town. (Perhaps taking advantage of the traditional 'cultural cringe' exhibited in such colonies as South Africa and Australia.) No doubt, his 1930s isolation from the ferment of debate occurring in the US or in England, plus his earlier, but limited education at the LSE, helped support the unbending clarity of his vision. In his 1964 effort, *The Economics of the Colour Bar*, Hutt somehow turns his opposition to apartheid into an anti-union screed. The theory and practice of separation formulated in the post war period by the Afrikaaner National Party is entirely reduced to an anti-competitive urge by white labour to eliminate its black counterparts. Racism is equated, at least to some degree, with the sin of allowing labour unions to flourish. (Those interested in Hutt's racial views might want to delve into Darity, Camara and MacLean 2023).

Hutt though was likely to have been crucially influenced by another LSE product (Arnold Plant) who was selected as the first Commerce Professor for the newly created field at the University of Cape Town. Arriving to take up the position in 1924 (before departing in 1930), Hutt would have overlapped with him for a potentially vital two years. It is difficult to dismiss the possibility that Hutt's work on the 'Colour Bar' was heavily influenced by a much earlier paper by Plant, written while still in South Africa. In it, Plant presented an argument which though valid, was reductionist in nature. Namely that the attempt by government in the 1920s to favour one race was driven purely by economics. In essence, the purpose behind such a policy was simply to stifle job competition by excluding the native population. Though such thinking can be seen as a driving force behind the Afrikaaner post war insistence on implementing a policy of white job reservation, this one aspect hardly comprehends the full extent of thinking behind the notorious *apartheid* program. However the logic originally provided by Plant, when filtered through Hutt, provided a convenient base for condemning unions as essentially a racist and anti-democratic institution.

In his defense, Ronald Coase, Plant's most famous acolyte, manages to clarify Plant's intention which appear to have been more narrowly economic in character than Hutt, though still too sweeping in judgment.

> The only one of his writings in South Africa which he decided to reprint in *Selected Economic Essays and Addresses* was one dealing with the economic

> relations of the races, a subject which one dealing with the economic rela-
> tions of the races, a subject which could hardly be ignored by someone seri-
> ously interested in the economic problems of South Africa. The article, "The
> Economics of the Native Question." Was writing in 1927 and published in
> the journal *Voorslag* (May-July 1927). It was a trenchant attack on the policy
> of the South African government of separation of the races. Plant argued that
> the policy arose from a desire to stifle competition from the native peoples
> and was economically injurious to South Africa. It was competition that
> forced individuals to co-operate in an efficient way. What the South African
> government ought to be doing was, by providing educational opportunities
> and in other ways, to bring the natives into Western society. It was wrong to
> justify its policy by arguing that the natives were uncivilized while withhold-
> ing the means which would enable them to become part of Western civiliza-
> tion (Coase 1994:178–79).

Friedman, buoyed by his own rhetorical devices, manages to snowball this dubious starting point into a vehicle that helps him reach a pre-established goal. Reasonably, this bit of prestidigitation should cause anyone not completely under his spell to question the extent to which he had mastered a basic degree of background research prior to arrival in South Africa. For instance, was a country lumbered with an apartheid regime really the most appropriate platform from which to denounce a 1970s equal pay for equal work campaign in the US by committed feminists? The natural extension of such logic would justify a marked differential between black and white wages as well. Unfortunately, such an approach is strictly consistent with the idea that market outcomes are inevitably optimal, or if not, competition would force changes in the status quo to achieve those results. Friedman's poison apple, in this case, is his starting claim that he only wants to prevent blacks (or woman) from self-inflicted wounds. Once his audience swallows this, the rest of his argument is more easily ingested. The suspicion that another (and sharply different) agenda might be at play is rhetorically a nonstarter.

> They do not realize it is anti-feminist legislation because if they insist that by
> law you have equal pay for equal work they are going to end up having
> reduced employment opportunities for women in jobs in which, for one rea-
> son or another, the males have an advantage, whether that reason be irrational
> prejudice or valid differentiation (Friedman 1976:29–30).

Friedman here is making what can at best be described as a contentious statement. But note has to be taken of the relevant audience in this instance. (A good marketing agent always knows how to tailor arguments to the sympathies of their targeted listeners.) In which case, Friedman's rhetorical flourish (justifying the status quo) would inevitably soothe the attending ears of businessmen representing that place and that era. They would not be likely to object to the idea that they were benefiting women (or blacks) by paying them less. (Friedman implicitly paints his audience as kindly philanthropists who benefit others while simultaneously benefiting themselves.) Perversely however, he also seems driven to levy the curious charge of irrationality (when describing those misbegotten feminists). This description appears to be a jot more than peculiar when coming from someone who, like Gary Becker (1971), subscribes meticulously to the idea of rationality in decision making. (This hardline Chicago approach comes close to concluding that decisions are definitionally.) According to this mode of thinking, there would be no place in competitive markets for irrational prejudice. Such bias, as Friedman ascribes to those pushing for equal pay, could not be indefinitely sustained given this theoretical perspective. To persevere would require those women to stubbornly persist in their irrationality, seemingly incapable of recognising the glaring self-harm endured. In fact, if we were to follow Friedman's logic, this campaign for equal pay should have vanished into well-deserved obscurity decades ago. (In a strict sense, Friedman is unintentionally lumping women together with children who are by definition not capable of completely rational thought.)

51   The wit of Robert Solow summed up Friedman's particular obsession.

> Another difference between Milton [Friedman] and myself is that everything reminds Milton of the money supply. Well, everything reminds me of sex, but I keep it out of my papers (Solow 1966:63).

52   There can be little doubt that Milton Friedman was hardly unacquainted with Laughlin Currie's work in the 1930s, despite having displayed a clear reluctance to acknowledge the obvious importance of that work in his own research.

> Even more relevant to the question at issue … is the fact that in November 1933 Laughlin Currie published an article in the *Quarterly Journal of Economics* in which he provided annual estimates of the money supply for 1921–1932 whose year-to-year percentage changes during the Great Depression are also similar to those describe by Friedman and Schwartz. And in April 1934 Currie used this series as the basis of an article which he published in the *Journal of Political Economy* on 'The Failure of Monetary Policy to Prevent the Depression of 1929–1932'. Indeed the major conclusion of this article was that 'The [Federal Reserve] policy followed throughout 1929, so far from tending to prevent the depression, actually operated, in the view of this paper, to bring it on …' Later in that year, Currie published a book on *The Supply and Control of Money in the United States* in which he reproduced the monetary data of his 1933 article (Patinkin 2003b:381).

53   The idea that the Meiji Restoration in Japan somehow represented the triumph of free, entrepreneurial markets seems to rest entirely on Friedman's

strongly felt need to validate an unvarying degree of wish fulfilment. Again, his audience has already been fed and has swallowed one (out of an extensive catalogue) of Friedman's abundant poison apples. In essence, this assertion stems directly from the obligatory logic locked into Milton Friedman's rhetorical flourishes. Since the Meiji Restoration resulted in the industrialisation of Japan, such unquestioned success could have only been the result of instituting a system of free markets devoid of government interference. Such an idea is entertaining, but entirely fanciful. At least that conclusion holds, except for those lacking any useful knowledge of that period, such as his then South African audience.

> While private industrialists were weak the government itself had to play the role of industrialist. Had the Meiji Revolution come a little later Japan might well have become a socialist state, or a national socialist state. At that time, however, socialism was no more than a theoretical programme. Japan made her start as a country run on the lines of state capitalism (Morishima 1982:90).

Moreover, the contrast briefly explored between Singapore and Indonesia is also curious, even if Friedman does somewhat cavalierly opt to deliberately overlook the difference in the size and economic structure of those two countries. Singapore is a classic 'nanny state' where the government is clearly a textbook example of the Big Brother variety. Within its bounds, citizens tend to reflexively self-censure. The key difference between the two countries, in terms of government, is that Indonesia has been cursed with corrupt and incompetent governments while Singapore has not. That bad government leads to bad results is hardly earthshaking or worth debating seriously.

54   Successfully diminishing Keynes as an economist would to a meaningful extent neutralize Keynes' attempt at instituting a theoretical (and possibly policy) upheaval. By attacking Keynes' reputation as a theorist, Friedman would hope to mortally undermine the validity of much of Keynes' work. That at least appears to be the strategic architecture within which Friedman operated.

> To understand my [Keynes'] state of mind, however, you have to know that I believe myself to be writing a book on economic theory which will largely revolutionize – not, I suppose, at once but in the course of the next ten years – the way the world thinks about economic problems. When my new theory has been duly assimilated and mixed with politics and feelings and passion. I can't predict what the final upshot will be in its effect on actions and affairs. But there will be a great change, and in particular, the Ricardian foundations of Marxism will be knocked away.
>
> I can't expect you or anyone else, to believe this at the present stage. But for myself I don't merely hope what I say – in my own mind I'm quite sure

> (John Maynard Keynes in a letter to George Bernard Shaw, 1 January 1935 quoted in Shaw 1988: vii).

55   Wily Odysseus in Homer's *Illiad* devises a strategy to end a costly and lingering war by decisively destroying the Trojans. The posed problem is how to successfully infiltrate a walled and armed city. The proposed solution initially involves lulling the defenders into a state of complacency. This step is accomplished by staging an apparent departure of the Greek forces. Next, the departing Greek forces make an unanticipated act of contrition to propitiate the Gods before they ship off. A magnificent wooden statue of a horse is left, which the Trojans (without any serious examination) proceed to wheel naively into their walled city. In this manner, the Greek army manages to worm its way into the heretofore impregnable fortress of Troy. The Trojans, buoyed by their seeming success, ignore any possible sounds emanating from within the horse (let alone the direct warnings from Cassandra). The fate of Troy is sealed. Consequently, in a more modern day version, Don Patinkin, with his ear firmly pressed against Friedman's proffered theory, identifies something that fails to ring quite true. Friedman's strategy of torpedoing Keynes, at least to some substantial degree, is temporarily thwarted by Patinkin's sharp sensibility. Moreover, unlike Helen of Troy, when placed in a similar position, Patinkin failed to keep his valid suspicions completely mum. Instead he vividly portrayed his doubts directly to the economics profession. In contrast, Helen allows the Greek's strategy to proceed in its deadly course. In fact, once she is restored (willingly or not) to Sparta, Helen has her midnight equine adventures described by her husband Menelaus, spotlighting Helen's own mischievous nature.

> Helen – roused, no doubt,
> By a dark power bent on giving Troy some glory,
> And dashing Prince Deiphobus squire your every step.
> Three times you sauntered round our hollow ambush,
> Feeling, stroking its flanks,
> Challenging all our fighters, calling each by name –
> Yours was the voice of all our long-lost wives! (Homer 1996:133).

56   Friedman was never quite as explicit in his dismissal of Keynes as Samuelson was in his damning categorization of Marx as an economist. "A minor Post-Ricardian, Marx was an autodidact cut off in his lifetime from competent criticism and stimulus" (Samuelson 1957:910). However to paraphrase Newton, Friedman does want to reduce Keynes to a dwarf standing on the shoulders of giants (the pioneers of the quantity theory of money).

57   Intentions are a basic analytical quicksand, since playing therapist places an examining economist in dangerous and often uncharted territory. Even seemingly unequivocal statements on the matter of intentions fails to shift

an investigation onto necessarily more solid ground. What an economist thinks of as his or her objective, may be a less than accurate calculation. Even when such an individual is apparently candid, the murky realms of the subconscious inevitably raises issues of intent and motivation. All that can be safely observed is what an economist actually does, rather than any announced motivational claims. Intent can be indirectly argued based on the individual's career and any clear overarching goals reflected by his or her writings and actions. But to emphasize, economists are not psychologists. (One wonders if even psychologists are psychologists.)

> This is absolutely essential in my field. And George would use it. If however I saw data based on responses to questions like: 'How do you feel this morning? What do you feel about Richard Nixon? Did your wife and you have an argument this morning?' I don't pay attention to *that* kind of data. There is this definite bias in Economics. You see what people *do,* not what they say. Because, you can never competently judge their motives, or what is in it for them. [laughs] You've got to study their behaviour, pure and simple (Conversation with Sherwin Rosen, October 1997).

58   Given their closeness of thought and approach to economics, much that could be said about George Stigler also applies to Milton Friedman. Both were skilled at a certain type of mental jujitsu. Opponents might, for instance, naively think that they had discovered a flaw in Chicago price theory. But when examined from the appropriate perspective the reality became quite otherwise.

> As far as George was concerned, I would think that the system building had already been completed by Adam Smith and there was not a hell of a lot of room for him or for anybody else to do that. He was interested, I would say primarily, in a particular sort of puzzle and it's a typical Chicago puzzle. And I don't mean that in any bad way, it's the sort of puzzle that the Chicago School's presuppositions require. Show me an apparent anomaly, something that does not seem to be explicable using the Smithian apparatus or the Marshalian apparatus and I will show you that it can be explained that way. That was exactly the sort of thing that George went looking for (Conversation with Robert Solow, October 1997).

59   Denigrating opposing theories was a strategy unquestionably endorsed by George Stigler. In practise, Milton Friedman often opted to do the same.

> *In several places he pushes this idea of the need to attack opposing ideas without exception in order to push your work. I suppose he is saying that you have to really be a salesman to be successful. What's your reaction to that sort of approach?*
> Sherwin Rosen: I don't know. Look, intellectual activities are a kind of business. Marketing is part of that business. There's no doubt that some people

> are able to market their work better than others. Or perhaps, it somehow catches on for reasons that are hard to say. I *hope* it catches on when it has something to it. I don't think marketing is all there is to acceptance (Conversation with Sherwin Rosen, October 1997).

60   As will be emphasized, Friedman creates a deliberate low bar by assuming Keynes had little to add to the existing canonical work on monetary theory. Part of Friedman's poison apple depended on shrinking Keynes into a position of insignificance. Accepting this particular poison apple allows Friedman to plough the road for his own monetary thoughts.

61   Milton Friedman never shied away from controversy. He would much prefer to be torn apart than to be ignored. But the point made here is that sometimes, it might be better not to immediately put the profession's collective backs up. Typically, irate opponents seem to miss (all too frequently), the purpose or essence of a presented theory. Such misapprehension can accordingly shove subsequent discussion off-track. For most communications, this result would be entirely counter-productive. In contrast (as discussed later in the article) Friedman in his 1953 methodology essay clearly wants to deliver a directed punch in the head to other economists and their concerns. He creates a veritable Molotov cocktail, which he hopes will inflame (or even explode) subsequent discussion. Whether such debate remains focused on the essay's thesis (or wanders down other unproductive digressions), may in this instance be simply a moot point.

> Because George Stigler, who was very critical of people, was almost worshipful of Milton Friedman. And I remember that one of his dicta was that a Milton Friedman theorem was more credible than any other theorem, because everybody picks on Milton. It's an unfair world and so forth, which means that he gets a more rigorous testing than anyone else (Conversation with Paul Samuelson, October 1997).
>
> The sterility of the early Walrasian system arose because it was ignored by most economists and adopted by a few but criticized by almost none. Milton Friedman's work is bound to be spread rapidly in the science and to achieve a wide scope and high rigor because of his wondrous gift of eliciting the probing attention of eminent contemporaries (Stigler 1982:111).

62   Notice that oral traditions conveniently leave no indisputable record. As subsequent debate between Don Patinkin and Milton Friedman demonstrated that the notion of an oral tradition can easily descend to the intellectual level of 'he said – she said'. As a consequence, and quite noticeably, in the relevant exchanges between the two, it would become clear that neither evidence, nor logical argument, could completely budge Friedman from his initial stance. When hard pressed, he would fall back on obfuscation and a weak appearance of acceptance (a non-concession, concession).

63   At about this time, Jacob Viner, a former mainstay of the Chicago faculty during those same interwar years, wrote to Don Patinkin about the decidedly ideological shift he couldn't help but noticing when later attending a conference sponsored by the Chicago department.

> It was not until after I left Chicago in 1946 that I began to hear rumours about a 'Chicago School' which was engaged in *organized* battle for *laissez faire* and 'quantity theory of money' against 'imperfect competition' theorizing and 'Keynesianism'. I remained sceptical about this until I attended a conference sponsored by University of Chicago professors in 1951. The invited participants were a varied lot of academics, bureaucrats, businessmen, etc, but the program for discussion, the selection of chairmen, and everything about the participants were so patently rigidly structured, so loaded, that I got more amusement from the conference than from any other I ever attended. Even the source of the financing of the Conference, as I found out later, was ideologically loaded (Jacob Viner quoted in Patinkin, 2003a:112).

64   For those readers who have suffered a dysfunctional childhood, namely spending their youthful years being inadvertently separated from the entrancement of A.A. Milne, the woozle reference comes from the tales that incisively chronicle the history of one Pooh Bear.

> Christopher Robin came slowly down his tree.
> "Silly old Bear," he said, "what *were* you doing? First you went round the spinney twice by yourself, and then Piglet ran after you and you went round again together, and then you were just going round a fourth time –"
> "Wait a moment," said Winnie-the-Pooh, holding up his paw.
> He sat down and thought, in the most thoughtful way he could think. Then he fitted his paw into one of the Tracks … and then he scratched his nose twice, and stood up.
> "Yes," said Winnie-the Pooh.
> "I see now," said Winnie-the Pooh.
> "I have been Foolish and Deluded," sad he, "and I am a Bear of No Brain at All" (Milne 1961:42–43).

65   In an almost Hegelian fashion, Friedman and Stigler seem to have identified the real with the idea. In essence, their theoretical models, especially when tested in the fires of their preferred statistical methods, were deemed to necessarily reflect the observable world (at least from their perspective). In nurturing this approach, they decisively broke away from their teacher, Frank Knight. In contrast, Knight saw the limits of theoretical constructs when piecing together actual policy. By adopting this method, Knight travelled co-temporaneously (at least mentally) with a tradition that characterized classical liberalism. The benchmark adopted, within that particular methodology, refused to allow economic practitioners the luxury of jumping from theory to policy based solely on their own constructed

imperatives. In contrast, Friedman and Stigler desired to expand the realm of economics to include any variety of human choice. In essence, they shared a predilection for constructing a universal science of decision making. (Others would extend this perspective to include the evaluation of animal behaviour as well.) Rational decision making, under such a universal canopy, explained not just a useful portion of some observables, but the entirety of all human decision-making. Not for Friedman, or for Stigler, the considered caution of Knight.

> ... in the present writer's judgement, theorists of past and present are to be justly criticized not for following the theoretical method and studying a simplified and idealized form of competitive organisation, but for not following it in a sufficiently self-conscious critical, and explicit way (Knight 1971:10).

66   Curiously enough, this interwar policy instance contradicted the subsequent Chicago post war strategy. As stated, the unswerving belief widely entertained was that defeating objectionable economic policy largely rested on eviscerating the theoretical basis underlying it. However, during the 1930s, destroying either Chicago or Keynesian style theory would have still left deficit spending policy unbowed.

67   An enduring mystery is Friedman's reluctance to credit Lloyd Mints (1888–1989), the faculty member who taught money and banking at Chicago from 1928 till his retirement in 1953. (His lengthy Chicago career commenced in 1919.) Instead of resorting to an ambiguous oral tradition of classroom lectures, Mints had a solid publishing record upon which to build. For some reason, Friedman is reluctant to accord credit for his ideas to Mints, perhaps in something of the same fashion that he tended to ignore the aforementioned Laughlin Currie. (Though Currie and Mints entertained very diametrically different political views.) Reasons here are difficult to pin down, let along confidently provide. It might appear though that Friedman wanted his work to flow from the past received wisdom of the economics profession. Doing so would allow him to assume the heroic role of resurrecting long standing theory and restoring these theories to their rightful dominant position. Consequently, he might have been equally loathe to have his wisdom classified as simply a close derivate of specific work that was already amply provided by a well-known economist. (Taking this tack would hardly have boosted his reputation or allowed his work to make the impact that he desired.) Mints himself proved wise enough to ditch economics upon reaching the age of 65, move in with his sister outside Fort Collins in Colorado and spend the rest of his life doing something useful. He transformed himself into a cabinet maker, spending almost as much time pursuing this vocation as he had in those days when he was mired in the intricacies of economics.

68   To repeat, I'm not a psychologist, let alone a mind reader. I am unable to ascertain what Friedman's conscious thoughts or intentions might have been. Instead I am co-opting Friedman's own device here and stating that he acted 'as if' these were his conscious intentions and strategies.

69   The simple minded idea driving this strategy is that people are less likely to be suspicious of the familiar and ordinary. Cloaking more outré notions with such convenient camouflage can be a clever way to slip in what would otherwise be more controversial theories and ideas.

70   No doubt, trying to piece out what an economist actually meant is a frustrating (and often unrewarding) process. But an honest effort to do so is easily distinguishable from those who simply force a work into a pre-existing framework.

71   Producing false equivalencies is a long cherished rhetorical trap. The aim is to muddle any inquiry by shifting the focus away from the question at hand. Thus, if a reader can be convinced that Keynes' thoughts on monetary issues remained consistent throughout his career, then it would be possible to glean the essence of that insight from his much earlier writings. This strained judgment would quite coherently form a suitable basis for analyzing *The General Theory* (1936). Once this supposition is accepted (acting as a well-polished poison apple), then the actual published content can be forcefully shoved into an approved template that automatically validates the desired interpretation. When carefully fitted with these pre-specified lenses, a reader is then eased through a carefully constructed theoretical tour of *The General Theory*, one ably piloted by Milton Friedman.

72   Keynes mentions the idea of a liquidity trap (not so labelled by Keynes himself) as a purely theoretical possibility ('I know of no example of it hitherto' – Keynes 1964:207). For Keynes, this concept would hold the same position as a Giffen good would for a micro-economists like George Stigler (1947). However, the preciseness of this formulation (and its undeniable tractability) held much more of a deadly allure for Keynes' subsequent apostles. Keynes' central idea of lender's risk, though simple to comprehend discursively, could more easily slip through attempts at theoretical construction, eluding the nuts and bolts process of model building.

It might be interesting to note, at least relative to concepts that caught fire only at a later stage, that Keynes couples lender's risk with that borne by the borrower ('the intermediate cost of bringing the borrower and the ultimate lender together' – Keynes 1964: 208). The persistence of such a cost is then identified as a persistent factor that effectively prevents an interest rate falling low enough to sustain a full employment level of investment. Keynes, in defining such a cost, was almost anticipating the work of Ronald Coase, an approach articulated only one year later (1937). Operating in the micro realm of markets, transaction costs inevitably prevent the optimal (or frictionless) operations of markets. Keynes' supposition of ineradicable risks attached to both lender and borrower is only a particular version of the transaction cost category. These specific obstructions are inherently located within any conceivable money market.

73   If Friedman doesn't harbour an ulterior motive, such as forcefully diminishing Keynes, then his relegation of Keynes to the fraternity of quantity theorists become inexplicable. Keynes couldn't be clearer in stating that in his evaluation, the quantity theory was no more than a special case, and not a particularly interesting one.

> For the purposes of the real world it is a great fault in the Quantity Theory that is does not distinguish between changes in prices which as a function of changes in output, and those which are a function of changes in the wage-unit. The explanation of this omission is, perhaps, to be found in the assumptions that there is no propensity to hoard and there is always full employment. For in this case, O [output] being constant and M_2 {money held for speculative reasons] being zero, it follows, if we can take V also as constant, that both the wage-unit and the price-level will be directly proportional to the quantity of money (Keynes 1964:209).

> For Keynes, this lack of any real applicability renders the quantity theory as being, by definition, basically pointless.

> If we had defined V, not as equal to Y/M_1 [money held for transactions or for precautionary purposes] but as equal to Y/M, then, of course, the Quantity Theory is a truism which holds in all circumstances, though without significance (Keynes 1964:209 ftn. 1).

74   Those who remain fastidious, or those who pride themselves on being professional doubting Thomases, can plough their way through Freedman (2006), where Friedman's flights of fancy on this issue are sufficiently detailed.

75   Friedman's obsession with Keynes' idea of a liquidity trap is highly reminiscent of a previously reported passing remark made by his contemporary, Robert Solow. "Another difference between Milton [Friedman] and myself is that everything reminds Milton of the money supply. Well, everything reminds me of sex, but I keep it out of my papers." (Solow 1966:63).

76   Let me re-emphasize that there is scant, if any, evidence that Milton Friedman was in fact aware that the economics he was practicing might in fact be no more than a rhetorical sleight of hand. Rather, the more likely conclusion is that he possessed a strong, if not unbreakable, *a priori* vision that was not vulnerable to either evidence or arguments. Harry Johnson's frustration (to the point of categorising him as a charlatan) when Milton Friedman proved to be utterly unmovable in the face of fact or logic,

remains quite understandable. However, Johnson's charges nonetheless are basically unproven (though amusing).

> The problem in the case of both counter-contentions was a basic difficulty in establishing a plausible linkage with pre-Keynesian orthodoxy. The solution to this problem was discovered by exploiting two lines of reasoning. The first was the invention of a University of Chicago oral tradition that was alleged to have preserved a fundamental truth among a small colloquium of the initiated during the dark years of the Keynesian despotism. The second was a careful combing of the *obiter dicta* of the great neo-classical quantity theorists for any bits of evidence that showed recognition (or could be interpreted to show recognition) of the fact that the decision to hold money involves a choice between holding money and holding wealth in other forms, and is conditioned by the rates of return available on other assets (Johnson 2003:170).

77   The ongoing economic perplexity centering on dynamic versus static analysis, often gets bogged down in an unresolvable definitional game.

> For more than twenty years I have been telling my students that one widespread uses of "Statics" and "Dynamics" was to distinguish a writer's own work from that of his opponents against whom he tried to argue. Typically, "Statics" was what those benighted opponents have been writing; "Dynamics" was one's own vastly superior theory (Machlup 1959:100).

78   Projective geometry incorporates as special cases: elliptic, Euclidean and hyperbolic geometry. These differ based on the nature of their rejection of Euclid's parallel postulate. Euclid had provided the prevailing definition of parallel lines for many centuries.

> As lines, so loves oblique may well
> Themselves in every angle greet;
> Though ours, so truly parallel,
> Though infinite, can never meet (Andrew Marvell (1621–1678), *The Definition of Love*).

That Keynes (like mathematicians or physicists), shared this common aim in constructing what he conceived of as a general theory is hard to argue against. Doing so would seem to require the skeptical individual to harbour an overwhelming imperative to deny Keynes' own words in order to advance an alternative agenda. What Keynes categorises as classical theory (Keynes 1964:3 ftn. 1) must, given his perspective, be reduced to a special case which remains applicable only when certain constrained conditions hold. For Keynes, involuntary unemployment is part and parcel of any market economy, as opposed to the sort of short term aberration envisaged by Simons and the Chicago School of the interwar years. There is also no mistaking Keynes' evaluation of the applicability, or the usefulness, of classical theory, bound as it must be by its limiting assumptions.

> Obviously, however, if the classical theory is only applicable to the case of full employment, it is fallacious to apply it to the problem of involuntary unemployment – if there be such a thing (and who will deny it?). The classical theorists resemble Euclidean geometers in a non-Euclidean world who, discovering that in experience straight lines apparently parallel often meet rebuke the lines for not keeping straight as the only remedy for the unfortunate collisions which are occurring. Yet in truth, there is no remedy except to throw over the second postulate of the classical doctrine and work out the behaviour of a system in which involuntary unemployment in the strict sense is possible (Keynes 1964:6–7).

79   John Maynard Keynes self-consciously, if not didactically, recognized the need to expand his vision.

> The difficulty lies, not in the new ideas, but in escaping from the old ones, which ramify, for those brought up as most of us have been, into every corner of our minds (Keynes 1964:viii).

80   Economists might soothe themselves with bedtime stories featuring true theory slaying badly misguided thinking, but as in most endeavours, timing is everything. Theories must be closely geared to the preferences of the profession when offered, if they are going to gain a credible foothold. Cases of premature presentation are not difficult to discover in the history of the economics discipline, or in sexual relations for that matter.

> *It certainly wasn't by appealing to the empirics.*
> Ronald Coase: No, it wasn't. The monopolistic competition versus perfect competition controversy really swept economics at that time. That was just due to a feeling that, you know, the existing theory was not particularly good, so they switched over (Conversation with Ronald Coase, October 1997).

81   In the *General Theory*, Keynes was content to assume perfect competition (his own ad hoc poison apple) as the operative foundational assumption behind his systemic view. Keynes does so, not because such a structure reflected the existing state of any economy, but for its rhetorical power. Any other suggested structure would have inevitably raised professional hackles and wariness. Subsequent discussions or debates would likely to have been diffused or diverted. Specific questions dealing with precise economic structures would dominate instead. The project of constructing a general theory (under such circumstances) would permanently flounder. Consequently, by accepting the perfect competition ruse, readers might prove more willing to consider, if not entirely swallow, the more revolutionary content of Keynes' message. In essence, in Keynes' brave new

world, failure to achieve full employment stemmed not from any traditional market frictions or economies of scale. Even markets devoid of the variety of market power defined by monopoly and oligopoly could still, given the underlining logic, fall into less than optimum equilibriums. To compel this conclusion, Keynes constructed his theory so that discussion and debate would not be waylaid by questions focused on the degree of competition within a given structured economy. He wanted, as much as possible, to thwart any attempt to shift the terms of debate onto less fruitful grounds. Attempted diversions that would shift debate to less fertile territory, needed to be imagined and subsequently thwarted in advance. Thus perfect competition served as his conceived poison apple.

82   Sraffa's (1926) article disrupted the familiar and fundamental assumptions that had faithfully buttressed an independent and operative supply and demand curve. These curves served equally well for both theoretic and policy derived purposes. Removing this requisite condition underpinning partial equilibrium analysis left Marshall's Economic Bible (especially as viewed through the vision of his prophet, Arthur Pigou) in tatters (at least theoretically). This conclusion seemed to reign supreme among the conclave of some of his most devoted critics. Considering his demolition work now complete, Sraffa's reconstructed resolution of this seemingly intractable issue necessitated a progressive path forward that lay steeped in the precepts of market power. Consequently, the logic of the critique produced those downward sloping demand curves which are attached, in standard economic analysis, to monopolists. Namely, they represented a shorthand for firms fostering some degree of market power. Chamberlin's perspective is just one of many roads that logically extend from Sraffa's mode of thought. (In Joan Robinson's world of imperfect competition, obedient demand curves slope downward reflecting her own specifically expressed commands or the relevant preferred necessities of theory. Bowing to the needs of model building strongly contrasts with a response triggered by observing operational markets.)

> It is necessary, therefore, to abandon the path of free competition and turn in the opposite direction, namely towards monopoly. Here we find a well-defined theory in which variations of cost connected with changes in the dimensions of the individual undertaking play an important part ... Everyday experience shows that a very large number of undertakings – and the majority of those which produce manufactured consumer goods – work under conditions of individual diminishing costs. Almost any producer of such goods, if he could rely upon the market in which he sells his products being prepared to take any quantity of them from him at the current price, without any trouble on his part except that of producing them, would extend his business enormously (Sraffa 1953:187).

83   Keynes is employing his own tailor-made version of a poison apple. Although, for those ultimately convinced by Keynes' analysis, his strategy could be labelled as tempting the profession with a candy apple. In either case, Keynes surely realised that abandoning marginal analysis would make marketing his theory extremely difficult, if not impossible. Keynes' clever end run (slipping a radical approach in while seeming to endorse the use of standard analytical tools) was intended to avoid ruffling feathers unnecessarily.

84   This recognition is hardly novel. When constructing theoretical structures, measurable and tractable variables are the preferred ingredients. Though here the distinction between theory and policy applications should be noted. Given that his father, John Neville Keynes (1891) wrote the ultimate nineteenth century guide to economic methodology, his son would be well acquainted, by necessity, with the classical prohibition against jumping directly from theory to policy. (A stroll through Colander and Freedman (2019) on this topic might be relevant despite incurring the increased potential for coma-like sleep.) Such a distinction would, unfortunately, be largely lost during the post war explosion of quantitative (scientific) methods defining economists of all hues and beliefs.

> Political economists generally and English political economists above others, have been accustomed to lay almost exclusive stress upon the first of these agencies, to exaggerate the effect of competition, and to take into little account the other and conflicting principle [custom]. They are apt to express themselves as if they thought that competition actually does, in all cases whatever it can be shown to be the tendency of competition to do. This is partly intelligible, if we consider that only through the principle of competition has political economy any pretence to the character of science (Mill 1965:242).

85   The post war profession was left with an obvious Achilles heel that Keynesians actively ignored. (Or perhaps it was on his 'to do' list when he died at a relatively early age, at least relative to other famous economists.) Attempts to displace standard price theory after the war failed. (Machlup (1967) provides a useful retrospective of this battle. However, it should be noted that the Machlup article is clearly written from the victor's side of the conflict. Something not unlike a complementary counterpoint is provided by Freedman (1995).) These alternatives, seeking to contribute a sensible coupling for Keynesian theory, was successfully resisted by the more conservative elements of the profession, including eminent members of the Chicago School. The unresolved disparity caused by this post war, theoretical mix and match approach would provide anti-Keynesians with a powerful micro-foundations lever. In fact it would prove sufficient to overturn the prevailing macroeconomic paradigm as the 1980s neared.

86   At least as far as Keynes is concerned, he was reversing the course of standard analysis. From his perspective, what he terms the classical school was fixated on the supply side of the economy. Within that narrow approach, the mechanics of a price adjusted labour and capital market was entirely constrained by the existing level of technology (the production function). Capacity determined output. The production of output in turn generated aggregate income with which the produced output could then be purchased. Consequently, insufficient aggregate demand was not an issue worthy of any serious discussion or investigation. Certainly in the short run, individual markets could face excess or deficient demand, but these ripples would be price adjusted over time. Resources would be efficiently shuttled between one market and the next according to shifts in market demand. Faced with this closed system, Keynes started his analysis by rejecting the formulation (or at least Keynes' sketch) of what is generally known as Says Law. (The exact nature of this supposed law remains a subject of debate.) Instead, Keynes posits that demand is not automatically or mechanically generated, but rests instead on unreliable expectations. Certainly Keynes' own formulation of this key relationship is spun in a rhetorically convenient fashion. This is to be expected. His aim is to demonstrate that the hitherto preoccupation with aggregate supply yields a rather limited level of analysis, one that only holds under a set of very constrained assumptions. But doing so, does supply Keynes with a powerful wedge. Through its strategic use, he would be able to redirect professional attention toward the more precarious task of restating the essential role performed by an expectation riddled level of aggregate demand.

> Thus Say's law, that the aggregate demand price of output as a whole is equal to its aggregate supply price for all volumes of output, is equivalent to the proposition that there is no obstacle to full employment. If, however, this is not the true law relating the aggregate demand and supply functions, there is a vitally important chapter of economic theory which remains to be written and without which all discussions concerning the volume of aggregate employment are futile (Keynes 1964:26).

87   The real wage is simply defined as the nominal wage over the price level. If the real wage is equated to the marginal product of labour, then that factor is dependent on the level of employment.

88   A lengthy investigation by Akerlof, Dickens and Perry (1996) provides evidence that workers do in fact resist nominal wage cuts.

89   For Keynes, perfectly flexible wages created the possibility for deflationary spirals.

> If, on the contrary, money-wages were to fall without limit whenever there was a tendency for less than full employment, the asymmetry would, indeed,

> disappear. But in that case there would be no resting place below full employment until either the rate of interest was incapable of falling further or wages were zero. In fact we must have some factor, the value of which in terms of money, if not fixed, is at least sticky, to give us any stability of values in a monetary system (Keynes 1964:303–304).

90   Harold Demsetz, something of a protégé of George Stigler, certainly reflects this view. In doing so he represents not simply the Chicago standpoint, but that held by most of the profession.

> And so what you say, is certainly consistent with the way he [George Stigler] approached problems and I don't know how to think about problems in a non-equilibrium way either. I know there are people that do think about problems in that way, but I find it very powerful to have an equilibrium concept in mind when you are looking at these problems (Conversation with Harold Demsetz, October 1997).

91   In a letter, Roy Harrod warned Keynes against deviating from the world of price adjusted equilibrium markets.

> The effectiveness of your work … is diminished if you try to eradicate very deep-rooted habits of thought *unnecessarily.* One of these is the supply and demand analysis. I am not merely thinking of the aged and fossilised, but of the younger generation who have been thinking perhaps only for a few years but very hard about these topics. It is doing great violence to their fundamental groundwork of thought, if you tell them that two independent demand and supply functions won't jointly determine price and quantity. Tell them that there may be more than one solution. Tell them we don't know the supply function. Tell them that the *ceteris paribus* clause is inadmissible and that we can discover more important functional relationships governing price and quantity in this case which render the s. and d. analysis nugatory. But don't impugn that analysis itself (Harrod warning Keynes against his approach to the labour market, quoted in Chick 1983:132–133).

92   The continuing inability, or outright refusal, of economist to read carefully is taken up in Freedman 2008.

93   In the quantity adjusted world that Keynes constructs, flexible wages are a performance hindrance, rather than acting as the central source capable of insuring full employment.

> If, on the contrary, money-wages were to fall without limit whenever there was a tendency for less than full employment, the asymmetry would, indeed, disappear. But in that case there would be no resting place below full employment until either the rate of interest was incapable of falling further or wages were zero. In fact we must have some factor, the value of which in terms of money is, if not fixed, at least sticky, to give us any stability of values in a monetary system (Keynes 1964:303–304).

94   In the same way that Doyle's dog didn't bark (in the relevant Sherlock Holmes story), economists became easily fixated on the price (the wage) that didn't adjust. In this formulation, sticky wages could easily be shoved into a familiar pigeon-hole labelled 'market failure'. A systemic failure is transformed into a remediable glitch, using traditional wage theory as a poison apple which could effectively undermine Keynes' theoretical intent. By buttressing this style of theory renovation, the domestication of Keynes' revolutionary approach could proceed unhindered. Meanwhile, the import of Keynes' *General Theory* could then be successfully side-tracked.

95   Frank Knight at least attempted to resist the appeal of muddling theory with policies that were aimed at the observed economic world. As a Classical Liberal, he understood that the limited insights gleaned from theory (such as perfect competition) were not usefully reified into a portrait of how actual markets operate, especial in terms of all the inevitable transmutations that would occur over time.

> ... if we merely assume that all the "dynamic changes" ... are foreknown for a sufficient time before they take place, or that they take place continuously in accordance with laws generally and accurately known, so that their course may be predicted as far into the future as occasion may require, then the whole argument based on the effects of change will fall completely to the ground (Knight, 1971:35).

96   In his 1933 *Yale Review* paper on international trade, Keynes speaks favourably of gradual changes and the grit in the market wheels, which beneficially acts to slow down this vaunted adjustment process.

97   George Akerlof certainly recognised this key element of Keynes' theory and the way in which it had been distorted (Akerlof and Yellen 1987). Yet somehow, when convenient for unreeling a specific story, this reality could be not so much denied, as simply overlooked (Akerlof, Dickens and Perry 1996).

> *The General Theory* makes clear that money wage stickiness is not in Keynes' opinion the ultimate cause of involuntary unemployment; indeed, due to the adverse effect of falling prices on demand, involuntary unemployment might possibly be more severe in its absence ... What to Keynes was a minor assumption in a theory rationalizing business cycles is now interpreted as the key assumption (Akerlof and Yellen, 1987:137).

98   Keynes was clearly insightful enough to realise that employing market structures deviating from perfect competition would allow his analysis to be unfairly tied to the special case category. The aim was to construct a general theory, not one that only operated within a specific market organi-sation. Otherwise unemployment could be simply explained away by the

presence of market power rather than existing as fundamental to competitive capitalism.

99   For Keynes, sets of investment plans rested on whatever variable expectations happen to dominate a given economy. Unfortunately, such expectations are not simply matters of probabilistic calculations. Keynes insisted that investment rests on shaky foundations given the inherent uncertainty attached to such judgments. These decisions about the future, and the accompanying risk of monetary loss, needed to be made in the present although the relevant outcomes resided in the future. Moreover they by necessity had to be based only on at best a rough estimation of future events. Some of these key outcomes are fundamentally unknowable, at least in the Knightian sense of uninsurable risk.

> By 'uncertain' knowledge, let me explain. I do not mean merely to distinguish what is known for certain from what is only probable. The game of roulette is not subject in this sense to uncertainty; nor is the prospect of a Victory bond being drawn. Or, again, the expectation of life is only slightly uncertain. Even the weather is only moderately uncertain. The sense in which I am using the term is that in which the prospect of a European war is uncertain, or the price of copper and the rate of interest twenty years hence, or the obsolescence of a new invention, or the position of private wealth-owners in the social system in 1970. About these matters there is no scientific basis on which to form any calculable probability whatever. We simply do not know (Keynes 1937: 213–214).

100   Harking back to the chapter on Coase, a similar problem appears to have derailed anything approaching a full understanding of *The General Theory*. Namely, economists focused almost exclusively on the MacGuffin that helps propel *The General Theory* (perfectly competitive markets) rather than the intent underlying the book. In essence, readers clamped down heavily on whatever appeared to be the most recognisably familiar aspect of the theory, declaring this comfortable bit of rhetorical persuasion to comprise the entirety of the book itself. Consequently, the fundamental importance of quantity (rather than price) adjusted markets was consistently overlooked.

101   Self-identified Post Keynesians would later denounce what they categorized as the Neo-Keynesian Synthesis (an approach that dominated the first few decades of the post war period) as having betrayed the spirit of Keynes. This trespass was supposedly committed by transforming the ideas expressed in *The General Theory* into a variant of Neo-Classical thought. These supposedly erring economists might be best described as having been gulled (or accidently mislead) by the rhetoric that drove the theory. In this fashion, early promoters would be judged as being guilty of

overlooking Keynes' true intent and purpose. Even one of the progenitors of this neo-classical approach, John Hicks, would later see fit to denounce the more traditional approach he pioneered. He condemned such thinking for its failure to recognise Keynes' attempt to use a static framework to capture dynamic uncertainty. To signify his own transformation, he became John Hicks leaving the young J.R. behind.

102   As a reminder, no significant difference should be imagined to exist between the employment of the term 'poison apple' and the alternative formulation of 'Trojan Horse'. Unfortunately, some readers may become uneasy when faced by this unexplained switching between these two labels. However, with a sufficient dollop of imagination, any seriously troubled soul should be able to fabricate a sufficiently useful distinction between these terms, thus relieving any accumulated discomfort so generated. But in practice, I simply became somewhat tired of repeating the term 'poison apple' over and over again. 'Trojan Horse' works well enough as an appropriate substitute. In this fashion, Homer gets to rub shoulders with the Brothers Grimm, which makes for an interesting (and unanticipated) juxtaposition.

103   George Stigler launched a sustained 'take no prisoners' campaign to destroy the basis of monopolistic competition, much in the same way that weed killers attack the very root of the perceived problem. One aspect of his unrelenting strategy was the convenient construction of a poison apple, which he tirelessly offered to the less discriminating members of the profession. Namely, he presented a comfortable alternative theory, an approach which rescued traditional market structures from becoming victims of grand theoretical upheavals. Judging by the usual presentation of monopolistic competition in most textbooks, his efforts did not go entirely unrewarded. By labelling it as a deviation from perfect competition, due to some identified market imperfection, Stigler diverted attention away from Chamberlin's claim of having constructed a general basis for all and any dollops of micro-analysis. Keep in mind that poison apples are inevitably constructed with the sole intent of shifting professional interest elsewhere, particularly away from a posed (and controversial) question. The shiny poison apple provided by Stigler presented monopolistic competition as an equivalent, namely no more than an alternative to perfect competition, a classic false equivalence. This sleight of hand attempted to shift perception away from Chamberlin's intention whereby monopolistic competition encompassed perfect competition rather than vied with it on an equal footing.

> It cannot be overstressed that, although "imperfect" (monopolistic) competition has in fact come to be widely accepted as either more general than pure

> competition, and hence designed to replace it *in part*, it is none of this to Stigler. It merely refers to the "literally infinite number of possible deviations from perfect competition" … Far from being the explanation of those "departures from competition" which economists have discussed in recent times, consumer ignorance has played virtually no part at all in explaining them. Important as it may be, and especially in connection with the particular subject of advertising, it is a fact that by far the greater part of the literature on 'imperfect' and monopolistic competition has been written without reference to it, *and would remain intact under the assumption of perfect consumer knowledge*. Product differentiation is explained, not by consumer ignorance, but … by the conscious production of variety in response to the demand for it, a demand arising from the diversity of tastes and needs (Chamberlin 1947:416–418).

104   George Stigler honed in on Chamberlin's apostasy as he did with any challenge to the carefully re-enforced edifice defining Chicago price theory. At least he chose to take such an adversarial approach when faced with alternatives that fostered the potential of gaining a toehold of acceptance within the profession. In the discussion quoted above, Milton Friedman is referring to Stigler's attempt to completely eviscerate Chamberlin's theory. This effort composed one of the five lecture's he presented (in 1948), for the further edification and delectation of the notables assembled at the London School of Economics. The title of his fundamental attack betrays Stigler's intention. ("Monopolistic Competition in Retrospect" (Stigler, 1949b) conveys the idea of a forensic autopsy on a work long dead and no longer considered viable.) However Stigler, in this directed onslaught, also takes aim at the potentially explosive claim that the reality, or legitimacy, of assumptions germinated theoretical validation. In essence, economists might need to allow reality to creep into any professional analysis. Or specifically, such core theoretic assumptions as 'profit maximising' were clearly being seriously debated at the time of Stigler's presentations. His close friend, Milton Friedman, would later make this same combative approach entirely his own. Friedman struck by publishing his famous 1953 essay detailing a conveniently constructed rationale for Chicago style assertions. What might have seemed obvious (theories should not depend on a bogus foundation), is turned upside down. Friedman needed only to boldly claim that theories work 'as if' such assumptions were true to exile an ongoing controversy onto the very farthest of back burners.

> Often a theory is criticized or rejected because its assumptions are "unrealistic." Granting for a moment that this charge has meaning, it burdens theory with an additional function, that of description. This is a most unreasonable burden to place upon a theory: the role of description is to particularize, while the role of theory is to generalize – to disregard an infinite number of

differences and capture the important common element in different phenomena (Stigler 1949b:23).

105   Economists over time have been trained to substitute textbook versions of monopolistic competition in place of those proffered by Chamberlin himself. (A similar misapprehension can be observed with models of Paul Sweezy's 1939 kinked demand curve.) For instance, the standard tangency condition (between the demand and average cost curve), one that yields a unique equilibrium devoid of economic profit, exists only as a heuristic simplification in the actual theory proposed by Chamberlin. The purpose motivating this abstraction simply aims at highlighting the essential core relationships established within the model itself. Such a tangency relies, in Chamberlin's words, on a heroic assumption concerning both of those specified curves. In essence the model highlights the necessary conditions for such an equilibrium to hold.

> For the present, then, advertising as a competitive activity is put to one side, and attention confined to the two variables of price and 'product'. This may be done by proceeding explicitly on the assumption of given wants and perfect knowledge concerning the means available for satisfying them. We therefore proceed under the heroic assumption that both demand and cost curves for all the 'products' are uniform through the group (Chamberlin 1933:72–73).

Stripped of those heroic assumptions, the surety provided by a textbook unique equilibrium must inevitably vanish.

> It is the notion that monopolistic competition is concerned only with situations where the demand and cost curves are tangent, hence where there are no monopoly profits, whereas any situation where there are such profits is to be classed as a monopoly. A moment's reflection will show that this is an artificial distinction … It may perhaps be accounted for by the over-prominence given to this solution in my own statement of the theory. All that need be done here is to call attention to passages where it is made clear that the solution of tangency flows from certain heroic assumptions which are later dropped, and is to be regarded as of only limited direct applicability, being mainly an expositional device, which represent an intermediate state in the development of the theory (Chamberlin 1937:561).

106   By the 1980s, Chicago price theory seemed not only triumphant but unassailable. The Friedman/Stigler duo felt comfortable in not only dismissing monopolistic competition as long past its due date, but also in administering the final rites to John Maynard Keynes. On the publication of George Stigler's 4th edition of his Price Theory textbook, Friedman could (in a comment heavily laced with snark) congratulate his friend Stigler on his targeted editorial choices.

> I congratulate you on restraining yourself from including a picture of Keynes and even more on not even mentioning him in your index (Letter from Milton Friedman to George Stigler, December 16, 1986).

107   The Friedman/Stigler dismissal of monopolistic competition didn't necessarily mean that the theory would disappear simply by fiat, as even one of Stigler's colleagues and unabashed admirers, Harold Demsetz, was willing to concede.

> Now, there's been more recent work that I haven't followed on monopolistic competition that seems to be using it, but I'm not sure whether what I have just said would be refuted by this more recent work or not. *Because in fact in his autobiography George Stigler refers to monopolistic competition as dead and buried.*
> A bit premature.
> *Never pronounce a death sentence on anything.*
> No, no that's right (Conversation with Harold Demsetz, October 1997).

108   Claims of this sort, often favoured by those at Chicago, of being loyal and true believers, question the extent to which either one of these self-proclaimed adherents really understood Marshall's project. Certainly Friedman and Stigler saw themselves as defending the last redoubt of Marshallian economics at Chicago.

> If any single action led to the overthrow of the Marshallian system, it was Pigou's establishment of the equilibrium firm as the central instrument of analysis; for it was now a simple step (though not one taken by Pigou) to define an industry in equilibrium as a collection of equilibrium firms ... and this exaltation of the equilibrium firm was the work, not of a critic, but of a 'loyal but faithless' Marshallian. The phrase is D.H. Robertson's ... but it has to be admitted that Robertson was also faithless. In his criticism of Pigou's analysis of the welfare gains supposedly attainable by subsidizing industries which were subject to increasing returns, he had insisted that these returns were the results of time and progress of organization yet in the symposium which followed the publication of Sraffa's (1926) article, he accepted Pigou's definition of perfect competition as a correct (if uncomfortable) interpretation of Marshall's competition ... Mrs. Robinson would therefore have been entitled to claim that, if she took the wrong turning, the diversion signs were erected by Marshallians (Loasby 1989:76).

109   Those with finely-honed memories will recollect that this was the central theme of a previous chapter.

110   George Stigler subscribed to the methodological reality incorporated in this letter. He would later enthusiastically expand on this approach, aided by his close friend and colleague, Milton Friedman. Yet when convenient, such qualifications would lose their application. (Or to paraphrase Cole Porter,

'Stigler knows, anything goes.') As a result, iron clad dicta could be safely ignored whenever convenient. Instead, their importance became situational. For instance, Stigler's 1947 attack on Sweezy's (1939) kinked demand curve did occur prior to the methodological styled note received from Milton Friedman. Yet in that Sweezy-centric paper, which surreptitiously defended Chicago price theory (see Freedman 1995) against targeted attack, there resides a discordant section titled 'The Validity of the Assumption' (of a kinked demand curve) (Stigler 1953/1947: 423). Within that discussion, Stigler felt quite comfortable in deriding Sweezy's model (1953/1939) (while personally residing in a world where the assumptions of a theory never mattered) by concluding:

> On the other hand, here are seven industries in which the existence of the kinky demand curve is questionable – a list that is longer by seven than the list of industries for which a prima facie case has been made for the existence of the kink (Stigler 1953/1947:425).

However, if we are to adhere to the dictates of the Friedman/Stigler methodological code, none of that evidence matters a single jot. Consequently, the very fact that it departs sharply from reality should not serve as a barrier in verifying its worth as an assumption (except when Stigler deems that qualification necessary).

111   The Ptolemaic system, in practice, depends upon a dual system of poison apples. As stated, the first is the assertion that the sun appears to revolve around the earth. The second though insists that celestial bodies describe a circle when they revolve around a fixed point like the earth. The rationale for that case is that circles, being the most perfect of geometrical forms, would be the only possible path that God would choose for such observed heavenly bodies. (Though reading the mind of God always involves skating on the very thinnest of egotistical ice.) This second assumption can be easily dismissed, because faith in God implies an acknowledgement that not only is God's knowledge infinite, but also unknowable. (The Book of Job drives this insight home with what can only be designated as a heavenly sledge hammer.) Consequently, despite self-assured assertions, there are absolutely no irrefutable reasons for any observed celestial body to describe a circle in each of its revolutions. The implicit sleight of hand underlying this perspective is the need to turn (however unconsciously), what is no more than an assertion into something resembling a Euclidean common notion. The same motivation (deployed by exercising another sleight of hand) can be recognized in the insistence of categorising the Earth as the unmoving centre of the universe by appealing to some common sensation. (Again, in marketing a theory, the first step can sometimes consist of the creation of an enticing poison apple. Assert a seemingly obvious

observation, such as a geocentric world consisting of circular pathways. Tested only by the most superficial of examinations, assuming an insight into God's intentions, such statements appear unexceptional. Namely, God by definition is perfect and is associated with only all that is perfect in creating the world. Once swallowed, the subsequent theory building is more easily accepted.)

112   The fundamental problem with a project of 'saving the appearances' was pointed out (or should have been pointed out) by Schopenhauer. As a passing thought, he raised the question of what the appearances on Earth would be if we all agreed that the Earth was actually moving around the Sun. In other words, the notion that geo-centrism accorded with casual observation was basically an assertion. It was obvious only to those who insisted that it was obvious, or needed it to be so.

113   Some theories, far past their used by date, manage to impede any future progress by increasing the difficulty of nurturing new ideas and alternative theories. Often these germinating ideas are effectively sunk by a combination of objectives. One focuses on protecting any sunk costs that might be invested in a given idea. The other reflects a determination to suppress (if not eliminate) potential threats to a given ideology. Certainly theories should not be discarded at the same rate as used facial tissues. But if one's sunk cost investment is high and ideological proclivities are entrenched, then almost no conceivable evidence is capable of actuating a change in view. Rationalisations to shore up leaky foundations will always be found, a sort of entrenched form of epicycle building.

> That's right, given my investment, given what I've read over the years. When somebody tells me now that an increase in the minimum wage increases employment, there's just been a study out on that, I'm very skeptical of that claim. I don't believe it! (Conversation with Sherwin Rosen October 1997).

The relevant investment is not limited to the most obvious range of items. Certainly an academic isn't keen to radically revise his research or even his teaching notes (a certain status quo bias). But, in a process creating an even more formidable barrier, the required ideological adjustment can prove far too intractable. For instance, the response to the empirical evidence that seemed to question the negative effects of imposing a minimum wage generated a furious, and at times, vicious rebuttal. Work by David Card and Alan B. Krueger (1994:1995) on minimum wage policy drew pointed and negative responses (see for instance, Neumark and Wascher (2000)). The resulting animosity rose to such a level that Card became loathe to bear the brunt of the continuing controversy, especially given his perception that these heated exchanges largely missed the point of their work.

I've subsequently stayed away from the minimum wage literature for a number of reasons. First, it cost me a lot of friends. People that I had known for many years, for instance, some of the ones I met at my first job at the University of Chicago, became very angry or disappointed. They thought that in publishing our work we were being traitors to the cause of economics as a whole (Clement 2006:3).

Consequently the judgment that Paul Samuelson has ascribed to Max Plank seems far from an overstatement.

As the great Max Planck, himself the originator of the quantum theory in physics, has said, 'science makes progress funeral by funeral': the old are never converted by the new doctrines, they simply are replaced by a new generation (https://quoteinvestigator.com/2017/09/25/progress/).

114   Given Chicago's joy of pointing out unintended consequences, as well as the attendant ability to explode apparent market anomalies, at times the approach provided by this School, seems based on proving that everything that everyone thinks they know, is actually wrong.

115   When referring simply to an entity as 'Chicago', this label represents a lazy shorthand for the Chicago School of Economics. For these stalwarts, opposing economists (who were seemingly obsessed with hypothetical market failures and other pesky anomalies) were simply would be collectivists, or at least dangerous fellow travelers. Such would be theorists, either knowingly, or even unknowingly, were determined to undercut the market institutions that preserved freedom of choice and provided the joys of liberty as well. Only by opening one's vision (by allowing in the Chicago brand of sunshine) could the fog and uncertainty created by such wrong-headed opponents possibly be dispelled. The disinfectant power of Chicago's insights may today seem to border on the clichéd or the over-weening. Namely, the extent to which there actually was an intense focus on openness and transparency at Chicago can always be questioned. The idea of sunshine being the best disinfectant might have depended too heavily on a particular, designated brand of that cleansing agent, rather than an all-purpose detergent. (In fact this idea of throwing light on the darkest of issues, is widely attributed to Justice Louis Brandeis whose objective in this instance seems admirable. He is reputed to have committed this sentiment to print in the form that would become his most famous statement "sunlight is said to be the best of disinfectants". The source would appear to be a 1913 Harper's Weekly article, entitled "What Publicity Can Do.") In practice, there is nothing defunct or out of date with shining light on a problem to uncover vested interests or misplaced incentives. The problem Chicago continued (and sometimes failed), to face was in thinking they held the patent to the only available working light source.

116   Both Milton Friedman and his close colleague George Stigler insisted that their theories, based on rational decision making, didn't just explain some reasonably high percentage of observed results. From their perspective, if only examined more closely, if the data was only to be sufficiently bludgeoned with the right rubber hose, any empirical observations would, in their view, always yield and submit to the undeniable force of rationality, as being their sole and proper progenitor.

> It's getting more and more, more and more part of him as he got older actually, this whole view. He [George Stigler] insists it's rational. He would tell you, 'There is some rational explanation for it. It's just that you haven't looked completely into it and found it (Conversation with Sam Peltzman, October 2020).

117   In essence, without a good spoonful of sugar, some more skeptical economists will find that this assumption sticks in their craws (or perhaps claws). The motivating idea of a poison apple strategy is to quite casually slip an idea through critical defenses. Pushing through controversial theories is best accomplished by ultimately disguising them. Advertising theories as highly controversial tends to put up everyone's hackles (wherever these may be located). Consequently, these less than palatable ideas and theories are instead presented in a fashion that allows the substance they contain to appear in a more acceptable guise. Such controversial assumptions have to be marketed in such a way that adverse reactions are not instantly and dangerously tripped.

118   Allen Wallis, the third of the three Chicago musketeers (Friedman, Stigler and Wallis) taught Armen Alchian statistics at Stanford. Whether Wallis acted as something of a conduit that helped bring Alchian to the attention of Stigler and Friedman is not easily determined. In any case, Stigler and Friedman greatly admired this early work by Alchian (1977/1950). Alchian, if anything, was willing to push the idea of the role played by markets even further than Stigler dared. (Alchian somehow managed to be "more Catholic than the Pope" – Conversation with Paul Samuelson, November 1997). He remained the rare individual who proved capable of taking George Stigler to task for failing to be sufficiently market oriented.

> But I do admit to an inability to detect the "moral responsibility to society" that you attribute to a university. I also admit to no privileged position for a shoe producer, a butcher or an advertising agency. The university has a product to sell. I care not if some of these universities propose to suppress certain ideas of their employees (who can go elsewhere) nor if the university has an ax to grind. I care not so long as the university is not a monolithic monopoly of the state – as it threatens to be. The access to the market for education, truth, falsity, shoes, was, and what you will is what gives truth a chance to

survive. Nor is it necessary – not even desirable possibly? – that truth be the goal of the agents that get it revealed. Your position strikes me as perilously close to advice to a paternalist agency. On the same grounds I see no reason to expect newspapers to have a responsibility to be honest. Let them lie as they will. I rely on access of others to expose the lie and to cater to the public's desire for truth – to whatever extent the public and individuals wish it (Letter from Armen Alchian to George Stigler, March 25, 1967).

In much more recent days, Alchian's assertion that 'the truth will out', has been sorely tested. His claim that the public has any clear desire for truth is debatable given a burgeoning market for conspiracy theories, plus the anti-scientific slant of much of the popular content on social media sites. The tendency of people to accept statements congruent with their pre-existing ideas and emotions, shouldn't be underestimated. Alchian, quite naturally, could not have anticipated the current strain of competition that prevails within the marketplace for ideas. But, even back in the 1960s, his fundamentalist belief in the sanctity of markets was more than a bit exaggerated, a true form of over-indulgence. The unyielding 'a market is a market is a market' perspective tends to muddle crucial differences between the wide variations that define existing markets.

119   Stigler (1982) considered this particular phenomenon in a short, but interesting piece, using Robert Merton's work on multiple discoveries as a useful jumping off point to mull over this issue.

> But there is only one reason why full multiples – completed and tested – should occur and that is incomplete knowledge of who is working on a problem and what his achievement will be. The better the information network of a science, the fewer will be true multiples that are separated by a significant period of time (Stigler 1982: 102–103).

120   In other words, in order to validate the assumption of profit maximisation, blue ribbons are doled out to the winners based solely on results. As Alchian (1977/1950) points out succinctly, "Success is based on results not motivation (1977/1950:19). Quite pointedly, this statement implies that the process by which the ends are achieved matter little, if at all. To underline the centrality of this hypothesis, Alchian pushes this idea to its extreme. He does so by examining the result of a competitive market process, if the decisions made by its participants were strictly random. (The result, for instance of flipping a coin.) The observed result under these circumstances would not vary. Successful firms would still be those that boasted the best results. Firms would appear to be profit maximising even when dependent on random events (the flip of a coin).

> For example, at a horse race with enough bettors wagering strictly at random, someone will win on all eight races. Thus individual random behaviour does

not eliminate the likelihood of observing "appropriate decisions" (Alchian 1977/1950:24).

By getting the desired result even in the context of an extreme assumption (random decision making), what consequently must be the case is that the appearance of profit maximisation must also follow when managerial decisions are much more definitive. By accepting the seemingly axiomatic statement, which insists that success is based on results, the 'as if' importance of accepting profit maximisation becomes self-evident. By offering a seemingly obvious definition as a basis for analysis, Alchian cleverly structures his poison apple strategy.

Moreover, the underlying perspective Alchian employs conveniently focuses on analysing outcomes of the classic 'representative firm'.

> A "representative firm" is not typical of any one producer but, instead, is a set of statistics summarizing the various "modal" characteristics of the population. Surely, this was an intended use of Marshall's "representative firm" (Alchian 1977/1950: 26).

In this world of economic analysis, the fate or actions of individual firms over time never comes to the attention of the 'representative economist'. Thus the reality of assumptions employed when applied to a 'representative firm' is essentially a moot question. The point of embracing the 'as if' formulation is that such methodological issues become largely, if not entirely, meaningless.

121 To construct a logical argument, Alchian muddles the passive nature of natural selection with that of firms competing in a market. The key error is to forget that firms do not passively accept their economic environment in the same fashion that species can simply be well matched to their natural environment. Firms (and humans) attempt to both change that environment (and change themselves) in conducive ways and manners. The fundamental error is to somehow fail to distinguish the inherent passive and active aspects of this process.

122 The 'as if' strategy effectively stymies evidence presented by Hall and Hitch (1939) which directly undercuts the profit maximising assumption, rendering it unrealistic. But as stated, if firms when tested, act 'as if' they maximised profits, any evidence similar to that provided by Hall and Hitch becomes simply irrelevant. In essence Alchian's approach runs parallel to that of both Stigler (1948) and Friedman (1953). Small wonder that both these rising young economists (using the term 'young' loosely) were enthusiastic about Alchian's effort.

123 By describing the outcome as representing 'the survival of the fittest', the status of those holdovers forcibly becomes (to an extent) glorified. More exactly, the result could be better described as survival of those who fit. In

Darwinian terms, different environments are not ranked (lacking any basis to do so). Therefore, happening to fit a prevailing environment displays no sense of superiority.

124 What cannot be repeated too frequently is that price theory deals with statistically representative firms, not anything resembling an actual organisation. Inner workings (as is the case with consumers) of such hypothetical creatures lack any weight or importance as far as recording the actual outcomes. The observed results are what justify the 'as if' aspect of the ad hoc assumptions.

125 For those readers whose Snow White eschatology runs no deeper than Disney animated revelations, the apple proffered by the Evil Queen (and failed step-mother) has only one of its sides poisoned. The Queen disguised as an old crone bites into the safe side of the apple convincing the naïve and unreflective Snow White that the apple is completely safe. Ms White commits this clear faux pas despite the same disguised (or deranged) Queen having already made two previous attempts on Snow White's life. This is to say nothing of the fact that she had twice been taken to task by all seven dwarves for succumbing to the Queen's obvious ruses. When indulging in this bit of gullibility, Snow White too closely resembles those (less than perspicacious economists), who perpetrate rather alarmingly naïve reading habits.

126 The inexorable path leading to Alchian's foreordained conclusion is further greased by mixing in a sufficient amount of assumed observables, which make the poison apple even more tempting. Consequently, Alchian, when possible, doubles down on his parallels between Darwinian evolution and market competition. Not only is a mention of Marshall's representative firm explicitly summoned from its previous gravesite, but there is an implicit reference to Marshall's suggestion that biological dynamics offers the best analogy to economics.

127 In their influential paper, among the most cited of any published economics article, Alchian in collaboration with Harold Demsetz (1972) employs a similar strategy. Namely, an assumption is simply asserted with a key term left undefined. By presenting a doubtful conjecture in the same terms as a Euclidean common notion, the trap is successfully baited. (In no sense is it possible to conclude that such a strategy is deliberate. Every bit of available evidence stubbornly concludes that these authors believed such an assumption was too obvious to dispute.) However, the path provided by the authors is smoothed only in one direction. (Alternative routes would require a machete to clear.) The hook embedded in the innocent appearing bait of the proffered apple in this case, is fashioned so that once swallowed, the path to their preferred conclusion becomes almost irresistible. (The unacknowledged sense is one of being pulled along by a conveyor belt or a tractor

beam.) The attractive yank of the argument is due to the core assertion within that proffered bait. The bold claim made is that any standard labour contract inevitably reflects an absence of anything resembling economic power that could be potentially exercised by the employing party. Consequently, both employer and employee are equally capable of breaking the existing contract and simply departing without occurring a substantive opportunity cost.

Therefore, by definition (or courtesy of the Alchian and Demsetz' logic) neither employer nor employee can exercise any power. To underline their position (the key poison apple introducing their argument) the authors proceed to compare the labour contract to a shopper's decision to buy a can of tuna fish. According to this analogy, just as neither customer nor grocer can exert economic power over one another, neither can employer or employee. The intrinsic problem in this seemingly innocent example begins with its failure to define what economic power specifically means. This fundamental absence is followed by a skillful avoidance of any discussion involving the relevant opportunity costs involved in the ending of an employment contract. For there to be no possibility of one party to a contract having more influence (power) than the other (an absence of leverage), the opportunity cost of ending that contract has to be equal for both parties. This equality is unfortunately simply asserted by the authors. The inconclusive tuna fish analogy is all they apparently have to offer. Instead, they boldly avoid specifying the nature of this unlikely condition (equal opportunity costs), or bothering to present any grounds for its existence, at least in the case of labour contracts. (The problem may be that such an assertion, no matter how confidently asserted, when scrutinized by employing available empirical observations, would at best only generate sincere doubts.) Nor does it seem credible that entering into the 'as if' territory of Milton Friedman could possibly provide any necessary validation that might create cover for this claim. As in his prior work (1950/1977), Alchian is once again involved in transforming an assertion into a common notion for the convenience of his argument (or more precisely the claim subscribed to by both Alchian and Demsetz).

> Telling an employee to type this letter rather than to file that document is like my telling a grocer to sell me this brand of tuna rather than that brand of bread. I have no contract to purchase from the grocer and neither the employer nor the employee is bound by any contractual obligations to continue their relationship. Long-term contracts between employer and employee are not the essence of the organization we call a firm. My grocer can count on my returning day after day and purchasing his services and goods even with the prices not always marked on the goods – because I know what they are – and he adapts his activity to conform to my directions to him as to what I want each day … he is not my employee (Alchian and Demsetz 1972:777).

In essence, what is presented as a paper explaining the origin and organisational shape of the representative firm, is actually a dogged defence of free enterprise markets (or more specifically, an implicit exaltation of private property). The firm in itself then becomes no more than an optimal internal market system, since it proves capable of nurturing superior information flows. This strategy (seeming to examine the nature of capitalist firms while actually defending private property) necessarily lies at the heart of this specific poison apple rhetorical approach. By diverting attention from the ulterior purpose behind employing such a simplistic starting point, the authors in this case create a far more palatable mouthful to swallow. Given that the Alchian and Demsetz paper was written at a time when capitalism, markets and standard economics were being widely challenged, meeting such opposition through misdirection would appear to be far more strategic than meeting those very same challenges in a head-on confrontation. Consequently, the end result of Alchian and Demsetz' journey marches the reader to the only pre-determined conclusion possible. As shaped by the authors, their defined free enterprise markets are necessarily not only efficient, but must also be entirely equitable. Such a conclusion largely takes the wind out of any collectivist criticism.

128   The argument pursued (in a rather roundabout fashion), throughout the remaining pages is largely focused on Milton Friedman's methodological creation (a work which was also built on the efforts of George Stigler). The conclusion presented, after exploring possible motivations for delving into this area, is that neither individual was particularly mesmerized by methodological issues. Instead, methodology offered something of a convenient poison apple that if accepted to some degree by the profession, or at least taken seriously, could help to undermine the idea that the reality of economic assumptions has consequences. Unfortunately in these closing pages, those who are not overly familiar with the approaches commonly adopted in exploring the History of Economic Thought might be expecting the obviousness of a smoking gun, or the bluntness of a suicide note, to support such a contentious claim. The idea that documents of this precise category exist, or are entirely capable of being magicked up to satisfy all and any Doubting Thomases, remains stubbornly ingenuous. Imagining that such a strategy was consciously explicit in the minds of these Chicago collaborators also requires a major leap of wishful thinking. (Although strictly speaking, Stigler was physically, though not spiritually, at Columbia during the relevant period.) That there would be some sort of convenient written, or even oral, record where Friedman and Stigler were carefully examining options to curtail the curse of collectivism seems absurd. (Those explanations are best left to conspiracy aficionados.)

Undeniably, Friedman and Stigler both saw themselves as rigorous scientific thinkers, rather than as ideological strategists. However, what we do know is that they both haboured an intense focus, if not an obsessive concentration, on torpedoing whatever might be considered as offering a serious threat to the legitimacy of Chicago style price theory. (Each one considered this framework as providing the only reliable firewall against those eager to expand government interference into the economy.) Consequently, their obsession with burgeoning collectivist threats should by now be sufficiently established as something of an underground stream nurturing their critical attacks on alternative economic theories. Given this context, their sudden interest, and even fixation, with methodology is best seen as growing out of these deeper concerns. Otherwise, a random and inexplicable fancy for outré explorations must be randomly posited. In essence, for no clear or discernible reason, the duo of Stigler and Friedman, arch enemies of collectivism, somehow, almost randomly, find themselves captured by a debate that is entirely unrelated to their chief concerns.

Such a peculiar stance would be required to support this particularly whimsical idea (a sudden and intense interest in methodology). Like a virus, academic focus could just magically flare up. Accepting this premise, would simply deliberately ignore the consistent opposition that both economists seemed to nurture to views encompassing monopolistic competition, as well as other alternative theories. Somehow, the implied supposition is that mysteriously, a sudden, insatiable interest in methodology dominated their academic labours. However, the resulting focus was at the same time entirely unrelated to their continuing battle against a perceived onslaught of heterodox alternatives. This conclusion would need to somehow hold, despite the duo commonly deeming all such theories as being virtual floodgates. These heterodox theories, in practice, allowed collectivism the necessary thin edge of the wedge which could not help but breed ever greater government intervention. In other words, it is well documented that Friedman and Stigler already had repeatedly taken aim against such theories that dared to persistently champion more realistic, core assumptions.

In an important sense then, we can choose either to assume a reasonable degree of coherence in their published work, or conclude that their attempt at methodology can, or even should, be dismissed as something of an inexplicable will-of-the-wisp. (Here, we need to be willing to explain their sudden shift of attention to something equivalent to a Scrooge-like bit of indigestion. "You may be an undigested bit of beef, a blot of mustard, a crumb of cheese, a fragment of an underdone potato" (Dickens 1946:28).) Moreover, after Friedman's published effort (1953), neither one ever evinced the slightest interest in ongoing methodological debates. They acted 'as if' in this one peculiar case, all doubts had been entirely eliminated. Either we need to locate and give full credence to an explanation which would be consistent with their life's work, or we desperately expose ourselves as willing to cling on to whatever deus-ex-machina might lend credibility to this curious methodological excursion on their part.

129   When I see tactics like this employed, I am for some reason reminded of a 1970s satirical group that performed as The Firesign Theatre. In 1974 they put out an album that sported the intriguing title, *Everything You Think You Know Is Wrong*. In a rather uncomfortable fashion, that phrase perfectly sums up, at least at times, the approach pursued by Stigler and Friedman. This characterisation particularly applies to their one foray into the unfathomable swamps created by prescriptive methodology.

130   The problem posed here is the use of a false equivalence, which as a sub-species of argument acts as a subset defining the poison apple category. To persuade a reader to swallow a dubious proposition, an attempt is made to equate that desired conclusion with some convenient assertion that sports a much more impregnable (an even unshakeable) foundation. Thus natural selection (and its populist trope of 'survival of the fittest') is equated to market competition. If Alchian can convince his audience to accept this particular sleight of hand, chomping away at the rest of the apple is rendered much simpler. Firms are set up to act as passive responders to market signals, whether they are aware of such a reality or not. Only those firms that successfully maximize profits will survive. Consequently, what can only be observed over the long run are profit maximizing firms, since by definition, all other firms have failed to survive. What must follow is that all firms behave as if they were consciously maximizing profits without needing to be explicitly aware of doing so. This, in the Alchian/Friedman view, is no different than leaves on plants and trees behaving as if they consciously and continually sought rays of sunlight. In this fashion, a dubious assertion can be accepted by splicing it to a much more robust proposition using fundamental horticultural principles. The perfect poison apple, in this fashion is grafted and formed.

131   Alchian confidently used the trope of plants growing toward the sunlight, not because of some conscious desire on their part, or some unalienable attempt to optimize a given environment, but because of a natural selection process that provides survival conditions. (The parallel equivalent is then constructed between natural selection and market competition.) Curiously, the same biological metaphor appeared two years later in Friedman's 1953 methodological attempt. Given that he had read Alchian's earlier 1950 effort, the influence displayed between the two papers can hardly be discounted.

> Consider, first, the simplest type of biological evolution. Plants "grow" to the sunny side of buildings not because they "want to" in awareness of the fact

> that optimum or better conditions prevail there, but rather because the leaves that happen to have more sunlight grow faster and their feeding systems become stronger (Alchian 1977:21).

132 Edith Penrose (1959), who wrote a potentially seminal, but largely ignored, volume on management and the firm, strenuously objected (Penrose 1952) to Alchian's acrobatic leaps in defense of price theory.

133 The essence here is that to an observer, firms may appear 'as if' they were actively seeking to maximise profits, but in reality, such firms are only responding passively to market forces. The illusion, according to Alchian, is due to the fact that only those that succeed in maximising profits survive.

134 Though recent research indicates that plants respond to sound and even communicate with one another. Perhaps even the fabricated plants in Alchian's 'as if' stories may possess a consciousness that Alchian failed to consider.

135 To be more exact, firms make contractual promises to a given set of constituent parties. These can only be met by generating a sufficient flow of cash, or by extending their borrowing requirements. Meeting such contractual responsibilities allows firms to re-contract for another productive cycle. Consequently, any continual failure to generate sufficient funds over time eventually leads to an inability to meet necessary re-contracted responsibilities. The term 'profits' in Alchian's case, is simply a method of referring to sufficient levels of cash flow.

136 Alchian was even emboldened to dredge out his version of the Marshallian representative firm. This construction, which again could support his hypothetical argument, would require the reader to take a definitive bite out of the proffered poison apple. The initial hard swallow provided by the fruit would leave such an individual bereft of the ability, and too far gone, to still sport a pair of critical examination lenses. An average or representative firm would mean that a collection of such identical firms would be able to yield the same outcome as that which is in fact observable. But here an analyst faces the problem of which group of actual firms to include when circumscribing a given, as opposed to a theoretical, market. Curiously enough, Stigler (1949b) had already mercilessly derided Chamberlin for making something of a parallel assumption in his construct of monopolistically competitive markets.

> This may be characterized by the "representative firm," a purely statistical concept – a vector of "averages," one dimension for each of the several qualities of the population of firms. A "representative firm" is not typical of any one producer but, instead, is a set of statistics summarizing the various "modal" characteristics of the population. Surely, this was an intended use of Marshall's "representative firm" (Alchian 1977:26).

137   In Alchian's theoretical geography, even innovation is downgraded to conform to the curvatures of his objectives. In his retelling of evolutionary transformations, survivors gain imitators. Fortunately, some firms will fail in their attempts to precisely imitate such survivors. These apparent failures are analogous to natural mutations, at least in the logical landscape drawn by Alchian's brushstrokes. Inadvertently, only a portion of these will by accident earn positive profits and survive. Once again, managerial direction of firms is largely illusory (an 'as if'), at least at the deeper levels of insight and cognition, where price theorists abide and actively thrive. 'As if' thinking is not only rescued from this perspective, but achieves a certain apotheosis. Those who obsess on issues of underlying reality, according to this account, are consigned to the limited satisfaction of superficial dogpaddling on the surface of an infinitely deep theoretical ocean. The conscious designs of agents are logically deemed irrelevant since upon any further application of analysis, firms are judged to simply perform 'as if' they were actively guided by the dictates of Chicago style price theory. Only such thinking effectively pierces the veil of appearances.

138   Again, once a reader accepts Alchian's all-encompassing vision of market competition, what relevant agents need to know operationally narrows substantially. In this case, his carefully constructed poison apple (once swallowed) manages to shift the terms of debate onto more copacetic terrain.

139   Once you break away from having a need for believable or empirically based assumptions, recognizing uncertainty, as an actual issue, provides only unnecessary complications when constructing analytical models. Inviting in theoretical demons, makes the modelling exercises less tractable. If demonstrated as providing negligible gains, then the engaged pains remain largely unrewarded. At least that lesson becomes ingrained in economic thinking if Friedman's poison apple is appropriately digested.

> *Milton Friedman*: I believe that it uses a false theory of probability. I believe that the only theory of probability that can hold water is personal probability, the kind of thing that Jimmy Savage (1948) helped develop. If you take that approach, you can't distinguish uncertainty from risk. There's no break point. But also, you see, it means that Knight implicitly was working on a definition of probability as a relative frequency. And that misleads people into thinking that there are objective probabilities that you can know. Therefore it leads to a distinction between risk and uncertainty in terms of costs. Knight assumes you know some probabilities and that there's no way you can know others. In a personal probability sense, nobody really knows any probability. There are no objective probabilities. Well, if I can experiment with your willingness to bet, I can determine your probabilities. There's going to be a war next year. Knight would say that's uncertainty. But in principle, if I can experiment with you, I can find out at what odds you are willing to take a bet that there will be a war next year. And thus I can extract your subjective probability of there

being a war and in that sense there's no distinction between risk and uncertainty. At any moment of time, you will in principle have subjective probabilities of any strategic event. I think it is a dead end. It's received a lot of attention and a lot of people talk about it. But I think it is very, very hard to make a logical distinction. Where does uncertainty begin and where does probability end, risk end? How happy do you think Knight was about that distinction?

Aaron Director: I don't know. I thought he drew his distinction from the fact that you can insure one and you couldn't insure the other. Period (Conversation with Milton Friedman, Rose Friedman and Aaron Director. August 1997).

140   To be perfectly fair, from the fifties through the seventies, the very mission of the Chicago School of Economics might be reduced to one of saving the appearances, much like the task afforded to those geocentric astronomers. The hidden assumption being that appearance was consistently (and coincidentally) a close match to the Chicago perspective. This goal, at least, seemed to require defending the essential centrality and validity of price theory in all aspects of economic analytics.

141   Becker's 1991 article basically confirms the thrust of Friedman's 1953 methodological essay. Reconfirmed is the set of belief structures defining the Chicago School. These ideologically tainted tenets had remained relatively unscathed for almost four decades.

142   I was fascinated during this exchange by the total lack of interest Gary Becker displayed in any explanation I might be able to offer that could sufficiently explain his stylised case of restaurant behaviour. (Perhaps a hint of a peculiar Chicago fault. Once a puzzle is solved, subsequent interest vanishes.) I, of course, only had empirical observations and experience to offer, having worked five years in the industry. However, from the Chicago perspective, my potential contribution could be easily dismissed as offering mere anecdotal evidence. My specific knowledge could only be seen as negligible when compared to an abstract theoretic framework uncovered by the foremost authority on pricing behaviour. Becker had clearly revealed exactly how markets are forced to operate in this (and other) instances by providing a universal (and generalizable) structure that could potentially be widely applied. Moreover, he did so in an impressively clever fashion. (Within the profession, cleverness carries more weight than is explicitly acknowledged.) I myself could make no such competing claims. However, my explanation did provide the advantage of simplicity, and if the legwork was undertaken, at least a limited universality, one that is steeped in basic economics. My alternative to Becker unfortunately could not be extended beyond the boundaries posed by restaurants.

Nonetheless, my less sophisticated alternative was soundly based on profit seeking, or more specifically, the benefit to be gained from increasing the marginal profitability of individual customers. In essence, many restaurant goers who wait for an hour or more before being seated, will indulge in a round or two of drinks at the bar or in the provided lounge. Well trained staff will clearly suggest that convenient possibility. (Becker wrote his article and I worked prior to the focus on drink driving and the attached legal liability.) The price mark-up for alcohol far exceeds that for food. Selling drinks is where restaurants most easily make their profit. Moreover, consumed alcohol impairs judgment. Arriving at their table after a lengthy wait, hungry customers will often order far more items, especially if subtly nudged by a waiter. Consequently, compelling reasons existed for any restaurant not to discourage customers from waiting for a table. Raising food prices might solve the supposed overflow problem. But my contention is that restaurants do not view such circumstances as a problem to be solved.

Nonetheless, my strictly restaurant based explanation doesn't discount Becker's far more original and complex response. But at the same time, my simpler explanation can't be completely swept off the board. The fact that all but the dullest of restaurant managers would be quite cognizant of this strategy doesn't automatically void its validity. If sufficient evidence (judged my version as operative) exists, then perhaps managers are not entirely unaware of how their particular market functions. (Straining our imaginations, they my even understand their own specific markets better than an academic economist can.) If so, managers would regain something of an active problem solving status even if they would continue to lack the sophistication of Chicago style training in the intricacies of price theory. It is not inconceivable that though elegant, Becker's solution is arbitrarily imposed on, rather than representative of, restaurant pricing regimes. It might even be valid, that despite developing piercing insights into abstract pricing structures, Nobel Prize winning economists would still be basically incapable of running a successful restaurant.

143   The justified temptation when examining such articles is to become aware of this convention, namely the willingness to tether an abstract theory to a simple empirical observation. This strategy could be easily discerned as composing yet another devised Chicago style poison apple. 'As if' assumptions regarding market prices are endowed with at least a flavour of reality when they are understood as having their origin in the mundane reality of everyday life.

144   In this article, Becker (1991) crafts the epitome of a cleverly constructed poison apple. Readers are drawn in by his immediate posing of a seemingly inscrutable problem. Pricing observations in the case cited seem to defy standard demand and supply theory. The appearances are saved with the assistance of a complex pricing model that not only predicts the specific case observed, but one that can be generalised much more widely to cover

other seeming anomalies. (By appearances is meant strictly the way in which the denizens of Chicago view markets.) But this was a method that in some ways defined the Chicago School of this era. Certainly, George Stigler, Becker's close friend and colleague was a fierce proponent of this approach.

> He [George Stigler] was interested, I would say primarily, in a particular sort of puzzle and it's a typical Chicago puzzle. And I don't mean that in any bad way, it's the sort of puzzle that the Chicago School's presuppositions require. Show me an apparent anomaly, something that does not seem to be explicable using the Smithian apparatus or the Marshalian apparatus and I will show you that it can be explained that way (Conversation with Robert Solow, October 1997).

But something of a Chicago style sleight of hand is also performed. Readers unconsciously swallow a set of core assumptions hidden within this polished poison apple. Namely that markets operate as if economic agents followed a set of prescribed theoretic prescripts. The core assumption is that economic agents simply respond to market dictated prices. As such, at least in economic terms, they are passive nonentities. In essence, the goals or strategies consciously devised and recognised by these agents are essentially nugatory. Thus, after enjoying a convoluted journey devised by Gary Becker's logic, we arrive back at a methodological 'as if' paradise. Again coincidentally, the very one charted by Friedman in his 1953 attempt to construct an effective, methodological dead end to economic reasoning. However, the apple Becker's provides is so tempting that readers are unlikely to recognise the assumptions that they so carelessly swallow during their rhetorical travels. Moreover, no handsome prince is likely to provide the kiss that lifts the imposed spell, after the apple is pre-emptily consumed. (Though in the Brothers Grimm version, it is the careless shifting of Snow White's glass coffin by royal servants that effectively dislodges the apple.) In essence, nothing perceivable in Becker's story, can prove capable of taking these readers out of this induced ideological swoon.

145 A reasonable assumption to make is that those who would argue that a case by case examination fails to define the core of Coase's work, would likely also be those who have not bothered to read Coase with any care. Such readers have simply lumped Coase together with their understanding of the Chicago School. This perspective is elucidated in a delightfully lengthy presentation that serves as this volume's first case study. Coase's distinctly idiosyncratic analytic approach is why it is accurate to conclude that though Coase was at Chicago, he was not necessarily of Chicago.

146 Many readers may find this claim hard to swallow, given the seeming enthusiasm of Friedman and Stigler for employing quantitative methods in

their research. Both insisted that any proposed theory must be tested before it could be granted any level of validity. Evidence, not ideology, was solely decisive. Such faith in quantitative methods became a point of faith within the Chicago School itself. Yet testing was limited to only highly generalised theories with data which was incapable of speaking for itself. (Data has a well-earned reputation for being inconveniently mute.) As Ronald Coase remarked about George Stigler, the lingering suspicion remained that these practitioners employed quantitative methods as simply a form of rhetorical persuasion.

> But he [George Stigler] certainly was a professed believer in quantitative methods. On the other hand, he knew what the answer was going to be in advance. He just regarded it, then, as a way of persuading other people (Conversation with Ronald Coase, October 1997).

147 Steadfastly believing that one's own insight into how the world works remained irrefutable, was never a trait limited to the post war stalwarts at Chicago. Unfortunately, though possessing some of the sharpest minds in economics, both Friedman and Stigler were adamant in their unswerving belief in market efficiency. That faith was embedded to such an immovable degree that it is difficult to imagine the type of evidence that could raise the slightest doubt in either one of their minds.

> You have probably observed this kind of thing. People take particular stands early in their career and they're steadfast, I have to admit that. They are not wishy-washy. No amount of empirical evidence will persuade them to change to a different point of view. Would there be some evidence that would have persuaded George on this? I'm not sure. He believed, he really believed that prices responded to short-run market demand. Was there any evidence that would have caused George not to believe that prices responded to short-run market demand? I can't help you on this. I don't have any reason to believe that he did believe there was any evidence for that (Conversation with James Kindahl, October 1997).

148 In this regard Friedman, as well as Stigler, depart sharply from their once revered teacher, Frank Knight. "But he [Stigler] came to feel that Knight was flawed … and that was my opinion, independent of Stigler." (Conversation with Gary Becker, October 1997). Knight persistently recognised the limitations of pure theory rather than simply promoting its broad applicability. But professed sceptics don't often claim to be perfectly conversant with the inner workings of the world, as some of his students seemed eager to do once their careers blossomed.

> The theorist not having definite assumptions clearly in mind in working out the "principles," it is but natural that he, and still more the practical workers building upon his foundations should forget that unreal assumptions were

made, and should not take the principles over bodily, apply them to concrete cases, and draw sweeping conclusions from them. The clearly untenable and often vicious character of such deductions naturally works to discredit theory itself (Knight: 1971 11).

Essentially Friedman and Stigler broke from Knight by taking an unacknowledged Hegelian turn of mind where the idea was transmuted into the real. Rational decision making, or the parallel version of profit maximising, was in this perspective more than a heuristic assumption that could operate as a useful theoretical tool. Somehow, such assumptions (in their 'as if' universe) came to resemble and reflect reality. The difference in stance from Knight becomes difficult to dispute.

> ... in the present writer's judgement, theorists of the past and present are to be justly criticized not for following the theoretical method and studying a simplified and idealized form of competitive organization, but for not following it in a sufficiently self-conscious critical, and explicit way (Knight 1971:10).

149   Friedman takes a very different approach to liberty than someone like Hayek, and perhaps even more so than other Austrian School economists. For Hayek, liberty is required given the ineradicable uncertainty defining the environment economic agents inhabited. (Hayek's (1945) article is well worth a look. To grasp this implied difference, help is provided by distinguishing between the more Austrian perspective and that defining the strictly Chicago view.) The unknown, for the Austrian coterie, is what creates opportunity for entrepreneurs and provides a certain stability to a market system. For Friedman, as indicated previously, this sort of fundamental uncertainty, emphasised by such disparate figures as Knight and Keynes, was simply mistaken. This proposed concept was entirely contravened by the indisputable work of Friedman and Savage (1948).

> I believe that the only theory of probability that can hold water is personal probability, the kind of thing that Jimmy Savage help develop. If you take that approach, you can't distinguish uncertainty from risk. There's no break point (Conversation with Milton Friedman August 1997).

Thus for Hayek, liberty maintains, at least in part, a purely functional role in facilitating market effectiveness. Freedom of choice fuels market effectiveness in an uncertain world. For Friedman it become an end in itself, a reworking of the Holy Grail, but redefined for the sphere of economics and politics.

> Liberty is essential in order to leave room for the unforeseeable and unpredictable. We want it because we have learned to expect from it the opportunity of realizing many of our aims. It is because every individual knows so

little in particular, because we rarely know which of us knows but that we trust the independent and competitive efforts of many to produce the emergence of what we shall want when we see it (Hayek quoted in Kirzner 1979:15–16).

150   When he was an undergraduate at Chicago (and they were graduate students), Paul Samuelson knew both Friedman and Stigler. Based on this intimate knowledge, he is able to draw a link between the Chicago reaction to Chamberlin's work and Friedman's 1953 essay.

> Knight always said, all that's good in Chamberlin he got from me and there isn't anything good in him. You know, something like that. And, there's no reason why this should have been of any importance, but it really riled Knight that Chamberlin was a Catholic convert. 'The man believes in the Immaculate Conception. What can you do with him?' Knight would say. So from the start, of course, they didn't like the notion that if you were analysing imperfect competition, you were analysing cases of market failure. They always played this down. Now, the early Stigler wasn't as strong on this as he was later on. But Friedman was from early on. And I think that part of the reason for it, was this development of his, was it 1953, his version of positivism?
>
> It's partly a licence for self-indulgence. You don't have to have a correspondence between a theory and the facts, or a close correspondence. In fact, the theory is all the better if it doesn't fit the facts, closely. And I think that there are some profound errors in that form of positivism, but it is there for a purpose. It serves a purpose. Do you think the cigarette industry with only four big producers in it is not competitive? Well, if one raises its price, another one will and so forth. That's the same paradigm of comparative statics that would happen under competition. So under the doctrine of 'as if', we can use the competitive theory. (Conversation with Paul Samuelson, October 1997).

151   The brunt of, if not the total, force of the attack was directed at Chamberlin. Joan Robinson's 1933 effort (*Imperfect Competition*) was not viewed as being at all disruptive.

> My recollection is not worth much, but for what it's worth is that the Robinsonian emphasis on individual firm economics, the analysis of marginal revenue and marginal cost, fitted in very well with what we were otherwise thinking. There were no problems about that (Conversation with Milton Friedman, August 1997).

152   The suggested parallels drawn by Stigler's claims easily collapse by applying only a minimal application of logical thought. The physicists enlisted by Stigler to prove his point can ignore friction because in some instances there are situations or locations that are characterised by an absence of friction. In other cases, the effect of friction can be precisely calculated. Nor are mathematicians taking liberties with perfect circles since all of

mathematics deals with objects that no one can see, let alone touch. The entire field is simply a series of mental constructs. Economic man (when examined rationally) is no more than a heuristic, a logical, rather than a tangible, element enlisted to facilitate one possible economic framework. This imaginative creation is, by definition, never observable, unlike the absence of friction which can either be simulated or detected as a phenomenon occurring in outer space. In contrast, pure mathematics is not meant to be about observables. To Frank Knight, Economic Man (and his travails within the world of perfect competition) is also entirely unobservable. Boiled down, this construct becomes a pure heuristic that is not directly transferable to any actual observable world. However, for Knight's student, George Stigler, the abstract world of economic science seems to increasingly bleed into the observable world the more he distances himself from Frank Knight. The problem politely ignored by Stigler is the necessary path leading from the theoretical bounds of the Economic Man (the rational decision maker) to the observable world of application and policy.

153   To emphasize, labelling Friedman's effort a landmark is not meant to reflect on its importance purely as a harbinger of future productive debate. Considering it to be a potential pioneering paper on methodology, or even a foray into applied philosophy, would be a misleading estimation. The essay did, however, help to transform the nature and structure of methodological debates within the profession for decades to come. Unfortunately, achieving this rare level of impact within the profession, does not automatically classify Friedman's effort as being either beneficial or even benign.

154   Surprised, if not shocked, at failing to gain a promised position at Chicago, George Stigler instead spent a pleasant year at Brown (1946) before shifting to Columbia in 1947. Chicago did not manage to entice him back until 1958.

> Sherwin Rosen: Stigler just didn't have that much power. For Christ sake, he wasn't even in a great university until ...
> *Until 1958.*
> Sherwin Rosen: No. [laughs] Well Columbia was pretty good. It took him a long time to get power and I don't think he ever had that much influence (Conversation with Sherwin Rosen, October 1997).

155   Chamberlin's 1933 book was a cause célèbre during Stigler's years at Chicago (1933–1936). Graduate students such as Friedman and Stigler poured over it minutely.

> We also studied Edward Chamberlin's then – new book on *Monopolistic Competition* We graduate students considered that this work would revolutionize economics. The faculty, however, gave it no attention: literally none. So George and a group who resided at International House, among whom I

remember especially Albert Hart and Kenneth Boulding, organized a seminar including me that met every Saturday morning and worked through – or debated – Chamberlin's book line by line and diagram by diagram. The judgment of history, I believe, would side more nearly with the appraisal of the book by the faculty than with that of the graduate students. But it is a significant work and the exercise had more lasting value than verifying Pareto's mathematics (Wallis 1993:776).

To be more exact, the Chicago faculty at that time didn't ignore it (despite the claims made by Wallis), but did not accept Chamberlin's efforts as a valid replacement for existing price theory. But unlike Knight, Stigler came to evaluate the market structure of perfect competition, not simply as a heuristic, but as a close reflection of existing reality. Stigler, like Friedman, detached himself from the classical liberal dictum separating theory from applied policy. Thus as early as his 1937 piece condemning the validity of imperfect competition (more a defense of perfect competition than a serious analysis of imperfect competition), Stigler makes an early, 'as if' argument.

> It is elementary to all scientists that certain methodological assumptions, which everyone admits are contrary to fact, are indispensable to theoretical reasoning. No one begrudges the physicist the right to ignore friction, and the mathematician is permitted perfect circles no one will ever see. The case for the economic man is just as strong, and had he not been imported into economics, today there would be no science worthy of the name (Stigler 1937:713).

Similar strained analogies would appear in Friedman's classic 1953 essay. But these represent concocted attempts to defend existing price theory, rather than providing thoughtful comparisons between alternative systems. A physicist can observe particles within a vacuum or gaze to the heavens. Friction can be reasonably ignored or added back into an equation. Mathematicians, on the other hand manipulate mental objects, rather than physical ones. The material world is outside the interest of the mathematician. These dealers in the abstract are not usefully confused with engineers. The essential point however, is that Friedman's 1953 line of attack was aimed at deflecting challenges to Chicago style price theory. Such a methodological defense would prove to be of continuing use.

156   In the same sense that those defending a geocentric astronomy claimed to be saving the appearances, so Friedman and Stigler sought to save the appearances (outcomes of competitive markets) by using an 'as if' formulation. Notice how this approach is not unlike the endless epicycles employed to maintain an earth centric celestial system. Whether in fact any appearances were maintained in either case is a matter of speculative opinion.

157   If anything, Stigler seemed to develop an allergic reaction to methodological issues after this short and somewhat mysterious foray. In the 1952 edition of his textbook, Stigler takes great pains to emphasize that theories must be tested by evidence, not just by logic, thus incorporating the methodology championed in his 1948 LSE lecture. His apparent intention in that revised edition of his textbook was to introduce his reader to methodological issues by paradoxically eliminating any concern for such considerations. The evisceration and absence of methodology became his distinctive version of applied methodology (at least that was the implicit message conveyed.)

> That Stigler was not much of a fan of quantitative jugglery or economic jargon is evident from his apologetic introduction to the chapter on basic concepts, where he says, "In economics … there is a language to be learned. And as elsewhere, the language is probably carried to excess: it is possible to have one's ideas snubbed merely because they violate the grammar of the profession" … In fact, in this book the chapter on methodology is dropped. In its stead, "A few mathematical notes are placed at the end where they are easier to ignore" (Kamerschen and Sridhar 2009: 187).

158   The term *outré* would seem quite appropriate when our commandeered focus shifts to the methodology of economics. True, more attention, at least indirectly, was ladled out in the nineteenth century. (John Neville Keynes (1891) wrote a potential (but mostly ignored) classic on economic methodology during this formative period. Potential is employed to mean that under more nurturing circumstances the volume might have had a much larger influence.) Still, it hardly seemed a fortuitous path to pursue for any ambitious young economist seeking to advance his career in those early post war years. Though it must be mentioned again, that neither Friedman nor Stigler chose to dwell on, or debate, the subject after their initial, short lived burst of enthusiasm.

159   It is unwise to simply dismiss the time and context in which an article is written as though conceived in some splendid hermetic isolation, a situation virtually unmoored from existing events or ideological imperatives. Alchian and Demsetz' (1972) often quoted article is ostensibly proffered as a reasonable explanation of why the existence of firms is socially beneficial. (If they didn't exist, workers would demand that they be established.) Capitalist firms are revealed to be both equitable and efficient because they perform as private rather than public markets. (Consequently, give three cheers for the ingenuity of markets.) The article though is written and appeared in print not only during a period when standard neo-classical theory was under attack, but also when capitalism and markets were as well. Thus the piece, when placed in its proper context, reveals itself to contain a hidden, or at least implicit, objective. The unannounced purpose

is one of beating back and taming what was then a rising tide of criticism of both capitalism and conventional economic analysis. In essence, the two authors were employing a classic poison apple strategy. By considering the article, the reader opened him or herself up to a seemingly well-reasoned investigation centered on the classic role of the firm. But buried within that explicit debate, possibly slipping through a reader's critical defenses, were some fairly rigid ideological beliefs and principles.

160   Friedman was determined not only to argue that there was no basis for government intervention, but that such intervention would in fact aggravate any existing situation. Here he pulled out his economic 'ace in the hole' namely the counter-intuitive case of unintended consequences. Buried within his argument was a nearly toxic injection of suspicion. Such government intervention (no matter how well-intentioned) clearly undercut essential individual liberty, but even more importantly, such actions only aggravated what it sought to correct. Accordingly, there was no need for direct intervention, since the consequences were predictably dire. If governments have the temerity to intervene, given Friedman's impeccable logic, they will only manage to damage what ostensibly they seek to cure. This poses a sort of double whammy attached to any government action. (The 'cure is worse than the cause' has been more recently trotted out during the 2020 pandemic. At its more extreme position, this perspective argues for allowing the virus the right to be 'free to choose'.)

> The distribution of income is still another area in which government has been doing more harm by one set of measures than it has been able to undo by others. It is another example of the justification of government intervention in terms of alleged defects of the private enterprise system when many of the phenomena of which champions of big government complain are themselves the creation of governments, big and small (Friedman 1962:176).

161   Much of George Stigler's adamant rejection of government intervention is grounded in the anticipated effect such actions inflict on income distribution. (All such policies must inevitably affect any existing distribution.) By undermining market incentives, Stigler was convinced that these misguided interventions ultimately weakened an individual's moral fibre.

> But we are persuaded that an economic system will not help us to move in the right direction unless it grants both opportunity and responsibility to the individual: the very uncertainty of our ultimate ethical goals dictates a wide are of individual self-determination. We are not able to supply a blueprint of the ideal life, but we are persuaded that even if it were known it would be ideal only for the person who individually and knowingly and voluntarily accepted it. It is not necessary, however to know what is best; it is enough to know what is better (Stigler 1949a:8).

162   Perhaps Friedman's 1953 essay was even more daring. His effort generated a storm of controversy. But the debate shifted to the more conducive territory of recondite methodology, a region that neither Friedman nor Stigler cared to explore intensively. Meaningful discussions that focused on the need for valid or observable assumptions were largely left in the lurch. Details of Friedman's hypothesis were discussed, much in the same way that troop placements at the Battle of Austerlitz might be pondered over with someone claiming to be Napoleon. Doing so, was not without interest, but nonetheless time consuming and ultimately fruitless. Friedman's goal appeared to be one of obfuscation, rather than clarification. The possibility exists that Friedman's aim was to end methodological discussions focused on the nature and role of assumptions in economics.

163   Friedman, perhaps even more than Stigler, innately knew how to provoke. He would almost willfully adopt stances which he intuited as potentially outraging his audience or readers. He would then proceed to defend his stance with an almost infuriating calm.

> Milton went down there and with a sweet smile on his face, he said that we ought to legalize drugs. You've got to picture this in your mind. All over the world, there are conservative professors and radical students. The students are yelling, "We have to make marijuana legal." That's as far as most of them are willing to go. Their professors are taking on this stern parental view. Here's Milton going to this very conservative college [Chapman College] and taking a very extreme view in favour of legalizing drugs. The students were *shocked!* The whole thing was riotously funny. Milton was just taking it all in, in his wonderful, easy-going way and debating with them. It was just a lot of fun (Conversation with Claire Friedland October 1997).

164   Fifty years later, Milton Friedman hadn't budged an iota from his initial solution (nothing to see here, move on your way). An AEA session (at that year's 2003 annual conference in Washington D.C.) celebrated the fiftieth anniversary of the publication of that influential 1953 essay. In a live phone hook-up, Friedman simply dismissed the possibility that his approach, as conceived, needed any further correction or adjustment.

165   Liberal and liberalism can generate confusion in the mind of a typical reader since the term seems geographically determined. In the US, liberal has become attached to left of center views in a country where political affiliations and memberships are more often claimed than explained. In the UK, and most other countries, liberal is viewed as following in the tradition of John Stuart Mill and perhaps Edmund Burke. To some extent, simple ideas of right, center and left fail to accurately describe the idea of liberalism, or what may be more exactly termed, classical liberalism. Friedman and Stigler, joined together in promoting and marketing an economic restoration project. Though when reduced to its barest essentials, they had no

intention of restoring the principles of classical liberalism to a position of political and economic dominance. Instead, they intended to claim a liberal lineage, while decisively pressing their own agenda forward in classic poison apple fashion. Friedman and Stigler offered what they considered to be a modern version of liberalism, one that was properly updated for the new, post war era. Readers however should attempt to recollect the distinctions covered in the first case study. Namely that an unrestrained urge to classify and pigeonhole often and easily becomes a method for dismissing opponents and embracing allies.

166   An effective place to gain a thoughtful analysis of the Mont Pelerin meeting (and the context within which it operated) is Burgin (2012).

> Long isolated in home environments where they were "forced constantly to defend the basic elements of their beliefs," the participants now found themselves among others who shared an "agreement on fundamentals" (Burgin 2012:103).
>
> At the outset there were several basic assumptions on which they could agree: a rejection of totalitarianism, a defense of the market mechanism, a connections between economic and intellectual freedom, and an acknowledgment of the importance of moral absolutes (Burgin 2012:105).

167   The bill for not establishing an alternative to neo-classical price theory would come due in the 1970s. Not only would Keynesian theory be deemed to lack a viable explanation for stagflation, but would also be judged guilty of being inconsistent with canonical price theory. By the seventies, this micro-economic foundation of price theory had entirely transformed itself into the incontestable core of economic thinking. An enticing opening for the theory of rational expectations (and New Classical Economics) was predictably created by pointing out the inconsistency between micro and macro components. These had previously been fudged together to compose an inconsistent theoretical sandwich.

168   Though strongly identified with macro-economic theory, it is well to remember that Friedman did teach the key graduate price theory course at Chicago until he retired in 1975 (not his close friend and colleague George Stigler). When Friedman arrived at Chicago in 1946 as an Associate Professor, one of his tasks was to take over Economics 301 from the departed Jacob Viner (who had taught both Friedman and Stigler). He would later use his notes from that course (as many teacher do) to write his own textbook (1962) for classroom use. Gary Becker would in turn succeed Milton Friedman.

> Although Friedman did allow that decisions regarding what goods and services to purchase involve "a deliberate act of choice," he went only as far as to say that in making these choices, "we shall suppose that the individual is

> making these decisions *as if* he were pursuing and attempting to maximize a single end" (1962:37). This characterization of the problem is present in student notes on his lectures from 1947, and is repeated verbatim in the 1976 revision of his text (1976:35). Of course, this "as if" approach to theorizing is a centrepiece of Friedman's methodological perspective (Friedman 1953) (Medema 2011: 156).

169   As a final point, let me emphasize that this examination of Friedman's methodology has nothing to say about the methodology's legitimacy. Nor does it exist as an evaluation of the validity of Friedman's theoretical contributions. Instead, it views Friedman's venture into the realm of methodology as simply the consequence of inexorably pursuing a specific marketing campaign. Selling his theory depended in part on attempting to destroy the persuasive underpinnings of opposing theories. In essence, Friedman's efforts are what has been labelled here as being a classic poison apple strategy. Consequently, I feel personally obliged to try to clarify the purpose of this chapter at this point since I am curious as to whether anyone cultivates the intellectual tenacity required to actually pay attention to endnotes. An essential question inadvertently attached to this chapter, may be whether those who automatically feel obligated to defend Milton Friedman will misclassify this article as an attack on Friedman's work, simply by ignoring the many disclaimers and detailed explanations provided. However, if read more carefully, the purpose of this chapter is simply to employ Friedman's own attempt at methodology as a humble example of a common form of obfuscation committed by economists, at least in their role as authors. Friedman may have used the technique skillfully, but he is far from unique in employing it.

170   Put very simply, Friedman conducted a successful sleight of hand (the poison apple strategy). The desire was to shift the conversation away from examining evidence that questioned some of the fundamental assumptions supporting economic theories. Instead, the proffered focus became the predictive reliability of theoretical results. In which case assumptions could perform 'as if' they were true. Though the 1953 article was offered as a foray into proscriptive methodology, the goal was to blunt any serious examination of the validity of assumptions. With the economics profession largely accepting the article at face value, the alternative investigation was essentially derailed. The poison apple had been bitten, swallowed and digested.

171   Friedman (1953) offered seeming valid and simple analogies of leaves acting 'as if' consciously seeking the sun. Whether there was such a motivated action was, at least in Friedman's terms, irrelevant. Starting with an 'as if' statement, building a useful, predictive model became achievable. Results, not assumptions, mattered. At first glance, such a thesis sounds palatable.

But perhaps the ingredients yielding an observed result do matter. The taste of a dessert may be pleasant and even delicious. But the mixture of components themselves, especially over time, might prove lethal.

172   Milton Friedman's 1953 effort almost instantly generated what became known as the can opener joke (or tin opener if you are exiled in the UK or Australia). There are variations on the basic theme composing the heart of this joke, with the trio of individuals often exiled to a desert isle where they most probably belong. But the contrast persistently presented is that of an economist faced with the contrasting thinking of two scientific disciplines, the sciences where assumptions do matter and controlled experiments are more easily conducted. The humour stems from the incongruity of the Friedmanesque idea that assumptions don't matter when faced with dire necessity. This veritable pre-drawn bullseye, as a centrepiece of the 'as if' world, proved fertile ground for this classic joke. The operative plot placed economists squarely in the position of being the butt of the intended humour. (Imagined can openers only work on imaginary cans. People in possession of such theoretical tools starve to death once imaginary sustenance proves to be insubstantial.) Attempts at this version of economical humour goes back at least as far as 1970 (possibly originating with an economist of the British persuasion). The first known written account appeared in a book by Kenneth E. Boulding (1970:101). Though one suspects that oral versions were extant back in the 1950s.

References

Akerlof, G. and Janet, Y. (1987). "Rational modes of irrational behavior", *The American Economic Review – Papers and Proceedings*. 77(2): 137–142.

Akerlof, G., William, D., and George, P. (1996). "The macroeconomics of low inflation", *Brookings Papers on Economic Activity*. 1: 1–76.

Alchian, A. (1977/1950). "Uncertainty, evolution and economic theory", in *Economic Forces at Work*. Indianapolis: Liberty Press, pp. 15–37.

Alchian, A. and Harold, D. (1972). "Production, information costs, and economic organization", *The American Economic Review*. 62(4): 777–795.

Austen, J. (1818/1936). "Northanger Abbery", in *The Complete Novels of Jane Austen*. New York: The Modern Library, pp. 1063–1211.

Becker, G. (1971). *The Economics of Discrimination*. Chicago: University of Chicago Press.

Becker, G. (1991). "A note on restaurant pricing and other examples of social influences on price", *The Journal of Political Economy*. 99(5): 1109–1116.

Boland, L. (1987). "Boland on Friedman's methodology: A summation", *Journal of Economic Issues*. 21(1): 380–388.

Boulding, K. (1970). *Economics as a Science*. New York: McGraw-Hill.

Burgin, A. (2021). *The Great Persuasion*. Cambridge: Harvard University Press.

Caldwell, B. (1980). "A critique of Friedman's methodological instrumentalism", *Southern Economic Journal*. 47(2): 366–374.

Card, D. and Alan, B. K. (1994). "Minimum wages and employment: A case study of the fast-food industry in New Jersey and Pennsylvania", *American Economic Review*. (84 94): 772–293.

Card, D. and Alan, B. K. (1995). *Myth and Measurement: The New Economics of the Minimum Wage*. Princeton, NJ: Princeton University Press.

Clausewitz, C. von (1918/1832). *On War*. Graham, J. J. (trans.). New York: E.F. Dutton and Co.

Chamberlin, E. H. (1937). "Monopolistic or imperfect competition", *The Quarterly Journal of Economics*. 51(4): 557–580.

Chamberlin, E. H. (1947). "Book review of the theory of price", *American Economic Review*. 37(3): 414–418.

Chamberlin, E. H. (1957). *Toward a More General Theory of Value*. Oxford: Oxford University Press.

Chick, V. (1983). *Macroeconomics after Keynes*. Cambridge: Cambridge University Press.

Clausewitz, C. von (1918/1832). *On War*. Graham, J. J. (trans.). New York: E.F. Dutton and Co.

Clapham, J. H. (1922/1953). "Of empty economic boxes" in Kenneth, B. and Stigler, G. J. (eds.) *Readings in Price Theory*. London: George Allen and Unwin Ltd., pp. 119–131.

Clement, D. (2006). "Interview with David Card – October 17", *The Region – Federal Reserve Bank of Minneapolis*. 1–10. http://www.minneapolisfed. org/pubs/region/06-12/card.cfm (20/08/2008).

Coase, R. (1937). "The nature of the firm", 4 *Economica*. 386–405.

Coase, R. (1960). "The problem of social cost", *The Journal of Law & Economics*. 3(1): 1–44.

Coase, R. (1994). "Arnold plant", in *On Economics and Economists*. Chicago: University of Chicago Press, pp. 176–185.

Colander, D. and Freedman, C. (2019). *Where Economics Went Wrong*. Princeton: Princeton University Press.

Darity Jr., W., M'Balou, C., and Nancy, M. (2023). "Locking in racial disadvantage in libertarian political economy: The case of W. H. Hutt and South Africa", *History of Economics Review*. 85(1): 7–19.

Descartes, R. (1701/1966). Crapulli, G. (ed.) *Rules for the Direction of the Mind*. (*Regulae ad Directionem Ingenii*), Critical Text with the 17th-Century Dutch Version, La Haye: Martinus Nijhoff.

Dickens, C. (1850). *David Copperfield*. London: Bradbury and Evans.

Dickens, C. (1843/1945). *A Christmas Carol and the Chimes*. Melbourne, Australia: Oxford University Press.

Fisher, F. (2011). "The stability of general equilibrium – What do we know and why is it important?" in Pascal, B. (ed.) *General Equilibrium Analysis: A Century After Walras*, New York: Routledge, pp. 34–45.

Freedman, C. (1995). "The economist as mythmaker – Stigler's Kinky transformation", *The Journal of Economic Issues*. 29 (1): 175–209.

Freedman, C. (2002). "The xistence of definitional economics – Stigler's and Leibenstein's war of the words", *Cambridge Journal of Economics*. 26(2): 161–178.

Freedman, C. (2006). "Not for love nor money: Milton Friedman's Counter-revolution" *History of Economics Review*. 42(Summer): 87–119.

Freedman, C. (2008). "Why economists can't read", in Freedman, C. (ed.) *Chicago Fundamentalism: Ideology and Methodology in Economics*. Singapore: World Scientific Publishing Co., pp. 283–320.

Freedman, C. (2016). "The Chicago School of anti-monopolistic competition", in *In Search of the Two-Handed Economist*. London: Palgrave Macmillan, pp. 165–343.

Friedman, M. (1953). *Essays in Positive Economics*. Chicago: University of Chicago Press.

Friedman, M. (1962). *Price Theory: A Provisional Text*. Chicago: Aldine.

Friedman, M. (1976). *Price Theory*. Chicago: Aldine.

Friedman, M. (2003a/1956). "The quantity theory of money – a restatement", in Robert, L. (ed.) *Keynes, Chicago and Friedman – Volume I*. London: Pickering & Chatto, pp. 31–52.

Friedman, M. (1962). *Capitalism and Freedom*. Chicago: The University of Chicago Press.

Friedman, M. (2003b/1972). "Comments on the critics: Patinkin", in Robert, L. (ed.) *Keynes, Chicago and Friedman* Vol. 2. London: Pickering & Chatto, pp. 145–166.

Friedman, M. (1976). *Milton Friedman in South Africa*. Feldberg, Meyer, Kate Jowell and Stephen Mulholland (eds.) Cape Town and Johannesburg: Graduate School of Business, University of Cape Town and the Sunday Times.

Friedman, M. and Leonard, S. (1948). "The utility analysis of choices involving risk", *The Journal of Political Economy*. 56(4): 279–304.

Grimm, B. (1992). *The Complete Fairy Tales of the Brothers Grimm: Translated and With an Introduction by Jack Zipes*. New York: Bantam Books.

Hall, R. L. and Hitch, C. J. (1939). "Price theory and business behaviour", *Oxford Economic Papers*. 2(1): 12–45.

Hammond, J. D. and Hammond, C. (2006). *Making Chicago Price Theory*. London: Routledge.

Homer (1996). *The Odyssey*. Robert, F. (tr.). New York: Viking Penguin.

Hayek, F. (1945). "The use of knowledge in society", *The American Economic Review*. 35(4): 519–530.

Hutt, W. H. (1964). *The Economics of the Colour Bar*. https://mises.org/library/ economics-colour-bar.

Kamerschen, D. and Deepa, S. (2009). "The theory of [competitive] price according to George J. Stigler", *Journal of the History of Economic Thought*. 31(2): 181–200.

Keynes, J. M. (1923). *A Tract on Monetary Reform*. London: Macmillan.

Keynes, J. M. (1933). "National Self-Sufficiency", *The Yale Review*. 22(4): 755–769.

Keynes, J. M. (1936). "Letter to Gerald shove", in Donald, M. (ed.) (1973). *The Collected Writing of John Maynard Keynes, Volume XIV, The General Theory and After, Part II, Defence and Development*. London: Macmillan, p. 2.

Keynes, J. M. (1937). "The general theory of employment, interest and money", *The Quarterly Journal of Economics*. 51(1): 209–223.

Keynes, J. M. (1964/1936). *The General Theory of Employment, Interest and Money*. New York: Harcourt, Brace, Jovanovich.

Keynes, J. N. (1891). *The Scope and Method of Political Economy*. London: Macmillan.

Kirzner, I. (1979). *Perception, Opportunity and Perception: Studies in the Theory of Entrepreneurship*. Chicago: The University of Chicago Press.

Knight, F. (1971/1921). *Risk, Uncertainty and Profit*. Chicago: The University of Chicago Press.

Leeson, R. (2003). "Toward a resolution of the dispute", in Robert, L. (ed.) *Keynes, Chicago and Friedman*, Vol. 2. London: Pickering & Chatto, pp. 293–314.

Leibenstein, H. (1966). "Allocative efficiency vs. X-efficiency", *The American Economic Review*. 56(2): 393–415.

Leibenstein, H. (1978). "X-inefficiency xists: Reply to an xorcist", *The American Economic Review*. 68(1): 203–211.

Loasby, B. J. (1989). "Joan Robinson's 'wrong turning'", in *The Mind and Method of the Economist: A Critical Appraisal of Major Economists in the 20th Century*. Cheltenham: Edward Elgar, pp. 71–85.

Machiavelli, N. (1532). *The Prince*. Florence: Antonio Blado d'Asola.

Machlup, F. (1959). "Statics and dynamics: Kaleidoscopic words", *Southern Economic Journal*. 26(2): 91–110.

Machlup, F. (1967). "Theories of the firm: Marginalist, behavioural, managerial", *The American Economic Review*. 57(1): 1–33.

Marcuzzo, M. (2020). "Richard F. Kahn: A disciple of Keynes", *History of Economic Review*. 76(1): 2–57.

Mariyani-Squire, E. (2017). "Critical reflections on a realist interpretation of Friedman's 'methodology of positive economics'", *Journal of Economic Methodology*. 24(1): 69–89.

Mayer, T. (1993). "Friedman's methodology of positive economics: A soft reading", *Economic Inquiry*. 31(1): 213–223.

Medema, S. (2011). "Chicago price theory and Chicago law and economics: A tale of two transitions", in Robert, V. H., Mirowski, P., and Stapleford, T. (eds.) *Building Chicago Economics*. Cambridge, Cambridge University Press, pp. 151–180.

Mill, J. S. (1947/1859). *On Liberty*. New York: Appleton-Century-Crofts.

Mill, J. S. (1965/1859). *Principle of Political Economy*. New York: Augustus M. Kelley.

Milne, A. A. (1961). "In which Pooh and Piglet go hunting and nearly catch a woozle", in *Winnie-The-Pooh*. New York: E. P. Dutton & Co., pp. 34–43.

Morishima, M. (1982). *Why Has Japan "Succeeded"?* Cambridge: Cambridge University Press.

Neumark, D. and William, W. (2000). "Minimum wages and employment: A case study of the fast-food industry in New Jersey and Pennsylvania: Comment", *American Economic Review*. 90(5): 1362–1396.

Opazo, T. (2016). "The boys who got to remake an economy", *Slate*. January 12, http://www.slate.com/articles/business/moneybox/2016/01/in_chicago_boys_the_story_of_chilean_economists_who_studied_in_america_and.html (31/01/2017).

Orwell, G. (1945). *Animal Farm*. London: Secker and Warburg.

Patinkin, D. (2003a/1969). "The Chicago tradition, the quantity theory and Keynesian economics", in Robert, L. (ed.) *Keynes, Chicago and Friedman*, Vol. 1. London: Pickering & Chatto, pp. 87–120.

Patinkin, D. (2003b/1974). "Friedman on the quantity theory and Keynesian economics", in Robert, L. (ed.) *Keynes, Chicago and Friedman*, Vol. 2. London: Pickering & Chatto, pp. 123–143.

Patinkin, D. (2003c/1974). "Keynesian monetary theory and the Cambridge School", in Robert, L. (ed.) *Keynes, Chicago and Friedman*, Vol. 2. London: Pickering & Chatto, pp. 315–344.

Patinkin, D. (2003d/1979). "Keynes and Chicago", in Robert, L. (ed.) *Keynes, Chicago and Friedman*, Vol. 2. London: Pickering & Chatto, pp. 373–392.

Penrose, E. (1952). "Biological analogies in the theory of the firm", *American Economic Review*. 42(5): 804–819.

Penrose, E. (1959). *The Theory of the Growth of the Firm*. New York: John Wiley and Sons.

Robertson, D. (1973). "Letter to John Maynard Keynes, October 1933", in Donald, M. (ed.) *The General Theory and After – Part I Preparations;*

Volume XIII of The Collected Writing of John Maynard Keynes. London: Macmillan, p. 319.

Robinson, J. (1933). *The Economics of Imperfect Competition*. London: Macmillan.

Robinson, J. (1974). "Notes on Marx and Marshall", in *Selected Economic Writings*. India: Centre for Development Studies.

Samuelson, P. (1957). "Wages and interest: A modern dissection of Marxian economic models", *The American Economic Review*. 47(6): 884–912.

Samuelson, P. (1963). "Discussion", *The American Economic Review – Papers and Proceedings*. 53(2): 232–236.

Schumpeter, J. (1934). "Robinson's economics of imperfect competition", *The Journal of Political Economy*. 42(2): 249–257.

Shaw, G. (1988). *The Keynesian Heritage*, Vol. I. Aldershot: Edward Elgar.

Shove, G. (1936). "Letter to John Maynard Keynes", in Donald, M. (ed.) (1973) *The Collected Writing of John Maynard Keynes*, Vol. XIV, *The General Theory and After, Part II, Defence and Development*. London: Macmillan, p. 1.

Simon, H. (1957). *Models of Man: Social and Rational*. New York: John Wiley and Sons.

Solow, R. M. (1966). "Comments", George, S. and Aliber, R. (eds.) *Guidelines: Informal Controls and the Market Place*. Chicago: University of Chicago Press, pp. 62–66.

Sraffa, P. (1926/1953). "The laws of returns under competitive conditions", in Kenneth, B. and Stigler, G. J. (eds.) *Readings in Price Theory*. London: Allen and Unwin, pp. 180–197.

Stigler, G. J. (1937). "A generalization of the theory of imperfect competition", *Journal of Farm Economics*. 20(3): 707–717.

Stigler, G. J. (1947). "Notes on the history of the Giffen paradox", *Journal of Political Economy*. 55(1): 152–156.

Stigler, G. J. (1949a). "The economists and equality", in *Five Lectures on Economic Problems*. London: Longmans Green and Co., pp. 1–12.

Stigler, G. J. (1949b). "Monopolistic competition in retrospect", in *Five Lectures on Economic Problems*. London: Longmans Green and Co., pp. 12–34.

Stigler, G. J. (1953/1947). "The Kinky oligopoly demand curve and rigid prices", in Kenneth, B. and Stigler, G. J. (eds.) *Readings in Price Theory*. London: George Allen and Unwin Ltd., pp. 410–440.

Stigler, G. J. (1960). "The influence of events and policies on economic theory", *American Economic Review, Papers and Proceedings*. 50(2): 37–45.

Stigler, G. J. (1976). "The xistence of x-efficiency", *American Economic Review*. 66(1): 213–236.

Stigler, G. J. (1982). "Does economics have a useful past?" in *The Economist as Preacher*. Chicago: University of Chicago Press, pp. 107–118.

Stigler, G. J. (1983/1984). "Self-interest, parties and ideology", Chicago: Special Collections, Regenstein Library, University of Chicago, pp. 1–7.

Stigler, G. J. (1988). *Memoirs of an Unregulated Economist*. Chicago: University of Chicago Press.

Sweezy, P. (1939/1953). "Demand under the condition of oligopoly", in Kenneth, B. and Stigler, G. J. (eds.) *Readings in Price Theory*. London: George Allen and Unwin Ltd., pp. 404–410.

Leo, T. (1869/1957). *War and Peace*. Rosemary, E. (tr.). Harmondsworth, Middlesex, England: Penguin Classics.

Viner, J. (1937). "Mr. Keynes on the causes of unemployment", *The Quarterly Journal of Economics*. 51(1): 147–167.

Viner, J. (2003/1963). "Comment on my 1936 review of Keynes' General Theory", in Robert, L. (ed.) *Keynes, Chicago and Friedman – Volume 2*. London: Pickering and Chatto, pp. 417–430.

Wallis, W. A. (1993). "George J. Stigler: In memorium", *Journal of Political Economy*. 101(5): 774–779.

Saint Milton of the Blessed Markets – A Hero's Journey

In a famous Cook County debate on wage-price controls, Solow declared, "What Sydney Smith said to Thomas Babington Macaulay, I say to you, Milton: "I wish Babington, I was as sure of anything as you are of everything" (Samuelson 2011a:617).

The recent December (2023) death of Robert Solow reminds me that all the towering figures of post-war economics are now gone. Apparently not every economist manages to automatically pass the centennial barrier.[1] Perhaps now we are forced to acknowledge that the academic remnants of the profession consists largely of a multitude of pygmies astride the shoulders of elusive giants. Consequently, I would not be surprised if the ongoing impact and recollection of Milton Friedman continues to unfortunately fade, despite his well-deserved recognition as one of the most renowned economist of his time, as well as the most skilled publicist and promoter of his profession.[2] "If John Maynard Keynes was the most influential economist of the first half of the 20th century, then Milton Friedman was the most influential economist of the second half" (Summers 2006:1).[3]

Given though his remarkable professional position and accomplishments (plus the sheer force of his personality), Milton Friedman does deserve a sympathetic, but probing examination of every facet of his career. Without a doubt, Jennifer Burns has done a remarkably intensive piece of research. The result is a well written (and easily read) biography.[4] Though written for the general reader, it would be the obsessive economist who did not learn something new by reading this volume. Consequently when I opened these pages, I was hoping that Burns would accomplish for Friedman what Caldwell (2003) did for Hayek.[5] Sadly she has failed to do so.[6]

No matter how much admiration you come to hold for the subject of your investigation, sympathy should never bleed into hagiography (a word I never thought I'd be able to employ). All humans have feet of clay. No useful end is ever accomplished by trying to bronze them over.

> When the *Journal of Political Economy* asked me to write an obituary of Viner's Chicago days, I [Paul Samuelson] was in a quandary. *Nihil nisi bonum* was not Viner's own credo, but *nisi verum* (Samuelson 2011b:596).

I. Lost in Translation – The Elusive Art of Economics

> One man and the truth is a majority (Milton Friedman quoted in (Samuelson 2011a:617).

Putting together a biography is much like constructing a jigsaw puzzle. There are countless bits and pieces that must be put together. Only judgment can decide exactly how such pieces fit and which of the multitude to use. (Providing too much information can be as confusing as too little.) However, Burns (2023) appears to have started with a pre-conceived picture and either moulded the various pieces to fit, or simply tossed aside any unwelcomed bits. Thus what might initially resemble harmless (and even trivial) mistakes, tend to induce genuine suspicion as they mount up. The suspicion arises that they actually might be knit together by a prior purpose.

Certainly, Burns starts off with a decided disadvantage. She is a historian of economic ideas, not an economist.[7] In certain cases, this particular foundation would not be a draw back. I have read efforts by both Burgin (2012) and Amadae (2003). In each case, neither one could be considered to be a card carrying economist. But in some instances, a detailed knowledge of economics is to a degree superfluous. While writing their volumes, both desired to stay at the level of ideas in an attempt to trace out their implications. In pursuit of their objectives, Burgin delivers a fascinating book, while Amadae's efforts are disappointing. (She has a peculiar hobby-horse that she rides to exhaustion.) But in contrast, Burns is attempting a biography of one of the outstanding (if not most notorious) economists of the 20th century. His theories and promoted policies inevitably (at least partially) define the man. This stricture implies that a sufficient understanding of positions that were sternly opposed to those of Friedman, composes a requirement for any in-depth evaluation of his work. Demanding this level of competence does not reflect some simple instance of wishful thinking.

But instead, Burns constructs a colourful quilt of a life, which almost always places Friedman on the side of the angels, or at least in Friedman's words, 'the good eggs'.[8] I have to admit that this unwavering approach fuelled suspicions of what would otherwise appear to be no more than an innocent mistake. Certainly being a year off on an event could happen to anyone. However, while discussing a seminal period of Friedman's graduate education, Burns is eager to highlight the year (which is a significant one) in which Friedman, Stigler, Wallis (and sometimes Director and Simons) held court in what was previously a disused storeroom. Dramatically, she has all the comrades cinematically disperse in 1935 (certainly Friedman, Stigler and Wallis). However, as Stigler (1988) relates in his autobiography, he left for his Iowa State job (one of the few then open) in 1936. It would seem that boring accuracy had to surrender to the needs of story-telling in this case and perhaps in too many others.

To a degree, such accumulating slips create a need (even at this early juncture) to point out similar unaccountable errors that Burns commits as she traverses Friedman's life. A reputable biography (which this certainly is) should not let easily detectable mistakes seep into the narrative fabric of its pages. Whatever the reasons for these missteps by Burns, the impulse behind them must remain a continuing mystery, meaning open to speculation but not to satisfactory explication. I mention them not in order to nit-pick but rather to reveal a troubling pattern that nurtures suspicions.

Thus on other occasions, there is a consistent (and parallel) problem whenever Burns is forced to sketch out some basic details surrounding George Stigler. If the issue was only being off a year on Stigler's departure from Chicago that in isolation would remain trivial. But she never does accurately pinpoint Stigler's implicit collaboration with Friedman, as well as his key role in building the Chicago School. Perhaps she doesn't want any overshadowing of Friedman, but Burns in my view, consistently depicts Stigler as something of a shadow of himself. For instance, Burns describes Stigler as jocular. He did have a rapier wit and a well- developed sardonic sense of humour. He was funny, not for an economist, but simply humorous, although his wit could verge on being cruel. He consistently came out with what Rose Friedman described as 'zingers'. But Santa

Claus is properly described as jocular, not George Stigler. Thus a single descriptive word provides an instant, but misleading picture.

There are other parallel, though minor curiosities, surrounding her depiction of Stigler. None of which seem justified. Burns, for unspecified reasons, feels compelled to discuss the Knight-Douglas feud of the 1930s. She finishes her examination by insisting "Stigler concluded that Simons has not met the tenure bar, yet he still painted Knight in a sympathetic light" (Burns 2023:79). She backs this up with a short quote from Stigler's (1988) autobiography. (Her use of short quotes eventually means that if the reader's trust in Burns is eroded, the suspicion grows that the quote may be taken out of context.) But Stigler's actual description doesn't sufficiently jibe with what Burns wishes to convey. Curious, because in her notes, Burns indicates that she has read Stigler's autobiography. She further uses a direct quote concerning Simons from that same source. Yet Stigler's actual evaluation of Knight's role is not so sympathetic, if read in its entirety. Why Burns would insist on this particular form of spin remains simply a matter of speculation. However, no useful purpose would be served by pursuing this thread. I can only suppose that this approach may display Stigler in a less than flattering light. But surely, her purpose shouldn't be to enhance Friedman by making his surrounding cast look inferior. Or at least, such an intention is best not entertained by any serious biographer.

> Frank Knight was my thesis chairman, and he befriended me all his life. Yet, as I read these letters I deplore the degree to which he associated his own position and dignity with that of Simons: That is a tactic which if often used would make departmental decision making utterly impossible. Of course, professors still push "their" candidates hard, but manners are important, even essential, to civilized discourse (Stigler 1988:189).

In addition, some of her other claims seem inexplicable and easily corrected. She dramatically introduces Paul Samuelson, then an undergraduate at Chicago, into her 1935 narrative of graduate life. He would become one of Milton Friedman's decades-long opponent as Burns later describes. According to Burns' account however, Samuelson was "pulled into the group's orbit after acing an introductory economics course taught by Aaron Director" (Burns 2023:66).[9] (Meaning the graduate student group whose core was Friedman, Stigler and Wallis.) But both Allen Wallis and Paul Samuelson tell the same (but different) story, one distinct from

Burns' more dynamic tale. Their mutual claim is that Samuelson had a make-work University job, which entailed dusting off the portraits of famous economists in the Department's Record Room. In this telling, the connection with the trio was made in a much more accidental fashion. Certainly this element of randomness contrasts with Burns' account. In that more dramatic construction, an almost tractor-beam inevitability pulled Samuelson into the heart of the mother ship.

> That was a strange interlude in his career. The reason that I saw them, and a good deal of them, was that to make some money during the Great Depression I had what was called an NYA, (National Youth Administration), scholarship supplement. I suppose the Department secured that for me. I don't know how much an hour I received, maybe twenty-five cents an hour, but they had to find some perfunctory work for me to do. And just as in *Pinafore*, I polished up the brass on the door.[10] I was given the job of dusting off in that Department Records Room the pictures of the great economists, Böhm-Bawerk, John Stuart Mill, David Ricardo, Adam Smith, and maybe Knut Wicksell. So I would be in that storage room doing my little 'make work job' and talking to George and Allen who were, of course, exalted graduate students. Well, you must have an impression of what George was like. I thought of the two of them then as being closer together to one another than either was to Milton Friedman (Conversation with Paul Samuelson, October 1997).

Moreover, for whatever reason, Samuelson, like a number of Friedman's other opponents, tend to be portrayed as slightly blemished. There was clearly an edge of aggression and tension between Samuelson and Friedman, although remaining friends for more than seventy years. Some of Samuelson's remarks reflect this frustration. But Friedman also would let his feelings about Samuelson show in his private letters.

> I wish you had a tape of your debate with Samuelson. I would love to hear it when I got back. Your reference to his ambivalence hits the nail on the head especially since I had never thought of putting it that way. The kind of tactics you describe unquestionably lost an audience. One reason why people like Samuelson are driven to them is that they are so unaccustomed to meeting serious intellectual opposition (Letter from Milton Friedman to George Stigler, February 22, 1963).

To emphasise the previous point concerning the way in which opponents are drawn, as Burns does point out, Harry Johnson certainly attacked Friedman's integrity quite viciously. But I fail to see why that bout of aggression could justify Burns in referring to Johnson as Friedman's half-colleague. Again, I am focusing on a very minor point. Moreover, in one sense, this description is true. Johnson had been granted the singular honour of a joint appointment at Chicago and Cambridge. Strictly speaking, he spent half his time in each place. But Burns doesn't mention these details. For the general reader, talking about Johnson as a part-time Chicago professor leaves the impression of holding an inferior position to that of Friedman. Perhaps I am reaching here for a vanishing implication, but as previously stated, the accumulation of slights to those opposed to Friedman's ideas does create suspicion. Her strict fairness in sketching others (particularly those who were not strictly aligned with his thought) becomes questionable.

Even more so, there is an almost miraculous coincidence between policy (ideology) concordances with Friedman and the fashion in which other individuals are evaluated. Those who stray from the true path (Friedman's market fundamentalism) fail to shine brightly. Even Arthur Burns, Friedman's long time mentor and friend, gets short shrift when he wanders toward 'false belief' during his term as Federal Reserve chairman. Burns (2023) burdens him with some armchair psychology, while pinning the onerous label of 'institutionalist' on his bowed shoulders.[11] (In essence, at a crucial juncture, Arthur Burns revealed himself as not being a true believer.)

> Friedman had always venerated Burns, continuing to treat him with deference even at his career transformed them into equals. In turn, Burns perpetually regarded Friedman as some sort of overgrown undergraduate; a welcome contributor to research, but certainly not someone with meaningful ideas that might alter his own. He may even have perversely resisted his former student's advice, just to keep the hierarchy intact (Burns 2023:350).

However, her questionable treatment of major economic figures are far less a problem than the shallowness of her economic grasp.[12] (In essence my apparent nit-picking has some more serious implications.) On the micro side, to start with the obvious, it seems clear that Burns failed to actually either read or perhaps understand what Ronald Coase (1960) intended to do in his article *The Problem of Social Cost*.

> Making moves similar to Friedman, Coase argued these costs [externalities] could in fact be priced and then traded. The key was a stable legal framework supporting private property. In an ideal environment of no transaction costs – which Coase admitted was impossible – regulation would not be required at all. In the existing world, the theorem suggested much economic activity that was regulated could instead be handled by courts or markets. Bargaining was key (Burns 2023:197).

The problem with this analysis is manifold. It was George Stigler who devised what textbooks refer to as the Coase Theorem. (How Coase may have been making moves similar to Friedman (as Burns claims) continues to elude me.[13]) Coase made it clear that he had no issue with the Coase Theorem as theory. But by focusing only on his constructed theorem, Stigler misunderstood the intention of Coase's article. The stated example of zero transaction costs was meant to be a deliberate McGuffin, necessary, but not the point of his lengthy exposition.[14] Coase was focused on countering the standard textbook (Pigou-like) understanding of externalities (unpriced costs or benefits). In essence, from Coase's perspective, externalities would cease to be a problem if transaction costs were zero. Under such deliberately impossible circumstances, externalities could then be ignored. In essence, the problem potentially causing markets to stumble was not externalities, but positive transaction costs. Once this was established, policy focus could shift to the realm of positive transaction costs, rather than remaining in some traditional understanding of externalities. But this specified approach meant that nothing could be said *a priori* about whether a given situation could be improved, or made worse, by government regulation. Only by examining the existing transaction costs (providing a contextual examination) could any useful conclusion be reached.

> I do not disagree with Stigler. However, I tend to regard the Coase Theorem as a stepping stone on the way to an analysis of an economy with positive transaction costs. The significance to me of the Coase Theorem is that it undermines the Pigovian system. Since standard economic theory assumes transaction costs to be zero, the Coase Theorem demonstrates that the Pigovian solutions are unnecessary in

these circumstances. Of course, it does not imply, when transaction costs are positive that government actions (such as government operation, regulation or taxation, including subsidies) could not produce a better result than relying on negotiations between individuals in the market. Whether this would be so could be discovered not by studying imaginary governments but what real governments actually do. My conclusion: Let us study the world of positive transaction costs (Coase 1994a:10–11).

Even more distracting than Burns' Coasian stumble, is her version of what lies at the core of the post-war Chicago School, namely the Chicago version of price theory. This construct underlies the way in which Friedman, Stigler, Director or many of the rest, understood how markets regulate an economy. The importance here does not lie with the way in which the version expounded in Chicago during those years was similar to that found in almost any microeconomics textbook. (This concordance is largely what Burns supplies.) But even worse, she seems to confuse the way in which Chicago applied price theory to the theory itself. Once you transform price theory into a rough equivalent of a decision making science, applications open up, engulfing what traditionally remained in the clubhouse of other social sciences.

> At the most basic level, Chicago price theory – named after its roots in the University of Chicago, where Friedman was educated and taught for decades – was simply microeconomics, the analysis of rational human choice under conditions of scarcity.[15] It approximates what any economics student still encounters in college. But the "Chicago" version was different, for it refused to keep economic analysis within its traditional boundaries. Taking price theory out of the classroom, Friedman crafted a dizzying array of policies with a consistent theme: setting prices free (Burns 2023:12).

Instead of blurring theory with application, a more valuable understanding can be gained by looking at Melvin Reder's (1982) account (himself a former member of the Chicago department) and in particular his insistence on a 'Tight Prior Equilibrium' composing the core of the theory. Whether his perspective is accepted, or not, it does succeed in raising at least a few questions.[16] Even more curious is that at this early stage, Burns appears to be examining Chicago Price Theory without any real discussion of the 'rational economic man'. Doing so is like watching a performance of the play *Hamlet* without Hamlet actually appearing.[17] Driven hard by Becker and Stigler, but supported by Friedman and Director, the transcendence of this central character, transformed price theory into the essential (and all-purpose) model of human decision making. At the heart of this view is the individual as a rational calculator. Returning momentarily to Ronald Coase, the incipient confusion that arises by not stipulating this condition allows Burns to blur Ronald Coase into nothing more than a generic Chicago style economist. However when properly understood (meaning Friedman's price theory stylistics), Coase's approach to economics differed decisively from that of Friedman or Stigler. Though Coase was certainly at Chicago for almost half of a very long life, he was never (in a fundamental fashion) of Chicago.

> I don't say people are wholly irrational. I have said that almost the only thing we can say about consumer behaviour is, if you raise the price of something, people will demand less. And that we know, but it doesn't follow that because a person does less foolishness when the price is high for foolishness that you don't have foolishness. The foolishness follows the universal law of demand. The greater the price you have to pay for being foolish, the less you do (Coase 1997:3).

What Burns chooses not to explore is the pivotal role played by making a strict rationality assertion. This particular incarnation of economic theory made it feasible for the economic method to then creep into and dominate (to varying degrees) other social sciences. Given this formidable foundation, the focus inevitably shifts ever more resolutely to the decision making process, one which is clearly not only relevant to the field of economics. Burns cannot avoid highlighting this approach in a biography that exalts Milton Friedman. What does seem puzzling (and unnecessary) is that Burns proceeds to tar Friedman's teacher, Frank Knight, with the same rationality brush. Placing the sort of academic imperialism that developed at Chicago as being consistent with Frank Knight's thinking on this matter indicates either a thorough misunderstanding, or lack of familiarity, with Knight's thoughts and writing.[18] In some curious fashion, Friedman's thought must flow backwards as well as forward. Knight through some unstated transformation must be turned into a rough forerunner of Friedman, performing as his John the Baptist. This connection seems more than a bit strained, given Friedman's distinct break with Knight.[19] However, I'll return to this topic when I examine Friedman's approach to markets, as well as the way in which Burns (2023) simply accepts the magic of markets without a single significant demur.

But much more puzzling in what becomes to some degree a cavalcade of misrepresentations is the way in which Burns deigns to treat Keynes. Key debates are inevitably misrepresented if opponents are handicapped to enhance the status of one's designated hero. In this instance, many of Friedman's battles (at least in the first part of his career) revolved around his attempt to topple John Maynard Keynes from his perch as the dominant figure in economics (even when he was long dead). A biography of Milton Friedman would accordingly ring hallow without the appearance of Keynes (or at least his ghostly presence). Thus a basic understanding of Keynes (1936/1964) *A General Theory* would seem to be required. (Though there is an attached warning. Namely, never bring up a subject in a biography without understanding enough about it to at least sound plausible.) Doing so is not admittedly a straightforward task. As an endnote in the biography reveals, there has been an endless controversy over what Keynes actually intended to say. But some issues are simply there to be found by any willing reader. Meaning that obvious faux pas will be easily spotted by anyone sufficiently conversant with the *General Theory*.

Unfortunately, Burns' (2023) numerous attempts to refer directly to the book must leave any perceptive reader of the original with the distinct impression that her knowledge comes from secondary sources, despite endnotes which cite the work. (The alternative would be worse, that she read the *General* Theory, but simply couldn't grasp its message.) Coincidentally, the seeds of my growing suspicions surrounding the entirety of Burns' work began to blossom, given her inexplicable failure to explain the basic (Hicks devised) IS-LM model.[20] She attempts to squeeze it into a standard supply and demand model, which would leave even an amateur macroeconomist feeling queasy.

However, a more glaring own goal arrives with an offhand comment attached to her botched discussion of Hick's model. For reasons unknown, she boldly claims that the *General Theory* lacks any diagrams. "Keynes's *General Theory of Employment, Interest, and* Money (1936) contained no graphs, but soon IS-LM came to summarize American Keynesianism" (Burns 2023:138). Perhaps she just became entranced by the contrasting picture she wished to draw. None might sound more dramatic than just one. But, as anyone who had actually read the book would know, there is definitely one diagram tucked within the pages of that work. The fact that there is only one, should make (if anything) that diagram more memorable. Sadly however, as her comments on Keynes accumulated, I was forced to conclude (with a degree of assurance) that she had never opened that particular book, or if opened, the work had baffled her. In any case, the only valid explanation I could reach was that her remarks on Keynes came through second hand sources, which she had simply (and uncritically) swallowed. The attached problem remains. Without sufficient economics training, it seems unlikely that an author can properly evaluate and judge contrasting interpretations of Keynes. As will be discussed later, Friedman's questionable claims concerning Keynes' work go largely unchallenged by Burns.

In discussing Keynes (and *The General Theory*) the terms aggregate demand and aggregate supply almost never appear. Instead, Burns chooses to transform the work into a framework that accords more closely with her predetermined aims. She does so by focusing only either on consumption or monetary theory. These are (not coincidentally) two of Friedman's great areas of research, but the attempt to transfer these concerns unadjusted, provides a much distorted vision of Keynes' intentions. His focus was instead on the instability of aggregate demand and why this periodically led to a recession or depression. (This contrasts sharply with Simons who believed that such moments were not an inherent (or inevitable) trait of market systems, but more of an aberration.)

In contrast to Friedman's future approach, Keynes assumes that consumption is a relatively stable percentage of total income. (As opposed to claims made by Burns, Keynes does discuss the psychological reasons behind saving – or non-consumption). Since all income isn't spent on consumption the remainder (at least in a simple model), must be composed of investment. For Keynes, investment is the underlying root cause of insufficient aggregate demand. Investment, in this approach, tends to be much more variable than consumption. The implication is that there can be periods where the level of investment (and thus aggregate demand) is insufficient or less than the economy's capacity (aggregate supply) to meet it. In which case, the economy can achieve a recessionary equilibrium featuring a high level of unemployment. But investment is seldom, if ever, mentioned by Burns, as if it is a matter not worth consideration, simply because it lay outside of Friedman's specific fixations.[21]

Instead, perhaps because one of Milton Friedman's unarguably major contributions to economic theory was his work on consumption theory, Burns disregards the key role investment played for Keynes. She doesn't deny it. To be strictly accurate, Burns just ignores these fundamentals.

(Specifically, no mention is made of how it is determined, or why such an investment function lacks stability. Nor does Burns display a sufficient level of interest in why monetary policy may be an unreliable source in boosting investment level.) Instead, Burns appears comfortable with simply transforming Keynes into a pale shadow of Milton Friedman.

This goal is easily accomplished, just by limiting discussion to Friedman's intense focus on consumption. Or perhaps Burns' insistence is driven by a perceived need to muddle the role[22] played by the multiplier in Keynes' thinking. (That's another key concept that largely falls through the cracks when Burns sketches out her version of *The General Theory*.) And yet the constituted multiplier is undeniably at the very centre of Keynes' fiscal policy and a backbone of his analysis. But despite Burns' strategic spin, Keynes assigned investment, not consumption, the lead role in his constructed drama. This interpretation of Keynes is hardly deniable. Nor will a quote from Hansen demolish the intent of an entire volume. Without exploring the relative context in depth, a single sentence quote carries little weight. Moreover, by this point, Burns has burned down any remaining bridges of good-will.

> At the crux of their conversation [Brady, Reid, Mack and Friedman] was the Keynesian consumption function. This was the mathematical relationship at the heart of the Keynesian revolution, which showed the relationship between money earned and money spent … As Alvin Hansen put it: "it has been my conviction for many years that the great contribution of the General Theory was the clear and specific formulation of the consumption function" (Burns 2023:222).[23]

Keynes, of course, did not regard *The General Theory* (1936) as in any sense his last word on either consumption or investment. His ideas on monetary theory (despite Friedman's opinion) had distinctly evolved throughout his career and would have undoubtedly continued to change and adjust. He had gone from a standard Marshallian view, as spelled out in his *Tract* (1923), to the exposition in his *Treatise* (1930), all before making his last comprehensive effort in *The General* Theory (1936).[24]

Given Keynes' record of being open to other (and even opposing ideas), the glitch noticed in his consumption theory (by Friedman as well as others) would have not posed some insurmountable stumbling block for his evolving ideas. The problem with Keynes' original consumption expectation is sufficiently discussed by Burns. Though mentioned in passing, she does manage to largely skirt a bit of more obvious evidence in this case. Namely that the problem which ended up gaining the ever intrepid Friedman important recognition was equally recognised by a host of Keynesians. Modigliani (1949, 1953 and 1957) had been developing his life cycle hypothesis during the post-war period. Duesenberry (1949) in turn focused on a ratchet theory of income.

This is not to belittle, or even for a moment demean, Friedman's crucial contribution to consumption theory (his permanent income hypothesis (1957)).[25] But, given Burns' predictable twist on all things Friedman, pointing out that Friedman was not swimming against the tide (in this case) remains an important point. Despite his drive and accomplishments, Friedman never tried to be more heroic than he had to be (and even at times was given to pettiness). Equally important, this discovered flaw in Keynes' simple formulation, one which was widely discovered during the immediate post war period, hardly threw a fatally damning spanner (one capable of utterly demolishing *The General Theory*), into the economic works. Burns does, however, insist on providing a subtle slant to the actual events, with Friedman acting as an implicit pioneer in discovering the fatal flaw in Keynes' theory. (In some strange and parallel fashion, Friedman appears in a Luke Skywalker mode, zeroing-in on the Death Star's point of weakness.) In doing so, Burns becomes too closely aligned to those would be critics, who suppose that discovering an error in Darwin's *Origin of the Species*, somehow effectively demolishes evolutionary theory once and for all.[26]

As pointed out, weighing up economic material, particularly contending theories, can pose difficulties even for the practised economist. For those without that peculiar background, the task is much more fraught. Right out of the gate, Burns stumbles due to her loose grasp of basic economics. But when it comes to the role that ideology plays in academic endeavours, a historian of intellectual ideas should prove more than capable of exploring this aspect of Friedman's work (particularly when the juncture between theory and policy is examined.) Especially since Friedman, unlike his close friend George Stigler, accepted the influence that ideology might have on an economist's professional work. But ultimately, Burns proves more intent on laying out and painting her vision of Friedman's heroic journey, than in grappling with these seamier aspects of his life. (She does provide a passing air kiss to the issue as her volume closes.)

II. Good Eggs and 'Our Kind' – The Role of Evidence and Ideology

> I doubt there is a truly unbiased academic. If you think the [Chicago] GSB is an unbiased environment, think again. They are recruited for their views. I wonder how many free marketers would get jobs in anthropology of sociology … It's true of any institute. You state a mission, attract funders. They expect the mission to be fulfilled. Very rarely do people fund pure knowledge (James Hickman quoted in Nik-Khah 2011b:380).

Simply ask a hard-core ideologue what would conceivably change his or her mind. That innocent question remains a basic, but effective, test for ferreting out committed, true believers. No such evidence can be imagined (or uncovered), which would be able to shift these one track minds (whether they are found to belong to the Right or to the Left). Academics who readily fit into this category implicitly think they know exactly how the world works. This firm conviction shields them from being convinced otherwise. Milton Friedman, for instance, was never filled with self-doubt, or grappled with acute indecision. Like more than a few of his Chicago colleagues, Friedman was blessed with a wonderful talent that allowed him to ask the right questions. But, he was simultaneously cursed with the unfortunate habit of knowing the answers to those posed questions in advance.

In fact, if asked to visualise the face of ideology in economics, an immediate photo of Milton Friedman might pop up in the minds of a good chunk of the profession. Consequently, it can only be disappointing to discover that Burns largely fumbles what should be a key focus when evaluating Friedman. Burns (at best) performs a sort of modified hokey pokey in this regard, barely putting her right leg in before quickly pulling it back out. Throughout the biography, whenever the ideological issue appears on the verge of erupting, she deftly side-steps whatever influence was clearly exerted by Friedman's rock-steady beliefs. (I can only suspect that the cause may lie in being overly sympathetic to her subject, or sharing too many of his specific beliefs.)

Only in a sketchy afterword, almost as an after-thought in the dying pages of the volume, does Burns take up the issue, if only briefly. She then appears to evaluate this singular issue of ideology, but her aim in doing so is to largely exonerate, not to fairly judge, him. His rock-ribbed beliefs (in Burns' eyes) did not lead to any detrimental bias in his work. Instead, such unalterable positions only spurred him on to further greatness. "But what, really, is at stake in this question? [The 'lucky consistency' between his research and his ideology.] Surely it would matter if Friedman suppressed evidence, faked his results, or refused debate and argument on his central points. Does it matter that a clear set of ethical and political commitments guided his work?" (Burns 2023:479). My counter-response is that it does certainly matter. Policy is partly a matter of persuasion. Whether ideology leaves such persuaders with clean hands remains questionable. Consequently, just as in a courtroom, Burns verdict of 'not guilty' doesn't leave Friedman innocent of all charges. (Burns' urge to act as prosecutor, defence attorney and judge is perhaps debatable.) Despite this broad acquittal, there is still the distinct possibility that Friedman's unambiguous policies might have been inferior (or even badly flawed), when compared to other alternatives. Or to put the matter bluntly, his fervour as a true believer might have persuaded, where persuasion was unwarranted. Given this biographical absence in Burns' efforts, I feel compelled to take up some of this slack in this and future sections.

In essence the question that has to be raised is whether either data or evidence was capable of changing Milton Friedman's mind.[27] His nemesis, John Maynard Keynes is reputed to have remarked that 'When the facts change, I change my mind. What do you do, sir?'[28] One is tempted to reply that when similarly challenged, Friedman just excavates and finds more agreeable facts. But like others, he seldom considers the possibility that he might be uncomfortably wrong in supporting his theoretical constructs. Ideology can then unbalance an economist's judgment. Not that it is possible to erase every shred of such a belief system, even amongst the most earnest.[29] Instead, the more pragmatic option is to be modest in one's professional endeavours. (Perhaps taking advice from John Stuart Mill in trying to be more open minded is still solid reasoning.) Fair minded economists might instead strive for usefulness. Keynes once characterised the desired professional aim as seeking to become similar to dentists, rather than setting oneself up as a seer and prognosticator.[30] Admitting the limits of one's knowledge, though uncomfortable, can maintain that necessary balance between beliefs and evidence.

Unlike his close colleague, George Stigler, Milton Friedman did acknowledge the potential role that ideology might play in the field of economics.[31] As always, Friedman was convinced that he had managed to maintain the appropriate balance, escaping the pitfalls that befell others in his trade. This judgment comes as no surprise. Even Burns' long exploration of Friedman, at no point, attempts to quibble with his own evaluation. When it comes to her subject, she is no fault finder. Unfortunately, in striving to become a competent biographer, this perspective (perhaps) leaves Burns in too compliant a position. Admiration is always possible without slipping into adoration.

> During my whole career, I [Milton Friedman} have considered myself somewhat of a schizophrenic, which might be a universal characteristic. On the one hand, I was interested in science, *qua science*, and I have tried – successfully I hope – not to let my ideological viewpoints contaminate my scientific work. On the other, I felt deeply concerned with the course of events and I wanted to influence them so as to enhance human freedom. Luckily, these two aspects of my interests appeared to me as perfectly compatible (Friedman quoted in Cherrier 2011d:535).

Though ironically failing to see the ideological mote in his own eye, he grew to see those motes elsewhere in the discipline. Yet despite the inherent audacity of such a position, both Friedman and Stigler, as well as others in the profession, firmly believed they knew exactly the way in which the world works (particularly the economic world). From this perspective, policy recommendations, derived from stated theoretical investigations, inevitably achieved a remarkable agreement with any prejudged opinions. If then Friedman (unlike others), was able to balance his ideological imperatives in order to avoid biasing his scientific work, his opponents (by definition) must accordingly have failed to properly fend off their own winds of ideology. Such a viewpoint would strike many observers as at least tinged with a touch of arrogance.

> As he explained in 1998, he had begun to doubt the possibility for rationalization in politics largely because he had "repeatedly experienced attacks on what I regarded as scientific findings by economists who seemed driven more by their values than their objective judgment". Self-interest and ideological blindness – not legitimate difference in judgment – blocked the acceptance of the truths of positive economics (Friedman quoted in Stapleford 2011:29).

Those truths of positive economics that Friedman continued to honour, appear to lack any tinge of ambiguity, trading at times accuracy for conviction. Nonetheless, Friedman long blamed policy differences as being ideologically driven, in essence leaving his opponents no other option than to cling on to badly misinformed alternatives. "Tellingly, Friedman concedes that there is not a 'one-to-one relation between policy conclusions and the conclusions of positive economics,' but he attributes the divergence solely to normative economics" (Friedman quoted in Stapleford 2011: 20 ftn. 13). In practise, he seemed to find accepting ambiguity to be difficult. This reluctance held whether examining policy differences, or when considering the truths of positive economics.

> Value judgements ended up playing a role in your assessment of parameters and of the evidence we consider … and there is no question that Milton and I, looking at the same evidence, may reach different conclusions as to what it means, because to him, it is so clear that government intervention is bad that there cannot be an occasion where it was good! Whereas, to me government discretion can be good or bad (Modigliani quoted in Cherrier 2011d:354).

The reality in which Friedman operated was structured by the first Mont Pelerin meeting. That conclave helped open his eyes to what was at stake in this new post-war world (the battle for freedom against collectivist tyranny). Henceforth, Friedman's scientific work took on a meaning that transcended the simple academic pursuit of economics. Friedman was transformed into (and continued to be) a crusader, a missionary espousing the miracle of markets. For him, the post-war period revealed life and death outcomes at play. He saw himself deliberately posed against the enemies (unwitting or not) of freedom and liberty. Someone playing for such high stakes should inevitably find it difficult to be fair minded when opposing collectivists who stubbornly persisted in pushing government (instead of market) remedies. (As with every true believer, his most accomplished bit of evangelising came in convincing himself of his own devised truths.) Even with the best of wishes, the collectivist designed vision, though paved with good intentions, still led directly to hell in his view. Thus the public, as well as the economics profession, had to be persuaded at all costs, even if at times whiffs of rhetorical sophistry seemed to enter into the arguments he presented. (The extent to which Milton Friedman was aware of such occasional evasions must remain an open question.)

If then you are motivated in the manner of Milton Friedman, seeing any small deviation from the truth becomes the first step down a slippery slope to perdition. Under these conditions, you are obliged to take no prisoners when dealing with opposing viewpoints. In his Manichean created world, you either struggled to maintain freedom and liberty, or you bowed down (knowingly or not) to some constructed authoritarian government. The dangers Friedman saw might well have prompted him to adhere so fiercely to his ideological perspective. Government intervention (collective action), despite its intentions, must (almost) by definition, always be dangerous. To underline this inevitability, Friedman practically doted on the idea of 'unintended consequences'. Such an approach could successfully blow any well intentioned policy out of the water. (This underlying fierceness, beneath Milton Friedman's apparent reasonableness and good humour, is an area of personal geography that Burns (2023) almost consistently shies away from.)

> The sincere fanatic has done vast harm in the course of human history. But in our time and our country, the major flaw that has converted doing good into doing evil is very different: it is the temptation to solve every problem by spending somebody else's money. Only government has the power to do that on a large scale. So the standard cliché for every social ill has become … more government spending, more government manpower. The result has almost always been that the money ends up being spent for very different purposes than those intended by the do-gooders, and makes the problem worse rather than better (Friedman 1971:3).

This is not to dismiss Friedman's work (and others at Chicago) in exploring government failure. Prior to these efforts, too much confidence was placed in the ability of government to solve problems in the fashion of some friendly engineering company building a badly needed bridge. The ruling policy consensus had arguably veered into an almost unexamined optimism. Yet, Friedman's examples of cases, where government agencies clearly fluffed its stated objective, fails to dismiss actual examples of success, even if such outcomes don't exactly meet plans or predictions.[32] Instead, his arguments were engineered so that once some seeming innocuous premise was accepted, even ostensible opponents found themselves incontrovertibly on an express train rocketing toward Friedman's preferred destination.[33] The bedrock of this argumentative railway (paving the way for these final stops), at least implicitly accorded with Friedman's libertarian impulses (though he shied away from embracing such a label). The core of such beliefs insisted that individuals were necessarily solely responsible for their outcomes. (Each one being the captain of his or her individual ships.)[34] It is therefore somewhat ironic that when turning autobiographical, Rose and Milton deemed themselves to be, *Two Lucky People*. In Friedman's world of extreme individual responsibility, luck had nothing to do with it (nor for that matter, did the uncertainty – that prefigures a realm of luck – actually exist).

But for Friedman, policy flowed with a one to one precision from constructed theory. (Beatrice Cherrier (2011d) does a thorough job of examining the remarkable concordance between Friedman's ideologically sound policy recommendations and the theory that underpinned it.) For some of his more sceptical professional brethren, such agreement might seem to strain credulity. But theory (or scientifically) based policy that was empirically tested formed the bedrock of his modernised version of liberalism. It further implied that faith in Keynesian style policies could be undermined by torpedoing their theoretical basis. This logic provided Friedman (and others) with a strategy by which a restoration of liberal (conservative in US speak) positions could be accomplished. (Or to be more exact, Friedman's conception of a new classical liberalism.)

Friedman chose to take this route in the aftermath of the Mont Pelerin conference. (Burns, for whatever reasons, doesn't give this event in Friedman's career sufficient importance in her narrative.) Moreover, heading down this direction, meant an increasing break from his Chicago teachers, particularly from Frank Knight, Henry Simons and to a lesser degree, Jacob Viner. To varying degrees, they were all liberals, but in the older, classical mode that Friedman was foregoing. As a group, his mentors tended to be more sceptical (and more tolerant) than Friedman, who persistently acted not purely as an academic, but also as a dedicated crusader. This approach strictly countered the classical liberalism of John Stuart Mill. For Mill, an open minded debate was the equivalent of a positive sum game that allowed individuals to improve their thinking, producing stronger and better grounded theories. (Friedman, in contrast, championed a winner take all approach, where good theories must predictably triumph over lesser offerings.)

In essence, Mill advocated listening carefully to opposing views, but not merely to discover ways in which an opponent could be vanquished. The goal was to thoroughly understand alternative ideas, not to simply grind them into the mud.[35] In the zero sum approach adopted by Friedman, the idea which somehow survived a bout of intellectual combat, would be deemed correct, having remained unvanquished during this battle of wits.

Though it is important to add that ultimately, only the test of time would reveal its inherent truthfulness. A theory would have to survive untold battles over a number of years before gaining full acceptance. Knowledge in the Friedman world was then viewed as being equivalent to unarmed combat, with outcomes inevitably boasting a stark winner and loser. Consequently, proponents of this perspective rejected environments that actively promoted academic collaboration (a positive sum game) where alternatives might yield a more fruitful outcomes.[36]

> Instead, Professor Kahneman favoured an alternative that he termed "adversarial collaboration." When people who disagree work together to test a hypothesis, they are involved in a common endeavour. They are trying not to win but to figure out what's true. They might even become friends (Sunstein 2024:1).

To frame the broader context, for Friedman, as for Stigler, the market for ideas was just another, undifferentiated marketplace. Competition would inevitably produce the best result in an almost Darwinian struggle. Unfortunately, the underlying confusion embedded within this approach is that the evidence for actual operative markets was never so bold in supporting these claims. Nothing in theory, or in practise, consistently insists that market competition must yield some optimal outcome. Like evolution through selection, markets yield the result that best meets consumer demand (at least given some optimal scenario). Pushing this approach in a parallel fashion only yields the idea that any market for ideas will best promote those theories which meet the expectations (beneficial flows minus user cost) of its academic consumers. The relationship of this process to some idea of actual truth is, at best, always oblique.[37]

> It may be that in the long run good ideas do surface but they surface faster, if written in a persuasive fashion. Moreover, bad ideas may be put persuasively. And they may gain the necessary threshold. However, taking that same analogy in competition among ideas, there is a presumption, although not a certainty, that in the longer run, the good ideas are going to compete out the bad ideas. But that may take a long time and may not even always operate. There's nothing necessary about that. Nothing guaranteed about that (Conversation with Gary Becker, October 1997).

This absolute ideological sense of virtue and correctness was to a large degree nurtured by the first Mont Pelerin meeting and absorbed by the attending, would be acolytes. Not that Friedman, prior to this date, lacked solid conservative principles, but that his work and policy efforts became far more focused after this event. A careful examination of his output, post Mont Pelerin, will I think display this marked departure. Burns though, chooses to give what is arguably insignificant weight to this event. She opts instead to shine an enhancing light (and by doing so, perhaps over emphasising their importance) on Friedman's actual actions there. Once again, Burns transforms Friedman into a prime mover, a position maintained no matter what the context or historical situation.

In a similar vein, this ideological refining, which occurred post Switzerland, namely Friedman's recognition that classical liberalism needed a serious updating, inevitably led him to break with such Chicago stalwarts as Knight, Simons and Viner. Friedman sensed that the old ways were insufficient to cope with the modern, post-war world. This increasing distance would become obvious over the passing years. Burns doesn't entirely overlook this discarding of his teachers' thoughts and approaches, but it is underplayed and not satisfactorily illuminated. In essence, the nature of the break and its importance isn't precisely grasped. To take a key example, Knight, for instance, cast a serious spell over the Chicago graduate students of the 1930s (as well as such junior members of the faculty as Director or Simons). Breaking away was not so easily accomplished. (Where is the struggle in Burns' bout of story-telling?)

> In Chicago everybody knew the answer, economics was a completed science. Allen Wallis never got a Ph.D; Homer Jones never got a Ph.D.; Al Hart had terrible problems in getting his Ph.D. past Knight because he wrote about the period of production. George Stigler told me that everything good in economics was already in Frank Knight (Samuelson 2011f:981–982).

Knight, though like many of his students fiercely critical of government programs, was equally critical of markets. Burns never makes this key difference clear. "Even Frank Knight was never your simple conservative in the sense that Milton Friedman was, or even in the sense of Henry Simons. He just was against any government action, but he really was also cynical about the market at that time" (Samuelson 2011f:982). In addition,

Knight worried about such things as uncertainty and the ethics of competition, both of which could make such outcomes imprecise and less admirable.[38] Markets, in his estimation, contained no regulatory mechanism to ensure anything resembling an ethical outcome. Instead, economies were buffeted by random outcomes and shocks, with individuals flourishing to some degree due to sheer luck alone. Burns, when speaking of Knight, fails to specify this fundamental difference. In contrast (and largely unexplored by Burns) competitive market outcomes, for Friedman, required no externally provided improvement. Meaning that tinkering with this mechanism was difficult (if not impossible) to justify. Burns simply fails to identify the implicit ideology lurking behind such definite claims.

> Frank Knight was skeptical of the moral and intellectual content of political behaviour and particularly hostile to central economic planning, but he was also severely critical of the ethical basis of a competitive economy. No doctrinaire defender of private enterprise would find him a source of strength (Stigler 1988:148).

The break with Knight was far more decisive than Burns allows. She chooses to approach the issue only tangentially, to an extent minimising its importance. But Friedman's post-war insistence in jumping directly from theory to policy (a rejection of classical liberalism) reveals his significant change in direction. In other words, this shift is not an area that should be left largely unexplored. (Though Friedman's approach to policy did become a strategy that unfortunately became widespread in post-war economics. The universal move was to make economics scientific, and this direct line from theory to policy was seen as the path that directly led to that goal.)

The result was an almost universal drive to substitute policies that were time and place specific with policies that were universally valid, holding sway indefinitely. Clearly this could be considered an unwarranted departure from Mill and Marshall, certainly one that Knight would be unwilling to commit. (Note that as even Burns highlights, Friedman claimed to be continuing in the Marshallian tradition, at least according to his own lights. "He [Milton Friedman] had begun with the battle against the Cowles Commission and the rehabilitation of Alfred Marshall" (Burns 2023:235). With friends like these, Marshall had no need for enemies.)

Like Marshall, Knight and Viner did not see economics as offering virtually inviolable laws. Instead, they looked at theories as tendency statements as when Knight said that "economic laws like other scientific laws state a *tendency*, a result which would follow if certain conditions are present (Medema 2011c:154).[39]

Though the major (and more widely acknowledged) breaks were with Knight and Simons, Viner should also be included in their number since his classical liberalism contrasts sharply with Friedman's modernised version. (Despite Friedman thinking that he was somehow restoring the essence of liberalism, the result was quite at odds with such an intention.) For instance, though Jacob Viner was not as immediately influential as either Knight or Simons, he did leave an initial mark on Friedman (as well as on George Stigler), via his infamous price theory class that could bring students to tears.

But while holding very conservative views himself, Viner avoided the realm of strident ideology and was more tolerant of those holding opposing views.[40] Burns describes an early Chicago conference (1951) funded with Volker money as, "In many ways the conference represented the ultimate Chicago ideal, featuring vigorous debate and a genuine clash of views" (Burns 2023:201). Jacob Viner's perspective and objections are mentioned by Burns, but she releases just a few snippets. "Viner found it 'rigidly structured' and was shocked to learn 'the financing of the conference, as I found out later, was ideologically loaded'" (Burns 2023:201). Such selected excerpts tend to water down (intentionally or not) the full force of Viner's response. A fuller recounting by Viner in a letter to Patinkin drives the observed problem home more clearly.[41]

It was not until after I left Chicago in 1946 that I began to hear rumours about a 'Chicago School' which was engaged in *organized* battle for *laissez faire* and 'quantity theory of money' against 'imperfect competition' theorizing and 'Keynesianism'. I remained sceptical about this until I attended a conference sponsored by University of Chicago professors in 1951. The invited participants were a varied lot of academics, bureaucrats, businessmen, etc, but the program for discussion, the selection of chairmen, and everything about the participants were so patently rigidly structure, so loaded that I got more amusement from the conference than from any other I ever attended. Even the source of the financing of the Conference, as I found out later, was ideologically loaded (Jacob Viner quoted in Patinkin 2003a:112).

Viner, unlike Friedman, was a Chicago academic who avoided sliding into a comfortable dogmatism. He had the grace of being able to say 'maybe' to alternative views, instead of just dismissing them. "Viner was studiously non-dogmatic on policy views … like the rest of the economics profession – none (except Viner) had serious reservation that his understanding of economic life was incomplete or mistaken" (Stigler 1982:170). Unfortunately, this touch of Chicago arrogance (notable perhaps particularly in Knight) is the one aspect the Friedman clung to most fiercely throughout his career. Burns seems willing to only skirt the border of Friedman's dogmatism without really exploring the consequences. However (in contrast to Friedman for instance) what both Viner and Simons vigorously supported, was a fiercely active anti-trust program. The implication squarely was that private economic power (monopoly) was a distinct problem. (Otherwise anti-trust seems a bit superfluous.) Simons, in essence, deduced that an economy needed active government intervention to achieve a sphere that resembled the world of competitive markets and the semblance of a liberal society that he recommended.

> With it [liberal society] however, he joined an extensive and intricate set
> of tasks for the state:

1. The positive pursuit of competition by limitist laws as well as by antitrust policy.
2. Public ownership and operation of 'natural' monopolies (preferably by local governments where possible).
3. Severe restriction of advertising and merchandising (Stigler 1982:168).

To underline this particular doctrinal break, a Simons like approach would become anathema to Friedman, who chose to be guided decisively by Aaron Director instead.[42] "If you look at parts of the *Program for Laissez Faire*, it doesn't look that interesting at this stage", (Conversation with Gary Becker, October 1997). In fact in Friedman's first unified collection of policy positions and recommendations, he effectively dismisses private power (and implicitly the use of anti-trust action) as posing a serious problem. What does not exist cannot impede the working of competitive markets. Or at least Friedman prefers to focus on one aspect of monopoly power. Predictably in his perspective, it is labour (not business) that creates the classic problem of monopoly power.[43] "In one respect, there is an important difference between labour and enterprise monopoly. While there seems not to have been any upward trend in the importance of enterprise monopoly over the past half-century, there certainly has been in the importance of labour monopoly" (Friedman 1962:124).

Burns (2023) mentions only in passing Friedman's views on monopoly, preferring to yield more print to his monetary theory, as well as his permanent income hypothesis. She is not wrong to do so, but some analysis of his monopoly position is vital in revealing Friedman's policy positions and market ideology. An assumed absence of any serious monopoly issues denies government (aka Friedman's dreaded collectivism) the thin edge of the wedge needed to increasingly clamp down on individual freedom and liberty. Examined, we find once again a happy coincidence. The empirical reality needed to support Friedman's ideological preferences are discovered once again. In a twisted Hegelian imperative, what is ideal for Milton Friedman turns out to be actual, or more precisely, what Friedman discovers to be actual concords with his ideal constructions. (To be crude, what Friedman wants, Friedman gets.)

In Friedman's perspective, freedom is both narrowly and ambiguously defined as a function of the absence of coercion. Fortunately for his formulation, competitive markets are deemed to yield both efficient and fair outcomes. Intervention (namely government coercion) is forestalled in order to preserve freedom, which can only be supplied when underwritten by competitive markets. The result of applying this specific ideology in this fashion is that freedom continues to be maintained as long as markets operate in an untrammelled fashion. Friedman's happy coincidence is preserved almost miraculously by this undeniably asserted connection between markets and freedom. Such unbreakable links appear almost fortuitously in the extent of their convenience.

Freedom though is the single, strongest motif throughout the biography and certainly throughout his scientific research and policy imperatives. Moreover, maintaining liberty and freedom drives his missionary work, whether attempted in the US or abroad. Hypothetically, if it was possible to fantasize about Milton Friedman deigning to tattoo his arm (or some other bodily region) the one word inscription of freedom (or perhaps liberty) is what would almost necessarily be discovered. Given Friedman's obsessive focus, Burns cannot help but touch on this particular salient fact of Friedman's recurring conception and employment of freedom (and the fear of its ever persistent loss). Meaning that she is almost forced to mention the lack of clarity surrounding the concept that forms the foundation of Friedman's ideology. This idea of individual freedom could even be viewed as forming the central motivation of his life's work. But unfortunately, she seems to simply accept Friedman's stance without anything other than a superficial examination.

The problem is that for someone who claimed to undertake scientific work, Friedman's ideas centring on freedom are largely devoid of precision.[44] Mostly, Friedman seems to equate any collective undertaking with coercion, meaning that in his vocabulary collectivism equates to a lack of freedom. This stance implies that since governments may force people to do what they would prefer not to do, government action can be defined as coercion that yields a distinct lack of freedom. Once that starting point is accepted, the only logical response is to minimise what governments can do. (The danger of accepting Friedman's initial assumptions has been previously mentioned.) Or in Friedman's words, "the scope of government must be limited" (1962:2) and "government power must be dispersed" (1962:3). But these statements, shorn of any obfuscation, tracks uncomfortably close to a five year old proclaiming, 'you can't tell me what to do'.[45]

Consequently, in a world where people are free to choose (unless somehow paralysed), an insistence on freedom as some absence of coercion is more a rhetorical device than an applicable notion. More sensible is thinking in terms of degrees of coercion. Take an extreme case to highlight this bit of flawed logic. A gun is thrust into one's face and money is demanded. The opportunity cost of refusal is extremely high, but choice is still possible. Governments can regulate and enforce, but for some individuals, the opportunity cost of not obeying is insufficiently high to prevent them from breaking the law. In both instances, they are free to choose.

Even in cases where there is a conflict of interest, both in government and in private enterprise, overcoming this impasse generally attracts a standard response. A viable resolution depends on changing the opportunity cost of disobeying through negative or positive incentives. Where a mutually beneficial result dominates, is coercion still present? At times, Friedman seems to be speaking of a hypothetical world where all opportunity costs are zero, more science fiction than fact. Yet for Friedman (or Stigler) the workplace is by definition not a site of coercion, a geography where firing or being fired surprisingly encompass the same opportunity cost. Remarkably, while markets are coercion free (defined in that fashion), government regulations or restrictions inevitable conjure up an abhorred situation where someone's will is bent to a set purpose.[46] But coercion, if it is to be an applicable concept, should logically be tied to the perceived opportunity cost of making a specific choice, not tied to some vague notion of being forced to do something disagreeable. Instead, Friedman seems to imply that he knows (and will recognise) coercion when he sees it (a response sometimes given to define pornography). Such a stance is not particularly viable.

Certainly the existence of a free or authoritarian society is not an either/or alternative. Such an option fails to reflect actual choices (market or otherwise) that are made in daily life. Societies exist along a continuum, rather than being restricted to either end. But even if a more sophisticated approach is accepted, the definition of the extremes that define the continuum remain largely debatable. There is a temptation of thinking of Friedman's free society in terms of the old Janis Joplin song, where freedom is just another word for nothing left to lose. In essence a low opportunity cost for any choice leaves the chooser largely indifferent. In which case, simplistically defining freedom as a lack of coercion is not at all helpful. Burns though fails to find Friedman's idea at all problematic. She falls into the trap of being unwilling to question what 'everyone knows'.

Perhaps though, the definition merely reflects a deep-rooted trait. Friedman clearly doesn't like being told what to do. He almost reflexively pushes back against authority. In the post-war period, economic authority initially consisted of mainstream, Keynesian thought. He is patently fond of asserting his views while steamrolling over that of others. Moreover, if Friedman's patterns of thoughts and actions are examined, his ingrained dislike of external authority (coercion) might be somehow connected to Friedman's firmly held belief that he was always the smartest man in any room, rather than someone capable of making mistakes. In which case, he would naturally resent being opposed or confronted by an opponent trying to convince him to act in a contrary fashion. Friedman certainly would dig in his heels, rather than being persuaded to accept what he knew (*a priori*) to be a false idea or theory. However, the notion of freedom that he nurtures and cherishes reveals a significantly different pattern than that which is more commonly recognised by the general public.

> True there have been developments that have widened man's freedom,
> but most of these owe little or nothing to govt & I believe you understate
> the extent to which freedom has been curtailed. The reason you do,

> I believe, is because the kind of freedom you & I think of have never
> been important to more than a small number of people and that kind of
> freedom has so far fared relatively well (Milton Friedman letter to
> George Stigler, September 1, 1965).

Certainly for someone who believes firmly in consumer sovereignty in the
marketplace, Friedman seems dismissive of what that majority might
want. If his goal is to be actually consistent in his market beliefs, then he
must apply that logic broadly (rather than tailoring it to meet his own
desires). Meaning that although he can define his ideas, in the case of
freedom, as being different from the majority, he cannot acknowledge
them as being superior to those of others. Or according to an influential
paper by Stigler and Becker (1977), 'De Gustibus, Non-Disputandem', he
should not place his preferences above others, given the professed sanctity
of consumer sovereignty. Perhaps surprisingly, an incisive response to this
seeming conundrum is provided by George Stigler in his autobiography.
Responsive to Friedman's discontent, Stigler incisively evaluates the failure of western countries to travel down Hayek's *Road to Serfdom* during
the post-war period.

> The proximate reasons that the darkly pessimistic prediction of con-
> servatives have not been fulfilled are two. First, the predictions were
> based on their special view of freedom: Freedom as consisting only of
> the lack of coercion by the state, so that the widening range of choices
> due to the growth of income and education is not an effective increase
> in freedom in Hayek's view, although it is in mine. The second reason is
> more interesting. Hayek denied that piece meal regulations of a hundred
> different industries and callings could survive. The conflicts and incon-
> sistencies would force the adoption of a single, centralized all-
> comprehensive plan – and that plan could allow little individual choice.
> But that multitude of inconsistent, partial interventions by the state in
> economic life is exactly what we have. Hayek's orderly mind could not
> comprehend the survivability of our disorderly world (Stigler 1988:147).

When looked at more broadly, the need to push back against government
over-reach, to point out the persistence of government failure, is both
reasonable and necessary. The problem again lies in Friedman's inability
to say 'maybe'. An economist who is absolutely self-assured will tend
to push toward black and white viewpoints. In her biography, this is

what Burns generally avoids discussing. Thus when in *Capitalism &*
Freedom (1962) Friedman discusses classic liberalism, the heart of
which he claims to be restoring, he sums up by stating a few absolute
points that fail to convey the complexity of Mill, Marshall or even Adam
Smith.[47]

> But what is revealed most of all by intensive examination of the libertar-
> ian weltanschauung is its coldness, particularly in its present day ver-
> sions which have frozen out the warmth of John Stuart Mill (*who put*
> *non-economic liberties first*) and of Henry C. Simons (*who did care*
> *about trustbusting and progressive taxation to equalize opportunity and*
> *mitigate inequality of living standards*) (Samuelson 1963:29).

Understanding Milton Friedman really does require diving into his rigid
ideological positions. Though personally, he did seem to be easily satisfied
with a happy coincidence that appeared to align his *a priori* positions with
his empirical results. The relentless persistence with which this almost
consistent justification occurred should raise questions for any painstaking biographer. Nor should his assumptions and declared correlations be
simply painlessly swallowed. But Burns, at best, manages only to edge up
to these roiling waters without ever taking anything like a full plunge into
this more questionable geography. For instance, Friedman's ambiguous
concept of freedom (as previously pointed out), is simply reduced to the
absence of government coercion. Such a brazen correlation seems
dubious.

Friedman is then emboldened to take his next step, namely that only
a prescribed, minimalist government can properly limit coercion. By
default, that leaves the existing government in the position of having
slowly, but surely, stifled freedom for decades. Once this assumption is
accepted, Friedman is able to take a parallel leap when evaluating private
enterprise. He somehow fails to locate any coercion in this private sphere.
Once that backdrop is firmly erected, Friedman can simply conclude that
only competitive, capitalistic markets can deliver economic freedom.
Once his base assumptions are fortified in this fashion, Friedman can
proceed to label this valued degree of economic freedom as necessary for
yielding the political variety. His argument however appears to be largely
bootstrapped, driven mainly by his ideological viewpoint. Again, a difficulty that Burns uncritically avoids until revealing Friedman's own
doubts, a wavering that apparently arrived only in his very last years.

> Libertarians fail to realize that the price system is, and ought to be, a method of coercion. Nature is not so bountiful as to give each of us all the goods he desires. We have to be coerced out of such a situation, by the nature of things. That is why we charge prices, which are high enough relative to limited money to limit consumption. The very term "rationing by the purse" illustrates the point. Economists defend such forms of rationing, but they have to do so primarily in terms of its efficiency and its fairness. Where it is not efficient – as in the case of monopoly, externality, and unavoidable uncertainty – it comes under attack. Where it is deemed unfair by ethical observers, its evil is weighted pragmatically against its advantages and modifications of its structure are introduced (Samuelson 1963:36).

Samuelson's counter-argument (which involves sketching out some market limits) clearly indicates why George Stigler (and others of the Chicago School) were so determined to erase any perceived conception of market failure from the realm of economic literature. Friedman and his gang required markets to behave responsibly and judiciously. Not to stray (or be lured) into uneconomic corners. Given Chicago's perceived battle against collectivist urges (which were necessarily freedom denying), the crafted response developed there comes as no surprise. The Chicago School came to cleverly explain why what appeared to be a market limitation was actually otherwise. But though the freedom provided by the marketplace may be clearly preferred to the overreach and monitoring of dictatorial regimes, markets themselves, by this reasoning, do not transform society into the means for achieving some level of absolute good. Like democracy itself, it may very well be better than the alternatives, without being good in itself. Markets as a form of economic governance may just be the best of a bad lot. However, without adopting a radical Ayn Rand approach of sovereign individualism, where each person is entirely responsible for his or her outcome, it is difficult to overlook the fact that everyone's freedom of choice, as provided by competitive markets, is far from equal. Just as the freedom provided politically may be something of an illusion, so are the choices provided by the Chicago endorsed markets. Not bad, but not free from some form of coercion.

> They [the poor] have to labour in the face of the majestic equality of the law, which forbids the rich as well as the poor to sleep under bridges, to beg in the streets, and to steal bread (France 1894:Chapter 7).

For the most part then, Burns would prefer not to grapple with Friedman's acknowledged ideology, or even question whether such an unwavering perspective could significantly influence his work. What does seem clear is that given his fierce ideological beliefs, it becomes understandable why Friedman had an almost religious calling to proselytise. Spreading the gospel of free markets was more of an obligation than an option to him. (Surely his constant travel wasn't solely motivated by an urge to visit new places and foreign lands.) The very strength of an ideological foundation can sometimes simplify the way the world is viewed, namely strictly black and white with all choices well defined. This perspective would partially explain why Friedman, almost doggedly, made himself into a well-known public figure. (Granted he did have a large ego that could have required constant stroking. But such speculation lies more in the realm of armchair psycho-analysis.)

Friedman, like some latter day Karl Marx, not only wanted to change academic understanding of the economy, but wanted to change the world as well. A true believer in his mission, he consequently never shied away from what he viewed as his responsibility to propagate the truth. In this sense, his visits abroad were not unlike a series of revival meetings. One can imagine those embracing Friedman's creed as being born again into the true libertarian spirit. Though Burns sees no need to emphasise this driving passion, these facts can be carefully excavated from her biography, if one chooses to read carefully. But once again, this identified ideological conviction needs to be placed in the context of Milton Friedman's other great need.

As previously mentioned, he had a definite compulsion to prove that he was the smartest man in a room. This missionary approach was an aspect of his polemical career, which revolved around a controversial issue. (Friedman's stance would place him in the rare position of opposing his close friend, George Stigler.) Namely, should an academic (an economist) actively seek to have a public persona? (Stigler wondered whether an economist, when giving expert testimony or acting in a public sphere even deserved the title of 'economist'. "I conclude – and perhaps I am alone in concluding – that when the economist goes to Washington, he deserves no more credence, and no less, than any other political appointment, and it is mildly deceptive to address him as Doctor or Professor (Stigler 1988:135–136)). Friedman, of course, was never able to separate his evangelical quest from buttressing his growing notoriety.

> And he [George Stigler], on more than one occasion asked me the question - he never gave the answer himself and I never knew how to answer

the question myself - 'Did I think that Milton Friedman would be remembered most for his polemics on policy or his scientific work on things like the consumption function?' He never gave the answer himself and I didn't know what the answer to that question was. I still don't know what the answer to that question is, but he obviously thought about this issue. This was an issue in his view and I would have to infer from his own behaviour that he was of the opinion regarding his good friend and respected colleague, that Milton's scientific work would be the hallmark by which he was most remembered. But that remains to be seen. The real issue, you know, is whether that's in fact going to be, whether that's going to hold up or not. On one other personal occasion I remember something related to this question coming up. I was at lunch with Milton Friedman and George Stigler at the Quadrangle Club in Chicago and I was then a very young man. And somehow the younger you are, the more evangelistic you are. So I would debate and argue with people about policy issues and as I recall Milton asked me if I would be interested in going on a tour of some campuses, I think in the Southern United States, to talk on these policy issues. Milton said, 'What have you got to lose by doing this?' And George said at the table to me, 'Only your anonymity.' So, on that occasion, I think he was hinting that maybe I ought to stick to my scientific work. But he was always very respectful of Milton and very seldom, in fact I can't remember an occasion, in which he and Milton engaged in open debate on some issue (Conversation with Harold Demsetz, October 1997).

As mentioned, whether an academic (an economist) should play a public role remained one of the few points of contention between Friedman and Stigler, an area largely unexplored by Burns. Though perhaps in this instance, the basic personalities (of these two colleagues and friends) were determinative. Friedman was charismatic and voluble. Stigler more saturnine with an acerbic wit. Also as indicated by some of his closest friend and colleagues, there was an underlying shyness or reserve that defined Stigler. In contrast, no one had probably ever thought of defining Friedman as shy. Thus basic motivations were likely to differ.

Aaron Director: I don't find that very difficult to explain. He [George Stigler] just thought there were two different functions to perform. One is just simply to understand. You don't have to be interested in changing anything.

But, was he interested in changing ...
Aaron Director: No, I'm certain …
Milton Friedman: Of course he was.
Aaron Director: He would always insist he was not.
Milton Friedman: But of course he was.
ron Director: Well …
I mean why else was he ...
Milton Friedman: Why would he accept a post on the price - what was it?
Aaron Director: Oh, yeah, well the price index I think.
Milton Friedman: Why would he chair a price index committee?
Aaron Director: Somebody asked him.
Laughter.
Rose Friedman: He didn't do everything somebody asked him to do.
Aaron Director: No, no, but I don't really think you can make something out of so very little. You can believe that your role is really - has very little to do with wanting to change the world. Yet, you know, if somebody wants to re-examine the price index; and they ask you to ... I don't think that's really a problem.
Milton Friedman: There's no problem. It's true, that George did want to change things.
Aaron Director: But he preferred to study them, not to change them.
Milton Friedman: He preferred to say that he preferred to study them.
Rose Friedman: He preferred …
Aaron Director: He preferred to study them. I should quit the argument.
Milton Friedman: It was partly a long-running difference between him and me.
Aaron Director: You're right.
Milton Friedman: And he liked to stress, 'I just want to understand the world and Milton wants to change it.'
Aaron Director: That's right. And predominantly I think that is correct.
Rose Friedman: You would have to have them both psycho-analyzed.
Aaron Director: Yes. That's right.
Milton Friedman: You see, George is …
Rose Friedman: Or hypnotised.
Milton Friedman: Added to that, well a lot came from Aaron. I think you had a lot of influence on what he said.
Aaron Director: I don't think so.
Milton Friedman: Between you and me … But of course, you know, people get into patterns of what they say and it doesn't always correspond to what they do.

Aaron Director: Yes (Conversation with Milton Friedman, Rose Friedman and Aaron Director, August 1997).

Only in the final pages of her extensive biography, does Burns recognise this ideological elephant in the room. Nonetheless she refuses to wade too deeply into such murky waters. She asks if 'Friedman was seeing only what he wanted to see?' (Burns 2023:479). But she misses the point. The issue wasn't whether Milton Friedman was dishonest. Such charges are left to those with a visceral hatred of the man. But far more likely, Friedman only saw data and evidence in one convenient manner. He simply wouldn't allow for the possibility of being wrong. This perspective led him to battle and attempt to destroy views that saw those same facts differently. Burns also is willing to ask whether it mattered "that a clear set of ethical and political commitments guided his work?" (Burns 2023: 479). Friedman often scoffed at those on the left who wanted to do good by imposing their ideas on society. The problem which Friedman somehow missed wasn't that they wanted to do 'good', but that their arrogance led them to think that only they understood how the world worked. Meaning that listening to, or entertaining, alternatives had to be a waste of time by definition. Given at least a partially (if not entirely) closed mind, Friedman wouldn't sense that seeking to improve the status quo by trying to push back government overreach attracted its own potential problems. By being so single-minded in his approach, Friedman almost automatically refused to see that he could have overstepped in the opposite direction, simply by his belief in the superiority of individual action over its collective alternative.

Friedman's fight for individual freedom, his constant battles against government intrusion, was crucial in an era when government was often seen as being able to exercise an almost magical ability to right wrongs and to fix what was broken. He brought scepticism and empirical evaluation to test the validity of many of those post-war claims. Friedman focused (if not obsessed) about the loss of freedom, as well as the requirements for encouraging its growth. Burns then is more than justified in making the reader aware of this fundamental characteristic driving much of what Friedman sought to accomplish. But as previously mentioned, Burns merely wades in these very deep waters. Friedman's very limited (or black and white) notion of freedom formed something of an Achilles heel for both him and his work. His seeming abhorrence of ambiguity seeping into any of his principles is a discussion that should have enticed any biographer, though its forbidding nature might equally create caution. Unfortunately for Burns and her endeavours (at least for the most part), this acceptance of Friedman's definition of freedom as a given brings to mind a response Jacob Viner is said to have offered to a nervous graduate student in his infamous price theory class. Perhaps it is not an entirely inappropriate response when summing up Burns' attempt to deal with Friedman's ideology. "Sir, you drown in shallow waters." (Samuelson 2011d:597). Again, perhaps the fierceness of his ideological views reduced Milton Friedman to viewing other, more social and political issues through a lens that tended to simplify. Certainly he established a position that was more conducive to an inveterate crusader for competitive markets and freedom of choice than a scientific researcher. Or perhaps to a certain degree he was also just very much a man of his generation.

Friedman and his acolytes failed to understand an essential feature of freedom. There are two kinds, positive and negative: freedom to do and freedom from harm … as Isaiah Berlin put it, freedom for the wolves has often meant death to the sheep (Stiglitz 2024:1).

III. Shallow Depths – Family Man, Feminist, Civil Rights Advocate and Freedom of Speech Advocate

Milton was a conveniently hands-off parent. When a visiting teenage cousin requested a drink at cocktail hour, he handed her a stiff one. One Halloween he instituted a completely laissez-faire policy on candy consumption, under the theory the children would eventually become sated (Burns 2023:230).

In his intermediate textbook, David Friedman (1986) tells what he seems to think is a charming story of the education of a proto-economist. As a young boy he would travel to Seattle with his family (Rose, Milton and his sister, Jan Martel) to visit his maternal grandparents. Back in the early 1950s such trips were accomplished using train travel. David Friedman relates how his father would give him the choice of either enjoying the comfort of the sleeping car, or sitting up in a standard seat. (Of course small children can snuggle in a chair with greater dexterity than an adult.) If the second option was chosen, David would receive the difference between the two tickets in cash. With a touch of pride, he relates that he chose to retain the money rather than enjoy the extra comfort. The impression given is that he was raised at an early age to make rational decisions and that his father respected individual choice. However, the idea of using children as guinea pigs to verify one's own theory is far too reminiscent of the apocryphal story of B.F. Skinner raising his daughter in a Skinner box and subsequently being sued when that daughter became an adult.

In contrast, his close friend and colleague, a true believer in Chicago price theory and what it entails never confused theory with personal relationships and responsibilities. Thus the younger Stiglers were not viewed as subjects in an ongoing experiment. To begin with, theories of child development, or choice theory in economics, rest entirely on a mythical average child. Unfortunately, all parents are tasked with raising their own specific child.

> *Can I just ask you one last question before we go because this is part of my own personal fascination? I note that some economists like to use economic theory in child raising. Was your father an economist that.....*
> I don't think so. Not that I can recall.
> *Do you recall appealing to your narrow self-interest ....*
> No. Not really. He was conscious of economic incentives and the like. He may have offered us pennies to do certain jobs and the like. This was not an experiment where I can speak of a control. [laughter] Fundamentally, I suspect it wasn't significantly different from other families and other childhoods. As a family, we were not as economically thorough in our upbringing as some people might be. I know some families that would think *everything* was economic. But that's not our family. In many ways my father was, if you wish, inconsistent in some respects. He was very generous with his time, with his money, with his expenditure on his family and towards his friends. He was not somebody who approached most of life with – his personal life – with any narrow, economic constraint (Conversation with Stephen Stigler 1997).

I'm not sure that parents would think of hiring Milton Friedman as the director of a day care centre. But this type of mental shrug at Friedman's various social stances and actions tends to typify the manner in which Burns maintains a steadfast arm's length distance from these more ambiguous issues. If anything, she even manages to sugar frost a few less savoury instances. Perhaps the only distinct condemnation (or as far as she comes to one), arises when assessing Friedman's generational views regarding race. These prove too out of step with current thinking to be easily swept under even the most obliging carpet.

Friedman's views on childcare (and other social issues) are clearly spelled out in Capitalism and Freedom (1962), a volume largely derived from his past lectures and speeches. In it, he seems to have a distinct view on just about anything and everything. When considering all matters great and small, Friedman manages to find space in which he can squeeze children manfully into a conveniently constructed category. Not wanting to appear as an unwary proponent of child abuse. Friedman manages to locate an exception (or loophole) for some type of protective government intervention (of an unspecified variety). For once such action is legitimised on paternalistic grounds, but only in the case of children. But even when dredging up this case, the potential need consists only in conserving the child's freedom, insofar as that child exists as an independent individual. To put this in economic terms, Friedman might conclude that children are not entirely their parent's private property. But you might say as much about a pet cat.[48]

> To put this in a different and what may seem a more callous way, children are at one and the same time consumer goods and potentially responsible members of society. The freedom of individuals to use their economic resources as they want includes the freedom to use them to have children – to buy, as it were, the services of children as a particular form of consumption. But once this choice is exercised, the children have a value in and of themselves and have a freedom of their own that is not simply an extension of the freedom of the parents (Friedman 1962:33).

This Friedman styled approach seems mostly a muddle. Human societies have a number of options when it comes to child-rearing. As early as Plato's *Republic*, this task was potentially allocated to specialists, rather than birth parents. In Israeli kibbutzim, children are to some degree raised by the entire community. The option of employing parents perhaps shares the same judgment that Churchill made concerning democracy. To paraphrase, parental guidance is the worst way to raise a child, except for all the rest. For many centuries, children (like women) were regarded as the property of their parents, perhaps catalogued as not dissimilar to durable consumption goods. Thus even today, reflected in ongoing educational battles, some parents respond to any intervention (such as mandatory vaccination) by insisting that you (the authorities) can't tell me (the parent) what to do with my child. In contrast, the more recent societal trend is to see parents more as agents who are tasked with the responsibility to raise children. At least, they are no longer simply parental private property. However, for Milton Friedman, such a conception might still smack too loudly of an unwanted collective approach. But the necessity to delegate judgmental tasks remains the backbone of any operative economy, as well as its societal envelope. Instead, Friedman wants to skip over such inherent difficulty by performing somewhat of a straddle. Not that he would ever intend to be cruel to his (or any other) children, or (intentionally) misguide them.[49] But veering significantly away from his fundamental beliefs could never provide a viable alternative. Instead, Friedman's preferred approach follows his baseline recommendations for resolving even the most ambiguous issues. He consistently opts to hop directly from theory to policy. In essence, he favours a one size fits all approach without considering any possible shifting contexts over time or place.[50] Thus he offers optimal applications for a hypothetical average child.

Though Jennifer Burns only refers to his role as father briefly (applying a somewhat amused tone to the subject), Friedman's relation with his wife Rose and other women are considered extensively. But in burnishing his credentials, Burns tries to place Friedman in a somewhat favourable light, by strongly emphasising any positive that might be captured.[51] Burns can certainly award Friedman a plus for the way in which he respected Rose's advice and opinion when it came to his work and career. He was never too stubborn or proud to incorporate worthwhile thought. Though there are times when a reader gets a feeling that Burns is deliberately shying away from any outright condemnation, even when seemingly justified. This desire to project Friedman in the best light leads to a curious bit of obfuscation. Clearly only Friedman's name is on the cover of his *Capital and Freedom* volume. But she adds that Rose's name does appear on the inside along with Milton's. This statement is true but misleading, as it implies that Rose's contribution is not ignored but (almost) equally rewarded. Yet, the internal acknowledgment isn't one recognising his wife as a co-author, but just that she assisted in its writing. This attribution is not a complete dismissal. But such labelling, though not reducing Rose to the level of a mere secretary, certainly elevates her no further than acting as some sort of editor. Even Alfred Marshall shared the credit of his first book with his wife Mary. (Though his subsequent track record was less admirable.)

Even George Stigler gave his long time research assistant full credit on some of his papers. Had she wanted, it is apparent (according to Clair Friedland) that Stigler would have expanded this to an additional number of his output. Why then was Milton Friedman so reluctant when it came to Rose? Jennifer Burns mentions that in her later years Rose received an honorary doctorate from Pepperdine University. But US universities seem to give these honorary degrees out like the meretricious prizes stuffed in boxes of Crackerjack. Why for instance couldn't Milton Friedman use his considerable influence to get the University of Chicago to grant a deserved degree to Rose Friedman? While at Chicago, Harry Johnson tried to do this for Claire Friedland (Stigler's research assistant). Had she actually wanted such an honour, the degree might have been awarded. Like Rose, she had certainly done enough to deserve it.

However, what remains difficult to ignore in the biography, is the way in which Jennifer Burns tries (in this case), to display Milton Friedman in the best possible light. Any potential feminist issue is resolved simply by highlighting his treatment of a few key female colleagues. But these instances come across more as transactional moments, instead of principled decisions. He was good at spotting those whose work and efforts would advance his career. Thus he didn't allow pure prejudice to stand in his way. In the same manner, General MacArthur's staff included a female officer. She was there because she had earned it and was super-competent. This hardly transformed MacArthur into a rampant feminist. From a broader perspective, MacArthur remained (as did Friedman) very much a man of his generation, with the views and prejudices commonly held at that itme.

Thus when married, Rose automatically became a mother, housewife and assistant, not someone pursuing her own career. Certainly she didn't perform as an academic or economist in her own right. Countless men and women of that wartime generation had similar attitudes, making Friedman no exception. No surprise that in the 1970s his views hadn't altered. Friedman felt perfectly justified in lecturing misguided women against demanding equal pay for equal work. That he considered such campaigners incapable of realising the unintended consequences of their aims (at least those appearing in his analysis) effectively sums up his attitude. Note that he has no solid evidence to back up his professed certainty, only his inflexible theory, backed by a rigid degree of ideology. But by assumption, in Friedman's rulebook, market results are deemed to be efficient, otherwise they would change.

> We have our poor, misguided women labourers saying: "We have to
> have governmental laws to make sure that there is equal pay for men and
> women in the same job." They do not realize it is anti-feminist legisla-
> tion because if they insist that by law you have equal pay for equal work
> they are going to end up having reduced employment opportunities for
> women in jobs in which, for one reason or another, the males have an
> advantage, whether that reason be irrational prejudice or valid differen-
> tiation (Friedman 1976:29–30).

Understandably Burns is a bit more uncomfortable with Friedman's civil
rights stand and particularly his attitude to blacks. These are much harder
to swallow, while being certainly difficult to justify. But like many of his
generation, (including his friend William F. Buckley[52]) there is no legitimate way to ameliorate his stated stance.[53] As the author states, Friedman
considered that individuals had the freedom, or right to discriminate. "I do
not question the right of individuals to be anti-negro or anti-Semitic and
to choose their friends and associates and even schools for their children,
accordingly (Friedman quoted in Burns 2023:265). Like his devotee,
Margaret Thatcher, this economist was never one for turning. Friedman
may have gone quiet in later years, when such sentiments were simply
unfashionable as well as downright unacceptable, but he was never in any
sense a civil rights advocate.

The attitude may have come from his deeply entrenched sense of
individual responsibility. Each individual is (in this view) entirely responsible for one's own fate. Milton Friedman, born into very modest circumstances had won fame and fortune. If Blacks largely had failed, it must
reflect their own lack of effort. But such a judgment would seem to be too
harsh for Burns to calmly digest. In one instance, she tries to lessen the
impact of Friedman's stance a bit by contrasting it with a very dubious
piece written by his close friend George Stigler in 1965. In 1965, Stigler
argued the 'basic problem of the Negro in America … is that on average
he lacks a desire to improve himself' (Burns 2023:265). Burn's almost
desperate attempt to ameliorate Friedman's stance (by pointing her finger
elsewhere), is entirely undermined by Friedman's wholehearted admiration of Stigler's efforts in this regard. Milton Friedman embraced Stigler's
stance wholeheartedly.

> Your piece on Negro unrest is magnificent. David and a friend of his
> who is an active student conservative politician were here over the

weekend and I read it aloud to them. They thought it magnificent (Letter from Milton Friedman to George Stigler, August 1964).[54]

The point isn't that Friedman should retrospectively be scolded for holding views common to his generation. The rationale for such views is made sufficiently clear in the biography. But there is no indication that he ever indicated any regret for that earlier position. The same difficulty holds when the biography examines the McCarthyism of the 1950s. At this point, a selective stance rears its unfashionable head when evaluating right-wing versus left-wing extremes. Burns offers a single piece of evidence demonstrating Friedman's opposition to (or at least disapproved of) Joe McCarthy and his tactics. (Her argument rests on a set of letters written to Fritz Machlup in 1952). Machlup saw McCarthy as 'the second coming of Nazism' (Burns 2023:183). As Burns sums up, the academic reality of that time was that "McCarthy's zealous crusade against Communists, which was roiling universities across the nation as leftist professors lost jobs and worried administrators pushed loyalty oaths on faculty" (Burns 2023:183) certainly to Machlup represented an imminent danger. In this period of fear and uncertainly, Burns feels compelled to somehow exonerate Friedman from even a lighter charge of passive collaboration (not actively supporting, but not even privately condemning McCarthy's actions.)

Burns wants to claim that "Friedman's opposition to McCarthy was sincere" (Burns 2023:184). But even by her account, Friedman expressed his supposed objection in a very roundabout (even difficult to discern) fashion. Friedman's habit of downplaying the threat posed to individual freedom from the right was balanced by excoriating any perceived threat from the left. Danger from the left of the political spectrum was far more pressing and immediate than anything the right might offer. In his estimation (at least when responding to Machlup), the election of Eisenhower was somehow the most effective method for keeping McCarthy and his fellow extremists under control. (Once elected, however, neither Eisenhower, nor Congressional Republicans initially demonstrated the courage to rein in McCarthy. They were simply too scared.) Nor did Friedman during this period ever seem too fussed by McCarthy's actions, even if he didn't explicitly applaud his methods.

Therefore in a series of letters written to Fritz Machlup, Friedman argued against voting Democrat in 1952. In essence, McCarthy was not the threat that some saw.

> "McCarthy is not a new phenomenon" … Eisenhower was no Hindenburg, no puppet: he was "imbued with American ideals." These ideals held by mainstream Republicans, Friedman suggested, acted to constrain those in power … "You need not only a Hindenburg – Hitler – Von Papen: you also need a Hegel." Here was a clue to how Friedman conceived his own purpose and mission as a thinker (Burns 2023:184).

Sadly, I am forced to differ with Burns in this case. Such a conclusion only demonstrates, at least to me, that Friedman lacked deep philosophical insight, as well as having cultivated a rather shaky grasp of history.[55] You might as well say, that McCarthy lacked a Wagner as well or a Schiller. Too much counter-evidence fails to provide Friedman with the exoneration Burns prefers. Despite her attempts, there were never any subterfuge attached to his Cold War views. Friedman even went so far as claiming (or merely asserting) that the University of Chicago during the interwar years was a hotbed of communism. The scourge for Friedman always came from the collectivist left. Meaning that sometimes rough tactics were justified even if the deliverers were a bit crude. Despite Burns' efforts, washing Friedman completely clean of the McCarthyite stench proves a bit too overwhelming even for her lavatory efforts.

> Friedman calculated that by 1934 'close to a majority' of faculty and students within the social sciences at the University of Chicago were 'either members of the Communist party or very close to it' (Leeson 2003a:288).

Contrary to Burns attempt to ameliorate Friedman's position, Mark Blaug's speculative jabs may come closer to the actual position embraced by Friedman (and Stigler). Blaug, who was Stigler's student (and well acquainted with Friedman), may come closer to zeroing in on their reaction to McCarthy. (Certainly the academic cleansing of Leftist/Communist faculty provoked not a hint of protest from either one. However, caution under those circumstances, though not particularly admirable, is entirely understandable.)

> A lot of right-wing people must have found McCarthy to be vulgar, brutal but basically less of a problem than the alternative. Basically he was on the right side of the issues. Not unlike what you read that people said about Hitler in the early 30s, when he was on the rise. Yes, he's a gangster. Yes, he's a hooligan but he's anti-communist. He's going to

keep back the communists and control trade unions. These are benefits. And they didn't realise that they were rearing a Frankenstein's monster who would eventually chop off their own heads. A lot of people were sympathetic, who would have been horrified if they had foreseen what would happen. Nevertheless they went along with it as being better than nothing. You have to stop these damn communists, etc. etc. I've met a lot of people who took a very quietist attitude. It didn't mean they loved him. But, as far as they were concerned, he was on the side of the angels. I dare say, I think that would have been Milton Friedman and George Stigler's attitude to McCarthy. One would have wished he didn't do it so loudly, he didn't do it so vulgarly, but they would have said that he was essentially right. In the same way that a lot of people said you know, you have to put up with McCarthy to keep communism in check (Conversation with Mark Blaug, April 1998).

But speculation is mere opinion and never entirely convincing. Actions will always speak louder. So best to flip the pages forward a decade or so. In contrast to his McCarthy stance, Milton Friedman was quite clear during the campus Vietnam War protests, that there existed a dire necessity to defend academic freedom, including free speech. This principled defence was expressed quite vociferously (by Friedman as well as his close colleagues). He even went so far as claiming (in a letter to George Stigler) that the numerous Jewish students leading the campus protests were 'bad for the Jews'.[56] In contrast, none of his actual actions demonstrate that during the McCarthy years, Friedman was at all perturbed about the quashing of free speech, or that ongoing witch-hunts were intimidating academics of that earlier era.[57] Seemingly more important for Friedman was the object of the hunt, rather than the tactics of the hunters.

Now, Aaron Director, for example, would never have written a good letter of recommendation for somebody who wasn't a staunch conservative, but neither would Milton. And I remember for years after I left the University of Chicago, when they were contemplating influential appointments they would ask me about the person, 'Is he really sound?' In fact, Milton once showed his naïveté to me, but it wasn't about appointments. He said, 'Tell me the truth, is Galbraith a Commie?' You know the amount of naïveté that's in that. I've done a lot of thinking about my old ... I can't say my old religion, although I was trained by the Jesuits, so I know it. But I once did a little informal investigation of whether people who were economic libertarians and tended to favour low taxation and low regulation and laissez-faire, were also people interested in civil liberties and freedom of expression, and that sort of thing. So I would ask innocent questions. 'Now what do you think of this group?' Of course, I had a placebo question control group. 'What do you think of the fact that this professor at the University of New Hampshire, the one who invited Paul Sweezy in the McCarthy era to give a lecture, is losing his job because neither he nor Paul Sweezy will testify as to what was the content of the lecture?' And Milton said, 'Gee, it's a simple case. It's a free speech society. If a man will not do what he should, this professor should be fired. Society has a right to know.' I said, 'You don't understand. They've got the notes on the lecture, verbatim. It's not a question of information' (Conversation with Paul Samuelson, October 1997).[58]

Lastly, Friedman (1962) retrospectively downplayed (actually dismissed) the damage done to the victims of McCarthyism. For Friedman, doing so was perfectly legitimate since the argument served to extol the virtues of a competitive market system. If by 1962, he couldn't exactly approve of the Hollywood blacklist that had caused writers, actors and other accused of communism to lose their jobs, he could overlook the actual damage. Overt support of such action would see Friedman treading on dangerous ground. A stance of approval would run directly against his bedrock principles of the primacy of individual freedom and choice.[59] Yet he chooses the well-known case of Dalton Trumbo (screenwriter) to condemn government monopolies, rather than McCarthyism. Namely, he focuses on the fact that Trumbo, forced to write under a pseudonym, achieved an academy award for screenwriting in 1959. Somehow the fact that the blacklist failed to be 100% effective is a triumph for competitive markets.[60] Friedman blithely waves away the harm inflicted on those blacklisted individuals like Trumbo. Reading his remarks, it is far from clear that Friedman would be interested in discovering those afflicted writers' individual histories. In his opinion, they had voluntarily assumed a risk (and volunteered for their subsequent treatment) by becoming communists. But Friedman then compounds this indifference by strangely hauling in Winston Churchill. Here he employs all the rhetorical stops connected with exaggeration and false equivalency. Though I would be surprised if he recognised any overreach in doing so.

From 1933 to the outbreak of World War II, Churchill was not permitted to talk over the British radio, which was, of course, a government monopoly administered by the British Broadcasting Corporation. Here was a leading citizen of his country, a Member of Parliament, a former cabinet minister, a man who was desperately trying by every device possible to persuade his countrymen to take steps to ward off the menace of Hitler's Germany. He was not permitted to talk over the radio to the British people because the BBC was a government monopoly and his position was too "controversial" (Friedman 1962:19).

This is an exaggeration, but one few of his readers at the time was likely to check. Churchill's time on the BBC was limited but not zero. At that period, he was out in the political wilderness and considered a war monger. I'd be surprised if the BBC allowed Oswald Mosley to broadcast his views during crucial periods. Churchill was then just a back bencher considered by many to be a has-been. However, he was free to voice his views in the British Press, which did not operate as a monopoly. He also pursued a lucrative career speaking on American radio. Nor was Churchill some sort of free speech supporter. In government in 1926 he had unsuccessfully attempted to strong arm the BBC into pushing the official line condemning the upcoming General Strike. Churchill was at most somewhat muffled during the period Friedman describes. He wasn't deprived of his livelihood as was Trumbo and others that were targeted by McCarthy and his allies. An argument can be made that the BBC problem, if there was one, was that it was a monopoly, not so much that it was government owned. A privately run radio monopoly at that time may not have chosen differently (conceivably even worse). The point being that if Friedman truly considered McCarthyism (even retrospectively) a serious incursion on the individual freedom that he treasured, he would not in 1962 been so cavalier about the blacklist that was a reflection of the shadow cast by McCarthy at that time. Nor would he have made a false equivalency between the blacklist and the 1930s foibles of the BBC. (Insisting that the BBC was equivalent to, or even worse than, the Hollywood blacklist.)

Blaug then may not have been entirely misguided in his suppositions. Friedman was vehemently anti-communist. Being so he most likely accepted the adage that you had to break a few eggs to make an omelette. Namely, that McCarthy's objectives were not out of line, but in pursuing them he may have stepped over the mark. This was, after all, the stance adapted by his friend William F. Buckley in his 1954 book defending Joe McCarthy. Buckley is often lauded for condemning the extreme right of his movement, but this approbation is not entirely deserved, nor is Friedman's.[61]

Pragmatism is not necessarily the same as principled action. Burns is almost certainly correct that Friedman had little truck with the ultra-extremists and conspiracy theorists on the right. But it is difficult to find instances where he took public stances against this group. My guess is that Burns papers over the negatives as she does with some of his less admirable views. As previously pointed out, the unshakeable nature of his ideological views made him more willing to overlook trespasses by those on the political right, while eagerly condemning any overreaching by those on the left. Thin edge of the wedge arguments were saved for those seen as pushing collectivist views.

IV. Methodology and Market Fundamentalism

> I sometimes think some of the Chicago people are hopeless. Well, I wouldn't include Milton as among the hopeless because he was smart enough to punch his way out of a paper bag sometimes. But in the end he didn't want to do so (Conversation with Paul Samuelson, October 1997).

In 1953, a perhaps unexpected methodological essay appeared in Milton Friedman's book on positive economics. (I will sidestep any discussion on positive versus normative economics since I have never found those categories particularly fruitful, though others obviously have.) His extended effort would have a decided effect on the economics profession. Burns (2024:156)) boils down this essay that launched untold articles in one sentence. "In a celebrated essay, 'The Methodology of Positive Economics,' he tied together his various critiques of Cowles and offered a new standard for economic theory: prediction." Her assertion here can be debated.

Larry Klein, who gets the short end of Burns' biographical stick whenever possible, was also known to insist upon the importance of prediction. But more important is the dog that doesn't bark here. Burns downplays and misses the point of Friedman's efforts, or at best simply accepts Friedman's efforts to camouflage his aims and objectives. (Namely, by focusing only on what is floating in full view, rather than exploring the treacherous depths that defines this attempt at formalising an economic method.) She ignores the curious fact that the essay seemed to come out of nowhere. Friedman had never published anything that remotely touched directly on methodological issues. Moreover, after the 1953 piece he would never do so again. And despite a veritable tsunami of criticism raised by his essay, he never responded to critics. The subject seemed to hold his attention momentarily, when compared to his true passions. In fact, in a typical Milton Friedman fashion, he would claim fifty years later that he had nothing to add to or subtract from the original. In his unwavering opinion, the essay was still correct as it stood.[62]

Once again, in mentioning Friedman's foray into methodology, almost mysteriously, his close friend and colleague George Stigler is overlooked. But as Friedman freely admits, no Stigler, no 'Methodology of Positive Economics'.

> Milton Friedman: I had written the methodology paper, which was later formally published. This preceded, by three or four years, the earlier versions. And he refers in one of those lectures to the fact that we had been talking about it.
> *Yes. And how influential were you in each other's thinking on this matter?*
> Milton Friedman: We were very influential. I think there's no doubt that my work would have been different if I hadn't been influenced by George and George's work would have been different if he hadn't been influenced by me (Conversation with Milton Friedman, Rose Friedman and Aaron Director, August 1997).

The origin of this methodological foray actually started with conflicts faced by George Stigler, rather than directly through Friedman's Cowell battles. Stigler's 1946 textbook had been blatantly trashed by Chamberlin for not providing sufficient attention to his own theory of monopolistic competition. Though offered a right of reply, Stigler decided to temporarily hold his fire.[63]

I am not inclined to do this [write a reply] because

(1) Of a general feeling against replies to reviews, and
(2) The inappropriateness of a short note in dealing with this matter (and the disinterest in a long one). All I gain by a reply is creation of doubts in the minds of those economists (numerous, alas) who think Chamberlin is a great man (Letter from George Stigler to Milton Friedman, August 1947 in Hammond and Hammond, 2006:61).

This Chamberlin tempest (whether or not occurring in the proverbial teapot) initiated a series of letters leading to Stigler's second lecture at

LSE in 1948. Certainly neither one of them had read deeply in the field of methodology. Friedman would admit that he had read only Karl Popper at that time.[64] But in their correspondence, leading up to Stigler's lectures, the framework of Stigler's efforts and Friedman's latter 1953 essay took shape.

> I should like to offer the general proposition that every important scientific hypothesis almost inevitably must use assumptions that are descriptively erroneous. It is of the very nature of a really important scientific generalization that it provides a simpler rationalization of a mass of facts than was available before. It is likely to obtain its objective by an inspiration about the particular basic elements of the situation that are important and by discarding what after the event can be shown to have been irrelevant complicating assumptions. In a way, the better the hypothesis the greater the extent to which it simplifies, the more sharply will its assumptions depart from reality (Letter from, Milton Friedman to George Stigler, November 1947 in Hammond and Hammond, 2006:65).

At stake was a larger issue (not mentioned by Burns), which would determine the direction that economics (and particularly microeconomics) would pursue in those immediate post-war years. As Friedman would admit, Chamberlin's theory was revolutionary (and thus dangerous).[65] By reducing perfect competition (and Chicago price theory) to a special case of a more general theory (a la Keynes), monopolistic competition (and other non-traditional approaches) threated to overthrow the status quo. Price theory depended on a Hobbesian style implicit contract within an economy. Individuals surrendered private power to the market place. Only by accepting a passive role of responding to market prices could they be free to choose, in Friedman's words. Thus challenges to Chicago price theory boiled down to attacks on freedom (or at least if Friedman's perspective was embraced.)

Chamberlin's approach had attracted attention given its inherent realism. The theory seemed to make more sense than did a realm where small representative firms maximised profit. But even worse, from the Chicago viewpoint, Chamberlin's approach allowed the heresy of multiple equilibriums and even a lack of any market equilibrium. Economic agents were bent on actively marketing and differentiating their products, rather than robotically adjusting to given market prices. But, by shifting the emphasis from the reality of assumptions to the realm of pure prediction, the gospel according to Friedman and Stigler could be preserved. Key here was to distract economic debate away from discussing the reality of assumptions. Instead, discussion was cleverly diverted to the dust storm created by Friedman and Stigler. Once accomplished (and with debate shifted), both lost interest as the focus of debate shifted primarily to the predictive validity of theories.

However somehow, through a fortunate consistency (once again), Friedman's independently derived methodology was the one that best saved his version of economics. But his solution (or the Stigler/Friedman solution) is problematic at best. Prediction is an important aspect of economics, but not the only one. The goal (as in any discipline), is to gain understanding, not just to roll out predictions like some gifted astrologist. Otherwise it is impossible to ever know why the prediction held, or whether it will only hold for a particular time and place. It is not so much (at least at times) a forest for the trees issue, since in certain instances Friedman seems instead to burrow underground. His vision, occasionally, seems limited by his own tunnelling. Burns either fails to see the implications of Friedman's methodology, or finds that further exploration might disturb the portrait she is constructing. Still, a methodology where an economist can simply assume a can opener is a bit too Humpty Dumpty to supply much in the way of reassurance.[66]

The problem, within the biography itself, is that Burns largely ignores one of Friedman's most well-known and much cited papers. Though gaining fame, if not always accolades, it is an effort that clarified little methodologically. A result that was not surprising, since its intended impact was to effectively obscure issues. The actual methodology of outcomes employed, the always fortuitous use of finding results 'as if' the underlying assumptions were valid. This approach, as pointed out, was a sort of defiant Humpty Dumptism. The approach proved most noteworthy for generating perhaps the most notorious of jokes (entirely at Friedman's expense) namely the aforementioned can opener story. But Friedman's unexpected, once off dive into a philosophic wilderness, ended up failing on two essential counts. Methodologies can either be descriptive or prescriptive. Friedman's ad hoc construction manages to offend on both counts. It fails to adequately describe what economists tend to do when either theorising or testing. Nor does it provide a useful pathway for productive research.

> The view that the worth of a theory is to be judged solely by the extent and accuracy of its predictions seems to me wrong. ... a theory is not like

an airline or bus timetable. We are not interested simply in the accuracy of its predictions. A theory also serves as a base for thinking. It helps us to understand what is going on by enabling us to organise our thoughts. Faced with a choice between a theory which predicts well but gives us little insight into how the system works and one which gives us this insight but predicts badly, I would choose the latter, and I am inclined to think that most economists would do the same (Coase 1994b:6–17).

Or we could look to the bluntness of Sam Peltzman, George Stigler's star pupil, who in many ways represents the next generation of the Chicago School.

When I was a graduate student we were taught a paradigm of how you do research. I've got to tell you, it's all wrong. It's not the way we operate. We don't sit up here and develop hypotheses and go out and test them. That's just not what we do. George taught me that. Milton taught me that. They're wrong! And I understand that. I'm older enough now to figure out that's not the way we do work. There's a lot of salesmanship, there's a lot of taking positions, defending them. Right. The facts will win out. I'm not saying that we're not in that sense correct. The facts do win out. But the process by which that happens is not the clean one of scientific method rigorously applied all the time (Conversation with Sam Peltzman, October 1997).

Consequently, the approach proves no more useful when examined from a prescriptive standpoint. Friedman's method does not represent what economists should aim for if they are seeking to accomplish fruitful work. Burns fails to grasp the full purpose driving the essay, by strictly limiting her exploratory evaluation. Instead she chooses to view the essay through the same narrow lens she uses to explore the Friedman-Cowles dispute. But more to the point, to obediently follow the dictates described in Friedman's approach would stultify, rather than improve, the research ability of the profession. The essay, essentially, collapses on its own terms.

If choosing theories in accordance with Friedman's criteria is to be treated as a positive theory, economists would need to adopt a procedure somewhat similar to the following. When a new theory is advanced, economists would compare the accuracy of its predictions ... with that of the predictions of the existing theory and would choose that theory

> which gave the best predictions. An insistence that the choice of theories be made in accordance with Friedman's criteria would paralyze scientific activity. … There is little profit in undertaking an investigation that is expected to show that a theory in which no one believes yields incorrect predictions, and I doubt whether any editor of a professional journal could be found who would be willing to publish a paper giving the results of such an investigation. If all economists followed Friedman's principles in choosing theories, no economist could be found who believed in a theory until it had been tested, which would have the paradoxical result that no tests would be carried out. This is what I meant when I said that acceptance of Friedman's methodology would result in the paralysis of scientific activity. Work could certainly continue, but no new theories would emerge (Coase 1994b:24).

Burns almost deliberately seems to artfully glide over Friedman's actual methodology, although it is an essential foundation for the market fundamentalism that he so fervently championed. Like religious evangelists, for Friedman, ambiguity finds not the smallest handhold in the world he so carefully constructs. Friedman harboured no doubt that he was capable of clearly grasping the way in which markets actually operate. Consequently, heretics, those wishing to undermine his unshakeable truths, must (almost logically) be efficiently and fundamentally crushed. Burns does accurately describe this particularly rigid perspective when relating the travails of Friedman's early work with the NBER. But without explicitly spelling it out, she gives that specific incident a certain favourable spin. Namely, she constructs her story so that Friedman appears in the role of the brilliant maverick fighting against hide bound obstructionists. This narrative imbalance is triggered by labelling his opponents as institutionalists. Unfortunately, when Burns throws some unwitting economist into the institutionalist bin, that individual always comes out worse for wear and certainly second best to Friedman. Though employed extensively, these identity tags (like institutionalist) consistently fail to clarify any of the nominated debates she covers. Burns appears to use the label as a signal. When Burns assigns an economist to that arid territory, the relegation is equivalent to an implicit condemnation. Only those professionals that she rates as retrograde and biased achieve that particular unwelcome status. Though the term is consistently negative, the exact meaning she intends continued to elude me, especially since the same label was tattooed across the foreheads of dissimilar economists.

For example, in the incident surrounding Friedman's work with Kuznetz (which eventually gained him his PhD.), Friedman wants to ignore the reality and differences between dentists and doctors. He prefers instead to carelessly jump from an abstract market model to a definite prediction. Burns is sympathetic to Friedman's plight when faced with objections from NBER established economists. She labels these obstructionists as narrow-minded institutionalists, as discussed shortly.

> Then came the leap, Friedman argued that approximately half of the increased income was due to "restriction" in entry, or the difficulty in gaining admission to medical school and then passing boards. In other words, there was a medical cartel – the American Medical Association (AMA) – that artificially raised incomes. Given the "free working of the much abused law of supply and demand," doctors would only earn about 17 percent more than dentists (Burns 2023:88).

Clearly, the AMA has the decided interests of its members in mind when restricting the flow of doctors. That should come as no surprise. The result being, that in contrast to what Friedman seems to prefer, not everyone is free to set up a medical practise. But locating an element of self-interest doesn't imply that there are not some positive aspects flowing from such restrictions. Friedman either ignores, or simply assumes away, the existence of asymmetric information in the medical market. Prospective patients are unaware of how competent a given doctor may be. The requirements to become licensed are not only there to increase medical incomes but to insure a minimum level of competency. The potential danger from an untrained or badly incompetent doctor would be quite serious. (I will return shortly to the question of information.)

Instead, Friedman simply jumps from theory to policy, ignoring the fact that policies must be time and place specific to be effective. A successful policy must depart from the methodological land of 'as if' and deal instead with numerous specifics. There needs to be real can openers if actual cans are ever to be opened. Neither Friedman (nor Burns) seem to acknowledge that in making that leap, Friedman is breaking with a basic tenet of classical liberal economics. (Whether such a leap is legitimate is a distinctly different question.) Instead Burns makes the dubious claim then that Friedman's approach reflected "the legacy of Simons and Knight" (Burns 2023:90). This particularly broad claim doesn't reflect well on Burns whatsoever. A judgment of this kind, only indicates a remarkable lack of understanding of Knight, if not Simons as well.[67] Friedman unequivocally broke with them both by insisting on a different approach to economics, departing greatly from their methods. Because, as Burns correctly says, Friedman:

> … had taken his basic framework and applied it not simply to economic dynamics within a profession but to the process of choosing a profession itself. It was taking Chicago price theory out of the classroom and applying it to the real world … But like a termite burrowing from within, he took up institutionalist preoccupations and turned them to his own purposes (Burns 2023:90).

What Friedman actually accomplishes in his initial NBER work (dealing with the professions) is to greatly simplify a more complicated market outcome into a single residual, one that is solely due to government licensing. His natural (scientific) urge is to drastically abstract from his observations in order to come up with a broad generalisation. Instinctively he views all markets as operating fundamentally in a similar fashion, if not exactly identical. Contrary matters, which serve to distinguish and differentiate markets, represent distractions for Friedman. Focusing on such details only tend to obscure greater truths.

Thus the young Friedman self-righteously bristles when his sweeping NBER conclusion is criticised by elder statesmen in his profession. Burns, in contrast, seems compelled to fit this episode into her 'Hero's Journey' portrait. She chooses to frame the disagreement as a principled battle with obstinate institutionalists (a seemingly code-word for obstructionist reactionaries). But Burns has to an extent written herself into a corner by doing so. She is faced with a dilemma. Showing Friedman's full limitations here would ultimately distract from the heroic tale that Burns is determined to relate, sketched together from a grab-bag of carefully selected pieces. In this customised telling of Friedman's saga, the hero must ultimately sunder all opposition and smash dangerous falsehoods. Nothing less would be acceptable in a cinematic portrait. Consequently, initially misguided opponents must ultimately see the light (if only partially) and confess (to some extent) their previous sins. But this style of story-telling is neither what Friedman (nor the reader) deserves. The actual (rather than mythical) Friedman remained a one-handed sceptic throughout his career (not unlike some of his opponents). His insistence on government failure was a needed corrective to the overly optimistic post-war enthusiasm for interventionist fixes. In essence that period was sometimes too quick to spot a market failure, while simultaneously assuming that regulation automatically offered a better alternative.

This one-sided scepticism made Friedman's disdain for collectivist solutions fundamentally unbalanced. Instead, his judgment was ruled by a fervid belief in the sanctity of markets. Ideally, they are no more than a governance structure that can, given very stringent conditions, always resolve an impressive array of economic problems. Markets are, after all, where the great majority of economists start their analysis. It is their trusted default position. The Chicago School differs from this standard, primarily in the weight they place on such solutions. The Chicago School of Friedman, Stigler and Director start and end with the marketplace (or at least nearly so). Purported failure (like externalities) could simply be internalised. "He [George Stigler] knew that they were out there, that externalities were out there. However, he said, 'Look, the market's rushing in every moment to take care of them'" (Conversation with Claire Friedland, October 1997).[68] The brutal reality, however, is that both governments and markets are no more than governance institutions invented by humans. They are human contrivances. By almost definition, flawed humans do not construct divinely inspired, or flawless, structures. Distorted market incentives, for instance, are unlikely to lead to optimal outcomes. That is why Friedman's more extreme market suggestions are no more than articles of faith, rather than fact. Asymmetric information, as has become increasingly obvious in the internet age, can badly distort operative markets.

That is why Armen Alchian's pronouncements of faith can today seem quaint, a relic from a more innocent time and place. Alchian, deemed by Samuelson to be 'more Catholic than the Pope', hewed to his market faith so strictly that he could actually chastise George Stigler for any slip away from the true path. When confronted by his logic, one can only admire the purity of Alchian's thought. He consistently hugs his principles tightly, causing him to rigorously reach conclusions that adhere to an impeccable line of reasoning. Yet, when viewed in the light cast by actual events, his claims can be tinged with the ludicrous. Much as Christians believe that all outcomes reflect God's goodness, so all market results (in Alchian's world) need be beyond question. In this Chicago world, economists start (and almost finish) with the assumption that economies (in order to promote freedom and choice) need to reflect consumer sovereignty. Markets are uniquely capable of providing what consumers want. Freedom is then forever welded to economic markets. Debate concluded, markets triumph. Plus a market is always fundamentally the same as any other market, indicating (at least to Alchian or Friedman) that any observed difference must be trivial. "Nor do I see anything unique in the fourth sentence … replace 'university' by 'gasoline service station'" (Letter from Armen Alchian to George Stigler, March 25, 1967.

Yet, the question remains, whether consumers always do know what is best for them (relative, at least, to any alternative source). This particular puzzle is intensified if consumers are easily provided with and often accept bad information. The importance of such flows rests on the fact that the world of rent-seeking, scams and much worse is dependent upon the propagation of misleading or false information. Yet, absorbed by his own language, Alchian sees this information issue as posing little or no problem. The point is that Friedman also thinks along similar lines. This problematic position has some controversial implications for Friedman's policy positions. Yet instead of underlining this issue, Burns strategically chooses to look away.

> Your position strikes me as perilously close to advice to a paternalist agency. On the same grounds I see no reason to expect newspapers to have a responsibility to be honest. Let them lie as they will. I rely on access of others to expose the lie and to cater to the public's desire for the truth – or to whatever extent the public and individuals wish it (Letter from Armen Alchian to George Stigler, March 25, 1967).[69]

Burns tends to slide over the fact that once Friedman convinced himself of some specific idea or view, he found it almost impossible to admit that he might have been wrong or had overstated his position. "He doesn't particularly announce changes in positions, but instead, lets them just decay away" (Conversation with Paul Samuelson, October 1997). His animus toward licensing (and particularly the AMA) struck upon early in his career never faded, or was later even qualified. By 1962 it blooms into a fully developed scenario where competitive markets can provide medical care more efficiently (and equitably) when devoid of any shred of regulation. Notice, in this case, how these idealised markets are magically capable of producing optimal outcomes. As always, lurking somewhere in the background (explicitly mentioned or not) is an equal phantasm of a legal system that insures efficient performance. Operating with zero trans-action costs, this Chicago style system seems to escape the problems of onerous fees or expensive delays. (Judicial incompetence, corruption and outright rent seeking have somehow become forbidden and economically erased.)

> Suppose that anyone had been free to practice medicine without restriction except for legal and financial responsibility for any harm done to others through fraud and negligence ... These medical teams – department stores of medicine if you will – would be intermediaries between the patients and the physician. Being long-lived and immobile, they would have a great interest in establishing a reputation for reliability and quality. For the same reason, consumers would get to know their reputation. They would have the specialized skill to judge the quality of physicians; indeed, they would be the agent of the consumer in doing so, as the department store is now for many a product (Friedman 1962:158–159).

Many of such potential legal issues are scoured away through the supposed force of market reputation. The self-regulation supplied by reputation, the applicable gold standard accepted by Friedman (and much of the Chicago School), is not without merit, but as in too many moments in Friedman's work, exaggerated. The core assumption deployed assumes that the cost of damaging a reputation far outweighs the gain of cheating, or cutting corners. In fact, Klein and Leffler (1981) sought to rigorously model such behaviour. Yet if you examine their resulting construction, good information has to travel rapidly, while consumers need to possess unbounded rationality. Unfortunately, relevant and immovable historical evidence (plus observed human behaviour) refuses to validate this supposition completely. People are cursed with extremely bounded rationality, no matter how much economists assert otherwise. (Using Friedman's methodology, theorists grant themselves the freedom to treat individuals 'as if' their rationality was unbounded (or nearly so)). But in fact, the general public (time and time again) fail to remember scandals and misdeeds over long periods, especially when an onslaught of other such events tend to muddle memory.[70] Moreover, those corporations, hospitals and other venues where corners are cut, do not for a moment believe that they will be caught (or that the imposed punishment will be particularly onerous). Again, history demonstrates that this is usually a safe bet to make.

Friedman, for his part, is correct when he insists that licensing overly restricts the supply of doctors. Nor does the practise necessarily insure a high quality of care. But it may tend to keep the very worst (and most dangerous) would be medicos away from the public. (Especially those whose marketing skills easily outstrips their medical knowledge or training.) Believing that anyone should be able to set up and practise medicine, more closely reflects a state of faith rather than evidence. Moreover, claiming that the previous, unregulated period of medical practise in the United States (19th century) was admirable, with quacks running free, seems more than a touch ludicrous. Consequently, his medical excellence through open competition scheme, is largely kept afloat by pure assertion. Then there is a remaining problem that pops up predictably in almost all of Friedman's free market constructions. Friedman never seems to bother exploring what conditions must hold in order for markets to properly self-regulate, to produce those favoured and optimal results. Instead, he just assumes that they will. From Friedman's perspective, markets by definition are imbued with incentives causing them to discover preferred solutions. Producing the convincing scaffolding required for a story of dominating self-regulation seldom poses many difficulties for true believers. Unfortunately, an actual application of this market constructed scenario may prove disappointing.

Given Milton Friedman's self-confidence, his unwavering belief in his perceived truths, it is not surprising that he concluded that markets were capable of resolving any difficulty they faced. This supposition is based (unmentioned or explored by Burns), on a rather surprising, but simple idea. Markets reward those who make profitable improvements. This extends not only to shifting assets to their most profitable use, but also to solving observed difficulties. Such rewards are believed to consistently provide sufficient incentives to achieve purported ends. Notice however that this logical argument is mounted on shaky foundations. Decision makers must have available adequate and accurate information (unbounded rationality). Unfortunately, any consideration of these required suppositions remain missing in Burns policy evaluations. At fault is the key, unexplored connection between methodology and policy, a subject she prefers to ignore whenever possible. Friedman's methodology was developed to form an essential foundation for the market fundamentalism he championed. (Not to mention providing a distraction from issues surrounding the validity of assumptions.) Similar to any religious fundamentalist, ambiguity finds not the smallest shred of shelter in the Manichean world Friedman creates. From this perspective (being assured of knowing precisely how the world works), those wishing to undermine these unshakable truths can be nothing less than inherently dangerous. They are heretics who must be crushed at all cost.

Despite these glaring pitfalls, Burns turns her face away from claims Friedman made, scenarios that could rightly be described as embarrassing. As previously mentioned, his obsession with letting markets roam completely free, made him an adamant foe of any form of licensure or regulation. Yet in some cases his claims seem paper thin.

> All can agree that trade associations do always have selfish monopolistic motives to pump up their incomes. But only Milton Friedman could argue – argue seriously – *that therefore everyone should be able to practice surgery*. That is a bizarre stretch, bred out of Friedman's libertarian gut rather than his syllogistic brain. Proof is that Friedman seriously opposed legislation requiring drivers on public highways to pass a competence test.
>
> Once conservative Bill Buckley dialogued with conservative Milton Friedman. I paraphrase this discussion:
>
> > B.B Yes, some public regulation can be necessary. Suppose the democratic legislature made prostitution legal. Surely then requiring prostitutes to pass a monthly test for venereal disease is a worthy idea.
> >
> > M.F. Not at all. If a woman on the street, professing to be disease-free does infect a customer, that will hurt her reputation. If, nevertheless she does infect you, then there is a *tort* that you can sue her for in court.
>
> When Friedman's conservative Chicago colleagues chided him for such extremisms, he was unrepentant. Someone in each generation must go all the way with truth, however much that dissipates his influence – that was his credo.
>
> Darwin gave Friedman every good gift of I.Q. and originality. But withheld from him was the precious gift of "maybe" (Samuelson 2011c: 863–864).

Looking at market alternatives is undeniably useful and should not be carelessly dismissed. Which means that Burns is half right in asserting that "Friedman's response was to ask another question: What would it look like if the market decided? At first using market mechanisms for governance seemed crazy. Then it seemed like common sense" (2023:481). But the problem is that Friedman didn't just play with the possibility. He would always insist that the market option was the only sensible one to choose. So Burns is not entirely correct in her unstinted praise for Friedman.

The crucial element in this discussion, one which she glides past, is that there needs be an examination of the conditions necessary for markets to work in any given instance. Simply assuming a can opener, Friedman's preferred methodological solution, won't open any tins of tuna fish. Such an approach is bound to be insufficient, not necessarily wrong, but too facile in creating unresolved issues. Burns though almost wilfully ignores an inherent and fatal fault in Friedman's market proselytising. Overselling the magic of the marketplace can lead to disappointment. This result can be expected whenever anything is badly oversold. Historically, such practises can lead to a somewhat equal and opposite reaction, an overcorrection which leaves a society too far on the opposite end of the spectrum.

For instance, Larry Summers fantasy of self-regulating financial markets yielded far greater (and perhaps more intrusive oversight) than would have otherwise occurred once a subsequent meltdown struck. Over eagerness in promoting globalisation managed to trigger a subsequent regime of tariffs, subsidies and industrial planning. Perhaps this was simply an unintended consequence of Friedman's unwavering self-belief and need to preach the truth. But, a better, and equally conservative option was offered at much the same time by Ronald Coase. Namely, it was impossible to concoct a one size fits all policy by jumping from some theoretical conclusion or ideological stance. Instead, he suggested a case by case approach dependent on empirical evidence. Unfortunately, few economists of Friedman's era proved eager to get their hands dirty by grubbing into the actual working of a given market at a given time. As noted, attributing a purely rules based monetary policy to a self-regulating system of financial markets was perhaps a poignant example of hope triumphing over experience. If anything, his stubborn unwillingness to modify his approach to monetary theory (despite contrary evidence) does display the way in which ideology can permanently skew one's perspective.[71]

V. Money Makes the World Go Round – The Road to Monetarism

Another difference between Milton [Friedman] and myself is that everything reminds Milton of the money supply. Well, everything reminds me of sex, but I keep it out of my papers (Solow 1966:63).[72]

Monetarism may be largely dead and defunct. Though it is hard to think of any economic theory that has been so thoroughly staked through the heart that it subsequently became incapable of resurrection, at least when given a bit of updating and a veneer of the contemporaneous. Economists have traditionally been wonders at intellectual recycling. But no matter what its current status, Friedman's views by the late seventies were given wide credence, though perhaps not quite the dominance that Burns would like to extend to them. Certainly the unforeseen oil shocks of the seventies provided something of a fortunate opportunity for Friedman's theories and obsessions to shine. In a space constructed by an alternative history, absent those shocks, the economy of the seventies might have been quite different. What Friedman was consistently loathe to acknowledge is that policies (and even theories) may be time and place specific.[73]

Given that he established his reputation with the meticulously researched volume co-authored with Anna Schwartz (1963), any biography that fully presents Friedman as an economist would need to simply explain this theory, as well as its policy implications. Yet, although monetarism is spoken of at great lengths by Burns (almost vindicating Solow), I am left lacking (after carefully reading her extensive efforts), any credible explanation of Friedman's theory. Certainly I am unable to locate one that incorporates a realistic transmission mechanism (or evidence of the same). (Namely, Burns fails to construct a bridge linking those favoured stocks of money with the real economy where goods and services are bought and sold.) Instead, I am left with the same feeling that stubbornly persists after reading an introductory macroeconomic textbook. Too much hand-waving (in place of any detailed explanation) reflects the imprecision and obscurity of key theoretical connections. In contrast, in most first year textbooks, price theory (microeconomics) fails to display similar logical gaps that require ad hoc jumps. The defined theoretical steps composing the whole, are clearly expounded. One ball bearing strikes the next until some conclusion is reached. At least in that case it is much easier to understand what you are arguing for (or against).

Instead, readers of Burns' biography are faced with an almost single-minded obsession with money stocks and the asserted need for them to grow, or shrink according to some simple rule. The deference to a rule is, in Friedman's approach, a necessary reflection of an insufficient level of knowledge. This crucial lack must subsequently rule out the possible success of any discretionary policy.[74] But questions arise, even initially, as to the appropriate money stock that should be observed.[75] But even more importantly, there is a direct necessity to understand exactly how changes in this stock might impact the actual economy. This insight would provide the required connection that could be clearly identified as the transmission mechanism. The problem is not that such explanations are necessarily lacking in Friedman's work, but that his theory and positions are not sufficiently explained by Burns. (Perhaps a direct problem for Burns herself given her insufficient economics background. (But this would be only speculation on my part.) Certainly Friedman's thinking extends beyond a simple version of the Quantity Theory of Money that Burns is eager to describe. (Though that remains an important component.)

The essential problem in Burns' account is that she conveys Friedman's obsession with monetary stocks without properly explaining how that focus connects to the real economy. That is the realm where theory must be applied and effective policies derived. Particularly, there remains a natural inclination (which Burns embraces) to dodge the issue by simply repeating the Director-Friedman dictum that inflation is everywhere a monetary problem (and then repeat it more than once again).[76] But that fails to detail the linkages between money stocks and accelerating prices that must exist if any sensible economic analysis is to be accomplished. Such a statement does not even go as far (or hint at something approaching a root causation) as the more popular slogan of too much money chasing too few goods. (That in itself does not provide the rationale for there being either too much money or too few goods, but exists as a sloppy way of describing the relative relation between aggregate demand and aggregate supply.)

Grounding inflation within the bounds of the real economy (one usefully determined by aggregate demand and supply should yield a better foundation than the alternative that Burns is willing to offer. (Once again, note that this fundamental concept is barely mentioned by Burns throughout hundreds of pages crammed with information, anecdotes and rough economic sketches. The choice seems counter-intuitive since aggregate supply and demand do form the basis of any economy.) Largely ignored in her discussion is the core idea identifying inflation as basically symptomatic in an economy, much as a temperature indicates bodily sickness in humans. Examining the actual causes would seem to be the best way to treat emerging symptoms. (Though such an approach would seem to contradict Friedman's 1953 methodology piece previously examined, where 'as if' dominates.)

In battling inflation, the usefulness of understanding why there is insufficient supply, as well as the reason for excessive demand, would appear logical, if not vital. Because of these two factors (and what may be driving them) all inflationary instances are not created equal. The problem may lie with certain bottlenecks in the supply system, as for instance when the wartime economy of 1945 transitioned to a peace time version. Added onto that issue were the abnormal level of savings accumulated during the wartime period, as rationing and bond drives deliberately curtailed consumer spending. (Government programs imposed these conditions as a means for countering any incipient inflation.) In a somewhat differentiation fashion, supply shocks and excessive government spending may, given the right circumstances, also fuel inflationary trends. Money enters the picture through the level of credit creation when allied with lending and borrowing.

Monetary policy (via central banks) can accommodate increased demand or hinder it. (In the space of a longer period, interest rates discouraging investment might eventually effect an economy's capacity.) But a government (or central bank) is not the main engine of money creation. That responsibility lies clearly with the actual banking system. Banks create money by lending. Monetary policy can act as a drag on aggregate demand, but cannot conversely force people to borrow, or banks to lend.[77] Consequently, as both Friedman and Keynes would agree, monetary policy can't be effectively employed to counter-act a recession. ('Pushing on a string' is a phrase often attributed to Keynes when describing the ineffectiveness of monetary policy.) However, Friedman contended that keeping a close watch on the pertinent stocks of money was sufficient, since such observations were predictive of future inflationary results. In either case, knowing a bit more about Friedman's monetary theory, beyond the simple quantity theory would have constituted a welcome appearance in this biography.[78]

To gain a more insightful perspective on Burns' shortcomings, going back to the start of Friedman's monetary journey might prove useful. In particular, when dealing with this topic, the author's economic shortcomings are at times painfully apparent. For instance, she seems unaware that the inverse relation between bond prices and interest rates is a necessary artefact of the mathematics of discounting.[79] It has nothing to do with economics. If bond prices fall, interest rates must rise and vice versa in anything resembling a rational world. And it is difficult to explain how bond prices would not fall given an increase in supply by a central bank.

Instead, Burns describes the working of bond prices and interest rates in a nearly incoherent fashion.

> First, foreign buyers rushed to U.S. Treasurys amid uncertainty. This pushed interest rates lower because buyers wanted security, not a high return … In order to raise interest rates, they had to make money scarce (Burns 2023:337).

I suppose that this description (above) is more interesting for the general reader, but its explanatory power is no less than mysterious. Translating, Burns simply says that U.S. Treasuries are viewed as riskless (repayment is not questioned). Therefore, they must have a lower attached interest rate (less risk means less reward) than other offerings with more doubtful repayment. Consequently, if demand for bonds increased, the price of those bonds would rise. At this point arithmetic takes over. As bond prices rise, interest rates must fall. The last sentence says that the Fed could raise rates by selling bonds. (Selling bonds removes money from the economy.) But to once again emphasise the obvious, an increase in the supply of bonds must cause the price of bonds to fall. Once again arithmetic dictates that when the price of bonds fall, interest rates must rise. Admittedly, this description is a bit lugubrious, but it at least attempts to explain the steps. Reading Burns' version of the bond market, I am left wondering how much of the basics she understands.

But for the moment, let's leave that specific Burns' quagmire and instead flip back to 1956 when Friedman first presented his particular version of monetary theory. If read carefully (or even not so carefully) his underlying aim is to clearly supplant the then ruling theory that claimed as its heritage Keynes' liquidity preference theory, first expounded in *The General Theory*. Friedman is clearly trying to supplant the then dominant (and perhaps ruling) theory based on Keynes' work. Burns might, at this point, have usefully provided the reader with some notion of what that monetary position might have been. But a general reader would need psychic powers to even vaguely conceptualise the basic composition of liquidity preference theory, or its more direct descendants. Instead, we are presented with her standard trope. Milton Friedman battles against misguided opponents, who in the end recognise the validity of his position. The hero triumphs with his defeated opposition admitting their failings, via very short (usually one sentence) quotes in her narrative. In a sense, this constant insistence that Friedman was always at the centre of every economic debate (at the eye of each whirlwind) trivialises his importance. He was not some cinematic *Zelig*, an almost miraculously ubiquitous academic. More significantly, he didn't always triumph in the end. Even his successes have in the ensuing years been re-evaluated, as often happens in the discipline. Essentially, Friedman's major importance and significance doesn't depend on reflecting an almost Hollywood sheen.

But to turn briefly to Keynes. His is a monetary theory based on the demand for money. The issue then turns on why someone might want to hold assets in the form of money, which remains the most liquid form or variety of wealth.[80] Thus what Keynes describes as a liquidity preference is grounded on a number of reasonable objectives. He simplifies by dividing the motive into two categories. The first (creating a demand for money) is largely dependent on output/input levels. Consumers need liquid funds for consumption while businesses incur costs before receiving revenues. Thus there is a direct connection between cash holding and the level of spending. Lastly, he adds to this category a precautionary category which consists of a 'just in case' motive, which attempts to provide for unforeseen expenses. As Keynes claims, "For the demand for money to satisfy the former motives it is generally irresponsive to any influence except the actual occurrence of a change in general economic activity and the level of incomes" (Keynes 1964:197). Keynes lumps these reasons for holding money (being liquid) into what he refers to as M_1 or sometimes L_1.

Keynes' major innovation is to add a speculative category, which largely turns on the expected rate of interest. This particular motivation for demanding money rests on the desire to achieve short term gains and avoid losses. (If there is an expectation of a rate increase, bonds are dumped and money is held to avoid losses. In the same sense, a counter expectation would see bonds bought to reap future gains. Notice how strong expectations one way or the other ends up reinforcing outcomes.) Naturally expectations will vary among speculators. Interest rates will then adjust to balance those who wish to hold bonds with those who wish to hold money. Keynes refers to this speculative driven money as either M_2 or L_2. This allows Keynes to make the standard quantity theory of money a special case of his more general theory.

The logic of this special case is straight forward.

In a static society or in a society in which for any other reason no one feels any uncertainty about the future rates of interest, the Liquidity Function L_2, or the propensity to hoard (as we might term it), will always be zero in equilibrium. Hence in equilibrium $M_2 = 0$ and $M = M_1$ ... Thus if it is practicable to measure the quantity, O [output], and the price, P, of current output, we have $Y = OP$, and therefore, $MV = OP$; which is much the same as the Quantity Theory of Money in its traditional form (Keynes 1964:209).

Contrary to Keynes particular liquidity story, it is clear that if one instead assumes that output is determined by physical capacity (and income velocity is stable), then price levels will simply depend on the existing quantity of money. That takes us directly to the Friedman-Director dictum that inflation is everywhere a monetary problem. But as Keynes insists, that approach fails to distinguish changes in prices (inflation) that are promoted by jumps in aggregate demand from those pushed by cost of living adjustments to wages. (The seventies oil shocks led to labour unions pushing (and usually winning) such adjustments.

> For the purposes of the real world it is a great fault in the Quantity Theory that it does not distinguish between changes in prices which are a function of changes in output and those which are a function of changes in the wage-unit. The explanation of this omission is, perhaps, to be found in the assumptions that there is no propensity to hoard and that there is always full employment. For in this case, O being constant and M_2 being zero, it follows, if we can take V also as constant, that both the wage-unit and the price-level will be directly proportional to the quantity of money (Keynes 1964:209).

In any case, the monetary theory appearing in the *General Theory* was far from Keynes' final word on the subject. Keynes considered all his theories to be provisional. His approach had always assumed that when his available evidence changed, his position would as well. After the 1936 publication of the *General Theory*, Keynes continued to tinker with his monetary theory.[81] Naturally after his death, others would expand and alter what he did. But Milton Friedman, for reasons unknown (though speculation here is possible), seemed to consistently misinterpret that theory. But then again, any evidence (or interpretation) that ran contrary to Friedman's *a priori* objectives could, at times, be discarded. "... the categories of "honest" and "dishonest" are quite irrelevant. What is instead relevant is the far more subtle phenomenon involved in human failing (to which we are all subject of sometimes suppressing that which it would be more convenient for us not to note or remember – with reference to questions to which we are strongly involved" (Patinkin quoted in Leeson, 2003b:258).[82]

Jumping ahead in years (at least momentarily), Friedman's position on Keynes would change very little. His persistent stance on monetary theory (and particularly its historical roots) would provoke Harry Johnson to make savage attacks, some even questioning his honesty. In 1971 Friedman would still give Keynes almost no credit in terms of the development of monetary theory. Instead, he continued to insist that Keynes in the *General Theory* deviated little from his ideas in the much earlier (1923) *Tract*. This interpretation could only be described as heroic in a misguided fashion. The *Tract*, as Keynes himself acknowledged, was very much in the Cambridge Quantity Theory tradition. Friedman, at least implicitly, insisted in essence that Keynes' "struggle of escape from habitual modes of thought and expression" (Keynes 1964:viii) was either a case of severe self-delusion or an instance bordering on outright and deliberate fraud.

> The major points which Milton made is that there is nothing particularly Keynesian about the liquidity preference function, and that the demand for money sections of the *General Theory* are simply a slightly inferior version of Keynes views in the *Tract* (Stanley Fisher quoted in Leeson 2003c:512).

Consequently, a useful understanding of Friedman's crucial attempt to supplant Keynesian monetary theory (starting in 1956), depends on what would appear to be two different strategies. (Burns, at best, chooses to skim over what at that time were major issues.) Namely, when his initial historical sally ran into a brick wall of contrary evidence, he fell back on an alternative. Both though shared the same objective of undercutting the stature of Keynes' work.

As an initial attempt, Friedman managed to stir up a continuing controversy by manfully trying to embed his theory in some ill-defined Chicago oral tradition. In doing so, there is at least an implicit implication that Friedman wished to provide his approach with some classically rooted gravity. As opposed to Keynes' revolutionary imposition, he tried to create an impression that his theoretical offering was historically based, an approach fundamentally grounded in generally accepted economic thinking. His modelling was best viewed as a continuation, rather than a disruption, of both classical and neo-classical thought. Unfortunately, Friedman's claim of building upon some instantly recognisable historical tradition exposed him as the tyro he was, someone dipping an uncertain toe into the history of economic thought. In fact, his lack of experience in this particular nook of the profession proved, in some way, to be his undoing. (Nor did he display much of an interest in such matters throughout his career.)[83]

His historical contentions were immediately challenged by an economist accomplished in this field, namely by Donald Patinkin. As opposed to Friedman, who was at Chicago for only two years, Patinkin received his doctorate from the Chicago Department. Plus in the early 1940s, he was taught by (and talked to) the same staff who had been there during Friedman's time. Moreover, Patinkin could rely on the extensive class notes he had taken during those Chicago years. After a thorough investigation, he was able to discover nothing to support Friedman's claim of some mysterious Chicago oral tradition. In some ways, Friedman's constructed story provided remarkably convenient (or possibly too convenient) support for his preferred theory.

Many decades later, Friedman would opt to simply skirt this issue entirely by dismissing it. "I was baffled at the time, and have been ever since, at what all the fuss was about. So far as I could see, very little was at stake" (Friedman quoted in Leeson 2003d: x). Such a statement, even retrospectively, has to be treated as somewhat ingenuous on Friedman's part. His attempt, in this instance, to slip away from what had become a heated controversy, doesn't ring particularly true. A response of this nature doesn't answer why Friedman insisted on providing his theory with this particular historical patina. Patinkin not only found fault with Friedman's historical memory, but wondered if Friedman was quite happy in his essay to "let [policy] wag ... theory" (Patinkin 2003b:126). As opposed to Friedman, Patinkin's objections were solely focused on the theoretical aspect of the issue.

> ... what interests me now is monetary theory, not monetary policy. These represent two different spheres of discourse. And whatever the relationship between the two, it is clearly not a one-to-one correspondence: different policy recommendations can emanate from the same conceptual theoretical framework; and different frameworks can lead to the same policy recommendation (Patinkin 2003c:319).

Put bluntly, Friedman's claims simply contradicted first person evidence. Nor did Chicago's chief monetary theorist during the interwar years, Lloyd

Mints, ever come to Friedman's defence on this point. Samuelson's lengthy quote on this matter would seem to be at least somewhat conclusive.

> Before comparing views with me on Friedman's disputed topic (and after having done so), Don Patinkin denied that in his Chicago period of the 1940s any trace of such a specified oral tradition could be found in his class notes (on Mints, Knight, Viner), or could be found in his distinct memory. My Chicago years predated Friedman's autumn 1932 arrival and postdated his departure for Columbia and the government's survey of incomes and expenditures. I took all the macroeconomic course on offer by Chicago teachers: Mints, Simons, Director, and Douglas. Also in this period, I attended lectures and discussions of the Great Depression involving Knight, Viner, Yntema, Mints, and Gideonse. Nothing beyond the sophisticated account by Dennis Robertson, in his famous *Cambridge Handbook on Money*, of the Fisher-Marshall-Pigou MV = PQ paradigm can be found in my class notes and memories.
> More importantly, as a star upper-class undergraduate, I talked a lot with the hotshot graduate students – Stigler, Wallis, Bronfenbrenner, Hart – and rubbed elbows with Friedman and Homer Jones. Since no whisper reached my ears, and no cogent publications have ever been cited, I believe that his nominated myth should not be elevated to the rank of plausible history of ideas (Samuelson 2011e:560–561).

Early on, even Milton Friedman felt compelled, when faced with Patinkin's evidence and logic to supply a half-hearted reversal regarding this will-of-the-wisp oral tradition. However, despite having his story exposed, Friedman simply refused to explain why he felt compelled to include this misleading assertion as part of his monetary essay. Claiming that he wasn't at that time focused on illuminating any history of thought aspects, fails to provide anything like a satisfactory defence of his actions.

> I find your description of the oral tradition entirely acceptable and much better and more acceptable than mine. In extenuation, I can only say that the 1956 essay did not set out to be an essay in the history of thought but an introduction to a collection of studies (Friedman quoted in Leeson 2003b:257).

Yet this extensive side of the debate seems not to have impressed Burns. Instead, she allows this controversy (perhaps given that Friedman fails to triumph) to be largely brushed aside, remaining impervious to counter-arguments. To justify her curious decision, she simply relies on evidence provided by Tavlas (2003), both in his written account and in discussions she undoubtedly had with him. Unfortunately, when discussing controversies surrounding Friedman (particularly theoretical and policy debates) Burns seems to be predictably convinced by whatever perspective conveniently coincides with her picture of Friedman's heroic journey. To seriously consider Patinkin's viewpoint would hardly burnish Friedman or the battles he fought. But daring to claim that he won this particular conflict would require an unwarranted stretch.

Burns then is completely mum on Friedman's second attempt to eviscerate Keynes' monetary theory. However by his subsequent actions, Friedman showed himself to be completely undeterred by his initial failure. The ambiguous Chicago tradition previous cited was unceremoniously dropped since waiting in the wings was an alternative line of attack. Burns' response is just to ignore the details with which Friedman builds his subsequent attack on Keynes' monetary theory. At this point, she might have taken this golden opportunity to examine Friedman's controlling motivation. Burns could have seized this opening to analyse Friedman's recurring passion, one that drove his attack not only on opposing monetary theories, but on many others as well. Predictably, Burns lets this moment slip carelessly by. She ignores even compelling evidence, which explained that like some subterranean river, Friedman's underlying motivation could usually be traced back to his perceived struggle against collectivist forces. In this depicted scenario, freedom and liberty were perpetually in a death struggle with the dark forces of collectivism.

> According to his disciples, Keynes trusted to human intelligence. He hated enslavement by rules. He wanted governments to have discretion and he wanted economists to come to their assistance in the exercise of that discretion. In Aaron Director's [Milton Friedman's brother-in-law] judgement, Keynes' work provided the foundations for 'collectivism' while Simons' work provided the foundation for 'freedom and equality' (Leeson 2003d:308).

In his second attempt to dismiss Keynes, after failing to demonstrate that his theory evolved from some secret oral tradition, Friedman sought to trivialise Keynes' contribution to monetary theory. He tried manfully to shrink Keynes' all-encompassing shadow to a state of near invisibility. In essence, Friedman wants to reduce Keynes to no more than a minor quantity theorist whose only contribution to monetary theory was his conception of absolute liquidity preference (more commonly referred to as the liquidity trap).

> There is one respect – and I believe only one – in which the discussion of the demand curve for money in the *General Theory* is distinctly Keynesian and that is the importance attached to 'absolute liquidity preference' or a high-interest elasticity of the demand for money. This element is distinctively Keynesian in the double sense that it is, so far as I know, introduced for the first time in the *General Theory* (Friedman 2003b:157).

If one bothers to read the *General Theory* (and apparently few do) the idea of a liquidity trap ('absolute liquidity preference') appears briefly on page 202 (1964). Keynes draws attention to the purely theoretical possibility that at a very low interest rate, the probability of a capital loss from rising rates is greater than the loss of a small yield from remaining liquid. In which case, holding bonds would lose their purpose, rendering monetary policy ineffective. For Keynes, this is purely a hypothetical possibility that had not occurred, nor does he indicate that it is likely to occur.[84] But Friedman proves determined to find in the *General Theory* exactly what he needs to find.

> Patinkin objects to my treating 'the case of "absolute liquidity preference" – as part of "Keynes's basic challenge to the reigning theory".' He cites as counterevidence Keynes's own statement ... that 'whilst the limiting case might become practically important in the future' he knew 'of no example of it hitherto' ... More important, Patinkin does not quote the sentence immediately following Keynes's disclaimer, to wit, 'indeed, owing to the unwillingness of most monetary authorities to deal boldly in debts of long term, there has not been much of an opportunity for a test' (Friedman 2003c:157–158).

Friedman appears here to be supplying a decisive reply to Patinkin's objections. But if seriously examined, it turns out to be a reply without any real substance. He fails to quote the next sentence which negates to a large degree the importance of Friedman's obsession with "absolute liquidity preference". Keynes points out the following: "Moreover, if such a situation were to arise, it would mean that the public authority itself could borrow through the banking system on an unlimited scale at a nominal rate of interest" (Keynes 1964:207).[85] Friedman further ignores the fact that Keynes was consistently much more interested in actual empirical observations than he was in mere theoretical possibilities. Yet Friedman is determined to soldier on with his claims. "One consequence of my rereading large parts of the *General Theory* in the course of writing this reply has been to reinforce my view that absolute liquidity preference plays a key role" (Friedman 2003c:158).

Such a claim, when seriously considered, is largely inexplicable. Friedman tries to support his contention through a planned distraction. He attempts to overwhelm any objection by simply listing a sizeable number of instances where he insists that Keynes refers to "absolute liquidity preference". But in each case, the supposed proof is either taken out of context or has nothing to do with Friedman's curious obsession.[86] The only speculative answer is that by reducing Keynes contribution to one dubious addendum (absolute liquidity preference), his statue would be much reduced. Whatever the motivation, this dispute certainly demonstrates Friedman's standard response to legitimate criticism. Mainly, he can be seduced by the power of obfuscation. Yet Burns doesn't find this particular debate over Keynes worth noting, even though it provides a sharp insight into Friedman's tactics. But even more so, a careful examination might underscore the way in which ideology and its imperatives can influence and dominate one's economic analysis.

But Burns refuses to be fazed, no matter what direction Friedman's journey takes. Her judgment in these matters fails to inspire a requisite degree of confidence. For instance, general readers would gather from this biography that Friedman correctly reduced macroeconomics to his version of monetary theory. Namely that tracing money stocks is not only necessary, but perhaps sufficient in understanding economic events. (Friedman's falling back on his convenient methodology, one that relies solely on prediction, seems to fortify this approach.) Such a carefully situated perspective allows Friedman to conclude, for instance that the Great Depression was simply a monetary policy fiasco on the part of the Federal Reserve.[87] Certainly, no one would be tempted to applaud the bank's actions (or lack of) during this period. But Friedman's narrow focus at times lacks complete credibility. Money stocks did drop during the early crucial period as Friedman noted. But this is hardly because the Fed tightened its policy. The most prominent event monetarily was the massive failure and closure of banks during these years.[88] The natural response by potential depositors was to avoid using banks (hoarding their money under the proverbial mattresses). The consequent result was a drop in the level of money stocks. The Fed could have intervened to bail out banks, but Friedman would have hardly concurred with such an approach. (He saw no need for a Central Bank and would have opposed any such bail-outs. Doing so would have stoked moral hazard in Friedman's eyes.) Burns simply accepts the drop in Friedman's nominated money stock as a sufficient explanation without delving any deeper.

Given a financial crisis, the Federal Reserve could have attempted to drastically loosen its monetary policy, but how successful such an approach would have been is far from certain, though it might have less-ened the subsequent severity of the depression. Keynes instead noted the rising borrowers and lenders risk during such periods, which basically put the kibosh on lending (and by that means, the growth of money stocks). In essence, perceived risk of a loan being repaid made lenders demand a higher rate from potential borrowers. While fear of being capable of repaying implied that borrowers would want a lower rate. Under such conditions, loans would quite naturally be drastically cut back.

For Friedman, however, the root of all outcomes, given his focused microscope, must be entirely monetary in nature. Consequently, it is not altogether (but still somewhat) surprising when the 1937 downturn in the US is reduced by Friedman to no more than a case of monetary misjudge-ment. Again, the issue, as related in the biography, comes down to the size of money stocks. Burns is easily satisfied with this single-minded approach. She just rejects the more obvious (and generally accepted) demand based explanation as some convenient coincidence. The undis-puted facts are that Roosevelt (in 1937) undertook an ill-advised attempt to consolidate federal debt. Pulling in fiscal spending would be expected to reduce aggregate demand and hence economic growth. This deduction doesn't require complex economic thinking. That is what in fact did hap-pen according to the available evidence, but not if we are tempted to accept Burns' judgment. For her, as for Friedman, the downturn reflected money stocks and attached Federal Reserve errors. Burns even throws in a few maybes and what ifs to further confuse what would otherwise be a straightforward analysis employing aggregate demand figures.

> More spending was not the only possible solution to the downturn. After
> all, deficit spending had been policy for five years, perhaps it had not

worked, or perhaps deficits themselves were the problem, as traditional economic thought held. Indeed, the moniker, "Roosevelt recession' was hung on the president by opponents who wanted to undermine the New Deal. Nor was the monetary explanation exhausted. In later years, Friedman and others would point to new reserve requirements for banks mandated by the Federal Reserve as a potential cause of the slump (Burns 2023:98).

To be blunt and unkind, Burns in the quoted paragraph simply doesn't know what she is talking about. Earlier in her narrative, she had admitted that Lachlan Currie, at the time a Roosevelt advisor who later Friedman would scorn as a Communist, had discovered 'for the first time since 1931, the government's net contribution to national spending had fallen (Burns 2023:95). Simply put, a recovering economy suddenly faced a significant drop in aggregate demand via a cutback in government spending. There was no reason to believe that the private sector would magically take up the slack at a time when demand was falling. The Federal Reserve might not have helped, though it is a reach to say that a drop in lending and borrowing was fundamentally due to a change in a bank's reserve requirement. This alteration might (with all else unchanged) lead to a minor tightening of lending. But with a drop in aggregate demand, reflected by a drop in borrowing (the constraint on bank activity seems essentially trivial). The bulk of her statement simply distracts by pointing in a variety of contrary directions.

Even more conclusive in burying the narrative Burns pushes, is the fashion in which the Great Depression was finally buried. America was forced to switch over to a war economy, even before the attack on Pearl Harbor. The high level of fixed government spending, plus the draft of young men into the military, insured that unemployment ceased to be an issue. For those war years, supply became the overriding issue with domestic consumption deliberately constrained. What is apparent is that in both cases (1937 and the war years), aggregate demand was unsurprisingly the key driver. Yet Burns, following Friedman's lead, blithely ignores demand issues throughout the volume. She takes notice of the peanut shell strewn rooms, while simultaneously ignoring the lumbering elephant. However, being Friedman's biographer shouldn't automatically put the author in the position of being conscripted as his enabler as well. Reading (and even being befuddled by) the book, I was never clear whether the reason for her approach lay with her unclear hold on economic understanding, or with her ideological preferences. If neither, I am at a loss to supply a viable explanation for what appears. In any case, simplifying Friedman does him no service. He may not have been a lauded philosopher, or a famous theoretical physicist. But his career is underlined by his complexity of thought, a quality that should not be sacrificed to achieve some sought after narrative convenience.

Burns of course should (and does) discuss the Friedman and Schwartz seminal work on money at length, but again she does so uncritically. She applauds rather than evaluates. In her biographical world, not only is the work universally acclaimed, but every significant opponent recognise its enormous worth. Faced with genius, they are forced to bow down before the unarguable clarity and insight. In contrast to this vision of sweetness and light, Friedman's sometime contentious interchanges with Harry Johnson may be of some use.

To backtrack, the IS-LM model (only haltingly discussed and hardly displayed by Burns), might be of use when exploring some implications of the Friedman and Schwartz work. Essentially, Friedman asserted (and would continue to claim), that the demand for money didn't respond to interest rate changes. Or to use the appropriate terminology, that demand was perfectly inelastic to rate changes (or close enough for modelling purposes). In terms of the graphical model, this must produce a perfectly vertical LM curve. Meaning that shifts in the IS curve, due to fiscal policy (more government spending), would be entirely ineffectual. Such a measure would only crowd out investment leaving not net gain. In which case, only monetary policy would have a chance of being effective. But since, according to Friedman, relevant knowledge was limited, a rule based growth for money stocks was the only viable option. Rules must serve to ameliorate ignorance. In any case, the question of whether the demand for money was at all responsive to interest rate changes (whether the LM curve was vertical) became one of the touchstones of the Keynesian-Monetarist (or the saltwater versus the clear-water: Harvard/MIT versus Chicago) battles of the 1960s which oozed to some degree into the early 1970s. Only in the 1990s (in one of his very rare moments) did Friedman concede that he had erred to some degree on this issue. Burns chooses not to tarnish her image of Friedman by delving into such (at least to her) peripheral matters.

As Burns does underline, Johnson reviewed the Friedman-Schwartz opus and was appreciative. However, contrary to what Burns expresses,

Johnson did hold some reservations. He was in no way a converted monetarist. As Johnson contended:

> If interest rates do not affect velocity, monetary analysis can be divorced from analysis of the real sector, since the quantity of money will affect money incomes in the short run and prices in the long run without interference from the real forces. If, on the other hand, interest rates do affect velocity, monetary analysis much incorporate interest rates, velocity, real income and prices ... to admit interest rates into the demand function for money is to accept the Keynesian Revolution and Keynes' attack on the quantity theory (Milton Friedman in a letter to Harry Johnson, July 15, 1965).

Writing to Johnson in response, Friedman falls back on the same obsession previously highlighted. Every time he see the name of Keynes, Friedman can only see the term 'liquidity trap' played out in flashing neon letters. I've already discussed how mystifying this insistence was. Certainly, given what might appear to be (at least a tendency toward) deliberate obfuscation on Friedman's part, Johnson's wider scepticism (focusing on Friedman's methods and motives) becomes more understandable. Though kinder souls might judge such attacks to be not entirely justified.

> In my theoretical essay, "The Quantity Theory of Money – A Restatement", I certainly emphasize the role of interest rates in the demand function for money without in any way accepting either the Keynesian Revolution or Keynes' attack on the quantity theory. I believe you are confusing two things: admitting interest rates and admitting the special liquidity trap for which Keynes gave to the demand function in deep depression. Admitting the latter is indeed to accept the Keynesian attack on the quantity theory. Admitting the former has no such implications (Milton Friedman in a letter to Harry Johnson, July 15, 1965).

Thus Johnson would subsequently conduct an extended war of words with Friedman, even describing him as something of an outright charlatan.

> [Friedman] has frequently trapped and sandbagged critics of reputation and integrity by the technique of under-disclosure of analysis and evidence of apparent overstatements of the strength of his results (Johnson quoted in Leeson 2003b:261).

Johnson would have his chance to level the playing field with Friedman when Tobin dropped the privilege of delivering the 1970 Ely address at the 1970 meeting of the American Economic Association into Johnson's eager embrace. This address is traditionally second in importance to the president's speech, which Tobin would naturally provide. Tobin appeared to be yearning to strike a blow which would forcefully respond to Friedman's confident 1968 presidential speech. But Tobin preferred not to dirty his hands. Better in that case to contract out the responsibility to an accomplished mudslinger like Harry Johnson.

His well-earned reputation would be subsequently upheld at the meetings as Johnson refused to shy away from controversy. Though Burns does spend a few pages detailing the animosity between the two, this key clash goes unmentioned. (Perhaps both Johnson and Patinkin did think that Friedman received an unwarranted amount of attention, due more to his marketing skill than strictly to his economic brilliance. Meaning that it is possible to dismiss the attacks, to a certain degree, as being borne largely out of jealousy. Though there are enough bullseyes landed so that the issues raised should still be taken seriously.) In essence, Johnson was primed to reveal the posing wizard behind the curtain. Particularly, to demonstrate how Friedman skilfully manipulated various levers in order to mount his monetarist counter-revolution.

> My concern, specially, is with the reasons for the speed of propagation of the monetarist counter-revolution; but I cannot approach this subject without reference to the reasons for the speed of propagation of the Keynesian revolution, since the two are interrelated. Indeed, I find it useful in posing and treating the problem to adopt the 'as if' approach of positive economics, as expounded by the chief protagonist of the monetarist counter-revolution, Milton Friedman, and to ask: suppose I wished to start a counter-revolution, against the Keynesian revolution in monetary theory, how would I go about it – and specifically what could I learn about the technique from the revolution itself? (Johnson 2003:171).[89]

Johnson, in these attacks, is hoisting Friedman by his own peculiar petard of positivism, as almost a form of academic sport or play. But Johnson's piece is not a simple exercise in cynicism, or a slash and burn personal vendetta. The subsequent vehemence of response by what might be call 'Friedmanites' and fellow travellers, was perhaps due to the accuracy with which Johnson constructed his attack. He was certainly rash enough to openly and clearly identify Friedman's polemical objectives.

> A counter-revolution, however, has to cope somehow with a problem that a revolution by definition can ignore … the problem of establishing some sort of continuity with the orthodoxy of the past. Specifically, the monetarist counter-revolutionaries were burdened with the task of somehow escaping from the valid criticisms of the traditional quantity theory, which the Keynesian revolution had elevated into articles of dogma and self-justification (Johnson 2003:178).

This attack would have had to hit hard, since it provides a precise motivation for Friedman to insist upon a mysterious 'Chicago oral tradition'. After initially introducing his version of a monetarist creed, Friedman had studiously tried to dismiss his original continuity claim as a slip of his memory, in any case, composing no more than a trivial misstep. But Johnson, much more savagely than Patinkin, shattered Friedman's attempt to camouflage his intentions. More specifically, from Johnson's perspective, monetarists tried to ease away the difficulty of continuity by making two counter-contentions. Both aimed to steamroller any objections by shifting attention elsewhere. First, they mounted a claim that the response of an economy (via output or price level displacements) to monetary changes could be reduced to nothing more than an empirical (rather than a theoretical) problem. Thus any vulnerability, presented by a questionable theoretical construction, would be automatically eliminated.

Second, they moved to quash the puzzle of whether velocity (in a demand for money model) was stable. Such a question might be successfully transformed into a something more tractable. Namely, the possibility existed of seeking (instead) a stable functional dependence linking velocity to a limited number of variables. Employing either of the two options would leave smaller targets to attack. In other words, potential theoretical weaknesses could be finessed by presenting a new and improved quantity theory with roots still firmly anchored in the centuries-ripened original (or classical) version.

> The problem in the case of both counter-contentions was to establish a plausible linkage with pre-Keynesian orthodoxy. The solution to this problem was found along two lines. The first was the invention of a

University of Chicago oral tradition that was alleged to have preserved understanding of the fundamental truth among a small bank of the initiated through the dark years of the Keynesian despotism. The second was a careful combing of the *ober dicta* of the great neo-classical quantity theorists for any bit of evidence that showed recognition (or could be interpreted to show recognition) of the fact that the decision to hold money involves a choice between holding money and holding wealth in other forms, and is condition by the rates of return available on other assets (Johnson 2003:170).

My problem with Burns' accounts of these monetary matters is that serious and controversial opposition to Friedman's single-minded marketing of his theory is never seriously explored. Instead, the substituted impression is a version of St. George (or St. Milton) slaying the dragons impeding his inevitable triumph. Readers are met with too strong a whiff of the recurrent hero's journey that Burns faithfully sketches for Friedman in this particular narrative. This same barely audible spin describes Burns' account of the 1970s, when Friedman went from reputational strength to strength. (Burns isn't obvious or crass, but an accumulation of how scenes are contrived, or the way in which non-Friedman allies are portrayed, betrays her need to structure a pre-conceived, specific presentation of Friedman.) Starting with her description of the 1970s stagflation, she provides a precise perspective without striving for strict historical accuracy.

No doubt the Federal Reserve's performance during the 1970s inflationary period was less than stellar. But other central banks also failed to excel. (In fact, Federal Reserve options were more constrained at that time, since avoiding a serious recession – rising levels of unemployment – wrestled more directly with maintaining price levels.) The obsessive focus on inflation would only gain dominance during the following decade. Moreover in the 1970s, Reagan had yet to break the backs of trade unions (via the air traffic controller's strike). Consequently, during Friedman's rise to dominance, cost of living adjustments occurred with much greater frequency and ease. Undoubtedly in addition, oil played a more central role in developed economies fifty years ago, leading to a larger shock effect from the 1973 and 1978 crises. (Burns tries to dodge the oil issue by minimising its importance. Of course in the carefully constructed world in which Friedman dwelt, only the money stock mattered.) But inflationary problems slugged all the then developed economies. Burns is simply incorrect in implying that the US could have largely avoided the worst of the problem by presenting Germany and Japan as two countries that successfully finessed these shocks. Here she is simply incorrect.

Looking at Japan in the 1970s, any fair-minded observer would be unable to conclude that the country was unaffected by the inflationary wave of that decade. Relevant figures are as follows: 1973 (11.6%), 1974 (23.2%), 1975 (11.7%), 1976 (9.4%), 1977 (8.2%), 1978 (4.2%), 1979 (3.7%). Given that Japan imported almost all its oil, the 1973 price shock hit Japan harder than the US. At that period, there was even a notorious run on toilet paper as the Japanese public became fearful of inflation induced shortages. (Panic of course inevitably validates such fears in a self-justifying prophecy sort of way.) Japan did handle the second shock better, but by then it had developed a strategy to combat the impact. Basically, wage rises were kept below productivity increases. Thus prices were controlled by squeezing the work force. Lower export prices then allowed Japan to finance the noticeably higher cost of imported oil. Germany, on the other hand is the odd man out of developed countries. Like other such countries, Germany as the 1970s opened was already suffering rising prices. However, the 1920s spell of hyper-inflation produced a morbid inflation obsession within the Bundesbank in the post-war period. But unlike Japan, its growth record was spotty at best during the 1970s. Choking off growth might be a method for controlling inflation, but hardly an entirely admirable option.

This leaves us to examine Burns' treatment of an apparent moment of triumph for Friedman. Toward the end of the 1970s, the central banks of England and the United States announced the commencement of a monetarist experiment. Burns is sufficiently painstaking to admit that these attempts were short lived. (Thus rendering any judgment on Friedman's approach to be entirely inconclusive.) Certainly Paul Volker, when heading the Fed, was never a genuine convert. Though there is a vague impression (left by Burns) that Central Bankers somehow betrayed the wisdom encapsulated by Friedman's rules versus discretion dictum. Burns does strongly hint that these bankers went astray by not focusing sufficiently on the money stock. However, at least in my memory, her report doesn't ring exactly true. There was certainly a public relation's push behind the announced policy change. But the reality, when applied, hinted strongly of a dominant pseudo policy. In application, a turn toward a monetarist approach only managed to create something of a cottage industry among financial firms. Each, at that time, had their own select Fed watchers. These acolytes would be instructed to conscientiously observe the ups and downs of a preferred money stock, in order to accurately forecast a central bank's future monetary moves. But this effort was soon abandoned when the supposed policy was revealed to be more of a charade than a reality.[90] Whether any central bank attempted to seriously control money stocks remains an open question. The entirety might have only been an exercise of smoke and mirrors, a strategy that central banks were not loathe to use at that time.

The idea that some simple rule could function effectively, even as financial technology changed and money itself constantly transformed, came to be seen as naïve. Volker certainly used his discretion in charting policy, with interest rate adjustments playing the role that Friedman had slated for his favoured money stocks, though such administered changes did not vary according to a fixed (or any discernible) rule.

> I belabour this ancient history because what those gods were modifying was much that Milton Friedman was renominating about money around 1950 in encyclopedia articles and empirical history. It is paradoxical that a keen intellect jumped on that old bandwagon just when technical changes in money and money substitutes – liquid markets connected by wire and telephonic liquid "safe money market funds," which paid interest rates on fixed-price balances that varied between 15% per annum and 1%, depending on price level trends – were realistically replacing the scalar M by a vector of (M_0, M_1, M_2, ... M_{17}, a myriad of bonds with tight bid-asked prices, ...). We all pity warm-hearted scholars who get stuck on the wrong paths of socialistic hope. That same kind of regrettable choice characterizes anyone who bets doggedly on ESP, or creationism, or ... The pity of it increases for one who adopts a simple theory of positivism that exonerates a nominated theory, even if its premises are unrealistic, so long only as it seems to describe with approximate accuracy some facts. Particularly vulnerable is a scholar who tries to *test* competing theories by submitting them to *simplistic* linear regressions with no sophisticated calculations of Granger causality, cointegration, collinearities and ill-conditioning, or a dozen other safeguard econometric methodologies (Samuelson in Barnett 2011:556).

A recurring problem throughout this comprehensive biography is that Burns appears to shy away (deliberately or not) from any controversy that fails to leave Friedman basking in a positive light. This tendency unfortunately undermines (if only subtly), Burns' discussion of the rules versus discretion debate. As applied to Friedman's monetary growth rule, logical problems (even when ignored), won't conveniently disappear. However, an alternative approach does exist, although it is one which Burns ignores and Friedman (given his ideology) would automatically reject. Namely that evidence of flawed judgment doesn't rigorously mean that exercising judgment should be summarily abandoned. A logical option would be an attempt to improve that judgment, rather than simply dismissing the option as inferior by definition.

In essence, even though the judgment of the Federal Reserve and other central bankers are far from perfect, there has certainly been some improvement in its practises over the last century. Claiming that nothing has been learned seems a far reach. Certainly, the idea of targeting inflation rates at 2 percent is applauded in the biography, though Burns neglects to provide a sound foundation for that applause. But targeting can't be practised without employing judgment. Namely, decisions as to when rates should be raised or lowered is (even with the best data and econometric modelling) always going to come down to informed judgment rather than being purely rule based.

But in talking about inflation targeting clarification is required. For the media and the political class, a 2 percent inflation rate has been generally accepted as an approved target. To such an extent that the public, encouraged by the media, labels anything else as a high rate. But attempts to provide evidence for such a rate have simply failed. Proof is lacking that a 2 percent level is in any way superior to a 3 or a 4 percent rate (from a purely economic stance). Nor despite Burns' suggestions, a rate higher than 2 percent does not automatically lead to accelerating inflation. Historically (and Burns is after all an accomplished historian) the 2 percent figure evolved accidentally. The number is due to an off-the-cuff remark made during a 1 April, 1988 televised interview by then New Zealand Finance Minister Roger Douglas. He was the driving force behind 'Rogernomics', the attempt by the newly elected Labour government to reform and restructure the New Zealand economy.

When asked what the country's inflation rate should be, Douglas responded that he was aiming for a number between 0 and 1 percent. The Bank of New Zealand adopted that number and adjusted it, since at that time, the current inflation measurement overstated the actual rate. That brought the preferred number up to a rounded figure of 2 percent. The psychology behind announcing that rate as a target depended on a specific hope. If all the pieces fell into place, business, labour and the general public would come to believe that the Bank operated under that fixed rule, which would trigger a determination to insure that particular stable level would always be met.[91] As a result, wage and price demands did subsequently ease. Throughout the 1990s, other central banks followed suit by adopting the same 2 percent target (with some banks allowing a bit more latitude). Unfortunately, the idea that there was something either empirical or theoretical to support this number (which was basically pulled out of a hat) was largely embraced. It became so rooted within the media and the political class that it is virtually now impossible to alter that specific bulls-eye.[92] Once everyone seemed to unquestionably know that 2 percent was the magical target, the figure became something of a self-fulfilling prophecy.

But rules always produce something of a quandary. Even if Burns is satisfied with accepting Friedman's dictum of increasing money stocks each year by a given percentage, the question left unasked is whether that percentage is fixed for all times. The fixed option seems unlikely in a world where financial technology is constantly changing, as well as the financial habits of both business and the general public. But deciding on a new goal, a new rate of increase, would involve judgment and thus discretion. Logically, even a rule based approach avoids the automatic implementation of rules. At some point, decisions are made as to when and how a rule is applied (and needs to be remade from time to time).

Change is an inevitable component of economic thinking. Policy, despite Friedman's idea of inviolate markets, is always time and place specific. No policy should be viewed as a once and for all option. What applies to policy must logically apply also (in varying degrees) to theory itself. In this regard, Friedman conveniently used his empirical research to bulwark his work on the Phillips curve. By doing so, he purported to provide universal (and unbending) theoretical links. The simple underlying idea was that in the long run (over time) there was no trade-off between inflation and unemployment (or could ever be). This certainty implied that the long run curve had to be vertically anchored at what Friedman termed the Natural Rate of Unemployment. (More innocuous terminology was later substituted, transforming the vertical Phillips curve into a representation of the Non Accelerating Inflation Rate of Unemployment or NAIRU). This change merely reasserted that trying to push unemployment lower than this mysterious rate might work in the short term, but over time, unemployment would return to this natural rate. In essence, further economic stimulation would simply induce inflation. The only manner in which prices could remain stable was if unemployment did not stray from this natural rate.

Friedman's fame (and in part his Nobel Prize) came by predicting, through his monetary theory (and the allied vertical Phillips curve), the 1970s bout of inflation. Given his methodology, such prediction was all that was required to verify his theory and justify his preferred policy. At the time, little debate was given to whether such a theory might only be specific to a certain post-war policy period, rather than reflecting some more fundamental relationship. Events of the 1990s certainly raised questions about the asserted stability of this relationship. The estimated natural rate wouldn't stay still. In response, explanations arose citing 'hysteresis' whereby certain economic events fed back onto and shifted the vertical Phillips curve. The old natural rate of 5 percent unemployment no longer seemed to hold. Estimations had to be downgraded to fit more current data. The frenzy of work instituted, trying to explain this deviation, mirrored to an uncomfortable degree, the Renaissance attempt to save Ptolemaic geocentric astronomy by introducing epicycle after epicycle. Though still estimated laboriously, unwavering faith in the NAIRU has in more recent times faltered, at least to some extent. In contrast to Burns' sentiment, Friedman's ideas have not always continued to dominate. Facts do have a way of changing, even occasionally getting in the way of, hardened ideology.

But Burns feels compelled (almost compulsively) to strengthen her case further. The danger in doing so lies in going at least a few steps too far in one's insistence. To unarguably display Friedman's ideas as still dominating in current times, Burns insists on nominating the Taylor rule as some sort of direct linear descendant of Friedman's monetary dictum, a sort of close offspring. "Taylor positioned himself explicitly in the lineage of Henry Simons and Friedman. His namesake Taylor rule, which dictated the appropriate interest rate as linked to macroeconomic indicators, was a reborn monetary-growth rule that soon became a widespread heuristic in monetary policy. Although monetarism did not become the new orthodoxy, central bankers learned much from Friedman" (Burns 2023:450). Such conclusions are debatable, not so much wrong, but lacking in precision.

In Evelyn Waugh's satirical novel *Scoop* (1938), set in the 1930s, the obsequious foreign editor of a major British newspaper (*The Daily Beast*), when asked to agree with his publisher's (Lord Copper's) erroneous statements, would reply that he 'agreed up to a point'. ("Up to a point, Lord Copper.") He was wise enough not to specify what that point might be. So I am forced to say that yes, the Taylor rule is linked to macroeconomic indicators. But it is meant to be a heuristic, not a rule dictating interest rate. If truly a Friedman-like relic, it would operate as an automatic, 'input/output mechanism. But instead, it is intended to be only a rule of thumb, or a reasonable starting point for decision making, i.e. not a rule in the Friedman sense.

To clarify Burns' assertions still farther, monetarism (again as formulated by Friedman), never become the new policy orthodoxy. (Though Friedman was without a doubt influential, what exactly bankers learned from him cannot be so easily defined.) However, the stumbling block preventing the implementation of his dictums lay in the fact that such an approach was neither practical nor workable. But if defensively, Burns is determined to drag in Taylor's rule no matter what, perhaps it might prove helpful to at least specify what that rule is and how it is usually applied. Readers who chose not to investigate are reduced to simply trusting Burns on this point. However, when the Taylor rule is examined, the actual estimations of its key values can seldom (only accidently) be at all accurate. In addition, the two key coefficients also have to be estimated, which only augments the lack of accuracy in automatically employing such a rule to set interest rates. Ultimately, there is a lack of evidence that applying this heuristic guideline can be accomplished without considerable slices of discretion and judgment. No responsible central banker would mechanically employ this rule of thumb to implement actual policy. Doing so would be a willing engagement in sheer folly. Perhaps it is best viewed as a type of warning signal, helping rates from becoming too skewed.

Given then Burns' unqualified admiration for Friedman's monetarism, it is almost ironic then that Friedman harboured a similar admiration for Alan Greenspan (who led the Federal Reserve between 1987 and 2006). In 1992, Friedman was moved to almost unexpectedly praise the Chairman of this central bank. "As you know, I have long advocated abolishing the Fed," he told *The Chicago Maroon*. "If it must exist, however, I can think of no one I would rather have running it than Alan Greenspan" (Friedman quoted in Burns 2023:442).[93] Excusably, economists are not, nor have ever been seers. John Kenneth Galbraith once claimed that economists predict, not because they know but because they are asked. I suspect that Friedman did not even need to be asked before staring into the future. He made his career, at least in part, by predicting the 1970s' inflationary difficulties. (But in some alternative universe, there is some sneaking doubt as to his fate had the world not been hit by two oil crises.

And yes, I do acknowledge that Burns does find the need to dismiss the importance of these two key events of that decade to construct a consistent story.) As it turned out, Greenspan would later admit his unwitting complicity in allowing the 2008 global financial crisis to blossom. (Though he did conveniently leave the Fed before the storm hit.) His faith in financial markets (once the crisis erupted) appeared to rest on very dubious beliefs, information (and theory). Greenspan's instituted policy (and his misguided judgment) too closely resembled Rick Blaine's decision to settle in Casablanca. In the film of the same name, he claims that he came to Casablanca for the waters.[94] Greenspan, when pressed against a wall, proved willing to acknowledge a few personal fault-lines. Friedman did die prior to the financial crises. But once again, the suspicion is that Friedman would chose to embrace ideology over evidence, as had been his habit.

To sum up, Burn's seems to take pride in the iconic figure Friedman cut throughout the 1990s, and not merely due to the triumph of monetarism. (In fact by the nineties, his monetary theory had been largely supplanted by others.) "In Mongolia, the new finance minister planned a statue of Friedman overlooking the capital of Ulan Bator – a counterpoint to the existing statue of Lenin" (Burns 2023:475). But it would seem in that cited case that the choice was to replace one ideologue with another. (Not entirely a moment of truth triumphant.) Burns though insists on seeing the sunny side of every instance connected to Friedman. No surprise then that in a final accounting or summation of Friedman's monetary theory and policy, Burns impulse of uncritical admiration could use some serious tempering.

Friedman did help push the economics profession away from simpleminded Keynesianism of the immediate post-war years, what Samuelson refers to as Model T Keynesianism. Here I am thinking in terms of the Keynesian Cross, once found in many introductory macroeconomic texts. The faults in this approach quickly appeared. Quite correctly, such models focused on the fiscal side of policy alone, especially on the world of fiscal multipliers. By doing so, such treatment was condemned to be overly one-sided. But Friedman wasn't the only economist interested in the role of money at that time, not the only professional who noticed the flaws in the more simple-minded formulation. Nor was he even the first. Keynesians soon returned their attention to their monetary model and greatly expanded Keynes' version. After those early years, few, if anyone who actually opposed Friedman, would ever be so bold as to insist that money didn't matter. The debate over the demand for money (and the interest rate) couldn't occur within a discipline where only one side saw the important role played by money. What that role might be was what ultimately spurred debate. The difference between Friedman and his opponents is that he repeatedly boiled all of macroeconomics down to matters of money in an almost obsessive fashion. This fixation is what Burns (for whatever reasons) fails to capture.

The profession has definitely moved on from Friedman's version of monetarism. Whether the more recent theoretical direction of economics is a positive advance remains, as always, open to debate. But Burns still wants to construct a discipline that is forever haunted by the ghost of monetarism, as Marx once described capitalism as shivering in the face of the spectre of communism. But in always forcing Friedman's thoughts to assume a dominant position, Burns has stretched credibility too far in her pre-fabricated form of story-telling.

> Before and after the Friedman-Schwartz, *A Monetary History of the United States* (1963) macroeconomists understood that Money Matters. Jim Tobin was the Hans Christian Andersen child who pointed out that it does not follow from this that *only* Money matters. Great "quantity" theorists like Fisher and Wicksell, before they died, lost confidence about V's constancy. Before Friedman died, no scrap of writing known to me registered regrets for his mono-monetarism (Samuelson 2011:864).

VI. The Kaleidoscope of History

> He [Milton Friedman] doesn't particularly announce changes in positions, but instead, lets them just decay away (Conversation with Paul Samuelson, October 1997).

When peering through a kaleidoscope, what you see depends on the way in which the tube is held and turned. In this respect, Jennifer Burns adopts a very peculiar setting when viewing Milton Friedman's long life. All too often (at least for this reader), Burns lets her inner Milton Friedman loose in a far too unconstrained fashion.[95] (Writing a biography on Friedman does not require the author to adopt the same perspective and conclusions that her subject would hold. The objective should be not to channel Friedman, but to understand him.) As previously mentioned, she has a tendency to either shape (or toss away) historical moments. Though my guess would be that such actions are accomplished entirely unconsciously. Burns just seems to let her expectation of what she will discover in her research influence her judgment. As previously mentioned, Burns appears to have a picture she wants to present. To achieve her goal, she willingly reshuffles the relevant Kaleidoscope fragments until a desired end result is viewed. Throughout the volume, I was too often left wondering who influenced her in making those choices and why. Difficulties arise in comprehending the reasons behind choosing and emphasising certain points, but not others.

Naturally writing any biography is quite impossible without sketching in the historical background through which the individual in question necessarily traipsed. (Not to speak of the key personages who were instrumental in defining his personality and influencing his progress.) But that landscape cannot be depicted in an entirely arbitrary manner. It is true that the historical judgments of those times will vary. But only to a given degree. In which case, I find some of the history described by Burns to be unduly problematic. Having myself lived through the sixties, seventies and eighties in the US, at points I find the country described by Burns to be unrecognisable.[96] In a peculiar fashion, her historical constructions are analogous to Friedman's authoritative stabs at the same subject, especially in his popular talks and works. The inevitable result is something akin to a series of fractured fairy tales. These unfortunately appear constructed in order to bolster favoured arguments.[97]

Burn's tendency is to place Milton Friedman at centre stage no matter what the event, with these starring roles beginning in his early high school years and lasting until his death.[98] In many instances Friedman did (in fact) play a central role, but for that very reason there is little need to burnish his image into that of a young Lochinvar who slays dragons and defeats his enemies in open combat. Sometimes, adopting a sceptical perspective (ala Frank Knight) can be more refreshing and accurate.[99]

The sense in this biographical recounting is that Friedman was an unstoppable force who would have broken through, no matter what. Because this perspective is fostered, the key role (for instance) played by his fellow Chicago graduate student and friend, Allen Wallis, is badly downplayed. Through Wallis, he gained his first government job working for the National Resources Committee, compiling a cost-of-living index. Later (1943–1945), when Wallis commanded the Statistical Research Group,[100] Wallis would hire both of his former classmates (Friedman and Stigler). The career impact Wallis exerted was not simply negligible.

Friedman's career as an economist was made possible, in a minor irony that he readily acknowledged, by economic programs of the New Deal. As his second year at the University of Chicago drew to a close in the spring of 1935, he had limited prospects for academic employment. "Absent the New Deal, it is far from clear that we could have gotten jobs as economists," he recounted in his autobiography. "Academic posts were few. Anti-Semitism was widespread in the academy" (Burgin 2012:164).

This historical over-reach continues when describing the inception of the volunteer army in the U.S Decades after the war years, Burns (demonstrating that Friedman was everywhere, conjuring up reforms that covered everything), focuses on Friedman's role in promoting a volunteer army during the Vietnam War. Such efforts did culminate in Nixon pushing that idea into law. The biography eagerly narrates this event (placing Friedman expectedly within a central spotlight), but in doing so, essential details and points are left missing, or at least rather fuzzy. The account lacks sufficient (and balanced) explication. Nixon certainly saw this volunteer army option as a way to partially defuse the anti-war movement. Undoubtedly, some of the energy of that movement was driven by young men not wanting to serve in what they considered to be an unjust war (as well as not wanting to die in one). But much is made by Burns, in terms of neutralising a conservative anti-draft movement. While not denying its existence, it would be surprising if such a movement held any significance in the widespread anti-war movement of that time. The motivation behind Nixon's wily strategy (of pushing for a volunteer army) was not to pander to a handful of libertarians, but to take some of the heat out of a left-leaning (and growing) anti-war movement. To some extent, this approach could be judged successful, especially if we limit its impact to the near future.

But when Burns retells this tale, Friedman doesn't just have a role to play in the attendant process. He becomes the dominant figure behind this policy push, while Wallis is nowhere to be seen. It is true that in *Capitalism and Freedom*, Friedman (1962:36) comes out squarely against conscription (as an assault on individual freedom). But this stipulation applies (as discussed in that volume) only during peacetime. Not stated in his 1962 discussion is any parallel wartime position. Somehow Burns glosses over this original imposed constraint. (Though Friedman seems to have later amended his position in an opportune moment.) However, there is a crucial aspect to this story that is casually omitted from her discussion.

Counter to Burn's Friedman influenced narrative, is the key role Wallis played. His orchestration of the policy process is at least equally important and perhaps more credible than Friedman's contribution. (Wallis being more of an inside player when it came to government policy.) But Burns (having a particular story to unfold), insists on casting Friedman into a central (and solo) role. Not only is her description of events a bit one-sided, but she concludes this curious recounting by leaving the impression that the move to a volunteer army was an unquestioned success. This conclusion has always been questioned, certainly recently with recruitment failing to meet requirements.[101] In any case, Burns succeeds in leaving out the nuts and bolts that actually explain this historical event.

> How many people can identify the father of the all-volunteer army? Ask around and the sophisticated answer heard most frequently is Milton Friedman. In fact, it was largely the doing of his friend, W. Allen Wallis …In his Armistice Day speech in 1968, Wallis put his objections to conscription this way: "First, it is immutably immoral in principle and inevitably inequitable in practice. Second, it is ineffective, inefficient and detrimental to national security."[102]
>
> A month later, Wallis saw Arthur Burns, who was head of Nixon's transition team. Burns told him that if it could be shown that a volunteer force could be instituted for less than $1 billion in its first year, he would put the matter before the president. Wallis quickly assembled research team of Rochester scholars including Martin J. Bailey, Harry Gilman and Walter Oi (from whose account these details are drawn) (Warsh 2003:3–4).

The author's urge to always put Friedman under the direct glare of a spotlight, too often implies that history must be bent so that the role played by others is minimised. This repeated tendency has been previously sketched out in providing the details surrounding Friedman's methodological escapades. Despite his central role in bringing to life this effort, George Stigler is nowhere to be found. This strange disregard for actual events extends whenever Stigler needs to make a cameo appearance. Consequently, when Friedman unexpectedly snags the 1946 faculty position at Chicago, Burns almost automatically describes this moment as yet another expected triumph for Friedman. For Burns, a hero must always be a man of destiny.

> It was a thick summer day when Milton bumped into Henry Simons on the street in Hyde Park. It should have been a joyful encounter. Milton

had threaded the needle, beating out a formidable roster of rivals –
including George Stigler and Paul Samuelson – for a coveted tenured
post at the University of Chicago (Burns 2023:131).

Yet it is a stretch to claim that Friedman had beat out Stigler, rather than
being installed by default.[103] In this instance, Friedman had been the unintended beneficiary of a random event, namely, the common cold. The
economics department chose Stigler (not Friedman) who only had to go
through the motions of an interview with the Chancellor, Robert Hutchins.
The story of that fateful event has been related in Stigler's (1988) autobiography and repeated elsewhere.

> In the spring of 1946 I received the offer of a professorship from the
> University of Chicago, and of course was delighted at the prospect. The
> offer was contingent upon approval by the central administration after a
> personal interview. I went to Chicago, met with President Ernest
> Colwell, because Chancellor Robert Hutchins was ill that day, and I was
> vetoed! I was too empirical, Colwell said, and no doubt that day I was.
> So the professorship was offered to Milton Friedman, and President
> Colwell and I had launched the new Chicago School. We both deserve
> credit for that appointment, although for a long time I was not inclined
> to what it with Colwell (Stigler 1988:40).

In this retelling, Stigler deflects the felt injustice of this event with a joke.
(Plus the lingering irony that in any known universe in 1946, Friedman
had the well-earned reputation for being more empirical than Stigler.)
Stigler did maintain his hurt and nurtured his resentment of that decision
during his (almost) self-imposed exile at Columbia.[104] He shrugged off
efforts to bring him back to Chicago until 1958. At that time he was over-
whelmed when the key unlocking the Walgreen trust-money was dangled
in front of his face. Unsurprisingly, this offer comprised a move engineered by his old friend Allen Wallis, now Dean of Business at Chicago.[105]
That Stigler felt the unfairness of the previous decision, but was too generous to mention it, was typical of his character. But this side of Friedman's
appointment remains largely unmentioned in Burns' sketch.

    This seemingly odd roll of the dice actually played a key role in steer-
ing future events. Indulging in a smidgen of alternative history may shed
some drops of useful light on the importance of this largely random event
on Milton Friedman's career. The subsequent formation and direction of

the Chicago School might have been altered, as well. (In other words, this instance can't be reduced to a trivial moment, nor should it be viewed as a clear triumph for Friedman.) Burns' oversight (in providing an incomplete account) distorts the larger context surrounding this moment. To indulge in a few alternative scenarios, but for Hutchins opportune illness, Stigler may have very well have been appointed. Friedman would likely not have so easily found another high level academic job, at least not in the immediate future. As mentioned previously, Milton Friedman had some undeniable handicaps that tended to render him unemployable in those immediate post-war years. His compulsion to demonstrate that he was the smartest person in the room did little to endear him to hiring committees. His proverbial combativeness failed to win him many friends.

> Now Milton had certain troubles, because of two things. Anti-Semitism, but also people were afraid of him. His corrosiveness and so forth. Gottfried Haberler wanted Milton Friedman to be appointed to Harvard and somebody like Ed Chamberlin, who was a very conservative person was the department member most violently opposed (Conversation with Paul Samuelson, October 1997).

Moreover, George Stigler was not Milton Friedman. Had he gained the position, conducting a life and death struggle against the Cowles Commission would seem a bit less likely. (The commission was largely focused on macroeconomic issues, an area Stigler steered clear of. "I think George said, in effect, I'm a micro-economist and not a macro-economist" (conversation with Paul Samuelson October 1997).) Nor in Friedman's absence is it remotely obvious that Samuelson would still have changed his mind in 1948, and rejected the proffered Chicago offer. As Burns (2023) points out, the presence of Friedman in the department (the potential future conflicts) might well have influenced Samuelson's decision, at least to some degree.[106] Given Samuelson's presence and Friedman's absence, the Chicago department might have foresworn the path that Friedman was determined to construct. Without Friedman engineering his favoured project, the Cowles Commission would be left without the same compulsion to decamp. All of which is naturally no more than speculation. But even ignoring this bit of dabbling into alternative history, Friedman did fear that the Chicago Department would drift inevitably into the Keynesian camp had Samuelson became a mainstay there.[107] Moreover, Friedman was not given to paranoid spurts of anxiety or fear.

> The Samuelson matter was again forced to a head – by Douglas - & thanks mainly to his efforts we lost badly. The dep't has voted to make Samuelson an offer. We don't yet know the end of the story. But whatever it is, I am very much afraid that it means we're lost. The Keynesians have the votes & mean to use them. Knight is bitter & says he will withdraw from active participation in the dep't. Mints, Gregg, & I are very low about it (Letter from Milton Friedman to George Stigler, November 27, 1946 in Hammond and Hammond 2006:46).

In essence, the story of Friedman's Chicago appointment, demonstrates that while he may have often played a central role in any drama, he was not always the prime mover, or the only major player. Unfortunately, Burns' imperative to always keep the limelight targeted on his diminutive figure can serve to shape and distort the actual historical picture. Unsurprisingly then, when Burns discusses the fateful Mont Pelerin adventure, what Friedman did and said overshadows the seminal effect the conference had on him (as well as his close friend, George Stigler.)[108] Consistent with other moments in the biography, Milton Friedman would have been vocal at that meeting, as he was everywhere. His compulsion to distinguish himself as 'the smartest person in the room' would not have been constrained by the distinguished company attending the meeting. But his influence, in those early years, would have been limited. The occasion was more important (as it was for George Stigler) for helping to shape and formulate his future work, His publications and his policy prescriptions would take on a sharper focus and direction following Mont Pelerin. The vision he would share with Stigler of formulating a modern liberal agenda, one that would build upon earlier, classical roots was planted and certainly nurtured on that mountain top. The hope of these young gunslingers was that this new style of liberalism would be imbued with a scientific basis that could match, if not conquer, the collectivism of Keynesianism. The guiding principle for his research and subsequent policy prescription can be pinpointed as only really getting off the ground when first defined on those slopes of Switzerland.

> He [Milton Friedman] credited the gathering in Switzerland as "what really got me started in policy and what led to *Capitalism and Freedom.*" The society was important less for the particular ideas that arose in its discussions than for the community of supporters it was able to establish. ... The Mont Pelerin Society provided a culture in which it was

possible to express an appreciation for free to express an appreciation for free markets that was undiluted by acts of rhetorical moderation. "Its great contribution," he maintained, "was that it provided a week when people like that could get together and open their hearts and minds and not have to worry about whether somebody was going to stick a knife in their back" (Burgen 2012:169).

The energy and focus Friedman (as well as his compatriot Stigler) would have drawn from the Mont Pelerin Conference could not but help shape Friedman's subsequent joust with the Cowles Commission. (The battle ended in the retreat of those at Cowles to the less contentious grounds of Yale University.) Milton Friedman came back from the conference as contentious as ever, but more of a crusader determined to defend the endangered redoubts of freedom and liberty. Even though those at Mont Pelerin may have found difficulty in finding concordance, they had no similar problem in agreeing on what they opposed. Namely, any act that smelled of collectivism, no matter how seemingly innocent, represented the first step down that proverbial slippery slope. (This conclusion at least, was one of the major lessons drawn from Hayek's (1944) *Road to Serfdom*.)[109] Given this perspective, one that focused on the need to revive a modernised Classical Liberalism, the enemy could be quickly recognised as the then dominating post-war Keynesian consensus.

The Cowles boys, in essence, epitomised everything against which Friedman was crusading.[110] He almost instinctively distrusted complex econometrics, saw general equilibrium theory as a dead-end and certainly would have strenuously resisted any attempt to provide the Keynesian consensus with a more rigorous, more scientific basis. Strengthening the collectivism underlying Keynesianism was the very thing Friedman was attempting to undermine and destroy. On an ideological and policy-political basis, Friedman saw the battle in terms of a do or die basis. (Reflecting the philosophy of Hollywood Westerns, 'Chicago wasn't big enough for the two of them'.)

In discussing this piece of early Friedman knight-errantry, Burns shies away from examining an essential part of his psychological character. Doing so, might just divert attention away from his mandatory hero's journey. Perhaps to build up Friedman's character, or instead for reasons unknown, Burns chooses to draw two of Friedman's opponents (attached to Cowles) in strangely dark (or negative) hues. To set this moment up, Burns makes an interesting link between one of Friedman's unfortunate results, while he was beavering away at the Statistical Research Group during the war. The incident helped to form his subsequent scepticism when it came to any strong dependence on complex econometrics. Friedman's disappointment appeared after a previous triumph with statistical testing. He had become convinced that "it might be possible to summarize the test data from all the separate experiments by calculating a single equation" (Burns 2023:135). What worked in theory, failed to work in practise, a result that often leads to further investigations and even, ultimately, a sought after, positive result. But Friedman responded differently.

> The episode left a deep mark on Friedman. And its lessons were readily transferable to economics. The simultaneous equations he had used for his alloys were the very same ones economists were beginning to use in constructing general equilibrium models.[111] He had already been a policy-maker, without such complex tools.[112] And ever after, when he thought about the predictive power of regression analysis, he would see F-1 and F-2, burning up amid the high temperatures they were designed to withstand (Burns 2023:135–136).

The question at this point, which insistently poked its way into my head, though apparently not into that of Burns, is why Friedman was so traumatised by this one failure. Most readers (including me) would find his fear of being proved wrong again (perhaps hinting that he might not be the smartest person in the room), entirely baffling. But if we accept Burns' narrative, this incident apparently coloured the way in which he saw econometric modelling. In essence, he feared that such overly ambitious attempts would inevitably fail. Consequently, he decided to do whatever was necessary not to be associated with predictable failure. This curious position was subsequently (again, according to Burns) reflected in Friedman's response to Larry Klein's model while both were at Chicago. Friedman's test of that model showed that it was flawed, or at least flawed from his perspective. Burns then claims that it was Friedman who first promoted the idea that models could not self-validate. "Economists couldn't use statistical criteria to judge their models: they had to test them against the real world, against inputs not already incorporated in the model" (Burns 2023:141). Her implication is that Klein, until awakened by Friedman, ignored the value of prediction. Yet, Klein is on record as stressing the undeniable importance of prediction. Burns also seems to forget that 1946 was early days in econometrics. Displaying the faults these models had when taking their first uncertain steps didn't mean that use of econometrics couldn't be improved in the future.[113] Moreover, the output of any model would always need to be interpreted. Only a very naïve econometrician would accept the raw results as a final conclusion.

But this is not the only instance where Burns displays a distinct animus toward Klein. Remaining something of a mystery to me, is the reason why she feels a need to choose sides when describing the academic combat between Friedman and Klein. Burns, however, does more than just choose a side. She positively edges uncomfortably close to character assassination in order to boost the stature of Friedman. She not only insists on branding Klein as displaying a collectivist mark of shame, but also tars him as some sort of unrepentant Marxist.[114] Even if true, the need to vigorously label Klein seems inconsistent with her preferred role as a historian.

> During his time at Chicago, Klein was a member of the Communist Party. This was both a mark of the political gap between Friedman and Cowles and a sign that Klein inhabited the political fringe. It was long past the high tide of popularity for organized Communism in America; in the wake of the 1939 Nazi-Soviet pact, most intellectuals had deserted the party. Even the wartime alliance between Russia and the United States had not restored the party's good name (Burns 2023:141).

Getting the actual facts would not have been difficult. Klein joined the Communist Party during the 1946–1947 academic year. He was thus a member for all of one year, which by sheer coincidence happened to be the year when both Klein and Friedman were at Chicago. The fact that Klein was only a member for one year could be discovered from any of the many obituaries printed at the time of Klein's death. A little further investigation would have found Klein's own explanation, which he detailed in a 1976 interview (to *People* magazine). Klein claimed that he had agreed to present a talk on Marxism organised by the Chicago branch of the Communist Party. He was pressed by an organiser to join prior to his talk. He agreed to do so, but let the membership lapse after that year. Did this one act place Klein on the political fringe? More easily argued would be that in 1946, Friedman's views were more on the political fringe than those of Klein. Remember that articles on Marx still appeared in the most prestigious economic journals. In 1946 Churchill had just given his 'Iron Curtain Speech'. The 'Cold War' was only at its beginning. But Burns goes even further and makes claims that seemingly have no foundation. Did most intellectuals actually leave and/or shun the Communist Party after 1939. Undoubtedly some did, but I fail to see the basis for claiming most chose to scamper then. (By most, does Burns mean 50% plus one, or perhaps she even means 95%. The impression though is that she wants to exile Klein by deliberately placing him out on the political fringe.) True, Friedman was hell-bent on removing the Cowles Commission. But the tactics once beloved by the House Un-American Committee seem to be highly unjustified in a sober biography.

Nor for that matter does the swipe at Klein seem entirely coincidental. Tjalling Koopmans is transformed into something resembling a stage villain. He may have had an acerbic tongue, but he would run a distant second to Friedman's close friend and colleague, George Stigler, who Burns surprisingly describes as being jovial. However, such negative descriptions appear largely beside the point when discussing those historical events. I am forced to wonder whether denigrating the member of the Cowles Commission is somehow intended to allow Milton Friedman to shine brighter in comparison.

> Thin, bearded, and serious in person-Rose found him "cold and authoritarian" – Koopmans poured his passion into an attack upon the NBER. "Measurement Without Theory" was ostensibly a review of Wesley Mitchell and Arthur Burn's *Measuring Business Cycles*. Its larger goal was to undermine the NBER approach to economics. In condescending tones, Koopmans characterized the rank empiricism of Burns and Mitchell as "the spirit of inquiry groping for guidance," accusing the authors of studying economic variables "as if they were the eruptions of a mysterious volcano whose boiling caldron can never be penetrated." The institutional economics of the NBER, Koopmans implied, was of the past; the future lay with his own mathematically driven approach (Burns 2023:142).[115]

But from villainising, Burns swings toward the opposite pole of narrative strategies (or nearly) when describing the 1964 Goldwater presidential campaign. Somehow the events become Margaret Mitchellised (Gone with the Political Wind), when Goldwater and his supporters are transformed into romantic (but doomed) cavaliers, the victims of unfair tactics employed by the dastardly Democrats. Though when Burns' narrative turns toward the Goldwater campaign, the questionable issues nurtured by her biography cover not so much Friedman's role in this political episode (which was essential), as Burns' depiction of those actual events.[116] Again, it is not that any of the statements or views expressed are strictly false, but that they shaped by a particular (and rather rigid) perspective. The result yields a somewhat distorted vision of that historical period.

Burns starts with the Kennedy assassination. "In truth, Goldwater's fate had been sealed seven months earlier, in November 1963, by the murder of President Kennedy. The assassination, widely misattributed to a radical right-winger, cast a pall over Goldwater's once quirky conservatism. … Goldwater was suddenly portrayed as a dangerous extremist" (Burns 2023:271).[117] Again, not strictly untrue, but not precisely accurate. After the assassination, conspiracy theories were flying right and left. Cubans, communists, mafia hitmen, as well as right wing extremists were tagged with responsibility. And everyone did not doubt that Lee Harvey Oswald was the lone assassin, at least those not addicted to conspiracy theories. Universal mistrust was not yet the norm. Nor was there a sudden labelling of Goldwater as a dangerous extremist at that moment. Those ideas were flying around when the possibility of a Kennedy-Goldwater match was bruited. I remember hearing and reading such remarks at the time. His extremism was always going to be at centre stage of any campaign. Predictably, those perceived weaknesses were going to be exploited and ramped up as the actual campaign unfolded. Kennedy's assassination hardly shoved the Democratic campaign in a new direction. The truth was that in 1964, Goldwater's ideas (and those of Friedman) were clearly outside of the American mainstream. Goldwater was not generally seen in the same way that Friedman viewed him, as some sort of embodiment of principled and truthful thinking.

> When he looked at Goldwater, Friedman liked what he saw: a man of firm principles who was willing to be unpopular in their defense, but who also responded to reasoned argument. In short, Friedman saw in Goldwater many of the qualities he prized in himself (Burns 2023:262).[118]

More mysteriously, Burns avoids discussing the heavy-handed Republican convention of 1964, which at moments was downright ugly. It was there that Goldwater essentially slit his own throat, helped by his fervent supporters. Don't forget that in 1964, all three television stations covered the two conventions gavel to gavel. There was nothing else to watch. Audiences were reasonably large and conventions themselves were not the pale, largely unwatched, productions of more recent times. Goldwater's core supporters were a mix of libertarians and very right wing conservatives.[119] At the convention, the Goldwaterites behaved badly. They booed down mainstay speakers of the Eastern Establishment, like William Scranton and Nelson Rockefeller. An NBC reporter, John Chancellor was thrown out of the convention floor (escorted out by two beefy security guards).[120] But the decisive moment of the convention came in Goldwater's acceptance speech, notable for just one unfortunate quote.

> I would remind you that extremism in the defence of liberty is no vice! And let me remind you also that moderation in the pursuit of justice is no virtue! (Accepting the presidential nomination, 16 July, 1964 in *New York Times* 17 July 1964, p. 1).[121]

Goldwater had labelled himself as extreme and did little, if anything, in the campaign to disabuse the general public of that one idea. That which most appealed to Friedman (seeing himself reflected in Goldwater's ideas) held little appeal for the mainstream of American opinion. Only after Friedman's death would such ideas gain traction.

> I find economic libertarianism – which is the Friedman version of Goldwaterism – more extreme from the standpoint of the mainstream of American political tradition that the real thing itself (Samuelson 1964:28).

In her defence, Burns does entertain at least one interesting discussion, defined by this same election. She refuses to flinch when describing Friedman's indefensible rejection of the Civil Rights Act, a 1964 election issue. Despite Friedman's reasoning, Burns desperately tries to excuse his race views as simply reflecting mainstream America of that time. In her justifying argument, Burns transforms the extremism charges against Goldwater into a mere fabricated strategy intended to distract attention away from Johnson's unpopular Civil Rights stand. Evidence for this radical claim is lacking. But even if true, Friedman's stance is hardly validated by pointing a finger at Democrats. "Johnson understood that Goldwater's tortured views on race were widely shared" (Burns 2023:271). Burns may be on shaky ground here. Outside of the South, conscious support of overtly racist views in 1964 would not have been so easily validated. This was not 1968. Though, in that earlier Republican stand (unremarked by Burns) lay the embryonic start of Nixon's southern strategy, marked by dog whistles and a complete writing off of the Black vote.

Her biography strongly indicates, that Burns harbours distinctive views regarding elections, with the Goldwater debacle failing to be an exception. But it is a perspective that seems to lean heavily on belief rather than on evidence. Not that Burns attempts to intentionally mislead when detailing a seminal election, but that her selection of facts and the way she presents them too often seems moulded to fit a certain scenario. So no surprises are discovered when the Nixon victories are described in an idiosyncratic fashion.

Friedman was rightly suspicious of Nixon, as Burns does indicate. "Unlike Goldwater, it was impossible to ignore Nixon the politician, impossible to understand him as a man of principle" (Burns 2023:308). Then again, it would have been difficult to discover anyone, at that time, who considered Nixon to be a man of principle. As it turned out, Nixon swerved right and left during his presidency, before being projected out of office, ultimately propelled by his own paranoia. Friedman of course, would have disapproved of much of what Nixon did. His Damascene moment (unmentioned by Burns) arrived when Nixon declared that 'we are all Keynesians now'. This is a confession that Friedman would certainly not applaud. On a more practical note, Nixon's wage and price controls were predictably an anathema to Friedman's more fundamentalist way of thinking. But despite all the easily available evidence, Burns can't resist making an unsupportable assertion about monetary policy in the lead-up to the 1972 election.

> In retrospect, it is easy to draw a link between Nixon's political anxieties and the surge in monetary growth that unfolded across 1972. But if there were no election, and no pressure campaign, would Burns have conducted monetary policy differently? Given the overall pattern of his eight-year tenure, presidential pressure cannot be the root explanation of his monetary policy, or of the Great Inflation it started (Burns 2023:339–340).

The measured response to this claim would have to be 'yes' and 'no'. Burns unfortunately chooses to bury one question when answering another. The idea that during Nixon's time in office, whatever pressure he may have tried to exert, would have been the impetus (and sole guiding light) for monetary policy can properly be rejected. But the buried question is whether Nixon did exert pressure (prior and during the 1972 campaign), which might have augmented the subsequent loosening that occurred. Here we have the Theory of the Political Business Cycle as a useful support. The argument against Burns' stance is that it was the observed pressure exerted by Nixon (and by others), which would form the foundation of (and undergird the movement toward) independent central banks in developed economies. (Clearly the same political pressure asserted itself in other countries as well.) Moreover, a president who was willing to engage in the Watergate shenanigans (and other dubious adventures) would not have blinked at attempting to strong arm Arthur Burns (then Chairman of the Federal Reserve). In other words, political pressure may not provide an explanation that is particularly decisive over the long run. But during the Nixon administration such pressure was not necessarily absent.

But as for the actual Nixon elections, Burns does not, for instance, write anything that is incorrect about the 1968 election, but she does leave out, for reasons unknown, some key aspects. (Certainly not for reasons of compressing space.) Nixon did run on a 'law and order' approach (which no Republican has not emphasised since). People reliably think that crime is much worse than can be supported by actual evidence. So it is not hard to play on a confected mountain of fears. Therefore, the recent riots plus the war protests fed into this scenario, perhaps even illustrated by the ill-fated Democratic Convention in Chicago. Yes, Humphrey was hurt by his connection to the Johnson Administration. But after the convention, he was steadily gaining ground. Had Nixon's agents not conspired with members of the South Vietnam government to stall any peace negotiations, Humphrey might have benefited even more. As stated, the vote was close. (As Burns well knows, listing the percentage of electoral votes won says little about the closeness of these peculiar presidential contests.) It is unknown what the outcome might have been had not a chunk of the left wing of the Democratic Party sat out, or decided instead to vote for third party candidates. Burns' description is not then incorrect, but curiously incomplete, which means not quite on target.

In much the same way, Burn's chapter on Friedman's Chilean adventure is once again, not largely incorrect in what she states (though it is always possible to quibble). The problem arises more in the issues she approaches, but ultimately veers away from. Burns acts as though such issues were too hot to handle.[122] However, in one respect she is undoubtedly correct. Armold Harberger was clearly (and always) the figure behind the Chicago Boys, not Friedman. Milton Friedman had more of a walk-on role. But it was ultimately his nurtured notoriety that did him in.

Well, I think I can give you a little story. We in Chicago spawned the so-called 'Chicago Boys', who in turn spawned the revolution of economic policy in Chile, which in turn led to major economic revolutions in other countries in Latin America (Conversation with Arnold Harberger. October 1997).[123]

The important point Burns tries to make, if only by implication, lies in determining exactly what Friedman might have been doing in Chile. Yes, he did have the missionary habit of going anywhere to spread his gospel. Certainly he was invited. But he had nothing really to contribute to this cause (or to the Chicago Boys' policy agenda) by making a whirlwind visit there. However, Friedman would have been stubbornly naïve not to realise that a visit would be seen as a stamp of approval for the Pinochet regime. Why not, for instance, have Harberger go, given his close identity with the program. Burns never really wants to explore why Milton Friedman had a need to always be centre stage, continually recognised as the smartest man in any room. I, at least, am left wondering if Friedman could rationalise such a visit as being somehow productive. So though he hardly deserved the controversy and opprobrium he garnered in this instance, from another perspective, he entirely asked for it and should have known it was coming.

Keeping consistent with the political agenda underlining the biography, I would be deliberately perverse to argue that the Reagan years didn't represent the triumph and absolute height of Friedman's decades-long campaign. His struggle, one that commenced in the late 1940s (seeking to push back the tide of post-war collectivism) appeared to have finally succeeded. The Kitch (1983) article conveys the appropriate mood of celebration, by having the principle academic participants trade war stories at an arranged roundtable meeting. (And there is an accordance of this triumphant mood with Burns' description of the general apotheosis of Reagan into a national saint.) But at least one curious absence in her biography is any real mention of the new Chicago thinking on monopoly and anti-trust. This shift accords with an older idea that whatever is, is efficient. (Or else it would predictably change.)

Thus mergers result in efficiency gains or they wouldn't survive. Errors are inevitably corrected. The germ of such thinking really lies with Friedman's cantankerous brother-in-law, Aaron Director, who diligently spread this gospel during his reign at the Chicago's Law School.[124] This approach represents one of the key ways in which Friedman (and both

Stigler and Director) broke from Simons in the years following his demise. Burns overlooks this key, but dramatic, departure. She proves to be uninterested in exploring the subsequent economic concentration that this loss of interest in anti-trust action encouraged.[125] Though the following quote refers directly to George Stigler, it is perfectly applicable to his close colleague and friend, Milton Friedman.

> I think he [George Stigler] is maturing as a person. He's getting away from Simons. He begins to understand that there must be good reasons why Eastman Kodak dominates the film industry. Obviously there must be market forces involved. Why wasn't capital flowing into an industry with high basic returns? He is asking himself the kinds of questions that just didn't occur to Simons. A guy like Simons would just say, 'Well, they're too big. Break them up! The text books tell you, the more firms, the better.' And that's it. Simple. End of story. Advertising screws up people's minds. Tax advertising and it'll be fine. So, he is beginning to understand that market forces are deeper than simple textbook stories (Conversation with Sam Peltzman, October 1997).

Thus the historical references within the biography can prove disappointing. Herodotus was quite content to define history as story-telling. And in some ways that focus is still not too far off the mark. A good historian today can and should still spin an engrossing narrative. Reaching out to a perspective audience should never be dismissed. In this regard, Suzanne Burns clearly qualifies as an accomplished historian, not only for her assiduous research, but also for her compelling ability to tell a fascinating tale. But any such project is bound to start slipping sideways if the type of story the historian desires to tell starts shaping the available evidence. For this unfortunate reason, I ended up sharply disappointed by Burns' painstaking labours in her quest to present Milton Friedman's eventful life. Perhaps I was just expecting too much from a justifiably talented historian.

VII. Legacy – Milton's Chickens Come Home to Roost

> An amazing, amazing guy. But a madman, a madman. One of the few people I could strangle with my bare hands. I feel I could actually do it (Conversation with Mark Blaug, April 1998).

Jennifer Burns ends her lengthy, but well researched and written, biography by exploring Milton Friedman's legacy. Doing so is covering perhaps necessary, but dangerous ground. Personally it would be enough to simply discuss how Milton Friedman helped to transform economic thinking, as well as many of the notions about government policy. He could duly be labelled a genius in his own field (an overworked, but not an entirely undeserved description). Friedman was also an intuitive genius in marketing his views to his own profession and more widely to the public at large.[126] Exploring that aspect alone would entail a sufficiently satisfying conclusion to Friedman's journey. More dangerous, however, is Burns' choice to speculate and project that legacy onto even the near future. Here Burns might have taken advice from an economist on the other side of the ideological fence. As pointed out before, Galbraith once said, "Economist predict, not because they know, but because they are asked."

Jennifer Burns, to her credit (though not without some strong caveats), goes rushing out onto the thin ice belonging to the future, despite her demonstrated lack of skill when skating over economic concepts. Somehow, she feels that Friedman must be shown to be right in his economic thinking, despite the fact that monetarism, as a dominant macroeconomic theory, is decidedly moribund. [127]

> Positivists measure a theory's merits by its degree of agreement with empirical economic history. Walter Wriston – head of Citigroup, the world's largest bank[128] – abolished overnight his monetarist economic staff when even by specifying epicycle after epicycle, $MV = PQ$ could not approximate to the imperfect accuracies of Greenspan, Eckstein, and Federal Reserve bank forecasting. Friedman's monetary proved to be neither tasty nor nutritious (Samuelson 2011d:864).[129]

Moreover, she falters by giving in to temptation while trailing through her final pages. Finishing up her volume in 2022, with inflation in the US at levels unseen since the 1970s (and early 1980s), Burns is quick to claim that Friedman has (once again) been clearly vindicated. She hauls out (for a final adieu) the very bedrock upon which his monetary theory was built. Doing so, causes Friedman's mantra that "inflation is everywhere a monetary phenomenon" to pop up once more in this concluding chapter. The implication is that the post-covid bout of inflation demonstrated that those often redefined money stocks matter. (Yet again, how money stocks translate into inflation is left to prosper in Friedman's 'as if' hothouse of predictive foundations.) In essence, those that doubted the validity of Friedman's approach have been proven wrong, convicted by overwhelming evidence in front of everyone's eyes. Those playing on non-Friedman teams would, according to Burns, have to admit defeat. She seems to take a quiet delight in seeing those opposition forces laid low.

> A high-profile group of economists and officials, soon known as "team transitory," batted away its significance. Yet inflation steadily rose to heights not seen since the 1970s. By the summer of 2022, financial leaders from Treasury Secretary Janet Yellen to Powell – the inspiration for team transitory – had identified inflation, then running around 8 percent, as a major economic problem. "I was wrong," Yellen told the media (Burns 2023:471).

If Burns had waited to send her draft sheets in, she would have witnessed inflation falling, while unemployment remained low and consumption continued at a healthy rate. Once again, these precipitous claims were based on an accelerationist view of inflation. Such constructs were rooted in a particular analysis of the 1970s. But theories and explanations are often time and place specific. Inflation, for instance, reigned in the immediate post war period as US economic capacity had to shift from a war time to a consumer based structure. In essence with war over, the economy could not instantly meet the now unleashed consumer demand that had pent up during the wartime struggle. Mandated rationing, linked to a vibrant economy, had created passive savings. When unleashed, a few years had to pass before the appropriate adjustments were made.[130] That post-war inflation problem was primarily supply based.

The best estimations of the burst of recent inflation was that supply adjustment accounted for at least half of the price boost in the post-covid period. Certainly the covid relief money created an increased savings level, wealth just waiting to be spent once the pandemic was declared over (or at least officially ignored). Nor was the unexpected Russian invasion of Ukraine without its inflationary effects. (Who knew so much grain and sunflower oil came from those Ukrainian farms.) It can then be argued that team transitory was not so much wrong as simply impatient. Economic adjustments are far from instantaneous. As mentioned before, you can't begin to understand the underlying issue of inflation without examining the relation between aggregate supply and aggregate demand. The insistence by Jennifer Burn of only looking at money stocks, without

explaining an appropriate transition mechanism linked to the real economy, sends any analysis hurdling toward a dubious cul-de-sac. Perhaps in
this case, it is not inappropriate to drag William Shakespeare in to deliver
a closing word. "For 'tis the sport to have the engineer Hoist with his own
petard" (Hamlet, Act 3 Scene 4).[131] Or to put it bluntly, canonisation isn't
the job of a biographer. Though I do refrain from swinging quite so heavy
an axe as his professed friend, Paul Samuelson, is willing to do.[132]

> People in our profession have always been kind of scared of Milton
> Friedman as a polemicist. So, he gets away with a certain amount of
> murder. And when he's safely dead and when they've salted his grave
> against any revival, the daggers will come out. I'm flogging the point.
> That doesn't change his overall status (Conversation with Paul
> Samuelson, October 1997).

Whatever his long range frustrations might have been, Samuelson was
never willing to begrudge Friedman his ability as an economist, nor
should any reputable biographer. Friedman was without quarrel, no matter
what faults may be found, a top-notch economist. If I was not so tentative
about using such terms, I would even argue that he was a brilliant economist. (To be clear, the word makes me edgy. I am even nervous when it
comes to describing Einstein as a brilliant physicist or Shakespeare as a
brilliant writer.) But he was not a character out of a Hollywood Bio-pic.
His life wasn't a hero's journey as reflected in far too many cinematic
screenplays.[133] Meaning that Friedman should not be reduced to the formula that describes a hero of humble origins, one who pulls himself up by
his bootstraps, while championing a noble cause (but only to be met by
derision and calumny). The hero then battles against all odds and adver-
sity, only to triumph in the final frames. By doing so, he (or occasionally
she) leaves the world a better place. The narrative is tidily concluded as
the credits roll. Milton Friedman deserves better than this.

Endnotes

1   Though Solow just missed hitting a century, others managed to hurdle pass
    that mark including such Chicago stalwarts as Ronald Coase and Aaron
    Director. Apropos of nothing much, I've often wondered whether econo-
    mists, on average, outlast those of other academic disciplines. Perhaps

economics is the eagerly sort elixir of long life. But such speculation remains, for me, yet another research project that will remain ever in limbo, at least as far as any resolution depends on me. Yet, the instances of promising economists tragically dying young seem strictly limited.

2   So many of the major movers and shakers of the past are pensioned off to the margins of the economics profession. While names like Smith, Keynes or Friedman will be recognised, few modern day practitioners will have read the works of those stalwarts. At most, they are relegated to the obscure regions where historians of economic thought toil. Such efforts may be respectable for the elderly assigned to gardening duty, but any extensive loitering in these regions remain devoid of any honour.

> Beginning with the 1930s, there was a period of very active work on economic theory, macro and micro, in both areas. What became prestigious was work in a kind of economic theory, namely pure and largely mathematical oriented. And it did not really have any considerable history. Now that period of change and development, that excitement, has disappeared. We are now in, what I [Milton Friedman] would say is, a relatively flat period of additions to the structure. So today, you either have to be an extraordinarily good mathematician, or else there is nothing else for you to do but the history of economic thought. I'm saying that there is sort of a balance wheel here. If there are exciting things being done in a theory, an interesting and exciting thing to do with the structure of the body of economics, that's what will attract the top young economists. They'll be drawn away from the history of economic thought or similar such fields. On the other hand, if it's a dry period, so far as really adding to the structure of economic thought is concerned, all of a sudden, everybody is interested in such things as the background of Stigler of Keynes, of Samuelson (Conversation with Milton Friedman, Rose Friedman and Aaron Director, August 1997).

3   Summers goes on to gush, "Not so long ago, we were all Keynesians … Equally, any honest Democrat will admit that we are now all Friedmanites" (Summers 2006:1). This is the first and last time Summers will be dragged into this review. (Jennifer Burn, the author of the biography was clearly unable to restrain herself in welcoming yet another loudest voice in the room.) To be honest, I've only mentioned Summers, in order to wonder why he has been so constantly quoted. Clearly, those on the right are delighted to quote a supposedly left of centre voice that agrees with them. But quite seriously, judging by his oracular statements over the past three decades, Summers is mostly consistent in his inability to get anything right. His record includes working to deregulate financial markets, without putting in place any effective oversight. The result was the 2008 financial crisis, which welcomed in a subsequent recession. Nor was his advice to Obama to aim relatively low on any fiscal stimulus package the correct call. In

pressing these views, he managed to out-talk Christina Romer, then head of the Council of Economic Advisors. Her reputation had been built (in part) on her extensive research on the Great Depression. Logically, Roemer should have been relied on to know more about the relevant issue than Larry Summers. But Summers relentlessly projected the image of being the smartest man in the room through his total sense of confidence, rather than what he actually knew. In a similar fashion, not a shred of doubt clung to his more recent insistence that the post-covid inflation could only be tamed with high interest rates and a ten percent unemployment rate. As is always the case with Summers and his predictions, we still patiently await an admission that he was wrong. Perhaps his depiction in the film 'A Social Network' as a smug, self-satisfied President of Harvard was not that far off. (No one was surprised when he was forced to resign from that position.) Arrogance can only take you so far.

4   Though applauding her thorough research, I remained baffled as to why she didn't seem to dip a toe into the Stigler archives at Chicago. There is, in my opinion, a treasure trove of useful information there. Perhaps not exploring that archive is the reason why her scant picture of Stigler seems off at some points. No one who knew, or even met, him would ever describe him as being 'jocular'. Endowed with a sardonic wit, certainly capable of producing extremely clever (and often cutting) remarks, but hardly landing in the jocular category.

5   I did in fact have the pleasure of interviewing Friedman in 1997. (Actually the occasion was a chance to discuss his close colleague and friend, George Stigler with not only Milton Friedman, but also with Rose Friedman and Aaron Director as well.) Even at the age of 85, having been saddled with a few heart attacks, he could only be described as charismatic. He never stopped asking questions, continuously trying to drill down to the underlying meaning in any discussion.

6   I am in fact saddened to be unable to write a positive review. My only consolation is that few, if anyone, will read this particular effort.

7   One way to emphasise the difference this makes is to point out that had I not read the blurb about her, I would have still concluded that the author was not an economist. Not only because it is very well written and extensively researched, but it is clear that Burns (2023) has at best a superficial (or downright foggy) idea of economic theory. Going further, there are times when I am far from reassured about her understanding of the history of the discipline.

8   Burns is almost forced, these days at least, to pull back when faced with his civil rights views. She is also brave enough to include Milton Friedman's reaction to Rose Friedman's rape, which hardly earns him a gold star in any feminist handbook. But these are the rare exceptions. That any economist

can always be on the right side seems an imposition of logic, yet somehow in Burns' construction of the Friedman story, the light of truth almost always shines on him. His opponents end up looking like Hamilton Burger, the district attorney in the old Perry Mason series.

9   As one of Friedman's long-time theoretical and policy oriented opponents, Samuelson does not come off particularly well in Burns' biography. Though again there seems to be no reason to burnish Friedman's reputation by cleverly chiselling down that of others. Friedman's well-earned reputation can stand on its own.

10   For those unfamiliar with 19th century English operettas, the reference is to *HMS Pinafore* by Gilbert and Sullivan.

> When I was a lad I served a term
> As office boy to an Attorney's firm.
> I cleaned the windows and I swept the floor,
> And I polished up the handle of the big front door.
> (He polished up the handle of the big front door.)
> I polished up that handle so
> That now I am the Ruler of the Queen's Navee!
> (He polished up that handle so carefullee,
> That now he is the ruler of the Queen's Navee!)

11   I should signal, that after reading the entire book as carefully as I could, I still have no idea of what Burns (2023) means when she uses the term 'institutionalist'. I garner it is not a particularly good thing to be, but why exactly this is the case is hardly clear. I don't know if she thinks they died out with Arthur Burns, or whether she is aware of a more recent revival of the term in the group defining themselves as the New Institutionalists.

12   I defer till later the area of monetary theory and policy where the problems are worthy of their own section.

13   Coase himself questioned whether such people as Stigler or Friedman actually understood fully what he was attempting. "But I often wondered how far he [George Stigler] agreed with what I was saying. I think he thought I was all right, but a little odd" (Conversation with Ronald Coase October 1997). Both Stigler and Friedman abstracted away from any details in order to generalise. For them, in an almost Gertrude Stein fashion, a market was a market was a market. They searched for the broad statement (rules not discretion), largely ignoring specifics. In contrast, Coase focused on the nitty gritty of actual functioning markets, how they operated in practise as opposed to theory.

14   A McGuffin is a term familiar to fans of Hitchcock films, since he in fact devised the concept. Cinematically, it is a device that although necessary, remains in its specifics largely arbitrary. Thus in the film *The Maltese Falcon*, the falcon of the story is essential to drive the plot forward, but it

could have been almost any other object that could cause its possessor to become wealthy. In the case of Coase, an economy defined by zero transaction costs is necessary to clear away the supposed importance that was usually awarded to an appearance of market externalities. But for Coase, its centrality relies upon an acknowledgment. Readers are asked to realise that the imposition of these conditions eliminate any measurable impact that externalities could have. In such an imagined economy, such potential impasses can be negotiated away between opposing parties. Coase's theoretical strategy switches the analytic focus to where he believes it belongs, namely to the world of positive transaction costs. This is the point Coase is trying to make in his lengthy article. Policy depends on the relevant transaction costs which vary from case to case. In contrast, Stigler's encapsulation of Coase's thought only captures a bridging step toward the article's actual goal. Clearing away the confusion previously nurtured by externalities was a necessary requirement before any advance could be accomplished. Doing so, at least from Coase's perspective, created the conditions for future productive analyses. But to emphasise, the world of zero transaction costs was definitely not the intended focus of the article itself.

15 Though later clarified, Friedman's graduate work at Chicago incorporated only two years of his education and not even two consecutive years. He did additional graduate work at Columbia University and eventually that would be the university that granted his PhD. Undoubtedly he was greatly influenced, at least initially, by Knight and Simons, but he left Chicago in 1935, not to return until granted an associate professor position in 1946. That return to Chicago was only granted because his close friend, George Stigler (who was intended for the job) got shafted by the university administration. Again a bit of nit-picking, but Burns' description is unnecessarily sloppy. Perhaps by nature I am unnecessarily suspicious when such inexplicable errors pop up.

16 Reder's (1982) analysis is controversial and not accepted by all Chicago acolytes, but it is crucial to gaining an understanding (at least to some degree) of the specific Chicago approach to price theory.

> Who was it, Mel Reder who wrote a piece in which he said 'the distinguishing characteristic of Chicago economics is 'the tight prior equilibrium'. That was wrong. I told Mel it what wrong, but it is easy to see how somebody could come to that conclusion (Conversation with Sam Peltzman October 1997).

17 Readers can come close to an imagined Hamletless Hamlet by attending a performance of Stoppard's *Rosencrantz and Guilderstern are Dead.*

18 I would have been happy had I been presented with some evidence supporting this view of Knight. The break with Knight by the modern stalwarts at

Chicago (Friedman, Stigler, Becker, Director) was sharp and conclusive. However, Burns never delves into the implications and ramifications of this break. Perhaps, once again, Ronald Coase makes this difference quite clear.

> I hold the view of Frank Knight: In certain areas rationality is enforced; in other areas it's weakly enforced … When you say it is un-Chicago, you mean that it is an unmodern Chicago view. Because Frank Knight was at Chicago, and I was brought up more on Knight than I was on any of the others. And my views were quite consistent with what he says. They're not consistent with what George Stigler, Gary Becker, and Richard Posner say. Posner condemns me because I don't think people maximize utility (Coase 1997:3).

19 George Stigler, Aaron Director and Milton Friedman broke fundamentally with Frank Knight even while continuing to respect him. Friedman, for instance dismissed one of Knight's core ideas, uncertainty (defined as uninsurable risk).

> Milton Friedman: See I'm a great admirer of Knight. But I think his distinction between risk and uncertainty is untenable. In the aspect of, I believe that it uses a false theory of probability (Conversation with Milton Friedman, Rose Friedman and Aaron Director, August 1997).

20 "This [the IS-LM model] was the basic supply-and-demand graph, blown up for the entire economy" (Burns 2023:137). Here we stumble upon a classic tyro mistake, committed by those lacking a proper knowledge of economics, or perhaps individuals less than adept at interpreting graphic models. The error perhaps comes from spying a downward sloping IS curve and an upward sloping LM curve. A careless beginner might then latch onto the fact that in microeconomics, supply curves slope upward and demand counterparts the other way. But to begin with, the IS-LM model will not yield an aggregate supply curve. With some sophistication an aggregate demand curve could be derived. Nor as the quote seems to imply is the aggregate supply or demand curve simply an adding up of individual cases. The quote itself remains incomprehensible.

21 Burns shares Friedman's odd disregard for investment. In a letter to George Stigler, Friedman seems confused between the state of Europe post the Second World War and that of the US. A devastated Europe needed to rebuild its capacity. Adequate consumption would ideally have to await the stage when the ability to meet such demands had been achieved. An obsession with investment would insure the 1960s European miracle or the later Japanese growth spurt.

> In the realm of economic ideas, one of the most interesting phenomena – which may not be new to you and should not have been but was to me – is the fetish of investment. Investment has become the magic word to solve all

problems just as gold or discount rate once was (or were? My English has gotten away from me.) The most obvious manifestation is the enormous value attached to high aggregate investment. The rate of investment by European countries is terrific considering their level of living. But everybody seems to take it for granted that more and yet more is required, that defense expenditures, for example, must come at the expense of consumption, not of sacrosanct investment (Hammond and Hammond 2006:119).

22   At points in her narrative, Burns seems to shadow Friedman's attitude toward Keynes. If Friedman is to undertake a hero's journey, then he will require a worthy enemy, and one who must be defeated if justice is to prevail. Keynes himself might be surprised to learn that he had championed some distinct form of collectivist domination. But nonetheless, if Friedman could be dismissive of Keynes, so could Burns.

> I can congratulate you on restraining yourself from including a picture of Keynes, and even more on not even having a mention of him in your index (Letter from Milton Friedman to George Stigler on the publication of the fourth edition of Stigler's textbook, 1986).

Perhaps this unexplored attitude explains a mystifying mistake committed by Burns. While still a graduate student, Milton Friedman's article discussing an aspect of Pigou's theory was rejected by *The Economic Journal*. (It was subsequently accepted by the *Quarterly Journal of Economics*, an equally staid and respected journal of the 1930s –and the two oldest economic journals in fact.) I can only suppose this rejection (perhaps unjustified from Burns' perspective) allows Burns to set up the future combat she described between Keynes and Friedman. (Though a struggle that seemingly involved a very dead Keynes.) Though Keynes was certainly the editor of *The Economic Journal* it was not (and is not) an adjunct of Cambridge University in a parallel way with *The Quarterly Journal of Economics* (Harvard University) or even *The Journal of Political Economy* (University of Chicago). *The Economic Journal* is published by the Royal Economic Society. This is without doubt the most minor of minor points. Entirely excusable except for the effort Burns makes to set up Friedman as the intrepid crusader battling a ruthless status quo that casually attempts to squash him. Suspicions inevitably arise with each of these perceived errors.

23   I may be unusually picky here, but as evidence of the role Keynes' consumption function plays, I would more readily hear from Keynes himself than from Hansen. The consumption function is there to highlight the variability of investment. For Keynes, it is insufficient investment that poses the problem, with consumption serving as a means through which to examine the role of investment. Of course, what Keynes offers is an

aggregate consumption function which makes the following statement by Burns a mystery (at least to me).

> Rose and Dorothy had been among the first economists to suggest that consumption did not have a clear and specific relationship to income, but rather varied with family location, family size, and, most critically, how much money a family made in comparison to its neighbors (Burns 2023:222).

But, unless I am badly mistaken, Burns entirely misses the boat, letting it sail completely away from her. Keynes is only stating that at any given time, a certain percentage of aggregate income will be consumed. Not that everyone will consume this percentage. Aggregates are not identical to individual observations. Keynes was also to some degree aware of the importance of relative income since he points out that relative wages are decisive when it comes to wage demands. The point is not to subscribe necessarily to Keynes' thought, but to get it right.

24 After publication (and prior to the war), Keynes (1937 and 1938) was deeply involved in discussions with such as Bertil Ohlin (1937a, 1937b) and others. His monetary theory would no doubt have continued to evolve had it not been for his early death in 1946.

25 Friedman's permanent income hypothesis is both elegant and useful. Unfortunately, Burns never adequately explains what Friedman's solution entails. Yes, her volume is meant to be approachable by the general reader. But his theory could have been simply laid out without delving into any frustrating technicalities.

26 Perhaps in a similar vein, Harry Johnson was fond of scoffing at his Cambridge colleagues for seeming to believe that finding errors in mainstream economic theory would cause capitalism to collapse.

27 The reluctance of Friedman and other Chicago colleagues to be moved by contrary evidence is somewhat contradictory, since a key selling point of their approach was that theory was empty until it had been empirically tested. Anyone might have a theory (like the Keynesians) but those developed at Chicago were fire forged. However, one wonders the degree to which the empirics were not employed more for their rhetorical power than as actual evidence. Facts and data don't speak for themselves, but have to be interpreted. Economists like Friedman and Stigler had a talent for training their facts to sing a Chicago tune.

> The interesting thing is he was a great enthusiast for quantitative methods. So, it doesn't seem altogether consistent. But he certainly was a professed believer in quantitative methods. On the other hand, he knew what the answer was going to be in advance. He just regarded it, then, as a way of persuading other people (Conversation with Ronald Coase, October 1997).

28   Pinning down these exact words have proven difficult. Perhaps it is sufficient to say that if Keynes didn't say, or write, these sentences, he should
have. Certainly he would not have disagreed with them.

29   Only the dead can reasonably claim to be in a state of complete objectivity.
As in many matters of judgment, Jacob Viner comes near enough to the
truth of the matter.

> I do not think it is practical to write an elaborate work on the working of
> economic process in a modern society on a completely "objective" basis …
> Anyone who could do so would be pathological and the pathology would be
> likely to extend to his selection of premises – it is always necessary to begin
> somewhere, but where one begins can have great influence on where one
> ends – and on his decisions as what are facts and what myths. In so far as is
> possible or desirable. They should not be elaborated or didactically pressed
> (Viner quoted in Van Horn 2011:291 ftn).

30   No one, of course, ever accused Keynes (or Friedman, for that matter) of
modesty. Nevertheless, he was on the mark when writing:

> But chiefly, do not let us overestimate the importance of the economic prob-
> lem, or sacrifice to its supposed necessities other matters of greater and more
> permanent significance. It should be a matter for specialists – like dentistry.
> If economists could manage to get themselves thought of as humble, compe-
> tent people, on a level with dentists, that would be splendid! (Keynes
> 1963:373).

31   Stigler dismissed factoring in ideology as an unproductive dead end.

> I don't know how important ideology is, but I think it is unimportant. You
> don't know how important it is but think it is important. My position is better
> because I try – feebly and so often unsuccessfully – to use a trusted theory of
> human behaviour to explain social phenomena. Your position is worse
> because you try – with marvellous ease – to explain the mysteries by a deus
> ex machine (Letter from Milton Friedman to George Stigler, December 24,
> 1987).

32   Friedman's strategy was always one of attack. Being quick on his feet, he
could shift the argument, making it difficult for an opposing view to respond.
Just when his opponent had formulated a response, he had shifted, attacking
another point of supposed vulnerability. Whether he had the stronger argument, or one that was evidence based, seemed to be of small account.

> I was totally opposed to American involvement. Milton was a firm adherent
> of the bombing Hanoi. We would have these incredible arguments. Now,
> I had read quite a lot about Vietnam. I don't think Milton had read anything.
> I was much better informed. Nevertheless, we would start these arguments at

> 9:00 o'clock and by 2:00 o'clock in the morning I would say, 'Milton, I just can't go on. I'm tired. I just can't take any more.' And he would say, 'Let me just give you one more argument.' He was patiently prepared to spend eight or ten hours trying to persuade me of the error of my ways. He knew nothing at all about Vietnam, or Communism. This was outside his knowledge. He was always patient, always polite, never got short tempered like I do in an argument, never got nasty. But he was a horrible person to argue with, just a nightmare. My idea of a nightmare is to stand on a stage and debate with him in front of the public. … An amazing, amazing guy. But a madman, a madman. One of the few people I could strangle with my bare hands. I feel I could actually do it (Conversation with Mark Blaug, April 1998).

33 Personally, I like to think of this as the poison apple strategy, after the incident in the fairy tale, "Snow White". The idea is to offer something that appears innocuous (or even enticing), but hides a more controversial objective.

> Let me advise you on how to conduct yourself if you ever have the misfortune to debate with Milton. He will begin by asking you to grant, say, three assumptions:
> 1. $2 is better than $1.
> 2. The law of diminishing returns.
> 3. Individuals do not have complete and accurate knowledge of the future.
>
> My fundamental advice is: do not grant these assumptions. If you do, you will find yourself led, by irresistible logic, to conclusions such as these:
> 1. The Federal Reserve System should be abolished.
> 2. The board of Governors of the Federal Reserve Board should be put on Social Security.
> 3. Social Security should be abolished (Stigler 1976:2–3).

34 His colleague, George Stigler (1971) had drilled home the point that government was merely a collection of individuals who were focused on maximising their own benefits. Consequently, the idea of a positive purpose for policy (including legislation and regulation) was merely a ruse to gain the support of the public. In its extreme form (the one toward which Chicago gravitated) government functionaries (and politicians) lacked any more generous purpose in what they did than any other decision-maker.

> Milton Friedman: No, no, he wouldn't allow for that. It has to be in terms of self-interest. Keynes now was the believer in the public interest theory. John Maynard Keynes was a strong believer in the public interest theory of regulation, and in the operation of government. Indeed I think it was his legacy on that subject which was much more damaging than his legacy on economics. *It struck me from my studies, from what I know of Keynes, that he had confidence in the ability of Cambridge economists.*

> Milton Friedman: And he had confidence not only in their ability, but also in their public spiritedness. In their willingness to serve, in a disinterested way, the greatest well-being of their society of the time (Conversation with Milton Friedman, Rose Friedman and Aaron Director, August 1997).

35 If John Stuart Mill, to some degree, epitomised classical liberalism, Friedman never seemed overly eager to follow in his footsteps. Though an announced crusader for freedom and liberty (unquestionably entirely sincere on his part), Friedman's views were hardly concordant with those of Mill, especially those expressed in his pamphlet, *On Liberty*.

> Unfortunately for the good sense of mankind, the fact of their fallibility is far from carrying the weight in their practical judgment, which is always allowed to it in theory; for while every one well knows himself to be fallible, few think it is necessary to take any precautions against their own fallibility, or admit the supposition that any opinion, of which they feel very certain, may be one of the examples of the error to which they acknowledge themselves to be liable ... In the case of any person whose judgment is really deserving of confidence, how has it become so? Because he has kept his mind open to criticism of his opinions and conduct. Because it has been his practice to listen to all that could be said against him; to profit by as much of it as was just, and expound to himself, and upon occasion to others, the fallacy of what was fallacious (Mill 1947:17 and 20).

36 As will shortly be explored, Friedman made a decisive split with his Chicago teachers in many fundamental respects. The one way, unfortunately, in which he kept faith with the dominant Chicago figure of the 1930s (especially Frank Knight), was in retaining a fierce level of combativeness. Opponents existed only to be defeated. Other views were by definition wrong. Crusaders on a mission don't waver, lest the prize slip away.

> Milton Friedman: I think you are getting something that is (a) the atmosphere at Chicago, and (b) intensified by Knight. That an academic is concerned not with being diplomatic, not with trying to avoid hurting people's feelings, but an academic is concerned with saying what's right. Telling the truth, or trying to get at it. And if you disagree with somebody you don't say 'well, now there may be something in what you say '
> Rose Friedman: You may be right
> Milton Friedman: You say that's a bunch of nonsense.
> Aaron Director: Exactly. That's not surprising (Conversation with Milton Friedman, Rose Friedman and Aaron Director, August 1997).

37 In the zero sum approach adopted by Friedman, the idea which survived would be deemed correct, having survived its own trial by combat. Subsequently, the test of time would reveal its truthfulness. But instead of approaching knowledge as equivalent to a legal battle with a stark winner

and loser, an environment of academic collaboration (a positive sum game) might yield a more fruitful approach.

> Instead, Professor Kahneman favoured an alternative that he termed "adversarial collaboration." When people who disagree work together to test a hypothesis, they are involved in a common endeavour. They are trying not to win but to figure out what's true. They might even become friends (Sunstein 2024:1).

38   Unlike Knight, Friedman was definitely convinced that he had demonstrated the non-existence of uncertainty. Again, Burns doesn't find this departure from Knight sufficiently compelling to explore.

> Milton Friedman: But I think his distinction between risk and uncertainty is untenable.
> *In what aspect?*
> Milton Friedman: In the aspect of, I believe that it uses a false theory of probability. I believe that the only theory of probability that can hold water is personal probability, the kind of thing that Jimmy Savage help develop. If you take that approach, you can't distinguish uncertainty from risk. There's no break point. But also, you see, it means that Knight implicitly was working on a definition of probability as a relative frequency. And that mislead people into thinking that there are objective probabilities that you can know. Therefore it lead to a distinction between risk and uncertainty in terms of costs. Knight assumes you know some probabilities and that there's no way you can know others. In a personal probability sense, nobody really knows any probability. There are no objective probabilities.
> *But is there a continuum of, for instance, how much you'd be willing to bet on one.*
> Milton Friedman: Well, if I can experiment with your willingness to bet, I can determine your probabilities. There's going to be a war next year. Knight would say that's uncertainty. But in principle, if I can experiment with you, I can find out at what odds you are willing to take a bet that there will be a war next year. And thus I can extract your subjective probability of there being a war and in that sense there's no distinction between risk and uncertainty.
> *In the sense of subjective probability.*
> Milton Friedman: At any moment of time, you will in principle have subjective probabilities of any strategic event.
> *Yes, potentially yes, okay ...*
> Milton Friedman: And I think George was influenced by that approach to probability as well.
> *So, he basically saw that distinction as a dead end.*
> Milton Friedman: That's right.
> *Taking you nowhere.*

Milton Friedman: I think it is a dead end. It's received a lot of attention and a lot of people talk about it. But I think it is very, very hard to make a logical distinction. Where does uncertainty begin and where does probability end, risk end?
Well, it all seems to me to ...
Milton Friedman: How happy do you think Knight was about that distinction?
Aaron Director: I don't know. I thought he drew his distinction from the fact that you can insure one and you couldn't insure the other. Period.
Hmm.
Milton Friedman: Well, but you can ...
Aaron Director: I'm only establishing his belief.
Milton Friedman: That was his belief. You can insure any of them in principle.
Aaron Director: Really?
Milton Friedman: And do.
Aaron Director: I understand that. But we are only talking about what Knight thought about it.
Milton Friedman: And Knight thought there were problems.
Aaron Director: You couldn't.
Milton Friedman: You couldn't?
That's right. That was his distinction. Uninsurable risk.
Aaron Director: Yep.
Milton Friedman: But if you say all risk is insurable, of course it means nothing.
Aaron Director: No distinction.
If you've got a zero set of uninsurable risks, then it's of no use.
Milton Friedman: If you ask somebody 'I want to make a bet with you' you'll find somebody who'll take your bet, if you Aaron advertise widely enough.
If you give them the appropriate odds.
Milton Friedman: Right. And at that point, you've insured the risk (Conversation with Milton Friedman, Rose Friedman and Aaron Director, August 1997).

39   This approach runs squarely against Friedman's policy preference for rules rather than discretion.

> None the less "the usefulness of history is not in giving us rules which can be made the basis of inference and prediction, it is not in this respect a science, but rather an art" (Knight quoted in Stapleford: 2011:26).

40   Though not necessarily mean spirited, Friedman would not, for instance, write a recommendation for someone who was 'not one of us'. Certainly suspected leftists or communists were clearly beyond the pale. In contrast, Viner looked only to ability and accomplishments, rather than to ideology.

> Although Jacob Viner had the reputation of a conservative economist who defended the orthodoxies of neoclassical and classical economics, he played a role of modest importance in Franklin Roosevelt's New Deal. Henry Morgenthau, Jr., secretary of the treasury, was no great intellect but he came to have respect for Jacob Viner. Through Viner, Harry Dexter White was called from Lawrence College in Wisconsin to begin his Napoleonic rise in the Treasury. Indeed not a few Chicago students of Viner, who were identified in the McCarthy hunts as communists or fellow travellers, were recommended by Viner (Samuelson 2011e:591).

41 While Burns does relate the perspective most of the profession had regarding the conference, she does her best to soften this judgment, by initially shedding a positive light on the proceedings. "The participants were genuinely diverse in outlook" (Burns 2023:201). Even when she accurately describes the way in which Friedman is subsequently viewed, she appears to have an underlying agenda up her sleeve. "A collective picture of Friedman was emerging: a retrograde thinker at best, a political hack at worst" (Burns 2023:201). This spot of darkness, in a larger context, seems to be strategically placed. What follows this apparent low is Burns' description of Friedman's lifeline path to total redemption. As an evangelical story, nothing could be more uplifting. But I am left with the idea (one I cannot shake) that the previous dire description is there only to spotlight his imminent triumph (well imminent after a few decades). Burns concludes:

> But Friedman had a secret weapon. Or rather, secret weapons. Already an outlier to the discipline's mainstream views on money and inflation, he took advantage of another vast blind spot in economics: male chauvinism. He would rebuild his intellectual reputation by harnessing the intellectual firepower of four overlooked women: Anna Schwartz, Rose Friedman, Dorothy Brady, and Margaret Reid (Burns 2023:202).

This (would-be feminist) description has more than a whiff of the arrival of a male saviour. As described later, Burns does during her narrative try to float the idea of Friedman as championing the rights of women. But recognising the usefulness of these women is not quite the same as recognising them as equals, let alone lobbying for their own goals and objectives. Though both sides would benefit, and Friedman would show his appreciation, rewards from these collaborations were heavily skewed in his direction. I wouldn't say that this was an intentional strategy, but in many ways Friedman was a man of his generation. Such actions would be done without any prior premeditation

42 Once positioned in the Law School, Director took aim at anti-trust policy as it was then administered. At the time (in the 1950s] being critical of how legal minds viewed anti-trust was genuinely open to question. But in his

self-appointed role of iconoclast, Director took an all or nothing approach. If the status quo wasn't working according to its promise, then the current system had to be rejected and removed. The idea that a non-functional policy could be fixed or improved, seemingly clashed with Director's take on iconoclastic thinking.

43   In this case, Friedman manages to be something of a historical throwback. The Sherman anti-trust act was first employed against labour, rather than the perceived concentrations of business power.

44   Both Friedman (and his close colleague and friend George Stigler) shared closely aligned ideas concerning freedom. Given that alignment, a simple definition of what the Chicago School means when they use that term can be found in one of Stigler's more public speeches. Notice the vagueness.

> A wholly free society is one which allows the pursuit of all values held by individuals and small groups where they do not impose large cost upon the remainder of the society. A wholly tyrannical society is one in which every permissible value is specified by some authority – a monarch, an oligarchy, or a majority ... I simply assume without argument that you and I wish to live in a free society. This governing assumption tells us little about what to do. It does *not* imply that the state should refrain from regulating any specific kind of behaviour ... A free society is to be defined by the spirit of magnanimity with which it treats minority views rather than by some fixed agenda of rights of individuals (Stigler 1971:3 & 4).

Like Friedman in his discussions of freedom, Stigler's statement sounds like it is conveying a specific idea, but falls apart when examined more closely. The free society described simply does not exist. Pursuing any value entails an opportunity cost. Certainly that cost (of pursuing freedom) is higher in an authoritarian society. But in both situations an individual is still free to choose. If the opportunity cost of pursuing certain values is raised sufficiently high, an individual has little incentive to choose to do so. We end up in a sort of Humpty Dumpty position where the way we define a situation determines whether it is free or not.

45   Viewed in everyday life, this paleo-libertarianism, turns into a refusal to accept vaccines or wear a mask. For that matter, when at its most arcane level (especially in the US where individualism can be adhered to in a naïve fashion) this imperative can transmute into outrage at not being able to buy incandescent light bulbs.

46   The myth that workplaces allow unimpeded free choice for both employer and employee is asserted in the well cited article by Alchian and Demsetz (1972). But this equal lack of power (or absence of coercion) between these individuals implies that losing a job or losing an employee has an equal opportunity cost at all times. As the article explains, employees are free to stay with their current employment or to quit, much in the same way as they

could buy (or not buy) a can of tuna fish. But upon examination, such an assertion turns out to be a classic false equivalence.

47 Friedman easily describes classical liberalism in ways conducive to his ideas. His method is to list a not untrue, but one-dimensional cataloguing of this position.

> As it developed in the late eighteenth and early nineteenth centuries, the intellectual movement that went under the name of liberalism emphasized freedom as the ultimate goal and the individual as the ultimate entity in the society. It supported laissez faire at home as a means of reducing the role of the state in economic affairs and thereby enlarging the role of the individual; it supported free trade abroad as a means of linking the nations of the world together peacefully and democratically. In political matters, it supported the development of representative government and of parliamentary institutions, reduction in the arbitrary power of the state, and protection of the civil freedom of individuals (Friedman 1962:5).

As always, the problem occurs when points are stated as being absolute, with such hedges as 'usually', or 'under these conditions', simply being erased.

> Classical economists, like Malthus always understood this coercion [by the market system]. They recognized that fate dealt a hand of cards to the worker's child that was a cruel one, and a favourable one to the "well-born". John Stuart Mill in a later decade realized that mankind, not fate with a capital F, was involved. Private property is a concept created by and enforced by public law. Its attributes change in time and are man-made, not *Mother-Nature* made (Samuelson 1963:36).

48 This restriction only implies that parental child abuse, like cruelty to animals, is no longer entirely condoned.

49 In at least one way, Milton Friedman appeared in the role of the typical doting father when questioning the *Journal of Political Economy*'s rejection of one of David Friedman's articles.

> That paper [by his son David], which I have read, is a hell of a lot better than most of the stuff you publish in the JPE. It has both more economics, and better English, than most, though it has less parade of econometric scaffolding (Letter from Milton Friedman to George Stigler, December 9, 1983).

His trust in the market for academic papers seems to have faltered, as well as his faith in a simple exit or loyalty approach to market decisions. In fact, his discovery of 'voice' would reoccur six years later with respect to his own efforts. (Though it always seemed somewhat peculiar that someone so focused on persuading others, should have ever been satisfied with a simple 'buy or don't buy', 'accept or reject' response to market outcomes.)

> I suppose all things must come to an end. Herewith ends more than 4 decades
> in which the JPE has been the first & last schol. [scholarly] journal to which
> I initially submitted my scholarly output! (Letter from Milton Friedman to
> George Stigler March 31, 1989).

50 Thousands of experts happily offer advice on child development. Each cohort of new parents eagerly look for the secret of successfully raising a child. Such books and advice can provide some initial rules of thumb. But they all discuss a mythical average child (on par with the representative agent beloved by so many economic theoreticians). Unfortunately, no one is blessed with an average child. Just as it is not valid to jump from theory to policy in economics, strictly raising a child, by the book (or by some theory) is not advisable.

51 One thing I wish I hadn't learned from ploughing through this volume is Milton's reaction to his wife's rape. An intruder committed this heinous crime in the Friedman's Chicago (Hyde Park) home. According to Jennifer Burns, Milton was away on yet another missionary trip, this time in India. His friend and mentor, Arthur Burns had to practically browbeat Friedman long distance to get him to end his travels and return home. Then in the aftermath, Milton refused Rose's understandabe request to find a new Chicago home. What I infer from this description (and the fact that it took him years before any move was made), was that Milton Friedman didn't want to surrender the nearby convenience of his Hyde Park residence.

52 I'm not sure why Burns tries to ameliorate Buckley's clear pro-South leanings, by claiming that they occurred only early in his career. I would not consider the 1960s as being early in his career. In fact, his 1965 Cambridge debate with James Baldwin laid down a case for Black inferiority. (Buckley was, and remained, an elitist believing that only a small remnant of the population deserved to rule, an effective recipe for any authoritarian government.) Buckley continued to believe that in that debate, he had lost the vote, but won the debate. (Egos never sleep.) Nor does his defence of Alabama state troopers and local police (who beat peaceful protestors on the Edmund Pettus Bridge outside of Selma (March 7, 1965)) shed any honour on his racial views. Buckley claimed that the troopers had exercised some considerable restraint.

53 At one level, Milton Friedman always stiches together arguments that on the surface seem logical and rational. But there is often a whiff (mild or otherwise) of rhetorical sophistry about them. The articulated iron constraints of markets can serve to paper over what would appear to be blatant racism. Thus employers must discriminate in hiring practises to keep their businesses afloat.

> Nevertheless, he is harmed, and indeed may be the only one harmed appreciably, by a law which prohibits him from engaging in this activity, that is, prohibits him from pandering to the tastes of the community for having a white rather than a Negro clerk (Friedman 1962:112).

Readers, far less sophisticated than Friedman, might make the mistake of thinking that those boxed out of employment (by allowing such discrimination) had been definitely harmed. But a stumbling block arises in Friedman's logic. If no one would continue to engage in such discrimination (because it is self-defeating), then it becomes difficult to see how such a law (though meaningless) would be harmful. Nor has the passage of such laws produced convincing evidence to the contrary. (Though racists might remain frustrated.) But Friedman will not be stymied once set out upon a determined path. Compelled to defend his dubious position, Friedman then seems to do an even deeper dive into the briar patch by attempting to defend discrimination as simply championing consumer sovereignty. He creates an example of why interfering with a preference for discrimination is irrational and ultimately counter-productive. In his concocted example, opera singers could be considered to be victims (harmed by prevailing tastes) relative to blues singers. This hypothetical outrage occurs when evaluated according to community preferences (discrimination).

> The potential opera singer is "harmed" by the community's taste. He would be better off and the blues singer "harmed" if the tastes were the reverse. … There is no case whatsoever for using government to avoid the negative kind of "harm." On the contrary, such government intervention reduces freedom and limits voluntary co-operation (Friedman 1952:113).

The clear lapse in this bit of reasoning is the unmentioned fact that a singer has the option of singing opera or blues. An African-American cannot choose the colour of his or her skin. Lastly in his popular pieces, Friedman sometimes assumes there is only a buy or don't buy (exit or loyalty) option in regard to consumer tastes, which is simply given. (A community has a taste for racism forcing sellers to either pander to it or go out of business.) However, when it is convenient, the idea of voice or persuasion significantly figures. Otherwise, perceiving that the economics profession lacked any taste for monetarism, he would have wisely desisted in his efforts rather than engage in an intensive marketing campaign.

54   The relevant article is Stigler (1965).

55   At an early junction in the biography, Burns reproduces names of philosophers that Friedman had scribbled down in a note, while still a graduate student. She seems to imply that Friedman, as a voracious reader, had naturally delved into the works listed. But there is no solid evidence for any

such conclusion. Contrary wise, Friedman's Hegel assertion raises more questions than it answers.

56   This statement is a bit dicey, since I have definitely seen it (and it is a memorable statement). But I simply can't lay my hands on the exact letter. Readers will have to trust me on this since it is otherwise a bit too weird to be a total fabrication.

57   Yet following the Goldwater defeat in 1964, George Stigler would complain that Warren Nutter was failing to win academic positions because of his previous support for Goldwater.

> It is depressing that at least two schools have not gone after him [Warren Nutter] because he supported Goldwater. He is of course an honest and basically unpolitical economist (Letter from George Stigler to Frank L. Keller acting chairman, Tulane July 1, 1965).

58   In a related issue, a Supreme Court case pitting Paul Sweezy against the State of New Hampshire (Sweezy v New Hampshire, 354 U.S. 234 (1957), the court found that Sweezy's rights under the First Amendment had been violated. As noted, such violations of individual rights and liberties in the fifties never seemed to upset (or even be noted) by Milton Friedman. Like his counterparts on the left, he seemed to have a one-sided view in regard to individual freedom of speech and liberty of expression. He wasn't adverse in expressing his deeply felt objections to the student left in the 1960s. This was especially the case when he thought that students had overstepped acceptable bounds by attempting to hamper conservative voices.

59   Support would contravene Friedman's core principle, though not in the obvious way. For Friedman, just as a writer should be able to write whatever he or she would wish, a movie studio had the right to hire or fire any writer it chose. The only problem for Friedman is that a number of movie studios (by employing a blacklist) had colluded against the rights of individual writers in their role as employees. Firing a 'commie' writer was perfectly acceptable. Forming a cartel to prevent that writer's employment was not.

60   Needless to say, no form of censorship is completely effective. *Samizdat* (self-publishing) allowed for an underground means to keep freedom of expression sparking even in the old Soviet Union.

61   Buckley's accolades stem from his stance against the John Birch Society in his conservative journal, *The National Review*. In matter of fact, the attack was aimed mostly at the leader and benefactor of the group, the candy executive, Robert Welch. He largely spared the members themselves as forming a crucial segment of the conservative movement Buckley hoped to build into a national force. Unhappily, that extreme element would become an increasing vital part of the Republican Party, even under the aegis of

Donald Trump swallowing the Republican Party whole. Meanwhile, I often wonder if the satire of the comic strip *Pogo* wasn't more effective in undermining the credibility of the John Birch Society.

62 The 2003 annual ASSA meeting was held in Washington DC and featured a session celebrating the 50th anniversary of Friedman's famous 1953 essay. He participated through a live phone hook-up.

63 Stigler did write a restrained letter to Chamberlin himself. However, he would hold his fire (and only consume his own plate of vengeance), when invited to speak before the assembled wisdom of the London School of Economics. Like the proverb, Stigler preferred his vengeance served cold. But this initial tempered letter contains the seeds from which the Stigler/ Friedman methodology would spring.

> In any event, it is not a sin to reject your orientation; in this I have very illustrious companions. I am prepared to argue (1) that your theory is indeterminate, and (2) that it is not useful (often in realistic analysis). I do not recall a single consistent application of it to a real problem, and this is the ultimate failure of a theory (Letter from George Stigler to Edwin Chamberlin, August 1947 in Hammond and Hammond 2006:62–63).

64 Both Friedman and Stigler offered a bit of a twist on Popper's falsification construct. (Prediction being the kissing cousin of falsification.) Strangely, Friedman never gave Stigler credit (or even cited his 1949 lecture) in his later essay. Though for whatever reason, Friedman at that time was not particularly given to sharing credit. These mysterious reasons Burns certainly declines to explore.

> And, he had already revealed the kind of attitude, which I subsequently realized influenced me enormously. It was a methodological position, which, only when Milton Friedman published his famous (methodology of positive economics) article in 1954 [1953] did I then realise he was using the type of argument that sounded exactly like the kind of things Stigler would drop in his articles. It was a kind of (what shall I call it) a poor man's Popperism. I mean it is basically Karl Popper's falsification with a tremendous emphasis on prediction, etc. And I later realised, discovered this because I asked him, that he and Milton Friedman talked about all these things. Milton however just ran away with it. George Stigler always slightly resented the fact that the entire world learned all this stuff from Milton Friedman, when in fact, if you look at the order of precedence, George Stigler was slightly ahead in this sort of attitude to the testing of hypotheses (Conversation with Mark Blaug, April 1998).

65 In contrast, for Friedman (and Stigler), Joan Robinson's (1933) effort was a simple extension of standard price theory, posing no challenge. The contrast was with Edward Chamberlin's (1933) work, which posed a distinct challenge to Chicago price theory.

Milton Friedman: My recollection is not worth much, but for what it's worth is that the Robinsonian emphasis on the individual firm economics, the analysis of marginal revenue and marginal cost, fitted in very well with what we were otherwise thinking. There were no problems about that. And that was clearly part of the agenda. But the Chamberlinian attempt to make it into a theory of the general equilibrium was not (Conversation with Milton Friedman, Rose Friedman and Aaron Director, August 1997).

66   The can opener joke is one of the best known among a limited repertoire of economic jokes. (With a few notable exceptions, the profession doesn't seem to attract naturally witty or humorous individuals. I leave it to the reader to hunt for those acknowledged exceptions.) The can opener joke deliberately makes fun of the idea that the reality of assumptions don't matter. 'As if' doesn't open any cans.

> *A physicist, an engineer and an economist are stranded in the desert. They are hungry. Suddenly, they find a can of corn. They want to open it, but how? The physicist says: "Let's start a fire and place the can inside the flames. It will explode and then we will all be able to eat".*
> *"Are you crazy?" says the engineer. "All the corn will burn and scatter, and we'll have nothing. We should use a metal wire, attach it to a base, push it and crack the can open."*
> *"Both of you are wrong!" states the economist. "Where the hell do we find a metal wire in the desert?! The solution is simple: ASSUME we have a can opener"*

To further clarify, Humpty Dumpty land is a territory first discovered by Lewis Carroll and revived during the Trump administration with the invention of alternative facts. Friedman's realm of 'as if' is a close neighbour to Humpty Dumpty's claim made to Alice.

> 'When I use a word,' Humpty Dumpty said in rather a scornful tone, 'it means just what I choose it to mean – neither more nor less.'
> "The question is,' said Alice, 'whether you can make words mean different things."'
> 'The question is,' said Humpty Dumpty, 'which is to be master – that's all'
> (Carroll 1974:193).

Just as Humpty Dumpty is his own designated master of meaning, Samuelson views Friedman's 'as if' as providing him with a remarkable lever. Using it, Friedman is able to force a correspondence between what he wants to observe and what he actually sees. Markets operate 'as if' they were competitive, allowing no room for government interference.

> So from the start, of course, they [Friedman and Stigler] didn't like the notion that if you were analysing imperfect competition, you were analysing cases of market failure. They always played this down. Now, the early Stigler

wasn't as strong on this as he was later on. But Friedman was from early on. And I think that part of the reason for it, was this development of his 1953 version of positivism. It's partly a licence for self-indulgence. You don't have to have a correspondence between a theory and the facts, or a close correspondence. In fact, the theory is all the better if it doesn't fit the facts, closely. And I think that there are some profound errors in that form of positivism, but it is there for a purpose. It serves a purpose. Do you think the cigarette industry with only four big producers in it is not competitive? Well, if one raises its price, another one will and so forth. That's the same paradigm of comparative statics that would happen under competition. So under the doctrine of 'as if', we can use the competitive theory (Conversation with Paul Samuelson, October 1997).

67   Throughout this biography, I increasingly wondered how Burns formed her understanding of Knight. In his most famous book, Knight subtly (or not so subtly) ridiculed the idea of taking theory as reality.

The theorist not having definite assumptions clearly in mind in working out the "principles," it is but natural that he, and still more the practical workers building upon his foundations, should forget that unreal assumptions were made, and should take the principles over bodily, apply them to concrete cases, and draw sweeping and wholly unwarranted conclusions from them (Knight 1971:11).

68   At its best, the Chicago School practised a certain sleight of hand. What you perceive as a market failure, when viewed properly from the Chicago perspective, actually confirms the efficiency of the marketplace.

… it's the sort of puzzle that the Chicago School's presuppositions require. Show me an apparent anomaly, something that does not seem to be explicable using the Smithian apparatus or the Marshalian apparatus and I will show you that it can be explained that way (Conversation with Robert Solow, October 1997).

69   Alchian's remarks brings to mind Rupert Murdoch and Fox News. His idea (and this certainty has been true of his other outlets) is to give a section of the public what they want (consumer sovereignty). Doing so is profitable. So profitable that he is willing to absorb any ensuing legal costs and battles. By his logic, Alchian would have to welcome this type of journalism (and others practising in a similar vein) and applaud the consequences of letting all hell break out.

70   The political realisation of this limitation has greatly changed the landscape of governance in a number of countries. Donald Trump (and his clones) willingly pile up so many scandals and malicious lies that most people simply have difficulty in remembering them and keeping such events straight. While in the past a single scandal, poured over by the media for

weeks at a time, would spell the doom of a given politician. By generating lots of confusing flak, such a strategy allows a calculating politician to skate over continuous eruptions and misdeeds. Moreover, constructed lies which flow faster than facts can overwhelm any sensible response.

71   It might be useful here, before plunging into all things monetary, to wonder why Burns never mentions the famous Kydland and Prescott (1977) paper in which they demonstrate the superiority of rules over discretion. Given the paper earned them a Nobel Prize (and is widely cited), it might have been worth noting.

72   Like his close friend George Stigler (composing with him an original odd couple), Robert Solow possessed a cutting wit. Though I have my doubts in Jennifer Burns claim that Solow was almost as famous for that crack (about Friedman's monetarist obsession) as he was for his Nobel Prize winning work. I am even less convinced (again according to Burns) that he seriously regretted making that remark. This was the sort of cut and thrust common to his generation. But Samuelson's remarks in this instance should also carry some weight.

> My point though, is that a wisecrack does not a science build. The refutation of unrealistic paradigms will come from prosaic scientific researches, and even from investigations carried on by rational expectationists themselves. It is not elder statesmen's wisdoms that kill off a young whippersnapper's foolishnesses, but rather another whippersnapper's regression data (Samuelson 2011c:619).

73   Burns tends to pooh-pooh those oil shocks citing some article to lubricate her aims. Clearly she hasn't studied, or thought deeply, about the relevant statistics. True incipient inflationary trends could be noticed in a number of developed countries as growing demand outstripped supply capacity. (The US was attempting to fight a large scale war without constraining domestic demand, while Japan promoted massive infrastructure programs.) But certainly the oil shock supercharged any inflationary trends. Notice how after the first one in 1973, the US economy was adjusting until hit by the follow-up shock in 1978. (Even the car market in the US was shifting back to large gas guzzlers.) The question remains as to whether Friedman would have been able to seize the high ground of economic discussion without Arab-Israeli enmity.

74   Once again, I was surprised that at no time did Burns refer to Kydland, Finn and Edward Prescott (1977) much cited paper which seemingly strongly supports Friedman's idea of rules over discretion.

75   According to Burns, when Friedman's inflationary predictions of the 1980s failed to eventuate he didn't doubt his basic theory that obsessively focused on money stocks. He simply shifted from focusing on M1 to instead

manipulating M2. Friedman's initial confusion was incapable of inducing a more general scepticism. "I was wrong, absolutely wrong. And I have no good explanation as to why I was wrong" (Burns 2023:441). In essence all he had to do was to find a money stock that now had better predictive possibilities. Given his stated methodology, any requirement for explaining the economics behind such a transition was purely voluntary.

76   Aaron Director's influence in shaping the Chicago School has until recently been largely ignored. (A reasonable suggestion would link Director's reluctance to publish to his lack of notoriety.) However, he largely laid the foundation for the study of Law and Economics while teaching at the Law School and editing *The Journal of Law & Economics*. His influence on such key Chicago players as George Stigler was indisputable.

> Milton Friedman: Added to that, well a lot of George's attitude came from Aaron. I think you had a lot of influence on what he said.
> Aaron Director: I don't think so.
> Milton Friedman: Between you and me, you were more influential (Conversation with Milton Friedman, Rose Friedman and Aaron Director, August 1997).
> By the last part of his life, whether in the last half or the last third, it was my impression that George [Stigler] was of the opinion that *laisse-faire* itself pretty much approximated to tolerably effective competition. And I think Aaron Director was the prime source of this view (Conversation with Paul Samuelson, November 1997).
> If a rigorous mathematical analysis is reinforced by an exemplary econometric study in asserting some relationship R, and Aaron Director on reflection denies the relationship, I would consider it rash beyond forgiveness to venture 5¢ on the existence of relationship R (Stigler 1976:5).

77   This particular reality was clearly demonstrated by Japanese Prime Minister Abe upon his return to that office in 2012. The Bank of Japan undertook a massive exercise in quantitative easing (purchasing outstanding Japanese Government bonds). In fact, the Bank of Japan ended up holding approximately half the outstanding total of those Japanese Government bonds. But in the absence of increased lending and borrowing (reflecting an insufficient boost in aggregate demand), the stock of money in the economy refused to noticeably rise. The desired increase in inflation to 2% (the Bank of Japan target), never occurred given the continuing level of flat demand. The basic flaw in this bout of quantitative easing was removing aggregate demand as the essential component of the equation. The goal should have focused on aggregate demand, rather than simply fetishizing money stocks.

78   As an identity, the quantity theory (PY = MV) must be true by definition. Nominal output must equal the money stock times the number of times that a given money stock turned over. But identity is not causation. Nor is point

fitting (by finding the right series of stocks of money), the equivalent of causation. Even the direction of supposed causation within the quantity equation fails to be uniquely specified.

79   I am reminded of one hard-headed class that I had the honour of teaching. Some of the students stubbornly refused to accept the basic arithmetic of discounting, no matter how many ways I attempted to demonstrate this necessity. Instead, many of these students insisted that the inverse relation between bond prices and interest rates only sometimes held. I momentarily regretted my past professional choices.

80   These days, since only the aged seem to use cash, it is hardly necessary to distinguish cash (a form of money) from money itself. But in Keynes' era, such a clarification could be useful.

81   As stated more than once, from the early post war period (certainly following the first Mont Pelerin conference), Friedman, with the assistance of Stigler and Director were intent on constructing a successful counter-revolution which would overturn the dominant Keynesian revolution. Though it might actually be more accurate to deem their project a restoration of a pre-existing theory (or their version of that). Hence Friedman's resurrection of the Quantity Theory of Money was presented as a restoration of a classic approach. In terms of British history the relevant difference lies between the ways that historians think about the Stuart restoration in contrast to the following Glorious Revolution. The first returned the country to the previous status quo, while the second overthrew the existing system.

Keynes did ignite a definite revolution. When *The General Theory* hit the American shores, soon after its publication, the volume was naturally much reviewed and much discussed throughout the US profession. Friedman, still a young man in his twenties (and a keen student of economics), would have undoubtedly been swept up in the debate, as were all the rising and would be young stars. Yet Burns claims (almost perversely) that the case was otherwise.

> In retrospect, *The General Theory* would set the intellectual agenda for Friedman's entire career, but when it appeared, he barely noticed. As Keynes's ideas were making landfall in American universities, Friedman offered a course through the Columbia University extension school that was a throwback to the early 1930s. Focused on individual demand curves, individual marginal utility, and individual economic decision-making, Friedman's course, Structure of Neo-classical Economics, made no mention of business cycles, national income or current economic conditions (Burns 2023:99).

Faced with this dubious claim, a practising economist becomes able to biblically divide the sheep from the goats. Burns' lack of economic training is on display when she insists on this flimsy style of claim. The extension school course she describes is easily classified as an undergraduate intro microeconomic course. The brief outline given would still fit such courses some 90 years later. It would be surprising to discover within such a course any mention of macroeconomic issues. Certainly the introduction of a radically new theory (one only starting to be discussed in graduate programs and faculty lounges), would be an unlikely component for a first year undergraduate micro course. Given his Chicago training, Friedman would have predictably set his face against any version of Keynesian teaching. But the claim that somehow Friedman was initially sheltered, or otherwise unaware of such widespread controversy, strikes a discordant and unnecessary note that clearly rings false.

82   For all his very impressive empirical work, it is difficult to argue that Friedman used such work as anything more than a rhetorical tool. Like his teacher Henry Simons, he did not need data to generate conviction. It is almost a hallmark of Friedman (and those captured by their own ideology) that they remain nearly immune to empirical evidence.

> It is hard to imagine an empirical observation that would convince most members of this department [University of Massachusetts] and the University of Chicago to change their minds. My personal view is that if someone holds a view it cannot be dislodged by any conceivable empirical data. Evidence from a data system doesn't convince them. These people have made their decisions already. They've become true believers and no amount of empirical evidence will ever convince them by definition (Conversation with Jim Kindahl, October 1997).

83   Friedman's attitude to History of Thought can only be described as dismissive. For him, it is what economists choose to do when no better alternatives exist.

> We are now in, what I would say is, a relatively flat period of additions to the structure. So today, you either have to be an extraordinarily good mathematician, or else there is nothing else for you to do but the history of economic thought. I'm saying that there is sort of a balance wheel here. If there are exciting things being done in a theory, an interesting and exciting thing to do with the structure of the body of economics, that's what will attract the top young economists. They'll be drawn away from the history of economic thought or similar such fields. On the other hand, if it's a dry period, so far as really adding to the structure of economic thought is concerned, all of a sudden, everybody is interested in such things as the background of Stigler of Keynes, of Samuelson (Conversation with Milton Friedman, Rose Friedman and Aaron Director, August 1997).

84   Nonetheless, the appeal of this theoretical toy hasn't entirely lost its explanatory glitter. During Japan's lost decade of the 1990s, Paul Krugman (1998)

dragged it out of his economics toolkit to explain Japan's seemingly hopeless situation. An easier explanatory option would begin with the boneheaded policy of the Bank of Japan during this period.

85   In this case Keynes was prescient. In the decade following the global financial crises, with rates scraping zero, a number of governments were happy to finance their budget deficits at these historically low rates, in order to prevent their economies from collapsing.

86   Those who are sufficiently cynical will here suspect that by citing so many examples Friedman hoped to effectively discourage less than diligent readers from verifying his multitudinous claims.

87   Friedman stirred continuing controversy (and gained recognition) from his insistence of linking Fed policy (of the 1930s) to the Great Depression. But a mystery surrounds his claims. Like many other dubious moments in Friedman's career (though not true of every single one) Burns artfully dodges one of Friedman's more regrettable practises. Friedman had the habit of sometimes not giving full credit where credit was due. The name Laughlin Currie does appear in Burns' biography, but only as one of Roosevelt's economic advisors, and moreover a rabid Keynesian. "In the moment, Hansen and Currie worked to establish a Keynesian interpretation of the Roosevelt recession – and the Great Depression – that supported increased federal spending. They held that a decline in federal spending had caused the recent recession and only an increase in federal spending could end depression once and for all" (Burns 2023:98). What Burns fails to mention is that Currie, earlier in that decade, had published a widely known article in the Chicago home publication (*Journal of Political Economy*), as well as publishing a book very favourably reviewed by one of Friedman's friends and mentors, Henry Simons. Currie, in those publications, used statistical analysis to highlight the failure of Fed policy during the early years of the Great Depression. Friedman would have certainly known and been aware of this work.

> Even more relevant in the question at issue ... is the fact that in November 1933 Laughlin Currie published an article in the *Quarterly Journal of Economics* in which he provided annual estimates of the money supply for 1921–1932 whose year-to-year percentage changes during the Great Depression are also similar to those described by Friedman and Schwartz. And in April 1934 Currie used this series as the basis of an article which he published in the *Journal of Political Economy* on 'The Failure of Monetary Policy to Prevent the Depression of 1929-1932'. Indeed the major conclusion of this article was that 'The [Federal Reserve] policy followed throughout 1929, so far from tending to prevent the depression, actually operated, in the view of this paper, to bring it on ...' Later in that year, Currie published a

> book on *The Supply and Control of Money in the United States* in which he reproduced the monetary data of his 1933 article (Patinkin 2003d:381).

In which case, to claim the work by Friedman and Schwartz to be entirely original would be to stretch the truth unnecessarily far. Yet this is the impression that Burns conveys. Why this lapse occurred (on the part of Friedman and Schwartz) is not unravelled within her biography. One possibility for this reluctance, at least one that has been claimed, is that since Friedman considered Currie to be a communist, such an allegiance meant that Curry had deliberately forfeited the right to be credited. If true, such a justification would provide Friedman with a convenient rationale for his obvious oversight.

> In 1966, as Brunner [Karl Brunner] was preparing the reprint [of Currie's *Supply and Control of Money in the United States*], Friedman informed him that 'Currie is a fugitive from justice somewhere in South America … Friedman did not initially acknowledge Currie's contribution' (Leeson 2003a:289).

88   The avoidance of massive bank failures should have been imprinted on every central bank's memory card after the great depression. But notice that the financial crisis of 2008 was triggered by the collapse of Lehman Brothers. The Federal Reserve assumed that markets had adequately adjusted in advance for such a demise, meaning that the impact of such a failure would be at best minimal. Thereafter, the Federal Reserve was no longer quite as cavalier. Banks were in one way or another kept afloat in some form.

89   To be fair, Johnson didn't limit his attacks and piercing criticism to Friedman and his monetarist project alone. He belonged more to the 'call them like he sees them' school of evaluation. Where he saw fraudulent marketing, Johnson never refrained from labelling it as such. Thus he was more than willing, when the occasion arose, to cast a critical eye on the Keynesian project as well.

> Nevertheless, one should not be too fastidious in condemnation of the techniques of scholarly chicanery used to promote a revolution or a counter-revolution in economic theory. The Keynesian revolution derive a large part of its intellectual appeal from the deliberate caricaturing and denigration of honest and humble scholars, whose only real crime was that they happened to exist and stand in the way of the success of the revolution. The counter-revolution had to endow these scholars, or at least their intellectual successors, with a wisdom vastly superior to what their opponents had credited them with. *Obiter dicta* and an oral tradition are at least semi-legitimate scholarly means to this polemical end (Johnson 2003:179).

90   The Bank of England and the Federal Reserve both stomped on the economic brakes in an attempt to cut the inflationary knot by throttling demand.

This would mark the first time that governments sought to deliberately midwife a recession. Their success in doing so almost saw the political demise of the then ruling governments. Both were saved by unforeseen events. Thatcher by the Falkland War and Reagan by an assassination attempt. Without these acts of God, the economic direction taken by each country might have been quite otherwise.

91 Ironically, during the Asian financial crisis of 1997, the New Zealand obsession with strictly following a rule (rather than using discretion), undermined its economy. The Bank of New Zealand in 1997 tightened rates in anticipation of inflationary pressures. Its neighbour Australia, using a degree of judgment, depended on a wait and see approach. Australia escaped recession, New Zealand didn't. Mindlessly following rules may not always be the informed option.

92 During post-covid bouts of inflation, rates of even 3.2 percent have been characterised by media outlets and politicians as too high. This claim is made confidently despite a distinct lack of evidence.

93 Just in passing, it may be appropriate to mention Friedman's stance on financial deregulation. Burns does have Friedman at least question his previous, simpler formulations.

> "Privatize, privatize, privatize" had been his mantra after the Berlin Wall fell, he told an audience at the institute [Fraser Institute in 2002]. "But I was wrong. That wasn't enough." Sounding a Hayekian note, Friedman asserted that "rule of law" was vital, in fact "probably more basic than privatization." It was a return to the ideas of the early Mont Pelerin Society: markets and freedom had to be constructed and supported by the state, not simply conjured into existence." Increasingly, Friedman observed that capitalism and freedom did not always go together – although he believed they should ... But the experience of Hong Kong and Singapore, he told the Fraser Institute, convinced him there were really three kinds of freedom at stake: "economic freedom; social or civil freedom; and political freedom." Unfortunately, it appeared that political freedom could be sacrificed without endangering the other two. That is, citizens could enjoy property rights along with freedom of expression and assembly, even as they had no choice of political ruler. But Friedman maintained that ultimately political freedom needed economic freedom in order to maintain "some independent source of authority" beyond the state (Burns 440–441).

Adjusting his views was of course admirable on Friedman's part, even if it took till his ninth decade for this revelation to occur. Perhaps it is a matter of better late than never. But history has pointed out (and Burns is a historian) that in the case of Hong Kong, economic freedom (in Friedman's terms) can continue without social and civil freedom (as well as a lack of the political variety). Why the centrality of "the rule of law" was (or is) a particularly Hayekian viewpoint (at least in Burns' opinion) remains unsettled. Moreover, despite Burns' insistence, the early Mont Pelerin Society was only united in being against what they perceived as a rising tide of collectivism. No specific positive program arose initially, given the different factions which composed the society at that time.

Extending these ideas to the realm of financial deregulation, Burns takes tentative steps to question the wisdom of simply wiping regulation off the board. But she determinedly refuses to face up to the full consequences of the debacles stemming from those actions.

> Domestic deregulation also took on a life of its own, now moving into the financial sector. Even a scandal in the savings-and-loan industry – more fallout from Regulation Q – did little to stem the tide. More pillars of the New Deal order rotted at the foundation and then toppled. As the tempo of bank mergers and acquisitions increased, laws like the 1935 Banking Act – otherwise known as Glass-Steagall – appeared to be fusty and inconvenient relics … After the object lesson taught by 1970s stagflation, policy-makers and voters alike had recovered the importance of profits, risk-raking, and incentives. These vital ingredients of prosperity came with their own internal checks and balances; the real danger was the dead hand of government choking off wealth … This meta-narrative had a large measure of truth. But if was defined not just by what was included but by what was left out. Bureaucracies might be sclerotic, regulation stifling, politicians dangerously self-interested. But what would capitalism look like without this drag? Increasingly, there were few voices who could still remember. The 1970s had displace the 1930s as the point of reference for a political culture hurtling into a limitless future (Burns 2023:447–448).

I am at times also guilty of employing fustian language. But Burns, in sketching out her vision of New Deal pillars rotting at the foundation, seems to get a bit carried away, intoxicated by her own created image. Financial technology over time did change. Regulations, which were once quite appropriate, became increasingly ineffectual. No longer useful, they were properly removed. But it is here that Burns hedges unnecessarily, so as not to distance herself too far away from Friedman. The saving-and-loan crises arrived once Regulation Q was removed. The end of Glass-Steagall ushered in the Global Financial crises of 2008. The problem was not in the removal of these basically moribund regulations, but in the failure to construct a modern day replacement. Historically (and repeatedly) financial markets have proven themselves incapable of self-regulation. The much anticipated 'internal checks and balances' always prove to be will-of-the-wisps, pushed by ideological economists and those bankers with a sharp eye for short term gains. Burns, though in this respect (as well as in others), will only go so far and not a step further, especially if it starts to fray her pre-determined tapestry depicting Friedman's journey.

94   For the very few who have not seen the film, Blaine claims that he came to Casablanca for the waters. When pointed out that the city is surrounded by desert, Blaine replies that he was misinformed.

95   This urge to inhabit Friedman's perspective dominates even when there is much to praise in Friedman's positions. By this I mean that when describing a policy or initiative, Burns seems to want to boost Friedman by implicitly dismissing his opponents. Such an urge is largely unnecessary. His policies, like his ideas, can stand on their own underpinnings. For example, Burns conducts an extensive discussion of Friedman's Negative Income Tax plan. Though never strictly implemented (and whether it could have succeeded remains arguable), this redistribution scheme has positively affected subsequent tax and poverty debate. However, while describing Friedman's ideas of the 1960s, there is no requirement or even productive reason for embracing Friedman's bleak attitude of the Kennedy-Johnson years. The economic numbers of those years confounds the impression that Burns seems determined to convey. Output grew steadily. Unemployment was low and prices stable. Income inequality shrank. Poverty didn't disappear, but counter to what Burns indicates, Kennedy's growth liberalism was only a key component, rather than the entirety, of the Democratic program. "A rising tide would lift all boats" (Burns 279). That was not untrue. Without such growth, poverty reduction would not have been possible. However, such growth did not necessarily reduce poverty, or at least did not do so sufficiently. Friedman thought he saw a way that markets alone could be properly harnessed to accomplish such reductions. In contrast, Johnson certainly saw a major role for government. Retrospectively, both sides of the debate were simply too optimistic. But Burns doesn't stop here. Burns' drive to find shadows rather than light extends to her evaluation of the Kennedy/Johnson (1964) comprehensive tax cuts. These cuts actually accomplished what they promised. Namely, unemployment fell as predicted. Unemployment in 1964 was 5.2%, falling to 4.5% in 1965 and then to 3.8% in 1966. Surprisingly, tax revenue actually rose in 1965. However, despite positive numbers and outcomes, Burns wants to blame the Johnson administration for not foreseeing the significant rise in defence spending that would help to initiate subsequent price increases. (I need not mention, but I will, Burns' insistence that the two oil shocks really were insignificant. For me at least, this position does lead me to question her competence in performing any accurate inflation analysis.) It is true that Johnson mesmerised himself into thinking he could fight a full scale war while keeping the economy at near capacity domestically. But Burns feels free to insinuate that in 1964 the administration knew that the Vietnam War would drastically expand, or that they deliberately ignored accurate and available forecasts of ever rising costs.

> The CEA [Council of Economic Advisors] feared that an irreversible tax cut would hamper future economic growth, preventing new spending that might be needed to stimulate demand. The CEA was right, but not for the reasons it expected. There had always been a bit of artistic leeway in the federal budget, no matter who was making the projections, but the figures Johnson fed to the CEA were unimaginably wrong (Burns 2023:302).

96   One simple example is the way in which Burns describes the hallowing out of Detroit. (She also doesn't seem aware of the simple fact that all developed economies shift from manufacturing to services. Automation also inevitably occurs driving down costs and prices.) Yes, Detroit did nearly collapse as its automobile empire faced new challenges, but this was not during the Kennedy/Johnson years of the 1960s. Few foreign imports were on the road during those years. If anything, the auto industry in Detroit often found it difficult to sufficiently staff its factories during those rapid growth years. (As opposed to the more recent romance surrounding manufacturing jobs, working on the factory floor, especially in the motor vehicle sector, was never some sort of dream job. Employment there was gruelling and mind numbing. See the 1970s film *Blue* Collar.) Henry Ford's supposed breakthrough in offering a $5 a day wage in the 1920s wasn't motivated by some enlightened desire to boost workers' demand. It was a bald strategy that hoped to lure workers to the Ford assembly line. The company had to offer bribes because assembly line work was so detested. (Picture the scenes in Chaplin's *Modern* Times). But Burns' depiction of the US car industry during the 1960s is simply off-kilter. American built cars had a stranglehold on the US car market. Jobs were not then shifting away. In 1965 only 3.5% of cars bought were from overseas. True, Burns had yet to be born back then, but that is hardly an excuse to confuse the oil shock decade with that of the sixties. But such dull facts doesn't seem to consistently interest her. Seeking ways to present the sixties with a negative twist she writes:

> During and after World War II, factories began to swap out manpower for machines, setting in motion a process of deindustrialization that had already hollowed out once proud industrial cities like Detroit (Burns 2023:279).

Rising income inequality in the US wasn't noted until the Reagan years, which came noticeably later (the eighties are not identical to the sixties). If anything, Johnson's 'War on Poverty', would signal a distinct attempt to reduce poverty and not simply depend upon raw economic growth. (Though growth remains a necessary, if not sufficient requirement to tackle that persistent issue.) Undoubtedly Burns is trying to boost the wisdom and potential effectiveness of Friedman's 'negative income tax'. But that goal could simply be accomplished without twisting history or denigrating the then governing Democratic Party.

97 Friedman is far from the only economist that succumbs to the allure of creating historical fables. Keynes (1936/1964) in *The General Theory* proves unable to refrain from contributing an entire chapter (23rd) of dubious historical reliability that serves to bolster his theory. For Friedman (1962), his first attempt at a popular work, *Capitalism & Freedom* has moments of pure poetic license. His argument against the late nineteenth century bimetallists blithely ignores a basic problem. The credit swings of that period made life difficult, and at times impossible, for the many farming communities. The then existing system (with State Banks issuing their own currency and the Eastern banking interests at loggerheads with most of the rest of the country), doesn't resemble a financial system capable of responding well to the frequent financial panics of that era.

> In retrospect, the system may seem to us to have worked reasonably well. To Americans of the time, it clearly did not. The agitation over silver in the 1880s, culminating in Bryan's Cross of Gold speech which set the tone for the 1896 election, was a sign of dissatisfaction. In turn, the agitation was largely responsible for the severely depressed years in the early 1890's. The agitation led to widespread fears that the United States would go off gold and that hence the dollar would lose value in terms of foreign currencies. This led to a flight from the dollar and a capital outflow that forced deflation at home (Friedman 1962:42–43).

Friedman's analysis in blaming Populists and Bryan for the subsequent depression years seems contradictory, since he is otherwise keen on extolling individual choice. These populists thought that their individual choice was being crushed by the prevailing (and private) economic power of that era. Also, though Friedman claims that the post-Civil War financial system ran reasonably well, its continuing vulnerability to numerous financial panics would seem to contradict such claims.

Friedman also wants to transform the post-Civil War 'Gilded Age' into a golden period when individual freedom of choice reigned supreme, the economy boomed and the depicted 'Robber Barons' of that period were actually heroic. A historian might point out to Friedman that the economy did not boom as it did in the post-World War II period. Nor was the life of the worker or immigrant anything but miserable for the generality of them. Even if Friedman wants to dismiss the novels, literature and journalism of the period, he would still be hard pressed to turn Jay Gould into a knight-errant. He also seems to have forgotten the subsidies, tariffs, and sheer corruption of that period. The Pennsylvania State Legislature of that period is often described as an adjunct of the Pennsylvania Railroad. Once the blatant spoils system was quelled to some degree with the Civil Service reform, outright buying of politicians by corporations exploded. Simply put, Friedman, like others, had a tendency to shape history to fit his ideological objectives.

> At that time [1892], a strange man called Thorstein Veblen lectured in economics at Chicago, who regarded the Rockefellers and Morgans as "barbarian freebooters", slaves of their own "savage human nature". ... Friedman too talked to me about that era. When I asked him what was his favourite period of history from the economic point of view he answered: "America from 1870 to 1914: It was a period of productive explosion in which huge masses of desperate, ignorant immigrants were absorbed. Friedman himself comes of a family of impoverished Jews from Ruthenia, who when they first arrived in New York worked for hunger wages for some robber-capitalist of the day: "If there'd been a guaranteed minimum wage then", he said, "I'd be a Soviet citizen today" (Levi 1973:37–38).

Like too many of Friedman's off-the-cuff arguments, on closer examination, this one fails to completely hold water. Entrepreneurs like Rockefeller were essential for driving growth (but not anything like the explosive growth of the post-World War II period). They were dependent on a rapidly growing population fuelled by a tsunami of immigrants. Without growing consumer demand, growing investment and capacity would not have occurred. There is no convincing evidence (besides that which exists as first year textbook diagrams) that hunger wages, which were widely paid during Friedman's golden period, were essential in guaranteeing growth and employment. Claiming that a minimum wage would have destroyed growth (thereby leaving Friedman a Soviet citizen) is simply an assertion. The effect of a minimum wage depends on the level at which it is set. There are simply too many differentiated labour markets to make a broad statement that giving employers an unhindered hand in setting rates, always maximises employment. In fact, the contentious empirical work by Card and Kruger (1995) negated the certainty of such a conclusion. But it is interesting to notice that this golden era, as described in Burns' biography, ended when Friedman was two. Though his life growing up in Rahway was poor, the Friedman family didn't survive on the hunger wages Friedman sometimes seemed to admire. (Though perhaps in his opinion, such wages provided migrants with a proper level of motivation.) But in essence, the US during his favourite period, would most likely still have been wide open to (while requiring), a flood of immigrants, even had some low minimum wage existed. I suppose to be consistent, Friedman might also claim that dangerous workplaces were equally essential to boost profit and encourage investment. (Perhaps it was a pity that his sisters were deprived of the opportunity of working in a shirt factory.) Then again, there is an assumption, common throughout the Chicago School (and best exemplified by an Alchian and Demsetz 1972 paper), that employers and employees have equal bargaining leverage. Namely, the opportunity cost of firing, or being fired, are the same.

98   Burns' insistence on this *Atlas Shrugged* approach suggested to me the Woody Allen film *Zelig*, where the main character is transported into the centre of all too many historical events.

99   Needless to add that there is no need for the author to achieve a Frank Knight level of scepticism, but being more vigilant so as to avoid reshaping history would be a definite bonus.

> Knight was a man of formidable character as well as intelligence. He was fiercely independent, and insisted upon a critical and searching examination of all matters intellectual. I suspect that he approached even the multiplication table with initial scepticism (Stigler 1991:1).

100   Again, to tell the story she wants to paint, the Statistical Research Group is depicted as a comradely place that allowed Friedman to shine. "In the SRG, Milton found the wartime esprit de corps he had been seeking, minus the political infighting and stifling bureaucracy … Shared intellectual interests, deep commitment t the war effort, and the feeling that their work truly mattered made the SRG an experience most remembered" (Burns 2023:125). This would naturally be the Wallis, Friedman, Stigler view of the matter. Others felt differently.

> And Wolfowitz in particular was incensed against the Friedman/Wallis group because he thought they were stealing Wald's stuff. And Allen Wallis, because this is the kind of a guy he is, got everybody very conscious about priorities. So people were keeping notes, 'I was sitting on the toilet and it was ten-o-three when I happened to look at my watch, which is when I got this idea. This was earlier than somebody else who was sitting in a bathtub and said 'Eureka!' That kind of thing is like AIDS or herpes. It spreads. You just need one rotten apple and then everybody is doing it to a characteristic degree (Conversation with Paul Samuelson, October 1997).

101   Besides cost and numbers, numerous other questions have since arisen including whether a volunteer army leaves the general public more indifferent about the wars pursued. Nor was the experience itself of fulfilling a civic responsibility so clearly the evil depicted by Friedman, who insisted in framing the question purely in terms of narrow self-interest. Retrospectively, one wonders whether for Friedman the sacrifices and imposed restrictions of World War Two served as an unwarranted trespass on freedom. Wasn't individual choice, no matter how arbitrary, more important than defeating the forces of facism?

> As a result, those who became involved in military service learned to attach a great deal of importance to respect for the opinions of others – even if it were grudging respect... Combat effectiveness as measured not in

> competence or loyalty, but by sheer willingness to fight, or at least remain in place. There was an abiding sense among those in uniform that all, soldiers and civilians alike, were somehow in it together (Warsh 2003:3–4).

102   Important to note here, is that Wallis' words come straight out of Friedman's (1962:36) work.

103   Stigler in 1946 was the more established figure. Milton Friedman had only that year been granted his PhD from Columbia based on his work with Kuznetz. Stigler managed in 1938 to grab a rare PhD completed under the supervision of Frank Knight. While Friedman in 1946 had yet to make his mark publishing (more known for his statistical analysis at this time), Stigler for his age had a more than respectable track record. As a replacement for Jacob Viner, George Stigler made more sense than Friedman (largely hired for his promise rather than current accomplishments.)

104   Stigler wasn't one to wear his heart on his sleeve. Like other men of his generation, he honoured the Henry Ford II's dictum of 'never complain, never explain'.

> Milton thinks it reveals a great deal about George's generosity of spirit that Milton's benefiting at George's expense never had the slightest effect on the closeness of their friendship (Rose Friedman 1998:153).

105   Burns' account of the Walgreen Foundation Professorship is covered by Burns with a distinct spin. In Burns' telling it was "Funded in the 1930s by drugstore magnate Charles Walgreen, who was upset by the radical doctrines his niece had imbibed" (Burns 2023:196). Not quite. Walgreen had charged the University of Chicago with communistic indoctrination, which prompted an investigation by the Illinois State Senate (hardly a hotbed of communist indoctrination itself).

> In his mention of the matter, *Time* reported that the committee, "after four weeks of chasing marsh lights, disgustedly called off its investigation for good." … Charges of communistic indoctrination adduced by Mr. Charles R. Walgreen, collapsed completely. The majority report says that "all oral and testimony offered by Mr. Walgreen and his witnesses does not prove the charges against the University of Chicago, even if his witnesses were uncontradicted" and adds that University witnesses "directly contradicted the testimony presented by Mr. Walgreen and his witnesses" (*The Alumni Bulletin – The University of Chicago* 1935:1 and 8).

The fund established was in the form of an apology given the embarrassment of the investigation. The Chair itself didn't remain empty, but was not permanently filled as long as it was in the hands of the history department. In the words of Walgreen's son:

> My Father established the Chair for the Study of American Institutions shortly before he passed away in 1939. Initially, the Chair was under the

auspices of the Department of History. Rather than filling the Chair, eminent individuals gave series of lectures from time to time. I am sorry to say that some of these individuals had beliefs that were extremely liberal and differing substantially from those of my Father's. Following discussions with Larry Kimpton, the Chair was moved to the School of Business. My Dad would have been delighted with the appointment of George Stigler (Letter from C.R. Walgreen to Hanna Gray, President, University of Chicago, March 16 1992).

As mentioned, behind this result (which delivered Stigler back to Chicago) was the deft hand of Allen Wallis. Burns' account isn't strictly wrong. She just turns the kaleidoscope of perspective sufficiently to relay the picture she prefers. Though perhaps it just accords with and is consistent with Friedman's retrospective view of the 1930s at Chicago.

> Friedman calculated that by 1934 'close to a majority' of faculty and students within the social sciences at the University of Chicago were 'either members of the Communist party or very close to it' (Leeson 2003a:288).

106   Samuelson most likely would have had the same trepidation shown by his colleague and friend, Robert Solow. Despite offers initiated by his Chicago friend, George Stigler, Solow was never tempted to accept. "but I don't think I would have been happy because being involved in intellectual conflict ... in controversy with one's colleagues all the time is never a formula for relaxation" (Conversation with Robert Solow, October 1997).

107   A related puzzle is whether Stigler would have been as adamant as Friedman in keeping Hayek out of the department. But then again, if there had been a Keynesian drift, the question of inviting Hayek may never have arisen. But it is important to note, nonetheless, that speculating within the muddle of alternative histories can help you draw peculiar (and sometimes barren) conclusions.

108   Stigler (1988) more modestly discusses the Mont Pelerin meeting in a chapter titled, "The Apprentice Conservative." Both he and Milton Friedman were at this time very much junior members within this assemblage. They were there only because of their connection with Aaron Director and the willingness of the Volker Fund to pay for their travel.

109   Perhaps lacking the same unflagging certainty as their student, Milton Friedman's most influential teachers were less enthusiastic about Hayek's dystopian vision.

> ... Viner write to a friend that the book "over argues his case" and was riddled with "dogmas," and Knight told the publisher that it insufficiently recognised "the necessity, as well as political inevitability, of a wide range of governmental activity in relation to economic life in the future," instead dealing "only with the simpler fallacies" (Burgin 2012:34).

110   Clearly, Milton Friedman's tactics succeeded in frustrating those on the Cowles Commission (some of whom also held positions in the economics department). One wonders how much of it was intentional and premeditated.

> On the whole, I admit I was wrong on Colin [Clark]. He is not the man you or I would want in that perfect University Arthur [Burns] wants to found, but he is personally nice, many of his instincts are on the right side, and he's much more interesting and provocative, and fundamentally no sloppier, than Kuznets or some other people in NY or Chicago. And he would be marvellous in infuriating the Cowles boys, although probably not your equal (Letter from George Stigler to Milton Friedman, December 1947 in Hammond and Hammond 2006:73).

111   This is a bit confusing. Burns must mean the structure of the model (simultaneous equations), rather than the actual equations. Friedman objected to the preferred structure.

112   This statement raises more questions than it could possibly think of answering. Friedman could easily consider himself adept at constructing policies even without the assistance of econometric analysis. But it doesn't follow that his ability was incapable of improvement. Nor does it effectively dismiss the role that econometrics might possibly play in assisting him.

113   The truth however is that in that post-war period, econometricians and Keynesian macroeconomists were initially overconfident in what they could accomplish. They believed that they had basically solved the fundamental questions of economics. (They had conquered the Great Depression, Nazism and now were able to control the business cycle by simply pulling the right levers at the appropriate times.) A more than touch of arrogance is too clearly evident.

> I asked Thurow, "What does the generation of young economists want?" He answered: "Most of us younger people think that the macroeconomic problem has been solved by the generation of Samuelson, Modigliani and Arrow. Our students have never seen a cycle. If there are cycles, it's because the governments are stupid enough not to follow the advice of the economists. In fact, the problem of control of cycles is political rather than economic. Even inflation doesn't worry us. I and others have analysed the problem sufficiently to convince ourselves that inflation doesn't harm either economic development or the poor; and so it doesn't interest us" (Levi 1973:103).

As a side note, Friedman, after talking to Arrigo Levi, couldn't resist putting him, as per usual, in a box distinguishing whether (or not), he was 'one of us'. "He [Arrigo Levi – journalist *La Stampa*] is not of our persuasion but also he is not hopeless" (Letter from Milton Friedman to George Stigler September 20, 1971). In contrast in the same letter, another mutual acquaintance apparently deserved a somewhat more propitious slot. "If he [Joseph Ben-David] were willing to work on this, however, he has the right abilities and the right ideology" (Letter from Milton Friedman to George Stigler, September 20, 1971).

114   To prove that he was an unrepentant collectivist at least (if not a flaming Marxist) Burns quotes a 1948 letter from Klein to Samuelson that appeared in an unpublished PhD thesis. "But Klein as a firm believer that "planning is superior to competition," as he put it in a letter to Samuelson" (Burns 2023:141). As stated before, given the constraints of writing for a more general readership, all quotes in the book are quite short (though all are not quite this short). Unfortunately, this means that unless each and every quote is tracked down (and I do not enjoy an unexpectedly long anticipated life), Klein's meaning is left uncertain. Planning is of course ubiquitous in any economy, whether market based or planned. (Corporation, businesses and individuals do not only react to market competition, they decidedly plan.) However, it would be a leap to conclude that Klein was admiring a Soviet-style, planned economy. A reader instead should remember that a number of economists in 1948 had an inflated notion of what could be accomplished through fiscal fine tuning. Klein, like Samuelson (and a great many other economists) in 1948 differed from the views firmly held by Milton Friedman. That neither made them Marxists nor on a slippery slope of becoming raving communists.

115   Yet, soon after the Reagan election, when the Chicago boys (and cronies) met to celebrate their triumph (Kitch 1981) institutionalists were roundly badmouthed by those attending. I doubt that their opinion of the Institutionalist School differed greatly from Koopman's blunt evaluation, despite the differences in economic perspectives between Cowles and Chicago.

> Not even my best friends have been institutional economists so I don't know the field well. … I would say the institutional school failed in America for a very simple reason. It had nothing in it except a sense of hostility to the standard theoretical tradition. There was no positive agenda of research. There was no set of problems or new methods they wanted to invoke. … they are never saying, "What shall we do next?" (George Stigler in Kitch 1983:169–170).

116   It is safe to say that the campaign disillusioned him.

> We came to his ideas, and not those of a "political dilettante", as he [Friedman] describes himself (the Goldwater episode left a good deal of bitterness: "never again anything of that kind", says his wife, Rose, herself an economist), but his ideas as a professional economist (Levi 1973:38).

He had previously chosen to stay largely apart from politics, though clearly he rejected the views of the Democrat Party. "The platform [of the

Democratic Party] is too transparent a fraud for even the gullible U.S. public ... I take that back, since I think the public is far more sensible & less gullible than our academic confreres ... to swallow" (Letter from Milton Friedman to George Stigler, July 27, 1960). But that was most likely due to the fact that prior to the Goldwater doomed campaign, his views (as spelled out in *Capitalism and Freedom* (1962)) were not only decidedly to the right of the Democrats, but also of the mainstream of the Republican Party. Like other enthusiastic ideologues in history, he nurtured an unrealistic view of Goldwater's chances, thinking that his ideas somehow came close to matching those of the voting public. He even tried to rope his close friend George Stigler into signing on to the Goldwater mania.

> The immediate pressure is to ask whether you would be willing and able to come to Washington for the day of August 18 to participate in a meeting of intellectuals to discuss what should be the major domestic issues that BG should discuss during the campaign (Letter Milton Friedman to George Stigler August 4, 1964).

117   In truth, conspiracy theories and rumours were alive during this period and thereafter. But there was far from only a single narrative being spread. Cubans and racketeers were equally targeted as the perpetrators of the Kennedy assassination.

118   True enough, Burns does qualify this statement, "What he did not see was Goldwater the politician, a man fundamentally oriented to the accumulation and maintenance of political power" (Burns 2023:262). In other words, Friedman was naïve when it came to politics. But though Burns is clear that Friedman's views on Civil Rights were extreme (unless you were a practising racist), she doesn't make it clear that almost all Friedman's ideas, at that time, were definitely outside the mainstream.

119   A number of these supporters were young, the result of the William F. Buckley created 'Young Americans for Freedom' movement on college campuses. The young seem more easily deluded about such things as the state of the world as well as chances for triumphing.

120   The interesting start (or emphasis) of the conservative claim that mainstream media is biased against them. A claim that has now flowered into the open war conducted by Trump and his supporters. This uprising would now also include the springing up of numerous media outlets like Fox News that resolves this supposed bias by being undeniably biased. But it was never clear how legitimate this decade's long claim was or is. At times, the charge seemed to be an unease created by the media holding up a mirror that simply reflected existing views. Nonetheless, Friedman shared a similar perspective.

> One of the topics we would like to have discussed has to do with the mass media and the trend toward collectivism. Why is it that almost everywhere the great bulk of the contributors to the mass media, the journalists, the radio commentators, the TV performers tend to be collectivists in their orientation? (Letter from Milton Friedman to Raymond Aron in preparation of the coming Mont Pelerin meeting, January 5, 1972).

Today, Donald Trump and the Republican Party (as well as many voters) would have no problem subscribing to such thoughts.

121 While Friedman would have no problem accepting this sentiment, he openly rejected Kennedy's even more famous word, "And so, my fellow Americans: ask not what your country can do for you - ask what you can do for your country" (Inaugural address, January 20, 1961). Friedman rejected this statement as being paternalistic. Perhaps he would say instead, "My fellow Americans: don't ask". But let me quote his actual words because in many respects this is for Friedman his sophistically most dubious argument.

> The paternalistic "what your country can do for you" implies that government is the patron, the citizen the ward, a view that is at odds with the free man's belief in his own responsibility for his own destiny. The organismic, "what you can do for your country" implies that government is the master or the deity, the citizen, the servant or the votary. To the free man, the country is the collection of individuals who compose it, not something over and above them. He recognizes no national goal except as it is the consensus of the goals that the citizens severally serve … The free man will ask neither what his country can do for him nor what he can do for his country. He will ask rather "What can I and my compatriots do through government" to help us discharge our individual responsibilities, to achieve our several goals and purposes, and above all, to protect our freedom?" (Friedman 1962:1–2).

The rhetorical tactic employed here by Friedman (which he trotted out elsewhere), is to initially misinterpret a quote in order to destroy it. The real clash here is between the idea of group identities and Friedman's Thatcher-like insistence that society does not exist. According to this perspective, it is only a collection of individuals. True that groups identities can be dangerous and incubate nationalism, racism, misogyny and a host of other stances. Collectivism, to some degree, can be utilised in order to simply dismiss those outside one's group. (Though it is interesting that Friedman himself was consistently keen on ideological group identities ('our kind', 'one of us').

Kennedy's statement simply calls on people to look toward their better natures. In other words, don't focus on what is owed you, on what your entitlements are. (Friedman seems to forget here that Kennedy starts with 'ask not') What is repugnant to Friedman is that Kennedy asks US citizens to focus not only on narrow self-interest. But to Friedman this is the alpha and omega of human experience. Focusing on what you can do for others (the second half of the quote), does not imply a sort of master/servant relationship of citizen to government that Friedman implies. Kennedy doesn't mention what you can do for your government, but for society. Friedman's substitute flirts with the childish idea of freedom (as previously stated) as basically stamping one's foot and declaiming that you can't tell me what to do.

Friedman's statement somehow suggests that pursuing individual goals never conflicts with those of others or could leave society (as a whole) worse off. To claim that an individual is completely responsible for that person's own destiny is to inhabit a mythical world. At the very least it is fair to say that Friedman's alternative to Kennedy's quote is flat and would prove incapable of stirring a flea. This bit of rhetoric on Friedman's part is simply Friedman attacking for the personal joy of attack. Libertarianism of this flavour seems to be the first cousin of anarchism – a system that works perfectly only in the minds of its creators.

Perhaps the underlying problem in his posed battle is the need to win his argument by presenting the issue as an all or nothing struggle. For Friedman, too much of his perspective is essentially an all or nothing approach. In his world, either you are elevated to a realm of freedom, or you are mired in the mud of serfdom. In essence, the smallest step away from Friedman's idealised Ayn Rand-type behaviour and goals, puts the unfortunate individual on that slippery slope down to collectivist hell.

122   While naturally mentioning the CIA role in deposing the Allende government in 1973, she is completely mum on the efforts of ITT and a major copper mining company (Anaconda) in ending the regime. Neither company was thrilled by expropriation measures. The reason for the omission is simply unclear.

123   Harberger is referring to a Chicago inspired set of policies and institutions that would become very controversial in the 1970s and 1980s, lingering even into the present era. Starting in the 1950s, a select group of Chilean economists did their graduate training at Chicago, aided by grants from the Ford and Rockefeller Foundations. The program shepherded by Harberger would only gain its notoriety after the September 11, 1973 Pinochet led military coup against the government of Salvadore Allende. The subsequent economic program was largely constructed by these Chicago disciples. Whether such an economic program favoured the Chilean people, or was heavily weighted toward US multinationals, remains a question of continuing contention. The coup itself was supported by funds made available by the CIA.

"Chile was not a jewel in 1995, but it's a jewel today," the economist Arnold Harberger says in the documentary *Chicago Boys*. Harberger, an American economist who taught at the University of Chicago from 1953 to 1991 alongside Milton Friedman, was a father figure to the "boys" – a group of Chilean economists who studied at the university in the 1950s. There, they became enthusiastic converts to Friedman's free-market economic philosophies, which they were then given free rein to implement on an unprecedented scale during Augusto Pinochet's dictatorship of Chile. The ideas they brought home from Chicago changed Chilean society forever and made it one of the richest countries in Latin America (Opazo 2016:1).

124   Since Director wrote very little (and published less), Bork (1978) is the place to go for those wishing to grasp his thinking.

125   The insignificance of private economic power (private monopoly) has long been a key element of Chicago School economics. The absence of such power drastically limits any need for government intervention, shifting the focus on government aided and abetted monopoly.

> They [Warren Nutter and George Stigler] conclude that, as of 1939, roughly one quarter of the economy could be regarded as governmentally operated or supervised. Of the three-quarters remaining, at most one-quarter and perhaps as little as 15 per cent can be regarded as monopolistic, at least three-quarters and perhaps as much as 85 per cent, as competitive. … Within the private sector, on the other hand, there appears not to have been any tendency for the scope of monopoly to have increased and it may well have decreased (Friedman 1962:122).

Theoretically, Friedman was equally convinced that any attempt at private collusion was unstable, since firms had a strong incentive to cheat on agreements which were not based on legal contracts. Though, as in too many cases, theory alone was deemed sufficient in making this case. In practise, collusive attempts tend only to become known via an inside whistle blower. Friedman however, was more concerned with the coercive power of labour via union monopoly. Unfortunately, Friedman's foresight has proven to be limited. Union power ebbed and the remnants were largely broken by the Reagan Administration. Moreover, his dismissal of private monopoly power could easily be questioned in more recent times.

> In four-fifths of America's big industries the top 50 firms had a higher market share than in 1997. Profit margins are at a near-record high, hinting at a lack of competition. The scale of dealmaking total transactions since Lehman's failure amount to 46% of American firms' current market value – points to more concentration, too. In the run-up to the financial crash many takeovers were by private equity firms which assembled vast portfolios of unrelated businesses. Now most ceals are 'strategic' with two firms seeking to combine similar operations, boost their price and cut costs. Food, cable, TV, telecoms,

airlines, computer chips and other industries all have consolidated in the past Half-decade (*The Economist*, December 12, 2015:56).

126   Friedman's marketing skills were so honed that he successfully sold himself on his own ideas. The one thing that Milton Friedman seldom, if ever, encountered in his long career was doubt.

127   I would, however, not be so presumptuous as to pronounce any economic theory dead. I would be hard pressed to name any economic theory as determinedly past its used-by date. Economists are great recyclers. So almost any construct, no matter how lame it might have been, has not been at some later time been resurrected, perhaps with a new coat of paint and some strategic glitter.

128   Samuelson's eulogy was written at the time of Friedman's death. Thus the reference to Wriston as the head of Citigroup and Citigroup being the world's largest bank.

129   Or perhaps more succinctly, we can once again turn to the razor sharp wit of John Kenneth Galbraith, "Milton Friedman's misfortune is that his economic policies have been tried."

130   I remember my father telling me how back from the service he was unable to buy a vehicle either new or used. Eventually he found an ancient car that had to be cranked to start. After some very limited use, the engine simply caught on fire.

131   Again the future is unknowable. Supply shocks may once again push up prices. But as previously stated, there is no research to show that a two percent inflation rate is non-acceleratory, while a three or even four percent level is. At what rate inflation becomes an economic, rather than a political, problem remains a mystery.

132   At least to his mind, Paul Samuelson did view Milton Friedman as a long-time friend throughout both of their very illustrious careers. But it does seem at times that Samuelson grew weary when dealing with Friedman's absolute certainty and unshakable polemics.

> Friedman and I – Milton and Paul – rarely agreed on substantive issues. However for 74 years since 1932, we have remained friends. That's a tribute to people (Samuelson 2023d:860).

133   The Hero's Journey was first constructed by Joseph Campbell (1949). These mythical steps have formed the backbone of many a Hollywood film, including most paint by numbers bio-pics. (One of the reasons I am not particularly fond of that genre.) In her biography, I would claim that Burns (2023) uses a modified version of this well-worn approach to vault Milton Friedman from his well-earned position as an extremely influential economist into an outright hero. The following enumeration is what are generally thought of as the steps depicted by Campbell.

1. **The Ordinary World:** We see the hero's normal life at the start of the story before the adventure begins.
2. **Call to Adventure:** The hero is faced with an event, conflict, problem, or challenge that makes him begin their adventure.
3. **Refusal of the Call:** The hero initially refuses the adventure because of hesitation, fears, insecurity, or any other number of issues.
4. **Meeting the Mentor:** The hero encounters a mentor that can give them advice, wisdom, information, or items that ready them for the journey ahead.
5. **Crossing the Threshold:** The hero leaves his ordinary world for the first time and crosses the threshold into adventure.
6. **Tests, Allies, and Enemies:** The hero learns the rules of the new world and endures tests, meets friends, and comes face-to-face with enemies.
7. **The Approach:** The initial plan to take on the central conflict begins, but setbacks occur that cause the hero to try a new approach or adopt new ideas.
8. **The Ordeal:** Things go wrong and added conflict is introduced. The hero experiences more difficult hurdles and obstacles, some of which may lead to a life crisis.
9. **The Reward:** After surviving The Ordeal, the hero seizes *the sword* – a reward that he's earned that allows him to take on the biggest conflict. It may be a physical item or piece of knowledge or wisdom that will help him persevere.
10. **The Road Back:** The hero sees the light at the end of the tunnel, but he is about to face even more tests and challenges.
11. **The Resurrection:** The climax. The hero faces a final test, using everything he has learned to take on the conflict once and for all.
12. **The Return:** The hero brings his knowledge or the 'elixir' back to the ordinary world (The Hero's Journey Breakdown: The Matrix – The Script Lab).

References

Alchian, A. and Harold, D. (1972). "Production, information costs and economic organization", *The American Economic Review*. 62(5): 777–795.

Barnett, W. A. (2011/2003). "An interview with Paul A. Samuelson", in Janice, M. (ed.) *The Collected Scientific Papers of Paul A. Samuelson – Volume 7*. Cambridge: MIT Press, pp. 553–557.

Bork, R. H. (1978). *The Antitrust Paradox*. New York: Free Press.

Buckley, W. F. Jr. and Brent, B. Jr. (1954). *McCarthy and His Enemies*. New York: H. Regnery Company.

Burgin, A. (2012). *The Great Persuasion*. Cambridge, MA: The Harvard University Press.

Burns, J. (2023). *Milton Friedman – The Last Conservative*. New York: Farrar, Straus and Giroux.

Caldwell, B. (2003). *Hayek's Challenge – An Intellectual Biography of F.A. Hayek*. Chicago: University of Chicago Press.

Campbell, J. (1949/1972). *The Hero with a Thousand Faces*. Princeton: Princeton University Press.

Card, D. and Alan, K. (1995). *Myth and Measurement: The New Economics of the Minimum Wage*. Princeton: Princeton University Press.

Carroll, L. (1974). *The Philosopher's Alice*. New York: St. Martin's Press.

Chamberlin, E. (1933). *The Theory of Monopolistic Competition*. Cambridge: Harvard University Press.

Cherrier, B. (2011d). "The lucky consistency of Milton Friedman's science and politics, 1933–1963", in Robert, V. H., Phillip, M., and Stapleford, T. A. (eds.) *Building Chicago Economics*. Cambridge: Cambridge University Press, pp. 335–368.

Coase, R. (1960). "The problem of social cost", *The Journal of Law & Economics*. 3(October): 1–44.

Coase, R. (1994a). "The institutional structure of production", in *Essays on Economics and Economists*. Chicago: The University of Chicago Press, pp. 3–15.

Coase, R. (1994b). "How should economists choose?", in *Essays on Economics and Economists*. Chicago: The University of Chicago Press, pp. 15–34.

Coase, R. (1997). "Looking for results", *Reason.com*, http://reason.com/archives/1997/01/01/looking-for-results, January 1: 1–8 (04/09/2013).

Duesenberry, J. S. (1949). *Income, Saving and the Theory of Consumer Behaviour*. Cambridge: Harvard University Press.

France, A. (1894). *Le Lys rouge*. [*The Red* Lily] Paris: Calmann-Lévy [French Edition].

Friedman, D. (1986). *Price Theory an Intermediate Text*. La Jolla, CA: Southwestern Publishing.

Friedman, M. (1953). "The methodology of positive economics", in *Essays in Positive Economics*, pp. 3–43. Chicago: The University of Chicago Press.

Friedman, M. (ed.) (1956). "The quantity theory of money – A restatement", in *Studies in the Quantity Theory of Money*. Chicago: University of Chicago Press, pp. 3–19.

Friedman, M. (1957). *A Theory of the Consumption Function*. Princeton: Princeton University Press.

Friedman, M. (1962). *Capitalism and Freedom*. Chicago: University of Chicago Press.

Friedman, M. (1971). "Doing good – Talk given at Commencement of University of Rochester, June 6", mimeo, pp. 1–5.

Friedman, M. (1976). In Meyer, F., Jowell, K., and Mulholland, S. (eds.) *Milton Friedman in South Africa*. Cape Town and Johannesburg: Graduate School of Business (University of Cape Town) and *The Sunday Times*.

Friedman, M. (2003a). "Preface", in Leeson, R. (ed.) *Keynes, Chicago and Friedman*, Vol. 1. London: Pickering & Chatto, pp. ix–x.

Friedman, M. (2003b). "Comments on the critics: Patinkin", in Leeson, R. (ed.) *Keynes, Chicago and Friedman*, Vol. 1. London: Pickering & Chatto, pp. 145–166.

Friedman, M. (2003c). "The monetary policy and theory of Henry Simons", in Leeson, R. (ed.) *Keynes, Chicago and Friedman*, Vol. 1. London: Pickering & Chatto, pp. 53–68.

Friedman, M. and Anna, S. (1963). *A Monetary History of the United States: 1867-1960*. Princeton: Princeton University Press for The National Bureau of Economic Research.

Friedman, M. and Rose, F. (1998). *Two Lucky People*. Chicago: The University of Chicago Press.

Hammond, J. D. and Claire, H. H. (2006). *Making Chicago Price Theory: Friedman-Stigler Correspondence 1945–1957*. London: Routledge.

Hayek, F. (1944). *The Road to Serfdom*. Chicago: The University of Chicago Press.

Johnson, H. (2003/1971). "The Keynesian revolution and the monetarist counter-revolution", in Leeson, R. (ed.) *Keynes, Chicago and Friedman*, Vol. 1. London: Pickering & Chatto, pp. 169–182.

Keynes, J. M. (1923). *A Tract on Monetary Reform*. London: Macmillan.

Keynes, J. M. (1930). *A Treatise on Money*. London: Macmillan.

Keynes, J. M. (1931/1963). "Economic possibilities for our grandchildren", *Essays in Persuasion*. New York: W.W. Norton Company Inc., pp. 358–375.

Keynes, J. M. (1936/1964). *The General Theory of Employment, Interest and Money*. New York: Harcourt Brace Jovanovich.

Keynes, J. M. (1937). "The 'ex-ante' theory of the rate of interest", *The Economic Journal*. 47 (188): 663–669.

Keynes, J. M. (1938). "Relative movements of real wages and output", 49(193): 34–51.

Kitch, E. W. (ed.) (1983). "The fire of truth: A remembrance of law and economics at Chicago, 1932–1970", *The Journal of Law & Economics*. 26(1): 163–234.

Klein, B. and Keith, B. L. (1981). "The role of market forces in assuring contractual performance", *Journal of Political Economy*. 89(4): 615–641.

Knight, F. (1921/1971). *Risk, Uncertainty and Profit*. Chicago: The University of Chicago Press.

Krugman, P. (1998). "It's Baaack: Japan's slump and the return of the liquidity trap", *Brookings Papers on Economic Activity*. 2: 1–69.

Kydland, F. and Edward, P. (1977). "Rules rather than discretion: The inconsistency of optimal plans", *Journal of Political Economy*. 85(3): 473–492.

Leeson, R. (ed.) (2003a). "The debate widens", in *Keynes, Chicago and Friedman*, Vol. 1. London: Pickering & Chatto, pp. 283–309.

Leeson, R. (2003b). "Patinkin, Johnson, and the shadow of Friedman", in Leeson, R. (ed.) *Keynes, Chicago and Friedman*, Vol. 1. London: Pickering & Chatto, pp. 249–279.

Leeson, R. (2003c). "From Keynes to Friedman via mints: Resolving the dispute over the quantity theory oral tradition", in Leeson, R. (ed.) *Keynes, Chicago and Friedman*, Vol. 2. London: Pickering & Chatto, pp. 481–526.

Leeson, R. (ed.) (2003d). "Towards a resolution of the dispute", in *Keynes, Chicago and Friedman*. Vol. 2. London: Pickering & Chatto, pp. 293–314.

Levi, A. (1973). *Journey Among The Economists*. London: Alcove Press Limited.

Medema, S. G. (2011c). "Chicago price theory and Chicago law and economics: A tale of two transitions", in Robert, V. H., Phillip, M., and Stapleford, T. A. (eds.) *Building Chicago Economics*. Cambridge: Cambridge University Press, pp. 151–180.

Mill, J. S. (1859/1947). *On Liberty*. New York: Appleton-Century-Croft.

Modigliani, F. (1949). "Fluctuations in the saving-income ratio: A problem in economic forecasting", *Studies in Income and Wealth*, Vol. 11. New York: National Bureau of Economic Research.

Modigliani, F. and Richard, H. B. (1954). "Utility analysis and the consumption function: An interpretation of cross-section data", in Kurihara, K. K. and Kenneth, K. (ed.), *Post-Keynesian Economics*. New Brunswick, NJ.: Rutgers University Press, pp. 388–436.

Modigliani, F. and Albert, A. (1957). "Tests of the life cycle hypothesis of savings: Comments and suggestions", *Bulletin of the Oxford University Institute of Statistics*. 19(2): 99–124.

Nik-Khah, E. (2011b). "Chicago neoliberalism and the genesis of the Milton Friedman institute (2006-2009)", in Robert, V. H., Phillip, M., and Stapleford, T. A. (eds.) *Building Chicago Economics*. Cambridge: Cambridge University Press, pp. 368–389.

Ohlin, B. (1937a). "Some notes on the Stockholm theory of savings and investment I", *The Economic Journal*. 47(185): 53–69.

Ohlin, B., Robertson, D., and Hawtrey, R. G. (1937b). "Alternative theories of the rate of interest: Three rejoinders", *The Economic Journal*. 47(187): 423–443.

Opazo, T. (2016). "The boys who got to remake an economy", Slate, January 12, http://www.slate.com/articles/business/moneybox/2016/01/in_chicago_boys_the_story_of_chilean_economists_who_studied_in_america_and.html (31/01/2017).

Patinkin, D. (2003a/1969). "The Chicago tradition: A comment", in Leeson, R. (ed.) *Keynes, Chicago and Friedman*, Vol. 1. London: Pickering & Chatto, pp. 87–120.

Patinkin, D. (2003b/1969). "Friedman on the quantity theory and Keynesian economics", in Leeson, R. (ed.) *Keynes, Chicago and Friedman*, Vol. 2. London: Pickering & Chatto, pp. 123–143.

Patinkin, D. (2003c/1969). "Keynesian monetary theory and the Cambridge School", in Leeson, R. (ed.) *Keynes, Chicago and Friedman*, Vol. 2. London: Pickering & Chatto, pp. 315–344.

Patinkin, D. (2003d/1969). "Keynes and Chicago", in Leeson, R. (ed.) *Keynes, Chicago and Friedman*, Vol. 2. London: Pickering & Chatto, pp. 373–392.

Reder, M. (1982). "Chicago economics: Permanence and change", *Journal of Economic Literature*. 20(1): 1–38.

Robinson, J. (1933). *The Economics of Imperfect Competition*. London: Macmillan.

Samuelson, P. A. and Stigler, G. J. (1963). "A dialogue on the proper economic role of the state", Selected Papers No. 7, Chicago: Graduate School of Business, University of Chicago.

Samuelson, P. A. (1964). "The case against Goldwater's economics", *NY Times Magazine*, October 25: 28.

Samuelson, P. A. (2011a). "Jacob Viner: 1892-1970", in Janice, M. (ed.) *The Collected Scientific Papers of Paul A. Samuelson – Volume 7*. Cambridge: MIT Press, pp. 588–601.

Samuelson, P. A. (2011b). "Robert Solow: An affectionate portrait", in Janice, M. (ed.) *The Collected Scientific Papers of Paul A. Samuelson – Volume 7*. Cambridge: MIT Press, pp. 613–620.

Samuelson, P. A. (2011c). "Milton Friedman: Nobel monetary economist", in Janice, M. (ed.) *The Collected Scientific Papers of Paul A. Samuelson – Volume 7*. Cambridge: MIT Press, pp. 860–865.

Samuelson, P. A. (2011d). "Paul Anthony Samuelson", in Janice, M. (ed.) *The Collected Scientific Papers of Paul A. Samuelson – Volume 7*. Cambridge: MIT Press, p. 969.

Samuelson, P. A. (2011e). "An interview with Paul A. Samuelson", in Janice, M. (ed.) *The Collected Scientific Papers of Paul A. Samuelson – Volume 7*. Cambridge: MIT Press, pp. 550–575.

Solow, R. M. (1966). "Comments", in George, S. and Aliber, R. (ed.) *Guidelines: Informal Controls and the Market Place*. Chicago: University of Chicago Press, pp. 62–66.

Stapleford, T. A. (2011a). "Positive economics for democratic polity: Milton Friedman, institutionalism, and the science of history", in Robert, V. H., Phillip, M., and Stapleford, T. A. (eds.) *Building Chicago Economics*. Cambridge: Cambridge University Press, pp. 3–36.

Stigler, G. J. (1946). *Price Theory*. New York: Macmillan.

Stigler, G. J. (1949). "Monopolistic competition in retrospect", in *Five Lectures on Economic Problems*. London: Longmans, Green and Co., pp. 12–34.

Stigler, G. J. (1965). "The problem of the Negro", *New Guard*. 5: 11–12.

Stigler, G. J. (1971a). "The theory of economic regulation", *Bell Journal of Economics and Management Science*. 2(1): 3–21.

Stigler, G. J. (1971b). "Modern man and his corporation", Graduate School of Business Selected Papers No. 39 (March). Chicago: Graduate School of Business, University of Chicago.

Stigler, G. J. (1976). "Birthday talk [George Stigler's birthday]", mimeo, pp. 1–10.

Stigler, G. J. (1977). "Birthday talk [Milton Friedman's birthday]", mimeo, pp. 1–3.

Stigler, G. J. (1982). "Henry Calvert Simons", in *The Economist as Preacher*. Chicago: The University of Chicago Press, pp. 166–170.

Stigler, G. J. (1988). *Memoirs of an Unregulated Economist*. New York: Basic Books.

Stigler, G. J. (1991). "Memorial service for Ethel Verry", mimeo, October 28.

Stigler, G. J. and Becker, G. (1977). "De Gustibus Non Est Disputandum", *American Economic Review*. 67(2): 76–90.

Stiglitz, J. (2024). "Time is up for neo-liberals", *The Washington Post*, May 13: 1.

Summers, L. H. (2006). "The great liberator", *New York Times*, September 19, http://www.nytimes.com/2006/11/19/opinion/19summers.html? pp. 1–2.

Sunstein, C. R. (2024). "The nobel prize winning professor who liked to collaborate with his adversaries", *New York Times*, April 1: 1.

Tavlas, G. (2023). *The Monetarists: The Making of the Chicago Monetary Tradition 1927–1960*. Chicago: University of Chicago Press.

The Alumni Bulletin – The University of Chicago (1935). "Senate ends "red hunt"; no hits, no runs, and only a few errors", August (1: 3): 1 and 8).

Robert, V. H. (2011). "Jacob Viner's critique of Chicago neoliberalism", in Robert, V. H., Phillip, M., and Stapleford, T. A. (eds.) *Building Chicago Economics*. Cambridge: Cambridge University Press, pp. 279–301.

Warsh, D. (2003). "A very short history of the volunteer army", *economicprincipals.com*, July 20, http://www.economicprincipals.com/issues/03.07.20.html (30/01/2007).

Waugh, E. (1938). *Scoop*. London: Chapman and Hall.

Index